THE INVASION WITHIN

I. The Invasion Within:
The Contest of Cultures in Colonial North America

The Invasion Within

*The Contest of Cultures in
Colonial North America*

JAMES AXTELL

OXFORD UNIVERSITY PRESS
New York   Oxford

Oxford University Press
Oxford   New York   Toronto
Delhi   Bombay   Calcutta   Madras   Karachi
Petaling Jaya   Singapore   Hong Kong   Tokyo
Nairobi   Dar es Salaam   Cape Town
Melbourne   Auckland

and associated companies in
Beirut   Berlin   Ibadan   Nicosia

First published in 1985 by Oxford University Press, Inc.,
200 Madison Avenue, New York, New York 10016
First published as an Oxford University Press paperback, 1986

Oxford is a registered trademark of Oxford University Press

Library of Congress Cataloging in Publication Data

Axtell, James.
The invasion within.

Bibliography: p.
Includes index.
1. Indians of North America—Cultural assimilation.
2. Acculturation—United States—History.
3. Acculturation—Canada—History.   4. Indians of
North America—Government relations—To 1789.
5. Canada—Social conditions—To 1763.   6. United
States—Social conditions—To 1865.   7. North America—
History—Colonial period. ca. 1600–1775.   I. Title.
E98.C89A93   1985   970.02   85-7260
ISBN 0-19-503596-8
ISBN 0-19-504154-2 (pbk.)

Printing (last digit): 9 8

Printed in the United States of America

Human life is reduced to real suffering, to hell, only when two ages, two cultures and religions, overlap.

ALBRECHT VON HALLER

As always, for Susan

Preface

I seek to bee short, howsoever my
Subject causeth mee to bee voluminous.
MARC LESCARBOT

Any book that takes nearly twelve years to write calls for an explanation. This book began in 1972 as a tidy seven-chapter outline, the naive inspiration of the author of a recent article on the New England colonists' education at the hands of their Indian neighbors. Having probed a few aspects of acculturation on one side of the colonial frontier, I was curious to know what impact the major competing cultures of eastern North America—English, French, and Indian—had had upon each other, especially when they set out consciously to educate or convert their rivals.

Five years later, having plunged into the research and come up sputtering, I finally conceded that a satisfactory answer could not be obtained in less than double the number of chapters and two additional volumes. That concession was made in full recognition of—and mixed admiration for—the work of Francis Parkman, whose eight-volume *France and England in America* still casts a shadow over the writing of colonial history. Parkman's questions, however, are not mine, so his majestically framed answers (and prejudices) do not speak to my concerns. Even if they did, modern readers would not be well served by his Olympian style, which is best read in morning coat and spats.

In history as in other disciplines, new questions invariably open new perspectives, which in turn uncover new strategies of research and new sources. While I happily (if more hesitantly) share Parkman's spacious geographical terrain, I am less concerned with military and political affairs on the grand scale than with social and cultural interactions on a broad scale. And I am interested in the educational and acculturative impact of *each* society upon the others, which has forced me to seek ways of understanding America's native cultures that are seldom used by historians of literate European groups. The best strategy I found was ethnohistory, an imaginative but disciplined blend of anthropological and historical methods, concepts, and materials. Demanding parity of focus, unusual sources, and tolerance for disciplinary tension, ethnohistory is perfectly suited to the moral and cultural complexities of frontier history, as I have argued and tried to show in *The European and the Indian: Essays in the Ethnohistory of Colonial North America.**

*New York: Oxford University Press, 1981.

The present volume, then, is an ethnohistory of the colonial French, English, and Indian efforts to convert each other. Its two sequels will carry forward the story of their cultural interaction over more than two centuries. The first, *American Encounter: The Confluence of Cultures in Colonial North America*, will examine the ways in which the three cultures became like each other or simply changed as a result of competing and occasionally cooperating. The second, *The European Presence: The Conflict of Cultures in Colonial North America*, will seek to explain how the English eventually won the eastern half of the continent from their native and European rivals, and at what cost.

It may be asked why the Spanish do not appear in these pages. Two historical reasons and one stylistic consideration must serve. First, by design and circumstances the Spanish in the Southeast were not serious contenders for continental hegemony east of the Mississippi; at most they hoped to safeguard their supply routes and bullion fleets in the Caribbean. Second, while Spanish arms and allies posed some threat to the southernmost English and (after 1700) French colonies, cultural intercourse was minimal, quite unlike the extensive exchanges between New France and the northern English colonies in both war and peace. And finally, even if historical marginality had not excluded the Spanish, the demands of stylistic economy might have. A cast of three main characters is manageable; any more would risk confusion. In the classroom I have long advocated "A North American Perspective for Colonial History," in which the Spanish, east and west, share the limelight with the English, French, and Indians.* But in books less ambitious than a survey text, selectivity based on historical relevance is a virtuous necessity.

Speaking metaphorically of diverse ethnic or national groups as "characters" might seem misleading and unfaithful to the complexity of the past. I have tried to avoid the danger of *over*generalization (some is desirable) by distinguishing as often and as clearly as possible individuals, interest groups, and communities within the three societies. Particularly in treating the Indians, I have heeded the warning of Father Paul Le Jeune, who in 1633 noted that "after having seen two or three Indians do the same thing, it is at once reported to be a custom of the whole Tribe. The argument drawn from the enumeration of parts is faulty, if it does not comprehend all or the greater part. Add to this that there are many tribes in these countries who agree in a number of things, and differ in many others; so that, when it is said that certain practices are common to the Indians, it may be true of one tribe and not true of another."† What Le Jeune said of Indians applies with equal justice to the French and the English.

I have also chosen to sin venially against my own preachment to view the geography of colonial America not as a political map crisscrossed by modern

---

The History Teacher 12 (1979):549–62.

†Reuben Gold Thwaites, ed., *The Jesuit Relations and Allied Documents*, 73 vols. (Cleveland, 1896–1901), 6:27.

state and national lines but as a topographical map marked only by the natural features of the continent. In the primary effort to reconstruct North America as it appeared to the natives and colonists who made it their home, I have indeed tried to follow my own advice. But for the sake of the reader I have freely used modern town, state, and provincial names, without the awkward prefix "present-day," to locate historical events. Inconsistency is sometimes the price of clarity.

Other choices have been less difficult. I have used "Indians" rather than "Amerindians," "Amerinds," or "Native Americans" to designate the American natives because the former is simpler, sanctioned by tradition, normatively neutral, and preferred by the vast majority of native people themselves, past and present. Most of the time I refer to members of specific tribes, which raises a possible point of confusion. Ethnological usage distinguishes between the Algonquin tribe (on the Ottawa River west of Montreal) and the Algonquian language family, which spoke closely related dialects (comparable, say, to the Romance language family). There was only one tribe of Algonquins, but most of the tribes in the Eastern Woodlands spoke an Algonquian language and were thus known collectively as Algonquians. The exceptions were the five (later six) nations of Iroquois in New York State and a few other tribes around the eastern Great Lakes (such as the Hurons and Neutrals), which spoke Iroquoian languages (equivalent to the Germanic languages). As the preceding sentence illustrates, I also refer to the collective members of the Huron tribe as "the Hurons," not "the Huron." The latter is a nonsensical ethnological convention left over from the nineteenth century; with good reason anthropologists steadfastly refuse to say things like "The Puritan were. . . ."

Three final notes on usage: I have silently removed indiscriminate italics from quotations when it was obvious that they did not contribute to the author's meaning but simply distracted the modern reader's eye. For the same reason I have been sparing in my own use of quotation marks to emphasize that normatively loaded words such as "pagan," "civilized," and "savage" should be taken not as my characterizations but as those of contemporary Europeans. The reader should bracket such words with mental quotation marks each time they appear; the context in which they appear will also help to avoid misunderstanding. Likewise, I have frequently used the native phrase "Black Robes" to designate Jesuit missionaries, and the uncapitalized "black robes" to indicate other missionaries, mainly Protestant. One relatively simple way ethnohistory can begin to give equal treatment to its cultural subjects is to allow them to judge each other through the value-laden language each used to characterize the others.

The task of writing frontier ethnohistory is difficult enough when only two societies are the subject. But maintaining a balanced focus on and special empathy for the diverse peoples of three societies, two of them at a very different stage of development than the third, poses a unique challenge to the historian. I therefore take some comfort from a colonial predecessor in tricultural studies and reiterate his plea. "An Historian's Views must be curious and extensive," wrote Cadwallader Colden in 1727 in his *History of the Five Indian Nations of Canada*, "and the History of different People and different Ages requires different Rules, and often different Abilities to write it; I hope therefore the Reader will, from these Considerations, receive this first Attempt of this kind, with more than usual Allowances."

Williamsburg, Va.   J. A.

Acknowledgments

History is not a problem.
The writing of it is.
SAVOIE LOTTINVILLE

While this book has been too many years in the making, one benefit of such tarriance is that I have accumulated a large number of happy debts to people and institutions who have smoothed the way of the researcher, freed the time of the teacher, honed the words of the writer, and tolerated the single-mindedness of the father-husband.

The most enjoyable aspect of scholarship is the shared discovery upon which it depends and toward which it is aimed. By their nature, libraries are perhaps the most generous institutions. I have received unflagging assistance and courtesy from the Yale University Library; the Dartmouth College Library; the Hamilton College Library and Walter Pilkington; the University of Maine Library, Orono; the Northwestern University Library; the American Philosophical Society; the New-York Historical Society; the Moravian Archives, Bethlehem, Pa.; the Connecticut Historical Society; the Connecticut Archives; the Massachusetts Archives; the Massachusetts Historical Society and its director, Leonard Tucker (who kindly supplied a reproduction of the portrait of Esther Wheelwright); the Library of Congress Manuscript Division; the Congregational Library, Boston; the Newberry Library and John Aubrey; the McGill University Library; the University of Ottawa Library; the Public Archives of Canada and Michel Wyczynski of the Manuscript Division; and especially from the staff of the Swem Library of the College of William and Mary, for which I am most grateful.

The ethnohistorian must go beyond the library into the museum and the field in order to recapture the living presence of his subjects. My education in material culture, Indian and European, has been greatly enhanced by visits to the Field Museum, Chicago; the Museum of the American Indian, New York; the Smithsonian Institution; the Cherokee (N.C.) Museum; the New York State Museum, Albany; the Caughnawaga Museum, Fonda, N.Y.; Plimoth Plantation; Colonial Williamsburg; Roanoke Island and Jamestown Island (National Park Service); Fort Ticonderoga; Fortress Louisbourg; the Micmac Museum, Pictou, N.S.; the New Brunswick Provincial Museum, St. John; La Maison Saint-Gabriel, Montreal; Ste. Marie-among-the-Hurons, Midland, Ont.; the Lawson Museum of Indian Archaeology, London, Ont.; and the National Museum of Man, Ottawa. I am particularly indebted to Ken Lister and Mima Kapches of the Royal Ontario Museum, Toronto, and Conrad

Graham of the McCord Museum, Montreal, for allowing me to examine their storage rooms at some length.

Even more generous (if somewhat more selective) have been several patrons of scholarship who have provided me with free time for the work at hand. In 1972 the American Council of Learned Societies awarded me a summer grant to launch the research for this book. Three years later the National Endowment for the Humanities kindly made me one of their Fellows for Independent Study and Research, which was followed by a second year as an N.E.H. Fellow at the ever-hospitable Newberry Library. Since then I have been fortunate to receive three summer grants and a semester research leave from the College of William and Mary, and, most gratifying of all, a John Simon Guggenheim Memorial Fellowship in 1981–82. Without the faith and generosity of these modern Maecenases, this tardy book would still be incomplete.

Two other institutions deserve special thanks: the annual Conference on Iroquois Research, for my ongoing education in ethnohistory and for helpful responses to my not-always-Iroquoian trial balloons, and the Institute of Early American History and Culture, for its monthly seminars in historical criticism and scholarly collaboration. Michael McGiffert and Daniel Richter of the Institute both improved Chapter 9 as well.

Because one must write alone, I am the more grateful for the company I have kept before, during, and after the writing of this book. Hanni Woodbury and John Steckley very generously supplied me with translations from Iroquois and Huron, respectively. The thought-provoking sermons and liturgical presence of Pickett Miles helped me to understand the inner spirit of Christianity and to measure the theological distance between Protestant and Catholic. In addition to serving up hospitality and stimulation in Ottawa, Cornelius Jaenen allowed himself to be used as an interlibrary copy service. And to Bruce Trigger I am greatly indebted for a critical reading of my Canadian chapters and his friendly agreement to disagree about the Jesuits.

At Oxford University Press, Sheldon Meyer, Leona Capeless, and particularly Tessa DeCarlo, my copy editor, have done me and my manuscript many kindnesses, not the least of which was to humor an author keen to meddle in book design. Even as a Cambridge man, I feel privileged to be associated with an ancient press of such consistently high standards.

Finding friends close enough to be frank about one's pet words and ideas is often difficult. Fortunately, during the writing of this and other books I have had the humbling benefit of four people who did not stint their expert criticism or their friendship. James Ronda and William Eccles have read every chapter, often more than once, and have straightened more cockeyed notions and sentences than either would care to admit. Their zest for learning and teaching, love of peripatetic research, and inimitable style have been a constant inspiration and goad. They alone give the lie to Carl Becker's complaint that "writing a book is a terrible job."

For many years I have taught my students to write for an "ideal reader," an actual acquaintance whose intelligence could appreciate tough-minded history unmarred by jargon or technical obscurity and whose familiar regard would demand nothing less than the author's best. I have been blessed with two ideal readers: my wife Susan and her late father, Howard Hallas. Before his death, my father-in-law's liberal learning, understated wisdom, and infinite care for expression nurtured all my writing. Fortunately, his daughter has inherited in full measure his literary sensibilities and editorial instincts. Moreover, in the midst of nurturing her own classes of preschoolers, our two teenagers, and a golden retriever, she has created the ideal environment for a writer: deep pockets of solitude surrounded by loving circles of meaningful engagement. To borrow a line, the thought of our past years in me doth breed perpetual benediction.

J. A.

Contents

THE INVASION WITHIN

THE EASTERN WOODLAND TRIBES
(At the earliest stages of European contact with each tribe)

The Skewed Triangle

*The anointed children of education have been
too powerful for the tribes of the ignorant.*

THOMAS ROLPH

France and England glowered at each other across the narrow channel that
kept them at arm's length. In the great arena of European power politics they
were inveterate enemies, forever concocting alliances with competitors and
launching military and economic adventures in hopes of gaining at least
temporary advantage. When these behemoths tangled, not only the European
continent but half the world was their battleground. Many of their sharpest
contests were joined in the wooded fastness of eastern North America, where
the allegiance of strategically placed native groups was often a crucial ingre-
dient of success as well as a principal prize.

In America, the Indian allies of the two powers, like their counterparts in
Europe, fought for their own interests, jumping from one side to the other,
standing neutral, or occasionally daring to take on all comers in order to
preserve their independence as long as possible. For the Indians the stakes
were particularly high. English farmers and speculators coveted their land
while French traders and military officers sought to reorient their material
life and labor. Colonial governors waved parchments claiming sovereignty
and eminent domain in the names of their distant kings. Perhaps most
dangerous were the missionaries of all persuasions who tried to remake the
natives in the image of European countrymen, inside and out, believing that
adherence to the national religion would entail religious adherence to the
nation. Whenever the competing colonies made plans for an offensive thrust
or a defensive parry, the Indians were obliged to reassess their goals and
resources and to initiate diplomatic, military, or cultural maneuvers appropriate to the situation. The fate of North America thus hung on a series of
shifting alliances and a closely calculated balance of power between the three
major competitors, French, English, and Indian.

Except in the earliest stages of colonization, none of the contestants was
capable of being physically obliterated; their demographic tenacity was simply too great. In the tangled forests and tumbling rivers of eastern America,
bulky European war machines broke down or became hopelessly mired,
forcing colonial armies to adopt native-style tactics against European and
Indian foes alike. These tactics, consisting largely of small-scale guerilla
raids, could deliver punishing stripes to segments of the population but never

a mortal blow to the whole society. Accordingly, the three competitors were forced to rely less on dreams of total military conquest than on the slower stratagems of diplomacy and cultural conversion. Despite a few famous outbreaks of armed aggression, especially during the intercolonial wars of the eighteenth century, the contest for North America was fought largely in times of declared peace, with weapons other than flintlocks and tomahawks.

During the 120 years of intercolonial peace (and many of the war years) between the founding and the fall of Quebec, the French and English colonists sought to capture native allies primarily by two means, trade and religious conversion. From one perspective, traders and missionaries were partners in the same business, although they frequently fell out over goals and tactics. Initially, both Catholic and Protestant missionaries sought to "civilize" the natives while (if not before) they converted them to Christianity. At its most extreme, the civilization process entailed the wholesale substitution of a European lifestyle for the natives' own, beginning with material artifacts—clothing, weapons, tools—and ending with deeply engrained habits of thought and feeling. Quite simply, traders provided the trappings of European material culture, whose technological superiority and beauty were expected to seduce the neolithic natives irrevocably. Missionaries were expected to build their spiritual edifices on the inroads made by copper pots, wool blankets, and glass beads.

While the European invaders enjoyed the advantage of offensive initiative, the native defenders of the continent were not devoid of resources. Although they quickly recognized the superiority of the Europeans' cloth and metal technologies, they could seldom be persuaded to buy more than the necessities of traditional life or to use the new items in other than traditional ways. While most tribes were soon outnumbered by French and English colonists, the Indians were adept at playing colonial governments who sought their economic and military allegiance against each other. In addition to keen insight into their own best interests, particularly in the short run, they possessed daunting self-confidence in their social organization and cultural traditions, an inclusive religion capable of adding elements from other religions without dissonance, and an uncanny talent for converting hostile enemies into loyal kinsmen. Armed with these defensive weapons, they were surprisingly well equipped to counter the cultural offensives of the Europeans by firmly resisting them, absorbing them, or threatening to transfer their loyalties.

The cultural warfare that pitted the European rivals against the Indians was also waged between the European colonies themselves, most often in wartime, when military and civilian prisoners were taken and attempts made to convert them to their captors' religion and polity. Like their Indian adversaries, colonial governments (particularly the French, who suffered from a relative paucity of people) realized the psychological and demographic advantages to be gained from enlarging one's own forces at the proportional expense of the enemy's. Although the English took very few French prisoners and converted fewer, substantial numbers of English colonists—

men, women, and children from the frontiers of Pennsylvania, New York, and New England—were carried to Canada, a large proportion of whom abjured their Protestant faith, received baptism in the Catholic church, took an oath of loyalty to the king of France, and settled down to lives of quiet contentment with French spouses.

Thus in the intense but nonmilitary struggle for eastern America, the three major contestants drew on different cultural resources and enjoyed unequal measures of success in converting their enemies. Although they had the largest population, the richest and most diversified economy, and unlimited confidence in the superiority of their way of life, the English compiled the least auspicious record in turning Indians and Frenchmen into Englishmen. The French, the smallest group of all, made the most of an ancient religion, a benevolent paternalism, and a comfortable sense of primacy in converting an impressive number of Indians to Catholicism and a surprising number of Englishmen to both Catholicism and political allegiance to French Canada. But the Indians, in the face of incredible odds, managed to convert several hundred English and French colonists not so much to native religion (which was an individual rather than a national affair) as to the whole native way of life. While being wracked by disease, war, and dislocation, the Indians successfully conveyed to large numbers of adversaries, through a remarkable process of education, their own ineluctable pride, social warmth, and cultural integrity.

In retrospect this is a strange concatenation of events because by 1763 the English had all but won the palm, France had been expelled from the continent, and the Indians faced a bleak future, having already lost many, in some cases most, of their lands, lives, and liberties. While hindsight is indispensable to the historian, it can also truncate the lived past by over-simplifying. Historians look backward, up the stream of time, but history's actors, in their own time, looked forward into the ill-charted flow of the future. If we are to capture their sense of life as it was being lived, of history being made, we must imaginatively ignore our knowledge of the denouement and seek to recapture the challenges they faced, the options they enjoyed, the choices they made, and the short-range as well as long-range consequences of their actions.

It is simply not enough for us to know that English politicians and armies won the battle for eastern America—we already knew that. What we need to take into account, now that history is more than past politics, is that in cultural attraction and educational sophistication the English were decidedly inferior to their French and Indian rivals, who lost what they did for other reasons. And since time is our master, we must also account for the specific course of events as they actually unfolded. If the competition for the most desirable part of the continent was not settled decisively until 1763, we are obliged to explain why then and not before. In short, we must explain how the eventual "losers" were able to persist as long as they did, what strategies they used to chase victory and, when that proved elusive, to postpone defeat.

While it cannot fully explain the outcome, the skewed history of conversion provides a major explanation for the temporal progress and duration of the contest for colonial North America. As if Clio had taken a page from Aesop, it describes how two slight but wily foxes, sometimes alone, often in concert, outmaneuvered and eluded the brute strength of the British lion for a century and a half.

CHAPTER ONE

Those Poor Blind Infidels

My Brethren, I think we are poor miserable
Creatures, we do not know what Ministers are.
ONEIDA SACHEM

They first came in tall-masted ships, festooned with billowy ash-white sails. Then they pushed up the sea-flowing rivers and through the forests of lakes in small pinnaces and borrowed canoes. By the end of the seventeenth century they had left their hard-heeled signature on America's geography from the Atlantic littoral to Lake Superior, from Hudson Bay to the Gulf of Mexico. And everywhere the French and English went, they were met by the natives with curiosity, apprehension, and fear.

The meeting of two peoples, two societies and cultures, is not only a physical conjunction but an interweaving of mental selves, and the images which those peoples have of one another are an important aspect of their encounter.[1] But on the face of it, the task of imagining the imaginations—of resurrecting the thoughts and emotions—of the Indians who first beheld the white strangers from another world is impossible. Although the myriad native groups had various first encounters at different times, they were unable to write down their impressions close to the event, and many of the first Europeans were also careless of the needs of future historians. Moreover, the Europeans who penned the first surviving descriptions of native reactions were not always the first white men actually encountered, nor were their interpretations of what they saw always perceptive. Yet if we read closely, we can observe some telling native behavior through the eyes of early—often the earliest—white observers, and better still, we can recapture some of the emotional ambiance of discovery through the oral memories of native descendants.

So awesome their strangeness proved to be, so cataclysmic their advent, that the Europeans appear to have first intruded upon the consciousness of many tribes not in the flesh but in dreams or premonitory visions. In the mid-nineteenth century the Micmacs of Nova Scotia and New Brunswick remembered that the French first appeared to a young woman who dreamed of a small floating island with tall trees and living beings, one of whom was dressed in garments made of snowy rabbit skins. Since her dream was so unusual, she consulted the tribal shamans and conjurers for an interpretation. But they were nonplussed by it until two days later a small island drifted

7

near to land. "There were trees on the island, and what seemed to be a number of bears were crawling about on the branches." Anticipating a great feast of bear meat, the Micmac men rushed to shore with their weapons, only to discover a wooden sailing ship disgorging a longboat of unbearlike men. Among them was a man dressed in a long white robe who made "signs of friendship" by "raising his hand toward heaven" as he came ashore and talking to the Indians in an "earnest manner." When the woman acknowledged that these were the things she had seen in her dream, some of the wise men were displeased because "the coming of these strangers to their land had been revealed to a young girl instead of to them. If an enemy had been about to make an attack upon them, they could have foreseen it and foretold it by the power of their magic. But of the coming of this white-robed man, who proved to be a priest of a new religion, they knew nothing."[2]

The power of an Ojibwa prophet on Lake Superior served him better. One night he had a dream so vivid that he prepared by fasting and sweating for several days before revealing it to his people. Then for half a day he described in great detail what he had seen:

> Men of strange appearance have come across the great water. They have landed on our island [North America]. Their skins are white like snow, and on their faces long hair grows. These people have come across the great water in wonderfully large canoes which have great white wings like those of a giant bird. The men have long and sharp knives, and they have long black tubes which they point at birds and animals. The tubes make a smoke that rises into the air just like the smoke from our pipes. From them come fire and such terrific noise that I was frightened, even in my dream.

At once a flotilla of trusted men was sent through the Great Lakes and down the St. Lawrence to investigate. On the lower river they found a clearing in which all the trees had been cut down, which led them to conjecture that "giant beavers with huge, sharp teeth had done the cutting." The prophet disagreed, reminding them of the long knives in his dream. Knowing that their stone-headed axes could not cut such large trees as smoothly, they were "filled with awe, and with terror also." Still more puzzling were "long, rolled-up shavings" of wood and scraps of "bright-coloured cloth," which they stuck in their hair and wound around their heads. Farther down the river they finally came upon the white-faced, bearded strangers with their astonishing long knives, thunder tubes, and giant winged canoes, just as the prophet had predicted.

Having satisfied their curiosity and fulfilled the prophet's dream, the Indians returned home with their trophies; each villager was given a small piece of cloth as a memento. To impress their neighbors, the Ojibwas followed an old custom. Just as they tied the scalps of their enemies on long poles, "now they fastened the splinters of wood and strips of calico to poles and sent them with special messengers" from one tribe to another. Thus were these strange articles passed from hand to hand around the whole lake, giving the natives of the interior their first knowledge of the white men from Europe.[3]

The nomadic Montagnais of the lower St. Lawrence had a similar recollection of the first Frenchmen. In 1633 a young Montagnais convert related the story his grandmother had told him of the Indians' astonishment at seeing a French ship for the first time. Like many natives before and after, they thought it was a "moving Island." Having seen the men aboard, however, the Montagnais women began to prepare wigwams for them, "as is their custom when new guests arrive," and four canoes bade the strangers welcome. The French gave them a barrel of ship's biscuits and perhaps offered them some wine. But the Indians were appalled that these people "drank blood and ate wood," and promptly threw the tasteless biscuits into the river. Like the Ojibwas, they were obviously more impressed by the white man's technology than his food, for henceforth they called the French *ouemichtigouchiou*, "a man who works in wood, or who is in a canoe or vessel of wood."[4]

The Indians regarded the Europeans' ability to fashion incredible objects and make them work less as mechanical aptitude than as spiritual power. When the Delawares, who once lived along the New Jersey–New York coast, met their first Dutch ship, they concluded that it was a "remarkably large house in which the Mannitto (the Great or Supreme Being) himself was present." Thinking he was coming to pay them a visit, they prepared meat for a sacrifice, put all their religious effigies in order, and threw a grand dance to please or appease him. Meanwhile, the tribal conjurers tried to fathom his purpose in coming because their brethren were all "distracted between hope and fear." While preparations were being made, runners brought the welcome news that the visitors were humans like themselves, only strangely colored and oddly dressed. But when the Dutchmen made their appearance, graced the assembly with a round of liquor, and distributed iron and cloth presents, the natives were confirmed in their original belief that every white man was an "inferior Mannitto attendant upon the supreme Deity"—the ship's captain—who "shone superior" in his red velvet suit glittering with gold lace.[5]

The earliest French and English explorers who were the objects of native awe corroborated native testimony, despite some suggestion that the Indians were struck most forcefully by other European characteristics. Some Indians appeared to be fascinated by the whiteness of European skin, but the close examination they occasionally gave the explorers' chests, faces, and arms may have been focused on the skin's hairiness rather than its pallor.[6] Most Indians were relatively hairless, and the little they grew was assiduously plucked or singed; understandably, European beards and tufted chests held an ugly fascination for them. Before they laid eyes on a white man, the Potawatomis and Menominees around Green Bay believed the French to be a "different species from other men" because they were "covered with hair," not because their skin was a shade or two lighter.[7] By the same token, the caresses Jacques Cartier received from Algonquians on the Gaspé in 1534 were given less because he was white-skinned than to thank him for the presents he had just given. By the time he reached the Iroquoian village of Hochelaga the following year, he had learned that "rubbing . . . with their hands" was a traditional native greeting, not one reserved for white visitors.[8]

The first Europeans, however, were no ordinary guests, and their friendly reception owed much to the native belief that they were spiritually powerful men, gods (as the Europeans put it) or *manitous* (in Algonquian parlance) like the Indians' own shamans and conjurers. The sources of their power were chiefly two. The first was their reputation among the Indians as purveyors or preventers of disease, exactly comparable to native shamans, who were also thought to wield powers of life and death. The palsied chief of Hochelaga begged Cartier to touch his shrunken limbs. "At once many sick persons, some blind, others with but one eye, others lame or impotent and others again so extremely old that their eyelids hung down to their cheeks, were brought in and set down or laid out near the Captain, in order that he might lay his hands upon them, so that one would have thought Christ had come down to earth to heal them." In playing his assigned role, however, Cartier took his cues from another script by reciting several Catholic prayers and reading the story of Christ's Passion in a loud, albeit unintelligibly French, voice.[9] In 1665 Father Claude Allouez found himself held in similar regard by the Indians of Michigan and Wisconsin. When he advised a Fox man to have his dangerously ill parents bled, the man poured powdered tobacco over the priest's gown and said, "Thou art a spirit; come now, restore these sick people to health; I offer thee this tobacco in sacrifice."[10]

At the same time, the Indians believed that all spiritual power was double-edged: those who could cure could also kill. Only powerful "spirits" possessed the ability to bewitch or to counteract another's witchcraft. When they inadvertently carried deadly European diseases into the North Carolina coastal region, the English colonists at Roanoke were deified by their hosts for their ability to kill Indians at a distance and to remain unscathed themselves. "There could at no time happen any strange sicknesse, losses, hurtes, or any other crosse unto [the natives]," wrote Thomas Harriot, the expedition's Indian expert, "but that they would impute to us the cause or meanes therof for offending or not pleasing us." The Indians had extra cause to worry when four or five towns that had practiced some "subtle devise" against the English were ravaged by an unknown disease shortly after the colonists' departure. The English allies under chief Wingina deduced that the havoc was wrought by "our God through our meanes, and that wee by him might kil and slaie whom wee would without weapons and not come neere them. . . . This marvelous accident in all the countrie," explained Harriot, "wrought so strange opinions of us, that some people could not tel whether to thinke us gods or men," particularly when no Englishman died or was even especially sick.[11]

The second and more important source of the white man's power in native America was his technological superiority. The Indians' acquaintance with it had certainly begun by 1524, when Giovanni da Verrazzano cruised the eastern waters from the Carolinas to Maine. On an "Arcadian" coast of beautiful trees somewhere south of New York harbor, a handsome, naked Indian man approached a group of the French sailors and showed them a burning stick, "as if to offer us fire." But when the Europeans trumped his hospitality by firing a matchlock, "he trembled all over with fear" and "remained as if thunderstruck, and prayed, worshiping like a monk, pointing his finger to the sky; and indicating the sea and the ship, he appeared to bless us."[12] Not without reason, European iron weapons continued to impress the natives who saw them in action for the first time. When Pierre Radisson and Nicolas Perrot traveled among the Indians of Wisconsin in the middle years of the seventeenth century, the natives literally worshipped their guns, knives, and hatchets by blowing sacred smoke over them, as a sacrifice to the spirits within. "If any tribe had some Frenchmen among them, that was sufficient to make them feel safe from any injuries by their neighbors" who were not blessed by the presence of such mighty "spirits." To Perrot the Potawatomi elders said, "Thou art one of the chief spirits, since thou usest iron; it is for thee to rule and protect all men. Praised be the Sun, who has instructed thee and sent thee to our country."[13]

Weapons were of paramount importance to the feuding native polities of North America, but metal objects of any kind, cloth goods, and cleverly designed or sizable wooden objects also drew their admiration. Appropriately, the most common Indian names for the Europeans meant "iron people" or "cloth makers."[14] The Sioux, Illinois, and Seneca Indians among whom the Recollect priest Louis Hennepin journeyed during the early 1680s frequently clapped their hands over their mouths in astonishment at such things as printed books, silver chalices, embroidered chasubles, and iron pots, all of which they designated as "spirits."[15] In the early 1630s the natives of southern New England considered a windmill "little less than the world's wonder" and the first plowman "little better than a juggler" or shaman. Being shown the iron coulter and share of the plow, which could "tear up more ground in a day than their clamshells [hoes] could scrape up in a month," they told the plowman "he was almost Abamacho, almost as cunning as the Devil."[16]

Thomas Harriot put his finger on the primary cause of the Indians' initially exalted opinion of the white strangers when he noted that

> most things they sawe with us, as Mathematicall instruments, sea compasses, the vertue of the loadstone in drawing iron, a perspective glasse whereby was shewed manie strange sightes, burning glasses, wildefire woorkes, gunnes, bookes, writing and reading, spring clocks that seeme to goe of themselves, and manie other thinges that wee had, were so straunge unto them, and so farre exceeded their capacities to comprehend the reason and meanes how they should be made and done, that they thought they were rather the works of gods than of men, or at the leastwise they had bin given and taught us of the gods.[17]

In such circumstances, the Europeans quickly realized that technological advantage could be turned to spiritual and political profit. As Captain

George Waymouth cruised St. George's River in 1605, he performed various feats of technological and scientific wizardry for the visiting Indians, such as picking up a knife with a magnetized sword, in order, he said, "to cause them to imagine some great power in us: and for that to love and feare us."[18] The heavy salesmanship of the fur trade, the religious proselytizing of the missions, and the political push of the farming frontier all depended for their initial success on that foundation of love and fear.

As the second wave of colonists and administrators discovered, however, the novelty of European artifacts and techniques was not enough to secure the natives' long-range allegiance; "the fresh supplies of new and strange objects" simply "lessened their admiration."[19] Whether the Indians were willing to submit themselves to European domination out of love or fear depended largely on their own religious and moral ethos, the way they ordered their world and structured their relationships with other living things. The place assigned to the white man in that cosmology would do nearly as much to determine the Europeans' initial success in overcoming the "native obstacle" as any of the invaders' own efforts, however skillful or determined.

Several of the early explorers and some of their less perceptive colonial followers thought that the Indians were entirely devoid of religion, just as they appeared to have no laws or government ("*ni foi, ni loi, ni roi*"). Because they were ignorant of the Indian languages and touched only briefly the periphery of Indian life, they too often mistook their own ignorance for native deficiency. Typical of the group was Verrazzano, who, at the conclusion of his four-month tour of the Eastern Seaboard, confessed that "we were unable to find out by signs and gestures how much religious faith these people we found possess." His presumption, however, was that "they have neither religion nor laws, that they do not know of a First Cause or Author, that they do not worship the sky, the stars, the sun, the moon, or other planets, nor do they even practice any kind of idolatry. . . . We consider that they have no religion," he concluded, "and that they live in absolute freedom, and that everything they do proceeds from Ignorance."[20] More than a century later, Thomas Morton, one of the better and more sympathetic English observers, still maintained that "the Natives of New England have no worship nor religion at all."[21] What these early observers missed in Indian life, of course, were the familiar signs of institutionalized religion that would have struck any foreign observer who walked into a contemporary French or English town: churches and meetinghouses; prominent crosses or other images; religious specialists whose demeanor, hairstyles, and dress distinguished them from the general populace; private or public acts of prayer, worship, or sacrifice; and printed texts—Scripture—that codified national beliefs and prescribed ritual observances.

Shortly, however, a closer, more sustained look enabled settlers and missionaries to realize that native religion could not be forced easily into a procrustean bed of Euro-Christian manufacture, and that the Indians did indeed possess a modicum of religious beliefs and practices. Yet even this admission was tempered by the Christian conviction that Indian religion was not only hopelessly variable from tribe to tribe but was shamelessly tied to the Devil. Captain John Smith noted of the Powhatans of tidewater Virginia that "all things that were able to do them hurt beyond their prevention, they adore with their kinde of divine worship. . . . But their chiefe God they worship is the Divell. Him they call Oke & serve him more of feare then love. They say they have conference with him, and fashion themselves as neare to his shape as they can imagine." Powhatan worship, lamented another first-generation colonist, consisted largely of "many Devillish gestures with a Hellish noise."[22] Apparently the natives of New England were no better off. According to Edward Johnson, a Puritan progenitor, the Devil had them in "very great subjection, not using craft to delude them, as he ordinarily doth in most parts of the World: but kept them in a continuall slavish fear of him."[23] From Canada to the Carolinas, the anti-Christian "evil one" held the benighted natives in thralldom, especially their shamans and conjurers, who were thought to be on speaking terms with him. By this token, of course, native religious customs could be seen by the Christian strangers as "only superstitions, which we hope by the grace of God to change into true Religion."[24]

But one man's superstition is another man's religion, as a glance at any dictionary will quickly reveal. According to the *Oxford English Dictionary*, the word *superstition* derives from the Latin *superstitio*, "soothsaying," by way of Old French and Middle English. By the early decades of the sixteenth century it had come to mean "irrational religious belief or practice . . . founded on fear or ignorance," with the connotation that the religion was "false, pagan, or idolatrous." Webster's first (and unchanging) American definition merely augmented the word's pejorative character by speaking of "an irrational abject attitude of mind toward the supernatural, nature, or God, proceeding from ignorance, unreasoning fear of the unknown or myste-rious." Religion, on the other hand, was seen by the European wordsmiths as the "service and adoration of God or a god as expressed in forms of worship." Many skeptics have seen through the illusion of difference, but none more clearly than Thomas Hobbes. The "fear of things invisible," he wrote in *Leviathan*, "is the natural seed of that, which every one in himself calleth religion; and in them that worship, or fear that power otherwise than they do, superstition."[25] In short, *superstition* has no objective reality; it is merely an aspersion used by one group to denigrate the religion of another. Accord-ingly, it is best dropped from the historian's descriptive vocabulary.

For all their novelty and variety, Indian religions were at once bona fide and culturally pervasive, capable of explaining, predicting, and controlling the world in emotionally and intellectually satisfying ways. The native groups of eastern North America each possessed a religion in that they performed "a set of rituals, rationalized by myth, which mobilize[d] supernatural powers for the purpose of achieving or preventing transformations of state in man or nature."[26] Despite their linguistic and cultural differences, they shared enough beliefs and practices to allow generalization and, to some extent, comparison with Christianity. For the Indians were not as far from the Christian invaders in religious belief as they seemed to be in practice (or ritual), which partially explains the successes of the European missions as well as their failures.

The religious life of the Indians was given shape by the dominant medium through which they learned and communicated. In the absence of alphabetic writing and print, native life revolved around the spoken word. In this predominantly voice-and-ear world, life was dynamic, communal, and traditional.

To oral man, a word is a real happening, an event of power and personal force. Sound is evanescent and irreversible, and words cease to exist as soon as they are spoken; they are rooted only briefly in the passing present. Therefore, while they are being spoken they are precious, mysterious, and physically efficacious. Contrary to the children's jingle about sticks and stones, words can hurt, even kill, in the form of charms, spells, and hexes. In oral cultures, sound is more real or existential than other sense objects. It registers an immanent, personal *presence*—a speaker—who, like all beings, is complicated and unpredictable. This, in turn, demands alertness and commitment from the listener. Speakers are respected and never interrupted, and the art of public speaking is regarded as an important qualification for social leadership. Even Europeans who did not yet understand the native languages were impressed by the dignified character of Indian councils and by the respectful silence between one speech and the next. Words did not come cheaply to people for whom speaking was as real as shooting a deer or lifting a scalp.

Because speech requires an audience, an oral culture is intensely communal. In face-to-face societies, the context and meaning of spoken words are ready-made by virtue of the largely verbal socialization process through which each member has passed and the immediate presence of an audience. Knowledge and truth are not an individual matter so much as a corporate possession. Accordingly, oral man psychologically faces outward, toward the community from which he derives the meaning and veracity of his thoughts; to break with social values is to feel the shame of popular disapproval. He also participates extensively in the total tradition of his culture because specialization is limited and traditional lore is passed on to succeeding generations in socially sanctioned rites of passage.

By the same token, oral knowledge is relatively authoritarian, depending on tribal consensus rather than personal analysis. Due to the difficulties of acquisition, memory, and recall, oral knowledge is designedly uncreative, nonindividualized, and slow to change. It is stored in flexible units of memory, such as adages, proverbs, and repetitive, thematic formulas, rather than being dependent upon verbatim recall. Mnemonic devices, such as condolence canes, wampum belts, and medicine sticks, release the memory of these units and help in their reconstruction.

The nature of oral memory has three social consequences. First, since conscious contact with the past is governed by what people talk about, oral man has little perception of the past except in terms of the present. Myth and history tend to merge. Second, although oral knowledge is tenaciously conservative, it is not changeless because it has a system of elimination—the "structural amnesia" of human pragmatism and forgetfulness. For example, "deities and other supernatural agencies which have served their purpose can be quietly dropped from the contemporary pantheon; and as the society changes, myths too are forgotten, attributed to other personages, or transformed in their meaning." Finally, traditional knowledge is fragile because its very existence depends on the memories of mortal people, often specialists who are entrusted with major portions of the corporate wisdom. Abnormally high death rates in one or more generations sever the links of knowledge that bind the culture together. In this oral setting, then, native religious life was formed and found its meaning.[27]

Behind all native religion lay a cosmology, a hierarchy of states of being and a science of the principles of their interaction. The most populous tier consisted of supernatural beings known as "spirits" or "souls," who were continuous "selves" capable of changing form. Though they were invisible, they were audible to humans, with whom they could interact directly (such as by shaking a conjuring tent) and by whom they were manipulable in the right circumstances. Possessing will and consciousness, they knew the future as well as the past because of their continuity. Human souls, for instance, could separate temporarily from the corporeal body in sleep, travel to other realms of experience, and return to inform or instruct the person in dreams. Consequently, dreams were regarded by many Europeans as the heart of native religion, for the Indians believed that the supernatural guidance of their lives came from these "secret desires of the soul," which had to be fulfilled if they were to enjoy health, happiness, and success.[28] In death the soul left the body permanently to travel to an afterlife, which may have been vaguely conceived before the Christians began to preach of Heaven and Hell, but which seemed to be an ethereal version of the happiest life they had known on earth, replete with good hunting, abundant fruits and crops, and fine weather. For the long journey to this spirit village in the Southwest, the soul, which had assumed a visible, anthropomorphic ghostly shape, needed food and proper equipment. So the deceased was buried with small pots of food and the tools of his or her calling, so that the souls of these items would separate from the physical artifacts and accompany the traveler's soul.[29]

Just as angels differed in power and character from the Christian God, so Indian spirits and souls differed from the more powerful "guardian spirits," who enjoyed the ultimate power of metamorphosis, and the "Master Spirit" or "Creator." According to native belief, every plant and animal species had a "boss" or "owner" spirit whose experience encompassed all the individuals of the species. Many Indian myths were narratives of the "self" adventures of these spirits. More importantly, a young man (less commonly a young woman) who sought a supernatural talisman of success underwent a vision quest alone in the woods in hopes of receiving instruction from a guardian spirit. If he was successful, the being he saw after days of fasting and sleeplessness became his personal helpmate for the rest of his life, during the course of which it would give additional counsel, usually when ritually called upon in time of need. So important was the possession of a guardian spirit or *manitou*, wrote a Moravian missionary late in the eighteenth century, that an Indian without one "considers himself forsaken, has nothing upon which he may lean, has no hope of any assistance and is small in his own eyes. On the other hand those who have been thus favored possess a high and proud spirit."[30]

The ultimate being in the Indian pantheon, just as in the Christian, was an all-powerful, all-knowing Creator, who was the source of all good but whose presence was seldom or never felt. More frequently encountered, especially after the advent of the Hell-bearing Europeans, was an evil god, a *matchemanitou*, who purveyed devilry and death if not appeased. Much to the chagrin of the Christians, most of the Indians' religious worship seemed to center on attempts to deflect the maleficences of this deity instead of praising the benefactions of the Creator.

In the native cosmology, living things, whether natural or supernatural (a distinction the Indians did not make), possessed different amounts of power (*manitou* in Algonquian, *orenda* in Iroquoian languages), but each had its own particular strength. Nonhuman "persons" had inherent power to live, whereas humans received it from more powerful spirits and retained it by offerings and respectful behavior. Power could be acquired and lost. Since a person's current power was always uncertain, the Indians avoided competition, fostered respect for other persons, and approached all encounters as if potentially dangerous. Public display, boasting, and external symbols denoting possession of power were sharply circumscribed in most Eastern Woodland societies. For the individual, a major goal was to be in control of oneself and of one's destiny. The ideal was not to be controlled by one's physical or human environment, and those creatures who enjoyed the greatest autonomy ranked highest in Indian eyes. Getting through life without mishap, especially reaching advanced age, was a sign of control and respectful relations with the higher powers. Perhaps most immediately helpful were guardian spirits, who conferred specific abilities (rather than general power for all time) upon their Indian beneficiaries to help them achieve autonomy. At the same time, power conferred responsibility, and those who enjoyed power were expected to limit its exercise so as not to impinge upon others' independence. Many native myths and folktales feature animal or human protagonists who are brought low for their arrogance, overweening pride, or assumed powers. To render another person helpless or out of control, by the use of love, hunting, or gambling charms, for example, was regarded as the unsociable use of "bad medicine."[31]

The Indians mobilized the supernatural in their world by a number of religious observances and rituals. Just as in the Christian churches, some of these rituals could be performed by any individual. Tobacco was frequently burned to appease or open communication with the more powerful spirits of nature, and pipe smoke was blown upon an object which seemed to be inhabited by a *manitou*. Prayers of thanksgiving might be offered to the sun at daybreak or to other spirits for personal blessings, such as good hunting, health, or crops. Natives often sought to control potentially dangerous situations by making sacrifices of tobacco, furs, food, or weapons to the spirits of natural impediments, such as river rapids or the "four winds" which controlled weather conditions. If the danger was bodily, a steamy session of recollection and chanting in a sweat lodge was thought to bring relief and purify the soul.

Many rituals, however, were efficacious only when administered in a communal setting by a specially qualified priest or shaman. The native priest was nearly always a male religious specialist who through apprenticeship and visions had acquired extraordinary spiritual power. Unlike his Christian counterparts, however, he possessed *personal* supernatural power that allowed him to manipulate the spiritual cosmology on his tribesmen's behalf; he was not a mere intermediary whose only strength lay in explanation and supplication. So individual was a shaman's power that it could be transferred or lent to an assistant, who would apply it on his master's behalf. But because all spiritual power in the native universe was double-edged, the shaman was as feared as he was revered. For while he could induce trances that made him impervious to pain, influence the weather, predict the future, and interpret dreams for the villagers, he could also cause as well as cure witchcraft, the magical intrusion of a small item into the body or the capture of a soul in dream by any person with spiritual power, which caused illness and eventually death. Bewitchment was the most feared calamity in Indian life because the assailant and the cause were unknown unless discovered by a shaman whose personal power was greater than that of the witch.

In the mixed-economy tribes south of the Canadian Shield, the primary communal rituals revolved around the annual agricultural-botanical cycle from which they derived a substantial portion of their diet. Among farmers whose major crop was maize, planting, green corn, and harvest festivals were important events in the ceremonial calendar.[32] Many tribes also gave communal thanks for the appearance of maple sap in late winter and of the strawberry in early summer. The first deer or bear shot by a young boy or of the season was also honored with a village feast thanking the animal's "boss" spirit for allowing it to be killed for human use. In all feasts scrupulous care was taken to enforce certain taboos on the sex and age of the participants and the treatment of the bones and other remains.

Another reason for communal rituals in these groups was to cure disease. Many tribes—the Iroquois and Ojibwa among them—had specialized medicine societies which operated largely in secret to cure potential members of physical and psychological ailments. But in groups where the dream was operative, communal feasts, sports contests, and even sexual orgies might be called to satisfy a sick person's dream and thereby effect his cure. In New England, at least, kinsmen and villagers crowded into the lodges of people undergoing treatment to assist the shaman in his drumming, chanting, and other physical exertions.

1. John White, artist and later governor of the Roanoke Colony, painted this Algonquian "conjurer" or shaman on the coast of North Carolina in 1585. Thought to be in league with the devil, the shaman wore a small black bird above his ear as a badge of office and a medicine pouch at his side. Reproduced by courtesy of the Trustees of the British Museum.

Finally, in all the woodland tribes, especially the northernmost groups that depended on large game animals for much of the year, tribesmen came together in lesser or greater numbers to prognosticate the location of game, changes in the weather, and even the outcome of war. If the prediction was unfavorable, shaman-led ceremonies might be held to alter the outcome. Hunters north of the St. Lawrence and Great Lakes often resorted to group rituals to bring heavy snow, which was conducive to tracking moose and elk and also slowed the animals' progress, and to prophesy the location of the animals through divination by fire, water, and bones. Their snowshoe dances honored the north wind for bringing the first big snow, just as farming tribes celebrated the warm spring rains from the south. The powerful "persons" of the natural elements were thanked when they helped the Indians achieve autonomy and supplicated for relief when they interfered.[33]

From this perspective, the Indians' initial reactions to the Europeans made eminently good sense. Apparently blessed by the gods with a preternatural technological capability, the white strangers clearly merited respect and even worship from the natives. But because they appeared to possess power surpassing anything the Indians had known, the Europeans were doubly unpredictable and therefore doubly dangerous. Not only were their customs and behavior bizarre, but the true magnitude of their spiritual power was difficult to measure. When it became clear, however, that the strangers were disagreeably boastful of their prowess and sought to compromise the autonomy of the natives in nearly every sphere of life, the Indians modified their initial respect and began to harden their resistance to the cultural blandishments of the Christians. In the face of still awesome white power, many natives launched a search for new sources of spiritual power with which to maintain control over their own lives and fate. In some groups this search led to nativistic revitalization movements, which sought to purge Indian culture of any European influence and to fortify it by a dedicated return to pristine aboriginal values and conduct. In still other groups, the incorporative, non-exclusive nature of Indian religion allowed them to add segments of Christian belief and practice to traditional observances. This syncretic blend preserved the most efficacious elements of the old religion while drawing on the demonstrable power of the new.

Whatever their response, the Indians soon found themselves locked in a permanent struggle for social and cultural autonomy, the outcome of which even their most powerful conjurers could not have foreseen. Although that struggle early took political and economic forms, for many natives and Europeans it remained primarily a contest between two concepts of spiritual power and the quality of life each promised.

BLACK ROBES
AND GRAY

CHAPTER TWO

Reconnaissance

*[He] much desired to see Adam's will
to learn how he had partitioned the world.*
THE CARDINAL OF TOLEDO, OF FRANCIS I

In the seventeenth century, French colonization in the New World was launched on waves of pious intent. Canadian schoolchildren still learn that New France was founded on "fur, fish, and the faith," and the tall ubiquity of Jesuit "Black Robes" in the national imagery of the past confirms the message. But in the sixteenth century, when the French exploration and tentative settlement of North America began, religious conversion of the natives was a tardy afterthought. In the minds of the French venturers who risked their lives on the unpredictable North Atlantic and of the monarchs who sent them, the faith—the shape of which was still being hotly contested in the French wars of religion in the last decade of the century—could not compete with salt cod, animal pelts, gold, and the Northwest Passage to the eastern spicery as an inducement to sail.

By 1540, however, an "ostentatious show of missionary zeal" began to color royal colonial commissions in an effort to "clothe the extra-territorial activities of the kings of France in apostolic respectability."[1] The monarchs' worldly and even papal counterparts were not taken in by these semantical tactics, nor should we be. But by the same token, we should carefully discriminate between the salient motives of one period and those of another. Samuel Champlain, the founder of Quebec, and Paul Chomedey de Maisonneuve, the progenitor of Montreal, were separated from Jacques Cartier, the first Frenchman to visit both places, by more than time. The historical context of the seventeenth century was simply different: the promising (if still fragile) implantation of commercial colonies in American soil allowed, even demanded, the serious promotion of Catholic missions. For once the French converted the fur trade from a coastal to a continental enterprise and dotted Acadia and the St. Lawrence with vulnerable settlements, they, like the other European colonial powers, were forced to solve their own version of the "Indian problem." All the major powers eventually learned that the missionary thrust for the salvation of the "savages" was indispensable to the sheer survival of "civility" in the wilderness, but the French absorbed the lesson fastest and best, due in no small part to their humbling Canadian experience in the sixteenth century.

The first official French voyage to North America was Verrazzano's reconnaissance of 1524. Rather than follow the northern Atlantic routes of French, Spanish, and Portuguese fishermen to the teeming banks off Newfoundland, Verrazzano set a more southerly course that landed him in late March on the Outer Banks of North Carolina. This was a disappointing landfall because he had set out to reach Cathay and the "extreme eastern coast of Asia," and the extension of *Terra Nova* north of Spanish Florida could only be regarded as a rude "obstacle." So for the better part of four months Verrazzano cruised north along the Atlantic littoral to Maine in fruitless search of "some strait to get through to the Eastern Ocean." Understandably, conversion of the various natives he happened upon—most friendly and receptive, a few hostile and suspicious—did not occur to the adventurer. Instead, he "baptized" several features of geography with Franco-Christian names, and compared an awestruck native man to a praying "monk" and native copper earrings to "paternostri" beads. The best hint he gave of the future direction of French colonization lay in his presumption that the Indians had no religion, a conclusion to which he seems to have been led in part by their courteous imitation of "everything they saw us Christians do with regard to divine worship, with the same fervor and enthusiasm that we had."[2]

Ten years later, after Pope Clement VII had assured Francis I that he might explore lands not discovered by other crowns, Jacques Cartier was sent to find a breach in the continental barrier and to "discover certain islands and countries where it is said there must be a great quantity of gold and other riches."[3] Probing the western coast of Newfoundland, Prince Edward Island, the Gaspé, and the eastern half of Anticosti Island, the experienced Malouin narrowly missed the St. Lawrence, which, while it was not the hoped-for cut to Cathay, led to treasures of a different kind. The crew erected crosses in several harbors, not to signal the conversion of the natives or even to claim French sovereignty, but as beacons and markers for future voyagers.[4] At the installation of a thirty-foot cross on Gaspé Bay, the assembled French knelt, lifted their clasped hands heavenward, and as best they could strove to suggest by signs to the curious natives that by means of the cross "we had our redemption." When the Indians later proffered furs for trade, the French exchanged a number of secular items but, apparently, no religious rings, crosses, or Agnus Dei medals. After being joyfully received by the local Algonquians and by a party of visiting Iroquoian fishermen from Stadacona (Quebec), who not only rubbed the strangers' arms and torsos in greeting but traded the furs literally off their own backs, it was easy for the French to believe that "they are a people who would be easy to convert." But nothing was done at the time for lack of priests, time, and motivation. Even the two young Iroquoians who were abducted and taken to France to learn French were not baptized during their one-year stay, nor were any of the Indian words solicited from them of a religious nature: *God* was missing, and *camet* was translated as simply "the heavens" or "sky." More characteristic entries were the native equivalents of *codfish, gold, sword, red cloth*, and *privy parts.*[5] Nevertheless, the religious seed dropped by Cartier on this first voyage to Canada did not fail to take root in the mind of his royal sponsor.

Since the 1534 voyage had not discovered an easy passage to the Orient, Francis sent Cartier and three ships to continue the search the following year. The crew of 110 included the two Indian interpreters, Domagaya and Taignoagny, but no Catholic priests. Knowing that his Indian guides had come down a great river to fish on the Gaspé, Cartier set out to probe the length of Anticosti Island, which he had previously taken for a peninsula. But not before exploring the coast of Labrador to "make sure that no strait existed along the north shore"; the spicy dream of Cathay lingered even as the air filled with the coniferous fragrance of a new world. On August 24 the French launched themselves up the river soon called the St. Lawrence, where they found the large native towns of Stadacona (home of their guides) and Hochelaga (now Montreal). They also listened wide-eyed to stories of a not-too-distant "kingdom of the Saguenay," blessed with "immense quantities of gold, rubies and other rich things," where the inhabitants were "white as in France and go clothed in woolens."[6]

By mid-September the French had grounded their two largest ships in the St. Charles River opposite Stadacona for the winter, established working relations with Donnaconna, the village headman, and determined to visit Hochelaga over the stubborn resistance of the Stadaconans. Almost at once, without priest or chaplain, the religious education of the Indians began. In an effort to dissuade Cartier from reaching their rivals at Hochelaga, the Stadaconans warned him that Cudouagny, their supreme deity, had predicted that Hochelaga would be plagued by "so much ice and snow that all would perish." In a response that would become nearly universal in the seventeenth century, the French all laughed at this transparent ruse and called the Indian god an ignorant fool. For they knew with certainty that "Jesus would keep them safe from the cold if they would trust in him." Whereupon the cate-chized interpreter Taignoagny asked Cartier if he had spoken to Jesus. The captain coolly replied that he had not but "his priests had done so and there would be fine weather."[7] And off he and fifty sailors went upriver to put the lie to the native prophecy.

Stepping ashore on Montreal Island, Cartier was greeted by a thousand Hochelagans who danced for joy, rained fish and cornbread into his boats, and brought their babies to be fondled. He reciprocated by distributing pewter paternoster beads, knives, and hatchets. In a traditional welcoming ceremony on the path to the imposing town, Cartier presented to one of the headmen a crucifix, "which he made [the Indian] kiss and then hung it about his neck." After passing through acres of cornfields and the single gate of a triple palisade, the party was seated in a public square surrounded by fifty longhouses. There the *Agouhanna* or chief asked Cartier to rub his limbs, which were completely paralyzed, in hopes that the stranger's touch could effect a cure beyond the capacity of his own shamans. As soon as Cartier had applied his hands—and received the chief's porcupine-quill "crown" in re-

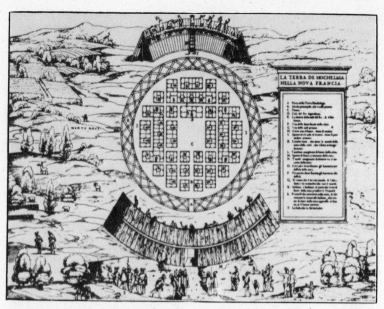

2. Hochelaga, a large Iroquoian village on the site of Montreal, was visited by Jacques Cartier in 1535. This plan was drawn by Giacomo Gastaldi in 1556 from Cartier's written description rather than the artist's personal observation. Although the palisades are inaccurate, the natives' fertile cornfields and amicable reception of the French are faithful to Cartier's account. From Giovanni Battista Ramusio, *Terzo volume della navigationi et viaggi* (Venice, 1565).

turn—a host of other invalids were brought in to receive the same treatment. "Seeing the suffering of these people and their faith," the captain prayed and made the sign of the cross over them before reading the story of Christ's Passion, "word for word." Although the natives looked up to heaven and imitated the French gestures, they were probably more grateful for the presents Cartier distributed—utilitarian tools to the men, decorative items to the women. The children scrambled for "little rings and pewter *agnus Dei*."[8]

When the French regrouped on the St. Charles for the winter, Cartier took the opportunity to show the Stadaconans their error in religion, calling their god "a wicked spirit who deceived them," and to preach a brief version of his own Christian faith. One crucial lesson that was probably not lost on the natives (assuming the interpreters were equal to the task) was the necessity of baptism, without which, Cartier emphasized, "we perish in hell." All this they seemingly accepted, for they immediately deemed their gods "nought" and asked to be baptized on the spot, which caught the lay proselytizers off guard. "Since we did not know their real intention and state of mind, and had no one to explain to them our faith," wrote the voyage's chronicler, "an excuse was made to them" that on a return trip the French would bring "priests and some chrism" to perform the service properly. The Indians had no difficulty accepting this because Domagaya and Taignoagny "had seen several children baptized in Brittany."[9]

By design the Stadaconans, who lived a league or two away, were also denied another ceremony that would have been, in its own way, equally edifying. When a severe outbreak of land scurvy afflicted the ice-bound French, killing twenty-five and incapacitating all but a handful, Cartier leaned an image of the Virgin Mary against a tree a bowshot from the fort. On the following Sunday, the able-bodied fell into a solemn procession to the image, singing the seven Psalms of David and the Litany of All the Saints and praying to the Virgin to intercede with her son for compassion. After mass even the rugged seadog Cartier, who remained untouched by the scurvy, vowed to make a pilgrimage to our Lady of Rocamadour, a famous French shrine, if God returned him home safely. Because native psychology was still largely indecipherable to the French, this parade of invalids was clearly something they did not wish the Stadaconans to see. Ironically, it was the pagan Domagaya who brought salvation to the Christians by showing them the curative secret of the white cedar.[10]

The final Christian act of Cartier's stay in Canada involved the erection of a thirty-five-foot cross to commemorate the festival of the Holy Cross on May 3, 1536. But the message for the Stadaconans, who flocked to watch the spectacle and to ponder the meaning of the royal escutcheon attached to the cross, must have been mixed. For Cartier proceeded to entice Donnaconna, the two interpreters, and two other headmen into the fort, capture them, and take them to France for an audience with the king. They and five children who had been given to Cartier as tokens of alliance never saw Canada again. When Cartier finally returned to Stadacona five years later, he told the villagers that Donnaconna had died and was buried in France but that the others "stayed there as great Lords, and were maried, and would not returne backe into their Countrey." But the unvarnished truth would have been much less comforting: nine of the ten had died, and several perhaps had not even received the timely consolation of a Christian demise. Three were not baptized until January 1539, perhaps on their deathbeds, and others, including Donnaconna, had to ask to be baptized after "a long time" in France. The Church eventually may have drawn these poor Canadian souls to its bosom, but certainly less warmly than the Crown received Cartier's offerings of Canadian gold (actually pyrite), however worthless the latter proved to be.[11]

Cartier left Canada in 1536 confident that the relatively sedentary natives he had met on the St. Lawrence "could easily be moulded in the way one would wish." Since he promised to return with ordained priests and consecrated oil, we might easily assume that the mold he envisioned would take a decidedly religious shape. Certainly the royal commissions issued to Cartier in October 1540 and the following January to Jean-François de La Rocque, sieur de Roberval, the nobly born commander of the third expedition, put a high verbal premium on religious conversion. Both commissions spoke of how Cartier and other French pilots had brought from Brazil and other parts of the New World "savage men living without knowledge of God and without usage of reason" for the purpose of having them instructed in the "love and fear of God and of His holy law and Christian doctrine." Thus catechized, baptized, and semicivilized, these new-made men were to be restored to their native lands "in company with many of our subjects who had good will thereto, the more easily to persuade the other tribes of those countries to accept our holy faith." Francis I was sending Cartier back to the elusive Saguenay, the source of "several good commodities," as he coyly put it, to "push further inland," to "converse with the inhabitants and to dwell among them if need be," and to "do what is agreeable to God our Creator and Redeemer, and to increase of His holy and hallowed name, and of our mother the Holy Catholic Church."[12]

While maintaining roughly the same religious course, however, Roberval's instructions took a somewhat different tack. His general goal was still the "sanctification of His holy name and the advancement of our Christian faith," but the means to be used had a distinctly Spanish flavor. Roberval was to plant in Canada a whole French colony—men and women, soldiers and citizens, liberal artists and mechanics—who would seek to "attract" the natives to Christian living by building "towns and forts, temples and churches." If the natives would not voluntarily put themselves and their lands in the hands of the French, however, Roberval was to employ French laws and "force of arms" to "make them live by reason and civility [police] and in the fear and love of God." Obviously, conquest was seen as the likeliest road to conversion.[13]

Initial doubt about the bona fide place of religion in the French plan is raised by the character of the instruments chosen: Cartier and Roberval were allowed to draw their pool of colonists from the nation's prisons—fifty convicts for Cartier, an unlimited number for Roberval. It is not difficult to imagine how the Indians responded to the religious lure of men who were murderers and thieves and women who had prostituted themselves, sold their daughters, and murdered their sons-in-law. Even stranger is the absence of any evidence that Catholic priests, especially missionaries trained to cope with aboriginal pagans, made the journey to Canada. An anonymous shopping list of men and supplies made in September 1538 does mention "six men of the Church" and the "things required for divine service." But three years passed before the first five ships under Cartier weighed anchor, and the record is silent about the presence of churchmen on board. In April 1541, just one month before Cartier's departure, a Spanish spy reported from Saint-Malo that "ten men of the church" were in Roberval's party. But Roberval did not leave until the following year, and again no priests appear in the chronicle of his voyage, although several gentlemen and pilots are listed by name. Moreover, Roberval was a prominent Protestant who, when he did sail, may not have been eager for Catholic company.[14]

Another reason to doubt the prominence of Indian conversion in French policy at this time was the utter absence of any mention of it by the Spanish and Portuguese spies, ambassadors, and officials who closely monitored the colony's progress to ensure that France did not encroach on their New World possessions. Surely the Spanish, whose pride in their own baptism of thousands of Latin American natives was unbounded, would have protested to the pope any infringement of their spiritual prerogative, especially if it happened to coincide with threats to their economic well-being. Yet the Iberian partners painted a single-stroke picture of French motivation: "they think, from what they learn," wrote the cardinal of Seville, "that these provinces are rich in gold and silver." A Portuguese informer had the same impression after a long talk with King Francis over sea charts and an astrolabe. Believing that Donnaconna was an "honest man" who spoke the "strict truth," the king had bought the Indian's story of "many mines of gold and silver" and an "abundance of clove, nutmeg and pepper" in the kingdom of Saguenay, and was financing a third expedition to collect the treasure.[15]

Even if the French had gone to Canada to convert the natives, their social relations there left room for little religious effort and less success. The arrival in August 1541 of Cartier's flotilla of several hundred colonists soon unnerved the Stadaconans, who in any case could not have swallowed the captain's excuse for not returning their kinsmen within a year, as he had promised. With the local tribe in "wonderful doubt and feare," Cartier wisely sailed past his old station on the St. Charles and settled on the western end of Cape Diamond, where the Cap Rouge River empties into the St. Lawrence. On the top and at the base of a high cliff, the French built two large forts for protection. Apparently they were not sufficient. Cartier pulled up stakes the following spring and sailed for France with several barrels of Canadian "gold," "silver," and "diamonds." When he unexpectedly met Roberval's three ships and two hundred colonists in Newfoundland, he excused his abrupt departure with the confession that "hee could not with his small company withstand the Savages, which went about dayly to annoy him." In September Portuguese fishermen from Newfoundland corroborated his tale of hardship. One had learned that the "fierce and valiant" Indians had killed several French carpenters who were building houses at Cap Rouge. Another, who had entertained a party of upper-river natives on shipboard in the St. Lawrence Gulf, was told that they had killed "more than thirty-five of Jacques' men." Between scurvy and short rations, which had to be supplemented with Indian fish and corn, Roberval's group fared no better and returned home the following summer. In these circumstances it is unlikely that the Indians succumbed to Catholic catechizing or the allure of the French lifestyle.[16]

After the failure of the Cartier and Roberval expeditions, the French monarchs all but gave up the search for a "New France" in the northern latitudes of North America. The south was even more unpromising. French attempts in the 1550s to establish a commercial beachhead in Brazil were firmly repulsed by the Portuguese, and in 1565 the Spanish delivered a deathblow to René de Laudonnière's fractious Huguenot colony in Florida. In these military responses and at the conference table, the Iberian powers made it clear that they would tolerate no trespass on their papal donations.

At the same time, France, though it pressed no territorial claims of its own, maintained that the seas were common to all and reserved the right to explore and trade in any New World lands not "populated and defended" by other Christian princes, positions that Spain and Portugal tacitly accepted.[17] Although the peace treaty at Cateau-Cambrésis in 1559 ended a half-century of Franco-Spanish conflict, the outbreak of the French wars of religion quickly turned French energies and attention away from the New World. Only two activities were capable of rekindling French interest in northern America— fishing and fur trading.

Throughout the sixteenth century, the Grand Banks were a steady magnet to Norman, Breton, and Basque fishing crews seeking to profit from the enormous Catholic demand for flake-dried and lightly salted fresh ("green") cod.[18] But the economic potential of Canadian fur developed only gradually during the course of the century. Cartier had brought home from his first voyage a number of furs traded by the Indians around the Gaspé, but he considered them all of "small value." The furry bounty of his second voyage was appraised somewhat higher. Francis I and the Portuguese cosmographer Lagarto were equally delighted that Canada bred "certain animals whose hides as leather are worth ten cruzados each, and for this sum they are sold in France."[19] Not until the 1580s did the French passion for furs begin to rival their earlier infatuation with gold.

Richard Hakluyt, the English cosmographer, was in France on a diplomatic mission when the French rediscovery of the St. Lawrence began to pay big dividends. According to Hakluyt, the Indian memory of the fate of Donnaconna and his fellow captives had closed the Laurentian trade to the French until 1581. In that year, fading memories and liberal gifts reopened the major artery to northern fur, and a small bark returned with a cargo profitable enough to launch a larger ship the following year. When the second vessel returned to Saint-Malo, the investors reaped profits of 1,400 to 1,500 percent. Valeron Perosse, the king's skinner, paid 4,000 crowns for "sables, bevers, [and] otters," and "great quantities of buff [elk or moose] hides" were sold into the Low Countries.[20]

The enormous profit margin of the second year prompted French merchants in 1583 to send at least three large ships to the St. Lawrence and another to Cape Breton and Nova Scotia. At season's end, Hakluyt (whose father was a skinner and presumably taught him the value of a pelt) saw in Perosse's Paris shop "precious furres" worth 20,000 crowns, a fourth of which had come from the enterprising Malouins. One of the seagoing merchants who did well for himself was Etienne Bellenger of Rouen, whom Hakluyt visited. From his four-month jaunt around Nova Scotia and the Bay of Fundy, Bellenger netted, from an outlay of only 40 livres (£4) in "trifles," a cargo valued at 440 crowns (£130), which included dressed and painted deerskins, sealskins, fisher, otter, lynx, and enough beaver to make six hundred hats. Although Bellenger lost two men and a pinnace to hostile natives, he planned to return to the area in 1584. His competitors from Saint-Malo did send five ships to the St. Lawrence, from which they received two

Indians and such a "swete" lading that they planned to double their sails in 1585.[21]

Bellenger's voyage was significant not only because it cast some French light on resources south of the St. Lawrence but because it was financed largely (and covertly) by Cardinal Charles of Bourbon, archbishop of Rouen, whose coat of arms Bellenger tacked to a tall Acadian tree. By the terms of engagement, Bellenger with twenty men was supposed to establish a trading station and spend the winter, but the Indian mishap scuttled that plan somewhere en route. This station may have been meant to grow into something more permanent. In January 1584 Hakluyt learned from Perosse and André Thevet, the royal cosmographer, that the cardinal, the duc de Joyeuse, admiral of France, and some friends "have had a meaning to send out certayne ships to inhabite some place for the north part of America, and to carry thither many friers and other religiouse persons." Although Hakluyt thought they were in "no haste," he may have been mistaken: perhaps they intended to establish a Catholic colonial claim before the current titleholder and viceroy of New France, the marquis de La Roche, could plant a Protestant refuge there. They may have been less anxious after La Roche's largest ship, bearing three hundred colonists, broke up off the coast of Saintonge later in the year.[22]

Despite this substantial setback, La Roche was determined to take advantage of the extensive powers he had been granted by Henry III in 1577 and 1578. His royal commissions, which expressed confidence in the "zeal and fervent devotion he bears for God's service as a Christian," endowed him with personal title to any new lands "he shall conquer and take from [the] barbarians" who happened to live there. The religious wars put a seven-year damper on his colonial projects when he was imprisoned by the Catholic League. After he was freed in 1596, however, Henry IV renewed La Roche's Canadian governorship and added to it exclusive rights to the fur trade, which had become so important in the intervening years, perhaps as consolation for depriving La Roche of personal title to Canada and the rank of viceroy. Recalling Francis I's confidence in Roberval for the work of Christian conquest, Henry conferred upon La Roche the same right to send convicts for "this holy work and advancement of the Catholic Faith." The marquis eventually chose forty hardy vagabonds from the streets of Rouen to populate his surprisingly long-lived colony on Sable Island, a thin bow-shaped spit of sand and rocks ninety miles off Nova Scotia's Cape Canso. In the absence of Indians, the colonists were expected to harvest the island's seal, walrus, sea lion, and fox populations by themselves, which they actually managed to do for a time. But by 1603, when the colony was five years old, only eleven settlers remained, and they were repatriated after murder and rebellion engulfed the post.[23]

The religious results of this Christian colony in the middle of the ocean were no better than those secured by Jacques Noël (Cartier's nephew) and Chaton de La Jannaye, who in 1588 were given a twelve-year trading and mining concession in Canada—soon withdrawn—to continue the work begun by Cartier. They, too, were to be allowed convicts, in their case sixty a year, with which to establish a colony, work the mines, and trade with the Indians "in every peaceful fashion, to attract and attempt to instruct and lead them to acquaintance with God and His Christian Faith."[24] But the partnership was stillborn, and no colonists were ever plucked from prison.

The official French faith in malefactors and murderers as missionaries to the Indians must be seen as either a severe case of noble dementia or, more plausibly, strong evidence that until the French could plant themselves securely in a New France, all talk of religious conversion was premature and disingenuous. When Champlain founded Quebec at the foot of a massive rock overlooking the St. Lawrence in 1608, the French at last had a suitable place and a genuine need for Catholic missions, which were not long in coming.

CHAPTER THREE

Beyond the Comptoir

. . . A country as large as half of all Europe.
LA CHAMBRE DU COMMERCE

The choice of the Quebec site came only after a four-year nautical search that encompassed the rocky promontories of Acadia (Nova Scotia, New Brunswick, and eastern Maine) and the gentler coasts of southern New England. Unlike the Spanish in Florida, the French in these early years were not obliged to erect a military stronghold against jealous European interlopers. Nor did they seek to plant prolific colonies of self-sufficient farmers, as the English were soon to do at Plymouth and Massachusetts Bay. The French rejected a series of actual and potential sites as far south as Cape Cod because they did not provide ready access to a profitable supply of prime furs, the only American product that in the short run could justify a settlement of any size and amortize its debts. The fisheries required little more than temporary summer flakes and stages on shore for the drying of cod, although a handful of winterers could prepare the facilities for an early spring start; Acadia's well-favored coasts harbored many such settlements during the late sixteenth and seventeenth centuries. The extraction of minerals would have to wait upon bona fide discovery and technological investment. Only a relatively small establishment of traders, strategically placed on a major river offering easy communication with fur-hunting natives, would serve French purposes. The four years before 1608 were spent in search of such a site. Although the lands south of the St. Lawrence did not yield one, the French gained invaluable knowledge of northeastern coastal waters, the durable friendship of the native Micmacs and Eastern Abenakis, and a permanent if tenuous foothold in Acadia.

By 1603 France enjoyed enough foreign and domestic tranquillity to look again to North America for mercantilist adventure. The Huguenot king Henry IV had begun to heal the nation's deep religious wounds by converting to Catholicism and granting toleration to the Protestants in the Edict of Nantes, and to unite the political kingdom against the usurpations of Spain, the Netherlands, and overmighty lords. In that year he appointed one of his faithful Protestant officers in the religious wars, Pierre du Gua, sieur de Monts, his lieutenant-general between forty and forty-six degrees latitude (approximately Philadelphia to New Brunswick), and gave him a ten-year monopoly of the Indian trade to help offset the expense of settling sixty colonists a year. The king instructed him to establish French sovereignty over the "Godless barbarians" of the area, by "open war" if necessary, in order to discover mines of gold, silver, and copper, profit by trade and commerce, preclude the English (who had been probing New England), and "summon and instruct" the natives in order to "provoke and rouse them to the knowledge of God and to the light of the Christian faith and religion" and establish its permanent "exercise and profession" among them.[1]

At the same time, a complementary commission from the admiral of France sounded a new note that would soon swell the official plans for New France to ungainly proportions. Unlike his predecessors, who had failed to found lasting settlements and garrisons, de Monts was now instructed not only to give the deficient natives a pew in the Holy Apostolic Church and a junior partnership in European capitalism but also to lead them to "civilization of manners" and "an ordered life." Although the means to implement this goal were not spelled out, the royal officers intimated that peace-giving alliances and treaties and the industrious example of civilized colonists would draw the Indians into the French fold. Like his sixteenth-century predecessors, de Monts was given the privilege of recruiting vagabonds and convicts. But, perhaps symbolizing the fresh start of the new century, he chose to leave them at home and took instead a large number of gentlemen, of whom "not a few were of noble birth," and a wide array of skilled craftsmen and mariners. Most conspicuous among this crew were Jean de Biencourt, sieur de Poutrincourt, a nobleman in search of an American home for his family and servants, and Champlain, de Monts's cartographer and geographer.[2]

In the summer of 1604, after exploring the Annapolis Basin and the Bay of Fundy, de Monts's three ships anchored four miles up the Ste. Croix River (the present border between Maine and New Brunswick) at an island about half a mile from shore. There the French built a winter settlement for seventy-nine men, hoping its strategic location would guard the river from competitors and provide a ready market for native furs. But the island failed to live up to its advance billing: it had no firewood or fresh water, it was too small and its soil too thin for farming, winter ice floes separated the colonists from their mill, charcoal pit, and wheat fields on the west bank, and, perhaps most discouragingly, the site was not a major Indian entrepôt for trade. When thirty-five men died from scurvy and another twenty came close to dying, de Monts decided to give the settlement more southern exposure.[3]

The following summer de Monts moved the settlement across the Bay of Fundy to Port Royal in the Annapolis Basin, where he had given Poutrincourt a favorite piece of land as a gift. This site was decidedly better than Ste. Croix: the buildings were framed in a closed quadrangle against the cold wind, hunting and fishing were bountiful, the local Micmacs under Membertou were hospitable and commercially cooperative, and only twelve of the forty-nine men who wintered there succumbed to scurvy. In the months before and the year after the move, however, the French reconnoitered the coast to the southwest in search of the perfect location. With gifts of knives, biscuits, and rosaries, they established amicable relations with the coastal villagers as far south as Stage Harbor (Chatham) on Cape Cod. But the coastal geography of New England did not meet their criteria, and short supplies and the lateness of the season prevented them from rediscovering the broad Hudson, with its easy access to the Iroquois, the Great Lakes, and the rich beaver lands beyond.[4] The harbors encountered were either landlocked or filled with dangerous shoals and islands. South from the Saco River in Maine the Indians' extensive cornfields and substantial palisaded villages indicated little interest in the gathering of furs. As a disappointed Champlain put it, "They are not so much great hunters as good fishermen and tillers of the soil."[5] Even the Abenaki hunters at the mouths of the Kennebec and Penobscot were keener on political alliance with the French than serious trading.[6]

On Cape Cod hostilities erupted in 1605 over a stolen kettle, and an Indian was killed. Only de Monts's forbearance prevented more casualties and obtained the release of an innocent native hostage. But the following year, when Poutrincourt and Champlain returned to the Cape to resume their search, four crewmen were attacked and killed at Chatham. When the victims were buried near a large cross, the natives razed the cross, desecrated the bodies, and made obscene gestures. Three days later, forced by contrary winds to remain in "Misfortune Harbor," the French revenged themselves on a few local Indians who came to trade and claimed to be unrelated to the troublemakers from the interior. Poutrincourt hatched a plot to capture and enslave them for "forced labor" at the Port Royal hand mill and at wood-cutting, but instead six or seven were "hacked and hewn in pieces" by hasty French swords.[7]

As these misadventures were turning French thoughts away from the southern coasts, word came in May 1607 that de Monts's monopoly was about to be rescinded and his trading company was on the brink of ruin. Partially to compensate de Monts for his heavy expenses in Acadia, the king granted him a one-year monopoly of the St. Lawrence trade for the following year. Glad to escape the "envious and intractable dispositions of the peoples along the coasts," de Monts regrouped his investors around the hope of "greater advantages in the interior, where the peoples are civilized, and where it is easier to plant the Christian faith and to establish such order as is necessary for the preservation of a country."[8] When Champlain was sent to build a fortified *habitation* where the river narrows at Quebec, de Monts and the French at last had a year-round establishment capable of intercepting native fur traders before they reached the competitive summer port at Tadoussac, of launching further discoveries into the mysterious *pays d'en haut*, and of growing into a sturdy scion of European culture and religion. For all these tasks, the French soon realized that Catholic missionaries were tremendous assets, if not actually indispensable.

Although the birth of Quebec signaled the advent of a permanent French presence in North America, neither was particularly auspicious. For its first twenty years, New France was so neglected and undernourished by the mother country that it resembled less a colony than a mere *comptoir*, a "storehouse for the skins of dead animals."[9] In 1627 only 107 Frenchmen resided in Canada; only 18 had come as settlers in the previous twelve years. The rest were soldiers, priests, or employees of the trading companies that dominated Laurentian life. The paucity of population owed to the economics of colonization at that time. The Crown was unable to finance American settlements because of the heavy cost of putting down civil disorder at home and keeping the Thirty Years' War from spilling over France's eastern borders. The only way to establish a firm French claim, therefore, was to grant a trading monopoly to a consortium of French merchants—typically Normans and Bretons—for a specified period, commonly ten or fifteen years. In exchange for the right to extract as much wealth from the country as they could and to import it at reduced tariffs, the company was obliged to transport a number of settlers each year. In 1615 the prevailing company also agreed to ship and feed six Recollect priests, who would begin to convert the natives to Catholic Christianity.

Receiving a parchment monopoly was one thing, enforcing it and capitalizing on it another. The early companies were beset by a host of obstacles they could never completely overcome: underfunding, feuds between Protestants and Catholics, the untimely death of partners and noble patrons, shipwreck and piracy, freebooting traders who ignored the monopoly, and crowned heads who truncated it. In such precarious circumstances the companies understandably were eager to minimize expenses, which they did largely by maintaining a bare-bones staff in Canada, ignoring their obligation to transport settlers (at 1,000 livres a head), and jealously guarding access to the fur-bearing natives who came downriver to trade. In other words, a *comptoir* was all they wanted at Quebec; settlement of Frenchmen and especially Indians was deemed counterproductive and strongly resisted.[10]

From the moment they arrived in 1615, the Recollects ran afoul of company policy. To the hardheaded traders who minded the Quebec store, the otherworldly mendicants were commercially naive and politically troublesome. The missionaries believed that before the Indians could be converted to Christianity they must be inured to French society and "civilized" by French laws and mores. "They must be fixed and induced to clear and cultivate the land, to work at different trades, like the French," argued Father Le Caron, none of which could transpire "unless the colony multiplies and spreads in all directions."[11] In company eyes, of course, this was bad economics because it sought to turn good Indian hunters into poor French farmers at the expense of the fur trade, and to introduce potential French competitors for the remaining pelts. So the company did its best to discourage French farmers from coming to Canada—so successfully that they were accused of having failed to clear "a single arpent of land" during their tenure.[12]

Equally stoutly did they resist Indian settlement and the missionaries who promoted it. "The lack of piety came to such a pass," complained Brother Gabriel Sagard, that an important Catholic investor in the company told the Recollects that if they thought of settling the natives of the north shore near the French at Quebec, the company would drive the Indians off "by force and make them withdraw to a far distance, away from any acquaintance with the methods of the trading." Even intertribal peace—another plank in the Recollect platform—drew company opposition. When Sagard tried to negotiate a treaty between the feuding Hurons and Iroquois so as to open both territories to the gospel, the company read him an elementary lesson in North American geopolitics: peaceful Iroquois would divert Huron furs to the Dutch at Albany, which was closer to Huronia than was Quebec.[13]

The era of bad feelings came to an end in 1627, when a rising chorus of colonial protest finally made itself heard at court. Not only the Recollects but Champlain, who as acting governor provided the most consistent leadership during the company period, and, after their arrival in 1625, the Jesuits had a vision of Canada very different from that of the companies. In the winter of 1617-18 Champlain presented a grandiose plan to—appropriately enough— the French Chamber of Commerce. In order to pour Christianity into an "infinite number" of thirsty souls, to give the king title to a country "as large as half of all Europe," and to follow the St. Lawrence to the Far East, Champlain asked for 15 Recollects, 1,200 colonists, and 300 soldiers to plant on the rock at Quebec a town "nearly as large as St. Denis." At a cost of only 45,000 livres, the king could expect to reap annually some 2 million livres from the sea, 1.1 million from the soil, 1 million from mines, 900,000 from the forests, and (as if to accentuate the positive) only 400,000 from the fur trade. Although the Chamber was enthusiastic about Champlain's proposal and sent it on to the king, His Majesty chose not to invest when astute businessmen were loath to risk their own capital.[14]

Three years later the Recollects and some of the principal inhabitants of Quebec sent their own remonstrance to the king to protest the dangerous weakness of company rule. Convinced that wandering about Canada were "more than 300,000 souls eager for agricultural pursuits and easily brought to the knowledge of God," the Recollects called for increased settlement, greater military protection at Tadoussac and Quebec, swift and impartial justice, the exclusion of Huguenots, twelve servants to cultivate the mission's land, and the funding of a seminary for fifty Indian children for six years, after which the land under cultivation could support even more.[15] Louis XIII was too busy reducing the Huguenot challenge in his western provinces to answer the Canadian call, but under his next two viceroys—Henri, duc de Montmorency, and the duc's nephew, Henri de Lévis, duc de Ventadour—New France entered an era of modest growth. Champlain built a fort on Cape Diamond overlooking the river, rebuilt and enlarged the *Habitation* in stone, established a court of justice and published the country's first ordinances, and made the rich meadows of Cape Tourmente a center of stock raising. Montmorency inaugurated the seigneurial regime in 1624 by granting Cape Tourmente, the Ile d'Orléans, and adjacent islands in fief to one of the company partners.[16]

But it was left to Ventadour to introduce the most powerful agents of change in seventeenth-century New France. When the understaffed Recollects issued a call for "new evangelical workmen" to assist them, Ventadour encouraged the already eager Jesuits, his spiritual advisors, to accept by paying the way of three of them to Canada.[17] This trio and the many who followed shortly were tireless supporters of full-scale colonization of the St. Lawrence, just as their predecessors in the short-lived mission to Acadia had been of Port Royal.

When Poutrincourt returned to Port Royal in 1610 to begin afresh, he was followed a year later by two Jesuits financed by a wealthy noblewoman. There Pierre Biard and Enemond Massé began to work among the seasonally nomadic Micmacs of Nova Scotia and Malecites of New Brunswick. Before a Virginia warship destroyed their mission stations in 1613, the priests concluded that only by teaching the Indians to cultivate the land could they be persuaded to remain in one place long enough to receive religious instruction. "The conversion of this country to the Gospel, and of these people to civilization," Biard warned, "is not a small undertaking nor free from great difficulties." But missionaries would have no chance whatever "if there is not established a Christian and Catholic colony" upon which the neophytes could depend for civilized models of success and even "provisions and temporal needs."[18]

On the St. Lawrence the Jesuits had been able to do little more than acquire a smattering of Indian languages and an inkling of native behavior when an English fleet seized control of the river and, in 1629, starved the small French garrison-*comptoir* into submission. During their three-year tenure, the English razed most of Quebec except the new fort, which they enlarged. They burned the Recollect chapel at Cape Tourmente, "scattering all the ornaments used in saying mass," and half the Jesuit convent, dismantling the rest. The Recollects' house was treated still worse. The Recollects' trove of altarpieces and sacramental furniture survived only because it had been carefully buried.[19] When Canada was restored to the French in 1632, the Jesuits returned alone. The Recollects were forced to abandon the Canadian field by Cardinal Richelieu, the head of the royal Council of State, who thought the Jesuits' superior wealth, discipline, and numbers could do the job better.

Just what that job entailed the cardinal made clear in 1627 when he chartered a new Company of the Hundred Associates, which was designed to inscribe "New France" indelibly on the map of North America. Louis XIII wanted a substantial colony in Canada, Richelieu wrote, because he sought, "with divine assistance, to introduce to the natives the knowledge of the true God, [and] to cause them to be civilized and instructed in the Catholic, apostolic, and Roman faith." According to Richelieu's lights, this could be done only by peopling the country with good "French-born Catholics, who will by their example, lead these nations to the Christian religion and to civil life." Of course, missionaries were indispensable; the Associates agreed to maintain at least three priests in every settlement for fifteen years or to give them equivalent support in cleared land. If anyone had doubted the sincerity of the French goal, the seventeenth article of the charter would have put his mind at rest: the king ordered that any Indian converts would be considered "natural-born Frenchmen" and would be allowed to settle in France, acquire property, and inherit or make donations and legacies like any other citizens. While the economic payoff of such a privilege was somewhat fanciful, its general spirit distinguished the French from all the other European colonizers of the New World.[20]

Just as the Jesuits were silent partners in the formation of the new company, so they agreed with its philosophy of settlement. "The French colony is the chief means and only foundation for the conversion of all these tribes," wrote the Jesuit superior from Quebec in 1643. "If I could see here a number of towns or villages, gathering enough of the fruits of the earth for their needs," his predecessor had written eight years earlier,

> our wandering Indians would soon range themselves under their protection; and, being rendered sedentary by our example, especially if they were to be given some help, they could easily be instructed in the Faith. As to the stationary tribes farther back in the interior, we would go in great numbers to succor them; and would have much more authority, and less fear, if we felt that we had the support of these Towns or Villages. The more imposing the power of our French people is made in these Countries, the more easily they can make their belief received by these Barbarians. . . .[21]

Fortunately, the three decades after the restoration of Canada were a time of ambitious plans and genuine, if uneven, social maturation. Both, however, were circumscribed by only a modest growth of population, due in large part to the periodic presence of Iroquois (mostly Mohawk) war parties.[22] According to their charter, the Hundred Associates were obligated to transport four thousand colonists by 1643. In 1640 Canadian census takers could find only 356 people, of whom 29 were Jesuit priests and 53 soldiers. As late as 1663, when the Crown stepped in to remedy the situation, Canada still had only 3,035 people, including 78 church men and women.[23]

And yet New France was, for the first time, more than a commercial *comptoir*. The Jesuit vision of a new Jerusalem of holy farmers seemed hopefully near. In 1633 the Associates, who had been granted all of New France in seigneury, began to parcel out long, narrow strips of land perpendicular to the river to the settlers they attracted to Canada and to older inhabitants and institutions. More than a tenth of the land went to seven religious institutions, most of it on prime river frontage; the Jesuits received nearly twenty concessions before 1663, which gave them sixty percent of the church holdings. By 1663 more than thirteen million arpents had been distributed in 104 seigneuries, spreading the thin French population over two hundred miles on both sides of the St. Lawrence.[24]

For economic as well as military reasons, towns were also needed. In 1634 the tiny outpost of Trois Rivières was ensconced at the mouth of the St. Maurice, some eighty miles from Quebec, to help secure the upper river trade from Iroquois attacks. But eight years later, seventy-five miles farther upstream, forty new immigrants and a dozen Canadians threw themselves into the teeth of the Iroquois when they planted Ville Marie on the island of

Montreal. Although this was clearly a reckless dispersion of resources, the king gave them a fort and a five-hundred-ton warship and private donors endowed a hospital, all of which were immediately pressed into service when the Mohawks resumed their assaults on the river. The population of Montreal hovered around fifty during its first decade, but substantial spurts of immigration allowed it to survive and play a key role in the Catholic investment of New France.[25]

The social and religious revival of New France after the English conquest owed much of its direction and vitality to a concomitant resurgence of spiritual energy at home. When the Jesuits were allowed to return to France in 1603, they launched a nationwide campaign of *collège* building for the middle and upper classes, while the Capuchins directed their efforts toward the rural peasantry and urban poor. Older orders, such as the Ursulines and nuns of Port Royal, assumed new habits of austerity, sacrifice, and mysticism, and a host of new orders and organizations—Sulpicians, Oratorians, Sisters of Charity, Priests of the Mission—sprang up to combat the moral laxity and secularization spawned by the excesses of the religious wars and the Reformation. The Queen Mother, Anne of Austria, bestowed her blessing upon the whole movement, cardinals Mazarin and Richelieu occupied the highest offices of state, and when the royal confessor, Jesuit Pierre Coton, spoke, the king listened.

Perhaps the most characteristic and powerful offspring of the revival was the aristocratic lay Compagnie du Saint-Sacrément, the inspiration of the young duc de Ventadour, Canada's viceroy. A secret organization with a powerful executive committee in Paris and numerous provincial cells, the company sought to put its members or sympathizers in all the key positions in church and state. Through them it pursued three kinds of work: persecution of perceived enemies of the Catholic commonwealth (Jews, Protestants, and Jansenists), philanthropy (hospitals, poorhouses, the royal galleys), and puritanical moral improvement (banning of exposed female cleavages, Molière's and all other comedies, and gambling). It was this company of wealthy *dévots*, in the guise of a smaller Société de Notre-Dame de Montréal, who underwrote the founding of Montreal in 1642, bequeathed the island to the Sulpicians in 1657, enjoyed the active sympathy of the Canadian Jesuits, and in 1659 secured the appointment of François de Laval-Montigny, a company member, as the first bishop of Canada. The spirit of their enterprise also brought the first Ursulines and Hospital nuns to New France in 1639 and inspired Marguerite Bourgeoys in 1653 to organize the secular Sisters of the Congregation on the model of the Sisters of Charity for work in primary education.[26]

Although Canada's religious institutions had gained wealth, numerical strength, and firm direction after 1632, the rest of the colony had not fared as well. By 1663 it was abundantly clear to the French at home and in Canada that New France would not survive if drastic measures were not taken on her behalf. The Iroquois continued to wage such relentless, unpredictable war all along the river that the French, as one chief boasted, "were not able to goe

3. In 1670 Quebec was a town visually and spiritually dominated by religious institutions. This unusual eagle-eye view of the town from the northwest shows the imposing buildings belonging to the Ursulines (9), Jesuits (7), Recollects (15), and Hospital nuns (4). Sillery is at the right (1). Reproduced by courtesy of the Bibliothèque Nationale, Paris, Département des Cartes et Plans.

over a door to pisse."[27] Effective countermeasures could not be taken for lack of manpower, administrative stability, and supplies. Governors came and, mostly, went, having found themselves in command of too few professional soldiers and too many farmers more used to hoes than to muskets. Unable to tend their crops in safety, the settlers retreated from the *côtes* to the towns to share food shortages, or took ship for France in despair. The Communauté des Habitants, in reality a clique of some fifteen businessmen which had assumed the Hundred Associates' obligations and trade monopoly in 1645, quarreled with the governor, the bishop, and each other, and scrambled to avoid bankruptcy when the fur fleets from the Great Lakes failed to appear year after year. And off to the south loomed some ninety thousand English and Dutch colonists, waiting to pluck the Canadian carcass as the New Englanders had picked off the Acadian peninsula in 1654.[28]

To avert certain disaster, the young king Louis XIV and his chief minister, Jean-Baptiste Colbert, transformed New France into a royal colony. Wielding the wealth and power of what had emerged as Europe's greatest nation, they temporarily subdued the Iroquois menace with a veteran commander and a thousand select troops; established a sound administrative system around a military governor, a civil intendant, and a Sovereign Council; strengthened the economy; and increased the population by promoting large-scale emigration and attempting to balance the sex ratio with marriageable *filles du roi*.[29] By the turn of the eighteenth century, Canada's fifteen thousand inhabitants were still grossly outnumbered by a quarter of a million Englishmen. But the English colonies lay pinned behind a vast French arc of military forts, fur posts, and religious missions from Louisiana to Detroit, all around the Great Lakes, and deep into the *pays d'en haut.* It was a thin line, as the British would discover at the Conquest, but for the intervening sixty years the French and their Indian allies would keep it tightly drawn around the lion's neck.

CHAPTER FOUR

The Art of Reduction

*The best mode of Christianizing them
was to avoid Frenchifying them.*
PIERRE DE CHARLEVOIX, S.J.

Despite the continued threat posed by its Indian enemies, at no point in its history would New France have survived without its Indian allies. So often yoked in common cause were the two peoples that cultural descendants of the English colonists still speak of "the French and Indians" in the same breath. Numerous native groups allied themselves with the French not only from a shrewd sense of self-interest but because the colonists managed to solve a series of "Indian problems"—the obverse of the Indians' various "European problems"—more promptly and usually more effectively than did their European competitors. The dominant explanation for the Indians' allegiance is the French aptitude for forest diplomacy, trade, and guerilla warfare. But this ignores the crucial role of the French missionaries, whose distinctive brand of gunless warfare decided countless close skirmishes and certainly claimed as many victims as their sharpshooting, smooth-talking countrymen did. In the contest for North America, religion was a major weapon for both the French and the English. But for nearly a century and a half, the French magazine was better stocked with spiritual hardware and software for the native market, and that competitive edge assured the survival of New France against tremendous odds.

The French in Laurentian Canada had not one but three main Indian problems, which were defined largely by the character and location of the tribes they encountered and by the goals the French missionaries and administrators sought to achieve. They also lacked one serious problem that plagued most of the other European colonies in North America: the French settlements along the St. Lawrence did not encroach on land claimed by any Indian group. Between Cartier's initial visit in 1535 and a summer reconnaissance by Champlain in 1603, the St. Lawrence Iroquois from Stadacona to Hochelaga had all vanished with hardly a trace. The best theory is that the men were killed and the women and children absorbed by Hurons in the Trent Valley of eastern Ontario and Mohawks of eastern New York, who found themselves barred from the growing river traffic in metal weapons and therefore at a military disadvantage.[1] Consequently, when Quebec, Trois Rivières, and Montreal were laid out, the French did not have to obtain Indian permission or risk ill feelings by paying purchase prices that, in native retrospect, appeared niggardly. On the contrary, the tribes that resorted to the north shore in the summer welcomed the French, their labor-saving trade goods, and their armed assistance against the aggressive Mohawks.

But the existing French problems with the Indians proved difficult to solve. From the French perspective, these various problems arose from the differing nature of the Indian groups with whom they had to deal. The first native peoples who constituted an administrative challenge for Champlain and a religious opportunity for the missionaries were the Montagnais and Algonquins of the north shore. The Montagnais were nomadic hunters whose thirty-five hundred to four thousand members were spread thinly throughout the boreal forest from Trois Rivières to southern Labrador. Ranking the three native "estates" of Canada, Gabriel Sagard placed the Montagnais with French peasants and "persons of low degree" because, he said, "they are as a matter of fact the poorest, most wretched and neediest of all. They . . . range the fields and forests in small bands, like beggars and vagabonds, in order to find something to eat. They have no stores of food, nor settled place of abode, and most of the time they are starving because they do not cultivate the ground."[2] The main reason for their precarious existence was that they were forced to scrape it from the scanty resources of the Canadian Shield, that vast outcropping of glacial moraine that covers most of eastern Canada. Because the soil of the Shield is poor, acid, and thin, agriculture effectively ends where the Shield begins. About twenty-five miles below Quebec, in the heart of Montagnais country, the Shield actually meets the river and retreats only gradually to a maximum of twenty miles near the St. Maurice, the western edge of their territory. With only 130 frost-free days a year at Quebec and less than 100 some fifty miles downstream, even maize agriculture was not a viable option for most of the Montagnais.[3] So, in an exhausting round of "removes," family groups of fifteen or twenty people pursued river eels in the fall and a wide variety of inland fish and game, preferably moose and caribou, the rest of the year. Only in the summer did the wintering lodges congregate in bands of 150 to 300 for fishing and political palaver along the St. Lawrence.[4] Thus one problem the Montagnais posed for the French was economic: that of feeding them when mild or snowless winters or scarcity of game frustrated their hunting.

A more serious problem stemmed from the role the Montagnais played in the fur trade. Thanks largely to geography, the Montagnais, especially the eastern bands, enjoyed the heady status of middlemen between the French traders who crowded the harbor at Tadoussac every summer and an extensive network of native trappers that stretched up the Saguenay to Lac Saint-Jean and across central Quebec as far as Hudson Bay and Lake Superior. While they did comparatively little fur hunting themselves, they could fill many ships' holds with precious cargo. At their fortified summer village at Tadoussac they cleverly played off the rival ships against each other to drive up the price for furs and lower the cost of trade goods. But when the company began to enforce its monopoly at Quebec and Tadoussac after 1614, the Montagnais found themselves paying more for trade goods, unable to drive as hard a bargain as previously by resorting to French, Basque, or Dutch freebooters. This naturally produced some hard feelings toward the Quebec colonists, which were mitigated only partially by the spotty presence of clandestine traders below Tadoussac, and by the Montagnais' need for the French as protection against the Iroquois and a year-round source of food. When collective feelings against the French ran high, individual Montagnais—who traditionally recognized no supreme authority—felt free to seek revenge for callous or ungenerous treatment by killing a colonist or two. The heavy-handed but vacillating way in which the French treated the culprits only engendered further resentment.[5] By 1624 Champlain was complaining that the French had "no worse enemies" than the Montagnais, who had boasted that if they were to kill off the French, they could obtain goods more cheaply from the Protestant Rochellais or Basques who would come. Having purchased guns illegally from such freebooters for at least four years, the Montagnais were capable of carrying out their threats.[6]

The other neighbors of the French on the north shore were the Algonquins, whom Sagard described as the entrepreneurs of native Canada "inasmuch as they are great traders, and undertake long journeys like good merchants."[7] Like their Montagnais allies, the Algonquins jealously guarded a middleman position in the fur trade. For French goods obtained at Montreal island or Trois Rivières they traded furs, corn, and hemp nets with the Hurons and a medley of pelts with their western neighbors, the Nipissings and Ottawas. Until 1615 the Algonquins managed to keep their French and native customers from making direct contact with each other, save for an occasional joint war party against the Iroquois. But when Champlain finally made his way to Huronia in 1615, the Algonquin monopoly was breached. For consolation the Algonquins even turned to the Dutch at Albany, but the Mohawks firmly rebuffed their attempts to operate south of the St. Lawrence.[8]

Although the Algonquins lost some of the carrying trade, at least one band preserved another source of revenue. The six major Algonquin bands stretched along the vital Ottawa River route that linked Montreal with Georgian Bay and Lake Huron. The lower three groups occupied the Ottawa's tributaries, probably to minimize contact with the Iroquois, but the upper three straddled the river. In the best position of all were the Kichesipirini, who made summer camp on Allumette (Morrison's) Island, a large natural tollgate in the river. Anyone wishing to pass up or down the Ottawa was obliged to pay his respects and a gratuity to the band's fearsome one-eyed sachem, Tessouat, which required a long circuit south of the island. To be caught by Tessouat's four hundred warriors trying to run the shorter northern passage was extremely hazardous, for the Kichesipirini were, in Sagard's opinion, "the most churlish, arrogant, and uncivil" Indians in New France (if also the "best dressed and painted").[9] As favored trading partners and allies who helped to keep the river free from Mohawks, the French were usually allowed free passage. But even they were not exempt from the demands of native protocol, as a Jesuit priest discovered in 1650 as he was returning from Huronia with the battered survivors of the Iroquois blitzkrieg. When he attempted to take the direct route home, Tessouat had him retrieved and hoisted from a tree by his armpits, "telling him that the French were not masters in his country, and that in it he alone was acknowledged as chief, and they were [all] under his authority."[10]

Although the upriver Algonquin bands could take an imperious tone with the French, some of the eastern groups seemed more amenable to French influence. Those who summered at Trois Rivières stirred French hopes because they cultivated maize traditionally and learned to plant French peas from the early traders.[11] No matter what their attitude toward farming, however, the Algonquins were expert hunters, intrepid fighters, and shrewd traders, skills that the French were eager to enlist, even if the Algonquins' peripatetic character posed serious difficulties for the missionaries.

Both the Recollects and the Jesuits took very little time in Canada to realize that the nomadic hunting tribes that surrounded the French settlements on the north shore were poor prospects for quick conversion to Christianity or French "civility." Unless every wandering lodge had its own hardy priest, the native languages could not be mastered, without which there was no way to convey Christ's message. And unless the natives and their sustenance could be planted in one place, there was no hope of taming their wild independence to French law and Christian order. In these circumstances, the missionaries understandably shifted their hopes to the "settled and sedentary peoples" of the interior, the "stable and permanent tribes" whose large populations and agricultural propensities seemed to meet the French goals half way. Villagers such as these, Father Paul Le Jeune predicted in 1633, will be "easily converted."[12]

When the early missionaries spoke of malleable townsmen, they were clearly thinking of the Hurons of southern Ontario. For Gabriel Sagard, who spent a short year with them, the Hurons—by which he meant the Huron men—resembled no one so much as the French aristocracy, "for they have a really noble carriage and bearing, occupy themselves only with hunting and war, do little work and always have something to live on."[13] But they were much more than Canada's *noblesse d'épée*, as Sagard well knew. The Hurons were also the quintessential traders of the eastern Great Lakes and the leading source of furs for the French. Between 1616 and 1629 the Hurons supplied two-thirds of all the beaver traded on the St. Lawrence. So commanding was their presence in the upper-country trade that Huron was the *lingua franca* for all exchanges with the Algonquins, Nipissings, Ottawas, Petuns, Neutrals, and Lake Superior Ojibwas.[14]

The Hurons owed their economic preeminence to the careful cultivation of geographical advantages. Huronia was pivotally located on the southern shore of fish-rich Georgian Bay, well below the Shield's "ugly surface of great rocks and barren mountains." Blessed with "open fields, very beautiful broad meadows," mixed forests, and well-drained sandy loam soils, the country was a settler's delight.[15] It had a 140-day growing season, and the Hurons took full advantage of it. They congregated in semipermanent towns of eight hundred to sixteen hundred inhabitants, their multifamily longhouses often surrounded by defensive palisades and always by ample fields. The men did very little hunting—meat comprised less than ten percent of the Huron diet—but they were resourceful fishermen, especially during the spring and fall spawning runs, and zealous canoemen who made long summer circuits of the northern lakes and rivers in search of vendible furs.

Yet it was the summer labor of the women that underwrote the Huron success in the trade. Every spring they would plant enough corn for two or three years as a hedge against drought and as a surplus for trade. To the nomadic hunters of the Shield, Huron corn was manna, for which they would pay handsomely in rich northern pelts. Flint and flour corn was sought so eagerly that the Nipissings and some of the Algonquin bands wintered in Huronia, and many of their tribesmen who did not swapped their winter catches for it as the Hurons passed to the French trading posts on the St. Lawrence. The women also collected and twisted Indian hemp into twine; from this the men wove fish nets, which traded as well as dried whitefish, tobacco (from the Petuns), wampum (from the Susquehannocks near Chesapeake Bay), and black squirrel skins (from the Neutrals on the Niagara peninsula).[16]

Initially the French missionaries were much taken with the stability of Huron life—what we now know to have been some twenty to twenty-five thousand natives living year-round in less than two dozen towns, dependent on the soil for eighty percent of their sustenance and on the women for the patterning of residence and inheritance. What the priests had not reckoned with was the noncoercive, consensual nature of Huron politics. Although the five Huron "tribes" were linked in a defensive confederacy, the loose hierarchy from clans and village councils to tribal and confederacy councils could be stymied at any level by dissent or indecision. This would prove a major stumbling block for the impatient missionaries who sought to turn whole towns to Christ or to mobilize the country against the unprecedented fury of the Iroquois.[17]

To the early missionaries, the Iroquoian-speaking Hurons were known as the "good Iroquois" for their many social virtues and seemingly unlimited religious potential. But the five culturally similar nations of New York Iroquois drew no such approbation. Although they, too, were populous, agricultural, and sedentary, inhabiting a genial environment much like Huronia, their very name stuck in the throats of the French throughout most of the seventeenth century. For the confederated Iroquois proper—the "bad" Iroquois—were from the beginning the archenemies of New France's Indian allies and therefore of the French, waging against all of them guerilla warfare of textbook classicality. From the distant safety of Port Royal in 1610, Marc Lescarbot could wax enthusiastic about the "greater [spiritual] harvest to be gathered" among the Iroquois than among the Micmac hunters of Nova Scotia. But he also knew that in 1603 Champlain had allied the French with the north shore Algonquians who dominated the fur trade, and in the past two years had helped his Algonquin, Montagnais, and Huron allies trounce two large Mohawk war-parties on Lake Champlain and at the mouth of the Richelieu. If the French wanted the thick, prime furs of the north, there was no alternative to a northern alliance, even if it earned them the enmity of twenty-two hundred Iroquois warriors.[18]

The early French successes deflected Iroquois energies toward the colonists' more vulnerable allies; before 1629 only one Frenchman was killed by the southern enemy. But during the rest of the century, New France enjoyed only fifteen years of peace with the Iroquois.[19] After abnormally large joint forces of Senecas and Mohawks laid waste to Huronia and put the dispirited survivors to flight in 1649–50, the French felt the full sting of Iroquois warfare. Well armed with Dutch muskets, eastern Iroquois war parties moved at will along the exposed *côtes*, to lie in wait for farmers and their families to come outdoors or drop their guard in the fields. Against such "uncivilized" tactics only Quebec was well defended; the scattered French *habitants* were virtually helpless. As the Jesuit superior despaired in 1660, the Iroquois "come like foxes through the woods, which afford them concealment and serve them as an impregnable fortress. They attack like lions, and, as their surprises are made when they are least expected, they meet with no resistance. They take flight like birds, disappearing before they have really appeared."[20] Perhaps the worst part of this war of nerves was the uncertainty. "It is not that these thieves are always all around us," wrote Father d'Endemare, "but that one is never sure either that they are there or that they are not, hence we have to beware of them all the time."[21] The only thing worse was to be captured and subjected to excruciating torture at the hands of Iroquois men, women, and even children.

By 1660, after numerous peace attempts and as many renewals of Iroquois aggression, even the missionaries and Bishop Laval had concluded that "these barbarians must be exterminated, if possible, or all the Christians and Christianity itself in Canada will perish." Marie de l'Incarnation, the mother superior of the Quebec Ursulines, expressed the religious predicament in starkly simple logic. If the Iroquois continue their "conquests and victories," she wrote to her son in France, "it will not be possible to carry on trade. If there is no trade, no more ships will come here. If ships no longer come, we shall lack all things necessary for life, such as cloth, linens, and the greater part of our food, . . . [and] the Savages, who stop here only to trade, will scatter in the woods," out of the reach of divine grace. "Only God, by a very extraordinary miracle," she thought, "can set them on the way to heaven."[22]

In seventeenth-century Canada miracles were in short supply. But in 1701 the Iroquois—after several daunting incursions by French regulars, over-extended empire-building in the west, Christian inroads upon their fragile unity, and deadly epidemics of imported diseases—agreed to peace with both the French and the New York English and to a pledge of neutrality in the white man's wars. For the price of peace with New France's seven western trading partners and promises of well-regulated trade with the English, the Iroquois countenanced the introduction of Anglican missionaries in the place of the Jesuits, who had begun their (frequently interrupted) work in Iroquoia in the 1650s.[23] For the French, however, expulsion from the cantons of the Five Nations was only temporary, and the resulting influx of the English into central New York provided French traders, government agents, and missionaries with a short but stubborn agenda for the eighteenth century.[24]

The configurations of problems and opportunities posed for the French by these three Indian groups were largely replicated, sometimes in slightly different patterns, by the tribes the French encountered later in the seventeenth and eighteenth centuries. When New France sought a profitable extension of its western boundaries under Governor Louis de Buade de Frontenac and later Lamothe Cadillac at Detroit, the firmest alliances were made with well-placed middlemen such as the Ojibwas and Potawatomis—the western analogues of the Montagnais and Algonquins. Until they were pummeled by the Iroquois in the 1680s, the gentle farmers of the Illinois embodied the religious hopes once placed in the Hurons, while the Ottawas easily picked up the Great Lakes carrying trade where the Hurons had left off. To complete the cast, the role of the dastardly Iroquois was now played with suitable malevolence by the Foxes of Wisconsin, whose implacable resistance to French trading posts and military garrisons was not put down until the 1730s.[25]

When the French looked south for native allies against the proliferating people of New England, the Eastern Abenakis who inhabited Maine's key river drainages seemed to combine the Algonquins' eye for trade, the fierce Iroquoian love of independence, and the Hurons' potential for Catholic conversion.[26] Not surprisingly, the goals, accommodations, and working solutions reached by the French missionaries in the first three or four decades of their experience on the St. Lawrence served as the dominant pattern of conversion efforts for the rest of the colonial period.

Despite the considerable differences between the character and situation of the three major Indian groups in New France, the goals of the missionary societies were not only strikingly homogeneous throughout the seventeenth century, but, with a single exception, immutable. Only the Jesuits, the order with the greatest physical and spiritual resources and the deepest Canadian experience, adjusted their sights to focus clearly on the changing reality of their cultural targets.

The first missionaries on the St. Lawrence, the Recollects, left France with a preconceived plan for the Indians' conversion which remained impervious to experience. When the first three priests and a lay brother landed at Quebec in 1615, they unloaded as part of their ideological baggage the success-laden history of their fellow Franciscans in Spanish America, where the Friars Minor (as the Recollects were known officially) manned some five hundred convents in twenty-two provinces for the greater glory of God and tens of thousands of baptized Indian converts.[27] Although they quickly discovered that Canada was not Mexico, in either native population or Christian forces, the Recollects set about trying to squeeze the local natives into a European mold.

Like all Christian missionaries in North America, the Recollects sought to
capture the Indians for God by saving them from themselves, by which they
meant from Satan's ubiquitous deceptions and from the countless deficiencies
of native culture. In the summer of 1616, after only a year in the field, the
missionaries gathered at Quebec with Champlain and six friends to chart the
future course of Christian Canada. Having wintered one priest at Tadoussac
and another in Huronia, the Gray Robes began by distinguishing between the
unpromising hunting bands of the lower river and northern Quebec and the
more sedentary tribes upriver and in southern Ontario and New York, who
appeared at this first glance "generally docile, susceptible of instruction,
charitable, strong, robust, [and] patient." But they concluded their delibera-
tions by casting all the natives as people "without subordination, law, or form
of government or system, gross in religious matters, shrewd and crafty for
trade and profit, but superstitious to excess."[28]

With time and experience the Recollect image of the Indians only grew
darker. In 1624 Father Le Caron reported to his provincial superior in Paris
that one of the "almost invincible obstacles" to the gospel was that the natives
"have nothing but what is extravagant and ridiculous" in the way of religion,
"so material and benighted is their intellect." When pressed on their beliefs
they remained "stupid and dull," incapable of defending their "insane" superstitions. So besmirched were their souls with sinful "darkness and insensibil-
ity" that "every inclination of theirs is brutal."[29]

The Recollects' forced retirement from the Canadian scene between 1629
and 1670 brought neither ameliorative second thoughts about the Indians
they had known nor a sympathetic assimilation of the richer experience of
their Jesuit replacements as described in the famous series of annual *Relations*.[30] The Jesuits' hard-earned and easily worn primacy on the St. Lawrence drew only carping jealousy from Recollect apologists. Among the most
captious were Governor Frontenac, who championed the returned Recollects
in order to "counterbalance the excessive authority the Jesuits have assumed"
in Canada, and a pair of unscrupulous court schemers who published two
volumes of trumped-up charges against the Jesuit record under the name of
unsuspecting Chrestien Le Clercq, a knowledgeable and generous-minded
Recollect who had served intermittently over eleven years on the Gaspé
peninsula.[31] In 1691 Abbé Claude Bernou, a *savant* interested in promoting a
new French empire in the Southwest (where he could obtain a bishopric), and
Eusèbe Renaudot, the editor of the *Gazette de France* and a popularizer of
Jansenism, hurriedly pasted together an account of the *First Establishment
of the Faith in New France*, which consisted largely of excerpts from Sagard's
Histoire du Canada and a variety of self-serving accounts of Frontenac's and
La Salle's western ventures. Although it was not written by the Recollect
missionary whose name graced its title page, it did reflect—albeit darkly—the
official Recollect attitude toward the Indians of Canada. "Exertions have
been made to civilize this barbarism," Renaudot allowed, "to render it
susceptible of laws, stop as far as possible their brutal outbursts, [and]
disabuse them of their vain superstitions." But "little progress is made," he

4. A Recollect missionary, in traditional tonsure, sandals, gray robe and cord belt. From Gabriel Sagard, *Le Grand Voyage du pays des Hurons* (Paris, 1632).

almost gloated, "these nations being yet so savage, so attached to their ancient maxims, their profane usages, gluttony, slander, pride, intoxication, cruelty, indocility." Contrary to the Jesuits' inflated reports, "the seed of the word falls in a barren and fruitless soil." And then, in a final pastiche of pessimism, Renaudot put the blame squarely where it did not belong, on the shoulders of the Indians: "If these nations do not correspond to the grace of redemption offered them, we have this resource of faith, that they are rendered inexcusable and God is justified in his condemnation of [them]."[32]

By 1703 it was common knowledge in both Canada and Europe that "the Recollects brand the Savages for stupid, gross and rustick Persons, uncapable of Thought or Reflection." If Bernou and Renaudot's denigrations were not sufficient proof, the popular works of Louis Hennepin, a Recollect priest who accompanied La Salle to the upper Mississippi in 1679–80, made the point even more bluntly. Whether he was ministering to the peaceful Iroquois at

RELATION

DE CE QVI S'EST PASSE'

EN LA

NOVVELLE FRANCE

EN L'ANNE'E 1638.

Enuoyée au

R. PERE PROVINCIAL

de la Compagnie de IESVS
en la Prouince de France.

Par le P. PAVL LE IEVNE de la mesme Compagnie,
Superieur de la Residence de Kébec.

A PARIS,

Chez SEBASTIEN CRAMOISY Imprimeur
ordinaire du Roy, ruë sainct Iacques,
aux Cicognes.

M. DC. XXXVIII.

AVEC PRIVILEGE DV ROY.

5. The title page of Father Paul Le Jeune's seventh *Relation* from Canada. This report to the French provincial of the order describes the Jesuits' activities in 1638, including the founding of Sillery.

Fort Frontenac on Lake Ontario or living with the mighty Sioux, Hennepin saw the natives as "miserable dark Creatures" whose "extremely stupid" faculties and naturally "savage, brutal, and barbarous" customs placed them "a prodigious Distance from God."[33]

But in the opening act of their mission in Canada, the Recollects had not yet reached the crippling conclusion that it was "to no purpose to preach the Gospel to a sort of People that have less Knowledge than the Brutes."[34] Before 1629 they wore the easy optimism of apostles everywhere, and placed their faith in a seasoned program of conversion.

According to the Recollects, the Indians in their current state of brutish savagery stood no chance whatever of being converted to Christianity. Unless their whole culture and mental outlook could be radically reformed, the sacred mysteries of the Catholic religion would be simply incomprehensible and the holy sacraments could not be placed safely in such polluted, unsteady hands. So in 1616 the assembled Recollects reiterated the common assumption of the day, that "none could ever succeed in converting them, unless they made them men before they made them Christians. That to civilize them it was necessary first that the French should mingle with them and habituate them among us, which could be done only by the increase of the colony." Eight years later, Father Le Caron elaborated on what the "civilizing" process entailed. The natives must be "regulated by French laws and modes of living," he said. "They must be fixed and induced to clear and cultivate the land, to work at different trades, like the French . . . , for all that concerns humane and civil life is a mystery for our Indians in their present state, and it will require more expense and toil to render them men than it has required to make whole nations Christian." Although the work depended ultimately on God's free grace, missionaries could prepare the way by "humanizing" the brutal natives, that is, by rendering them "men of order, more docile and tractable." "Until Christians are the absolute masters of the Indians," Father Hennepin put it with disarming candor, "missionaries will have scant success without a very special grace of God, a miracle which He does not perform for every people."[35]

The operative words in the Recollect philosophy—and in the thinking of the other missionary societies in New France—were "docile" and "tractable," which is understandable in light of the French predicament on the St. Lawrence.[36] For a miniscule population of interlopers surrounded by populous tribes of unpredictable and talented guerilla warriors, the best course was to try to bring peace to rival nations (lest revenge fights spill over onto the heads of newcomers), offend no potential customers, and gradually, through immigrant fecundity, military recruitment, and commercial shrewdness, establish French sovereignty over the region. If the object of French officials was to turn a demographical deficit into a political surplus, the missionary goals lent themselves perfectly to that end. For a good Christian was a docile Christian, a tractable, malleable being who saw that social order was essential and natural to man—fully humanized man—because it was a clear reflection of the divine order of the cosmos. Without order, the world was chaos and Lucifer's plaything.

On another, more mundane level, however, the missionaries drew the imperative for order from their own institutional lives. The three leading missionary societies in New France—the Recollects, Jesuits, and Ursulines, were "regular" orders (from the Latin *regula*, meaning "rule"), organized hierarchically and tightly bound by perpetual vows, the most important of which was obedience to one's superiors. Virtually the whole education of a regular priest or nun consisted of learning to annihilate one's self—one's pride, vanity, independence—in order to be subsumed completely by God's will, for a soul filled with the natural self had no room for the infusion of the Holy Spirit. Because of its inherent difficulty, self-abasement before God was learned in stages, before one's religious superiors. To renounce one's own judgment and to blindly obey the Church and its representatives was considered the most appropriate and most efficacious training for the spiritual life.[37] From their own point of view, the missionaries asked of their Indian neophytes only what the religious demanded of themselves. From the Indian viewpoint, of course, that was asking far too much: the Indians were expected not only to give up their former course of life, in all its habitual concreteness, but to assume new physical and spiritual habits that the vast majority of Frenchmen could never wear.

Yet it was the ordinary French *habitant* whose example was expected to seduce the natives from their wild, nomadic ways to bucolic civility. "To convert them," Father Le Caron reminded his superior, "they must be familiarized and settled among us. This cannot be done at once, unless the colony multiplies and spreads in all directions." In the opinion of Champlain as well as the Recollects, even in Huronia, some eight hundred miles distant by canoe, French "inhabitants and families are needed to keep [the Indians] to their duty and by gentle treatment to constrain them to do better." Indeed, after the visiting French governor and Recollect priest extolled the French lifestyle, the Hurons themselves obligingly asked for some living exemplars. "Thus judging our life wretched by comparison with yours," Champlain has them say, "it is easy to believe that we shall adopt yours and abandon our own."[38] What the missionaries could not see so early in the religious season was that the Indians could seldom be persuaded that the French lifestyle was superior to their own, except in a few areas of technology. Nor could they divine that when the natives did emulate the French, their models were more often keg-carrying traders and roistering soldiers than pacific priests and abstemious nuns.

When the Jesuits came to Canada in 1625 after a brief stint among the hunters of Acadia, they shared not only the Recollects' convent on the St. Charles for two and a half years but the essential tenets of their conversion philosophy. The first object of all the French, of course, was to "acquire an ascendancy" over the neighboring Indians, on the assumption that "the more imposing the power of our French people . . . , the more easily they can make their belief received."[39] Like the Recollects, the Jesuits believed that the imposition of French sovereignty in the St. Lawrence Valley was most easily achieved by reducing the Iroquois to peace and seating the wandering hunters of the north shore in permanent farming towns, where they could be kept under the watchful eye of the Church and their persons and subsistence subjected to legal or military retribution for misbehavior. But the Jesuits realized that unless French workmen actually cleared the land, sowed the crops, and built the houses, the uninitiated Indians would promptly fail as farmers and in discouragement revert to their roving ways. This was a lesson the Montagnais and Algonquins had tried to teach the Recollects. When Father Le Caron invited them to settle down so that the priests could learn their language, instruct them in the true faith, and inure them to the authority of the French, a Montagnais chief replied that the Gray Robe had no sense "because you yourself realize that we have not enough to live upon, nor you the means of giving us enough, while we are cutting down trees and clearing the ground. If the French had sufficient courage to lend us support for the year or two which we should require in order to put this land in order," he argued, "we should set to work at it willingly along with all our families. . . . If in that way we got enough to support us we should hunt and give back to the Frenchmen their food in the form of skins and furs, and more than they had lent us. Otherwise we could not remain in one place without dying of hunger."[40] The Jesuits thought that the help of French hands would not only help woo the natives from the hazards of the hunting life and bring them within the Church's reach, but would provoke such gratitude for "this miracle of charity in their behalf" that the natives could be "more easily instructed and won" to King and Christ.[41]

Settling the Indians in *reserves* in the midst of the French colony had the additional benefit of giving life to two other missionary institutions—a hospital or *Hôtel-Dieu* and sexually segregated *séminaires* for the education of native children. "Let these barbarians remain always nomads," Father Le Jeune warned, "then their sick will die in the woods, and their children will never enter the seminary. Render them sedentary, and you will fill these three institutions. . . ."[42] The Recollects before them had asked for royal support of a seminary for fifty boys, but the king realized that the understaffed friars were not the best people to underwrite in the schooling business; only twelve Recollect fathers and six brothers ever came to Canada in their initial fourteen-year stint, no more than four at any one time. Nevertheless, in 1620 the Recollect convent of Notre-Dame des Anges also became the Seminary of St. Charles, and a few Montagnais and Huron boys passed through briefly in search of literacy, warm clothes, and regular meals. But "hunting and the woodland air attracted them," even modest correction repelled them, and the mere promise of future utility could not keep them at their bookish labors. When the alms used to support the children dried up, the school closed its door after five years of fitful existence.[43]

Unable to acculturate the young natives at home, the Recollects resorted to the century-old tactic of packing selected boys off to France for a few years' stay in a brother house. There, in an unarguably civilized setting, they would learn the mother tongue—and perhaps Latin—with a proper accent, religion from a whole community of religious, and, with luck, no seductive sins from the *paysans* and *paysannes* outside the cloister walls. But life was more dangerous within the walls, at least for the body: of the six Indian students sent to France, only two survived to return home. One, Louis Amantacha, a Huron, was temporarily "ruined" by the English conquerers but later helped the French reestablish trade and religion on the St. Lawrence before he was captured by the Iroquois. The other, Pierre-Antoine Pastedechouen, a Montagnais, was more thoroughly ruined by his six years in France. Having forgotten his native language, he had to be forced to return to Tadoussac to relearn it; having lost any forest skills he may have had, he earned only ridicule from his tribesmen, took to drink, and went through four or five wives because he could not support them. After he threw off his civilized habits with a vengeance during the English takeover, the French, who had sought his skills as an interpreter and language instructor, washed their hands of him and he died of starvation in the woods, alone.[44]

During their first few years in restored Canada the Jesuits, too, sought native children to spend their junior years abroad, but they did not discriminate against girls or allow the students more than two years among the attractions of civilization. When they returned to Quebec, they were expected to stay with the Jesuits and to persuade their young native companions to do the same. The choice of students was discriminating. Children from the far tribes, like the Hurons, could be educated "with all freedom" in a seminary in Quebec, it was thought; their doting parents "will give them if they see that we do not send them to France." But the children of neighboring tribes had to be sent away because "the Indians prevent their instruction: they will not tolerate the chastisement of their children, whatever they may do . . . [and] they think they are doing you some great favor in giving you their children to instruct, to feed, and to dress. Besides, they will ask a great many things in return, and will be very importunate in threatening to withdraw their children, if you do not accede to their demands." To a people who exchanged children to cement trade and political alliances the Black Robes must have seemed peculiarly pinchpenny. But the Indians would have understood their desire for students from distant trading partners to serve as hostages for the safety of Frenchmen in their country.[45]

The lack of endowment for a school and the loving interference of local parents compelled the Jesuits to send Indian children to France until 1636, when a true *séminaire* or boarding school was founded just north of Quebec.[46] After some initial vacillation over which tribes would be served, the priests accepted boys from the Hurons, Montagnais, and Algonquins between the ages of ten and fourteen, sending the younger ones who were offered them—frequently orphans—to French families in Quebec. When bands from the three tribes camped nearby for summer trading or winter hunting, a few parents sent their children as day students for religious instruction in Latin and their native tongue and reading and writing in French. But the majority of students were Hurons, and the seminary was dedicated primarily to providing some young Christian leaven for Huronia. "We expect more fruit from these young plants," Le Jeune wrote in 1637, "than from the old trees almost entirely rotten."[47] So important were these particular children to the seminary that two of the three most experienced and fluent missionaries in Huronia, Antoine Daniel and Ambroise Davost, returned to Quebec to teach them.

From the day it opened with five young Hurons, however, the seminary was plagued by a host of problems that could not be completely overcome. Even with generous endowments from France, expenses threatened to overrun income. The students had to be dressed not only *à la française* but three times as often as French children, so hard were they on clothes. Free from forest scarcity for the first time in their lives, they ate the novel French cuisine with a gusto that exceeded normal adolescent voracity, which soon led their mentors to shift half their diet to Huron-style foods to prevent illness. Perhaps most important, presents had to be given to their parents and friends, who, if they lived nearby, also had to be helped to live part of the time. Although the students were given much of the afternoon for native recreations, the rest of the day was long—beginning at 4:00 A.M.—and restricted within four walls to rigorous lessons, prayers, catechism, and examinations of conscience. "To be born an Indian and to live in this restraint is a miracle," admitted the Jesuit superior.[48]

Only a miracle could have prevented the change of air, diet, dress, housing, and occupation from taking its toll on the homesick Indians. In the first two years pleurisy, slow wasting fevers, catarrhs, and colds laid several students low and carried off the two most promising Hurons. The prevailing European remedies of bleeding and purging only made matters worse. In 1638 three of the latest arrivals from Huronia sized up their chances of happiness or even survival, stole a canoe and supplies, and went home, having established reputations for "thieving, gourmandizing, gaming, idleness, lying," and an inability to endure the "paternal admonitions given them to change their mode of life."[49] The Jesuits were also disappointed by their own failure to obtain adequate replacements from Huronia or the north shore. When the Huron fear of bewitchment by the French or the reluctance of the politically powerful clan matrons to part with their youngsters did not keep native children at home, the Iroquois often captured them en route. Moreover, French trading partners resented the one-sidedness of the exchange. "One does not see anything else but little Indians in the houses of the French," fumed a Tadoussac captain, "there are little boys there and little girls—what more do you want? . . . You are continually asking us for our children, and you do not give yours; I do not know any family among us which keeps a Frenchman with it."[50]

These and similar problems encountered among the Hurons convinced the Jesuits that an abrupt change of plan was necessary. The first clue may have come in 1638 from a fifty-year-old Huron man who begged for admission to the seminary and would not be denied. To the Black Robes' off-putting references to his duller memory and advanced age he replied shrewdly, "It seems to me that you are not right to prefer children to grown men. Young people are not listened to in our country; if they should relate wonders, they would not be believed. But men speak—they have solid understanding, and what they say is believed; hence I shall make a better report of your doctrine, when I return to my country." Reminded of a fact they well knew to be true, the priests let him stay the year and in 1639 announced that their new religious targets were "Old Men, and the more prominent Heads of families," preferably stable Christians. As Father Le Jeune told his European readers, "the freedom of the children in these countries is so great, and they prove so incapable of government and discipline, that, far from being able to hope for the conversion of the country through the instruction of the children, we must even despair of their instruction without the conversion of their parents." Henceforth, the seminary would be reserved for "the children of our Christians" and for selected adults who wished to be instructed "at leisure and more quietly."[51] When none of these prospects materialized the following year, the school closed, just as the newly arrived Ursulines opened a seminary for Indian girls which was cast very much in the mold of the moribund Jesuit seminary.[52]

On the ship that brought the Ursulines to Canada were three nuns from the Hospital of Dieppe, one of the most religious and best-run hospitals in France. These "women in white" (as the Indians also called them) had come in answer to the Jesuits' plea for such an institution in New France to complement their own efforts. Seventeenth-century hospitals invariably ministered to the spirit as well as the body, partly because the state of scientific medicine could not prevent high patient mortality, largely because the nursing profession was almost exclusively the province of regular and secular nuns. The Jesuits thus felt that the gentle charity and religious instruction of a convent of *hospitalières* would do more for the conversion of the Indians than all their own journeys and sermons. When the sick Indians found themselves "in comfortable beds, well fed, well lodged, well cared-for," Le Jeune argued, "this miracle of charity" could not fail to "win their hearts."[53]

Indeed, it did not fail to do so. When the generosity of the duchesse d'Aiguillon allowed the erection of a hospital building in 1640 at the new Indian *reserve* at Sillery, a league and a half upriver from Quebec, the sisters nursed hundreds of patients every year, dispensing drugs and spiritual advice in equal measure. In 1642, for example, some three hundred natives were cared for, including the poor who needed food and a place to sleep and the mothers who would not leave their sick children. Some four hundred and fifty prescriptions were dispensed, exhausting the supply of medicine but perhaps to good effect because only six patients died. Equally remarkable was that the natives of Sillery learned the "practice of charity" by visiting the sick in the wards or in cabins built near the hospital's front door, shifting them, and preparing their *sagamité* (corn meal mush) better than the nuns could.[54] What made it remarkable in French eyes was that the northern hunters, who depended on speed and mobility to overtake their cloven-hoofed food supplies, were known to abandon the sick in the winter woods to die rather than endanger the whole group by dragging them along. "To be sick among these Barbarians, and to have already one foot in the grave, is one and the same thing," noted Father Le Jeune, who had followed them for a season and been appalled by their apparent lack of compassion.[55]

The custodians of this hospital dedicated to the merciful "Blood of the Son of God" also played a vital role in the religious conversion of their native patients. Assisted by a Jesuit chaplain, the sisters taught the inmates to pray, celebrate mass and take communion after they were baptized, confess their sins, say their rosaries several times a day, and sing spiritual canticles. The eagerness of the Indians, great and small, to learn the catechism and the prayers often made "a Chapel and a School of the sick ward." Those who were able and a few who were not even fasted the forty days of Lent in imitation of the "holy maidens" who tended them.[56] But annually on Maundy Thursday the Indians received the ultimate compliment of Christian compassion. Governor Charles Huault de Montmagny and the leading gentlemen of Quebec washed the feet of the male patients "very lovingly and modestly," while the nuns and leading ladies did the same for the women and girls. When the French explained that they took their lead from Christ and then laid out a grand feast, the natives were visibly touched.[57] To the French, it was small wonder that many former patients were "firmly won to God" and became "so many precursors of the Gospel" among their tribesmen.[58]

The Hôtel-Dieu of Quebec was instrumental in furthering the religious cause of the French in two additional ways. Directly, it gave strong support to the settlement of the Indians by reinforcing the resolve of those who wished to try the experiment of living near the French. Although Sillery was never very large, the Jesuits were confident that the location of the hospital there for four years guaranteed the town's survival. And indirectly, even the hospital's losses were considered gains, and not only in terms of the native souls saved from eternal damnation, for the Ursuline seminary and later schools often inherited the children of those who died there.[59]

Up to 1640, the Jesuit program of conversion closely resembled its Recollect predecessor. But with the collapse of the Jesuit seminary and the accumulated experience of thirteen priests in Huronia, the Jesuits veered sharply in an independent direction. Their goal still was to "bridle" the headstrong natives with French laws, economy, and most of all religion, but after 1640 they went about it in new ways. Perhaps a change of method was inevitable, since their basic attitudes had differed from the Recollects' from the beginning. The first noticeable difference was that the Jesuits believed that only by working arm in arm with the trading company could they achieve their religious goals. If the Indians ceased to hunt altogether in order to work hardscrabble farms along the St. Lawrence, warned a contemporary Jesuit historian, "nothing could be more disastrous for the tribes since it is through the trade that the knowledge of the Faith has been brought to them and it is from the profits of the fur trade that a contribution is annually made for support and extension of missions." But in the Jesuit view, farming and hunting were not incompatible, as they were for the Recollects, and everyone—Indians, priests, and traders—would benefit from settling the north shore hunters. "If they are sedentary, and if they cultivate the land," Le Jeune predicted, "they will not die of hunger, as often happens to them in their wanderings; we shall be able to instruct them easily, and Beavers will greatly multiply" because they will not be overhunted; each family would be allocated a hunting territory in the interior and counseled by the French to kill only fully grown males.[60]

The Jesuits also departed from Recollect thinking on the capacity of the Indians for social and intellectual improvement. While the friars thought them barely above the level of brutes, the Jesuits "intitle[d] them to good sense, to a tenacious Memory, and to a quick Apprehension season'd with a solid Judgment," whereby they "readily apprehend the meaning of the Scriptures." As early as 1632, the missionaries who worked with the Algonquins and Montagnais were convinced that they were "not so barbarous that they cannot be made children of God. . . . Education and instruction alone are lacking." Le Jeune compared the natives he knew to the uneducated villagers of France and concluded that, man for man, "the Indians are more intelligent than our ordinary peasants."[61]

Another area of disagreement was the suitability of French colonists as models of Christian civility. In the promotion stage of emigration, the Jesuits expressed hopes as high as anyone's for a new Jerusalem of saintly *habitants*, a Catholic city upon another hill capable of seducing the errant Indians from their dissolute lifestyle. But by 1635, as the French population inched upward, a note of ambivalence crept into the Paris-bound relations. On the opening page of Le Jeune's report for that year, he rejoiced that "the families who come over every year are beginning to change the barbarism of the Indians into the courtesy natural to the French." By the end of the first chapter, however, he was expressing fear that "vice will slip into these new colonies" unless the governor and company directors put God before Mammon and restricted passage to the godly. But as a keen student of human character this unworldly man of the world had to concede that "inhabitants of Cedar and Babylon . . . will surely slip in here" to spoil the religious plot and to require its rewriting.[62]

As much as the Jesuits needed the company to carry out their mission, they realized that the nature of the company's business created at least one major trouble spot: the traders who wintered among the far tribes in order to maintain good relations with the leading suppliers of fur. Commercial success often led to spiritual disaster. Gabriel Sagard defined the problem well when he observed that in Huronia "the evil life of some of the French is a noxious example, and in all these districts the natives, although savages, reproach us with it, saying that [the missionaries] teach them things the reverse of what are practiced by the French." The Jesuits no less than the Recollects could indeed "imagine what influence our words can have after that."[63]

By 1634 the Jesuits solved this problem temporarily by substituting among the distant tribes, particularly the Hurons, their own lay servants, *donnés*, for the company representatives. In return for food and wages, the *donnés* conducted the trade for the company. But they were bound to the Jesuit missions for life by private vows, and they were kept with the priests "in order that they may not become debauched with the Indians and show a bad example, as those did who were here formerly." Moreover, as seculars they were of greater service than brother coadjutors (lay brothers) would have been because they were allowed to haul supplies and carry firearms.[64]

All these changes were relatively minor and unobjectionable to colonists and crown alike compared to the major shift in Jesuit policy that occurred after 1640. This shift came about largely as a result of the founding of Sillery, "a new kind of seminary" aimed at "persons older and more capable of instruction." In 1637 Noël Brûlart de Sillery, former commander of the Knights of Malta and one of the Hundred Associates, endowed a village for Indian converts on some ten thousand arpents of land three miles upstream from Quebec. Using his funds, the Jesuits built a church, a residence, and eight French-style houses for the native leaders. The first residents were Montagnais and Algonquin neophytes, who lived in a number of temporary bark wigwams as well as the French houses. But contrary to Jesuit expectations, Sillery was seldom inhabited year round. Smallpox in 1639, Iroquois raids throughout the 1640s and '50s, and a costly fire in 1656 caused major evacuations, and annual hunting and trading expeditions left the village virtually empty for several months. Nor could the villagers be persuaded that maize agriculture was the economic wave of the future. Only a few Indian men dared to be caught undertaking the traditional women's work of farming, even when the personal example of Father Vimont, the new Jesuit superior, was provided. The result was no better after 1651, when the Company of New France granted to the Indians themselves the seigneury of Sillery and fishing rights in the St. Lawrence. By 1663 the few Indians who remained claimed only seven arpents of uncultivated frontage; the rest had been granted by their Jesuit guardians to seventy French families.[65]

In its first few years, however, Sillery was the Christian showplace of Laurentian Canada. At the Jesuits' urging, the villagers elected by secret ballot three magistrates, two keepers of duties, and a prayer captain, only one of whom was still a "Pagan." These officials enforced a new, adamantine code of morality, mostly against female independence, by resorting to such untraditional devices as prison, chains, and death threats. Two priests and the hospital nuns led daily religious exercises, which were performed with such devotion and order that the neophytes appeared to their teachers to have recaptured the spiritual quality of the primitive Church. By 1645 the parish counted among its inhabitants 167 Christian Indians, whose zeal for their new religion had reached the ears of numerous tribes in the interior.[66]

In 1640 the Montagnais residents of Sillery invited their Tadoussac cousins to join them, and the newly gathered Island Algonquins at Trois Rivières extended the same offer to the Attikamègues, a Montagnais band from the headwaters of the St. Maurice, when they came to trade. It was the unexpected response of these groups and the mixed success of Sillery that convinced the Jesuits to alter their conversion policy. The Attikamègues told

Father Buteux at the Trois Rivières mission that they had a "great desire to be instructed and to cultivate the land, but not with the Algonquins," who were of a different humor and language. The best place, they thought, was in their own country, about a day's journey upriver. Buteux agreed, and promised to send two priests the following spring. Likewise, when Father Le Jeune delivered the Montagnais invitation to Tadoussac, the recipients answered that they were resolved to pray as steadfastly as the Sillerians, but that it was more expedient for the Black Robes to "descend to Tadoussac, and set up a House there." Farming, of course, was out of the question in the rocky, windswept hills of Tadoussac, but it was obvious that the Montagnais would be at no loss for livelihood with their closely guarded monopoly of the Lac-Saint-Jean–Saguenay trade. In the three weeks that he spent with them, Le Jeune was impressed by their resolution to become Christians and agreed that henceforth a priest would be sent during the summer.[67]

In accommodating themselves to the Montagnais, the Jesuits determined for the future that seminomadic hunters and traders could still be good Christians, and that Christianity was compatible with many, perhaps most, aspects of traditional native culture. No longer would authentic Christians reside solely in Frenchified parishes along the St. Lawrence. After 1641 they could be found at dozens of "flying" missions for a few months of the year and deep in familiar woods for the rest. As long as they carried Christ's message in their hearts, prayed regularly, and honored the seven sacraments when they were available, the Indians of Canada were accounted *bons catholiques*, at least by their Jesuit mentors.[68]

By the same token, when other Indian *reserves* were established along the St. Lawrence or nearby on tributaries, Sillery no longer served as the prototype in all respects. Cornfields remained a prominent feature on most *reserves*, and as at Sillery they were planted traditionally, in hills, rather than being plowed with European draft animals, and were tended predominantly by women, who were the farmers in northeastern woodland societies. *Reserve* government tended toward the rigorous Christian pattern of Sillery, backed by resident priests and often soldiers, but never replicated its pristine authoritarianism. Likewise, the languages spoken were native, housing was largely traditional, and dress was freely chosen from both cultures. Most immune to change was the *reserve* economy, which demanded periodic male absences for war (usually as French allies), trade (much of it illegal), and hunting. In all these ways, St. François, Bécancourt, Lorette, Sault Saint-Louis, Lac des Deux Montagnes, St. Régis, and La Présentation bore a fair resemblance to Sillery. But in one important way they differed pointedly: they were established at arm's length from the French urban centers because the Jesuits considered exposure to the Canadian brand of French civilization not only unconducive but positively hazardous to the spiritual health of the Indians. The new Jesuit plan called for sedentary as well as nomadic missions, but both *segregated* from French society. The goal was to Christianize the pagans of Canada, but without Frenchifying them first. Unlike the Recollects who

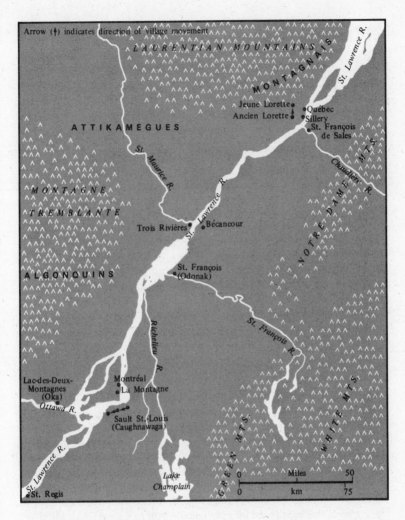

Arrow (↕) indicates direction of village movement

LAURENTIAN MOUNTAINS

MONTAGNAIS

St. Lawrence R.

ATTIKAMEGUES

St. Maurice R.

Jeune Lorette
Ancien Lorette
Québec
Sillery
St. François
de Sales

St. Lawrence R.

NOTRE DAME MTS.

Chaudière R.

MONTAGNE
TREMBLANTE

St. Lawrence R.

Trois Rivières
Bécancour

ALGONQUINS

St. François
(Odonak)

St. François R.

Richelieu R.

Lac-des-Deux-
Montagnes
(Oka)

Montréal
La Montagne

Ottawa R.

Sault St.-Louis
(Caughnawaga)

St. Lawrence R.

GREEN MTS.

WHITE MTS.

Lake
Champlain

St. Regis

0   Miles   50
0   km   75

FRENCH CATHOLIC RESERVES IN THE ST. LAWRENCE VALLEY

6. Caughnawaga, the fifth location of the Jesuit mission of Sault-Saint-Louis, in the mid-eighteenth century. The largely Mohawk villagers still lived in bark-covered longhouses and the women farmed the cornfields behind. The church (A) and missionaries' quarters are on the right. Reproduced by courtesy of the Bibliothèque Nationale, Paris, Cabinet des Estampes.

preceded them and the Sulpicians who followed them to New France, the Jesuits felt that the natives possessed innate civility and goodness which needed only to be plated and polished by Christianity to make them complete "men."

With the surge of immigration after 1663, several varieties of Old World vice were introduced into Canada by ill-paid soldiers, loose women, and men seeking a fast franc. But in the eyes of the missionaries, none was so inimical to the Christian missions as the reckless consumption of *eau-de-vie*—demon brandy. For decades, perhaps centuries, gentle Frenchmen had considered a nip or two of fine brandy the ultimate complement to a good meal, and their social inferiors in Canada knew the warming touch of a dram against the morning chill and the wintry blast. By European standards, brandy was at best a cordial benediction or a bracing medicine, hardly a social problem. But in the native cultures of North America it had uses far different and conse-quences far more serious. For the Indians drank alcoholic beverages only to become thoroughly intoxicated. "Social" drinking for taste or mildly pleasant sensations was rare. Inebriation served variously as an inflater of self-esteem in times of social and spiritual pressure from the invaders, as a socially sanctioned time-out in which aggressions could be released without conse-quence, and as a shortcut to a dreamlike state of religious possession, a means of sacred communication with one's guardian spirit and the innermost wishes of the soul. It took very little time for the French to capitalize on the Indians' seemingly unquenchable thirst.[69]

The consequences stretched the descriptive capacities of contemporaries and the credulity of royal officials at home. Drunken Indians too often turned into naked, howling "wolves," fighting with and killing each other, biting off ears and noses, and creating a living image of Hell. Firing guns and flashing knives, they terrified spectators, accidentally set fire to lodges, and killed domestic animals. Indian and French women were violated, and even wives and children were stabbed and thrown into roaring fires or boiling cauldrons. On occasion the madmen broke into French houses, but more often they sold their own family's food, tools, and clothing to buy another rundlet. When they had nothing left, they cozened French traders into extending them credit; when their debts grew too great, they fled the country.[70]

With considerable justice, the missionaries saw the brandy traffic and its behavioral products as "the general perdition of all the Indian missions," "almost the sole obstacle" to their labors. In 1671 Dollier de Casson, the Sulpician superior in Montreal, lamented that "if brandy were kept away from all the Indians, we should have thousands of conversions to report. . . . I do not doubt that the majority of the Indians who visit the French would all embrace the Christian religion, but for the fact that this liquor has so diabolical an attraction for them that it ensnares all the natives in proximity to the French, save for a certain number. . . ."[71]

Among the most successful in resisting brandy's advances were the native Christians of Sault Saint-Louis. Established in 1667 near a few French settlers at La Prairie, at the bend of the St. Lawrence opposite Montreal, the *reserve* attracted mostly Mohawk and Oneida Iroquois from New York by its religious decorum and strict temperance. Although the natives fled the drunken excesses of the Albany trade, temptation was everywhere. The village moved four times in fifty years, always farther away from Montreal, largely to escape the alcoholic enticements of French settlers and small-time tradesmen, whose illegal activities were winked at by Governor Frontenac.[72] So great was the natives' torment that by 1682 it could be said that they were "no longer guided by the French, whom they had hitherto considered good Christians." Twelve years later the battle for sobriety was far from won. Besides the forty casks of brandy sold to Indians at Montreal's three major trading fairs, the Saulteurs had access to fourteen or fifteen casks of their own a year. Understandably, Father Chauchetière and his two colleagues at the Sault mission were frustrated by their inability to dam the flow. "We all desire, as did St. Francis Xavier, to see ourselves so far away from the French with our beloved Indians that we may no longer have such stumbling-blocks," he wrote. Unlike the majority of their countrymen and most of their religious competitors in Canada, they saw in the natives "the fine remains of human nature which is entirely corrupted in civilized nations," and they fervently wished to preserve it from contamination by the brandy sellers.[73]

Although drunkenness hurt the Catholic missions by putting a severe strain on families and marriages, its religious damage was more extensive. By

7. Father Claude Chauchetière (1645–1709) came to Canada in 1677 and served for sixteen years at the mission of Sault-Saint-Louis. A few years after his arrival he began to draw and paint scenes from the founding of the mission to illustrate his *Narration annuelle* (1667–86). This scene shows the neophytes banning liquor from the *reserve*. In the priest's eye, brandy was obviously an instrument of the devil, seen crouching at the foot of the cross. Reproduced by courtesy of the Archives départementales de la Gironde, Bordeaux.

the 1680s brandy had played a major part in the destruction of the Algonquin missions as far north as the Nipissings, many of whom fled their country to avoid the hard sell of French brandy traders, and as far south as Sillery, which had lost its original Algonquian population by 1663. When a number of Abenakis fled Maine in 1671 to escape English land grabbers and rum peddlers, the Jesuits installed them in the houses of Sillery's former tenants. But the *reserve*'s proximity to Quebec was too tempting to native and vendor alike, despite watchful priests and intendants, a law prohibiting the sale of alcohol in Indian villages, and a bishop who did not hesitate to excommunicate violaters. Only a move of the whole mission to the Chaudière River, some fifteen leagues from Quebec, around 1685 saved it from being totally inundated by brandy.[74]

Yet no place in New France was beyond the long reach of the brandy men and bootleggers, no mission immune to their blandishments. As a consensus of missionaries stated the problem, baptized converts were seduced from moral order, unimpressed even when told that "brandy will be the inextinguishable fire with which you will burn in hell," and potential converts were repelled by the drunken decay they saw on the *reserves*, forced to flee from French debts to the heretical embrace of the Dutch or English, or put in early graves by the fiery spirits.[75] Since long experience had shown that the "neighborhood of the French" caused "manifest injury to the nascent [Indian] Church," the Jesuits were forced to conclude that only by moving their native charges out of that declining neighborhood could they lead them to Christ.[76] This departure, coupled with the innovation of flying missions for nomadic Christians, gave the Jesuit conversion program a look very different from what it had had before 1640.

Not everyone was happy with the new Jesuit program. Brandy sellers merely considered it a mild challenge, of course, but in Paris the young king Louis XIV and his ambitious minister of finance, Colbert, found it not to their liking. With the help of their Canadian intendant, Jean Talon, and, after 1672, their bumptious governor, Frontenac, they began to snipe at the altered Jesuit missions as soon as the Iroquois were quelled by the Marquis de Tracy in 1666. For the next fifteen years this cadre of armchair missionaries sought to turn back the religious clock to the hopeful beginnings of New France, when "civility" seemed destined to conquer all, and at the same time to curb what they felt to be excessive Jesuit power in both church and state.

After New France became a royal colony, the reigning idea at Versailles was mercantilism, the state effort to augment the wealth and population of the nation at the expense of world competitors, particularly the Dutch and the English, to maximize the economic potential of colonies, and to ensure state supremacy over the ultramontane Church. In the view from Paris, the Canadian Jesuits enjoyed too much influence in affairs of state and a dangerous monopoly of religious initiative. Therefore, Bishop Laval, the Jesuits' friend, was persuaded to leave his Sovereign Council seat empty except for ceremonial occasions, and the Recollects were reintroduced in 1670 to help the Sulpicians keep the Jesuits in their place. On the secular front, vigorous encouragement of immigration and the birth rate propelled the Laurentian population over ten thousand by 1683, which filled the river seigneuries from Quebec to Montreal with productive farms. In a search for even greater markets, the vast *pays d'en haut* was explored and presumptuously claimed, and whole villages of potential Indian customers were encouraged to relocate in French territory. Despite Colbert's unsuccessful efforts to diversify the Canadian economy, however, the fur trade remained dominant. This had the unwanted effect of overextending the colony's political limits, draining male laborers from the settled areas, and postponing the Indians' departure from their hunting grounds for less rigorous sites along the St. Lawrence.[77]

But it was the Jesuits, not the traders and their highly placed backers, who appeared to stand in the way of progress. Their flying missions removed the religious need for the far Indians to settle among the French (as the illegal *coureurs de bois*—"woods runners"—removed the economic need). Those tribesmen who could be persuaded to join the abstemious *reserves* were kept as far as possible from the most profitable trade of all. And perhaps worse, by allowing their neophytes to remain unfrenchified, the Jesuits blindly refused to bolster French sales. For this concatenation of political, economic, and religious reasons, the Jesuits were called to account almost annually from 1667 until Frontenac's recall in 1682.

By January 1666, only four months after landing in Canada, Talon had determined that the quickest and cheapest way to augment the colonial population was to "civilize" the Algonquin, Huron, and other Indians who had become Christians, to settle them among the French, and to bring up their children in French manners and morals. After ten months of trying to *police* the natives, however, he admitted to Colbert that numerous obstacles stood in his way, the most serious of which were brandy and the Indians' ignorance of the French language.[78] Clearly action was called for. If an administrator on the spot was unable to move, it behooved his superiors three thousand miles away to cut through the impasse with sharp decisions. Over the next two years Colbert and the king sent to Canada a set of missionary marching orders that would remain in effect—if not in force— until Colbert died in 1683. In order to promote the assimilation of the Christian Indians, they ordered Talon to attract whole families of them to French settlements, to oblige them to abandon their "idle and lazy form of life" for farming, and to encourage them to marry French *habitants* "in order that, in the course of time, having but one law and one master, they may likewise constitute one people and one race." Equally important was the education of Indian children, who must be reared according to "our customs" and taught "our language." To that end, Bishop Laval and the Sulpicians were instructed in 1667 to establish schools, *petites séminaires*, and by their example to encourage all the ecclesiastics and heads of prominent families to throw themselves into the Frenchification scheme.[79] What a strong sense of *déjà vu* the Jesuits must have had, seeing their "neglect" blamed for calling forth such belated and extensive efforts.

By the time Frontenac arrived in 1672, the meager results of all these plans were conspicuous. Especially disappointing were the Indian students taken in by the religious orders, even the reluctant Jesuits: they, especially the boys, ran away so fast and displayed such a profound lack of interest in learning the French tongue, dressing in confining French clothes, and sitting through sunny days in stuffy rooms that their frustrated mentors could only blame the children's nature or previous nurture for their own failure.[80] So the new governor, who had never before met an Indian, started all over again, acting as if he would undertake the conversion of pagan Canada single-handedly. He promptly sent back to Colbert, in detail, the minister's now venerable scheme as if it were a spontaneous invention of his own. He was shocked— just as Talon had been—to find that the Hurons of Notre-Dame-de-Sainte-Foi, only a league and a half from Quebec, did not *parle français*. When they moved to Lorette in 1673, he advised them to "build their huts regularly with French chimneys" and gradually to "adopt our manners and customs." He even proposed to learn some Huron during the winter to enable him to become "a good missionary, and perhaps help in Frenchifying the Indians as much as the next man." As a second step in that direction, he obtained eight children from the Iroquois when he conferred with them at Cataraqui in 1673. They were regarded as hostages for the good behavior of their tribesmen, and were supported by a thousand livres from the king. Four girls were sent to the Ursulines, two little boys were boarded with a French woman, and two boys between nine and ten years were "adopted" by Frontenac, who sent them to school daily with the Jesuits. We do not know how these children turned out, but they probably fared as well as the three youngsters taken in by Intendant Jacques Duchesneau in 1681. As soon as he had gone to considerable expense to outfit them, they all vamoosed because he "would oblige them to learn something."[81]

Try as they might, royal officials at home and in Canada could not persuade the Jesuits that their mission policy was misguided or to change their ways. With Frontenac under royal orders not to constrain ecclesiastics in any matter, the Jesuits told him civilly but firmly that their sacred calling was to carry the gospel to the natives in the farthest corners of America, if need be, and that when the Indians were settled in Christian villages they would continue to segregate them because "communication with the French corrupted [them] and was an obstacle to the [religious] instruction they were giving them."[82] In his blind egotism and hostility toward the order, Frontenac never saw the light of their reason, not even during his second gubernatorial term in the 1690s. In 1744 the Jesuit historian and former teacher at the Collège de Québec, Pierre de Charlevoix, noted dryly that in 1691 Frontenac had defended his hidebound philosophy of Frenchification on the strength of "twelve years' stay" in the country. "An experience, not of [twelve] years, but of more than a century," he retorted, "has taught us that the worst system of governing these people and maintaining them in our interest, is to bring them in contact with the French, whom they would have esteemed more, had they seen them less closely. In fine," he concluded, by the time Frontenac stepped ashore the second time, "there was no longer any doubt that the best mode of Christianizing them was to avoid Frenchifying them."[83]

The Jesuits' plans for converting native Canada to Christianity needed no apologies or justifications in 1744, nor do they now. For they were the considered result of the accumulated experience of a large number of perceptive missionaries, whose extensive work among a variety of native groups entitled them to respect, if not approval. But even the best-laid plans must stand the test of time. How well the Jesuits succeeded in their chosen task can be determined only by looking closely at the lengthy record of their Indian missions, flying and sedentary, in the colonial period.

CHAPTER FIVE

When in Rome

*I have become all things to all men
that I might by all means save some.*
1 CORINTHIANS 9:22

From the first fall of Quebec to the second, the Jesuits were forced by Indian demography and mission geography to adopt a culturally relative stance toward their prospective converts, a stance to which they were predisposed by worldwide experience and the doctrinal evolution of their order. Everywhere, in flying missions to the *pays d'en haut* or in Laurentian *reserves* that buffered New France from its more populous enemies to the south, the priests were greatly outnumbered, regarded as meddlesome inferiors, and prevented from using methods that might alienate their native neophytes. Without concentrations of armed countrymen nearby, the Jesuits could not hope to compel the Indians to convert. Nor did they wish to, knowing full well that the slightest hint of compulsion would undermine the foundations of faith. At best they could remind the natives of their vital and growing dependence on French trade and military assistance against traditional and colonial enemies. For the rest, the priests were on their own, forced to rely on their wits, tongues, and personal charisma to earn the Indians' respect and to purvey their alien brand of spirituality. As they found from their earliest contacts, they could do this only by adapting their lifestyle, their methods, and their message to the stubborn dispositions of native life.

This adaptation was in no way tantamount to a lapse in the priests' feelings of ethical or cultural superiority. While the enormous variety of peoples and cultures suggested to them that the natural world could be approached with a certain amount of flexibility and toleration, affairs of the supernatural—the realm of a single omnipotent, immutable God—demanded absolute fidelity to a unitary Truth, of which the Jesuits were devoted custodians and shining, if confessedly imperfect, paradigms.[1] But these special feelings had to adjust to, or at least confront, the striking opinion that the Indians held of their own superiority. Time and again, in countless cultural settings, the Black Robes were told by their native hosts that they had no "sense" because they did not think or act like Indians. Frequently the missionaries took the hint and adapted their approach to reflect more faithfully the native way—but only if they considered the issue a matter of cultural "indifference." For once they judged it to be a religious concern, the Jesuits, as resolutely as any of their Recollect, Capuchin, or Sulpician counterparts, set their mental jaws and dug

in their moral heels, entertaining no thought of compromise with the holy
Word of God, Pope, and Church. Even in accommodating themselves to
indifferent facets of Indian culture, the Jesuits sought with singleness and
tenacity of purpose to destroy native religion and to install Christianity in its
place. Clearly, this goal did not distinguish them from the other Christian
missionaries of the day. They stood out almost solely because of their
methods, which in sum were not only unique but in the end more efficacious
than those of their competitors.

Although sedentary *reserves* along the St. Lawrence were a prominent feature of Canadian mission life, the great majority of missionaries spent most
of their apostolic lives in periodic or long-term service to native bands and
villages far removed from the civil security of Quebec and Montreal. The first
Jesuits in Acadia worked among the Micmacs and Malecites without any
urban support save Poutrincourt's frail establishment at Port Royal. When
their successors joined the Recollects at Quebec in 1625, they rushed off to
Huronia and Tadoussac at the first opportunity to begin their apprenticeships in native mores. Once New France was restored by the English in 1632,
the now-dominant Jesuits lost no opportunity to recruit and send missionaries to nearly every tribe within several hundred miles of Quebec. Even the
Canadian superior, Paul Le Jeune, was not content to remain at his desk and
wintered with a band of neighboring Montagnais in the Appalachian High-
lands. By the 1660s Black Robes could be seen in native camps as far north as
James Bay and as far west as Chequamegon Bay on Lake Superior. By the
eighteenth century they had planted the cross in present-day Illinois and
Louisiana; in succeeding decades they inundated the Ohio Valley, central
Maine, and Nova Scotia, all of which had English claims written on them. As
they crisscrossed the length and breadth of New France, often in company of
fur traders and their native partners, the missionaries learned their first rude
lessons in Indian ways.

Traveling with the Indians was a dramatic and sobering rite of passage for
new missionaries. Although travel in Europe and across the Atlantic was
always taxing and often dangerous, it was easy work compared to paddling
paper-thin bark canoes on turbulent rivers or snowshoeing through trackless,
snow-covered forests, all at the direction of sullen strangers who spoke an
alien tongue. As an introduction to native life, canoe travel was the most
traumatic of all. Not only did it throw the missionary and several Indians
together in a tight and dangerous space for several weeks, but it could not
even begin until the missionary's order or the trading company had given the
canoemen a large traditional gift to reciprocate their generosity in taking
aboard the dead weight of the priest and his baggage.

Once the arrangements were made and the canoes left the French quays,
the missionaries quickly slipped into conditions guaranteed to "cast down a
heart not well under subjection." While the Indians paddled nonstop from
dawn to dusk, the priest crouched like a useless monkey among the baggage,
his long robes tucked around his bare legs and feet, his head dipping to avoid

the brain-rattling thump of a paddle as the sternman stood to negotiate obstacles and rapids. All day long, in every kind of weather, the passenger hunkered in cramped, perpetual silence, afraid to offend his sweaty hosts with obnoxious small talk or linguistic enquiries. If they took a dislike to him for any reason—and "a word, or a dream, or a fancy" was sufficient—they could jettison his precious altar kit or books, "borrow" his broad-brimmed felt hat and cloak, or abandon him altogether. An acquiescent, cheerful demeanor in all situations was the best policy. Even if the priest managed it, he could expect a daily barrage of "foul wind of the stomach," a token of their sparse diet of parched corn, water, and an occasional fish or glutinous bit of *tripes de roche*. He would also be invited to relieve himself in the wooden bowls that doubled as drinking cups; standing in a canoe was universally frowned upon.[2]

If the priest did not quickly learn two important lessons, his future invariably took a turn for the worse. One lesson was that the Indians put a high premium on first impressions. As Father Brébeuf warned newcomers headed for Huronia, "the Indians will retain the same opinion of you in their own country that they have formed on the way; and one who has passed for an irritable and troublesome person will have considerable difficulty afterwards in removing this opinion." Only a cheerful face could prove that the passenger "gaily" endured the fatigues of the trip. The second lesson was consistency: "Do not undertake anything unless you desire to continue it," advised Brébeuf. "Do not lend them your garments, unless you are willing to surrender them during the whole journey," but above all, "do not begin to paddle unless you are inclined to continue paddling."[3] Painful blisters, aching muscles, and native disdain were the amateur canoeman's sole reward, as Claude Allouez discovered en route to the western Great Lakes in 1665. Obliged by the Indians to paddle as an "honorable employment" of a "great Captain," he felt more like a "malefactor sentenced to the Galleys." For his inept pains he earned only the contempt and jibes of his sinewy partners, who registered their "slight esteem" by purloining most of his loose clothing and his blanket.[4]

Portaging around rapids or between lakes was another cross to bear. The route to Huronia alone had some thirty-five carries, and in some years more than fifty shallow places where the crew had to tow the canoe while walking barefoot over sharp rocks in icy water. The Indians, of course, had the strength of "mules" and could carry more than their own weight using tumplines across their foreheads; they expected nothing less from the French. If missionaries could "go naked" and "carry the load of a horse," Brébeuf promised, the natives would recognize them as "wise" and "great" men. Otherwise not, as poor Father Allouez learned. When his knees buckled under the loads he was given, his companions laughed and threatened to call an Indian child to carry him and his burden.[5]

Nightfall brought little relief, for sleep came with difficulty on a bed of bare earth and a pillow of stone or wood. Huddled beside his equally odoriferous guides under a canoe or a makeshift lean-to, the missionary confronted the fiercest enemy of all—the hordes of biting insects that are still synonymous with the northern woods. Lacking the half-protection of the Indians' animal-grease repellent or a choking smudge fire, the religious offered up their tender white flesh to insatiable legions of black flies, gnats, mosquitoes, and no-see-ums. Only boots, gloves, and headnets could have kept the insects at bay, and none were to be had. So every morning the priests found themselves covered with blood; sometimes their eyes were swollen shut. Perhaps worst of all, they were frequently prevented from finding the inner solace of prayer by the afflictive din.[6]

If the missionaries risked being drowned in swollen rapids or eaten alive by flying carnivores in their summer travels, in winter they prayed that they would not die from starvation or frostbite as they struggled to keep up with small bands of nomadic hunters. In an effort to learn the various native languages and to begin the gradual conversion of their speakers, the Recollects and Jesuits apprenticed themselves initially to wintering family groups of Micmacs, Montagnais, Algonquins, Nipissings, and Attikamègues, and later to Ottawas, Ojibwas, Naskapis, and Crees. These hunters spent the long subarctic winters moving over the frozen landscape north and even south of the Great Lakes and the St. Lawrence in search of large game animals, particularly moose and caribou. As their peripatetic food supplies moved in search of fresh browse, the natives donned their lozenge-shaped *raquettes* and gave pursuit, dragging their households and families behind them on narrow toboggans. Unless they sought premature martyrdom, the missionaries were obliged to follow.

This was no easy task for men whose mothers had not bound them as infants on cradleboards, toes in, as Indian mothers did to form expert snowshoers. As an envious Recollect noted, the natives "carry themselves better than Frenchmen, who always turn the point of the foot out, and thus make the tail of their snowshoes turn in, often entangling them and bringing about a tumble."[7] Moreover, in the chase itself snowshoes did not prevent Indian hunters from "jumping like bucks or running like deer."[8] Not only were the Indians fast on their feet, but driving snow could quickly obliterate their tracks. More than one missionary had to spend a terrifying night alone in the woods because he lacked native speed or discretion.

For all its difficulties, winter travel was no match for the living martyrdom that the priests endured in Indian lodges between removes. The whole extended family crowded into a dark, bark-covered wigwam, too low to allow any posture but sitting, lying, or kneeling. A hole in the roof vented the central fire, which emitted copious quantities of acrid smoke, and admitted snow and cold air. The extremes of heat, cold, and smoke severely tested the missionaries' fortitude. Their eyes watered constantly (which often led to conjunctivitis), they were forced to sleep "higgledy-piggledy" with all ages and sexes (unless they installed a one-log room divider), and the large and numerous Indian dogs walked on their faces and stomachs and upended their wooden eating bowls. Unable to shift position when their roommates were all present, the priests scorched their feet and gowns in the fire and froze their heads on the snowbanked periphery. Religious duties were nearly impossible:

reading a breviary was prevented by the smoke and commotion within and the glaring snow, wet, or cold without.[9] Father François de Crespieul, who had spent twenty-six winters with the Montagnais along the Saguenay, accurately described the winter existence of a roving missionary as an "almost continual practice of patience and of Mortification."[10] Like the initial phase of every priest's mission among the Indians, it was mortifying not only because of its extreme harshness but because the bookish priests who had come to teach spent most of their time absorbing hard lessons from their prospective pupils.

In his instructions to new priests being sent to Huronia, Father Brébeuf warned that, "leaving a highly civilized place, you fall into the hands of barbarous people who care but little for your Philosophy or your Theology. All the fine qualities which might make you loved and respected in France are like pearls trampled under the feet of swine. . . ."[11] For the Jesuits the contrast was all the more striking because of the extraordinary preparation they brought to their Canadian task.

The 115 Jesuit fathers who came to New France in the seventeenth century were among the best educated men in Europe, not only in philosophy and theology but in the classical humanities as well. On the average they were nearly thirty-four years old, having spent at least half their lives in Jesuit *collèges* and universities.[12] By 1624 the Society had established forty-five schools to educate France's noble and professional classes as well as to recruit promising boys for the religious life; by the end of the century upper-class education was dominated by seventy-seven Jesuit academies. The curriculum, standardized by the *Ratio Studiorum* of 1599, emphasized Latin grammar, rhetoric, poetry, and classical history, with complementary attention to stylistic grace and clarity in the native tongue. Frequent exercises in Latin—disputations, classical and religious dramas, and declamations—honed the forensic skills of an oral culture and an apostolic ministry.[13]

Having put on the black soutane of the Jesuit novice in their late teens, the candidates proceeded through a three-year course of philosophy (logic, mathematics, physics, ethics, and metaphysics) leading to a bachelor's degree, frequently at the elite colleges of Clermont in Paris and La Flèche in Anjou. This was followed by at least four, often six, more years of theological training, which gave them a deep familiarity with Scripture, canon law, positive and moral theology, and the varieties of religious psychology expounded and probed in "cases of conscience."[14]

Such a bookish existence might have produced erudite but ineffectual missionaries had Loyola and his successors not realized that the best way to reinforce and activate one's knowledge is to teach. Virtually every Jesuit who came to Canada had also spent several years teaching the humanities classes or the more advanced philosophy classes in the Society's colleges, typically before or during their theological studies.[15] This experience pitted them against the inventive minds and formidable wills of students ranging from boys of nine or ten to young men in their twenties, most of whom were socially favored lay externs deeply uninterested in the religious life. The cumulative problems of discipline and pedagogy posed by such worldly classes were a valuable and often lengthy introduction to many of the challenges of the missionary life. The students were not Indians but their teachers still had to gain their attention, respect, and affection in order to inculcate the Jesuits' particular brand of virtuous culture. Although the Jesuits could assume somewhat more of French neophytes, the essential educational task was the same one they would face in America.

Thus the men who committed themselves to the Canadian missions had prepared for their calling by a studious life of quiet gardens and meditation, punctuated by testing times in noisy classrooms and noisome hospitals, prisons, and almshouses. Eschewing the canonical hours, cloisters, and prescribed dress of the traditional monastic orders, the Jesuits practiced a kind of worldly asceticism, regarding study as a form of prayer and selfless charity as the ultimate imitation of Christ.[16] Though they were constantly busy *in* the world, they were definitely not *of* it. Indeed, most novices took their first vow expecting even less involvement with the world than they eventually came to have, or desire. Throughout the sixteenth century the Society was predominantly (though not exclusively) attractive to the sons of professional, merchant, and minor noble families who wished to leave the world altogether, to find a haven from moral temptation and the manifold misfortunes that seemed to befall laymen and secular clerics alike. While attending the Society's schools, they were drawn to the Jesuit lifestyle—the grace, modesty, and erudition of the fathers, and the collegial life of the mind, seemly, measured, and chaste. Saving souls in pagan lands was far down their list of priorities. At that early stage, avoiding the world was preferable to reforming it.[17]

But the two-year novitiate, during which the candidates were put through Loyola's strenuous *Spiritual Exercises* and were taught to submerge their own wills in the will of God, and their long educational apprenticeship turned most of the new priests to thoughts of mission. Small wonder when in their first month they were taught that Christ's will was "to conquer all the lands of the infidel."[18] Many caught the Canadian fever from reading Le Jeune's early *Relations* from Quebec or being taught in French colleges by fathers retired from American missions. After his return from Acadia in 1613, Énemond Massé inspired generations of future missionaries at La Flèche with vivid tales of Micmac and Montagnais souls perishing for want of Christian succor. Although members were not supposed to "scheme, directly or indirectly," for any particular post, many Jesuits secured assignment to Canada by subjecting their unworthy bodies to harsh mortifications and their worthy superiors to tenacious lobbying.[19]

Just as the Canadian missionaries had been thoroughly acculturated as novices by the rules, dress, and senior members of the Society, they also had been taught the value of adaptability in their spiritual labors. Part of their novitiate and all of their third and final year of probation before full admission were devoted to apostolic living on charity and a ministry of service to society's least fortunate. In this ungenteel "school of the heart" the Jesuits learned to take Christ's message to France's own *sauvages* by mastering the local vernacular (of which France still had many), "adapting themselves to the capacities of children [and] simple persons," and appealing to all five senses in their preaching and catechizing.[20] The tactics acquired in teaching school and begging alms were of immediate use to the missionaries when they approached an Indian village for the first time.

Having served long apprenticeships in France and survived the rigors of travel to Indian country, the missionaries were understandably eager to implement a series of religious goals, most of which were clearly defined only after the Jesuits collectively had gained some experience among the native societies of New France. This clarification of goals proceeded hand in hand with the priests' continuing education in Indian ways, indeed depended upon it. The general goals of the Society and an outline of appropriate methods—both derived largely from experience with Christianized European populations—had been set forth in Loyola's original *Constitutions* of the Society. But to be effective in pagan North America, both ends and means had to be adjusted to the conditions of native life, to the cultural exigencies of Montagnais hunting bands, Huron farming villages, and Ojibwa trading rendezvous. Fortunately for their ultimate success, the Jesuits were undaunted by this necessity. Their anthropology was based on a supple brand of cultural relativism and their ministry on Christ's admonition to "be all things to all men in order to win all."[21]

After a few years in Canada the Jesuits had established a stable program of operative goals appropriate to Indian life. The ultimate aim, of course, was to turn whole villages and tribes from their traditional religions to Catholic Christianity; by 1640 the Society's initial goal of remaking native culture in a French image had been put aside as hopelessly quixotic and largely unnecessary. But the Jesuits realized that this larger goal, which they shared with every other missionary group in North America, was contingent upon the achievement of several intermediate goals.

The first was to gain the active support of the political leaders in each native group, the more important the leaders and the larger the group the better. In the *Constitutions* Loyola argued that in choosing religious targets "preference ought to be given to those persons and places which, through their own improvement, become a cause which can spread the good accomplished to many others who are under their influence or take guidance from them. For that reason, the spiritual aid which is given to important and public persons ought to be regarded as more important, since it is a more universal good."[22] In New France the priests lost no time in identifying these key leaders with the civil chiefs, councillors, and trading captains of major villages and populous confederacies.

The missionaries' second goal was to supplant the native shamans as the religious leaders of Indian life. This entailed the doubly difficult task of not only discrediting these traditionally powerful physicians, soothsayers, and spiritualists but effectively replacing them in all their social and religious functions while subtly altering the content and methodology of their art. To be accepted by the Indians as bona fide shamans, endowed with *personal* spiritual power, was not easily done by the priests, who believed that they merely *interceded* with the spiritual forces of the universe on man's behalf. One of their initial tasks, therefore, was to persuade the natives that the intercession of a Holy Apostolic Church with an omnipotent God was in the long run more efficacious than appeal to the personal but capricious power of a shaman.

Leaders without followers were clearly worthless, so the Jesuits sought as their final goal the winning of the general native populations and the institutional and emotional support of their new converts. The first step toward this end was to create a rock-ribbed Christian faction among the tribesmen, preferably from leading families and lineages who could withstand the disdain of their more conservative neighbors. Then a trustworthy native cadre, if not clergy, had to be gathered and trained to carry on the new religion in the fathers' absence or in new locations. And to prop up the whole Christian community as it strove for complete hegemony over native life, the Jesuits sought to recreate in the North American wilderness the major institutions of Roman Catholicism—chapels and churches, sodalities and sacraments, calendars and choirs, ceremonies and services.

Though armed with a formidable array of personal and institutional weapons and fired by an uncommon zeal, the Black Robes did not conquer the lands of the Canadian infidels with anything like celerity. A major impediment was the disconcerting belief of the natives in their own superiority, to which many stubbornly held even after the French fathers had done their best to disabuse them. Indeed, they were convinced that the priests' very attempts to do so were further evidence of the priests' general imperfection.

To form a low opinion of the strangers the Indians had but to look them over and to observe their behavior for a short time. The long black and gray robes of the Jesuits and Recollects were not only effeminate but a positive liability in woods or on water. When wet they dried slowly and dragged sand into the canoe; when dry they caught on underbrush, attracted stinging insects, and absorbed the summer sun—along with the Frenchmen's distinctive scent of onions, salt, and garlic. Equally repulsive were the Jesuits' breeches, which would have slowed the hunter-warrior in pursuit of his prey and prevented him from squatting to urinate, as he was wont to do.[23]

Worse yet were the priests' beards and haircuts. The native idea of crowning beauty was long, stiff, black hair, "all lustrous with grease." To them, short-cropped hair on any part of the body was so repulsive that whenever a missionary fell into the hands of an Indian enemy his beard and tonsure were among the first objects of the torturer's rage. In the 1660s the Outagamis (Fox) killed any Frenchmen they found alone because they could not endure the sight of their beards. The French, in turn, their beards neatly trimmed in imitation of saints and royal ministers, were perplexed that in Indian eyes they seemed "very ugly," even "deformed." All over native Canada a beard was detested as a "monstrosity," "the greatest disfigurement that a face can have," a mark of weak intelligence and limited sex appeal. When the Hurons wanted to insult a Frenchman, they called him *Sascoinronte*, "Bearded, You have a beard."[24]

Another priestly oddity was their pointed disinterest in women. Although most of the northeastern tribes knew short-term continence among warriors before and during a war party, they did not immediately appreciate the missionary's vow of perpetual celibacy. Like most Europeans, they could not imagine a man without a woman; ignorant of the monastic tradition, they could imagine still less a life without sex. When the Recollects worked among the Hurons in the 1620s, they were bombarded with requests to marry. "In these importunities," wrote Brother Sagard with some embarrassment, "the women and girls were beyond comparison more insistent and plagued us more than the men themselves who came to petition us on their behalf." For reasons such as this, the missionaries who lived among the sexually liberated natives felt in need of truly "angelic chastity," for as Father Le Jeune put it, "one needs only to extend the hand to gather the apple of sin." When religious eyes could no longer support the sight of so much "lewdness, carried on openly," the priests moved to separate quarters, thereby earning even lower marks for sociability. Only with the advent of lonely French traders and soldiers did the fathers' lack of interest in Indian wives and daughters begin to win favor.[25]

Two other Jesuit rules also rendered the priests initially unwelcome in native camps and canoes. One was the vow of poverty that prevented the missionaries from owning personal property. The Society of Jesus was not a mendicant order like the Recollects and therefore enjoyed seigneurial rents and other endowments as well as royal and company subventions, which they applied to the work of the missions. But the problems of supplying the far-flung mission stations were not easily solved, particularly when small native canoes, laden with the owners' newly acquired trade goods, were the major means of transporting the missionaries and their annual necessities. In the early years, therefore, the priests were totally dependent on the hospitality of the natives for their food, shelter, and protection, with very few ways of reciprocating other than with the gift of salvation. As they quickly learned, however, to accept generosity from the Indians was "to bind oneself to return an equivalent," and in traditional Indian eyes gifts of a strange spirit were not the equivalent of familiar fruits of the earth.[26] Until the inauguration of the *donné* system, in which lay servants joined the missions to raise and hunt food for the fathers and brothers, the Black Robes were often regarded as ungracious freeloaders.

The *donnés* also helped to repair another Jesuit deficiency in the Indians' estimation. By constitution, candidates for the Society were required to leave all weapons behind when they entered the novitiate and, as men of peace, were prohibited from carrying or using them thereafter; one of the "mortal sins" that could lead to the dismissal of even the Society's Superior General was "the infliction of a wound."[27] When Indian traders at Quebec or Montreal were asked to carry the missionaries home with them, especially during periods of intensified Iroquois activity, the Indians were "very willing to take on board some Frenchmen who were well armed; but they did not want these long robes, who carried no arquebuses." Only a delicate mixture of threats and gifts from the French governor or company officials could persuade them to accept the pacific priests. The donnés, who worked under no such handicap, were less reluctantly received.[28]

Obviously, the missionaries began their work in Canada with several strikes against them. From the Indian perspective, their personal appearance was truly repulsive, their social behavior aberrant, and their clothes impractical and sexually confused. They could not paddle or portage a canoe, trot on snowshoes, or carry loads as well as an Indian woman. Raising a wigwam, trapping a beaver, or building a toboggan were clearly above them. If lost in the woods, they remained lost until rescued; if attacked by Iroquois, they did not flee or defend themselves. Even the black flies found them easy pickings. It should therefore not surprise us—though it was a source of endless incredulity for the priests—that the natives thought themselves "better, more valiant, and more ingenious than the French," indeed "by Nature superior to the rest of Mankind." Notwithstanding their "great lack of government, power, letters, arts and riches," as the first Jesuits put it, the Indians could not imagine a better life than their own. Like their Christian adversaries, they too believed that the supreme spirit had made them "the best people in the world" and given them "the best country" for their inheritance.[29] An opinion so firmly and universally held was not easily shaken, but it had to be before the missionaries could make any headway in propagating a faith grounded in man's natural unworthiness and the supreme sacrifice of the Son of God.

Against such odds the missionaries could only set to work with quiet determination and holy cunning. "As God made himself man in order to make men God's," a Jesuit superior counseled, "a Missionary does not fear to make himself a Savage, so to speak, with them, in order to make them Christians. . . . We must . . . follow them to their homes and adapt ourselves to their ways, however ridiculous they may appear, in order to draw them to ours."[30] The immediate object of the priests' efforts was to become accepted by the natives as men of "sense," people capable of "rational" discourse who shared at least the most basic native values and behavior. After experimenting briefly with various moods and miens, the Recollects discovered that the Indians preferred men of "gentle words, contentment in the heart, and a humble, serious and modest bearing."[31] The Jesuits needed even less time to make the discovery because these were qualities that they had cultivated and used to attract new members since their founding in 1540. In their Canadian "novitiates in [the] Nomadic life," Jesuit newcomers were advised by Paul Ragueneau, a veteran of the Huron mission, to cultivate a "tried Patience, to endure a thousand contumelies; an undaunted Courage, which will undertake everything; a Humility that contents itself with doing nothing, after having done all; [and] a Forbearance that quietly awaits the moment chosen by Divine Providence." But he also cautioned the reform-minded fathers against proceeding too fast with their tradition-bound hosts: "One must be very careful before condemning a thousand things among their customs. . . . It is easy to call irreligion what is merely foolishness, and to take for the work of the devil something that is nothing more than human. . . . It is difficult to see everything in one day," he noted wisely, "and time is the most faithful instructor that one can consult."[32] For the missionaries who wished to be accepted as men of sense, it was a point well and quickly taken.

Since social discourse must be conducted in a mutually intelligible language, the Jesuits had only two courses open to them when they entered their Indian missions: they could teach their numerous hosts to speak French or church Latin, or they could themselves learn a native tongue. All of them chose the latter, partly out of demographical expediency and partly because in the *Constitutions* of the Society Loyola had urged them to master the vernacular languages of their target populations. "Indian," he had written prophetically, "would be proper for those about to go among the Indians."[33]

The difficulty, however, was to learn without conventional teachers, books, or formal rules, "at an age already mature," languages that bore little resemblance to those of Western Europe. Once again, the process entailed a sudden drop in status for the learned priests. "Instead of being a great master and great Theologian as in France," Brébeuf warned his Huron-bound protégés, "you must reckon on being here a humble Scholar, and then, great God! with what masters!—women, little children, and all the Indians—and exposed to their laughter. The Huron language will be your saint Thomas and your Aristotle; and clever man as you are, and speaking glibly among learned and capable persons, you must make up your mind to be for a long time mute among the Barbarians." But if Christ's disciples wished to overthrow the "empire of Satan," they had no choice but to "attack the enemy upon their own ground, with their own weapons," the most important of which was an intimate knowledge of the native dialects.[34]

Not only were the missionaries far beyond the best years for learning languages, but their previous linguistic training, predominantly in Latin grammar, which they considered ideal, was weak in phonology, obsessed with dogmatic rules, and disrespectful of the integrity of linguistic systems.[35] The Algonquian and Iroquoian languages of the Northeast were very different from the classical paradigms of Latin and Greek. "When you know all the parts of speech of the languages of our Europe, and know how to combine them, you know the language," wrote Father Le Jeune after a winter with the Montagnais; "but it is not so concerning the tongue of our Indians. Stock your memory with all the words that stand for each particular thing, learn the knot or Syntax that joins them together, and you are still only an ignoramus."[36] Confusing letters with sounds, the missionaries found several "letters" missing from native languages, primarily the labial and fricative consonants b, p, m, f, l, v, x, z. When Sagard tried to teach the Hurons to say "Père Gabriel," the best they could manage was "T. Aviel." By the same token, the Indian languages were disconcertingly poor in abstractions, universals, and of course words from another world; no Montagnais or Huron had ever spoken before of sheep, salt, sin, cities, pewter, prisons, cannons, candles, kings, or Christ.[37]

On the other hand, the priests who applied themselves soon discovered in the native languages a number of entirely new sounds, mainly throaty gutturals, and a complex richness of grammatical forms that pushed their aging memories to the limit. Unlike Latin or French, most of the native languages of the Northeast had separate forms for animate and inanimate objects (which were just as arbitrary as the masculine-feminine distinctions in French), verbs that included information not only about the actor but the goal of the action as well, and long compound words resulting from the fusion of noun, verb, and pronoun elements, all fully conjugated (or declined) by tense, gender, and number. The Montagnais even used different words on land and on water.[38] But memorizing an "infinite" number of complicated words was only the missionaries' first step toward mastery of the Indian dialects. Far more difficult to capture for ears attuned to the sounds of Europe were the great diversity of native inflections, accents, breathings, and changes of tone. Frequently, "two words composed of the same letters [had] totally different meanings," a tailor-made trap for linguistic novices.[39] The Nipissing word *kidauskinne* meant "You have no sense" pronounced one way, but "You have lied"—a more serious accusation—pronounced another. While Father Massé was learning Montagnais at the Recollect convent near Quebec, he tried to ask a visitor, "Give me your soul," but gravely insulted the man when his inflection led him to predict, "You shall soon die."[40]

The priests had only one effective way to surmount the native language barrier, although initially they tried others. When the Recollects came to Canada in 1615, they resorted to the company interpreters for elementary instruction. A few were helpful and competent to teach, but others, particularly the Montagnais expert Nicolas Marsolet, refused to share their knowledge because of an oath to preserve the company's monopoly in all things. Even when the interpreters were forthcoming, their vocabularies were often shaped more by the economic life of the natives than by their religion, betraying minds that were, in the priests' estimation, "somewhat coarse."[41] Once a few missionaries were launched on their studies, they prepared short phrase books, dictionaries, and grammars for their successors. Copying these manuscripts became for new missionaries a standard part of their linguistic preparation. Brother Sagard and Father Le Jeune even began their studies of Montagnais in France, thanks to the labors of their Recollect and Jesuit confrères. But Le Jeune's little dictionary was "full of errors," and Sagard arrived in Canada "mute" without a knowledge of native intonation and accent. They and their colleagues soon discovered that "practice," as one of their best linguists put it, "is the only master that is able to teach us."[42]

Unlike the *coureurs de bois* who also pursued their calling in Indian country, the missionaries were denied the company of those female "sleeping dictionaries" who so quickly formed the strangers' tongues to native vocabularies, syntax, and accents. They turned instead to any villagers who would talk to them: men (including captives from other tribes), women (preferably those who were safely married), and children (who were always glad to swap their own words for priestly *bons mots*). If prayer did not bring instant fluency, the next best method was to have a teacher like the woman whom Pierre Laure engaged in 1730 to teach him Montagnais. When he satisfactorily pronounced his first word, she said to the others, "That will do; our father has spoken our language; I will no longer speak French to him."[43]

As difficult as the total immersion method might have been, more problems arose from a less rigorous approach. Since native teachers were not professional linguists, they were often stumped by the fathers' technical questions; even when they were not, they had to be plied liberally with food and tobacco to sustain their interest. When the lessons got boring, some teachers palmed off "vulgar words" on their eager pupils, which the Black Robes promptly "went about innocently preaching for beautiful sentences from the Gospels."[44] And throughout their long apprenticeships in the native tongues, the priests had to endure a steady barrage of ridicule for their halting speech. When Father Le Jeune's lodgemates wanted a good laugh for the evening they signaled him to make a speech in Montagnais, because, he admitted, "I pronounce the Indian as a German pronounces French." Even those who had progressed far in the languages were not immune from ribbing. After acquiring a remarkable facility in Nipissing, Jean Richer, a company interpreter, was told by his hosts that if he studied two or three more years—and cut his beard—he stood a reasonable chance of becoming a man of "sense."[45]

Despite their proven ability in Latin and Greek, a few missionaries were never able to subdue an Indian language, which their superiors took as a sure sign that they should be shipped home or relegated to humbler service among the French colonists or in a Jesuit residence. After four or five years with the Hurons, Noël Chabanel "could hardly make himself understood, although he was not deficient in either talent or memory—as he had shown in France, where he had taught Rhetoric with great satisfaction." Undoubtedly his "great aversion" to Indian manners and life had something to do with tying his tongue. Father Anne de Noüe was similarly handicapped—also by a feeble memory—and was sent back to Quebec after only one year.[46] But those who persevered and learned to speak as natives often went on to gain acceptance *as* natives, as men of probity and "sense" whose now-familiar words were worth listening to. Believing that "faith enters by the ear," the Black Robes did not hesitate to make the most of their new status.[47]

One of the earliest signs that the missionary had been accepted, at least provisionally, as a member of the tribe was that he was given an Indian name by which he would be known for the rest of his life. When he died, the name passed to his religious successor, exactly as the Indians "raised the tree of life" after the death of one of their own notables. In 1639 all ten Jesuit missionaries in Huronia went by local names. Father Brébeuf was called *Echon*, after a tree with medicinal properties, and his colleague Isaac Jogues was known as *Ondessonk*, a "bird of prey." Upon Brébeuf's death in 1649 at the hands of the Iroquois, the Huron survivors conferred his name on Father Chaumonot, who later served them at Lorette for nearly twenty years. Similarly, Jogues's name passed to Simon Le Moyne (who was originally known as *Wane*, because the Hurons could not pronounce the *m* in his surname) and then in 1666 to Thierry Beschefer, who was "baptized" at a great feast for eighty at which the name was drawn, Indian-style, "from the bottom of the kettle."[48]

The importance of receiving a name from the Indians—and at their initiative—was underlined in 1712 when Father Joseph Lafitau was posted to the Iroquois *reserve* of Sault Saint-Louis. To secure "accreditation" in native eyes, his fellow missionaries thought he ought to assume the Indian name of the late Jacques Bruyas, a noted linguist and missionary to the Iroquois. Since Bruyas had been dead only four months, however, the neophytes objected to "raising the tree too soon" and reproached the young priest for having usurped "their father's name." Nevertheless, Lafitau observed, "they unfailingly treated me as they would have him himself because I had entered into all his rights."[49]

Perhaps the villagers were upset because the Jesuits seemed to be taking for granted or arrogating to themselves a major native honor conferred only on those whose behavior and character merited it, namely adoption into the tribe. Being relatively new and untested, the thirty-one-year-old Lafitau was still under scrutiny when the fathers decided to ask the village elders to adopt him. The Jesuits were understandably, if not excusably, hasty because they knew from personal experience that unless a missionary was formally adopted he "would not be an acceptable person in the village." They knew that an Indian's identity was shaped as much by kinship as by language. Without bona fide membership in a recognized clan or family, a missionary could never receive a native name—traditionally drawn from a repertoire of distinctive clan names—or gain the trust of the villagers necessary to his religious work, no matter how well he spoke the language. When Father Luc Nau, one of Lafitau's successors at the Sault, was adopted at a grand feast in 1735, the council speaker repeated all the Indian names of former missionaries before drawing *Hatériate*, "The Brave, the magnanimous man" from the "kettle" of the Bear clan. Wrote Father Nau happily, "I now go by no other name in the village."[50]

A missionary's adoption in the relatively predictable environment of a Laurentian *reserve* was a "necessary formality," but in the distant and dangerous missions of the *pays d'en haut* it was a formal necessity. Among the nomadic hunting bands, even an Indian person without a family alliance stood little chance of survival. Since the priest traveled without food, shelter, or armed protection, one of his first tasks in launching a flying mission was, with "holy artifice," to get himself adopted by a prominent headman, preferably one whose extended family included a number of good hunters. If he was successful, the "captain" would henceforth regard him as a "son or brother," depending on his age and status, and the tribe would consider him "a native of their country and a relative of the chief." In his immediate family he would assume the rights and responsibilities of the deceased member whose name he bore.[51]

In a Laurentian *reserve* the responsibilities might outweigh the rights, as Father Jean de Quen, the superior of Sillery, discovered in 1644 when he accepted a few beaver pelts from an old woman and her kindred as a token of his adoption in the place of a relative who had been killed. All winter long his new kinsmen overwhelmed him with requests for food and lodging "as one who was expected to do for them all that the deceased was accustomed to do." But in the woods the priests always gained much more than they gave. When Gabriel Druillettes was "begot" by the Norridgewock Abenakis in 1651, not only was he fed, housed, and cosseted, but they carried his portable chapel everywhere, promised to clear land for planting, and invited him to their councils "for speaking, and for giving decisions in their affairs." Forty years later Pierre Millet's life was saved when his Oneida captor decided to adopt him as an elder brother and gave him the name *Otasseté*, after one of the founders of the Iroquois League. One moment a prisoner whose life hung in the balance, the next Millet found himself elevated to the status of a prominent chief, whose presence at council meetings was not only obligatory but a sharp pain in the side of the English, who wanted him dead.[52]

The ceremony of adoption was the first communal ritual in the priest's long passage to spiritual leadership among the natives. Marking his provisional acceptance as a man of "sense," adoption enabled him to request an audience for his ministrations wherever in the tribal territory he went. But alone it could not ensure that his listeners would return for a second session or admit him to their cabins for further talk. Only by a consistent display of three qualities could a missionary consolidate his sagacious reputation—oratorical skill, generosity, and moral integrity.

By virtue of their sacred office, the Jesuits' reputation for moral probity was perhaps the easiest to attain, in part because the standards of judgment were much the same in both cultures. Their clerical vows and the constitution of the Society virtually assured the molding of men who led lives that in the eyes of the Indians were blameless, if somewhat eccentric. Quite unlike the other Europeans with whom the Indians came in contact, the Black Robes, for all their initial ugliness and physical ineptitude, showed an admirable disinterest in native land, women, war, and pelts.

Unlike insatiable English and Dutch farmers, the missionaries asked for no land to plant their crops and therefore did not disturb the feeding patterns of local game. Even the rents from their large and numerous seigneuries along the St. Lawrence, which had been laid out on land swept clean of native inhabitants by the intertribal wars of the sixteenth century, were largely returned to the Indians in the form of missionary services.[53] As celibates who lived by themselves whenever possible, the Jesuits could hardly be suspected of corrupting Indian women. Nor were they a military threat, although their strategic interests and those of colonial officials normally coincided. But unlike the early trading companies, who fanned the preexisting hostilities between the Dutch-oriented Iroquois and their own native partners, the missionaries sought peace among the Indian nations to enable them to spread the Word as far as they could reach by canoe and snowshoe. Only the heretical obstruction of Protestant rivals called for military retaliation, a crusade for which native warriors were seldom wanting. And finally, in the presence of shimmering beaver robes the Jesuits acted very differently from the *coureurs de bois* and soldiers who sometimes accompanied them. It was obvious to the natives that the priests did not try to cozen them out of their furs with mind-boggling brandy or fiery rum, much less become inebriated themselves or launch into orgies of swearing under its influence. While they seldom refused skins when they were offered, they accepted them only on behalf of the Society or the Church, to help finance their religious work; certainly their austere attire and lack of personal possessions showed no evidence that the proceeds were being spent otherwise.[54]

Two other moral attributes served the Jesuits well in Indian country. Personal courage, especially in the face of death, was appreciated in Europe, but from the American natives it drew special respect. When the Jesuits ventured into Iroquoia for the first time after the destruction of the Hurons, the *sang-froid* they displayed when boastful warriors told them "It is I who killed such a black Gown" and "It is I who burned that other" gave their protagonists a favorable impression of their sustaining faith. The Iroquois were even more impressed when Father Jogues, his hands mutilated by torture during his previous captivity, returned to the Mohawks in 1646 to pursue the cause of peace and Christ. When gentle fathers endured the most hideous torments as stoically as the most hardened warrior, the Indians knew they were pitted against men of uncommon spirit. Bred to self-abnegation and strict obedience to a higher will, the Jesuits could with no dissimulation tell their native audiences that "people like us do not fear death. Why should we fear it? We believe in God; we honor, love, and obey him; and we are assured of eternal happiness in Heaven after our death."[55]

The other quality that raised the missionaries in Indian eyes was their relative immunity to the epidemic diseases that scythed through native villages with cruel intensity and frequency. The Indians were impressed with the anomalous health of the Black Robes because in their own cultures good health and longevity were signs of "right living," of strict attention to moral rules and proper respect for the spiritual forces of the universe. When powerful shamans not only could not stay the diseases but succumbed themselves, the natives could only regard the Jesuits, who worked among the sick and dying every day without becoming ill, as superior "spirits." Initially, in the disorienting chaos and sweeping mortality of the first wave of epidemics, they feared the black-robed strangers as "demons" and "sorcerers" who had spawned the diseases to conquer them. But the fathers quickly commandeered the argument and gave it a Christian shape by suggesting that they survived the Creator's just punishments because they strictly obeyed His moral law.[56] Since the Indians believed in a similar connection between god-given health and spiritual morality, their fearful "astonishment" at the Jesuits

8. When the Iroquois launched their mass attacks on the Hurons in 1648–49, Jesuit priests were among their victims. This composite painting (*ca.* 1665) by Hugues Pommier brings four martyrs together, although they died at different locations at different times. Father Jean de Brébeuf (right) receives a "rosary" of red-hot hatchet blades while another warrior prepares to "baptize" him with a cauldron of boiling water. Much of the authentic detail in the picture is based on a 1657 drawing by Father François-Joseph Bressani, who witnessed the destruction of the missions. Reproduced by courtesy of Le Musée des Augustines de l'Hôtel-Dieu de Québec.

eventually turned to grudging respect that credited the priests with still more native "sense."

Even when the results worked against them, the Indians also admired the Black Robes' ability to hold their own in the rhetorical give-and-take of native councils. It took no time at all for the Jesuits, virtually all of whom were former debate coaches and professors of rhetoric, to realize that "there is no place in the world where Rhetoric is more powerful than in Canada" and that, man for man, the native Canadians were "the greatest speech-makers in the world," fully equal to Cicero and the most renowned European orators of their own day.[57] An Indian chief or "captain" was chosen largely for his eloquence and "obeyed in proportion to his use of it." Lacking the European instruments of civil force, all of his authority rested in "his tongue's end." If he could not persuade his tribesmen to obey, they went their own

way. In the intensely oral cultures of America, reason had to be clothed in
"undisguised eloquence" before it would sway public opinion. Not unreason-
ably, the earliest Jesuits predicted that "any one who knew their language
perfectly . . . could manage them as he pleased."[58]

It was not that simple, however, as the fathers discovered when they
attended their first Indian council as passably fluent speakers. The best
orators, who were therefore the most influential politicians, cultivated a
special style of delivery in which "they raise and quaver the voice, like the
tones of a Preacher in olden times, but slowly, decidedly, distinctly, even
repeating the same reason several times." To add further interest to the
proceedings, the speeches were couched "almost entirely in metaphors" and
the speakers spoke "not less by gesticulation than by language," walking back
and forth like "actor[s] on a stage."[59]

The missionaries who wanted to translate the Word of God into a native
idiom lost no time adopting the native style of speaking. One of the most
successful imitators was Simon Le Moyne, who engineered a peace council at
Onondaga with four nations of the Iroquois in 1654. In a two-hour peripatetic "harangue," he astonished his hosts when they heard him, "speaking
slowly and in the tone of a Captain," name them all "by Nations, bands,
families, and each person individually who was of some little consequence."
Le Moyne's accomplishment was the more remarkable because he spoke not
in any of the languages of his audience but in the closely related Huron
tongue. The following year Father Joseph Chaumonot reaffirmed the treaty
in "a torrent of forcible words" and preached in what his colleague could only
call "the Italian style, having a sufficient space for walking about and for
proclaiming with pomp the word of God."[60]

Both missionaries were greeted frequently with chesty *Haau*s of approval
from their patient auditors, not only because the priests had mastered the art
of council speaking with proper panache but because they had also learned
how to use gifts to "interpret" their words. Just as no tribal business could be
done "without speeches," so not a word was said "except by presents," which
were thought to speak more forcibly than lips.[61] Every major item of discussion had to be represented by a gift of commensurate value, to serve partly as
surety for the speaker's sincerity and partly as a mnemonic device for his
audience. Since every proposition received a formal reply, gifts were exchanged in a setting of studied reciprocity; to go home empty- or short-
handed was to suffer a grave insult. Much of the diplomatic success of French
officials and of the Jesuits in North America was due to their conscientious
adherence to native protocol in matters such as this.

The native custom of conciliar gift giving was only part of a more general
pattern of generosity that the missionaries had to emulate if they wished to
consolidate their positions as men of "sense." In the precarious economies of
the Northeast, survival of the group depended heavily on an ethic of open
hospitality and open-handed sharing; the capitalist idea of accumulation for
a rainy day was totally foreign. For people who normally lived close to the
bone and whose daily consumption fluctuated wildly with the weather, the

seasons, and the fortunes of the hunt, one of the worst epithets was "stingy."
In the early years many of the missionaries were so branded. One reason was
that the mendicant Recollects and the pre-*donné* Jesuits were totally dependent on their native hosts for food and thus seldom in a position to repay the
numerous feasts to which they were invited. Knowing that for every favor the
Indians expected a return, the priests were forced to decline invitations,
which the Indians regarded as another sign of unsociability. Another reason
was that even when the fathers had a supply of food, usually at the start of a
trip from Quebec, they were visibly nonplussed when the Indians consumed it
all at the first opportunity. They soon learned, as did the Recollects among
the Montagnais, that "there is no remedy for that, and one must . . . not
speak a word, otherwise they would call you *Onustey*, miserly and stingy."[62]

Still a third reason for the unfavorable impression the missionaries initially
made was the general reputation of the French. The Hurons, among others,
despised the French merchants, who would "bargain for an hour to cheapen a
beaver's skin," because they themselves were "satisfied to take what one
honestly and reasonably offers them." They were also appalled to learn that
indigent beggars roamed the streets and highways of France. Since they, like
the other tribes of the Northeast, "shared everything" with anyone in need,
they blamed the French situation on the Recollects' lack of charity. When the
Jesuits succeeded the Gray Robes, the Hurons tarred them with the same
brush, even when the fathers were sharing the best of their meager provisions
with the sick. During the epidemics of 1636 a hostile Huron man handed
Father Le Mercier a slab of fish and a sharp "compliment": "Look now, how
people ought to do when they concern themselves to give," he said. "You
people, you are misers; when you give meat, it is so little that there is hardly
enough of it to taste."[63]

Though there was little the Black Robes could do to avoid criticism, they
made concerted efforts to earn indelible reputations for charity and liberal-
ity. They never went anywhere without distributing, especially to the women
and children, small presents that made up in novelty what they may have
lacked in value. They maximized the credit earned by the Hôtels-Dieu of
Quebec and Montreal, their own hospital at Ste.-Marie-among-the-Hurons,
and their assiduous care and feeding of their hosts during frequent illnesses
and epidemics. And they repaid the generosity of their adopted tribesmen
whenever possible with all the means at their disposal. At Ganantahaa in
Onondaga country, the Jesuits kept "open house for the Indians," though
they "brought no means of subsistence" with them and did not "possess an
inch of soil" for raising any. But they firmly believed that the Indians would
be attracted to the truths of the gospel when they saw them published with
such liberal "*éclat*." Similarly, whenever native delegations visited the French
settlements, the Jesuits treated them as handsomely as possible. Unlike the
officers and gentlemen who vied for the Indians' company, however, the
acculturated fathers entertained them "in the native fashion," as they did a
party of Onondagas in 1665, "by giving the chief wherewithal to give a good
feast to the Hurons and Algonquins," their temporary allies, and, in the

evening, "by taking to each of them a small loaf, some roasted eels, some prunes, and beer."[64] While the Indians had long memories for generous treatment, they had longer ones for errors of parsimony, and the Jesuits sought to avoid the latter at all costs.

Because of their great learning and the proven success of their proselytizing in Europe, Asia, and the Far East, the Jesuits were expected by many of their countrymen, particularly donors, to make quick and dramatic gains for Christ among the unlettered *sauvages* of North America. "Some are astonished," wrote Father Le Jeune in 1633, "when they hear nothing about the conversion of Indians during the many years that we have been in New France." But they should not have been, for after the Jesuits had been in Laurentian Canada only a year, Charles Lalemant had warned French readers that "the conversion of the Indians takes time. The first six or seven years will appear sterile to some; and, if I should say ten or twelve, I would possibly not be far from the truth." Le Jeune agreed, pleading for time in a homely metaphor: "It is necessary to clear, till, and sow, before harvesting," he said, immediately noting that "it was 38 years . . . before anything was accomplished in Brazil." "How long," he asked rhetorically, "have they been waiting at the gates of China?"[65]

Converting the Indians did indeed take time, largely because the Jesuits had to put themselves so long to school in native languages, customs, and manners. But once armed with a native tongue, an Indian name, a family alliance, and a steady reputation as a man of "sense," the Catholic priest was finally ready to challenge his shamanic rival for spiritual leadership of the tribe. And this too would give the Black Robes "no little trouble," just as they predicted.[66]

CHAPTER SIX

Harvest of Souls

*Those who think that one has only to show
a crucifix to an Indian to convert him
deceive themselves.*

CHARLES GARNIER, S.J.

From the first coastal assault on Acadia, the Jesuit invasion of pagan America was suitably cast in a military mold. Ignatius Loyola, the founder of the order, had been an audacious officer in the Spanish forces of Navarre before his conversion to the religious life while recovering from wounds suffered in a French attack. A noble son of Spanish chivalry, he fell naturally into the language of war when he penned the institutes for his new Society of Jesus. So did Pope Julius III, whose bull *Regimini militantis Ecclesiae* sanctioned the order in 1540. Having received a special vow of obedience from the Jesuits, he regarded them as "soldiers of God beneath the banner of the cross," "clad for battle day and night" in the "militia of Christ." Both men agreed that Christ's will was that they should "conquer the whole world and all [his] enemies" and that only uncommon men bound by a vow of unquestioning obedience to their superiors could successfully spearhead the attack.[1]

Once a beachhead was secured on the St. Lawrence, the Jesuits drew their battle lines with the ancient metaphors of evangelical Christianity and religious crusade. One of the first ashore in 1632 was Paul Le Jeune, who said he felt like a mere pioneer sent to "dig trenches" for "brave soldiers" who would "besiege and take the place." But after meeting the enemy in person, he began to talk more like a soldier at the front. As superior of the Canadian mission, he mounted linguistic "expeditions" to "attack the enemy upon their own ground with their own weapons," and designed "batteries" to "destroy the empire of Satan," over which the French would "unfurl the banner of Jesus Christ." His main target was the "infinite" number of Indian "superstitions," which, "like spoils carried off from the enemy," he hoped to consecrate to his spiritual redeemer. Appropriately, native converts were quickly christened "new soldiers of Jesus Christ."[2]

Le Jeune's successors and colleagues carried the same aggressive spirit to Canada. They saw the Jesuit residences in Huronia as so many "forts" and "citadels" from which they would launch "batteries of Sermons and instructions" aimed at the Demon's "fortress." In 1646 the beleaguered Huron Church was likened to "an army which is in the fight, and which, being separated into various squadrons [village churches], sees itself weakened on

9. Paul Le Jeune (1591–1664) was the Jesuit superior in Canada from 1632 to 1639, the editor of the first eleven *Relations*, and procurator of the Canadian mission after his return to France in 1649. From an engraving by René Lochon, 1665, courtesy of the Public Archives of Canada, Ottawa, Picture Division (Negative no. C 21404).

one side, but breaks through the enemy on the other; and, though it suffers losses, maintains itself invincible in its organization, and remains victorious in the field of battle, not exterminating its enemy, which still goes on renewing the combat, but strengthening itself with glory the more it is attacked." When the Jesuits were invited to the Iroquois cantons in 1656, they saw an opportunity to "wage war against the Demons in their very Stronghold." After a winter of peaceful moderation, befitting their status as diplomatic hostages, the Black Robes "openly declared war against Paganism" the following summer. Only a "Church militant" could hope to accomplish "the conquest of this new world" with anything like the speed and thoroughness demanded by the Jesuits and the post-Tridentine hierarchy.[3]

The extended military metaphor employed by the Jesuits to describe their missionary goals and methods was apt, not only because proselytizing Christians did in fact take the offensive in North America, but because the initial Jesuit goals were to attack and supplant the native shaman on his own ground and to nurture Christian factions within the native communities. Having infiltrated the enemy camp in the guise of men of "sense," the Black Robes sought to organize a native resistance movement against the unholy usurpations of the Devil and his gullible minions. How well they succeeded in these initial tasks largely determined the pace and penetration of their subsequent efforts to install a Christian master over native life.

The first target of the Jesuits' campaign to Christianize America was the native shaman, the sentry of "superstition" and custodian of cultural conservatism. Not unlike the French priests themselves, the shamans performed functions in their societies that far exceeded their strictly religious roles. In modern terms, they were thought to be not only doctors of the soul but physicians of the body who could diagnose, treat, and explain illnesses of all kinds; psychiatrists who could cause as well as cure psychosomatic illnesses and witchcraft; meteorologists who could control as well as predict the weather; and clairvoyants who could predict the future and find lost objects. Of these functions the most important were weather control (because hunting and farming depended so heavily on favorable conditions) and the preservation of individual and community health. By exercising so much personal power over the vital activities of the community, the shamans were able to become virtually indispensable in the eyes of their tribesmen and to extract high fees for their unique services.

To destroy these bulwarks of tradition the Jesuits mounted a three-pronged offensive. First, they sought to undermine the whole fabric of native belief that supported the shamans' influence. Simultaneously, they offered a personal challenge to the shamans' authority by attacking their practices as charlatanry calculated to separate weak patients from their wealth. And finally, they sought to persuade the native community that the Jesuits' own selfless brand of social religion was more efficacious than the shamans' mercenary "jugglery," and that they could successfully replace the shamans in all their roles with only minor adjustments in the daily life of the group. If at the same time they could persuade the shamans to renounce their diabolical art and to enlist their social influence under the Christian banner, so much the better. If they could not, they trusted in divine justice to remove those stubborn "idolaters" from the ranks of the living.

As people who had imbibed Christianity with their mothers' milk and later had severed nearly all natural ties for the religious life, the Jesuits were understandably ambivalent about the possibility of undermining native traditions of thought and action.[4] As evangelical missionaries who had to believe in the convertibility of all men, they tended, especially in the launching stage of a mission, to underestimate the tenacity of cultural habit. Undoubtedly, fewer priests would have requested posting to Canada if they had known just how obdurate native customs and character would prove to be. At the same time, the Jesuits' experience with cunning young students bred to a variety of family values and with the underprivileged of French society, who were preoccupied more with empty bellies than with unsaved souls, taught them not to expect quick results. Recalling the residual paganism of the European Christian community in their own day, they reminded each other—and their impatient French supporters—that "you cannot all at once eradicate the deep-rooted customs and habits of any people, whoever they may be." As for Indian customs, cautioned Father Le Jeune, "a disease of the mind so great as is a superstition firmly established for so many centuries . . . is not eradicated in a moment." At least in the beginning, no missionary had to be convinced that the majority of native habits were riddled with "superstition," which like sin itself was "a chain, very difficult to break."[5]

To cut the links of habit that bound the Indian people to their ungodly past, the Jesuits possessed two powerful tools: novelty and self-righteous audacity. The first drew a crowd and got the priests a hearing for their strange ideas; the second shook many natives out of their habitual complacency long enough for them to entertain the insidious possibility that the new views might be superior to their old ones. While the appearance or reputation of these newly minted men of "sense" could capture an audience, the Black Robes' resort to public ridicule and aggressive criticism of native beliefs, practices, and priests was dumbfounding to people who studiously avoided any behavior that would humiliate a tribesman. As a Jesuit historian admitted in 1710, "to jest in the victim's presence, or to make a verbal attack, face to face, is characteristic of [European] religion," not of Indian etiquette.[6]

Although later responses would show that the Indians were not devoid of resources to combat this shocking effrontery, they were initially at a disadvantage. Not only were they untrained in the martial arts of scholastic disputation, but they were thrown on the defensive by the very act of having their habits questioned, a process that no culture can long withstand. While many native habits may have had self-consciously rational origins deep in time, the essence of habits is that they are unexamined, and therefore largely indefensible, ways of thinking and acting. Only a people accustomed to rationalizing their every thought and motion would have possessed an armor of self-consciousness strong enough to repulse the Jesuits' unseemly irruptions.

That the Indians were not so clad left them vulnerable. Father Le Jeune set the standard for priestly pugnacity when he wintered with a Montagnais shaman and his kin in 1633–34. At every turn Le Jeune "ridiculed his [host's] sorceries" and the "foolish beliefs" and "superstitions" of his tribesmen. At a three-hour "shaking tent" conjuration, where silence was mandatory, Le Jeune did not fail to intrude "a little word" into the proceedings. On other occasions he made sport of the Montagnais' dreams and their taboos regarding the treatment of animal bones. When they refrained from throwing beaver bones to the dogs for fear that their future hunting would be spoiled, Le Jeune told them that the Iroquois and the French observed no such nonsense and yet captured more game than they. Because the Indians believed that puncturing the backbone of an animal with a stick caused intense pain in the spine of the perpetrator, Le Jeune did it purposely, in their presence, "to disabuse them." At their eat-all feasts, where everything had to be consumed by the participants to secure good hunting or the cure of a sick person, Le Jeune threw some of his meat to the dogs to "contaminate" the proceedings. And when his lodgemates were thrown into terrified silence one night by the approach of the "Manitou" or "Devil," Le Jeune laughed at them, boldly walked outside, and called the creature in a loud voice, announcing that as a man of God he was not afraid and challenging the Devil to appear in his presence.[7]

Whether exposing inconsistencies in tribal legends or ridiculing the "childishness" of religious rituals, the Jesuits kept up a steady bombardment against native tradition. Most of the attacks were verbal, but some priests eventually felt secure enough to commit physical acts of iconoclasm. In honor of the first Christian commandment, the main targets were religious "idols," especially those to whom "sacrifices" were made. In the western Great Lakes region Father Allouez encountered two man-shaped rocks near rapids to which the natives offered tobacco, arrows, and other painted objects to ensure a safe journey. To remove these causes of "idolatry," he had them carried away "by main force" and thrown to the bottom of the river. In the same spirit, Father Henri Nouvel desecrated a "sacrifice to the sun" while traveling with some Ottawas near Lake Erie in 1676. Coming upon a dog hung from a painted pole, he "overturned everything, broke the pole, and cast the dog into the river, with the scalp of an extraordinarily large and hideous bear which had also been immolated."[8]

If the Jesuits' assaults on native tradition were to succeed in opening the way for Christianity, the priests had to gain a native following of those who dared to break with popular opinion long enough to entertain the new option. In the face-to-face oral cultures of the native Northeast, where popular opinion was much more the arbiter of truth than it was in the larger literate cultures of Western Europe, finding such an adventurous group was initially difficult, for none of the Indians was eager to "take the dreaded first step, and venture to run counter to the customs of the Country." According to the Jesuits, the reason for the natives' reluctance was not total blindness to shortcomings in their own way or any major dissatisfaction with the Christian alternative, which appeared reasonable and consistent within its own terms. "It is strange that these Barbarians find our truths very adorable, . . . many of them approve our belief," puzzled Father Le Jeune in 1637, "and yet do not wish to receive it until they are dying." At the same time, he noted, "when one propounds to them some argument that overthrows their belief, they are the first to laugh at the simplicity of their forefathers for having believed such absurdities and childish notions." Even elderly Hurons who clung tenaciously to traditional ways could be made to "contradict themselves" and "admit their ignorance."[9]

Still, as the Jesuits discovered in village after village, precious few natives would risk being the first to break with tradition and take the exclusive part of the new way. The reason was simple: they were afraid of being "mocked by their fellows" and "receiving little bites from scoffers or impious people."[10] In these small communities, where survival demanded maximal cooperation, the need for internal harmony was too great, the fear of offending a potentially lethal spiritual enemy too strong, for individuals lightly to overthrow ancient habits for foreign novelties. So most villagers sat quietly on their mats to await the outcome of the spiritual contest between the Black Robe and the shaman, feeling it only sensible to side with a winner.

In attacking their shamanic rivals the Jesuits pulled out all stops. An early ploy was to force the shaman to lose his composure by humiliating him before his tribesmen and calling his work "child's play," a favor the shaman quickly learned to repay in kind. Adept at suppressing anger, the Indians at first were "greatly surprised when the Fathers censured their faults before the assembly; they thought that the Fathers were madmen, because among peaceful hearers and friends they displayed such vehemence." But the Jesuits' unexpectedly aggressive taunts and jibes so often shattered the surface of native civility that the shamans were hard put to restrain themselves and could hardly wait to unleash their tribesmen on the presumptuous Black Robes. Since "I was a great enemy of his impostures," Le Jeune wrote of his Montagnais lodgemate, "he did all he could to destroy me and . . . to make me the laughingstock of small and great," who were encouraged to heap upon the stranger "a thousand taunts and a thousand insults," such as "Shut up, shut up, thou hast no sense," "He is proud," "He is bearded like a Hare," "He has a head like a pumpkin," and "He is Captain of the Dogs."[11] Only fear of French retaliation or the loss of trade goods preserved the lives of the most obnoxious priests.

Name-calling was not nearly as damaging as the Jesuits' confident disparagement of the efficacy of the shamans' practices, for questioning a shaman's "medicine" was like "tearing his soul out of his body."[12] The Jesuits' greatest allies in this campaign were the lethal diseases they inadvertently brought from Europe. Against the strange ravages of smallpox, diphtheria, influenza, and measles, which careened unchecked through the "virgin soil" populations of the New World, the shamans' traditional songs, dances, incantations, and gyrations were totally impotent. Not only could the native physicians not cure their tribesmen, who tended to fall sick in inexplicably large numbers, but they often fell victim to the new diseases themselves. That the French, with their acquired immunities, were seldom brought low by the same disorders only put the natives' traditional medicine in a worse light. When the shamans' power thus reached its nadir, the Jesuits rushed forward with free nursing, comforting if not curative medicines, and a plausible theological explanation for the misfortunes that had taken the natives unawares.

The primitive state of contemporary European medicine was hardly capable of lending much real aid to the Jesuits' cause, but the priests' dedicated nursing of stricken villagers and the well-timed administration of a few placebos and cordials may have saved as many natives as did their constant prayers. Because the new epidemics commonly struck down whole villages, leaving no one well enough to fetch wood, water, or food for the sick or to shift them on their mats, the Jesuits and their servants cheerfully assumed these chores. Although the priests seldom had enough supplies for their own purposes, they spoon-fed weak soups, water sweetened with sugar or raisins, bits of lemon peel ("French squash"), and prunes to as many patients as they could reach. If they were available, small doses of theriac and senna were also given, especially to persons whose recovery was despaired of by the shamans. On other occasions, desperate faith in the strangers' medicine endowed placebos with temporary efficacy. Bleeding was the most popular one. During the Huron epidemic of 1636–37, Simon Baron, a Jesuit *donné*, bled more than two hundred inhabitants of Ossossané, who "emulated each other in holding out their arms to him—the well ones having themselves bled as a precaution, and the sick considering themselves half cured when they saw their blood flowing." Likewise, Father Le Moyne gained a favorable reception among the normally hostile Cayuga Iroquois in the cabins where a French surgeon had preceded with his lancet during another epidemic in the winter of 1661–62.[13] Among sedentary and nomadic tribes alike, the Jesuits' medicines often "dazzled the whole country," including some skeptical shamans, and served as "an introduction to the faith."[14]

Whether or not the missionaries could outperform the shamans in curing native illness, the Christians had a decided advantage in the equally important task of explaining the fearful epidemics and other calamities: they simply attributed all misfortune to an omniscient God's just punishment of native sin, individual or corporate. In the absence of any consistent or compelling native explanations, this quintessential piece of Christian logic, always argued with absolute conviction and considerable vehemence, soon secured a firm place in neophyte epistemology. The process might begin much as it did in 1637 with the mauling of a Montagnais-Algonquin war party by the Iroquois. When the survivors straggled into Quebec, Father Le Jeune publicly blamed the disaster on the shaman who had accompanied them. Before the party left, he charged, the shaman had "blasphemed," saying that God could not prevent the success of their war effort. To this the fallen shaman could not reply, but a perspicacious companion said, "He will never do that again; he does not know him who made all." After a few such incidents, particularly epidemics of shocking mortality, and several doses of catechizing on the meaning of Adam's fall, many natives were ready to believe that death, disease, and poverty resulted from their own sin, or as one group put it, "all our ill-luck comes to us because we do not pray to God."[15]

Whenever the Jesuits eclipsed the shamans in curing native patients, they attributed their success less to human medical skill than to their spiritual intercession with a merciful God. Unlike the shamans' haughty personal power, ironically, it was the priests' indirect purchase of spiritual authority from an omnipotent deity of ineffable justice and goodness that gave them supreme confidence in the righteous efficacy of their own work. This confidence served them well in all their assaults on native religion. It allowed them to take partial credit for the recovery of ailing Indians after baptism or special prayers, to deflect all personal blame for native deaths, and to challenge their shamanic rivals for tribal leadership with weapons of the spirit.

Much of the Indians' loyalty to their traditional religion was rooted in fear of the shamans' ability to bewitch or "charm" those who defied their wishes or challenged their authority. As Father Le Jeune noted, "I hardly ever see any of them die who does not think he has been bewitched" by "charms, or wishes, and imprecations, by the abetment of the Manitou, [or] by poisons" which the shamans concocted.[16] Even if the Christian Devil was not involved in the shamans' "deceptions"—and there was some disagreement among the missionaries about it—the fathers knew they had to liberate the natives from their thralldom to the sorcerers before they could place their necks in the more comfortable "yoke of Christ."[17] The best way to do this was to issue a direct challenge to the shamans' power to kill by sorcery, for if the Black Robes could not be harmed by the most awesome weapon in the shamans' arsenal, then the natives would soon see the wisdom of being brought under the priests' protection.

When Father Le Jeune tangled with a Montagnais shaman named Piga-rouich in 1637, this was the priest's first maneuver. After baiting the shaman by ridiculing his practices and accusing him of arguing in "horse-and-mule" fashion, Le Jeune wagered him that the shaman's shaking tent was not caused by khichikouekhi, "those who make the light," as the natives believed, but either by the fraudulent shaman himself or by deceiving Satan. "Now the Devil fears us," the priest announced to the excited gathering, "and, if it is he, I shall speak to him severely,—I shall chide him, and shall force him to confess his impotence against those who believe in God; and I shall make him confess that he is deceiving you. Now when he sees himself ridiculed, if he gets into a fury, . . . we will defy him to approach us, and . . . he will not be able to do it, because God protects us." After the shaman went off the next day to hunt rabbits rather than accept the priest's challenge, Le Jeune retained the upper hand. Many of the shaman's followers marveled that the French were "greater sorcerers than they were" and called them Manitouisiouekhi, "those

who are acquainted with the Manitou, with him who is superior to men."
When the shaman finally dared to show his face, Le Jeune, like many of his
brethren in other settings, "often defied him to exercise his charms upon us"
and continued to ridicule his *manitou*, "whom they fear as they do death."[18]

Having done their best to expose the shamans' feet of clay, the Jesuits
proceeded to call for their spiritual deposition if not their actual death.
Getting a shaman to burn his pebble-filled drum, his scorched prognosticating sticks, and his medicine bag of stone amulets was a step in the right
direction because it was a public admission of defeat; converting him to the
more powerful "medicine" of Christianity was even better because his example was influential among his tribesmen, whose "great love . . . for life"
bound them to their "ordinary superstitions in order to give health to the
sick."[19] But if the shaman showed much reluctance to capitulate to the new
religion, the Jesuits informed his followers that "it was a wicked thing to use
[the Devil's] help," that "in France they put Sorcerers and Magicians to
death," and that therefore "they ought to do the same with their sorcerers."[20]
Just how seriously the natives took this suggestion or how seriously the
missionaries meant it to be taken we cannot know, but it must have conveyed
rather vividly the deadly animosity between the religious rivals. It is possible
that the Indians invested it with more significance than was intended because
they, too, were known to execute witches who used their spiritual medicine
for malevolent purposes, and their shamans on occasion did call for the
death of pestilent priests.[21]

Although the pacific Black Robes were not themselves given to physical
threats, they were not averse to calling down divine vengeance upon blas-
phemers or drawing pointed lessons from the timely deaths of recalcitrant
shamans. The "wretched Sorcerer" who made Le Jeune's Montagnais winter
miserable was "burned alive in his own house" not long after they returned
from the woods; two of his loyal brothers died equally ignominious deaths,
one by drowning, having "lost his mind," the other by starvation in the
woods, "like a dog." In January 1637 Tonneraouanont, a Huron shaman who
had already lost a great deal of his credit when his cures for and prophecies
about the prevailing epidemic proved worthless, was "beset by all sorts of
misfortunes, or to express it better," wrote Father Brébeuf, "God began to
chastise his haughty spirit." He broke his leg in a fall on the ice before his
cabin and died from complications three weeks later. By 1730 Father Pierre
Laure had witnessed the terrible deaths of four Cree and Montagnais shamans on the Saguenay. "Through the admirable providence of God," he
wrote, ". . . these wretched sorcerers, . . . persisting in their scandalous obsti-
nacy, die[d] a miserable death, in the midst of their criminal actions, or as a
punishment for their foolish medicines." By contrast, their converted colleagues, who had once seen "extraordinary fires and supernatural monsters,"
confessed that they "no longer saw anything, although they frequently traveled at night."[22]

The missionaries used many tactics to overthrow the native shamans and
to advertise their own fitness to replace them as the spiritual leaders of the

community. Perhaps the most persuasive was their demonstration of technological skills, which included not only knowledge of contemporary Western
science and geography but an impressive range of spiritual techniques for
manipulating nature. Added to their putative superiority in treating and
explaining novel diseases, the Jesuits' technological expertise confirmed their
reputation as men possessed of extraordinary *manitou* or *orenda*, men to be
revered and feared at the same time, as the shamans once were.

The most useful skill the priests seemed to possess was the ability to
summon wildlife and to control the weather to the natives' advantage. As the
shamans formerly were thought to predict the whereabouts of game, ensure
the timely arrival of rain, and protect crops from vermin, the Jesuits seem to
have achieved the same results frequently enough by prayers and processions
that many Indians felt they had no further need for the shamans. On
Christmas Day 1633, after a particularly hungry week in the highland forests
south of the St. Lawrence, Father Le Jeune and his Montagnais companions
offered prayers to "the Great Captain who hast made the Sky and the Earth."
Before a makeshift altar decorated with a small crucifix, a reliquary, and a
religious picture torn from the priest's breviary, each of the natives, including
the shaman, knelt and promised the Black Robe's God that, "if it pleases you
to give us food, I will obey you cheerfully, . . . I will surely believe in you."
Before the day was out all of the hunters returned with a porcupine or a
beaver, and moose tracks had been spotted that would lead shortly to
another kill. The baptized Abenaki band accompanied by Father Gabriel
Druillettes enjoyed similar success in the Maine woods in the winter of 1647–
48. According to their spiritual mentor, "God assisted them beyond their
expectation. . . . Some Pagans, who confided in their Manitou, were four
days without eating, and barely found enough to drag on their poor and
miserable existence. They all admitted, in the Spring, that the Father's band
had suffered less than the others, though it had proceeded into the most
barren regions of all those countries."[23]

As prayers procured meat for nomadic hunters, so prayers and other
Christian rituals protected the vegetable crops of semisedentary farmers.
When the Hurons experienced an especially dry summer in 1635, most of the
villages resorted to their own *Arendiowane* ("sorcerers") to bring rain to their
sandy soil. But in vain, for "the Heavens were as brass to their foolishness."
The "docile" people of Ihonatiria, however, applied to their Christian advisors for help. After explaining carefully that only God could bring rain or
fine weather, the Jesuits offered to make daily processions and a novena (nine
daily masses) to St. Joseph, the spiritual protector of the Hurons, to implore
God's aid. "Exactly as the novena was completed . . . on the thirteenth of
June," Father Brébeuf reported with relish, "we could not finish the Procession on account of the rain, which followed very abundantly and lasted, with
several intervals, the space of a month, with a great improvement and growth
of the fruits of the earth." Needless to say, the Hurons were duly impressed,
especially after another novena to St. Ignatius instantly brought rain during a
dry spell in late July. The Iroquois of Sault Saint-Louis were no less edified in

1679 and again in 1685 when the prayers of their priest and sprinklings of holy water appeared to destroy the corn worms that had ruined several successive plantings.[24]

The Jesuits sought to confirm their reputation as powerful medicine men at every opportunity. Sometimes the simplest French artifacts made disproportionately large impressions on native audiences. Father Le Jeune put a Montagnais shaman to shame by moving some needles on a piece of paper with the help of a concealed lodestone. The Hurons of Ihonatiria were reportedly "astonished" by some of the priests' household possessions: a pair of carpentered doors, a flour mill which they loved to crank, an eleven-sided glass which "represented a single object as many times," a small phial in which "a flea appears as large as a beetle," joiner's tools, and a clock the Indians called "the Captain of the day." "They all think it is some living thing" and that "it hears," wrote Father Brébeuf, "especially when, for a joke, some one of our Frenchmen calls out at the last stroke of the hammer, 'That's enough,' and then it immediately becomes silent." In the opinion of the missionaries, all these things served to gain the natives' affection and to "render them more docile when we introduce the admirable and incomprehensible mysteries of our Faith; for the belief they have in our intelligence and capacity causes them to accept without reply what we say to them." In tribute to the prowess of those who made such wonderful objects, the Hurons called the Frenchmen *ondaki*, "demons."[25]

The Indians' admiration of French technology allowed the Jesuits to introduce the argument from design for an omnipotent God, as they did on many other occasions. Moving from the craftsmanship of man-made objects, Brébeuf proceeded to ask the Hurons why they did not similarly conclude that He who made the sky, the sun, and the changing earth "must be some beneficent *oki*, and some supereminent intelligence."[26] This kind of reasoning appeared to have the best chance of appealing to the native mind because, as Father Le Jeune recognized, the essential truths of Christianity are "historical," and "the mind which has no knowledge of him who has revealed to us these truths remains free to believe or not to believe." To convince an Indian, therefore, "he must be confronted with natural truths, which," the Jesuits were confident, "are in harmony with our belief, then he embraces the supernatural truths through faith."[27]

The Jesuits possessed two exceptional skills that simultaneously excited the respectful wonder of the Indians and prepared the way for their reception of "supernatural truths": the ability to predict eclipses of the sun and moon, and the ability to read and write. The prediction of eclipses, Thierry Beschefer told his French provincial in 1683, "has always been one of the things that have most astonished our Indians; and it has given them a higher opinion of their missionaries." When the Jesuits predicted a solar eclipse not long before, Beschefer continued, some "Infidels" attempted to conjure the sun "not to cast that shame upon them." Their failure to move the sun and the priests' success "greatly disabused them of their persuasion that there was some divinity in that heavenly body."[28]

Father Pierre Millet drew similar strength for his attacks on Iroquois tradition from his prediction of a lunar eclipse on January 21, 1674. For several weeks before the event Millet had talked about the eclipse with the Oneidas and had "challenged the elders and, in particular, some jugglers who claim to foretell events, to say in how many days it would occur." When they all hung their heads in silence, he pressed them further: "Are these men—who know fabulous stories so well, who relate such extraordinary things about the sun and the moon, who take these objects for divinities, and offer them tobacco to obtain success in war and in hunting—not aware when one or the other is to be eclipsed?" After mass on the following Sunday Millet publicly announced that the eclipse would occur the next night. Everything happened as the Black Robe predicted, and the Oneidas were "compelled to admit that we knew things better than they. For my part," Millet reported, "I derived great benefit from this, in instructing them and undeceiving them about their myths and superstitions."[29]

Astronomical predictions were useful for undermining native beliefs, but they could also serve more positive ends. When an eclipse of the moon began on January 31, 1646, just when the Jesuits had predicted, the Huron converts of Ossossané rushed from their lodges and awakened the village's remaining "pagans," urging them to "come and see how truthful are our preachers; and strengthen yourselves, by this argument, in the belief of the truths which they preach to us." One neophyte confessed that, although faith alone was sufficient to bind him to Christianity, he had gotten up to see the eclipse "to confirm himself in the belief which he had, that what we taught them of the future resurrection will one day prove just as true as what we had predicted to them of this eclipse before it appeared."[30]

So powerfully did the Jesuits' predictions augment their credibility that the results occasionally backfired when the Indians continued to interpret the Black Robes' skill exclusively in traditional terms. In 1639 Jérôme Lalemant wrote from Huronia that "because we predict to them the Eclipses of the Moon and Sun, which they greatly fear, they imagine that we are masters of these, that we know all future events, and it is we who order them. And with this idea, they address themselves to us to know if their crops will succeed; where their enemies are, and in what force they are coming,—being unable to persuade themselves that we are not wiser in all things than their sorcerers, who profess to discover such secrets." When the fathers proved unable to predict or to prevent future events of this kind, especially disasters, the Hurons—and later their Iroquois cousins—held them personally responsible for doing nothing themselves and interdicting the use of traditional remedies.[31] Normally, however, the priests' predictive powers were taken on their own restricted terms and regarded with the awe due superior "spirits."

For oral peoples whose only libraries were the collective memory of their elders, the second Jesuit skill—that of reading and writing—was perhaps more awe-inspiring than any other and may have contributed to the Indians' reception of Christianity as much as any single method or argument employed by the missionaries. We who take literacy and printing so much for granted may have difficulty recapturing the sense of wonder, the almost totemic reverence, engendered by a tribal, exclusively oral person's first encounter with a book. Fortunately, Gabriel Sagard, one of the early Recollects in Huronia, left us some vivid reminders of what it was like. Since the Hurons understandably chose not to learn French in their own country, Sagard noted, "they were satisfied with counting the leaves of our books and admiring the pictures in them, and that with such close attention that they paid no heed to anything else, and would have passed whole days and nights over them if we had allowed them to do so. But such frequent handling of our books, which they constantly were asking to look at, one after another, especially the Bible on account of its size and illustrations, ruined them and reduced them to tatters."[32]

The main reason these nonliterate people "read" the friars' books to shreds was that they were searching for the secret power that allowed the Gray Robes to know the thoughts of others at a distance, something they believed their shamans could do only on rare occasions when their souls left their bodies during special visions. As Sagard was on his way back to Quebec, he and his Huron companions discovered that one of their canoes was leaky. So he sent a note to his colleague back in the village, asking him to send a fresh canoe. "When our canoe arrived," Sagard remembered, "I cannot express the admiration displayed by the Indians for the little note I had sent to Father Nicolas [Viel]. They said that that little paper had spoken to my brother and had told him all the words I had uttered to them here, and that we were greater than all mankind. They told the story to all, and all were filled with astonishment and admiration at this mystery."[33]

When the Jesuits followed the Recollects to Canada, they inherited the natives' respect for writing and the writer's mantle of spiritual power. But, as they did so often, they turned these advantages to religious purposes by arguing before native audiences that the Christian way of life was superior to the natives' just as the written word of Scripture was superior to the human variability of the spoken word. Father Francesco Bressani reported that one of the three most compelling arguments used by the Jesuits with the Indians was that "Scripture does not vary like the oral word of man, who is almost by nature false." After admiring the excellence of handwriting and how much more accurately it could transmit words than could fallible memories, "they began to discern the certainty of the divine word."[34]

In 1647 a Huron convert argued the Jesuits' part with convincing authority when he stopped the mouth of a speaker at an important election council, where the Hurons traditionally related their tribal legends for the benefit of younger generations. "Where are the writings which give us faith in what thou sayest?" he asked. "If each one is permitted to invent what he will, is it strange that we know nothing true, since we must acknowledge that the Hurons have been liars from all time? But the French do not speak by heart; they preserve from all antiquity the Sacred books, wherein the word of God himself is written, without permission to any one to alter it the least. . . ."[35] With his shrewd grasp of native psychology, Father Sébastien Râle put the matter in terms no Indian could long resist. After explaining the major articles of the Christian faith to a group of Algonquians from the lower Kennebec, he added: "All these words that I have just explained to you are not human words; they are the words of the Great Spirit. They are not written like the words of men upon a collar [wampum belt], on which a person can say everything that he wishes; but they are written in the book of the Great Spirit, to which falsehood cannot have access." Small wonder that as early as 1638 "the art of inscribing upon paper matters that are beyond sight" was given no little credit for converting the natives of New France to Christianity.[36]

While the Jesuits were happy to capitalize on any external circumstances that heightened the natives' receptivity to their work, their main purpose was to convey a specific religious message. Even as they campaigned against the shamans, they began to catechize the natives in the meaning of Christianity on any occasion they could find—at the annual renewal of alliances; after funerals, when stories were traditionally told; at adoption ceremonies; during the torture of captives; in cabin visits to nurse the sick; and in special councils to discuss the new challenge to tradition.

One early line of argument that carried considerable weight with the natives, especially those villagers who had sent a kinsman to view the splendors of France, was that the French priests would not have left their fair country if they were not absolutely convinced of the accuracy of their religious vision. One well-taught Huron convert argued in 1646 that "it must be that those who come to teach us are more certain of [resurrection in Heaven] than of the things which they have seen in France; since it is only with a view to Paradise that they have abandoned their relatives, their native land, and whatever there can be most agreeable in the world, in order to come here to drag out a wretched life with us." When Father Bressani returned to Canada in 1645, having been captured by the Iroquois the previous year and suffered the loss of most of his fingers, the Hurons asked themselves, "If there were not a Paradise, could there be found men who would traverse the fires and flames of the Iroquois, in order to withdraw us from Hell, and to lead us with them to Heaven?" "No," one exclaimed, "I can no longer be tempted regarding the truths of the faith. I can neither read nor write, but those fingers which I see cut off are the answer to all my doubts."[37]

If the Indians were not convinced by native testimony, the Black Robes themselves did not hesitate to spell out the nature of their sacrificial mission. "It is not for purposes of trade that you see us appear in your country," Father Chaumonot told a great council of the Iroquois in 1656. "We aim much higher. . . . For the Faith, we have left our country; for the Faith, we have abandoned our relatives and our friends; for the Faith, we have crossed the Ocean; . . . for the Faith, we have given up fine houses, to lodge in your bark cabins; for the Faith, we deprive ourselves of our natural nourishment, and the delicate viands that we might have enjoyed in France, to eat your boiled meal and other food, which the animals of our country would hardly touch."[38]

Just what the Black Robes meant by "the Faith" was rather more difficult to explain than they anticipated, in part because they had somewhat ambivalent feelings about it themselves. On the one hand, at their most evangelical the Jesuits were convinced that the principal articles of Christian belief were few and easily grasped, "since God commanded us to do nothing which was not most reasonable."[39] On the other hand, they characterized those articles almost universally as "mysteries," which could not be fully explained to the natives without a sophisticated understanding of their languages. And maybe not even then, for "our truths," Father Le Jeune held, "are newer to these Barbarians than the operations of Algebra would be to a person who could only count to ten."[40] The Indians' intellectual capacity was never at issue; according to the Jesuits, who were old hands at evaluating brainpower, they compared favorably with peasants, rural villagers, and even "the shrewdest citizens and merchants" in France.[41] Only the novelty and complexity of the Christian credo imposed barriers to native understanding.

The novelty of Christian belief stemmed largely from the historical origins of the religion in a course of events surrounding the life of Jesus Christ (a man the Indians had never heard of) in the Near East (a part of the world they did not know existed) more than sixteen hundred years before (an inconceivable length of time for oral peoples). It was all news to the natives that the Great Spirit (God), after creating the universe from nothing, made the first man and woman on earth and promised them eternal life in Paradise for their faith and obedience (many of the northeastern Indians, particularly the Iroquoians, believed that a water-covered earth existed before a Sky-Woman fell from heaven to people a gigantic island, formed on the back of a turtle from mud gathered by a diving animal); that the first couple disobeyed God, thereby staining their progeny with original sin and condemning them to eternal punishment in a fiery Hell (the Indians knew only a beneficent afterlife and nothing of sin); that in His mercy God breathed the holy spirit into the womb of a virgin, who bore His Son, Jesus (the Sky-Woman, too, became miraculously pregnant by "the wind," but bore twins, one good, the other evil); and that after a blameless life of teaching God's commandments, Jesus took upon himself the sins of the whole world and sacrificed his life upon a cross so that man might live again in purity and merit the joys of Heaven.[42] Perhaps equally stunning was the news that the Indian peoples of America, a continent unknown to the Old World when and long after Jesus lived, were included in this divine plan, and that the Black Robes had been sent by Christ's captain on earth to convey the good news written in God's Book.

At the most elementary level, where the Jesuits began their instruction, the main articles of Christian belief may have seemed plausible even to Indians who heard them for the first time. As a Montagnais man told Father Le Jeune, who had just summarized the Christian story, "I cannot contradict thee, for I have no knowledge to the contrary; thou tellest me new things that I have never heard before."[43] But the history of Christianity and especially of the Roman Catholic Church extended far beyond the exemplary life and redeeming death of Jesus. By the time the Indians received the Word, the Church had grown enormously in size and complexity, the centuries-old product of schism, papal personalities, secular interference, conciliar reform, theological debate, and ritual innovation. Understandably, "the Faith" of the Church—its articles of belief and ritual underpinnings—had experienced a similar evolution. Although the missionaries could compress the Christian requirements into two—"to believe in [God], and to be firmly resolved to keep his commandments"—the catechism, creeds, and set prayers they taught the natives contained a host of more complicated ordinances to be learned and followed by the good Catholic Christian.[44]

From Brébeuf's twenty-six-page Huron translation of Father Ledesme's *Doctrine Chrestienne*, the native catechumen learned, among other things, the sign of the cross, the Apostles' Creed (which spoke of the "remission of sins" and the "resurrection of the body"), the triune nature of God ("Father, Son, and Holy Ghost"), the necessity for "faith, hope, charity, and good works," the *Pater noster* (Lord's Prayer), the intercessional use of guardian angels, saints, relics, and the Virgin Mary to release souls from Purgatory (neither Heaven nor Hell), four kinds of sin, seven sacraments (including the Eucharist, in which bread and wine become the body and blood of Jesus Christ), and ten commandments. At the other end of the Laurentian mission, Father Massé taught the Montagnais many of the same lessons, in addition to an Angelic Salutation to the Virgin, pre- and postmeal grace, and two confessions of sin.[45] Clearly, the burden of knowledge and belief laid on the shoulders of a new Christian was not light.

As if the natives were not required to make enough additions to their religious knowledge, they quickly learned that conversion also entailed several troubling subtractions. Even if they could get along without their traditional shamans, their new black-robed priests insisted that they not only keep God's commandments but "give up their superstitions." The natives' initial reaction to this demand was predictable. Every day among the Montagnais, Le Jeune noted in 1639, "we hear some who tell us that our doctrine is good, but that its practice is difficult." Pigarouich, the former shaman who desired baptism, was frequently saddened by the thought that "God does not love us, since he gives us commandments that we cannot keep." To Father Brébeuf's request in 1636 that the Hurons of Ihonatiria renounce their dreams, eat-all feasts, *andacwander* (curative sexual assemblies), cannibalism, and loose marriages, Onaconchiaronk, an old chief, replied, "My nephew, we have been greatly deceived; we thought God was to be satisfied with a Chapel, but according to what I see he asks a great deal more." Captain Aenons added, "I must speak to you frankly. I believe that your proposition is impossible. . . . When you speak to us about obeying and acknowledging as our master him whom you say has made Heaven and earth, I imagine you are talking of overthrowing the country."[46]

The Hurons were not wrong, for the Jesuits did plan to "overthrow the Kingdom of Satan" in America, where native customs were ranked with "stagnant, ill-smelling pools." In the eyes of the first Jesuits, very little in Indian culture was free from "superstition" or from condemnation by God's law. "For, indeed," said Father Lalement in 1639, "the greater part of their dances, feasts, Physicians, and medicines, ceremonies, and customs, being either manifestly diabolical, or filled with so many senseless ceremonies that it is almost impossible to judge or interpret them as being free from superstition or tacit pact and communication with the devil, we are obliged to hold all these under suspicion, and to raise scruples against them in our Catechumens and Neophytes."[47]

To native thinking, the Jesuit list of cultural proscriptions was alarmingly long. It included not only narrowly "religious" practices, such as sorcery, dreaming, and sacrifices, but also customs from nearly every aspect of Indian life: health care (curing dances, games, feasts, and sweats), warfare (revenge, killing of children, cannibalism, and torture, though not war itself), domestic relations (slander, nudity, polygamy, adultery, divorce, and premarital sex), and death (suicide, excessive mourning, fancy dress of the corpse, and indiscriminate mixing of Christian and pagan remains). While a liberal reading of the Ten Commandments was responsible for some of these injunctions, the rest were the products of French ethnocentrism. Although the Jesuits belonged to an international religious order, they were nonetheless creatures of their own culture.

By 1648 even some of the priests realized that they had gone too far in the direction of social reform. Paul Ragueneau, the superior of the Huron mission, advised new missionaries to "be very careful before condemning a thousand things among their customs. . . . I have no hesitation in saying that we have been too severe on this point," he confessed. The fathers' excessive scrupulosity deprived their native converts of not only "harmless amusements" but "the greatest pleasures of life." "In any case," he concluded, "we find that such severity is no longer necessary, and that in many things we can be less rigorous than in the past."[48] Unfortunately for native culture, Ragueneau's lead was followed imperfectly in the major Laurentian *reserves* and only of necessity in flying missions to Indian country.

Given the rigor and complexity of the Jesuit demands, it might be thought that Christian doctrine and ritual were simply beyond the Indians' grasp and that the intellectual and cultural requirements for conversion were too exacting for all but the most exceptional natives. A memoir to the king from an anonymous missionary in 1671 suggested as much. No friend of the Jesuits, this missionary—probably one of the recently returned Recollects—told His Majesty that the evangelization of the Indians in Canada enjoyed little success, largely because the Jesuits did not adjust the (exalted) mysteries of the Faith to the (limited) intellectual capacity of the natives, exposing them to religious concepts too difficult for them to grasp.[49] He was wrong on both counts: the conversion of the Indians proceeded with enviable success throughout the 1670s, no thanks to the Recollects' and Frontenac's outdated and unworkable schemes for Frenchification, and the Jesuits garnered the vast majority of converts because they were amazingly adept at making the Christian message palpable, relevant, and appealing to even the least intelligent Indian, who was always capable of more than the other missionaries believed possible.

The greatest problem the Jesuits faced in teaching the Indians the new concepts of Christianity was translation. Since the priests were forced to speak only in native tongues, they had to find ways to convey with some fidelity the full meaning and resonance of ideas largely new to Indian experience. Finding few native words equal to the task, they were forced either to "coin words approximating to their language" or to teach the meaning of French words, which were then incorporated into the native lexicon. The Hurons and Iroquois seem to have preferred familiar coinage to imported specie. With the exception of a few proper names, such as Jesus and Mary, all of the Christian concepts used by the missionaries were translated into an Iroquoian word or phrase. According to a Jesuit dictionary written in the last quarter of the seventeenth century, the Onondaga word for *Christian* (*Chrétien*) meant "He has caused me to be good," a *church* (*église*) was a "holy lodge," the closest approximation to *sin* (*peché*) was "mistaking one matter for another," and the *Virgin* (*Vierge*) meant, plainly enough, "She does not know a spouse."[50] By the same token, in the works of Sagard, Brébeuf, and Father Pierre Potier (1708–81), the Hurons referred to the *soul* as "our medicine," to the *Jesuits* as "they are called charcoal," and to a *rosary* as "Mary's necklace" (with connotations of a collar of wampum).[51] On the other hand, the Abenakis of the Kennebec incorporated a number of French words along with their meanings. Father Râle's extensive dictionary contained *angeri* for "my angel" (*mon ange*), *hostisin* for "communion wafer" (*l'hostie*), *kékékimeghé* for "catechism" (*catéchisme*), *neconfessé8i** for "I confess" (*Je me confesse*), *sañᶜté Marie* for "feast of the Conception" (from *saint* [*jour*] for *fête*), and *aramâiskañin* for "mass" (*messe*).[52]

As might be expected, not every Christian word or phrase could be translated adequately into a native tongue. As the Onondaga rendition of *peché* suggests, the Indian languages had no word to convey the idea of sin as an offense against God. The closest the Montagnais could come was a word for *wickedness* which meant "a violation of purity," a sexual indiscretion. The difficulty was short-lived, however, because the natives could easily be taught to feel remorse for having committed such an offense after the Jesuits convinced them that their familiar Great Spirit was in reality the Christian God—omnipotent, omniscient, and a stickler for moral details. Somewhat harder to solve was the lack of an Iroquois expression to render correctly the "In the name of" portion of the baptismal formula. In 1681, when a fervent Mohawk convert wished to accompany a war party to the Illinois to baptize the victims before death, Father François Vaillant was forced to teach him the formula in French for lack of a better solution. Father Brébeuf had more luck

---

*The French used the numeral *8* to indicate the native diphthong *ou* (*w*).

in translating "In the name of the Father, and of the Son, and of the holy Ghost" into Huron. Because the Hurons could not say simply *Father* or *Son* without a pronominal prefix indicating the person to whom the noun was related, Brébeuf thought he had biblical sanction for translating it as "In the name of *our* Father, and of *his* Son, and of *their* holy Ghost."[53]

Cultural habits could also raise barriers to the acceptance of Christian concepts, even those adequately translated. When the Micmac chief Membertou was learning the Lord's Prayer from Father Biard in 1611, he hesitated when the priest came to "give us this day our daily bread." "If I did not ask him for anything but bread," the old Indian protested, "I would be without moose-meat or fish." Among the Hurons (and most of the woodland tribes), Father Brébeuf observed, "to speak to them of the dead whom they have loved, is to insult them." Thus the priests could not teach "Our Father who art in Heaven" to those who had no father on earth. "A woman, whose mother had died a short time before, almost lost her desire to be baptized because the command, *Thou shalt honor thy Father and thy Mother*, had been inadvertently quoted to her."[54]

No matter what words were used, the Jesuits had to teach the meaning of their faith largely through homely metaphors and analogies to other aspects of Indian life. One of the fullest examples of this approach is an extended set of "Instructions of a Dying Pagan" in Huron, probably used by new missionaries in the seventeenth century as a copy text for learning the language; it was still being used in the 1740s and '50s by Father Potier, the missionary to the Hurons on the Detroit River. The instructions begin as the priest attacks the Huron idea that the "medicine" (souls) of all human beings, "whether they are 'straight' people or malicious shamans," go to a heaven in the direction of the setting sun. Certain that his "writing" contains the true Word of "Him who is master" (God), the Jesuit argues instead that those people who "do good" and have "correct thoughts" will "enter the sky" after death, and those who often commit "offenses" and have "bad thoughts" will suffer "inside the earth." To ensure the former fate, humans have only two essential duties: to "greet God with great respect" (pray), and to "show compassion" for their fellows. Honoring God also means avoiding "the things he hates for all time," such as adultery, wife-stealing, larceny, and "sorcerers who kill by spiritual means."

Those who do not honor the master "have no sense," the priest continues, because they make him "angry." Which is "frightening," for those who commit offenses are thrown into "a lake of fire . . . that does not go out." The suffering of a war captive is trivial compared to that of the poor souls in Hell. The pain "lasts only a short time for those who are tied up, tortured, and die," but God punishes offenders "forever." "They breathe fire. . . . They make their meal of fire. They drink fire. . . . Fire serves as their bed. . . . Blood boils in their veins. Brains boil inside their heads. The boiling will never end. . . . Ah, it is frightening inside the earth."

Fortunately, God has given "the men called charcoal" (Jesuits) the means of "effacing the offenses of human beings"—baptism with "pure water" and "praying." Through the supreme sacrifice of his son, Jesus Christ, God offered salvation to those who would repent of their sins. Toward this end the dying man is encouraged to pray: "Have pity on me, great master. Purify me of the corruption of my offenses with baptism. Let me enter your 'straight' group. . . . I will not shame those who taught me your words. . . . I will not disobey them in the many things they ask of me. I will follow them to the sky." If the Indian sincerely repents, the Jesuit promises, "the underground dweller who bore you ill will and was enticing you inside the earth will flee. At that time Jesus will adopt you" into his "true family of believers" and "will provide a village in the sky for you to settle in when your life ends."

Having traded the promise of obedience for God's promise of "happiness in the sky," the people "completely made new" by baptism are expected to behave in new ways. "After a number of days," warns the Black Robe, "I will know of the good you resolved to do. I will know by looking at whether you have completely abandoned your former corrupt habits. I will know by the fact that every day you will go to pray; that every day you will instruct your relatives; and that you will ask: 'If only they were believers.' I will know if you are a believer in earnest each time you oppose joking about fornication; when you do not applaud people speaking out against Christianity; when you do not feel hate when people bother you; when you are not ready to obey when people ask or command you to do that which is bad." As a final warning the Jesuit reminds his auditor that "prisoners are sometimes seized again, who once escaped. Then it is excessive, their retying, as they are tied up tightly. At the time they are tortured again, they fear that those who go about doing damage will again retie them. You escaped from the spirit [Devil], my brother, when you were baptized. You should always be on your guard in order that the one who lives inside the earth does not recapture you. Continually go about learning so that you will not offend."[55]

It is no coincidence that the most striking metaphors in this Jesuit catechism are military. The whole piece is set as a battle between opposing sides: God versus Devil, Jesuit versus shaman, converts versus pagans. But unlike the Jesuit writings for French consumption, the martial metaphors were not drawn from European sources. For the main themes of torture, recapture, and adoption (whereby a captive was granted life by being made a bona fide relative of a family that had lost a member) the Black Robes drew upon their extensive knowledge of native warfare. That their analogies spoke knowingly to the natives' familiar experiences, especially those that carried a great deal of prestige, was one measure of the Jesuits' superiority as purveyors of the new faith.

Another way the Jesuits made their religious wares attractive to the Indians was to allow or encourage a certain amount of syncretic blending of old and new beliefs and practices, hoping thereby to ease the natives' transition to the new faith. This tactic, too, depended on a deep knowledge of native culture, but it also required considerable cultural flexibility, which was made possible largely by the fathers' supreme confidence in the ultimate victory of their religion and their own righteous talents. In the 1630s, however, before they knew which methods worked best, the priests were relatively inflexible about their cultural and religious standards. Typical was the disapproval they showed in 1636 toward an old Huron man who, although he had been the first adult in his tribe to cross himself, later tried to "blend our creed with their superstitions and nonsense" and ended by dying in "unbelief."[56]

But as the Jesuits settled on the most effective techniques and began to win converts, they felt freer to allow the natives some latitude in building bridges to Christianity from their own customs. By 1648 even the mentors of rock-ribbed Sillery were pleased that the neophytes there were "beginning to give quite a Christian character to the harmless usages that they have derived from their infidel ancestors." The priests were referring to the ceremony in which a deceased person was "resuscitated" by the giving of his name and obligations to a promising kinsman, who then adopted the man's orphans as his own children. A Christian captain of Sillery used the occasion of the resuscitation of his deceased nephew to deliver a fervent harangue on death as a temporary separation, not a permanent loss. "I take this resurrection of my nephew, that I now accomplish," he concluded, "as a symbol of the true resurrection to which we look forward. Therefore, I adopt such a one for my nephew; and he will remind me that my nephew is not dead." When the boy received the traditional present from his new father, he, too, made a gratifyingly Christian speech, which was followed by a customary chant but to the words, "He who is to bring me back to life is he who consoles me."[57]

As at Sillery, the initiative for most syncretic practices came from the natives themselves, although the priests monitored every innovation closely. The Kiskakonk (Bear) Ottawa band that wintered at La Pointe (Wisconsin) with Father Marquette in 1669 Christianized their traditional feasts by omitting sacrifices and using the customary welcoming speech to ask God for health and other necessities. In order to foster changes of this sort, said their Black Robe, "I keep a little of their usage, and take from it all that is bad."[58] Marquette's colleague in the west, Claude Allouez, was somewhat less tolerant of native initiatives. When converted Ottawas offered presents to the "true God" at perilous places in the rivers to ensure a safe journey, Allouez "disabused" them about the appropriateness of cloaking a pagan ritual in Christian garb. He was a little easier on a recently baptized Potawatomi ancient who prayed to God by "continually throwing tobacco into the fire and saying 'Thou maker of Heaven and Earth, I would honor thee.'" Perhaps because the man was thought to be one hundred years old, Allouez contented himself with making him understand that "it was not necessary to honor God in that way, but merely to speak to him with the heart and the mouth." With the Illinois the priest was still more relaxed. He thought their efforts to see the Christian God in traditional vision quests greatly facilitated their conversion, and believed that he had only to teach them "how they must serve him in order to see him and be blessed."[59]

On other occasions the Jesuits took the lead in adapting traditional practices to Christian ends. Although he generally disapproved of the cult of dreams, Father Le Jeune used the Montagnais belief in them to beat his pagan rivals at their own game. In early January 1634, as the hunting band with whom he traveled made its ninth settlement, Le Jeune's host dreamed that they had all perished in the woods for lack of food. Fearing that his host might abandon him to prove himself a prophet, Le Jeune "made use of his weapons" and related that he had dreamed just the opposite, "for in my sleep," he said truthfully, "I saw two Moose, one of which was already killed and the other still living." Even the shaman greeted this revelation with applause. Three years later Le Jeune again resorted to native custom to disarm a group of Algonquins who were resisting evangelization. "If thou dreamest that no one will be converted," he warned, "we will dream that you all will be converted."[60]

Of greater frequency was the Jesuit adaptation of new Christian forms to old functions. One of the easiest and most successful techniques was to substitute a variety of sacramentals for traditional stone amulets. All of the northeastern peoples with whom the Jesuits worked used "charms," to which they spoke and made feasts in order to obtain from them what they desired. Whether "found" in a dream, inherited, or purchased, charms were a necessity and were considered almost the sole avenue to good luck. Since amulets smacked of idolatry, however, native converts were promptly instructed to empty their medicine pouches and throw the contents in the nearest river.[61] Henceforth, they were to seek their fortune from God alone by supplicating him with the aid of Christian amulets—crucifixes, medals, rings, rosaries, and relics. These icons were not only mnemonic devices, like wampum belts and medicine sticks, but sources of power in their own right.

When used by believers in the proper spirit, Christian sacramentals were thought to perform as well as—usually better than—their "pagan" counterparts had for traditionalists. A rosary hung around the neck of a sick child restored its health. The grabbing of an Agnus Dei medal worn by a captive precipitated a violent thunderstorm and saved him from further torture. And "if there was anything in the world capable of inspiring the demons [of disease] with terror, it was the cross." At Tadoussac in 1643 an old man, formerly given to "dreams and superstitions," was persuaded to abandon his "cursed instruments" in order to obtain God's blessing upon his stricken son. When Father de Quen hung a crucifix above the child's head in the place of the father's medicine pouch, the boy's fever lifted and he was cured.[62]

Perhaps most efficacious were the relics of saints and Jesuit martyrs. Membertou's dying son was miraculously saved in 1611 when Father Biard laid "a bone taken from the precious relics of the glorified St. Lawrence" on him. In 1636 a Huron woman, after twenty-four hours in labor, "brought forth a child happily" as soon as the Jesuits applied to her abdomen "a Relic of Our Blessed Father St. Ignatius [Loyola]." After Napagabiscou, an Algonquin shaman, had been given up for dead by his relatives and given over to the Recollects' care as a last resort, he renounced his diabolical art, relinquished his medicine stone and prognosticating sticks, and calmly awaited death. But Emery De Caen of the trading company lent him his gold cross containing "some wood of the true cross," and Napagabiscou recovered completely. In 1666 another Algonquin was near death when he was urged to touch some of the relics of Father Brébeuf, whose memory the Algonquins held in "extreme veneration." Predictably, on the next morning the priest returned to find the lad full of health.[63]

Nearly as important as the Jesuits' oral catechizing was their use of visual images to lay the foundations of faith. Loyola had directed the followers of his *Spiritual Exercises*, particularly the Jesuits, always to make "mental representations" of the places where the biblical events they were contemplating had occurred, and to praise the Church's use of relics, images, and adornments as aids to understanding.[64] With the partial exception of rosaries and relics (which came in many forms), all of the sacramentals had a strong visual component. The dominant image captured the central dramatic moment in the history of Christianity, Christ's redemptive crucifixion. Crosses and crucifixes, of course, were unambiguous statements, but rings and medals also spoke of Christ's love of mankind and his supreme sacrifice. Archaeological excavations of former mission sites and Indian villages all around the Great Lakes reveal that the Jesuits gave their native proselytes oval brass or bronze medals featuring Christ as an infant with Mary or as an adult and a Latin or French inscription, such as "Good and Infinite Jesus Have Mercy on Us" or "By your death and your burial deliver us Jesus." Rings came in a wide variety of styles, especially after the natives learned to reproduce them from pieces of metal trade goods, but three prototypes dominated: *L*-heart (which signified Christ's love and possibly Loyola's in sending his Black Robes to America), double *M* (*Mater Misericordia*, Mother of Mercy), and *IHS* (*Isus Hominis Salvator*, Jesus Savior of Mankind). Other common motifs were cleft hearts (indicating sadness over Christ's death and man's sins), three spikes (representing the nails used to pin Jesus to the cross), a tonsured priest holding a cross, and the crucifixion itself.[65] Obviously the priests' orders had been filled by their French procurators. When Father Jean Enjalran wrote from Sillery in 1676 to request some "things which may help us to win these poor Indians," he specified "medals; small crucifixes a finger in length, or smaller still; small brass crosses and brass rings, also some in which there is the figure of some saint, or the face of Jesus Christ or the Blessed Virgin; [and] wooden rosaries, very black and very thick, which they wear hanging from the neck or about the head."[66]

Images of another kind helped to etch in the Indians' already tenacious memories the central *negative* message of the priests' teaching—that the fires of Hell (or Purgatory) awaited those sinners who did not sincerely repent and turn to Christ's Church for the remission of their sins. Compared to the emotional drama of Hell, the ethereal joys of Heaven were given relatively short shrift in the Jesuit lessons, perhaps because the Indians regarded their traditional "land of the dead" as more sensually pleasant and physically gratifying. The Jesuits' aim was to jolt the natives out of their objectionable religious and cultural habits by threatening them with a fate far worse than any they had ever known. As Loyola had urged, sinners needed to be taught a "servile fear" of Divine Majesty before they were capable of a "salutary" or "filial" fear based on a "real and holy horror" of sin. In America as in Europe, fear was considered the "forerunner of faith." The Black Robes knew their end had been gained when native prayers concluded, "May I not burn eternally in Hell."[67]

Loyola had also instructed novices in their first week of spiritual exercises to draw a mental picture of the "length, breadth, and depth of hell" in which they could see "the vast fires, and the souls enclosed . . . in bodies of fire, hear "the wailing, the howling, cries, and blasphemies" of the damned, smell "the smoke, the sulphur, the filth, and corruption," taste "the bitterness of tears, sadness, and remorse of conscience," and touch "the flames which envelop and burn the souls."[68] His Canadian protégés, having mastered the technique in seminary, encouraged their Indian catechumens to do the same by placing before their senses unforgettable representations of the under-world.

According to an eighteenth-century Jesuit historian, many Indians initially withheld their belief of the gospel because they felt that a fire as extensive as Hell would require an incredible supply of wood, and the fathers had declared that the lower world possessed no wood but burned by itself. To stop their derision, an ingenious priest offered to demonstrate before the whole neighborhood—and particularly twelve leading men chosen to prevent fraud—that the earth itself could burn. So he passed a lump of sulphur around to the judges, who declared that it was certainly earth. Then, as the judges craned forward, he repeatedly shook some grains from the lump into a kettle of live coals. Each time, the sulphur burst into flames and "filled the curious noses with a stifling odor," at which the Indians placed their hands flat over their mouths to register their astonishment. Henceforth, the historian noted, they "believed in the word of God that there is a lower world."[69]

The missionaries worked the native ear as well as the native nose. At St. François in the 1680s, Jacques Bigot gave instructions on the infernal verities by means of "certain Mournful Songs," in which he tried to express, according to Indian notions, "all that is best fitted . . . to torment one damned, and the vices which are most common among them." A more comprehensive attempt was made in 1640 when Governor Montmagny sponsored a play in Quebec to celebrate the birth of the dauphin. In order that the local Indians might derive some benefit from it, Montmagny invited the Jesuits to insert something that might "strike their eyes and their ears." The priests obliged by adding a scene in which the soul of an unbeliever was pursued by two Algonquin-speaking demons, who finally hurled it, struggling and shrieking, into "a hell that vomited forth flames." As the priests admitted with ill-concealed satisfaction, more than one native spectator went home to terrifying nightmares.[70]

All of these performances were spectacularly effective, but they were not universally applicable to or available in the settings where most of the missionaries plied their calling. The Jesuits therefore placed their pedagogical faith in engraved or hand-drawn pictures of the major Christian characters and events. Hell was an especially apt subject for pictorial treatment because of the vibrant colors and heightened emotions it conjured up. And pictures of Hell were powerfully moving documents for New France's Indian allies because they stirred unquenchable memories of fiery torture at the hands of the Iroquois. When the natives caught an Iroquois and subjected him to like treatment, the Black Robes and their neophytes were quick to say that what the Iroquois was enduring was only a "very rough picture of the torments suffered by lost souls in Hell."[71]

The Jesuits began to use pictures in their teaching as soon as they landed in Acadia in 1611, and continued with growing sophistication throughout their tenure in Canada. As in many other aspects of culture, they became increasingly sensitive to native preferences in their choice of pictorial subjects and treatment. In 1637 Father Le Jeune was using pictures of Hell which featured enchained souls "mad with pain," a practice he recommended highly. "Heretics [Protestants] are very much in the wrong to condemn and to destroy representations, which have so good an effect," he told his French provincial. "These sacred pictures are half the instruction that one is able to give the Indians." Having ordered some portraits of Hell and lost souls, he was nevertheless disappointed that those sent were on paper, rather than cloth, and too confused. "The devils are so mingled with the men that nothing can be identified therein, unless it is studied closely," he complained. "If some one would depict three, four, or five demons tormenting one soul with different kinds of torture—one applying to it the torch, another serpents, another pinching it with red-hot tongs, another holding it bound with chains—it would have a good effect, especially if everything were very distinct, and if rage and sadness appeared plainly in the face of the lost soul."[72]

After several years among the Hurons, Charles Garnier became even more sensitive to the aesthetic preferences of the natives. Writing to his brother, a French Carmelite monk, around 1645, he submitted a long list of pictures badly needed by the missionaries, including a handsome, beardless Jesus at eighteen, Jesus on the cross, a damned soul, a happy soul, and an uncluttered Judgment. Because it was a favorite of the Indians, he requested several copies of a published picture of the child Jesus hugging the knees of the Virgin, who wears a crown on her head and holds a scepter in her right hand and the Earth in her left. Illuminated paintings were preferred to highlight the grandeur of the sacred mysteries; for the chapel hangings, rolled cloth on rods served better than the paper images given to the natives. But most important to Father Garnier were the cultural details in the pictures. Because many Indians for a long time thought that pictorial people were alive, capable of following them with their eyes to rebuke backsliders, portraits were to face front with open eyes. Bodies were to be only semicovered, heads uncovered, hair straight and well combed, beards absent. Distracting scenery should be minimal. Jesus, Mary, and happy souls should all be white; others should be dressed in bright red or blue, the natives' favorite colors of trade cloth, not green or yellow. The damned soul, Garnier concluded, should be "grilled and blackened" by the flames, his hair shaggy, his eyes flashing and his mouth open wide in agony, his hands, feet, and middle bound by red-hot chains. A horrible, scaly dragon should entwine his body while two powerful and frightening demons jab at him with iron harpoons and another removes his scalp.[73]

Rather than cope with inadequate supplies from France, two other Jesuits took artistic matters into their own hands by drawing and painting their own instructional images. At Sault Saint-Louis in the 1680s, Claude Chauchetière made illustrated books for the villagers by sketching "The Truths of the Gospel" and "The Practices of Virtue," a series of catechetical lessons invented by Michel Le Nobletz, a missionary in Brittany in the early seventeenth century.[74] Another book featured colored pictures of the ceremonies of the Mass "applied to the Passion of our Lord," while still others depicted the torments of Hell and the creation of the world. These books were read by the Indians with "pleasure and profit," said the artist, and served as their "mute teachers," especially when the Saulteurs dispersed to the woods to hunt.[75]

Nobletz also inspired the religious artistry of Jean Pierron, missionary to the Mohawks, in the late 1660s. In a series of hand-painted pictures, wrote Pierron, "our Indians see a graphic representation of what I teach them, by which they are more powerfully moved." One picture in particular drew a curious crowd and gave the father an opportunity to learn more of their language as they animatedly discussed the Christian mysteries. The main purpose of this study of "the deaths of the pious and the wicked" was to stop a number of old men and women from plugging their ears with their fingers the moment Pierron tried to speak to them of God. In one part of the picture he put a pious Christian, clasping a cross and a rosary, rising heavenward with the help of an angel. In the lower portion he painted an old woman, bent with age, who is stopping her ears before a Black Robe attempting to show her Paradise. "But there issues from Hell a Demon, who seizes her arms and hands, and puts his own fingers in the ears of this dying woman, whose soul is carried away by three Demons; while an Angel, coming out of a cloud, sword in hand, hurls them down into the depths." After the priest had explained his picture to the villagers, he asserted, "not another person was found who dared to say, 'I do not hear.'"[76]

A year later, in 1669–70, Father Pierron again capitalized on his artistic imagination when he invented a game of chance called "*du Point au Point*," meaning from the point of birth to the point of eternity. Very quickly, if the missionary can be believed, the Mohawks developed an "extreme passion" for it because it played to their almost fanatical love of gambling. The game consisted of painted card emblems, much like those pioneered by Nobletz, which represented "all that a Christian has to know"—roughly the contents of Ledesme's catechism. So effective were the drawings that Pierron felt that even the coarsest minds "have no difficulty in rising to the knowledge of things spiritual," and planned another game for "destroying all the superstitions" of the Mohawks.[77]

The Jesuit war on American "paganism" was total and unrelenting. Not only did the priests seek to destroy and supplant the shamanic curators of native tradition, but they trained a fifth column of faithful neophytes to lead the resistance to the old religion and, if the opposition proved too strong, an exodus to the Christian *reserves* among the French. Although the Jesuits did not target every aspect of Indian culture, their campaigns against native "superstition" left several gaping holes that could be filled only by imported replacements or syncretic inventions.

Partly because of the persuasive arsenal of Jesuit techniques, partly because of cultural needs that their own religions could no longer meet, many Indians in the Northeast did come to know a variety of new "things spiritual." At first the number of converts was predictably small; the new faith seemed to ask its disciples to shed their "old skin all at once," to begin a "new life" before the religious integument of their old life had completely atrophied, and few people can so easily erase their cultural habits.[78] But the persistence and skill of the missionaries, coupled with the social crises triggered by the multiple European invasions, eventually gathered enough catechumens and neophytes to form sturdy Christian factions within the villages and tribes where they worked.

At first, before chiefs and shamans led whole communities into the fold, conversion was largely a family affair. Parents and children, husbands and wives, brothers and sisters, aunts and uncles converted each other, often to avoid separation at death as Christians ascended to the Black Robes' heaven and traditionalists went to their western land of the dead. Typical was the answer of an old Huron woman when Father Brébeuf asked her whether she wished to go to Heaven or to Hell. At first she allowed that she would go "where her son wished." But having been told that her father, a late convert, had gone to Heaven, she said, "Then I wish to go there!" Later many of the Huron converts who had been adopted by the victorious Iroquois after 1649 led their new kinsmen to the faith. When a portion of this composite band of neophytes hived off to settle Sault Saint-Louis across from Montreal, their hunters frequently returned south to stalk human quarry, "their kinsmen and acquaintances," for the Church. Similarly, twenty-five lodgemates of an Abenaki woman traveled from Maine to Sillery in 1681 to join her in baptism.[79]

Naturally, the Jesuits did everything in their power to sustain and augment their embattled cadres, for in most communities the traditional reaction to the Christian threat was terrible and swift. At the outset, the resistance of chiefs, shamans, and elders "inspired the people, and even the children, to imitate them." They and the great majority of their followers resisted the new changes out of "fear of what others would say," which the Jesuits recognized as perhaps the most "potent factor" among those oral peoples.[80] "If a poor Indian becomes a Christian," Father Lalemant noted in 1639, "he is immediately assailed by all those of his acquaintance" and "incurs the hatred and desertion of his people." Acquaintances were one thing and might be safely ignored, but close relatives were another. Those who knew how complaisant the Indians normally were toward relatives were shocked by the anti-Christian behavior they witnessed. Traditionalist family members lamented and deplored the converts as if they were "already lost," predicting that all their hair would fall off, that a man would be unlucky in hunting, trading, and war, a woman would bear no more children, and all would be defrauded of feasts, which was tantamount to losing "all the rights and intercourse of friendship with their kinsmen and compatriots."[81]

If these "assaults of the affection of corrupted nature for kindred" (in the words of the de-familied Jesuits) did not halt the apostasy from tradition, the converts were subjected to "great persecution," "atrocious insults," and "ill treatment" from their relatives. The families of the saintly Kateri Tekakwitha and other Mohawk converts reproached them bitterly for abstaining from work on Catholic feast days, denied them food, pelted them with stones on their way to mass, and raised tomahawks over their heads to frighten them. When many of the faithful stole away to the Sault to "avoid occasions for offending God," their angry kinsmen—especially after war between the French and the Iroquois reignited in 1689—captured men and women alike, tortured them over slow fires, and lifted their scalps, telling them that "you sealed your own fate when you left to live among the Christian dogs."[82]

Since the neophytes believed that good Christians must suffer "many insults and calumnies" for their faith, loss of life was less alarming a prospect to many than loss of purity. Knowing this, Huron traditionalists in the 1640s "incited, even publicly and in the midst of their feasts, lewd girls to win the hearts of the [male] Christians—hoping that, having lost their chastity, their faith would no longer be so rigorous, and would perish in debauchery." These were no mean temptations for converts who rolled naked in the snow and applied to themselves coals and burning brands to smother in their loins a fire more horrible to them than Hell. And the danger persisted wherever the cross was raised. In 1681 three young Iroquois women plotted to debauch three Christian men of the Sault, including the leader of prayers, and to make them "fall into sin." The conspiracy misfired, but the sirens did manage to lure one recently married man to Iroquoia.[83]

Against the taunts, tortures, and temptations of the "infidels" the Jesuits sought to fortify their native converts by raising churches and chapels and by administering the holy sacraments. The churches appeared in every imaginable size and setting, from bark-covered lean-tos deep in the woods to graceful frame structures on the Laurentian *reserves*.[84] Flying chapels might consist of no more than a small crucifix and a picture pinned to a napkin. But given time, money, and workmen they could easily grow into impressive piles. The Huron church at Ossossané measured thirty by sixteen feet around and twenty-four feet high, and was built of squared timbers in the style of the Jesuit chapel of St. Julien in France. Even grander was the chapel at Sault Saint-Louis, which measured sixty by twenty-five feet and supported three bells. Perhaps somewhere between was Father Laure's log church at Chicoutimi. "Plastered with mortar, well glazed, with painted ceiling and altar-screen," the priest wrote, "it possesses nearly all its furniture—and, I might say, every convenience."[85]

Whether large or small, each church was decorated as lavishly as possible so as to make an indelible impression on the natives. The few exceptions only proved the rule. In 1730 the Tadoussac chapel was so bare that Father Laure thought it "impossible, for lack of ornaments, to inspire these nascent Christians . . . with either an idea of our mysteries, or veneration for the hidden sanctity which they represent." The constrast with Father Râle's church at Norridgewock on the Kennebec could not have been starker. With French workmen from Quebec, Râle had built a church at once "commodious and well adorned." "I thought it my duty to spare nothing," he reported, "either for its decoration or for the beauty of the vestments that are used in our holy Ceremonies; altar-cloths, chasubles, copes, sacred vessels, everything is suitable, and would be esteemed in the Churches of Europe." Most European priests would have envied Râle's abundance of homemade bayberry candles that washed the church interior in flickering light.[86]

A few decorations in the mission churches would not have been recognized in most of Europe. A great number of native-made collars of patterned wampum and articles worked with glass trade beads and porcupine quills graced the altar at St. François de Sales when the church was dedicated in 1684. One of the belts, extremely large and adorned with quills, was the most beautiful collar Father Bigot had ever seen. The Abenakis soon sent it to the tomb of their patron saint at Annecy, just as they sent to Chartres Cathedral in 1699 a six-foot belt as a *petit présent* to the Virgin Mother.[87] To encourage the people of the Sault in their faith, the Hurons of Lorette sent a large hortatory belt upriver in 1677. Thereafter its "words" could be "read" by the worshippers as it faced them on a beam above the altar.[88]

For priests and proselytes alike, the heart and driving force of the Faith were the Mass and the seven sacraments of the Roman Church: baptism, Eucharist (the only two shared with Protestant denominations), confirmation (by a bishop), penance (for sins), marriage, orders (clerical vows), and extreme unction (at death). With the partial exception of the first and last rites, which needed to be administered wherever death struck, the Jesuits restricted the sacraments to consecrated space—a church, the Jesuits' lodge, or a Christian cemetery. This was most easily accomplished in a semipermanent village or a *reserve*, where most celebrants were to be found in any event. In Huronia, except in case of necessity, the fathers baptized only in their cabin "to cause the Sacrament to be more highly respected." Similarly, at Sault Saint-Louis a half-century later, "sick people were carried to church on a litter of bark, when giving them the viaticum, in order to inspire [them] with the respect which is due to the Blessed Sacrament." Since the converts did not think that "Our Lord should himself take the trouble of going to seek them," the priests had to defy custom in 1680 to administer last rites to Kateri Tekakwitha in her cabin.[89]

As befitted the elaborately decorated interiors, church rituals were conducted with as much pomp, splendor, and dignity as circumstances would allow. Stately processions bore statues of the Virgin or Christ, crosses, banners, tapers, and the Eucharist beneath a rich canopy held aloft by four poles. At the head of the retinue marched a young acolyte swinging a censer to raise the prayers of the people on the sweet smoke, a custom that blended perfectly with the traditional native burning of tobacco for the same purpose. Emulating the priests in their ornate chasubles, native celebrants in the Laurentian *reserves* or in Quebec sometimes proceeded two by two wearing painted and figured skin robes or full battle regalia. At Sillery the native children imitated their elders by forming processions in their own fashion, complete with cross, banner, and homemade candlesticks. As they marched in twos, they sang the simple French airs and chants they had learned from the resident Black Robes.[90]

Singing played an indispensable role in native services. "As a class," wrote an admiring Jesuit, "all the Indians have much aptitude and inclination for singing the hymns of the Church, which have been rendered into their language." One priest who had recently arrived in Canada thought that most prayers were sung because the natives were "incapable of prolonged mental application," but he was mistaken. More exposure to the devout converts of his own Sault Saint-Louis would have removed any doubts about the Indians' capacity or penchant for sustained prayer. The main reasons for the native love of church singing were that the cadences and melodies of the chants and hymns were excellent mnemonic devices to lock the songs' religious messages in memory—the Sault women knew more than thirty hymns by 1679—and the Indians, especially the women, excelled at it. Recently arrived French colonists and priests attuned to the finest church music of Europe compared native choirs to "a hundred Cordeliers" or "some great community of nuns." After a year at Sault Saint-Louis, Father Nau went even further. "Neither cordeliers nor nuns ever sang as do our Iroquois men and women," he boasted to a French colleague in 1735. "Their voices are both mellow and sonorous, and their ear so correct that they do not miss a half-tone in all the church hymns, which they know by heart."[91]

As splendid as native voices were the brocade vestments and gilt altar vessels used by the Jesuits to "quicken the devotion" of their neophytes. In 1611 the first Jesuits left France well endowed with linen vestments and sacred furniture, the gift of two noblewomen. Thereafter, thanks to similar donations and the brilliant needlework of the Ursulines of Quebec, the mission churches of Canada lacked for little that would have graced the finest churches of France. Altars and stations about the church displayed elaborate gold or silver *soleils* or ostensories, chalices, crucifixes, candlesticks, communion plates, cruets, fonts, and censers, as well as gilt and painted statues of Christ, Mary, saints, and angels. The sacramental wine and wafers—made even in distant Huronia with an iron press that stamped "IHS" into each—were covered with beautiful brocade cloths, as was the altar itself. But perhaps the most majestic pieces of all were the priests' vestments, cut from red velour or fine white linen and covered with flowers, borders, and religious symbols in gold, silver, and colored silk thread.[92]

Some idea of the religious impact of these sumptuous articles can be glimpsed in the initial reactions of unconverted Hurons and Sioux. When the Recollects showed the beautiful chasuble that the queen had given them, the Hurons considered it "superior in richness to the greatest rarity they pos-

10. The handsome silver altar vessels from the Indian church at Caughnawaga. Believing that the Holy Spirit entered through the senses, the Jesuits spared no expense in decorating their mission churches. From Marius Barbeau, *Le Trésor des anciens Jésuites*, National Museum of Canada, Bulletin 153, Anthropology Series 43 (Ottawa, 1957); photo by F. J. Tropp.

sessed." "They used to come often and beg us to show it to their sick," wrote Brother Sagard; "the mere sight of it would comfort them and seem to alleviate their sufferings." Many years later, when Louis Hennepin was captured by the Sioux while exploring the Mississippi with La Salle, the warriors did not dare to touch the chalice from his portable altar because, he said, "when they saw the shining silver gilt, they shut their eyes, saying it was a spirit who would kill them." But they did not hesitate to wrap a dead man's bones in Hennepin's brocade chasuble, tie it with his red and white wool girdle, and present the valuable bundle to a distant tribe who had brought the calumet of peace.[93] By all accounts, the Jesuits' ornate furniture and dress cast a similar spell over the natives after the latter exchanged their errant "superstitions" for the mysteries of the faith.

The holy awe in which they held Church rituals and priests helped the native converts to learn to kneel before the altar and during the administration of the sacraments. When the Hurons paid their first visit to the Jesuit chapel in Quebec in 1633, they all squatted down "like monkeys" at the altar because kneeling was for them a posture "altogether strange and extraordinary," as it was for the other tribes of New France. By 1637, however, a model Huron convert was capable of praying on his knees for three-quarters of an hour. At the Christmas service two years later, he knelt during five consecutive masses. "This, for an Indian who has never known what that posture is," admired Father Lalemant, "might well pass for a petty martyrdom." Father Bigot was clearly dazzled in 1681 when, during the half-hour prayer given to all newcomers, not a single Abenaki rested against the benches or hunkered "as the Indians generally do."[94]

Although in kneeling the converts seemed to shrink before their enemies, the spiritual power and confidence they gained from the sacraments more than compensated for any temporary loss of physical advantage. For the natives the most important sacraments were baptism (by which they became Christians), marriage (by which they united with other Christians for corporate strength), and extreme unction (by which they were guaranteed salvation in Heaven).

Unlike the Franciscans, Dominicans, and Augustinians who established missions in New Spain, the Canadian Jesuits were distinctly uninterested in mass baptisms or other forms of ecclesiastical head-counting. As soon as they landed in Acadia in 1611, they were appalled by the lack of knowledge displayed by the hundred or so Micmacs who had been baptized the previous year by Poutrincourt's secular priest Jessé Fléché. Without the least instruction in Christian fundamentals—Fléché was ignorant of the language—the Indians had accepted baptism as a sign of friendship with the "Normans" (as they called the French), or to obtain a glass of brandy and a pipe of tobacco.[95] To distinguish themselves from their Spanish counterparts more firmly, the Jesuits maintained that they preferred "the conversion of one of these poor Indians to the conquest of a whole Empire." "The joy that one feels when he has baptized an Indian who dies soon afterwards, and flies directly to Heaven to become an Angel," exclaimed Father Le Jeune, "certainly is a joy that surpasses anything that can be imagined."[96]

The Jesuits claimed to have baptized more than sixteen thousand natives between 1632 and 1672, some twelve thousand in Huronia alone. But as Father Bressani observed in 1653, the priests might have baptized the whole country had they been interested only in "number and name." However, he continued, "we were not willing to receive a single adult, in a condition of perfect health, before we were very well informed about the language; and before we had—after long probations, sometimes for whole years—judged them constant in the holy purpose not only of receiving the Sacrament of Baptism, but of punctually observing the divine precepts." The first adult Huron was admitted to the rite only after three years of careful instruction and testing.[97] The reason for the Jesuits' caution was their fear of "making more Apostates than Christians," for they believed that Indian adults "would soon show a contempt for our holy Mysteries, if they had only a slight knowledge of them." On the other hand, those who were in danger of suffering pagan deaths and the fires of Hell were readily anointed with the holy waters. At least a third of the Jesuit baptisms during those forty years were of infants, children, and adults who soon expired, often from European diseases.[98]

The Black Robes' eagerness to sprinkle water, make signs, and mumble strange incantations over the heads of people who promptly died raised a major obstacle to the conversion of Indian survivors. Without any knowledge of epidemiology, they quite logically assumed that the suspicious act of baptism *caused* the death of their relatives and loved ones. On that assumption, many of them closed their ears to the priests and hid their sick and dying, which forced the Jesuits to resort to all sorts of stratagems to baptize them in secret. Having come to associate water and death, Huron parents even resumed their former custom of threatening to spit cold water in the faces of wayward children. As they scattered around the Great Lakes in succeeding decades, Huron, Ottawa, and Nipissing traditionalists cultivated a long memory of the "deadly" baptismal rites.[99]

Gradually, as the epidemics diminished and more of the baptized made "miraculous" recoveries, the natives came to believe that baptism, which was instituted to confer holiness upon the soul, often gave health to the body, as well as providing the best insurance against hellfire. Even at the height of the Huron epidemic of 1636–37, a "sorcerer's" apprentice used as one of his remedies a kettle filled with "a mysterious water with which he sprinkled the sick."[100] When the traditionalist opposition was forced to imitate the Christian sacrament, converts could take special comfort in their own spiritual transformation.

Native converts also took strength from the sacrament of marriage, which united them with Christian partners in a permanent bond of personal amity and spiritual support. Since the priests rarely allowed mixed Christian-pagan marriages, they sometimes postponed the baptism of deserving Indians because of a shortage of potential Christian spouses.[101] At the outset of missionary activity, the shortage was severe in all but the most devoted villages and *reserves*. While the priests regarded monogamous marriage as a sacrament and divorce as anathema, the natives of the Northeast had been "for many ages in possession of," as Father Vimont put it, "a complete brutal liberty, changing wives when they pleased—taking only one or several, according to their inclination." Understandably, "conjugal continence, and the indissolubility of marriage, seemed to them the most serious obstacles in the progress of the Gospel."[102]

When Father Le Caron explained the Ten Commandments at the public baptism of a Montagnais lad, the assembly burst into laughter at the sixth, which forbade adultery, saying that "it was impossible to keep that one." Earlier, in Huronia, Le Caron had confronted the classic Indian objection to the Christian prohibition of divorce. "Just see," a Huron man told him, "you have no sense. My wife does not agree with me, and I cannot agree with her. She will be better suited with such a one, who does not get on with his wife. Why, then, do you wish us four to be unhappy the rest of our days?" Among the Iroquois, Father Bruyas subjected his married catechumens to a longer probation before baptism because they were surrounded by the traditional ethos of easy divorce. In 1667 a drunken Mohawk pounded on Bruyas's chapel door and shouted, "I will kill him; he is a demon who forbids us to have several wives." Twenty years earlier, as the Iroquois were wreaking havoc all over New France, the Jesuits' war on polygamy was particularly hard on their battered allies. These remnant nations, Father Vimont sympathized, "consist almost entirely of women, widows and girls, who cannot all find lawful husbands, and who consequently are in danger of much suffering, or of committing great sins."[103]

When the native Christian population achieved some degree of sexual parity, the sacrament of marriage began to enjoy a measure of popularity. All but the most important, and obdurate, chiefs and shamans (whose obligations of hospitality required many hands) discovered that they could make do with a single wife and that facile divorces and adultery bred their own kinds of trouble, especially if children resulted. By 1638 the Jesuits were remarrying Indian couples from several different nations and blessing their new wedding rings. In 1674 the inhabitants of Sault Saint-Louis began to solemnize their unions according to the rites of the Church, having previously pledged lifelong fidelity to each other at baptism. Divorce was rare: in the first twenty years of the mission, less than twenty husbands abandoned their wives, and all returned after some years to die in the village. Father Crespieul's parishioners at Tadoussac were equally monogamous and constant in their marriages.[104]

Converts who had spent most of their lives in the faith approached death with Christian resignation, if not joyful anticipation. But relative newcomers sometimes experienced difficulties similar to the misgivings of traditionalists as they anticipated the last rites of the Church and Christian burial. The sacrament of extreme unction was never a concern because it was administered only to Christians in good and full standing. Of greater moment were the burial customs of the Roman Church as interpreted by the French priests: the bones of Christians and "pagans" could not be mixed in consecrated ground; pets could be buried near but not with their owners; excessive mourning, such as the fifty days observed by Huron wives, was frowned upon as "superstitious solitude"; corpses were to be plainly dressed if not wrapped naked in a linen winding sheet; grave goods were to consist of Christian symbols or to be transformed into alms for the poor; the dead were to be placed extended on their backs, preferably in coffins, rather than flexed on their sides, with their feet toward the rising sun; and dirt was to be cast directly onto the coffin or corpse, without the traditional protection of bark, branches, and logs. Taken together, these changes might seem to have altered traditional practices to an alarming degree, but in reality they left a great deal of room for syncretic blending of old and new. As the missionary at Lorette noted in 1675, "after removing from them all the superstitions which they had learned in paganism, we have left them the remainder, which serves but to maintain the mutual union which exists between them, and even to inspire devotion in those who witness the ceremonies."[105]

Receiving the Christian sacraments did much to make the natives "new men." But to help their neophytes make a clean break with the pagan world, the Jesuits sought to sacralize the time they spent as well as the space they inhabited. As the fathers buttressed the converts' faith with consecrated buildings, altars, and cemeteries, so they regulated each day, week, and year in an effort to leave no time for the Devil to gain an audience. Punctuality became a watchword for the Indians, whose days used to be, according to their new pastors, "nothing but pastime." Within a short time, the major Huron and Iroquois mission villages and all the Laurentian *reserves* had large bells to call the faithful from their sleep or labors for divine service at least twice and usually three times a day. On Sundays and feast days all "unseemly deeds" and "servile work" were prohibited to allow proper devotion to prayer, a regulation that worked some hardship on people who normally lived "from hand to mouth."[106] When the natives dispersed into the winter woods to hunt, they carried paper calendars made by the priests on which they could make daily crosses to determine the "days of honor and respect." Special devotion was reserved for the feast days of the saints for which they had been named at baptism.[107]

The net result of all the Jesuits' spiritual and moral support was the formation of cadres of devout, resilient disciples who could withstand the hatred of their unregenerate kinsmen while building little Jerusalems all over New France. Recapturing much of the tenacious fervor of the original Christians, the native converts threw themselves into the life of the Church Militant with abandon. Every congregation had its "prayer captain" or *dogique*, a man or woman responsible for leading prayers and hymns, counseling families, catechizing children, initiating newcomers, enforcing morality, and occasionally baptizing the dying in the priest's absence.[108] The major missions also had native acolytes to assist the priests. Even on the remote Kennebec, Father Râle trained a "minor Clergy of about forty young Indians, who, in cassocks and surplices," he wrote, "assist at divine Service; each one has his duty, not only in serving at the holy Sacrifice of the Mass, but in chanting the divine Office at the Benediction of the blessed Sacrament, and in the Processions. . . ."[109]

Perhaps the most extraordinary Christian fervor was displayed by the women (and occasionally men) of Sault Saint-Louis, Saint François de Sales, and Lorette. Both sexes subjected themselves to painful "austerities" and penances in an effort to tame their sinful bodies, which they had learned to regard as "their greatest enemy." Exceeding the temperate advice of Saint Ignatius and the disciplined example of Canadian priests and nuns, the neophytes scourged each other with whips and chains, wore hair shirts and iron-pointed belts, mixed ashes in their *sagamité*, stood naked in ice-covered ponds or snowstorms, put glowing coals between their toes, and rolled on mats of thorn. Enfeebled by such excesses, Kateri Tekakwitha died a lingering death at the age of twenty-six, and several of her spiritual sisters were also lost to the faith prematurely. Their Jesuit mentors were understandably torn between encouraging their holy sacrifices and reproving their excesses.[110]

11. The fervent religiosity of Indian converts to Catholicism has no better representation than Father Claude Chauchetière's drawing of several Caughnawaga women taking vows of perpetual continence before a statue of the Virgin Mary. To confirm her resolve, the woman at the right cuts her hair with a knife to make herself less attractive to men. Courtesy of the Archives départementales de la Gironde, Bordeaux.

A more salutary manifestation of conversion zeal was the female emulation of the Virgin Mary and the nuns of Montreal and Quebec. With the encouragement of the Jesuits, who simply followed Church doctrine, converted women in the *reserves* and in various Great Lakes tribes took and kept strict vows of virginity or chastity, deeming sexual purity highest in the eyes of God.[111] To discourage male advances, they disfigured themselves by cutting their shining black hair, forwent fancy dresses, jewelry, and makeup, and bloodied the noses of any who tried to seduce them. Young and old alike consecrated their bodies to Christ, eschewing sex and marriage altogether or, if already married, living "like brothers and sisters." "The fair mirror of chastity is so clean at the Sault," wrote Father Chaumonot in 1681, "that people there cannot endure the least spot on it."[112]

In the *reserves* the principal guardians of moral purity were a small number of elite sodalities or associations of the most fervent Christians, such as the Holy Family established in 1671 at the Sault after the original chapter at Lorette. Calling themselves "sisters," the members of these miniature monasteries devoted themselves to moral improvement, relief of the poor and the sick, chastity, and mutual support. The disciplined lives they led prepared a few of them to become nuns in the Hôtels-Dieu and Sisters of the Congregation, and the remainder to experience indirectly the highest calling for women in the Catholic Church.[113]

THE LIVELY LIQUOR
OF THE GOSPEL

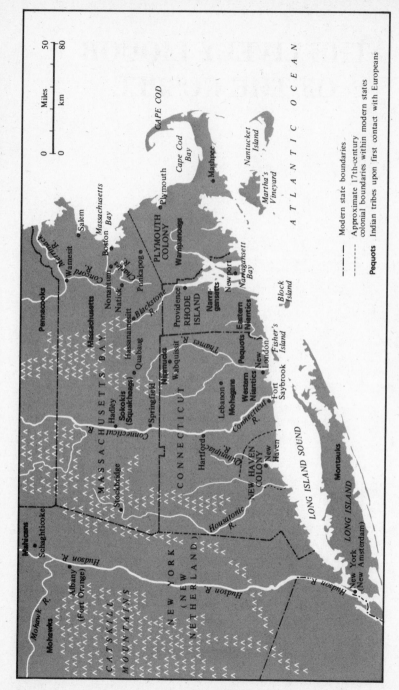

SOUTHERN NEW ENGLAND

CHAPTER SEVEN

Reduce Them to Civility

*In order to make them Christians,
they must first be made Men.*
REV. CHARLES INGLIS

The Catholics may have taken an early lead in the struggle for native American souls but, in the beginning at least, the English Protestants would not concede their rivals anything but a temporary advantage. For they were supremely confident—as only an insular people can be—that their way of life was superior to anything Europe (and therefore the world) had to offer and that the Indians, for all their deficiencies, would soon recognize England's preeminence. When they did, the blandishments and bribes of the French would be powerless to prevent the English harvest of souls that would follow the native rush to material and spiritual prosperity.

The English were sustained in their confidence by two articles of faith, neither of which was grounded in knowledge of Indian life. Although both were to be eroded somewhat by a century and a half of experience in the American field, their survival well into the nineteenth century testifies to their durability and perhaps to their indispensability to missionary enterprises of every stripe.

The first article proclaimed the essential educability of the American natives. For unless they were potentially convertible, they could never become Christian converts, a thought that no missionary could entertain for long and remain in his calling. From their map-strewn studies in London and Oxford, the cousins Hakluyt described the Indians as people "though simple and rude in manners . . . yet of nature gentle and tractable." Richard Eburne, a fellow promoter, agreed. His *Plain Pathway to Plantations* was lined with "exceeding[ly] tractable" natives who were "industrious and ingenious to learn of us and practice with us most arts and sciences."[1] Since none of these men had ever made the American voyage to take personal measure of the natives' capacity, they were drawing on the Protestant humanists' faith in the power of education as well as the optimism of early explorers for their assessments. In 1609, as the Virginia Company was outfitting its third fleet for western waters, the Reverend Robert Gray gave classical expression to that belief when he told potential investors, "It is not the nature of men, but the education of men, which make[s] them barbarous and uncivill." "Chaunge the education of men," he predicted, "and you shall see that their nature"—corrupted at the source by Adam's sin—"will be greatly rectified

131

and corrected."[2] Despite their late start, English missionaries armed with such a faith could expect at least as much success as their Jesuit rivals had enjoyed.

They could look forward to even more, perhaps, if their second article of faith had a foundation of fact. While the Indians were thought to be susceptible to English education, the possibility existed that the process of conversion might be long and laborious. But to admit as much would only dry up commercial investments and dampen religious ardor, either of which would be fatal to the missionary enterprise. The only sensible alternative was to banish the word "hard" from the promotional lexicon and substitute "easy." Thus a typical description might read, "This people believe not at all in God, but . . . they are very easie to be perswaded." According to the clerical blueprints for New Zion, the American natives were "apte to submytte them selves to good government" and "very ready to leave their old and blind idolatries and to learn of [the English] the right service and worship of the true God."[3] It followed as surely as night the day that they could be "brought to our Civilitie . . . in short time."[4]

Since this optimism had never faced any actual Indian reaction to Protestant proselyting, it was probably generated by the ease with which freebooting explorers and fishermen gathered armloads of valuable furs while cruising the Atlantic littoral. Nearly every sailor who put into an English port and pub must have crowed his own tale of how the Indians eagerly waved passing crews in to trade the furs literally off their backs for such "worthless trifles" as ship's biscuits, fishing knives, brass earrings, glass beads, rigging rings, even bolts and the metal tips from belaying pins.[5] After hearing how the Indians hankered after the Englishman's temporal goods, it was but a short step to assume that they also craved his spiritual wares.

Indeed, the connection in English minds may have been even more direct. According to the Reverend Mr. Gray, "men by nature . . . easily yielde to discipline and government upon any reasonable shewe of bettering their fortunes."[6] By this token, the Indians would acquire not only the superior material advantages of English life but the transcendent prize of Christianity as well. As the Virginia Company quaintly put it, the English would "buy of them the pearles of earth, and sell to them the pearles of heaven."[7] But one of the main reasons the Indians were expected to purchase the "pearles of heaven" was that they were expected to recognize, as the English did, the causal relationship between the English standard of living and the English religion. The Protestant ministry entertained no doubts that God rewarded his true followers with "externall beneficence and advancement, as well as spirituall grace and blessings."[8]

The firmness of the English faith that the Indians would covet the religion that engendered such affluence clearly registered in Cotton Mather's disappointment with New England's missionary efforts as of 1721:

Tho' they saw a People Arrive among them, who were Clothed in *Habits* of much more Comfort & Splendour, than what there was to be seen in the *Rough*

Skins with which they hardly covered themselves; and who had *Houses full of Good Things*, vastly outshining their squalid and dark *Wigwams*; And they saw this People Replenishing their Fields, with *Trees* and with *Grains*, and useful *Animals*, which until now they had been wholly Strangers to; yet they did not seem touch'd in the least, with any *Ambition* to come at such Desireable Circumstances, or with any *Curiosity* to enquire after the Religion that was attended with them.[9]

So confident were the English of their cultural superiority that they could hear the Indians calling, "Come over and help us," which request they promptly emblazoned on the Massachusetts colony seal. If there was any question as to the nature of the help desired, the younger Hakluyt had answered it a half century earlier. "The people of America crye oute unto us . . . to come and helpe them," he told Queen Elizabeth, "and bringe unto them the gladd tidinges of the gospell."[10] With such a mandate, English missionaries would surely overtake their Catholic rivals and quickly win the natives to the Protestant Christ.

There was only one hitch: the Indians were still in a state of "savagery" or "barbarism," which every civilized man knew to be an "infinite distance from Christianity." While the Indians were potentially salvable, their savage condition was not felt to be fertile ground for the holy seeds of Christianity. They were much too "degenerate" for religion to prosper or for the Word to work its magic. The heart of the matter was that they could not be trusted with the holy church ordinances, baptism and communion, "whilst they lived so unfixed, confused, and ungoverned a life."[11]

The English missionary prospectus was thus drawn for the next century and a half. Until the 1760s it was the opinion of "the most sensible Writers on this Subject" that it was necessary to "civilize Savages before they can be converted to Christianity, & that in order to make them Christians, they must first be made Men."[12] Without a single dissenting voice in all those years, the Protestant missionaries in the Anglo-American colonies felt it their clear responsibility to give the Indians "*Civilitie* for their bodies" before "*Christianitie* for their soules," for while the second made them happy, the first made them "*men.*"[13]

In implying that the Indians were not yet "men," the English meant one of three things. The first meaning was that the Indians were the children of the human race, their passions still largely unrestrained by reason. The second meaning also emphasized their passions, but was much less charitable. Rather than innocent children, the Indians in this view were little better than animals, incapable of reason and enslaved by the most brutal passions. Thus in 1721, after nearly a century of mixed success, Cotton Mather advised the commissioners of the New England Company that "to Humanize these Miserable *Animals*, and in any measure to *Cicurate* [tame] them & *Civilize* them, were a work of no little Difficulty; and a Performance little short of what One of our most famous *Physicians* esteemed the *Greatest Cure* that ever himself had wrought in all his Practice; *To bring an Idiot unto the Use of Reason.*"[14]

12. The seal of the Massachusetts Bay Colony, designed in 1629, wishfully represents the American Indian as saying to the English Puritans, "Come over and help us." Reproduced by courtesy of the Archives Division, Office of the Secretary, Commonwealth of Masssachusetts, Boston.

The third and by far most prevalent meaning, however, was simply that the Indians had not mastered the "Arts of civil Life & Humanity," which is to say, the classical liberal arts.[15] In the European hierarchy of knowledge, Theology—the province of the missionaries—was the queen of the sciences, and Philosophy her handmaiden. To approach Theology one had first to master the seven liberal arts, the arts of humane living, much as one would progress through the trivium and quadrivium of Renaissance Oxford or Cambridge. While civilized Englishmen could be assumed to have acquired at least the rudiments of these arts through education or social osmosis, the Indians were thought to lack them totally. Consequently, the missionaries' perceived duty was to "*root out*" their vicious habits" and "national vices," and to replace them with a "civil, orderly & Christian way of living."[16] In sum, the purchase price of the "pearles of heaven" was inordinately high. It was nothing less than the Indians' "whole Way of Living."[17]

Whenever plans were drawn for "humanizing" the American natives, the missionaries chose a peculiar phrase that speaks volumes about their religious attitudes and cultural preconceptions. Time and again, from the sixteenth century to the American Revolution, it was said that the first goal of the English was to "*reduce*" the Indians from savagery to "civility." Without a hint of cultural modesty, the younger Hakluyt spoke of the glorious task of "reducinge . . . infinite multitudes of these simple people that are in errour into the righte and perfecte way of their salvation." When King James I put his seal on the great patent of New England in 1620, he seized the providential moment for the "reducing and Conversion of such Savages as remaine wandering in Desolacion and Distress [after the "wonderfull Plague" of 1616–18] to Civil Societie and Christian Religion." To the lay leaders of colonial Massachusetts, New Plymouth, and the United Colonies, wholesome laws and English schools for the natives were the chosen means to "Reduse them to Civillitie and the knowledge of God." The phrase had acquired almost a litanical quality by 1785, when George Washington told a friend that he saw no way of converting the western Indians than by "first reducing [them] to a state of greater civilization."[18]

The phrase is puzzling because we would expect a people with a superior self-image to attempt to *raise* their inferiors, rather than reduce them, to their level. To my knowledge, only two missionaries during the whole colonial period ever expressed their goal as one of elevation—both only once—and even their aberrance was wholly out of character.[19] In modern parlance, superiority connotes a high position and inferiority a low one. Heaven is high above, Hell far below in the Christian scheme of things. And until quite recently, social scientists used to measure high civilizations against more lowly primitive cultures on a scale of social progress. Why, then, did the colonial missionaries speak as if Indian culture needed a kind of degrading before measuring *down* to English civility?

The answer lies in the nature of the wholesale changes in Indian culture required by the English to render the natives worthy of religious conversion.

From the English perspective, the Indians were deficient in three essential qualities: order, industry, and manners. This meant in essence that they were not Englishmen, what they should be and should want to be.[20] So with characteristic confidence, the missionaries proceeded in the heady decades after settlement to prescribe a veritable pharmacopoeia of remedies for their savage condition. Their diagnosis of the natives' deficiencies helps to explain why cultural health could be restored only by "reducing them to civility."[21]

The immediate concern of the English was to remove the Indians from their "disordered riotous rowtes and companies, to a wel governed common wealth," from what they took to be civil anarchy to the rule of English law. For of all "humane Artes," the missionaries knew, "Political government is the chiefest."[22] To men accustomed to kings and queens, administrative bureaucracies, standing armies, police, courts, and all the punitive technology of justice known to "civilized" states, the Indians seemed to suffer from unbenign neglect. If they were acknowledged to have any government at all, it was often the capricious tyranny of an absolute theocrat, such as Powhatan or Uncas.[23] More prevalent was the view that the "common rules of order in the administration of justice"—the rules followed in Parliament or the Dutch Estates General—were not observed in Indian society. Indeed, so subtle and covert were the workings of Indian justice that the colonists were "astonished to find that such societies can remain united" at all. Cast in such a light, these "wild people" obviously needed the English to "bring them to Political life, both in Ecclesiastical society and in Civil, for which," the missionaries assured themselves, "they earnestly long and enquire."[24]

In retrospect, the English rhetoric of disorder might seem to be merely an elaborate verbal feint to draw attention away from an illegitimate grab for racial domination. There was such a grab, and it was, by any standard of justice, illegitimate, but before 1675 it carried no racial (as opposed to cultural or religious) overtones.[25] If there was deception, the English themselves were the victims, but they were at least consistent in attempting to control "anarchy" wherever it flourished. In 1643, for reasons again not wholly disinterested, the Massachusetts authorities cracked down on a handful of heretical Gortonists in Narragansett country. Their offenses to Puritan sensibility were numerous, but the one most publicized was that they "denied all magistracy and churches" and lived "without any means for instructing them[selves] in the wayes of God, and without any civil Government to keep them in civility or humanity."[26] Some years later the Plymouth General Court ordered three men to attend church and "live otherwise orderly" or to leave the colony. Their crime had been to live "lonely and in a heathenish way from good societie," out of the ken of watchful saints. The centrifugal flow of frontier settlements was especially disturbing to the colonial governments because many settlers were "contented to live without, yea, desirous to shake off all yoake of Government, both sacred and Civil." In this regrettable circumstance they resembled nothing so much as "the Indians they lived amongst."[27]

Whether Indian or Englishman, those who erected sovereign standards outside the walls of the "City upon a Hill" posed a challenge which the authorities within could not ignore. For in the strange material and moral wildernesses of America, established rules of order were all too easily questioned, and new challenges might push them to their limits, perhaps beyond the breaking point where confusion and anarchy lay. To preserve self-control and moral certitude in such a tenuous environment, the English denied themselves the possibilities of the unfamiliar and clung to the warm securities of the known. The only acceptable notion of order, accordingly, was the order they had known at home, the all-encompassing order of institutions, written law, and hierarchy. Any other possibility, such as the Indian form of suasive government, was literally unthinkable. The implication for the Indians of this search for order was that the sway of English sovereignty over those intended for conversion would have to be complete. They would have to be shorn of the last vestiges of independence before the missionary program could ideally begin. When the goal was to "change their whole Habit of thinking and acting," anything less than complete domination would not serve.[28]

Another disturbing symptom of disorder was the Indians' "scattered and wild course of life."[29] Anyone could see that they did not live in fixed communities like London, Bristol, or even Swaffham Bulbeck, but there were at least two ways to interpret that obvious fact. The first, almost always the choice of promoters attempting to remove any Indian claim to the lands slated for settlement, was to picture the natives as little more than foraging animals, clearly incapable of owning land. "Their land is spacious and void," promised the Reverend Robert Cushman, "and there are few and [they] do but run over the grass, as do also the foxes and wild beasts." According to international law (which the Indians had no part in making), such a "vast and empty chaos" was free for the taking because it was always lawful "to take a land which none useth, and make use of it."[30] So John Winthrop, the Cambridge-trained lawyer, reasoned when justifying the planters of Massachusetts Bay, of which he was one: "That which lies common, and hath never beene replenished or subdued is free to any that possesse and improve it." "As for the Natives in New England," he wrote in 1629 before ever setting eyes on any of them, "they inclose noe Land, neither have any setled habytation, nor any tame Cattle to improve the Land by, . . . soe as if we leave them sufficient for their use"—in the judgment of the English—"we may lawfully take the rest, there being more than enough for them and us."[31]

The second way to interpret the peripatetic Indian lifestyle was more common and, being based on personal observation, certainly closer to the truth. This was to admit that the Indians did indeed fail to live in conventional English houses affixed to one patch of ground, but to offer legitimate reasons for their seasonal movements and even to emphasize (if inadvertently) some of their advantages. John Josselyn noticed that the natives of Maine, who were too far north to rely much on garden crops (or to be included in the missionary plans of the English until the eighteenth century), commuted between forest and seashore in search of fresh meat and fish. "Towns they have none," he wrote after two long visits down east, "being alwayes removing from one place to another for conveniency of food."[32] From Florida to Massachusetts, however, their more southerly neighbors congregated for longer periods around their corn fields and gardens in villages that ranged from just a few families to more than two thousand inhabitants.[33] When they moved, usually after five or six months of summer community, they did so to be near their seasonal food supply, to escape the winter winds in "warme and thicke woodie bottomes," and to find more wood for their fires, more land for their fields, or simply relief from the fleas of summer.[34]

It was obviously disconcerting to Englishmen accustomed to finding towns in the same place year after year to discover a village of a hundred wigwams gone within a day or two for parts and reasons unknown. Not only were such a people physically uncontrollable, but, perhaps worse, they were unpredictable, and surprise was the last thing the English wanted in the New World. Still bred in the twilight of chivalry, they were equally shocked to learn that it fell to the Indian women, "troubled like snails to carry their houses on their backs" to the various locations, while their congenitally idle husbands— "their loggerships"—led the way under the staggering weight of perhaps a bow, pipe, and tabacco pouch.[35]

But the most galling discovery (though probably few ever consciously made it) must have been that the natives, in all their basest "savagery," dared to break God-graven class lines by usurping the privileges of the English aristocracy, who were held the more in deference by the colonists in proportion to their absence.[36] Forever tweaking the nose of authority, Thomas Morton of Merrymount all but visibly rubbed his hands over his observation that when the Indians "are minded to remoove," they "remoove for their pleasures . . . after the manner of the gentry of Civilized nations." The same glee cannot describe the pious Edward Johnson of Woburn, who nonetheless volunteered that the Indians' wigwams bore an uncanny resemblance to gentlemen's "Summerhouses in England."[37] To have viewed the Indians as America's noblemen, commuting conspicuously between winter "castle" and summer cottage-by-the-sea, would clearly not have served. Better that their movements be seen as the vagrant shiftings of dissolute barbarians. For then, in the name of English civility and Christian religion, such flagrant disorder and chaos could be reduced, and the Indians brought under control.

The cure for the Indians' disorder was a strong dose of English order. Of primary importance to the missionaries (and, for slightly different reasons, to the colonists as well) was the extension of English sovereignty over the natives. It is no coincidence that the first conversion attempts (as opposed to proposals) in the Massachusetts colony were made only after March 1644, fourteen years from its founding. In that month five local sachems "volentarily" placed themselves, their subjects, and their lands under colonial jurisdiction "to bee governed & protected by them, according to their just laws & orders, so far," read their articles of submission, "as wee shalbee made capable of understanding them." In exchange for protective custody, five red coats, dinner, and a "potfull of wine," the Indians parted with fifty-six fathoms of wampum (worth some £14 sterling) and pledged their willingness "from time to time to bee instructed in the knowledg & worship of God." But before accepting the word of pagans at face value, the English explained the articles as well as the Ten Commandments of the English God to whom the natives were submitting themselves. According to the court's record, the Indians "freely assent[ed]" to everything, including injunctions "not to swear falcely" and "to honor their parents & all their superiors," chief among whom now stood the English.[38]

There is, however, some reason to doubt that the Indians fully understood the Christian commandments at least. Nine months previously, two sachems from Narragansett, allegedly seeking protection from land-grabbing Gortonists, signed away their sovereignty and lands to Massachusetts and answered a religious quiz in words and phrases nearly identical to those later used by the Massachusett sachems. It would seem that either the Massachusetts learned their catechism at the feet of the Narragansetts—which seems highly unlikely—or that they both learned to parrot an English minister's prepared text. At the same time there is no doubt that the English recognized the significance of the native submission to colonial sovereignty. When the Massachusett sachems had "tendered themselves to our government," wrote Governor John Winthrop, "we now began to conceive hope that the Lord's time was at hand for opening a door of light and grace to those Indians." In carefully restricting his hopes to "those Indians," he revealed how dependent the Protestant missions were upon the complete political and social domination of the proselytes, however willing the latter professed themselves to be "yoked to Christ."[39]

The paper reduction of Indian disorder was one thing, its actual accomplishment another. After more than once expressing its earnest desire for the Indians' conversion and calling upon the colonial clergy for advice, the General Court finally hit upon the policy that would be responsible for whatever success they achieved in the future. In November 1646 a committee of the court and three ministers, including Roxbury's John Eliot, was appointed to purchase land "for the incuragement of the Indians to live in an orderly way amongst us." As the *reserve* did in New France, the "praying town" in the English colonies gave the missionaries some hope of segregating their converts from the raw example of the frontiersmen and the seductive paganism of their native neighbors. Moreover, it would severely cramp the Indians' mobile style by encouraging them to build heavy English-style houses, to surround themselves with the cumbersome trappings of English technology, and to remake their civil polity in the English image. The Massachusetts authorities could boast that "we compell them not to the Christian faith, nor to the profession of it, either by force of armes or by poenall laws"—which was not strictly true—largely because the praying town was the next best thing.[40]

Fourteen praying towns were founded before King Philip's War made a severe dent in the mission program in New England, but none ever achieved the new-modeled anglicized quality of Natick, the first. Beginning in 1651

13. John Eliot (1604–90), minister of the First Church in Roxbury, Massachusetts, was the dominant English missionary in the seventeenth century. He translated a large array of Puritan religious and educational works into the Natick dialect and promoted the "praying town" as the best means of "civilizing" the natives. This 1659 portrait by an unknown artist hangs in the Henry E. Huntington Library and Art Gallery, San Marino, California, by whose courtesy it is reproduced.

under John Eliot's constant supervision, the Natick Indians laid out "3 fair long streets," divided individual house lots, planted orchards, plowed fields, and built a "Pallizadoe Fort," an eighty-foot bridge over the Charles River, a large meeting-and-store house, and a few square-timbered, stone-chimneyed frame houses on their six thousand acres.[41] The houses obviously represented a loss in comfort for the natives. Not only could they no longer pick up and move their dwellings to escape fleas and lice (and town laws forbade them to bite the bugs in revenge), but the English-style houses were more expensive to build and, when built, not as warm in winter or as cool in summer as the wigwam.[42] So the majority of praying Indians kept their "old fashioned houses," much to the chagrin of the missionaries. For the ministers rightly feared that the Indians were "not so capable to be betrusted" with the holy ordinances until they could be brought to a "fixed condition of life" because, as Eliot explained, "if any should through temptations, fall under [church] Censure, he could easily run away (as some have done) and would be tempted so to do, unless he were fixed in an Habitation, and had some means of livelihood to lose, and leave behind him." They knew that Indians traditionally voted with their feet whenever they had a falling-out with a sachem, and that the new issue of Christianity had sent many people packing. The only remedy was to encourage the building of permanent houses as symbols of personal status and friendship toward their new white sovereigns. If the natives should violate that friendship, the colonists had it "more in our power to Distress them . . . as we can revenge ourselves on their fixed habitations, & growing corn."[43]

Heavy houses and "Cohabitation" might reduce one mode of native disorder, but the general question of civil polity for the praying towns still remained. Since the praying Indians had universally submitted themselves to colonial authority, they expected to receive "just laws & orders" and they were not long disappointed. The colonial legislatures frequently passed special statutes for all the Indians within their jurisdiction (whose limits depended on their ability to enforce them), but the praying towns were subject to much closer attention, as befitted their promising initiation into Christian civility. Like most of the early New England towns, the praying towns were considered too special to depend upon English common law alone. They were to constitute native models of *The Christian Commonwealth*, Eliot's plan for the spiritual regeneration of the West. But Eliot's praying towns differed from even the most saintly English communities by being modeled upon an expression of theocracy so extreme that upon its publication in Boston it was burned by the public hangman.[44] Unlike English towns, Indian praying towns did not have to compromise with individual dissent, political tradition, or corporate imperfection. They could be new-modeled on the scriptural vision of essentially one man, a missionary, and neither his English neighbors nor his native constituents could complain.

"So that Christ shall reigne both in Church and Commonwealth," Eliot proposed to "fly to the Scriptures, for every Law, Rule, Direction, Form, or what ever we do." From the eighteenth chapter of Exodus he drew the pattern for a hierarchy of native leaders who would govern, respectively, ten, fifty, and a hundred of their fellows. Since the population of the praying towns seldom exceeded that number, the rulers of hundreds exercised the authority of chief magistrate and governor, while one of the rulers of fifties wielded the "black staff and power" of constable.[45] This was the ideal where the inhabitants chose their own governors, as in Natick. But in most towns, which had not achieved the "civilized" quality of the first, the chances were good that the missionary and a court-appointed Indian superintendent would impose leaders well affected to the English cause. Democracy may have been commensurate with the "anarchy" of Indian life, but it was anathema to Englishmen nursed on monarchy and teethed on Scripture.[46]

The first few praying towns resembled their English neighbors in another way: they were founded by the voluntary subscription of their inhabitants to a social covenant.[47] The people of Natick agreed that

> We are the sons of Adam. We and our fathers have a long time been lost in our sins; but now by the mercy of the Lord beginneth to find us out again. Therefore, the grace of Christ helping us, we do give ourselves and our children to God, to be his people. He shall rule over us in all our affairs, not only in our religion and affairs of the church, but also in all our works and affairs in this world. God shall rule over us. The Lord is our judge; the Lord is our lawgiver; the Lord is our king; he will save us. The wisdom which God hath taught us in his book, that shall guide us, and direct us in the way. . . .[48]

By their unanimous commitment to the Word of God (as far as they understood it), the praying Indians effectively surrendered final authority to the English missionaries, in whose keeping the translation of God's inscrutable Word lay. Although the natives seemed to resemble English townsmen in distinguishing civil rulers from religious, no English minister ever held such uncontested sway over his community as Eliot did over the early praying towns of Massachusetts. If true theocracy was ever practiced in Anglo-America, Natick was the place.

Eliot and his Indians allegedly flew to the Scriptures for two other props of praying town government: a written code of laws and economic support for civil rulers. Unlike the capital laws of early Massachusetts (to which the Indians were already subject), however, few of the praying town laws could ultimately be traced to Scripture. Most if not all of them derived from the cultural imperatives of English custom. Crimes, rather than being sins in the sight of God, were simply offenses to English sensibility. Accordingly, small fines or whippings were meted out for infractions ranging from idleness, drunkenness, sporting long hair (male) or naked breasts (female), body greasing, and louse biting to fornication, polygamy, gambling, powwowing, and pride.[49]

Scripture did seem to recommend the introduction of tithes for the support of public officers among the praying Indians. In the Massachusetts towns, native leaders were given the "tenths of their yearly increase of all sorts of grain and pulse," while the two Pequot governors in Connecticut collected five shillings in "current Indian pay" annually from "each Indian man above sixteen yeares of age." So scriptural was the practice of tithing that Captain Daniel Gookin, the Indian superintendent in Massachusetts, feared that the new custom would be censured by some as "savouring too much of judaism and antichristianism."[50] But few Englishmen seemed to mind, and the Indians were used to paying taxes. In fact, tithing must have seemed to them less an English novelty than the continuation of a venerable Indian custom.

The choice of Indian leaders for the praying towns was a central problem for the English, and tithing may have inadvertently helped to solve it. The missionaries were quick to realize that between them and even moderate success stood the traditional sachems. Only two years after Massachusetts was founded, an English supporter of the colony advised one of its leaders that "it is a rule in warre"—his choice of words was apposite—"to aime to surprise & captivate greate ones, and the lesse will soone come under, soe winn the hartes of the Sachems and you win all." When the missions were finally set afoot in the 1640s, such advice had been rendered gratuitous by the transparent political realities of the New England Indian groups. On the eve of King Philip's War, Captain Gookin could testify from long experience that "when a sachem or sagamore is converted to the faith, and yields himself up to embrace the gospel, it hath a great influence upon his subjects." The reason, as Eliot knew, was that their acceptance "doth greatly animate and encourage such as are well-affected, and is a damping to those that are scoffers and opposers."[51]

Traditionally, the New England sachems were supported by taxes in the form of tribute, such as corn, game, services, housing, furs, or fish. "It was a flower in the prince's crown and a royalty paid him," wrote the Reverend Jared Eliot of Connecticut's native customs, "all the skins of bears, every fifth bass, and as lord of the fee the skins of all deer killed by other Indians not of his own jurisdiction in his territories; and the whole of all white deer. . . . As to the subject," he continued, lest his reader pity the poor taxpayer, "their customs were esteemed so just, and their equity appeared in such a glaring light, that our English hunters have governed themselves by them in their fishery and hunting, and determined controversies by these old customs."[52] Payment was voluntary, as was most behavior in Algonquian societies, and the rate was fixed according to ability to pay—in effect, a progressive income tax. Those individuals and even whole villages who felt that the sachem was not providing protection or leadership commensurate with their tribute could simply transfer their mobile homes and allegiance to another band. This ability of even the humblest native to vote with his feet, as well as the universal fear of mortal witchcraft, usually sufficed to reduce the pretensions of sachems to something less than omnipotent autocracy.

Predictably, the missionaries viewed the giving of tribute in a much darker light. To them the sachems exercised unbridled "tyranny" over hapless subjects held in "absolute servitude." Whenever the sachem wanted anything, he would fall into a temper tantrum until his cowering subjects gave him all they had to "pacifie" him. If they refused, the tyrant would "suborne some villain (of which they have no lack) to finde some opportunity to kill" them. "This keeps them in great awe of their Sachems," Eliot believed, "and is one reason why none of them desire any wealth, only from hand to mouth, because they are but servants, and they get it not for themselves." Thus the missionaries could interpret the sachems' opposition to Christianity as a crude fear of losing their economic stranglehold upon the people, who would quickly recognize that Christian civility offered deliverance from many kinds of bondage.[53]

But to sachems already predisposed to convert, the availability of tithed support in the praying towns must have seemed at least a fair exchange for the loss of tribute from their traditional constituents. That many praying town rulers were former sachems "of the Blood" lends credence to this possibility.[54] Likewise, since the economic rewards were roughly equal for either course of action, sachems who were still hesitant to yield their independence to the English could decide solely on the social and political merits of the case. Most traditional leaders in Massachusetts feared the sheer loss of manpower to the praying towns far more than the alleged loss of tribute that might ensue. With their numbers already greatly reduced by European diseases and the deadly incursions of the Mohawks from the west, the native bands of eastern Massachusetts faced erosion of their distinctive ethnic identity or, worse, virtual extinction, if less than the whole population moved to the praying towns.

The English reading of their own motivations into Indian decisions led them to exaggerate the importance of economic considerations and the ease with which the conversion of native leaders could be bought. John Eliot offered a classic lesson in ethnocentrism in one of his semifictional *Indian Dialogues* between two praying Indians and a traditional sachem named "Philip Keitassoot." Philip had several objections to conversion, but only one sounded authentically native in origin, namely that if he converted, his people would go to other sachems and leave him "empty and weak.'" Two other objections bore the distinctive mark of missionary rather than native concerns. "You *praying Indians* do reject your Sachems, and refuse to pay them Tribute," Philip was made to say. "I must become as a common man among them, and so lose all my Power and Authority over them." Such equality of persons before God would be intolerable, he explained, because it "will lift up the heart of the poor to too much boldness, and debase the Rulers too low: this bringing all to an equality, will bring all to a confusion." Obviously grateful for an opening, Eliot's Indians rushed in with an English antidote for the sachem's anglicized concern: "Church-Order doth not abolish Civil Order, but establish it," they assured him. "Religion teacheth and commandeth reverence and obedience to Civil Rulers."[55] Indians who had submitted to English sovereignty had, of course, been well catechized by the missionaries in the elastic meaning of the Fifth Commandment. But natives who had known the personal independence of northern Algonquian society must have found their Christian brothers' concern for hierarchy and order yet another measure of the distance that had come between them.

Equally alien to traditional Indian thinking was the English assumption—based, no doubt, on considerable success at home—that gifts could buy the temporary vote if not the permanent allegiance of political leaders. In 1632 Edward Howes, a learned English friend of John Winthrop, Jr., passed on some free advice on how to secure the friendship of Indian leaders, which everyone knew to be the prerequisite to "civillizinge the meaner sorte." His suggestion had the simplicity of a lesson learned from the great in Parliament. "Guifts blind the wise," he wrote, "howe m[uch] more them that are ignorante & simple, as I thinke all the natives are." By this touchstone, Howes thought it best to give a "scarlet coate" or some other garment emblematic of their "place & dignitie" to selected under-sachems, with "which other Sachems (of greater command than [t]he[y]) hearinge & seeinge, may thereby be allured to love & respect the English, in hope & expectation of the like. . . ." Sixty years later, the appeal of Howes's kind of thinking was still much in evidence, though on this occasion the advice flowed in the opposite direction. When John Usher, a Boston merchant, visited London in 1692, he lent the New England Company his colonial experience by advising that "presentts of Laced Coates, Shooes, stockins, hatts & shirts with a Small Sword and beltt be given to the Sachems" of prospective tribes "as from the King."[56]

Assured of the soundness of such advice, the company made the giving of presents an essential part of its mission program throughout the next century. When schools were established, dozens of stroud blankets went to native leaders and "such as send their Children"; when a new praying town was carved out of the western Indian country, "Presents to the Indians" consumed more than thirty percent of the annual operating budget.[57] The irony in all this expense is that whenever an Indian leader decided to align himself with the Christian cause, the English naively assumed that their generous bribes had carried the day (in tandem, of course, with the glaring superiority of Protestant Christianity). Largely ignorant that Indians acted out of self-interest as much as they, the English failed to see that what they intended as special bribes the Indians accepted only as ordinary gifts, the expected exchange of civilities that preceded any serious exchange of ideas. Although many believed the Indians to be descended from the Lost Tribes of Israel, it did not follow that native leaders would sell their independence for a mess of pottage.

In light of the importance they placed on the "Christian submission" of traditional Indian leaders, it should come as no surprise that the English often went beyond mere bribes to secure it. Believing as they did in the mercenary foundation of Indian motivation, they also tried to threaten sachems indirectly with the loss of tribute, despite contrary advice from New England Company officials, and unconvincing protestations of innocence from the missionaries notwithstanding. Indeed, the Company's ordering of Eliot in 1654 to go "slow in With-Drawing Indian Professors from paying accustomed Tribute and performing other lawfull servises to theire Sagamores" suggests that the practice was well under way. Eliot's account of

October 1650 confirms that it was, for in that year he heard Cutshamekin, the head sachem of the Massachusetts, complain that "the Indians that pray to God . . . do not pay him tribute as formerly they have done." According to Eliot, the root of the problem was greed: "he formerly had all or what he would; now he hath but what they will [give]." To smooth the sachem's ruffled feathers, the missionary excused himself by saying that he had already lectured his praying Indians on the meaning of the text, "Give unto Caesar what is Caesars and unto God what is Gods." To which the Indian shrewdly replied that Eliot had indeed "taught them well, but they would not in that point do as [he] taught them. . . . This thing are all the Sachems sensible of," he warned.[58]

One of the sachems most sensible of these thinly veiled threats was Uncas, sachem of the Mohegans in neighboring Connecticut. Uncas had been a steadfast opponent of Christianity for thirty years when Eliot and Gookin crossed to the west side of the Mohegan river in the fall of 1674 to preach the English gospel at Wabquissit, a town of a hundred and fifty souls. On English maps the town lay about four miles within Massachusetts's southern border, but Uncas knew better. When Eliot began to preach, an Indian emissary stood up to warn the visitors that "Unkas is not well pleased, that the English should pass over Mohegan river, to call his Indians to pray to God." Eliot's reply was again somewhat shy of the truth. He told the messenger to assure Uncas that "he did not meddle with civil right or jurisdiction" and that his purely Christian mission was "not hereby intended to abridge the Indian sachems of their just and ancient right over the Indians, in respect of paying tribute or any other dues." (It is revealing that Eliot anticipated the sachem's complaints of loss of tribute before they were ever raised.) The main design of the English, he explained ingenuously, was only to "bring them to the good knowledge of God in Jesus Christ; and to suppress among them those sins of drunkenness, idolatry, powowing or witchcraft, whoredom, murder, and like sins. As for the English," Eliot hastened to assure him, "they had taken no tribute from them, nor taxed them with any thing of that kind."[59] After hearing such a catalogue of native sins, Uncas could hardly be blamed for harboring some suspicion that doing away with the payment of tribute to a notorious "tyrant" (as he knew himself to be regarded) was probably the next object of the Christians' crusading zeal.

Eliot's disclaimers notwithstanding, Indian opponents and English critics alike sensed that the missionaries condoned, if not inspired, their converts' refusal to pay tribute to "pagan" sachems. Although they had a grudge against the dissenting colonial clergy, the royal commissioners who reported on the state of New England in 1665 had obviously received testimony (or at least heard rumors) that Eliot and company were speaking of tribute with forked tongues. They told King Charles II that the Massachusetts missionaries "convert Indians by hiring them to come & heare Sermons" (an allusion to their gift-giving), "by appointing Rulers amongst them over tenns, twenties, fifties & c., and by teaching them not to obey their Heathen Sachims."[60] Whether wholly true or not, such evidence strongly suggests that the missionaries believed that most sachems would find a loss of tribute sufficient incentive to convert, or at least to cease their opposition to the missionary program.

When it was not sufficient, the Christians were apparently not above exerting other kinds of pressure upon the holdouts. Perhaps the most efficacious method was prayer to set the wheels of divine providence in motion. If God's chosen people were themselves unable to clear the path of Protestant progress, then divine agency would have to assist them, as it had during the land-clearing plague of 1616–18 and the Pequot War of 1637.[61] Because his ambitions were greater, Eliot needed more help than most. "There be two great Sachems in the Countrey that are open & professed enemies against praying to God," he told the New England Company in 1652, "namely Unkas & Nenecrot [Ninigret] & when ever the Lord removeth them, there will be a dore open for the preaching of the Gospell in those parts." For some inscrutable reason, the Lord did not see fit to remove them, and they went to their natural graves unrepentant and implacably opposed to the conversion of their people. The doors to Connecticut and Rhode Island remained firmly closed well into the next century.[62]

Apparently Eliot's prayers received better attention in 1670. The Penagwog Indians had built a "great Fort" at the upper Merrimack Falls, largely, it seemed, to frustrate the missionaries' pious designs upon their souls. "Their Sachems refused to pray to God, so signally and sinfully," Eliot noted, "that Captain Gookins and my self were very sensible of it, and were not without some expectation of some interposure of a Divine-Hand." Accordingly the English were not disappointed when, during a Penagwog revenge raid against the Mohawks, the divine hand "signally rejected" and "cut off" all those Penagwogs who had refused to convert. Now, since their impious sachems were all "reduced," Eliot reported with transparent satisfaction, "the People (sundry of them) . . . do bow the Ear to hear, and submit to pray unto God."[63]

When the English could not borrow the strength of the divine hand, they found substitutes that even the toughest Indians had to respect. One was the judicious application of legal force to enjoin attendance upon the preaching of the Word. They admitted that "tho' you can't compel the Indians to be of the Christian religion, you may oblige them to give the hearing unto a preacher that you shall send unto them."[64] A much less subtle use of force was the threat of outright war. When Roger Williams sailed for England in 1651 he was "importuned by the Narraganset sachems, and especially by Ninigret, to present their petition to the high sachems of England, that they might not be forced from their religion, and, for not changing their religion, be invaded by war; for they said they were daily visited with threatenings by Indians that came from about the Massachusetts, that if they would not pray, they should be destroyed by war." Although under Massasoit they had been strong enough to resist any English entreaties, by the 1670s the Wampanoags of the Plymouth Colony also were feeling the steady pressure of the Christian forces. When the Quaker lieutenant-governor of Rhode Island, John Easton, attempted to forestall the outbreak of King Philip's War by listening to the Indians' grievances, Philip and his council told him "thay had a great fear to have ani of the[i]r indians should be Caled or forsed to be Christian indians. Thay saied that such wer in everi thing more mischivous, only disemblers, and then the English made them not subject to ther kings, and by ther lying to rong their kings." The pacific Easton sadly admitted that "we knew it to be true."[65]

The exact inspiration and nature of the Christian application of force to their pagan neighbors is still a mystery. For one thing, the praying Indians of Massachusetts certainly enjoyed no numerical superiority at any time, even before King Philip's War reduced the Christian towns to four. According to Captain Gookin's census of 1674, the largest town could have held no more than twenty-five or thirty adult men, not all of whom were willing or able to bear arms. Even in concert (which they never were), the total number of warriors from the most reliable older towns could not have exceeded a hundred.[66] But what they lacked in manpower they may have compensated for in firepower. The New England colonies all passed laws to prohibit the sale of guns, powder, and shot to the Indians, but the laws were often honored in the breach. The natives most favored by the colonial traders were the praying Indians. When Mohawk war parties began to wreak havoc along the Massachusetts Indian frontier in the 1660s, John Eliot saw to it that mission funds provided his praying towns with "powder & shott"—they already had guns—for "defence" against their "professed Enimies." Although the New England Company severed Eliot's unholy supply line in 1669, he and Captain Gookin managed to keep their Indians so well armed that the natives were accused of selling surplus powder to Philip's men during the bloodiest war in American history.[67] We would like to know if before 1675 the praying Indians turned their guns upon their less-well-armed pagan brothers in an excess of conversion zeal, and if so, what role the missionaries played. At this remove an educated guess will have to suffice, but from what we already know of English missionary activity in America, virtually nothing would be surprising.

When the natives had been subdued to some semblance of civilized order, the time was ripe to introduce them to the English art of industry, without which their new town life would be superfluous and their conversion to civility incomplete. In one of his first meetings with the Massachusetts, Eliot told them that they and the English were already "all one save in two things," the first being that the English were Christians and they were not. The second difference was somewhat less obvious, but to English minds nearly as important: "we labour and work in building, planting, clothing our selves, &c. and they doe not." The key word in Eliot's comparison was *labour*. To the idealistic missionaries, many of whom had pursued the life of learning because their constitutions were "unsuited to labour," to "labour" did not mean simply to "work" (as Eliot's additional use of that word implies), for even the Indians could be said to work in the sense of expending energy and thought upon various tasks. Rather it meant to work laboriously, in the sense of severe, painful, or compulsory toil, the kind that a plowman knows as he walks behind a pair of huge oxen in the late spring heat. In that sense, of course, the Indians had never known work, a deficiency the English diagnosed as a congenital "national vice," idleness.[68]

From the descriptions of the first settlers, the Indians have been branded with an indelible reputation for laziness and lack of industry. "They are not industrious," said the Reverend Cushman, mincing no words, "neither have art, science, skill or faculty to use either the land or the commodities of it, but all spoils, rots, and is marred for want of manuring, gathering, ordering"— that word again. Nearly two centuries later, when the white frontier had shifted into western New York, the Reverend John Thornton Kirkland, the namesake son of the famous New England missionary at Stockbridge, assured the members of the Massachusetts Historical Society that the situation had not changed in all that time. The Oneida, Stockbridge, and Brotherton Indians, he wrote from personal observation in 1795, "have none of the spirit, industry, and perserverance necessary in those who *subdue* a wilderness. . . . They seem to have an insurmountable aversion of labour; and though they discover some energy in the chace, wholly want it in husbandry and the arts of life." Not that the natives failed to acknowledge the importance of industry to their "happiness, respectability, and even existence." They merely felt "fast bound by the power of their savage habits" and lamented the fateful fact that *"Indians can't work."*[69]

More than once the natives seemed to confirm the ministers' worst suspicions. In the first catechism administered when they submitted to English sovereignty in 1643 and 1644, the Narragansett and Massachusett sachems were instructed "not to do any unnecessary worke on the Saboth day, especially within the gates of Christian towns." To this proposition they purportedly replied, "It is a small thing for us to rest on that day, for we have not much to do any day!" Once they had their own Christian towns and began to wear the "yoke of Christ," the Indians confessed (as John Speene did) that before their conversion "I did greatly love hunting, and hated labor: but now I beleeve that word of God, which saith, Six dayes thou shalt labor: and God doth make my body strong to labor."[70] Without divine help, however, most Indians were hard pressed to make the transition. So tempting was their former way of life that the English saw many converts apostatize because "they can live with less labour, and more pleasure and plenty, as Indians, than they can with us." In fact, one of the reasons given by colonists who either ran away to the Indians or refused to return from captivity was that amongst the Indians they enjoyed the "most perfect freedom, the ease of living, [and] the absence of those cares and corroding solicitudes which so often prevail with us."[71] When it came to procuring a living, the natives simply "prefer their practice to ours" because they quickly recognized that English methods "require too much labour and care." Captain Gookin's prediction was appropriately gloomy: "I do perceve the sinne of idleness is so riveted in them," he told the Commissioners of the United Colonies in 1664, "that much patience and labour must be put forth and exercised before it can be expected to see the contrary vertue florish among them."[72] Those raised in the Protestant ethic could best appreciate the suitability of having to "labour mightily" to bring the Indians to even minimal labor.

The English campaign against idleness was not specially designed for the Indians of the New World. Like the English quest for order, the colonial promotion of industry was the overseas rehearsal of a familiar English theme. Since Henry VIII divorced the country into the Protestant Reformation, parish clerks and clerics had read the "Homily against Idleness" at least once a year throughout the land. Puritans, Catholics, and churchmen alike inveighed against this besetting "national sin" and the "general leprosy of our piping, potting, feasting, factions and mis-spending of our time." In the keen economic competition of the budding industrial world of the North Atlantic, England was thought to be at a disadvantage because her laborers still emulated too closely the continental Catholics, who observed more than five months of saints' days and festivals every year, and when they did work thought nothing of "late coming unto their work, early departing therefrom, long sitting at their breakfast, at their dinner and noon-meat, and long time of sleeping after noon." With wages pitifully low and malnutrition eating away at his energy, the common English worker could often do little to avoid the righteous censure of his better-fed superiors.[73]

It was upon the feeble backs of men such as these that the promoters of Virginia expected to plant an economic empire. With the colonial working day set by law at between three and eight hours, depending on the season, the planters—like the Spanish before them—expected to reap their fortunes largely from the labor of the American natives, who would welcome their "gentle government" and emulate their "industrious" example. In this land of plenty the English could not imagine that feeding themselves would be more than a temporary political or, at worst, military problem. The only flaw in this pleasing prospect was that the Virginia Company had "sent the idle to teach the idle."[74]

But New England was a different land and the Puritans a different breed. There a sterner environment and an aggressive religious zeal would unite to eradicate the idleness of the Old World while reducing a godforsaken wilderness to a garden divinely favored with moderate but wholesome abundance. To the objection that "competency to live" in New England "must bee purchased with hard labour," John White, one of the founders of the Massachusetts Bay Company, countered with a characteristic expression of the Protestant ethic: "If men desire to have a people degenerate speedily, and to corrupt their mindes and bodies too . . . let them seeke a rich soile, that brings in much with little labour; but if they desire that Piety and godlinesse should prosper, accompanied with sobriety, justice and love, let them choose a Countrey such as [New England] which may yeeld sufficiency with hard labour and industry: The truth is," White warned, "there is more cause to feare wealth then poverty in that soyle."[75] As the Puritans saw it, God could be found in glacial moraine more easily than black loam.

Not every New Englishman thought the same way, however. For some the idea of grubbing among stumps and stones for a spare existence appealed neither to their religious spirit nor to their national pride. If the descriptions of their detractors are any indication, they, too much like the Indians, made a virtue of idleness. The best known of these stylish shirkers was Thomas Morton of Merrymount, "Lord of Misrule" and master of a "School of Atheism," who erected an "idle or idol maypole" to symbolize his freedom from the tedious labors of his saintly neighbors. Finding more reward for less effort in trading with the Indians, he and his "dissolute" crew spent their "working" days enjoying flowing wine, Indian women, and ribald song. When their bellies began to growl, Morton hired some Indian men to "hunt and fowl for him." To prevent this artful dodger from seducing all their servants and the "vile scum of the country," the Plymouth authorities despatched an armed party under Miles Standish—whom Morton dubbed "Captain Shrimpe"—to pack him off to English in irons. When he boldly returned the following year to resume his careless life of gunrunning, the Massachusetts government shipped him off again and demolished his house, "that it might be no longer a roost for such unclean birds to nestle in."[76]

The pursuit of idleness was obviously attractive work (if you could get—or get away with—it), and Morton was not alone in drawing the moral fire of the colonial authorities. In 1655 the president of Harvard College condemned the licentious settlers who headed for the "howling wilderness" where "they may follow their worldly business at any time" (free from the constraints of the Puritan Sabbath) "and their children may drudg for them at plough, or hough [hoe], or such like servil imployments, that themselves may be eased." Almost from the beginning of settlement, as if to emphasize the cord of continuity between Old England and New, ministers fretted that "idleness would be the ruin both of church and commonwealth."[77] To forestall such an event, the colonial legislatures passed numerous statutes—which were rigorously enforced—to prod the idle into fruitful labor, and even church covenants resolved to shun "Idleness as the bane of any State."[78] By 1679, when the jeremiads following King Philip's War were in full throat, the New England clergy were united in their censure of the "abundance of Idleness, which brought ruinating Judgement upon Sodom, and much more upon Jerusalem . . . and doth [now] sorely threaten New-England." In the minds of at least the Boston Mathers, father and son, there was no doubt that the colonists had been "Indianized," for everyone knew that the natives were "*Lazy Drones*, and love *Idleness* Exceedingly."[79] It was a small but important measure of the power of their American experience that the colonists could so readily blame the Indians for so venerable an English trait.

On the other hand, the colonists fell back on an entirely European habit when they particularized their indictment of the Indians' idleness. When idleness was said to be endemic to Indian culture, the cultural norm they had in mind applied to only half the Indian population—the male half. For upon closer examination it appeared to English observers, almost all of whom were male, that while Indian men were indeed epitomes of slothful indulgence, the work done by Indian women came respectably, even pitiably, close to the missionaries' ideal of labor. Since such behavior ran counter to their civilized expectations, here was double cause for raised eyebrows.

As soon as the first settlers stepped ashore the stark contrast between the industry of Indian women and the idleness of Indian men was fixed forever in the national mythology, providing the colonists with still further cause for self-congratulation. George Percy, a gentle-born passenger on the first ship to Virginia in 1607, reported home that the native women "doe all their drug-erie. The men takes their pleasure in hunting and their warres, which they are in continually, one Kingdome against another." Captain John Smith, who was on Percy's ship, saw the Virginians with the same eyes. "The men bestowe their times in fishing, hunting, wars, and such manlike exercises, scorning to be seene in any woman like exercise," he noted ambivalently, "which is the cause that the women be verie painefull [laborious] and the men often idle. The women and children do the rest of the worke. They make mats, baskets, pots, morters, pound their corne, make their bread, prepare their victuals, plant their corne, gather their corne, beare al kind of burdens and such like."[80]

When Puritan parties landed in New England some years later, the Indians there exhibited similarly "barbarous" ways. The Reverend Francis Higgin-son, the author of a "true description of the commodities and discommodi-ties" of *New-Englands Plantation*, obviously reckoned as one of the discom-modities that the native "Men for the most part live idlely, they doe nothing but hunt and fish. Their wives," on the other hand, "set theire corne and doe all their other worke." Edward Johnson, who arrived with Governor Win-throp on the *Arbella* in 1630, could not have approved more of the minister's disapproval, for he too lamented that the Indian women were "generally very laborious at their planting time, and the Men extraordinarily idle." Not only did "the men follow no kind of labour but hunting, fishing and fowling," but they also made "their squawes to carry their Children and the luggage beside; so that many times they travell eight or ten mile[s] with a burden on their backs, more fitter for a horse to carry then a woman."[81] To hear the English tell it, an Indian woman's lot was clearly not an happy one.

When European observers sought an explanation for the Indian woman's misfortune (which they rarely did), they could only blame it on her spouse's unshakable belief in male superiority, which dominated because the "softer passions" had no place in a savage society. John Smith set the tone when he described Indian men as "scorning to be seene in any woman like exercise." Twenty years later, a Dutch official at New Amsterdam, Isaack de Rasieres, noted that Hudson River Indian men were "so inclined to freedom that they cannot by any means be brought to work." While their women were labor-iously planting, hilling, and weeding their corn fields, "the men would not once look to it, for it would compromise their dignity too much, unless they are very old and cannot follow the chase." William Wood, an early emigrant to New England, went his contemporaries one better. He not only charged that Indian women were lorded over by their lazy, "gourmandizing" husbands, but claimed that since the arrival of the English the squaws would no longer "rest themselves content under their helpless condition." For seeing the "kind usage of the English to their wives, they do as much condemn their husbands for unkindness and commend the English for their love." According to Wood, who was undoubtedly looking at his own people through rose-colored glasses, the much-maligned Indian women "resort often to the English houses" to "somewhat ease their misery by complaining" to their pampered equals (equals only "in sex," Wood was quick to point out). If their surly husbands came looking for them and besieged the houses with "bluster," the "English woman betakes her to her arms, which are the warlike ladle and the scalding liquors, threatening blistering to the naked runaway, who is soon expelled by such liquid comminations." Faced with such treatment, the warriors could only blame their English counterparts for "their folly in spoiling good working creatures."[82]

By the time the young missionary David McClure made his journey to the Ohio Shawnees in 1772, the stereotype of the lazy Indian and his squaw drudge had hardened into accepted fact, dignified by some impressive-sounding amateur ethnology. "The savage state has always been unfavorable to the female," offered the twenty-two-year-old Yale graduate. "The superior strength of the man is used, not in protecting & lightening the burdens of the weaker sex, but in depressing them. The men are *ashamed* of all kinds of labour, except war & hunting [and] the building of their miserable houses. . . . Such is the pride of these lazy lords of the wilderness!"[83]

Bred, like all people, to an ethnocentric world view, the English saw what they expected to see in Indian life. Initially jarred by the half-correct observation that native men were not responsible for the agricultural livelihood of their society, the English never recovered their visual focus enough to notice that what was normal behavior in England did not always obtain in America, that Indian men played a role in their economy every bit as important as English farmers did in theirs, and that Indian women did not view their social position in the light cast by the male observers from another culture.

The roving naturalist John Bartram inadvertently gave the first clue to a more accurate view of Indian "industry" when he noted that Iroquois men were "lazy and indolent *at home*." The colonists visited Indian villages most frequently in the summer months, when the women were busily occupied with farming. At this time of year, when groundnuts, berries, and fish were plentiful, Indian men appeared to spend "halfe their dayes in gaming and lazing."[84] Certainly their share of communal work fell upon them more lightly in the summer months after the long winter of hunting and trapping, often alone, far from home, and in frequent danger and discomfort. But white observers seldom saw their elaborate preparations for hunting, fishing, and fighting—which were vastly underrated—and for those even less frequently acknowledged activities, trade and diplomacy.

To prepare for hunting and its social analogue, warfare, the men had (as a minimum) to fashion bows and numerous arrows, chip flint or carve bones for arrowheads, spearpoints, and knives, carve wooden warclubs, weave or sew quivers and sheaths, and procure and mix paints for body decoration. For winter hunting and trapping, snowshoes and nooses for spring snares were essential; so too were toboggans if the catch was successfully large. Long journeys for trade and diplomacy required canoes (dugouts or bark) and wampum belts, strung from hundreds of tiny cylindrical beads laboriously ground from the quahog shell. All of these activities took the men away from their villages and families for considerable portions of the year, for which they had to leave sufficient stores of meat and fish and all man-made equipment so that the daily routines of life could be carried on in their absence. In short, when Indian men were at home they were either resting from or preparing for the energetic performance of their seasonal duties away from home.

Furthermore, if the white visitors had come to the Indian villages at the right time of year, they might have seen that native men did not universally shun the "woman's work" of farming (though they might disguise their involvement). Throughout the East, men were responsible for clearing the fields by girdling trees, extracting rocks, and burning underbrush, and often for breaking the soil. At this point they normally withdrew, leaving to the women the planting, hilling, and weeding of the "three sisters," corn, beans, and squash. "Yet sometimes," as Roger Williams observed of the Narragansetts, "the man himselfe, (either out of love to his Wife, or care for his Children, or being an old man) will help the Woman which (by the custome of the Countrey) they are not bound to." Again at the harvest the men would sometimes return to pick, husk, shell, or braid the corn for storage.[85] Although the Indian divison of labor differed somewhat from European expectations, native men were actively involved in every phase of the subsistence cycle, as were the women. In the eyes of colonists who knew them well, the Indians' work no less than their own could be regarded as "toyling labour."[86]

The European myth of the squaw drudge rings no more true than that of the idle warrior. While native women performed several tasks their colonial counterparts found slavish, their attitude toward their work had nothing of the slave mentality about it. After a long career as a missionary to the Delawares, John Heckewelder specifically denied that Indian women were "treated as slaves" or that their work was "hard or difficult." While he admitted that their labors were hard "compared with the tasks that are imposed upon females in civilised society" (which he probably underestimated), he recognized that "they are no more than their fair share." "They are not only voluntarily, but cheerfully submitted to," he argued, for "as women are not obliged to live with their husbands any longer than suits their pleasure or convenience, it cannot be supposed that they would submit to be loaded with unjust or unequal burdens." If the male missionary's word was suspect, however, that of the women themselves presumably was not, and the Delaware women acknowledged that "while their field labour employs them at most six weeks in the year, that of the men continues the whole year round."[87]

Still less assailable was the testimony of a woman who had lived the life of an English farm girl until she was fifteen and the rest of her days as an Iroquois mother and wife. At the end of a full life among the Senecas, Dickewamis (better known as Mary Jemison) said that "our labor was not severe, and that of one year was exactly similar, in almost every respect, to that of the others, without that endless variety that is to be observed in the common labor of the white people. Notwithstanding the Indian women have all the fuel and bread to procure, and the cooking to perform, their task is probably not harder than that of white women, who have those articles provided for them; and their cares certainly are not half as numerous, nor as great." Even the field work of summer was not as laborious as most white observers regarded it because "we . . . generally had all our children with us; but had no master to oversee or drive us, so that we could work as leisurely as we pleased."[88]

In contrast to the colonial woman whose work revolved almost exclusively around the care and management of her own home, which in many frontier settlements was physically isolated from its neighbors, the work of Indian women was "very trifling" within doors and was largely done outdoors in communal work parties, crowded with kith and kin, in a "vein of gaiety and frolic." Whether hoeing the fields, gathering firewood, or pounding corn, these mutual aid societies not only lightened the work with singing, gossip, and humor, but strengthened the bonds of kinship that were so vital to Indian society.[89] If the truth had been known, the lives of Indian women might have merited more envy than pity.

On their face the English criticisms of Indian "industry" were serious enough, but a number of less overt grievances reveal even more about the cutural preconceptions of the colonists, and therefore about the remedial prescriptions that could be expected from the missionaries. First of all, native farming was criticized not only because it was done largely by women, but because it did not employ the deep-cutting plow harnessed to animal power, fences to enclose the fields, or (particularly symbolic) fertilizer in the form of tame animal manure.

John Winthrop's legal rationalization concluded that a civil (as opposed to a natural) right to common land was conferred by "inclosinge and peculiar manuerance." Happily for the Massachusetts Bay Company, it was decided that the New England natives "inclose noe Land, neither have any setled habytation, nor any tame Cattle to improve the Land by," and so were devoid of any legal claim to their territory.[90] The Dutch in New Netherlands, who shared with the English many economic assumptions, entertained a similarly low opinion of Iroquois and Mahican practices. Adriaen Van der Donck charged that they "cultivate no wheat, oats, barley, or rye," the standard European crops, "and know nothing of ploughing, spading, and splitting up the soil." They left their common fields and private gardens "open, unenclosed, and unprotected by fencing." "Of manuring and proper tillage," he concluded, "they know nothing," which must have prompted his readers to ask just how they managed to raise such an abundance of corn and beans every year that the Dutch obtained "whole cargoes in sloops and galleys in trade."[91]

The English readers of Thomas Harriot must have been similarly puzzled. According to the Roanoke explorer, the native Carolinians "never enrich the soil with refuse, dung, or any other thing, nor do they plough or dig it as we do in England." Nevertheless, their corn reached prodigious heights and "the yield is so great that little labor is needed in comparison with what is necessary in England." Although the natives could watch an English plow "tear up more ground in a day than their clamshells [hoes] could scrape up in a month," still "they prefer their practice to ours," Van der Donck admitted in puzzlement.[92] To those who swore by the Protestant work ethic there was nothing more galling than to discover that wild savages reaped the proverbial fruits of the earth without working up a European-style sweat. Such an anomaly cast a shadow upon English pretensions to divine favor and upon the validity of their missionary design to reform every aspect of native culture.

Another criticism of Indian farming was implied by the fact that no more equipment was required than a crude hoe and a few handmade baskets. This meant that native technology was as portable as their housing, which rendered them still more difficult to bring to English order. Without horses, barns, carts, harrows, plows, halters, collars, and harnesses—in other words, without a substantial investment in the capitalist way of life—the Indians could not be securely anchored to one plot of ground where they could always be found. In addition, without an involvement in the encircling web of credit that husbandry entailed, the Indians could at any time pull up stakes and head for the hinterland, out of the reach of scriptural and English law.[93]

Trying to persuade the Indians, even the most Christian, to invest in the heavy technology of farming was a task of no little difficulty because it both raised their deeply engrained suspicions of anything that threatened to circumscribe their independence and offended their sense of utility. The English, keen entrepreneurs that they were, understood that the civilized citizen was "attached to his country by property, by artificial wants which rendered that property necessary to his comfortable subsistence."[94] So one of the first tasks of those who would attach the Indians to the English political interest was to "multipl[y] their Wants, and put them upon desiring a thousand things, they never dreamt of before." Thus "their wants will be encreased," reasoned "The Planter" in an eighteenth-century Philadelphia newspaper, "while on us they must in a manner wholly depend to have them supplied."[95] For a society of men uniquely responsive to the marketplace, it was a strategy with promise, but it failed to reckon with the alien psychology of the native Americans.

While the natives would gladly purchase portable goods, such as clothing, guns, kettles, rum, and ornaments, they could rarely be induced to incur long-term debts and responsibility for English-style farm equipment. In 1795, for example, after his father had spent nearly thirty years preaching and demonstrating the virtues of farming, John Thornton Kirkland found that of the six hundred and fifty Oneidas living in New York only in "two or three instances" did they "imperfectly adopt our husbandry, possess the most necessary farming utensils, and succeed in tillage. All the others in the nation get half or two thirds of their subsistence by raising corn, beans, and potatoes" in one field, "having no implement but the hoe; and the other part by hunting and fishing." Their remaining tracts they allowed to run wild or leased for a "small rent" to the neighboring whites.[96]

The Kirklands need not have been surprised by the native resistance to their designs, for two centuries of colonial experience might have taught them that "having few artificial Wants," as Ben Franklin put it, the Indians considered "our laborious Manner of Life, compared with theirs, . . . slavish and base." Merrymount's merry mercenary, Thomas Morton, had to commend his native customers in one particular, that "though they buy many commodities of our Nation, yet they keepe but fewe, and those of speciall use . . . They are not delighted in baubles, but in usefull things." The reason was plain to see if Englishmen dared to look. "They care for little, because they want but little," William Penn tried to explain to his English partners, "and the Reason is, a little contents them: In this they are sufficiently revenged on us; if they are ignorant of our Pleasures, they are also free from our Pains. They are not disquieted with Bills of Lading and Exchange, nor perplexed with Chancery-Suits and Exchequer-Reckonings. We sweat and toil to live; their pleasure feeds them, I mean, their Hunting, Fishing and Fowling. . . ."[97] The natives could be as industrious as any Englishman, as many colonists came to recognize, but they preferred to expend their energy in their own time and in their own way. Navigating a heavy plowshare behind a recalcitrant team of oxen who periodically released their "peculiar manuerance" simply struck them as grotesquely effeminate and quite mad, appropriate for the white man perhaps but beneath the dignity of true men.

Penn's characterization of Indian hunting as "pleasure" introduces a second group of English objections to the Indian division of labor. It was bad enough that women should manage the Indian fields without the aid of either their menfolk or the labor-inducing technology of the English, but almost worse was that the truant warriors misspent their days sporting in the woods or the water. Like the founder of Pennsylvania, colonists up and down the Eastern Seaboard felt that Indian hunting and fishing were more pleasant pastimes than real work.[98] While they could sometimes appreciate that native men took "extreame paines" in those pursuits, they could not forgive them for expending their energy in places other than plowed fields or fragrant cow barns. John Smith thought that since hunting and fishing were "their ordinary exercise from their infancy," the Powhatans "esteeme it a pleasure." The versifying minister, William Morell, regarded the New England natives in the same light. "Thus all worke women doe," he wrote, "whilst men in play, in hunting, armes, and pleasures end the day." The most that Adriaen Van der Donck could say of such men was that "to hunting and fishing [they] are all extravagantly inclined."[99] Clearly something was unseemly about such misplaced enthusiasm.

A southern gentleman put his finger on the true cause of English concern when he noted, after an extensive survey of the Indian country between Virginia and North Carolina, that native men were "quite idle, or at most employ'd only in the Gentlemanly Diversions of Hunting and Fishing." By this William Byrd II, the English-bred scion of one of the wealthiest families in Virginia, indicated that the Indians' greatest offense was the usurpation of aristocratic privilege, the disorderly jumping of class lines. For in England the only people who hunted were members of the upper classes, who did not kill to eat, and poachers, who did, and risked their ears—or necks—in the attempt. Forests were not public property but belonged to the nobility, who regarded them as private game preserves. Guns were expensive and their ownership was generally forbidden by law; paid soldiers used a clumsy musket far heavier and less accurate than a sporting rifle.[100]

These were the assumptions that the colonists carried to America, where the forests seemed to belong to no man, where guns became a household fixture, where hunting was often a necessity, and where English class lines failed to replicate themselves. In spite of all the social and environmental changes that should have engendered a different outlook toward hunting (and in some instances did, when it came to the colonists' own hunting), the colonists continued to view the economic activities of Indian men with Old World eyes. Regarded as the social inferiors of all Englishmen, the Indians were harshly judged by semifeudal standards that simply made no sense in the New World, much less in an alien culture. When the Great Council for New England granted John Pierce, a London clothworker, a land patent in 1621, it also conferred the "libertie to hunt, hauke, fish or fowle," as if he were a newly dubbed knight about to enter the king's private preserve.[101] To anyone who had lived in the American woods, however briefly, such a grant must have seemed superfluous, if not downright laughable. Surely the Indians who hunted to live would have found it both.

While these were seldom articulated, the English had other misgivings about Indian hunting that lay just beneath the surface of their vocal disdain. These revolved around the fearful fact that in Indian society, hunting and warfare were but two aspects of the same activity. Not only was warfare conducted by hunting patterns, but hunting was a sort of ritualized warfare, carried on under strong religious sanctions. The education for one was the training for both. David Zeisberger noted that, as soon as Indian boys were able to run about, "they learn to use the bow and arrow." To harden them for the rigorous life of the hunter-warrior, their parents "put them into cold water as soon as they are born, and afterwards in the cold of winter they make a hole in the ice and put them in."[102] From a tender age the boys followed their fathers in avoiding "hard labour," partly to keep their limbs supple for the chase, which might take them "twenty-five or thirty-miles" over "rough and smooth grounds," through creeks and rivers "whether shallow or deep, frozen or free from ice," in pursuit of "a wounded deer, bear, or other animal." And the English knew only too well that the practice of stealing through the woods to creep up on game served the warrior equally well in ambushing unsuspecting enemies.[103] Whether intended or not, the colonial reduction of Indian hunting to a harmless "diversion" served to disarm, at least mentally, a disturbing and dangerous alternative.

Wishful thinking had its uses, but the most effective way to remedy the natives' lack of "industry" was to "subdue them to labour," to subvert their traditional division of labor by imbuing them with an Anglo-Protestant work ethic and offering them a place in a radically different economy. For as Eliot had reminded the Massachusetts in 1646, an important difference between the English and themselves was that "we labour and work in building, planting, clothing our selves, &c. and [you] doe not." Consequently, one of the main goals of the New England praying towns was to provide "incouragements for the industrious" and "meanes of instructing them in Letters, Trades, and Labours, [such] as building, fishing, Flax and Hemp dressing, planting Orchards, &c."[104] On paper, "Letters, Trades, and Labours" seemed to promise the Indians a full share in the complex market economy of the North Atlantic community. But in reality the missionaries could never muster the cultural vision or the social resources to enable their converts to become anything more dignified than tawny husbandmen who scraped a bare existence from the grudging soil of their reservations.

The colonial failure to introduce the Indians to the full range of English economic skills has no better measure than the failure to place Indian youth in fruitful apprenticeships. Traditionally, at home and in the colonies, many English children prepared for their life's work by being apprenticed to a master of a trade or skill for a given number of years. By living in their master's family, they ideally received some formal education (the ability to read and write was sometimes stipulated in their indentures), social discipline, religious nurture, and especially on-the-job training at their chosen calling.[105] But even with a shortage of skilled labor in America, apprenticeship played a remarkably small role in the missionaries' attempts to "civilize" the natives.

Not that proposals were never made. Throughout the colonial period, numerous schemes were hatched for turning Indians into able artisans through apprenticeship. One duty of the colonial commissioners of the New England Company, the London-based missionary society that financed the majority of American missions before the Revolution, was to place "the Heathen Natives or their Children . . . with or under any English Masters in any Trade, Mystery, or Law full Calling." In 1660 the commissioners tried to encourage Indian parents to apprentice their children to "Godly English" masters by offering "one coate" upon presentation of the master's certificate that the child actually lived with him. Apparently the spirit was lost from the letter of the law, for in 1678 the offer was limited to children under the age of twenty-one who would serve "godly masters, such as will engage to teach them to read well, and bring them up in Christian nurture."[106] When John Daniel Hammerer devised his plan for "Civilizing the North American Indians" in the 1730s, he seemed to derive from the first generation of New England missionaries his touching faith in the reforming power of apprenticeship. He, like the Puritans, thought only of "lead[ing] on and tam[ing] the rude and undisciplined Minds of the Indian Youths," and failed to reckon the difficulty of enticing either skilled craftsmen or native apprentices to the experiment.[107]

Apprenticeship failed to be used to effect for several reasons. Indian parents were "so indulgent to their children, that they are not easily persuaded to put them forth to the English." Even when they could be persuaded, the children were reluctant servants at best and often ran away from the uncustomary "labour and order" of their English confinement. Their pronounced love of liberty, added to the normal pedagogical difficulties of working with young people of another language and culture, made many if not most English masters equally reluctant to take on Indian charges. Even the New England commissioners had to admit that "Their Nature is so Volatile, they can few or none of them be brought to fix to a trade."[108]

Accordingly, apprenticeship came to be seen less as an educational institution than as an instrument of social control. By the eighteenth century the only Indians who were bound out were the children of paupers and debtors or students who did not take to the life of English learning. In 1760 Gideon Hawley, the missionary of the Mashpee reservation on Cape Cod, complained that "there is scarcely an Indian Boy among us not indentted to an English Master" as "collateral security for [his] parents' debts."[109] The penal use of apprenticeship did nothing to enhance its attraction, nor did its character as a last resort for Indian students who failed to appreciate the finer points of Latin prosody or English grammar. Ben Uncas, the son of the Mohegan sachem, tasted the life of learning at the tables of two successive ministers but quickly lost his appetite. So he was bound to a cordwainer for three years "to learn that Handy Craft, & to read & to write." A promising but indolent Mohawk student of the Reverend Eli Forbes of Brookfield was relegated to a similar fate. Although he was "so well acquainted with farming Business that he is well able to maintain himself, without obstructing the benevolent design of his Education," yet "he is not willing to labour while he is supported from another Quarter [the Massachusetts General Court]." Unwilling to countenance native idleness, the court ordered him bound out for six months to "some good Sober family in the farming way" to be taught "Diligence and Industry."[110]

Perhaps the most important reason for the failure of Indian apprenticeship was the colonists' inability, or unwillingness, to encourage the natives in skilled trades. In 1609 the Reverend Robert Gray advised the English tradesmen and artificers in Virginia to "be warie in taking the Savages to bee apprentices" to teach them "our trades and mysteries," since there were more humble jobs "to set many thousands on worke." Manual labor, in other words, was good enough for the natives, who would save the colonists' backs in the bargain. In 1662 the New England Company promised its colonial commissioners that if their funds increased, "wee should consider of some . . . trade and manifactury to Imploy the Indians." Anticipating their need, John Winthrop, Jr., who was in London on other business, quickly submitted a proposal that called for an initial stock of £5,000 but failed to specify the uses to which it would be put. He did, however, assure the Corporation that the Indian people to be employed, those situated between Narragansett Bay and the Thames River at New London, were "more civil and active and industrious than any other of the adjacent parts" and "apt to fall into English employment." It is uncertain whether the company officers were aware that Winthrop's personal landholdings happened to fall in the very midst of those "industrious" tribes, but in any case the swift decline of their funds brought all plans to naught nearly at once.[111]

The most skillful trades to which Indians were ever apprenticed were carpentry, smithing, and printing, and only one or two natives are known to have plied each of them.[112] And the closest thing to a proper "manifactury" they ever saw was a "large and convenient work-house" that John Hoare built for fifty-eight Nashobah Indians (twelve men and forty-six women and children) in the center of Concord, cheek by jowl, appropriately enough, with the "town watch-house." According to Captain Gookin, "this house was made, not only to secure those Indians under lock and key by night, but to employ them and set them to work by day, whereby they earned their own bread." Had they not been marched off to windswept Deer Island in Boston Harbor as a security threat during King Philip's War, these peaceable Indians might, "with God's blessing, . . . have lived well in a short time."[113] That workhouses stood beside jails in the English pantheon of penal institutions could not have inspired the freedom-loving Indians with much confidence in the missionaries' concern for their economic salvation.

Far more typical of praying Indian trades were woodcutting, stonewalling, shingle splitting, basket weaving, broom making, and spinning.[114] The natives usually had little choice once English settlements had encroached upon their lands, driving game before them, and many of their traditional crafts had been lost to an increased dependence upon European trade goods. Reduced to economic straits for reasons largely beyond their making, they characteristically turned to occupations that minimized their labor and their need to learn new skills and maximized their income, independence, and ability to remain on their ancestral lands. In the process some traditional Indian sex roles were altered. Strenuous efforts were made to remove native women from their communal field work, for example, by isolating them behind spinning wheels and wool cards, which did not easily lend themselves to clan- or village-sized workbees. But since Indian women were traditionally responsible for their families' clothing, their transition to its English-style production was not as abrupt as the change faced by their menfolk in shifting from hunting and fishing to farming.[115]

The first natives to experience the transition were the eastern bands of New England, who were reduced to dependency upon the English not only by disease and demographic inundation but by their fear of Mohawk raiders from the west. Though the Algonquians greatly outnumbered the Mohawks, "the appearance of four or five Maquas in the woods would frighten them from their habitations, and cornfields, and reduce many of them to get together in forts; by which means they were brought to such straits and poverty, that had it not been for relief they had from the English, in compensation for labour, doubtless many of them had suffered famine." As providence would have it, just as the Iroquois were wrecking the native economy, English missionaries were beginning to preach a new gospel of work. The war thus came to have—in English eyes—a "good effect" upon some of the natives, "namely, to turn them from idleness; for now necessity forced them to labour with the English in hoeing, reaping, picking hops, cutting wood, making hay, and making stone fences, and like necessary employments, whereby they got victuals and clothes."[116]

Thus forced to rely increasingly upon the English for subsistence, the Indians quickly learned that the missionaries entertained a somewhat narrower idea of industry than did the rest of the colonial population. To the preachers and the politicians who supported them, industry meant farming, and farming meant tillage, not grazing.[117] Since the natives suffered from idleness, a constitutional disorder of the worst sort, they could be cured only by the heaviest dose of English labor, which the tending of a few cows and pigs did not constitute. As the Elizabethan adventurers had found in Ireland, a pastoral economy was not incompatible with "barbarism." The "wild Irish" maintained herds of cattle as shaggy as themselves, which might have betokened their potential for economic salvation, but their migrations between summer and winter pastures marked them as hopeless nomads and therefore as invincible barbarians in the invaders' eyes.[118] The American natives, of course, did not enjoy even so partial an advantage. "Tame Cattle they have none," observed John Josselyn, tongue in cheek, "excepting Lice, and Doggs of a wild breed that they bring up to hunt with." Which was true, despite the well-meaning credulity of some Englishmen who believed that the Indians domesticated deer and moose sufficiently to collect manure for their fields and milk for butter and cheese.[119]

Therefore, as soon as the missionaries were able to establish themselves among the Indians they began to introduce the idea of English-style farming. In 1647 John Eliot encouraged his native followers at Nonantum (Newton) to "fence their ground with ditches [and] stone walls" by offering them "a groat or sixpence a rod" and "promised to helpe them with Shovels, Spades, Mattocks, [and] Crows of Iron." But fencing was only a small preliminary to full-scale farming, and the natives had to live in the meantime. So they timidly entered the nascent market economy of Massachusetts with the resources at hand. Eliot noted proudly that they "find something to sell at Market all the yeer long: all winter they sell Brooms, Staves, Eelpots, Baskets, [and] Turkies," and during the other seasons a variety of game, fish, and berries. With the establishment of Natick, however, Eliot's vision of English-style Indian farms began to be realized. Apple orchards were planted, fences extended around both fields and orchards, cows, goats, and hogs introduced, hay gathered, barns and sheds built from hand-sawn planks, and most important, fields plowed with proper implements by men and tame animals, not by women with clamshell hoes. [120]

The official English preference for tillage showed itself every time a new mission was founded. The Housatonic Indians were so taken with Stockbridge when it was granted to them in 1736 that they planted three times more than they ever had. Two years later the New England Company allowed them £300 to purchase "husbandry tools—as axes, carts, ploughs." The following spring (1739) their missionary, John Sergeant, procured "four Ploughs" and they "plow[ed] their Land themselves, which they used to hire done" by local farmers. That farming was essential to Sergeant's plans for civilizing the Indians can be seen even in his design for a coeducational boarding school, which was to combine work and study on a two-hundred-acre plot. To ensure that "as little time as possible may be lost in idleness" between classes, he proposed that the students raise their own provisions, maintain a stock of cattle, sheep, and hogs, and manufacture the wool, flax, and milk by-products. This would, he felt, "form them to industry" and prepare them by the age of twenty to establish farms of their own.[121]

The idea of laboring while learning later caught on as well at Eleazar Wheelock's famous Indian school in Lebanon, Connecticut. There Wheelock's students, Indian and white, put in time working the master's farm because he thought it necessary that his pupils, designed for missionaries, interpreters, and schoolmasters, should be initiated in the "practical knowledge of husbandry." The idea was a sensible one, but in practice "husbandry" was only a dignified word for farm chores, as the vocal protests of several of his Indian students revealed. Word reached Boston that Wheelock used the Indians "very hard in keeping of them to work," treating them little better than "servants." The unusually qualified father of a Narragansett student complained to the master that "I always tho't Your School was free to the Natives; not to learn them how to Farm it, but to advance in Christian Knowledge . . . ; not that I'm anything against his Labouring some for You, when Business lies heavy on you," he added, "but to work two Years to learn to Farm it, is what I don't consent to, when I can as well learn him that myself and have the prophet [profit] of his Labour, being myself bro't up with the best of Farmers."[122]

If Sergeant and Wheelock had restricted their instruction to farming and forgotten all about book learning, Gideon Hawley believed they might have done some good for the Indians. The most astute and certainly the most successful English missionary in the colonial period, Hawley knew from over fifty years' experience that putting an Indian in a boarding school or teaching him the learned languages was "not the way to civilize, much less to Christianize" him. "An acre of Corn or even a yard of Potatoes will be of much more utility to him," he wrote in 1802, "than being able to translate Virgill or Cicero. And to teach a young female savage to spin a skaine of yarn, milk [a] cow, or even raise a brood of Chickens will do more toward civilization than all the fine learning . . . at any expence would do." The only way to civilize the Indians, Hawley had deduced from long experience, was to initiate them in "civil jurisprudence, evangelical knowledge, and habits of industry." And without the latter the whole scheme would topple.[123]

Hawley's inventory of acceptably industrious activities suggests that he may have been right in more respects than one. The only aspect of English-style farming the Indians adopted to any extent was not intensive tillage, which required burdensome and expensive equipment, but the maintenance of grazing stock, which they simply added to their traditional corn culture.[124] Such a minor adoption had two important advantages for the natives. First, the domesticated animals, primarily beef cattle and hogs, acted as a protein substitute for their diminished consumption of wild game.[125] And second, they required relatively little labor to maintain. If the Indians emulated the colonists' example, they allowed their livestock to forage in the woods and wastelands during most of the year on oak and beech mast, browse, and fallen fruit. At other times Indian corn sufficed, as it did for English cattle. Such careless methods did not produce maximum growth on the hoof, but they satisifed both Indian and colonial farmers in minimizing labor. They also satisfied—at least partially—the missionaries' requirements for a civilizing mode of industry. If the Indians could not become idealized English husbandmen, at least they could earn a respectable living from mixed farming, like their white contemporaries. Beyond that even the most acculturated natives would not go, despite the blandishments of smooth-tongued ministers who promised that greater labor would bring "worldly comfort" and the "comforts of [English] life."[126]

There were several reasons for the Indians' refusal to share the colonial dream of prosperity. One was their fierce pride and fear of ridicule, white and Indian. The natives must have had no difficulty in sensing that their English teachers held impossibly high standards to which they could never measure up. After boasting how well his Nonantum followers were adapting to a market economy, Eliot could not resist noting that "it's not comparable to what they might do, if they were industrious." Similarly, Captain Gookin described the considerable success the praying Indians of Hassanamesitt had in husbandry, horticulture, and "keeping cattle and swine," wherein, he continued, "they do as well, or rather better than any other Indians, but yet are very far short of the English both in diligence and providence." Many years later among the Oneidas, Samuel Kirkland expressed his hope that "some few of them will in time make œconomists, at least Indian ones. . . ."[127] No matter how industrious the Indians became in English terms, they never worked as hard or as well as their colonial counterparts. It would be strange indeed if such ethnocentrism had not made itself felt by the Indians.

They could no more easily escape the disdain of their native neighbors and enemies. In 1765 a Seneca war chief exhorted his brethren of the council to reject young Kirkland's offer of the Bible because they would become "a *miserable abject people*" by accepting it. "How many remnants of tribes to the East are so reduced," he asked knowingly,

that they pound sticks to make brooms, to buy a loaf of Bread and it may be a shirt. The warriors, which they boasted of, before these foreigners, the white people crossed the great Lake, where are they now? why their grandsons are all become *mere women! Brothers attend! This* will be the condition of our children & grandchildren in a short time if we *change* or renounce our religion for that of the white people. We shall soon lose the spirit of *true men*. The spirit of the brave warrior & the good hunter will no more be discovered among us.

We shall be sunk so low as to hoe corn & squashes in the field, chop wood, stoop down & milk cows like *negroes* among the Dutch people. . . .[128]

To a people who valued their freedom almost more than life itself, the possibility of becoming slaves to an alien economy undoubtedly turned many natives from a "civilized" course.

If the potential converts could withstand the contempt of their Indian brethren, they encountered still more serious obstacles from the English themselves. To the colonial farmer who sought to substitute land for labor in his search for easy prosperity, the extensive hunting grounds and cornfields of the Indians presented a powerful temptation, which the utopian plans of a few missionaries could not deflect. The idea of reserving inviolable tracts of land for the subject Indians was bruited by a few men of foresight, but the generality of colonists had other plans for the American soil. Thus arose the single most serious obstacle to the Protestants' conversion attempts: "the grasping disposition of the White people," as Gideon Hawley called it.[129] As soon as the praying Indians had reduced a parcel of woods to tillable fields, their English neighbors found a way—within or without the law—to gain possession of some or all of them.[130]

Atypical only in its blatancy, the treatment of the Groton Pequots provides an essential clue to the Indians' feelings about English "civilization." By 1735 the small band of Connecticut natives had cleared two hundred acres, partially cleared another two hundred, planted at least fourteen acres and numerous apple trees, and fenced much of their hilly, rock-bound seventeen-hundred-acre reserve. Despite the less-than-zealous protection of two white overseers, however, the farmers of Groton openly coveted the Pequots' land for pastures and much else, as the Indians' petition to the governor of Connecticut complained. "They Removed a great part of our Gennerrell feild fence to arrect their own fence," which allowed their corn to be "Destroyed by the English Cretors." Likewise their orchards were assaulted by the English swine that were allowed to "go in and eat up our apples and bed Down." When the hogs did not steal the apples, intrusive white tenants did to make "Sider." If the Indians protested the animals' trespass, their owners "Thretten us if wee dont hold our tongs to beat our Brains out" and "cut our Stoaks [stalks] some time when Corn is in the milk." After watching the English "bild houses upon our Land" and "Sowe whe[a]t," the Pequots had no difficulty in realizing that "there Chiefest desire is to Deprive us of the Priviledg of our Land and drive us off to our utter ruin." This naturally had a depressing effect upon their desire to "Live as the English do." For "it makes us Conserned for our Children what will be Com of them for thay are about having the gospell Preched to them, and are a Learning to read."[131] In countless cases like that of the Pequots, the colonial farmer slowly but effectively undermined the economic and religious dreams of the Protestant missionary, thus realizing Samuel Sewall's simple prophecy. "It will be a vain attempt for us to offer Heaven to [the Indians]," he wrote in 1700, "if they take up prejudices against us, as if we did grudge them a Living upon their own Earth."[132]

Even when the colonists allowed the native farmers to proceed unmolested, the English ideology of farming clashed with traditional Indian practices and beliefs. In English eyes a farm was the private property of an individual husbandman who fenced and hedged its boundaries to declare his ownership. Its products were the fruits of none but his own labor, and he could dispose of them as he saw fit. Its sole use he reserved for himself by a civil law of trespass. The Indians of the Northeast, on the other hand, held a communal idea of the land. Individual families, represented by their women, might "own" personal gardens, but fields of corn, beans, and squash were the possession of the whole village which tilled them and shared equally their fruits.[133] In the absence of corn-craving animals, the natives felt no need to fence their acres, an effort that in any event would have been wasted in their periodic removes to new ground. The southern Indians thought the colonists "childish" for confining their improvements, "as if the crop would eat itself." In the north, where denser European settlement and more numerous cattle posed a constant threat, fences often became an unwelcome necessity. Yet even there the Indians' fences were often described as "miserable" because they did not have the "heart to fence their grounds."[134]

Before the Indians could subsist solely upon the fruits of farming they had to jettison their traditional communal ethic of sharing and hospitality. For unless everyone in the community could shift *at the same time* to an individualistic, every-man-for-himself philosophy of accumulation, the provident exemplar of the "civilized way" would lose all incentive by being eaten out of house and home by his improvident friends and relatives.[135] Such a shift was doubly difficult to effect because the missionaries themselves preached a gospel message of charity that seemed to deny the meaner spirit of capitalism. Samuel Kirkland's encouragement of the Oneidas to a life of farming, for example, was met with precious little success and the entreaties of his impoverished villagers for food, requests that he could not in conscience deny. For as they reminded him, "You have often exhorted us to be charitable to our Neighbours and hospitable to our Foreign Brethren, when they came this way, and if it be near the end of the week invite them to tarry over the sabbath, and hear Christ's gospel, or *good news*." By sharing what they had with those in need, the Indians seemed to most Englishmen to have "no care for the future," to be squandering the wealth of the earth upon the lazy and the shiftless. But in the eyes of some, "they appeared to be fulfilling the scriptures beyond those who profess to believe them, in that of taking no thought of to-morrow."[136] It was this double obstacle—the ingrained communalism of the natives and the inconsistent philosophies of the missionaries— that in the end prevented farming from becoming the economic salvation of the Indians in the colonial period.

The English failure to reduce the natives to industry can have perhaps no more eloquent epitaph than the petition of the Mohegan Indians to the Assembly of Connecticut in 1789. Nostalgic for a golden past, their plea also bears witness to the powerful bonds of community that sustained them through almost two centuries of forced acculturation, political domination, and religious intolerance, but now could sustain them no longer. "The Times are Exceedingly alter'd," they wrote,

> Yea the Times have turn'd everything Upside down, or rather we have Chang'd the good Times, Chiefly by the help of the White People. For in Times past our Fore-Fathers lived in Peace, Love and great harmony, and had everything in Great planty. When they Wanted meat they would just run into the Bush a little ways with their Weapons and would Soon bring home good venison, Racoon, Bear and Fowl. If they Choose to have Fish, they Wo'd only go to the River or along the Sea Shore and they wou'd presently fill their Cannoous With Veriety of Fish, both Scaled and shell Fish, and they had abundance of Nuts, Wild Fruit, Ground Nuts and Ground Beans, and they planted but little Corn and Beans and they kept no Cattle or Horses for they needed none—And they had no Contention about their Lands, it lay in Common to them all, and they had but one large Dish and they Cou'd all eat together in Peace and Love—But alas, it is not so now, all our Fishing, Hunting and Fowling is intirely gone, And we have now begun to Work on our Land, keep Cattle, Horses and Hogs And We Build Houses and fence in Lots, And now we plainly See that one Dish and one Fire will not do any longer for us—Some few there are Stronger than others and they will keep off the poor, weake, the halt and the Blind, And Will take the Dish to themselves. Yea, they will rather Call White People and Molattoes to eat With them out of our Dish, and poor Widows and Orphans Must be pushed one side and there they Must Set a Crying, Starving and die.

So it was with "Hearts full of Sorrow and Grief" that they asked "That our Dish of Suckuttush may be equally divided amongst us, that every one may have his own little dish by himself, that he may eat Quietly and do With his Dish as he pleases; and let every one have his own Fire." Other tribes as well eventually succumbed to the necessities of a foreign economy and an alien work ethic, but seldom before the colonies gained their independence and began to hurl a missionary onslaught at the remains of native "idleness" and independence. But even then the time clock and the regular paycheck could not completely stifle the traditional Indian values of social generosity and personal liberty.[137]

When the Indians had changed their homes, their community, their liveli-hood, their government, and their allegiance, they still had not done enough to satisfy the English reformers. Nothing less than total assimilation to white ways would fulfill the uncompromising criteria of "civilization," nothing less than renunciation of the last vestige of their former life. For a Christian and a savage were incompatible characters in the English cosmology, and only a willing departure from all he had known, all he had been, could prepare an Indian for a life of Christ. In English eyes, no native characteristic was too small to reform, no habit too harmless to reduce.

Among the first objects of reform were the Indians' names. To English ears, inured to the peculiar accents of home and the sea, the Algonquian and Iroquoian languages of the eastern woodlands struck a discordant note. Native words, including names, were often long and seemingly undifferen-tiated, full of throaty glottals and short of defining labials. Understandably,

the colonists wished to abbreviate, translate, or anglicize the names of those
natives with whom they had any commerce, especially those tapped for
conversion. Perhaps the easiest way to bestow intelligible English names was
to intercept the native child at birth before an Indian name could be given. In
praying towns and villages with a resident missionary, this was done most
readily at the baptism of the child (if one or both of its parents were church
members). On such religious occasions, biblical names naturally found favor
with the ministers, though just as often Indian parents preferred common
English or Dutch names. When in 1754 Gideon Hawley assisted an Oquaga
Iroquois woman in delivering twin boys, he baptized one of them Christian
but, less modestly, named the other Gideon. A year later he christened three
Tuscarora children Mary, Abigail, and Cornelius, the last apparently in
honor of a Dutch acquaintance of the boy's parents. Other missionaries, lay
and clerical, obviously contributed to the nominal richness of the Indian
population, if the many Jobs, Abrahams, Isaacs, Aarons, Hoseas, Hannahs,
Ruths, Repents, Desires, and Mercys that punctuate the colonial records are
any indication.[138]

Baptisms were not the only occasions for conferring English names, nor
were children the only recipients. The eastern tribes shared a custom of
renaming in which an individual could give himself or be given a new name
whenever changed circumstances, personal fortune, or mere whim warranted.[139] One of the occasions that might call for a new name was the
realization that the friendship of the English could be an advantage in trade,
politics, or religion. If assuming a short English name would make it easier to
deal with the increasingly dominant colonists, many natives were willing to
make the change, especially if around their own fires they were still known by
their Indian names. On June 13, 1660, for instance, at the "ernest request" of
Wamsutta, the Wampanoag sachem, "desiring that in regard his father [Mas-
sasoit] is lately deceased, and hee being desirouse, according to the custome
of the natives, to change his name," the Plymouth Court ordered that for the
future "he shalbee called by the name of Alexander Pokanokett" and that his
brother, Metacomet, would henceforth be known as Philip.[140] In his English
guise the younger brother became a dreaded household word throughout
New England fifteen years later when he launched King Philip's War against
the encroaching colonists.

English persistence and Indian preference soon led to a Pandoran variety
of native names in the areas touched by European settlement. Some were
quaintly medieval (William of Sudbury), others reminiscent of black slaves
who lost their family surnames for a racial tag (Joseph Indian, Miriam
Negro, Charles Slave). Many were either legitimate translations of Indian
names (Cornplanter, Blacksnake) or fabricated "Indian" names given by the
colonists (Pipe, White-Eyes). Most were simply compromises between utility
and history, a union of English given names and native surnames (James
Wohquanhekomeek) or translations of surnames (Mercy Fish, Merry Por-
ridge). All, however, forced the natives to compromise their personal identity
for the convenience and ideology of the white invaders.[141]

If the intimacy of a personal name could be violated, it is small wonder that the missionaries did not hesitate to intrude upon even the most personal relations between the native sexes. The principal means of enforcing the English standards were the civil laws drafted for the praying towns by the missionaries and approved by at least the native leaders. In accordance with English custom, the adultery of married persons and the fornication of single persons were outlawed. Adultery, with biblical sanction, carried the death sentence in Massachusetts, though no Indian is known to have suffered the extreme penalty. (Connecticut more sensibly assessed the guilty parties forty shillings each.) The punishment for fornication was a fine of twenty shillings for the man and only half that amount for the woman, the civilized assumption being that men usually made the first advance. By implication the law on adultery as well as a separate statute also enjoined polygamy, though no penalty was published.[142]

To judge from early exaggerated descriptions of native polygamy, the English obviously expected the law against it to put a noticeable crimp in the Indians' lifestyle. But in fact the outlawing of premarital relations worked a greater hardship on native custom, adultery being already proscribed by tribal law. Very few northeastern tribesmen took more than one wife, and those who did were usually sachems or men of importance whose duties of hospitality required more female hands than two.[143] Significantly, it was Corbitant, a Massachusett sachem, and his councillors whose only objection to the Ten Commandments was the seventh, "thinking there were many inconveniences in it, that a man should be tied to *one* woman." On the other hand, the woodland Indians placed no great value on premarital chastity. Their young people took to sexual exploration early in their teens and found nothing shameful about their bodies or their amorous potential. Their scanty dress (another statute frowned upon "naked breasts") and mingled living quarters did nothing to disabuse them of those feelings.[144]

In addition to imposing their own sexual standards upon the praying Indians, the missionaries sought to reduce the temptations of the flesh by covering native bodies with more modest English clothes and altering wigwam interiors to shield the eyes of the innocent young from the legal passion of their parents. Thomas Shepard happily reported in 1648 that the converts' wigwams at Nonantum had been built "in good bignesse, the rather that they may have their partitions in them for husbands and wives togeather, and their children and servants in their places also, who formerly were never private in what nature is ashamed of, either for the sun or any man to see."[145] English houses with sleeping lofts for the young might have been an even better solution, but these were far from popular with the natives, Christian or pagan.

English officials did not stop at intruding upon the normal sexual relations of their Indian subjects. Their puritanical imaginations plunged on into the lurid thicket of the abnormal, the pathological frontier between their own experience and their worst projections. At the catechetical examinations of the Narragansett and Massachusett sachems who pledged their allegiance to the Bay Colony, the natives were enjoined "to commit no unclean lust, as fornication, adultery, incest, rape, sodomy, buggery, or bestiality." The Massachusett sachems admitted somewhat ambiguously that "though sometime some of them do it, yet they count that naught, & do not al[l]ow it." But the Narragansetts made it perfectly clear that although they too prohibited "fornication and adultery" (as they understood them), they were not familiar enough with the other English specialties to warrant swearing against them.[146] In all likelihood, the minister who prepared this lively list taught the natives a few things about vice they had been innocent of before. Unwittingly, he helped to reduce them to civility.

The intrusive lengths to which the English would go to "civilize" the American natives has perhaps no better measure than the praying town law that fined an Indian woman twenty shillings for following the "old Ceremony of the Maide walking alone and living apart so many dayes." This referred to the widespread native belief that a menstruating woman possessed malevolent powers, capable of poisoning food with her touch, scaring game with her scent, or injuring a man's health with her glance. In most of the tribes of the Northeast, such as the Massachusetts, women "in their courses" withdrew to a small hut in the woods (*wetuomémese* in Narragansett) for the duration, where they lived alone, cooked their own meals, and lowered their eyes when a tribesman came near. At the end of her period, "she washeth herself, and all that she hath touched or used, and is again received to her husband's bed or family."[147] Despite the taboo's intriguing similarity to ancient Jewish custom, the missionaries wanted not only to move the Indians away from a hunting economy, where the menstrual taboo was strongest, but to undercut the whole belief system upon which it was founded. But before they could reeducate the natives in personal hygiene, physiology, and metaphysics, they simply ruled that the Indian woman's time-honored way of dealing with her natural processes was taboo and subject to the scrutiny of foreign men. What the modern women's movement has called "vaginal politics" was clearly not unknown to the Anglo-Protestants who led the invasion within.

As interested in finding a ready market for English cloth as in reducing savage souls to Christianity, the colonists also resorted to sartorial tactics in attempting to change the native identity. If Indians could be persuaded to change their whole lifestyle, so that they looked as well as lived and acted like Englishmen, the chances were considered good that they would eventually think English thoughts and believe English truths. They would, in effect, cease to be Indians, the conversion process would be complete, and the colonial "Indian problem" would be solved. All that remained in the first stage of the missionary program, then, was to get the half-naked forest dwellers to look like seventeenth-century Englishmen. In some respects this proved to be the easiest task of all, but in the end the English enjoyed only partial success. For in the seemingly indifferent matter of personal appearance, they encountered the paramount symbol of Indian identity and the rock upon which most English efforts to "reduce" it were broken.

English plans for colonization early included the notion that the American natives could be readily induced to purchase English cloth and clothing, thereby creating a new market for a declining home industry. But in the sixteenth century there was no thought that English clothes would help the naked Indians acquire the Christian habit. The benefits of the trade would accrue solely to the underemployed English "cappers, knitters, clothiers, wollmen, carders, spynners, weavers, fullers, sheremen, dyers, drapers, hatters, and such like." With the advent of actual settlement, however, it was suggested that the Indians too might derive some benefit from the cloth trade. John Winthrop, Jr., not only told the New England Company that the employment of the Connecticut natives would be a "great benefit to the English people here in a way of vending store of their commodities," but suggested that clothing purchased by the Indians with their new-won wages would, in a small way, help in the "civilizing of them." "For there be many thousands which would willingly wear English apparel," he assured the Company, "if they knew how to purchase it."[148]

Winthrop's faith in the attractiveness of English clothes was touching, but it corresponded imperfectly to the natives' actual demand for them. Even after the Protestant missions introduced a new reason for adopting English garb, the majority of woodland Indians had small use for fitted clothes designed for briarless farms and open fields. In 1634, some fourteen years after the Pilgrims had landed in New England, William Wood noted that the typical Indian male costume—deer- or mooseskin moccasins, leather leggings attached by thongs to a leather breechclout, and a bearskin mantle—had been modified only by the occasional substitution of a coarse stroud blanket for the skin mantle, and then only "if their fancy drive them to trade." For the New England natives, and their southern counterparts as well, "love not to be imprisoned in our English fashion. They love their owne dog fashion better (of shaking their ears and being ready in a moment) than to spend time in dressing. . . . But the chief reasons they render why they will not conform to our English apparel are because their women cannot wash them when they be soiled, and their means will not reach to buy new when they have done with their old. . . . Therefore they had rather go naked than be lousy and bring their bodies out of their old tune, making them more tender by a new acquired habit. . . ." Eight years later, their reasons had not changed. "Our English clothes are so strange unto them," observed Roger Williams, "and their bodies inured so to indure the weather, that when (upon gift &c.) some of them have had English cloathes, yet in a showre of raine, I have seen them rather expose their skins to the wet then their cloaths, and therefore pull them off, and keep them drie."[149] Not surprisingly, then, the heavy European serges, baize, and fustians, cut into fitted garments that restricted movement and ventilation, found little favor in the native markets of North America— until the missionaries gave their proselytes reason to buy.

That reason was the English belief that an English appearance visibly segregated their converts from their recalcitrant pagan brothers and provided a ready sign in times of frontier unrest by which "friend Indians" could be distinguished from enemies. For the first few decades of settlement, this reasoning made some sense. But as the native resistance to foreign cloth weakened, more and more tribesmen could be found who adopted some articles of English dress for their decorative value or because the loss of game made traditional garb impossible. When the woods became a sartorial hodge-podge, native intentions and allegiances were much more difficult to discern. But even then the infallible mark of a "praying Indian" was his English appearance: short hair, cobbled shoes, and working-class suit.[150] So important was English clothing as a badge of civilization that an Indian's degree of acculturation could almost be read in his appearance. The more he wished to emulate the English and to become one with them, the more anglicized his dress became and the more pains he took to put aside his native costume.

Among the most eager students of English dress were the native leaders who chose to cast their lot with the colonial governments. Daniel, the deputy overseer of the Connecticut Pequots, was typical. In 1674 he lost his wigwam and worldly possessions in a fire. Although he was poorer by more than £100 in wampum and English plate, the deepest "melancholy impression" upon him was made by the loss of his "excellent Masathuset cloth cloke & hatt," a gift of the English which he sported on holidays and at the Pequots' general court sessions. Reduced to a short jerkin donated by one of his councillors, Daniel felt virtually naked until his delegated authority could be clothed in a new cloak and hat.[151]

Many years later in the same vicinity, a colonial physician on his way to Boston encountered a remarkable Niantic leader who had adopted a lifestyle even more "civilized" than Daniel's. On the road from Stonington, Connecticut, to Rhode Island, wrote Alexander Hamilton, "stands a house belonging to an Indian King named George [Ninigret], commonly called King George's house or palace." On his stock farm of twenty to thirty thousand acres, some of which he leased to tenants, he lived "after the English mode." His wife dressed "like an English woman" in the silks, hoops, and stays of high fashion, and he educated his children in European belles lettres. In the discerning opinion of the good doctor, the chief himself was a "very complaisant mannerly man." For when Hamilton stopped to pay his respects, "King George" treated him with a "glass of good wine," the true mark of a gentleman. On the other hand, the "English mode" may have been his only real choice of lifestyle, considering that his "subjects," as Hamilton put it, "have lost their own government, policy and laws and are servants or vassals to the English here."[152]

Other native leaders, possessed of more elbow room and sovereignty, displayed their political colors in much the same way. Dr. Hamilton arrived in Boston in time to witness a dramatic parade of Mohawk sachems who had come to help Massachusetts put the restless eastern Indians in their place. "The fellows had all laced hats, and some of them laced matchcoats and ruffled shirts," apparel so "a la mode François" that the tourist from Annapolis mistook them for French Mohawks. In reality they were native New

Yorkers, one of whom was Hendrick (Theyanoquin), whose elegant blue, gold-laced coat and cocked hat had been presented him by King George II when the sachem visited England for the second time in 1740. After more than a century of sartorial politics, the doctor's mistake was in some ways less excusable than that of the Boston children who mistook *him* for an "Indian king" because of *his* laced hat and sunburned visage. At least he knew that native leaders, especially the pivotal Iroquois, had long been forced to declare their cultural allegiance by choosing between traditional, French, or English clothes.[153]

Twenty-five years later the political importance of the native wardrobe had scarcely diminished. When Richard Smith visited the Susquehanna Indian communities in 1769, the average Mohawk and Oneida man was still dressed skimpily in native fashion, with only a shirt or blanket to indicate the proximity of English or Dutch settlements. Some of the chiefs, however, "imitate[d] the English Mode," and Joseph Brant, the not-yet-famous Mohawk sachem educated at Wheelock's charity school, was appropriately dressed in a suit of "blue Broad Cloth as his Wife was in a Callicoe or Chintz Gown."[154] When the British wrested control of Canada from the French in 1763, they removed only a complicating alternative for the Indians, not the decisive choice of dress itself.

Under even more pressure to anglicize their dress were the "praying Indians," for whom English clothing constituted a religious as well as a political statement. Less than a year after Eliot began to preach to Waban's people, Thomas Shepard "marvailed to see so many Indian men, women and children in English apparell, they being at Noonanetum generally clad, especially upon Lecture dayes." So happily was their appearance transformed that "you would scarce know them from English people." The other praying towns were cut from a similar pattern. As soon as a new town was founded, English clothing quickly made the scene. By 1651 "most if not all" of the inhabitants of Natick were "clad all in English apparell."[155] When an intrepid war party of five Mohawks was released by the Boston authorities in 1665, they were given English matchcoats and cautioned not to kill any of the praying Indians who lived within a forty-mile radius. Praying Indians, they were told, could be distinguished from other Indians by "their short hair, and wearing English fashioned apparel." And in 1698, when two ministers visited the Indian towns in Massachusetts for the New England Company, one of their criteria for missionary success was the degree to which the inhabitants had taken to English clothes. The fifty-five souls who attended Daniel Hinckley's ministrations at Cokesit "gave very decent attendance" at meetings and were "very handsomely cloathed in English apparel." In the other promising congregations on Martha's Vineyard and Cape Cod, the people were similarly "well clothed, and mostly in decent English apparel."[156]

A hundred years later, despite the decline in missionary attention brought on by the forced economies of the Revolution, many descendants of the original praying Indians still made an effort to dignify the Sabbath with proper clothing. In 1802 Gideon Hawley boasted that the women in his

Mashpee congregation not only clothed themselves and their families in "every-day-homespun," but on the Lord's Day appeared in "very decent and showy dress." A visiting minister from New York even testified that Hawley's Indians were generally better dressed than many white congregations he had encountered on the outskirts of New Jersey. That was in 1767, and according to their minister, "they have *since* greatly improved." But the Mashpees were exceptional in having such a steadfast (and durable) missionary, and being surrounded by Anglo-American settlements; they may have had little choice in their wardrobes. Native groups farther from white influence obviously enjoyed greater latitude in their dress, as in their politics and religion. In 1795, when John Thornton Kirkland visited the Oneidas who had once received the zealous attentions of his father, he noted that, among other deficiencies of civility, "they dress chiefly after the Indian manner; though several can make garments in the English fashion." Predictably, these were people who refused to farm English-style and gave only "faint assent" to the white man's religion.[157] In the northeastern woodlands, you could often tell a convert by his cover.

But dress alone was not an infallible guide to the Indian's political allegiance, much less to his religious convictions, unless it was accompanied by an equally decisive uncovering—short hair. If a colonist met a native American man who spoke English with a slight accent and wore hard-heeled shoes and English clothes, he might rightly have taken him for a hired servant, a visiting sachem, or a shrewd merchant who understood the shifting balance of trade. If that man also had closely cropped hair, however, there was little chance that he was anything but a praying Indian who had subjected himself to the laws of England and the "yoke of Christ." For nothing symbolized the Indian's identity—his independence, his vanity, his pride—more effectively than long hair. An Indian could change his clothes and even his moccasins for foreign articles and still retain his essential character; his bearing and his profile would still proclaim him an Indian. But a willingness to cut his long black hair signaled his desire to kill the Indian in himself and to assume a new persona modeled upon the meek, submissive Christ of the white man's Black Book. Since this was the missionaries' primary goal, they wasted no time in persuading their native proselytes to submit to the barber's shears.

When the ministers succeeded, the loss was dramatic. Eastern native hairstyles were infinite and various, and many of them would "torture the wits of a curious Barber to imitate." Warriors and young men, north and south, wore the left side long and the right cut short so as not to impede their drawn bowstrings. Other tribesmen, like the Mohawks, cultivated the roach, a streak of short hair down the middle of the head. Still others shaved their heads save for a circular patch of long, braided hair on the crown—the scalplock, which they painted and decorated with fur, jewelry, or wampum. Some were content simply to let their hair grow, binding it with fur or cloth strips when it reached their shoulders. Most, however, affected a studied fancy that to many English observers betrayed the "sparks of natural pride," a vanity that did not seem to be present in their clothing, houses, or material possessions. After carefully sleeking their hair with bear's fat and red paint, noted a Dutch minister with scarcely veiled contempt, "they look at themselves constantly, and think they are very fine."[158]

The English were no more fond of native coiffures. John Bulwer, the author of an early book on the cultural variety of the human form, characteristically yoked the "wild Irish" and the Indians in his criticism of non-English hair styles. The Irish, he said, use their shoulder-length hair as a napkin after meals, while the "barbarous Indians are condemned for never cutting nor regulating their hair, as suffering themselves to enter into a neerer alliance with beasts than Nature ever intended. . . ."[159] At the same time, some of Bulwer's contemporaries were worried that the barbarian plague of long hair was infectious. With the advent of the English civil wars, ministers of a reforming mind bent their zeal against the creeping fashion of long hair and powdered wigs in pulpit, court, and quadrangle. When "Divines of note" appeared to pray in "ruffianly haire," their Puritan brethren could no longer hold their peace and trotted out scriptural citations and prolix arguments to condemn the practice, insisting that a polled head was a holy head. One minister even blamed the New England Indians for the prevailing fashion of female bangs and "one locke longer then the rest" for gentlemen, a sure sign that God did not countenance such foolishness.[160]

More common was the use of New England to shame foppish Englishmen out of their curls. In 1644 the Reverend George Gipps shook his head at the godless London fashions before ending with a westward nod. "Certainly it was not so within these few years," he lamented, "when the poore fugitives posted to new England in another cut of haire and clothing." Even the pagan Americans were praised for their native modesty. Roger Williams told his readers that while the Narragansetts were given to scalplocks (*Wuchechepún-nock*) and long hair (*Múppacuck*), "I never saw any so to forget nature it selfe in such excessive length and monstrous fashion, as to the shame of the English Nation, I now (with griefe) see my Countrey-men in England are degenerated unto." And in a brilliant stroke to prove that even "meere civiliz'd men" condemned long hair, Thomas Hall, the pastor of King's Norton in Worcestershire, pointed out that "the Indians in New England have made a law, that all these men, which weare long haire, shall pay 5.s. and every woman that shall cut her hair, or let it hang loose, shall pay 5.s."[161]

Hall was referring, of course, to Waban's praying Indians at Nonantum, who had been the first to legislate the substitution of English fashions for their own. Almost at once, the converts at Concord published their own code of laws, one of which promised that "They will weare their *haire* comely, as the English do" or lose five shillings. When formal law could not reduce native hair to civilized lengths, the missionaries brought the weight of their authority to bear. William of Sudbury's heart was so puffed up with native pride that he was constantly angry at the English attempts to convert him. After hearing that Cutshamekin, the Massachusett sachem, prayed to the new god, he resolved to give it a try and accordingly sought the Reverend Mr. Brown. "I will pray to God as long as [I] live," he implored the minister, who only retorted, "I doubt it" and "bid me cut off my hair" as a sign of subjection to the Word. Monequassun, Natick's schoolmaster, received the same injunction, that "it is a shame for a man to wear long hair." His first impulse was to obey the ministers by lopping off his hair, but he quickly found it "very hard to cut" because he "loved" it so. Only another bout of sermons and prayer convinced him that his hair had been a "stumbling" to his conversion and had to go.[162]

Another obstacle to godly hair was the taunts of their "pagan" brothers. One pilgrim "complayned of other Indians that did revile them, and call them Rogues and such like speeches for cutting off their Locks, and for cutting their Haire in a modest manner as the New-English generally doe; for since the word hath begun to worke upon their hearts," observed John Eliot, "they have discerned the vanitie and pride which they placed in their haire, and have therefore of their owne accord (none speaking to them that we know of) cut it modestly."[163] Eliot may have been disingenuous in minimizing the colonists' encouragement of short hair in the winter of 1646–47. But within a matter of months, the English imbroglio over long hair erupted on American shores, making it unlikely that the eastern Massachusetts Indians, at least, could remain ignorant of the missionaries' designs on their heads.

When the synod of New England clergy reconvened at Cambridge on June 9, 1647, they were joined by a great confluence of Indians from all parts who had come to have Eliot show them "their miserable condition without Christ" in their own tongue. Before he did, however, the Reverend Ezekiel Rogers of Rowley treated them to a passionate diatribe against certain church practices, the decline of family government, gouging tradesmen, and "other things amiss, [such] as long hair, etc." In the same day the Indians were thus introduced to the two warmest champions of short hair in an increasingly long-haired colony. Both went on to prod their congregations, college, and governments into outlawing "proud fashions" and "the wearing of long haire after the manner of Ruffians," "wild-Irish," and "barbarous Indians."[164]

At the back of Eliot's mind, no doubt, was the nagging thought that the continued English sporting of long hair would "prove some stumbling block to the conversion of [the New England] natives." This fear was justified in some small measure in 1649 when an Indian asked, at a public lecture, "What if a Minister weare long hayre, as some other men do, what will God say?" Certainly Eliot himself need not have felt abashed, for no one in New England was better known for "Exemplary Mortification," especially in matters of fashion. Nor could he look askance at his pious neighbors in the Plymouth colony, whose hair was so short, jibed their nemesis Thomas Morton, that they had nothing to pull in anger when he eluded their grasp.[165] Even in the midst of tonsorial riot, however, the danger was small that English hair would stifle native conversions. In matters of hair as in most things indifferent, the praying Indians followed the scriptural counsel of their missionaries rather than the wayward example of urban divines, homespun courtiers, or callow collegians. Their desire to clothe themselves in the habit and demeanor of true Christians was so powerful that they could see only the missionaries in their midst and hear only the straitened version of English life they preached. With the faith of new converts, they never questioned the motives of the ministers who so urgently entreated them to cut their hair. Yet that very urgency about a matter of acknowledged "indifferency" bears scrutiny, for in a simple if roundabout way, short hair symbolized the essence of Christian "civility," the goal of native reduction.

Whether English or Indian, the principal sin of long hair was pride. And seventeenth-century Englishmen did not need reminding that pride was the original sin of their spiritual parents, Adam and Eve. In the innumerable laws, proclamations, and warnings that resulted from the colonial establishment's concern over long hair, overweening pride was the "badge" of those who refused to cover themselves with Christian "humility, sobriety, modesty, [and] shamefastness." Apostle Eliot found the Harvard students' long hair worse than the Indians' because the "sons of the prophets," above all others, were supposed to be trained up in a way of "mortification and humility," not in the "lust" of pride. According to the Reverend Michael Wigglesworth, long hair was either a "badge of pride and vanity," to be shunned for a host of scriptural reasons, or a sign of "effeminacy," and everyone knew that the "speciall sin of woman is pride and haughtiness." In Puritan thinking, it was poetically just that one of the "provoking evills" that brought God's wrath down upon New England in 1675 (in the form of King Philip's warriors) was the "manifest pride" of long hair.[166]

Even if long hair had had no significance to the Indians themselves it still would have offended the Protestants' fine sensitivity to personal pride and vanity, but not as grievously as it obviously did. For long hair aptly symbolized the Indians' deeper affront to Anglo-Christianity, which was their characteristic pride and independence. Whenever the European invaders took honest or hostile measure of the native Americans, these two qualities found the page with great frequency.[167] Faithless men on the frontier could appreciate and even emulate them, but Protestant Christians, especially ministers, could only be chagrined that some of God's creatures were not duly "mortified and humbled" before their creator. As God's servants on earth, they felt a strong obligation to ensure that the Indians, the "dregs and refuse of Adams lost posterity," were drawn from their "sinful liberty" into "Subjection to Jehovah."[168]

Setting the pace for those who followed, Eliot's goals were, as he expressed them, to "convince, bridle, restrain, and civilize" the Indians, "and also to humble them." Appropriately, when the praying Indians of Concord drew up a code of laws in January 1647, the tenth ordinance enjoined them to "labour after humility, and not be proud." In describing their religious goals, the missionaries most commonly used the metaphor of placing such "heady Creatures" in the "yoke of Christ" and teaching them to "bridle" themselves.[169] In other words, becoming a Christian was comparable to assuming the posture and character of tame cattle—docile, obedient, submissive. In another popular metaphor, the missionaries' goal was to reduce the Indians' prideful independence and godless self-reliance to the total dependence of a "weaned child," dependence upon God, his Protestant ministers, and his "Chosen People."[170] Since it was total, this dependence was at once political, social, and religious. In short, the Indians would become civilized. The savage would give way to the civil man by repressing his native instincts, habits, and desires, and quietly taking the political bit in his teeth and the religious yoke upon his neck.

Thus the meaning of the puzzling phrase "to reduce them to civility" becomes clear. As long hair symbolized pride for the English, so too did the long-haired Indian. In the Christian cosmology, the proud Indian—wandering, lawless, and unpredictable—occupied the higher place: he was puffed up with self-importance, inflated with a false sense of superiority, and unrestrained by law, labor, or religion, not unlike the Devil whom he was thought to worship. It was therefore an affront to God and his people that the Indians remained in such an unnatural and undesirable state. They must be reduced in pride and liberty until they exactly resembled the English Christians, who knew their place in the eternal hierarchy. By this token, if God saw fit to infect the Indians with a love of labor, they could in justice be said to have "a little degenerated from some of their lazy customs." And if they knowingly broke the colonists' civil law, they could most appropriately have their "haire cut round close" off their heads to remind them that only through humility and submission could they find the path to peace.[171]

It was a reminder that most of the natives in colonial America did not need. If they did little more in a century and a half, the Protestant missionaries left no doubt among the Indians that their goal of "reducing them to civility" was tantamount to cultural annihilation, total and uncompromising. Whether infused with high religious or low political meaning, the goal never changed. Only the means varied with time and circumstance.

CHAPTER EIGHT

The Little Red School

The letter killeth . . .
2 CORINTHIANS 3:6

The goal of the English missions was to convert the Indians from a traditional to a totally new way of life and thought. No aspect of native life, no native person, was too small to ignore. Throughout the colonial period, missionaries tried to reach Indian children and adults at the same time. But when the English became frustrated in their attempts to convert native adults, their emphasis shifted perceptibly toward the young, just the opposite direction taken by the Jesuits. This was a logical emphasis because from the beginning the English hoped to train native preachers, teachers, and interpreters to assume the task of converting their brethren to civility. The only feasible way to train this cadre of native agents was to catch Indian children early in their development, before the hereditary stain of savagery became indelible, and "bring them up English."

According to the book-learned ministers and officials who designed the missions, conversion was essentially a form of education—reeducation—and education was something that transpired largely in formal institutions of learning. The best way, then, to reduce Indian children, primarily boys, to civility was to send them to English schools and colleges—sexually segregated, morally guarded, classically oriented, rigorously disciplined, patriarchally dominated, and, until the eighteenth century, located in English territory, far from the contagion of traditional habits, families, and friends.

The English reliance on formal institutions was safe and convenient, but it failed to capture the imagination or the allegiance of the Indians. In stressing structure over example, compulsion over persuasion, duty over love, schools could never attain the influence wielded by charismatic missionaries living among the Indians. The English resort to schools constituted a surface attack on native habits, manners, and words, but not a deep thrust for conviction and loyalty. Schools touched the intellects of a few, but not the hearts of the many. Predictably, they failed.

Like nearly all the early English colonies, Virginia was founded with a professed interest in the "conversion and reduction of the people in those parts unto the true worship of God and Christian religion," to "human civility," and to "settled and quiet government." To help implement these goals, King James I authorized his clergy in 1617 to collect money in their parishes for the "erecting of some Churches and Schooles" in America for the education of Indian children. The appeal was a financial success; by 1619 the Virginia Company had been entrusted with £1,500 for the American mission. In the previous year the company had reserved more than ten thousand acres at Henrico, near the falls of the James River, as an endowment for an English university. Within that grant, a thousand acres was earmarked for a residential college for Indians.[1] Every sign augured well for the first English mission.

But the signs were deceiving. An abundance of land meant little in land-rich America unless it could be converted to rents or cash crops. Money in the London coffers of the ambitious Virginia Company meant little unless it could be converted to American dormitories, professorships, and books. And pious plans for Indian education meant nothing at all to the natives, who had never seen anything resembling a school, much less a college, and when they did had to be persuaded—or forced—to commit their children to it.

Like many subsequent plans for Indian conversion, the best-laid schemes for Henrico College went awry. In an attempt to establish an annual income from the college lands, the company sank enormous sums into the outfitting, transportation, and support of a hundred tenants to work the property at half shares. Several hundred pounds were invested in an iron foundry that foundered, and at least £700 was diverted by the company to the amortization of outstanding debts and other pressing business. One London benefactor donated £550 to educate several Indian children in reading and the "principalls of Christian Religion" from the age of seven to twelve years and in "some lawfull Trade" until the age of twenty-one. But seeing that his money was being put to dubious uses, he suggested to the company that his benefaction—augmented by an additional £450—could be better spent in bringing eight or ten Indian children to London, where they could receive a proper English education in the blue-coated livery of Christ's Hospital and be overseen by a tutor or governor of his choosing.[2] Nothing came of his plan, or of his money. The Indian uprising of 1622 and the dissolution of the Virginia Company two years later pricked the Henrico bubble as easily as it had been blown.

The results were disappointing. A rector for the college had been appointed (chiefly for his fund-raising prowess aboard an East India ship), but he never reached America. A carpenter and five apprentices actually sailed for Virginia to build a feeder school (not the college itself) in Charles City, but they arrived in the aftermath of Opechancanough's attack and found other work. Vast endowments of land and money were squandered or went unimproved. Henrico was an Indian college without buildings, without teachers, without books, and without students. Not a single Indian derived any benefit from the first English scheme for their conversion.[3]

There were only two tangible results of the Virginia fiasco. The first was an enduring hostility on the part of the colonists to further schemes for Indian education. "The way of conquering them is much more easie then of civilizing them by faire meanes," wrote a contemporary chronicler of the uprising, "for they are a rude, barbarous, and naked people, scattered in small companies, which are helps to Victorie, but hinderances to Civilitie: Besides that, a conquest may be of many, and at once; but civility is in particular, and slow, the effect of long time, and great industry."[4] Not until the final decade of the seventeenth century did Virginians again give thought or money to a project for Indian education, and even then much of the thought and most of the money had to come from England. For now the colonists, twice burned—the Powhatans rose again in 1644—knew that the mass killing of Indians was a cheaper and more permanent means of reducing them than "particular" conversion. Schools were simply irrelevant to the early southern strategy.

The other result, ironically, was the publication of a book on Indian education, a book that, although it was dedicated to them and was obviously pertinent to their American mission, the governors of the Virginia Company were too busy to read when it was presented in 1621.[5] The author of the book was the Reverend John Brinsley of Ashby-de-la-Zouch in Leicestershire, a "strict puritan" in religion, "very severe in his life and conversation," and one of the leading classical educators of his day.[6] His book, *A Consolation for Our Grammar Schooles*, was a short "incouragement" and annotated syllabus for English secondary schools, "more specially for all those of the inferiour sort, and all ruder countries and places," such as Ireland, Wales, Bermuda, and Virginia. Although it never served the education of the Virginia Indians, the book prefigured several key ideas and assumptions of later English missions, especially those in the northern colonies.

The first idea widely shared by the English was that conversion should begin ideally with the youngest generation of natives, "that so from the children, it may please God more easily to derive the same unto their fathers . . . and so in time, by some of themselves so trained up, to propagate it to all their posterity." Secondly, to help lighten the white man's burden, God "ordained schooles of learning to be a principall meanes to reduce a barbarous people to civilitie." A third feature of the English missions was the unthinking application of the traditional curriculum of English grammar schools to the novel needs of native education in America. The goal of such schooling was to ensure that "all may speake one and the same Language." That language, of course, was to be English initially but eventually (and ideally) the *lingua franca* of educated Europe, Latin. Accordingly, Brinsley's syllabus spoke of little but grammatical rules, parsing, construing, double translation, and copybook exercises for various classical hands. His ignorance of the possibility that different pedagogical strategies might be needed for different cultures was highlighted by his insistence that the book's suggestions were "without any difference at all from our courses received here at home." Educational traditionalism and cultural imperialism were felt to be the best weapons against the "industrie and restlesse plotting of the Jesuites," whose educational prowess was legendary throughout Europe in the seventeenth century. "We cannot be ignorant," warned Brinsley, "how our enemies the Jesuits, not onely in their Seminaries, but also in their lesser schooles, do bend their wits, to go beyond us in this verie kind." Indeed, the English were not ignorant, and their missionaries always had one eye cocked for the devious Black Robes, who would "bewitch all with an opinion of their learning, the more easily when their time serves to cut the throats of all, who truly and sincerely professe Christs Gospell."[7]

Brinsley's *Consolation* also forecast an enduring English interest in keeping young Indian students in "meete awe, and submission to their Maisters," but he sounded a distinctive note that separated him from most of his pedagogical successors. The methods customarily employed in English schools, Brinsley charged, resulted in the "endlesse vexation of the painfull Maisters," and the "extreme labour and terrour of the poore scholars, with enduring far overmuch and long severitie." To free the poor children from "that continuall feare, whereby . . . the greatest part have bene wont to be exceedingly dulled and to be made most unwilling to their bookes," Brinsley proposed that they be brought up in the "most loving and gentle manner, as it were in playing, and with ingenuous strife [competition] and emulation."[8] Unfortunately, in this instance he was no more a harbinger of glad tidings to Indian children than in any other. "Meete awe and submission" continued to be exacted by English teachers, but seldom in a "loving and gentle manner." The arduous task of reducing "proud" and "stubborn" native children to good order and obedience could be accomplished, it was thought, only by the traditional rod and birch.

The Virginia Company's plan for Indian schools suffered less from Opechancanough's uprising than from the colonists' scattered riverine settlements, tenuous economic existence, and pronounced lack of interest in the schooling of their own children. In the founding decades, at least, New England suffered from no such handicaps. By the time John Eliot tardily entered the mission field in 1646, southern New England had a population of nearly twenty thousand English inhabitants who lived in more than forty compact towns. They were served by numerous local petty schools, at least nine grammar schools, and Harvard College. Armed with the Reformation belief that it was "one chief project of that old deluder, Satan, to keep men from the knowledge of the Scriptures," the New English Puritans turned naturally to their schools and college when they decided the time was ripe for the conversion of their native neighbors.[9]

Never a people to think small, the Puritans' first instinct was to send Indian children to Harvard. In August 1645 two Massachusett boys, James and Jonathan, were sent to live with the Reverend Henry Dunster, the college president. But the experiment did not fare well, nor did the boys. James was sick for five or six weeks, Jonathan for a shorter time; their fourteen months with the president yielded them only twelve shirtbands, eight shirts, and a half year's schooling for James, Jonathan being but "a very childe." After spending £18 on his charges, Dunster begged the General Court to release him from his fruitless mission: "Wheras the Indians with mee bee so small as that they [are] uncapable of the benefit of such learning as was my desire to impart to them, and therefore they being an hindrance to mee and I no furtherance to them, I desire they may be somewhere else disposed of with all convenient speed."[10]

This setback did not daunt the Puritans. To their way of thinking, it was not the goal that was flawed—surely any Indian with a Harvard degree must be considered civilized—but their overestimation of "savage" capacities. This led them to think it better to prepare the natives for college in the established grammar schools of the Bay towns. After a year or two with a local dame learning the rudiments of the English language, therefore, "choice" Indian boys were placed under the expensive care of Thomas Danforth or Elijah Corlet in Cambridge, near the college, or Daniel Weld in Eliot's home town of Roxbury. For £18.8.0 a year, each boy roomed and boarded with his master and tried to learn the intricacies of English, Latin, and Greek that would secure his entrance to Harvard, where the cost of his support would be appreciably less.[11]

In spite of formidable obstacles, a few boys made "good proficiency" in these foreign studies and returned to the praying towns of New England as schoolmasters. But the majority found the change of diet, lodging, and clothing too radical, and the tedium of sedentary study unbearable. Those who were not "disheartened and left learning" died in alarming numbers. In the 1660s the cost of burials far exceeded the expense of tuition in the masters' accounts. By 1662 at least six Indian students had died. Two years later Master Weld asked the New England Company for another student to add to his current three "because they are much subject to consumptions whereof 4 have died [in Roxbury] within these few years." In all, the three masters took some twenty Indian students between 1658 and 1672; at least eight of them fell prematurely to tuberculosis, "hectick fever," and small-pox.[12] The cause of Indian education was clearly not well served by sending native children to English schools in the larger, disease-ridden colonial towns.

The more common course taken by the New English was to establish schools in the praying towns, where Indian teachers could instruct their younger brethren without undue risk of moral or viral contagion and the excessive cost of boarding schools far from home. Recognizing the economic and political value of English literacy, many praying Indians, particularly sachems and their councillors, readily offered their children to Eliot for schooling, even before schools were available. In the spring of 1651 the townsmen of Natick finally opened a school in their new central lodge. Two Indian teachers taught their scholars to read and write copies from a short catechism that Eliot had copied in the "Masters Book." The following winter Thomas Mayhew, Jr., established a school on Martha's Vineyard. Within a few months it was crowded with thirty children "apt to learn, and more and more" on the way. By 1662 at least thirteen native teachers were plying their newly acquired art in the praying towns of southern New England. In Natick and on Martha's Vineyard, at least, their classes were full: attendance was compulsory under pain of civil and ecclesiastical censure, "the offence being against both."[13] Like most aspects of their lives, the education of the praying Indians was not left to choice or chance.

The use of native teachers was a compromise for the New English missionaries, who were of two minds about the appropriate language of instruction. The Indians did not understand English, in which the new cultural values and religion were best expressed, and the English did not speak the Algonquian dialects, which could not in any event fully translate the concepts of Western European culture. Ideally, Eliot would have preferred to employ English teachers who spoke an Indian language. They at least could have been assured of understanding the English way of life and thinking, which Indian neophytes, no matter how intelligent, could never fully grasp. Since the ultimate goal was to help the natives substitute the English language for their own, an English teacher with an elementary grasp of an Indian dialect was considered the fittest instrument. But Eliot found that the Indians could not absorb a new religion and a new language at the same time. Moreover, English teachers willing and able to work in Indian villages were simply not to be found in sufficient numbers in the early years of the missions. College graduates, whose classical linguistic training might have been expected to prepare them to learn an Indian dialect, looked to greener pastures whose flocks spoke only English and paid well. Daniel Gookin recognized that young men would need to be "very much mortified, self-denying, and of a publick spirit" to pit their ambitions and talents against "poverty and barbarity," and was not surprised when few volunteered for the Indian service. Native teachers, moderately fluent in the English tongue and after 1671 primed with Eliot's crash course in the "Art of Teaching," were thus the only alternatives.[14]

Since native teachers were not ideal conduits of English civility, Eliot sought to augment their efforts with Indian translations of some of the primary religious and educational guides to English Puritan culture. With the aid of an Indian servant from Long Island, he translated fourteen works into the Natick dialect, which by his death in 1690 had become the written standard of the New England praying towns. Among them were books familiar to every New English schoolboy—catechisms, psalters, primers, grammars, dialogues, and, of course, the whole Bible, *Up-Biblum God*. Several were to be sent through multiple editions by eager native hands that literally read them to shreds.[15]

But the costs of printing sometimes lengthy and always difficult works in a strange language were very high. Added to the chagrin of seeing whole villages of "converts" turn from praying to preying in King Philip's War, this expense convinced the New England Company by 1679 that allowing the Indians to maintain their native languages only postponed their reduction to civility. The impetus for change, however, seems to have come from the field even before the war erupted. Superintendent Gookin, with Eliot's advice and the approval of "most of the principal rulers and teachers of the praying Indians," proposed in late 1674 to the company governors that a free school be established in Marlborough, an English town bordering upon an Indian reserve in the midst of the Massachusetts praying towns, to teach the New England natives to "speak, read, and write the English tongue." Endowed with a farm carved from Indian land, the school would depend upon company funds only for books and a blue coat for each student. The English master would support himself from the produce of the farm and fees paid by the English inhabitants who wished to send their children. To avoid the financial burdens and health risks of the Roxbury and Cambridge boarding schools, the parents of the Indian students would provide them with traditional clothing and diet, "mean for quality" by colonial standards perhaps, "yet best suiting their bodies in point of health."[16]

Although the outbreak of war the following year prevented his plan from ever being realized, Gookin's shift to an anglicized concept of education for Indians was complete. Eliot's translations would no longer be used in the classroom presumably, and an English master and English students would "much promote the Indians' learning to speak the English tongue." This in turn would have three important results. First, the Indians would be able to converse familiarly with the English colonists, whose pious example would inculcate "civility and religion." Secondly, they would be able to read even the most abstruse English book, "the better to teach them the knowledge of God and themselves" through the various arts and sciences. Finally, the natives would be able to understand the learned preachments of English ministers, who could better instruct them in "substantial and orthodox divinity, than teachers of their own nation." What all this amounted to was an articulate model of linguistic imperialism. Pointing to the Elizabethan failure to subdue the Irish as the exception to the rule, Gookin observed that "the changing of the language of a barbarous people, into the speech of a more civil and potent nation that have conquered them, hath been an approved experiment, to reduce such a people unto the civility and religion of the prevailing nation."[17]

Gookin's arguments, especially in the backwash of King Philip's War, were persuasive. In 1679 the New England Company adopted as its official policy for the remainder of the colonial period Gookin's idea that English schools among the pacified Indians were the "most probable" means to "Reduce them to Civillity." A few Indian language tracts were published after Eliot's death, but they were short and printed in small editions. When Samuel Sewall, the earnest secretary-treasurer of the Boston board, raised the question of reprinting the Indian Bible in 1709, he failed to engender any enthusiasm among his colleagues. Their objections were cogently voiced by Cotton Mather, who argued that the amount of time and money required to print the Bible " would go very far towards bringing [the Indians] to a sort of *English Generation*. It is very sure, the best thing we can do for our Indians is to Anglicize them in all agreeable Instances; and in that of Language, as well as others. They can scarce retain their Language," he wrote, echoing Gookin, "without a Tincture of other Salvage Inclinations, which do but ill suit, either with the Honor, or with the design of Christianity." Appropriately, Mather's

India Christiana was the last book published by the company to contain any translation from an Indian language. Published in English in 1721 for an English audience, the book's only contribution to Indian linguistics was a few phrases—translated by Rowland Cotton—to give the London commissioners a "taste of the language." When the native tongues had become mere curiosities to the English gentlemen charged with the Indians' conversion, their days were clearly numbered as the mode of instruction in Indian schools.[18]

Eliot's personal sway over the Massachusetts mission program ensured that no English factionalism marred the essential aims and methods of conversion in the seventeenth century. But the advent of competing missionary societies and colonial beneficiaries in the eighteenth century, and the consequent reevaluation of methods, engendered pronounced and sometimes fierce infighting over the use of schools which persisted as long as Christian denominations sought the redemption of heathen souls. One of the first areas of conflict was Connecticut, where the predominantly coastal and riverine settlement of the English allowed the inland tribes to maintain an unusual degree of political and cultural autonomy well into the eighteenth century. By the time the Connecticut establishment made its first concerted attempts to convert the natives, the descendants and neighbors of Uncas had established a firm tradition of anti-Christian independence, and the Boston commissioners of the New England Company had fashioned a pattern of funding that virtually ignored the New England colonies beyond Massachusetts, Plymouth (which was absorbed in Massachusetts in 1692), and Martha's Vineyard.

Connecticut did not begin to look to the spiritual welfare of the Indians in a serious way until 1725, when, following Massachusetts precedent, the governor and council assumed nominal jurisdiction over the tribes within its borders. Previously, only the Pequots had been subjected to English rule for their "insolent" attempts in the 1630s to revenge the murder of some of their people and to drive the encroaching settlers from Pequot land. In 1675, shortly before King Philip's War erupted, the Connecticut legislature imposed upon the subject Pequots a set of laws closely resembling the rules of the Massachusetts praying towns. In place of their native religion, which was of course proscribed, they were enjoined to give a "ready & comely attendance" upon the preaching of any English minister who might be sent among them. If later testimony is any guide, this burden was not a heavy one. When Mrs. Sarah Knight passed through Connecticut in 1704, she observed that the Indians in the towns along her route were the "most salvage of all the salvages of that kind that I had ever Seen; little or no care taken (as I heard upon enquiry) to make them otherwise."[19] Two years later the New England Company launched what would prove to be a prolonged assault upon Connecticut's Christian torpor. In a spirit of brotherly watchfulness, they reminded Governor John Winthrop, Jr., that "it is well known to you that you have a body of Indians within the very bowels of your Colony, who to this day ly perishing in horrid ignorance and wickedness, devoted vassals of Satan, unhappy strangers to the only Saviour."[20]

The engine of piety behind this effort was Cotton Mather, who continued to prick the conscience of the Connecticut General Assembly until it funded a school on the Mohegan reservation in 1726. In 1713 a fainthearted attempt to proselytize the Connecticut natives "came to nothing," so Mather renewed his campaign. Five years later he could still write that "it has appeared a matter of no little grief and shame unto many considerate minds, among us as well as among yourselves, that in the very heart of a colony renowned for the profession of Christianity, there should for fourscore years together be a body of the aboriginals persisting in the darkest and most horrid paganism."[21]

When Connecticut's mission zeal was finally kindled and the Indians "in general" brought under English law in 1725, its leaders expectantly turned to the New England Company for financial assistance. But Governor Joseph Talcott quickly discovered that, despite his colony's obvious geographical location in New England and his own (if only nominal) membership on the board of commissioners, the New England Company was unwilling and perhaps unable to bestow anything like an annual moiety upon Connecticut's fifteen hundred native souls. "I dont know that Even one penny of the money Raisd from that Bank," he fumed, "hath of Late years (if Ever) been Expended in this Coloney."[22] Perhaps stung by the justice of his suit, the company managed shortly to inaugurate the regular support of a teacher—Captain John Mason, the grandson of the colony's commander in the Pequot War—for the school built by the legislature at New London. Henceforth Connecticut's Indian missions bore a strong resemblance to those that preceded them in the English colonies of the seventeenth century.

If some of the leading missionaries had had their way, however, the result might have been different. Both Cotton Mather and Governor Talcott thought that for the scattered majority of New England's native children apprenticeship in "English and godly Families" was the likeliest mode of civilization. The advantages of such a plan were that the children would be self-supporting and the colonial education laws would oblige their masters to teach them to read English, both of which would relieve the pressure on the legislative and company treasuries. Obviously both men, being unacquainted with native culture, failed to reckon with the extreme reluctance of Indian parents to part with their children, especially in tribes which still enjoyed considerable freedom from English interference in their internal affairs. So the Connecticut missions, like their Protestant counterparts in other colonies, fell back upon English schools as the "only best if not advantag[e]o[u]s way" to reduce those tribes to "Christian civility."[23]

Since few native adults were willing to be gospelized, Governor Talcott decided to "begin with their children" in the hope of persuading and preparing a select few to be "teachers to their own Nation." Finding pupils would be no problem, he thought, because "most of the Chiefs of the 3 biger tribes"—

Mohegan, Pequot, and Niantic—"manifest a willingness to have their Children School'd," a disposition that could be expected to yield from twenty to forty "royal" candidates. The best way to eradicate their traditional habits and customs was to place them in boarding schools, "separate from their parents and under good government, Mixt amongst English Children." An unusual feature of the Connecticut plan was the wish that girls too should be sent to dame schools, lest male graduates seek "pagan" mates whose untutored calls were louder than Christ's. The English rightly feared that, without the moral reinforcement of "civilized" spouses, male converts would return to native villages and apostatize.[24]

During the next ten years at least four Indian schools were established in Connecticut, partly at the request of the natives themselves, who saw literacy as a powerful tool of survival in their increasingly anglicized world. This was a decidedly secular request—the Indians continued to display little interest in the Englishman's religion.[25] What they did not recognize immediately was that the road to English literacy was paved with religious literature. To the English, learning to read was synonymous with learning the elements of Protestant Christianity from primers, psalters, and catechisms such as John Cotton's *Milk for Babes* and the Westminster Assembly's *Shorter Catechism*.[26]

The children, as eager, curious, and bright as any new pupils, did not appear to mind—"they seem to love their books and to be desirous of learning"—but their parents caught on quickly. Some thought enough of the new skills to enroll themselves in the elementary classes, where they absorbed the new religion, willy-nilly, with the new language. But the suspicions of many adults were raised to such a height that the English could only resort to bribes and gifts to allay them. John Mason's first estimate of necessities for his Mohegan school included "3 Stroud Blanketts for the Sachems of the 3 tribes" and "27 Blanketts for the Councellors & other Chiefs or such as send their Children." By 1733 sartorial "encouragements" were standard equipment in Connecticut schools. The New England Company made this perfectly clear in a letter to Governor Talcott, telling him that an eighteen-year-old Indian boy who was inclined "to be bro't up to Grammar, and even Colledge Learning, with a resolution to become a Minister to the Indians" should be furnished at company expense with a "Homespun Coat, Jacket, and Breeches, two Shirts, Stockings, Shoes and Hat, after the English Fashion." They also gratified the governor's request for more blankets for the "encouragement of the Indian Lads or Girls" before adding a frank postscript: "If the Indian Youth does not desire to be bro't up to Learning and be a Minister, he is not then to be Clothed in the English Fashion, but only to have the largest Blanket." In the bullish economy of religious sales, altruism was clearly not good business, something the Indians quickly learned as well. The following year some Indian families near Hartford pretended "want of cloathing" as a reason for their neglect of public worship, but signified their willingness to learn to read. Ten blankets and twenty primers were voted with alacrity. The ebb and flow of native interest in English schooling prolonged such maneuvers well into the century. As late as 1767 the Reverend Joseph Fish was still haranguing his Indian flock for failing to send their children to school, and offering shoes to those who would.[27]

In spite of all the sparring between the adult generations over Indian education, the children themselves seem to have enjoyed at least their initial stints in the boarding schools, and pleasantly surprised their benefactors with their scholastic aptitude. Tolerably well clothed and well fed, warmed by fireplaces around which they slept in the "Indian mode," and treated with some degree of gentleness for fear of driving them home, the native pupils could devote their full attention to acquiring the rudiments of literacy, that infinitely complex process that all young children master with deceptive ease. To distinguish the arbitrary sounds of the alphabet, to link them into words, to attach meaning to the words, and then to manipulate them according to the often capricious calculus of English syntax and grammar—these the young Indians seemed to regard as child's play. When two ministers examined seven of Mason's beginning students in 1728, they were clearly impressed. After only eighteen months at their books, the children read with a "considerable degree of freedom, exactness and judgment. While some read in their Primers and others in their Psalters they all spelt well," reported Benjamin Lord, "and some of them I perceived were able to read off a Psalm roundly without spelling. And their dropping of the Indian and falling so readily into the English tone and pronunciation to such a wonderful degree of conformity made me think they might quickly become great proficients in the language and manners of the English, if followed with their present happy and faithful instruction." Happily, the new students seemed to "delight in their Learning & value themselves pretty considerably upon it."[28]

The enthusiasm of the students—all boys at the time—was infectious. Later in the year the Boston board informed the company governors that "The Females begin to think it hard that They are not taught, so that some girls are likely to be received in a Short time."[29] English education was in such fashion in the late 1720s and '30s that another of Talcott's hopes was realized when one of the first graduates became a "teacher to his own Nation." John Mettawan, the boy who presumably got to keep his "English Fashion" wardrobe by proceeding to higher education, taught among the Tunxis Indians off and on for two years or more. Having attended the Reverend Samuel Whitman's boarding school in Farmington and "attained to a considerable knowledge and understanding of the principles of the Christian religion," which he could express in stylish Latin letters, John in his turn "kept [the school] well and faithfully and as good orders in it as in any English School." The thirteen or fourteen pupils who attended regularly made "very good progress" in reading and catechism, for which their teacher received a gratuity from the colonial council.[30] In later years a few Connecticut boys went even farther along the English route of learning. When Eleazer Wheelock founded his Indian boarding school in Lebanon, several of his first students came from the shores of Long Island Sound, where English petty schools had set them on the road to literacy.[31]

While Connecticut was trying to catch up with Massachusetts in educating natives to civility, Virginia made a feeble entry in the schooling sweepstakes. Predictably, disinterested philanthropy was not the motivating force. Virginia's interest in the education of Indians was rekindled largely by a keen desire to share a noble English inheritance and fanned by an Indian uprising in neighboring North Carolina. Nor was the interest widespread; it was confined effectively to one ambitious college founder and a few safety-conscious royal governors. The rest of the population, particularly its elected burgesses, had long and bitter memories of the "troubles" of 1622, 1644, and 1675, in which Indians were cast invariably as treacherous villains. Extirpation, not education, was considered the best remedy for such dangerous miscreants, "people more like wild beasts than men."[32]

In January 1691, while the Reverend James Blair was in London seeking a royal charter for the College of William and Mary, the natural philosopher Robert Boyle died, leaving £5,400 for unspecified "pious and charitable uses." Commissary Blair, ever the astute church politician, persuaded the earl of Burlington, Boyle's nephew and executor, that a school for Indians at Virginia's new college would constitute a pious charity of the first order. Accordingly, Burlington invested the funds in a manor called Brafferton in the North Riding of Yorkshire, the annual rents and income from which would go to William and Mary after modest annuities were paid to Harvard College and the New England Company, who were also in the Indian business. By the terms of agreement the college was to keep Indian children "in Sicknesse and health, in Meat, drink, Washing, Lodgeing, Cloathes, Medicines, bookes and Education from the first beginning of Letters till they are ready to receive Orders and be thought Sufficient to be sent abroad to preach and Convert the Indians." Another item of expense, however, suggested that the course of Indian education would not be entirely smooth. Included in the £14 allotted annually for the maintenance of each student was the cost of "buying or procureing Such Children."[33]

The peculiar mind set that regarded Indian slave children as the most promising students was formed early in the colony's history and persisted well after better sources were discovered. In 1619 Governor George Yeardley informed Virginia Company officers in London that the Indians were "very loath upon any tearmes to part with theire children." He and his council were therefore giving serious thought to the invitation of Opechancanough's warriors to lend eight or ten armored soldiers to help them revenge the death of some Powhatan women at the hands of a Siouan group beyond the falls of the James River. For their assistance the English would share equally all captured corn, land, and "booty of male and female Children." The offer was attractive, Yeardley thought, because the male children taken might serve to "furnish the intended Collidge" at Henrico, especially since the Powhatans were "in noe sort willinge to sell or by fayer meanes to part with their Children."[34]

By 1700, however, the native population of the Tidewater region was reduced to less than a thousand, having been militarily crushed and shunted onto tiny reservations by the English planters, whose numbers had swelled to more than fifty-five thousand. Despised and legally discriminated against as "blacks," the local natives were no longer considered worthy, if capable, of higher education. So Francis Nicholson turned to remoter tribes to fill the newly endowed school. In May he instructed two Indian traders headed for western villages to inform the headmen that a "Great Man" had given the college enough money to teach nine or ten Indian children to "read, write & all other arts & sciences that the best Englishmen's sons do learn" and that in the coming summer rooms would be ready for them. If each "Great Nation" would send three or four children between seven and eight years old, they would be given "good, valuable clothes, books & learning" and be looked after "both in health & sickness."[35] Just how the learned college faculty proposed to deal with these seminaked, incomprehensible youngsters is a mystery. In the absence of even a special master of the Indian School, who was not appointed until at least 1706 (perhaps 1712), they obviously would have found themselves between a pedagogical rock and a cultural hard place. Fortunately, they seem to have escaped this challenge by the extreme reluctance of native parents to give over their children to be educated even in the manner of "the best Englishmen."

In 1711 a bloody uprising of Tuscaroras in North Carolina offered the Virginians a more promising source of students for the Indian School. Marching a large troop of militia to the southern border, Lieutenant-Governor Alexander Spotswood assembled deputies from the Tuscarora towns that were not party to the hostilities and from the tributary tribes of Virginia whose "Fears and Interests" bound them to the English. The treaty they concluded called for each tribe to send two sons of headmen as "Hostages" to be "brought up at the College," there to serve as "Security" for their tribesmen's fidelity and to take the first step toward the conversion of "whole Nation[s] to the Christian faith." In return the neutral Tuscaroras would not suffer Virginia's military retribution and the tributaries would be forgiven their annual payments of twenty beaver pelts to the governor. Although this plan entailed little expense to the colony, both the college governors and the burgesses resisted it. The burgesses had been asked only to modestly supplement the Boyle fund to support the twenty Indians who arrived at the college before the year was out. Instead, with a "violent disposition" for "exterpating all Indians without distinction of Friends or Enemys," they chose to pass a £20,000 bill for carrying war against the Tuscaroras in general. For their part, the college governors inexplicably continued to prefer "buying Indians of remote nations taken in war to be educated." It is small wonder that the tributaries showed some reluctance to accept Spotswood's offer, pointing to the "breach of a former Compact made long ago by this Government, when instead of their Children receiving the promised education they were transported (as they say) to other Countrys and sold as Slaves."[36]

Although they were well dressed and "kindly treated," the young hostages apparently were not persuaded that an English education was in their best interests. By 1716 Indian students were so few that their master sought permission to take English pupils as well and to erect a partition to separate the two groups.[37] Perhaps the main reason for the lack of native students was Spotswood's settlement of Fort Christanna in 1714. The fort had three public purposes. The first was to offer the Siouan tribes on Virginia's exposed southwestern flank—the Saponis, Tutelos, Stuckanox, and Occaneechis—a measure of military protection from their northern Iroquois enemies in return for their service as a peacekeeping frontier buffer. For this purpose a large pentagonal palisaded fort was built around five log bastions, each sporting a 1,400-pound cannon, on the southern bank of the Meherrin River, about seventy-five miles from Williamsburg. The second purpose was to exercise a twenty-year trade monopoly recently gained by Spotswood's Virginia Indian Company and to encourage the "Saponis" (as the tribes were known collectively) to settle near the fort for preferential trading treatment, which three hundred of them did. The third purpose of the fort was to promote the education and conversion of Indian children. In addition to maintaining the fort and garrison after two years, the company was obligated to build a schoolhouse and settle a master. To encourage the natives to send their children, Spotswood not only promised them goods at "cheap rates" but granted to any Indians educated at the college or the fort school places of "Trust or profit" in the company, which, "by former Laws of the Colony, they were prohibited to do." Out of his own pocket he paid Charles Griffin, an English-born Anglican lay reader from North Carolina, £50 to serve as teacher.[38]

By contemporary standards, Griffin was a huge success. A man of sweet temper and infinite patience, he had "so much the Secret of mixing Pleasure with instruction that he had not a Scholar who did not love him affectionately." "The Indians so loved and adored him," testified Hugh Jones, formerly professor of philosophy at William and Mary, "that I have seen them hug him and lift him up in their arms, and fain would have chosen him for a king of the Sapony nation." So delightful was his teaching that at one time he had seventy-seven students in attendance, nearly a quarter of Christanna's Indian population.[39] But whether the quality or durability of instruction matched the quantity of students is open to question. Certainly one man could give only slight attention to each pupil, who was, after all, engaged in the difficult process of learning a new language largely through writing and printed materials. That the children went home each day to their native-speaking families, who resolutely spoke only their native tongue in formal councils with the governor even when they understood English, did little to reinforce their school lessons.[40] We do not even know how many children attended regularly, how long the academic year, week, and day were, or how often the children accompanied their parents on seasonal hunting expeditions.

Perhaps somewhat easier to absorb were the oral lessons from the Book of Common Prayer. After little more than a year on the job, Master Griffin boasted to the bishop of London that "the greatest number of my scholars can say the belief, the Lord's prayer, & ten Commandments perfectly well, they know that there is but one God & they are able to tell me how many persons there are in the Godhead & what each of those blessed persons have done for them. They know how many sacraments Christ hath ordained in his Church & for what end he instituted them, they behave themselves reverently at our daily prayers & can make their responses. . . ." Again, we do not know how many scholars comprised "the greatest part." A few months after Griffin's buoyant report, John Fontaine, a Huguenot guest of Spotswood, saw only eight Indian boys answer the prayers well and appear to understand what was read. Spotswood believed that changing the "Savage nature" of Indian youth would provide two benefits, "the salvation of many poor souls & withal, the best of securities to our persons & Estates, for once make them good Christians & you may confide in 'em." Ironically, his own actions may have nullified much of Griffin's religious teaching. In his frequent visits to Christanna Spotswood sponsored archery contests among the boys and encouraged them to perform war dances, which featured elaborate panto-mimes of the "base way they have of surprising and murdering [one another] and their inhuman way of murdering all their prisoners."[41] While such exercises undoubtedly prepared the Saponis to defend Virginia's frontiers from foreign invasion, they did little to render the boys particularly trust-worthy, predictable, or meek.

In any event, the Christanna experiment in Indian education lasted less than four years. Ambitious Virginians excluded from the Indian trade and British merchants opposed to monopolies conspired to have the Indian Company Act disallowed in 1717, and Spotswood could not persuade the burgesses to assume the small cost of maintaining a secure frontier and profitable trade at Christanna. In the spring of 1718 the eleven student-hostages who had been placed at the fort the year before by the western Carolina tribes were sent home, the tributaries had their privileges and protection withdrawn, and Charles Griffin moved to the college as the Indian School master. Thus an enlightened and workable plan for intercultural relations was defeated, largely (as its author correctly noted) by "the preva-lence of a party."[42]

When Master Griffin was translated to William and Mary he failed to carry with him his large following of native students. As the frontier alarms over the Tuscarora war of 1711 and South Carolina's Yamassee uprising of 1715 diminished, Virginia's desire for young hostages cooled and places in the Indian School went begging. By 1721 the college had no Indian students and an Indian master who survived on the tuition of local English boys. Indeed, the college was a college in name only: one master "lately come over" and one usher taught grammar and writing to less than two dozen boys. Ever since Christanna had siphoned away most of the college's Indian students, how-ever, the Boyle funds had been accumulating so rapidly that in 1723 President Blair was able to make a grand if cynical gesture toward native education as his opening move in the resuscitation of his dying institution. For £500 he built opposite the future site of the President's House a handsome two-and-a-half-story brick house for the sole use of the Indian School. Still no Indians knocked on the new door of the Brafferton (as the building was shrewdly called, after the Yorkshire estate that built it). So in 1732, faced with another £500 in the Boyle account and a pathetically inadequate college library, Blair empowered a London agent to spend between £250 and £300 on books for the use of English candidates for the ministry and other professions. A model of casuistry himself, Blair rationalized this diversion of Boyle funds in two ways. First, he noted sarcastically that "as we do not live in an age of miracles, it is not to be doubted that Indian Scholars will want the help of many books to qualifie them to become good Pastours and Teachers. . . ." Then he promised that although the college students and faculty were free to use the books, each book would bear a special inscription and would be housed in the Brafferton in distinctly marked bookcases. Since the college would provide future Indian collegians with the learned services of its professors, said Blair, it was only fair that the Indian fund provide the college with a decent library for their mutual use.[43]

Such were the uses to which the Boyle funds were put until a resurgence of frontier unrest, predominantly during the intercolonial wars, brought a new handful of reluctant hostages to the Brafferton. Perhaps half a dozen arrived in 1743, eight Cherokees stayed from 1753 to 1755, and five boarded during the 1770s, joined in 1774 by four Shawnee hostages taken in Lord Dunmore's War. During the short time they spent in Williamsburg they were indoctrinated in the standard three Rs of English education—reading, writing, and religion. In addition to the Bible and the Book of Common Prayer, *The Whole Duty of Man* and Thomas Wilson's catechetical *Indian Instructor* were used to prepare the students for the first important step toward conversion, baptism. In 1714, however, the Anglican convention in Virginia felt that although several Indian students had mastered the church catechism and service responses, they should not be baptized until they were capable of giving public account of their faith, "not being born of Christian Parents." Fortunately, the clergy soon relaxed its standards, and native education at least had its ultimate rationale restored.[44]

What could never be restored was any sense that the Indian School served a useful purpose other than as a scholastic compound for military hostages. The observations of contemporaries, many of them friends of the college, and the actions of most native students suggest that Virginia's eighteenth-century venture in Indian education was no more fruitful than its seventeenth-century chimera. As in Massachusetts, the poor health of the natives in an urban environment frustrated the educational design at every turn. Hugh Jones lamented that, especially when the boys were boarded and lodged in the town, "abundance of them used to die, either through sickness, change of provision, and way of life; or as some will have it, often for want of proper necessities and due care taken with them." From surviving account books it is clear that the students never lacked medical attention. But from the lists of drugs administered it is equally clear that the cure was often worse than the disease. Peruvian bark (quinine) may have effectively cooled malarial fevers,

14. "The Brafferton" at the College of William and Mary was built in 1723 as a dormitory for Indian students, primarily those from the tributary tribes of Virginia and North Carolina. It saw only sporadic use as an Indian school and was soon dedicated to more traditional collegiality. Today it houses part of the college administration. Colonial Williamsburg Photograph.

but frequent "vomits" and "purges" must have drained the life strength from more than one infirm Indian body.[45]

When the Indian students did not pass away, they ran away. Their reasons were few and simple, as Governor Robert Dinwiddie revealed in a letter to the Cherokee headmen in 1756. "The Young Men that came here for Education at our College did not like Confinement . . . ," he explained. "They were too old" (older than eight years) and had "no Inclination to Learning" (at least the sort being offered by the English). Since "they could not be reconciled to their Books, they went away of their own accord, without leave." The naturalist Mark Catesby may have met one of them some years later in North Carolina, a boy who had fled from the school at the age of nine or ten, crossed the James River, and traveled home on foot three hundred miles while living on nuts and berries.[46] The reasons put in the mouths of the Iroquois by Benjamin Franklin for rejecting an offer from Virginia to send three or four boys to William and Mary, while they were not actually spoken, likely preyed on the minds of the young warriors from other tribes who had been sent against their wills. The Iroquois purportedly said that "some of their Youths had formerly been educated in that College"—which was patently untrue—"but it had been observed that for a long time after they returned to their Friends, they were absolutely good for nothing, being neither acquainted with the true methods of killing deer, catching Beaver or surprizing an enemy." What Canassatego, the Iroquois speaker, actually said at the Lancaster treaty in 1744 registered more faithfully the feelings of many Indian parents and children toward English schools. "We must let you know," he told the Virginia commissioners, "we love our Children too well to send them so great a way, and the Indians are not inclined to give their Children learning. We allow it to be good, and we thank you for your Invitation; but our Customs differing from yours you will be so good as to excuse us."[47]

It was the Indians' cultural tenacity and sublime self-confidence that spelled the ultimate failure of the Indian School. When native boys returned to their villages after only a year or two in Williamsburg, "instead of civilizing and converting the rest," complained William Byrd II, they "immediately Relapt into Infidelity and Barbarism themselves." Indeed, "as they unhappily forget all the good they learn, and remember the Ill, they are apt to be more vicious and disorderly than the rest of their Countrymen." What little they did learn they did not hesitate to employ "against their Benefactors." Four years later an English traveler supported Byrd's assessment: "most return to their old way of Life and Carry more Vices away with them than [their] fellows ever knew."[48] In Virginia as elsewhere, a little learning was a dangerous thing because it reduced the Indians to a level of civility unwanted and perhaps unseen by English educators.

Defense needs also called Indian schools into existence on the northwestern frontiers of New England, with only marginally better results than were obtained in Virginia. One of the longest experiments in native education in the eighteenth century was mounted in Stockbridge, Massachusetts, which lay astride a principal warpath from Canada. But a flawed design, the "prevalence of party," and English land hunger doomed it to mixed failure.

During the peaceful interlude between Queen Anne's and King George's Wars (as the English knew them), Massachusetts farmers and speculators received from the General Court and purchased from the Indians most of the southwestern corner of the colony. The native Housatonics, who had suffered severe depopulation from smallpox and had incorporated numerous Mahicans from the upper Hudson Valley, retained four villages, the most important of which were Skatekook and Wnahktukook. But boundary disputes with New York and the presence of Dutch farmers in the Housatonic Valley forestalled extensive English settlement until after 1736, when the mission town of Stockbridge was laid out on six square miles at a bend in the river. To give the ninety Indian townsmen visible models of civilized piety and industry, the government encouraged four English families to join John Sergeant, the resident missionary, and Timothy Woodbridge, the Indian schoolmaster. Almost inevitably, the advent of English farmers, led by the ambitious Ephraim Williams, resulted in the alienation of the Indians' land, the frustration of designs for their education in "civilized" ways, and their eventual removal to New York.

Stockbridge was founded largely to assist the missionary labors of Woodbridge and Sergeant, who since 1734 had divided their attentions between the two main Indian villages. Sergeant, a small, energetic man with a keen mind, lively black eyes, and a withered left hand, had been plucked from a comfortable tutorship at Yale College to answer the Housatonics' call for Christian succor. Blessed with a "catholick temper" and a "guileless spirit," he sought to avoid partisanship of any kind and to befriend everyone, Indian and white.[49] When he married Abigail Williams, the accomplished young daughter of Ephraim, however, he allied himself with one of the colony's most powerful and clannish families, thereby inadvertently raising the devil for his native neophytes and his ministerial successor. Unlike his son-in-law, Williams kept a sharper eye on the Indians' soil than on their souls. From an initial homestead of 150 acres, situated symbolically on a proud eminence overlooking the native village along the river, Williams parlayed his position as town moderator and selectman into 1,500 acres by the time he left Stockbridge in 1753. Most of it was acquired after the 1744 separation of Indian and English precincts, in which the natives—for whom the town ostensibly was founded—received less than a third of its land.[50]

Despite the unsavory machinations of his father-in-law and his own post-marital move from a plain cottage among the Indians to an imposing Georgian pile on the hill, Sergeant seems to have maintained the trust and affection of his native congregation throughout his ministry. A major spring of their regard was his constant concern for their secular education as well as their spiritual welfare, which manifested itself even before he was ordained and installed as their missionary. When Sergeant was invited by the New England Company in September 1734 to assume the Housatonic post, he wished to guide his senior class through commencement before leaving Yale. As a compromise, he visited the Housatonics for two months that fall, preaching and teaching with Woodbridge at a site midway between the two main villages. Returning to Yale in December, he was accompanied by two Indian boys, the eight-year-old son of "Lieutenant" Umpachenee, the headman of Skatekook, and the nine-year-old son of "Captain" Konkapot, the chief of Wnahktukook. Two years later these men would lead their tribesmen to Stockbridge and become its dominant Indian selectmen; although the Mahicans were matrilineal, Sergeant sought to equip their sons for future leadership roles by sending them to the New Haven free school. Living with Sergeant in college, these "very likely lads" learned English by day and taught an Indian dialect to their host by night. When their parents came to retrieve them in May, they must have been pleased to show off their new tongue, along with the college's library and "rareties." So promising was Konkapot's son that he was allowed to remain in school all summer, at the conclusion of which he had "learnt to speak and read English very well."[51]

After Sergeant settled among the Housatonics in July, he and Woodbridge both taught English and religion "in a catechetical way" to about forty children and a number of adults who wished to prepare for the brave new English world. As soon as the Indians moved to Stockbridge in 1736, however, the educational program received a tremendous boost from Isaac Hollis, a London clergyman whose recent inheritance allowed him to indulge his passion for missionary philanthropy. Hollis made a long-range commitment to underwrite the cost of lodging, diet, clothing, and tuition for twelve Indian boys. And about the same time another English benefactor contributed £100, which Sergeant earmarked for the domestic education of native girls.[52]

Within two years Sergeant had spent only £5 to board two young girls, one of them Konkapot's eldest daughter, with English families because, "thro' a childish fondness for home," as he called it, "they would not be contented to stay long enough where I sent them, to obtain any good by it."[53] The Hollis grant, on the other hand, helped to solve the serious problem of native absenteeism. For several weeks in late winter the Housatonics traditionally left Stockbridge and repaired in family groups to sugar camps in the bush to collect and boil down maple sap. In the summer similar migrations took them to planting grounds around their old villages or to work for Dutch farmers in New York. Hunting expeditions in the fall and late winter also removed children from school. The lack of continuity in their English lessons, the frequent and often lengthy intervals of traditional living and speaking, and the daily influence of Indian-speaking parents at home conspired to minimize the impact of Master Woodbridge. Hollis's benefaction made it possible for the English to tuck at least a dozen students firmly under their pedagogical wing for most of the year.

In January 1738 Sergeant took the twelve new Hollis scholars into his new bachelor's quarters, overseen by an Indian housekeeper, and began to instruct them in reading and writing. But the care and feeding of such a youthful horde severely taxed the preacher's domesticity, so after a year he placed them in English families, paying their living expenses from the Hollis fund while continuing to teach them. Those who could not or would not live with the English received only their clothes and were sent to the town school with Master Woodbridge. In the end, it was thought, "those who liv'd in English families made much the best progress in their learning, beside the benefit of gaining the English language."[54]

By 1741 Sergeant realized that the placement of Indian children in a variety of unsupervised English families might not improve the natives' moral or social fortunes as much as their language. In a letter to the Reverend Benjamin Colman of Boston, one of the commissioners of the New England Company and a staunch advocate of the Stockbridge mission, Sergeant proposed the establishment of a "Charity-House for the instruction of our Indian children, both boys and girls, in business and industry, as well as in reading and writing and matters of religion." Because such a plan would require the donation of two hundred acres of unappropriated Indian land, the missionary rightly "suppos'd the jealousies [suspicions] of the Indians would be a bar in the way," so for two years he kept it to himself. But by 1743 a "more than ordinary spirit of religion" appeared among his native congregation. Symptomatic (to Sergeant's thinking) was the personal request of two Stockbridge girls to be placed in English families to learn the English language and manners. As Sergeant explained to Colman in a letter that was soon published as a prospectus, his missionary goal was to change the Indians' "whole habit of thinking and acting," to "raise them as far as possible into the condition of a civil, industrious and polish'd people," to instill the "principles of virtue and piety," and "withal to introduce the English language among them instead of their own imperfect and barbarous dialect." For this he sought to build a boarding school, on the lines of an "Irish Charity School," to remove boys between ten and twenty years old from the corrupting example of their parents and friends. Under the direction of a study master and a work master, they would have their congenital "idleness," "vicious habits," and "foolish, barbarous and wicked customs" rooted out of them, the whole enterprise supported eventually by the profits from their own stock-raising and farming.[55]

Hollis, of course, was enthusiastic about the scheme and doubled his support. But the public subscription launched by Colman was only a limited success. A number of English dignitaries responded generously, but in the colony only ten English inhabitants of Stockbridge and Colman himself came forward with cash. Four American gentlemen subscribed but never paid, probably because the whole affair was thrown into doubt by the outbreak of King George's War in 1744. When that conflagration died on the frontiers four years later, Sergeant returned to the task. Hollis was champing to have his new donation spent specifically on twelve additional boys of "heathen parents, such as are not professors of Christianity," which effectively eliminated most of the local Housatonics. With Colman now dead, however, Boston was even cooler to the idea of supporting an expensive boarding school for distant and dangerous savages, and gave nothing. Only a testamentary bequest and two church collections in Connecticut raised enough money to enable Sergeant to complete the construction of his boarding school in the summer of 1749, days before he died of a nervous fever.[56] Although he had lived to see his educational dream materialize, death spared him the cruel sight of its misuse and eventual destruction at the hands of the master he had appointed and his own relatives.

Even before the frontiers were completely safe, however, the importunity of Isaac Hollis had persuaded Sergeant to send twelve boys of "heathenish" proclivities to the relative security of Newington, Connecticut, to be schooled for a year in civility by Martin Kellogg, a sixty-year-old army captain, farmer, and interpreter. When the boarding school was completed the following summer, Kellogg was persuaded to transfer the boys to Stockbridge and to assume their direction for another year. Had he lived through the summer, Sergeant presumably would have carried out his plan to visit the New York Mohawks in the company of Kellogg, who spoke their tongue after being twice captured by the Caughnawagas, to invite them to send children to the new Hollis school.[57] A number of Mohawk children—and their adult relatives—eventually moved to Stockbridge to board on the Hollis bounty, but the pedagogical incompetence of Kellogg and the internecine infighting of the English over the control of the town's various Indian schools soon drove them away.

At the unlikely center of this educational imbroglio was Abigail, the brilliant and beautiful widow of John Sergeant. In the eyes of her father, Ephraim Williams, her taking of a new husband would perpetuate the Williams dynasty in Stockbridge, particularly if the lucky man also happened to be Sergeant's successor as Indian missionary. Obligingly, Abigail cast her eye first on Ezra Stiles, a Yale tutor (as Sergeant had once been), though five years her junior, who proved acceptable to the Indians and the Williams side of the church. But Stiles had doubts about his own religious orthodoxy and sensed that a hornet's nest of intrigue awaited him in Stockbridge. When he announced to Abigail his withdrawal from ecclesiastical (and, by implication, marital) consideration in the fall of 1750, her anguished response must have confirmed the wisdom of his decision. She revealed that Deacon Woodbridge, a religious New Light, was pushing to have the Indian missionary post given to Jonathan Edwards, the brilliant theologian who had recently been ousted from his Northampton pulpit by another branch of the Williams clan. Her father and Captain Kellogg, of course, were "very Bitterly against" his appointment. But the crowning blow, she confessed, was that Woodbridge had told the Indians that "they must not have a young man, [for] if they do he will likely marry in to my fathers famely and then Be under his Direction."[58] Thanks to Stiles, and much to the chagrin of the Williamses, the elderly Edwards was duly installed nine months later.

Frustrated in love, Abigail sought to build her own Indian fiefdom by becoming mistress of the Indian girls' school, which did not yet exist. Although various English benefactors had contributed toward the education of girls, little had been done and their monies had been diverted. But in April 1750 her father had persuaded the General Court to spend annually £150 for seven years to educate twelve Indian girls, six Housatonics and six Mohawks, "according to the Plan of the late Reverend Mr. Sargeant." Although another Williams was to administer the funds, the legislators asked Colonel Williams and Captain Kellogg for their opinion of the plan and to inform the Mohawks, about twenty of whom had recently moved to Stockbridge at Sergeant's earlier invitation.[59] Apparently, the colonel successfully presented his daughter's credentials for the job. The following summer Elisha Williams, an American member of the London Board, persuaded the New England Company to pay his cousin Abigail £30 a year to serve as schoolmistress to not more than ten native girls, each of whom would also be credited with £7.10s for clothing and lodging. An extra £10 was drafted to enable Mrs. Sergeant to put her already impressive house in order.[60] Clearly, a widow with three children could do worse than to set herself up in the Indian business.

Abigail did even better in 1752 when she married Joseph Dwight of Brookfield, a forty-nine-year-old politician, speculator, brigadier general, and recent widower. They had undoubtedly come to a meeting of minds during the previous winter, when Abigail took some of her Indian girls to Brookfield and put them out to service rather than teaching them herself. From then on the Dwights moved to monopolize Indian affairs in Stockbridge, with no little hope of personal profit. The general assumed charge of provincial affairs in the west, the Hollis foundation, and the business of the New England Company, bypassing Edwards, the company's missionary, at every turn. Edwards could only conclude that the proud and domineering Abigail had twisted her courtly consort around her finger; nothing else seemed to explain the abrupt reversal of Dwight's lifelong admiration of Edwards.[61] It looked to Edwards as if the Williams clan was trying to duplicate its Northampton victory in Stockbridge. Although the stakes were much less theological, the aging missionary was determined not to lose another round. He unleashed the only weapon at his command—verifiable truth—in a barrage of letters to officials in London and Boston. In unambiguous detail, he described how the Dwight-Williams ring had wasted the Hollis fund, wrecked the promising Mohawk mission, and made a mockery of the girls' school.

The Dwights' interest in the Indian girls' school, Edwards revealed, was little more than a brazen attempt to pervert the public trust for personal profit. With funds and materials provided by the General Court, they proceeded to build a schoolhouse on the widow Sergeant's land, hoping eventually to sell the parcel to the province at a "high rate." In the meantime, two of their sons were maintained and educated at public expense, two daughters similarly enjoyed free rides in the girls' school, a Dwight relative served as Abigail's usher, their family servants were disguised as the school's workmen, and the whole family eventually moved into the school, which drove the remaining Mohawks straight back to New York. Although Abigail did provide a certain amount of care to the native girls, her three batches of children—his, hers, and theirs—monopolized her time and energies, just as Edwards warned the commissioners it would. And superintending all of this chicanery was the province's resident trustee of Indian affairs and two commissioners of the Boston Board—her husband, her father, and her cousin.[62]

The Hollis fund and boarding school were equally mismanaged, which in turn undermined the province's efforts to secure the Mohawks' critical allegiance through education. By the end of King George's War, if not long before, it became clear to New Englanders that their exposed northern frontiers could not be guarded without the keen eyes and ears of native allies, preferably those living in English territory. The Mohawks fit the bill nicely because they enjoyed an enviable reputation for martial prowess, had relatives in Canadian *reserves* who might act as unwitting spies or refuse to fight, could influence the other five nations of Iroquois to sever their French connections or at least to remain neutral, and were located nearby in eastern New York. If a substantial number could be induced to relocate in Stockbridge, western Massachusetts would have not only a mobile force of experienced guerilla warriors but a collection of young hostages to ensure the mete behavior of countrymen at home. In the boarding school and the ample funds provided by Hollis and the General Court the material means existed to attract the Mohawks to Stockbridge. All that remained was to give their children an educational experience that did not alienate their affections but also had some discernible payoff in improved behavior and literacy. This the aggrandizing army of General Dwight, Colonel Williams, and Captain Kellogg could not provide, no matter how earnestly they sought the Mohawks' allegiance.

The heart of the matter was the indisputable incompetence of Kellogg. Even Sergeant, who had appointed him, recognized his mistake, but he died before he could find a suitable replacement. Since the new boarding school was largely finished, Kellogg returned the Hollis boys to Stockbridge and carried on there as best he could. His best was simply not good enough for the parents of the few boys who remained in his charge. Early in 1750 twenty Mohawks who had moved to town for the sake of their children's education left, complaining that the boys were "not cloathed so well as they are at home." Only a great deal of verbal and material persuasion by provincial agents brought the Mohawks back to Stockbridge. In October 1751 nearly a hundred arrived to settle on prepared farm land around the boarding school, partly on the strength of Kellogg's promise that he now had clothes in abundance. What he meant was that he had clothes and room for twenty-four boys on the Hollis fund but not for the other Mohawk children, who numbered thirty-six by January. When the provincial committee asked him to take all of the Mohawk boys until a separate schoolhouse could be built, he refused, saying "he was Independent in his School, and inclined to keep it separately," conveniently forgetting that "his" school was built partly with government funds. Accordingly, Benjamin Ashley, Kellogg's assistant and brother-in-law, was ordered to teach the other boys.[63]

After watching Kellogg rapidly alienate the Iroquois, Edwards could hold his peace no longer. Speaking for the vast majority of Indian and English townsmen as well, he penned a series of frank letters to Hollis and various Boston officials exposing Kellogg's utter unfitness. First, as even the longhouse-dwelling Indians noticed, the boarding school was in a "miserable state"—unfinished, too small, and ill-equipped. Ceilings in two of the five rooms and a staircase were missing, as were adequate beds, writing tables, benches, and bedclothes. Still worse was Kellogg's care and government of the boys. Although he drew full pay from the Hollis fund for two years, he never made an accounting of his expenditures to Hollis or to Dwight, apparently with good reason, for the boys were poorly "dieted" and their clothes cost "but a trifle." Furthermore, he spent a third of the year away from school pursuing more pressing "avocations," which was perhaps just as well because when he was present his teaching and discipline left much to be desired. Barely literate himself, Kellogg managed to teach only mindless memorization. The children merely learned to attach sounds to clusters of marks "but know not *the meaning* of the words," said Edwards, "and so have neither profit nor pleasure in reading, and will therefore be apt soon to lose even what they have learned." And even though the Mohawks gave their children over for English-style "Correction & Discipline" as well as instruction, Kellogg's scholars made "no progress in civility & vertue," the townsmen accused, "but have rather declin'd, living an idle life, and much without government." Understandably, parents complained loudly of the "increase of unrulyness & disorder in their children" and would have withdrawn them and moved from Stockbridge altogether had Edwards, at the request of the Boston Commissioners, not hired in February 1752 an able master to teach the Iroquois not enrolled in the Hollis school.[64]

The new master, Gideon Hawley, was a twenty-four-year-old Yale graduate with a "happy talent in teaching" and a "good spirit of government." Within weeks of his arrival he was diligently teaching the colonial three Rs to about thirty-six pupils, several of them lured away from Kellogg. In addition, he was learning an Iroquois tongue (Mohawk or Oneida) and teaching it to a couple of English boys whom the province had placed in the school to prepare for future work as missionaries or interpreters. Perhaps most pleasing to the Iroquois parents, who "strengthen[ed] his hands" whenever possible, was his regulation of the children's "manners" and establishment of "good order."[65]

The advent of a successful rival soon drove Kellogg, Williams, and Dwight to distraction. Not only had their nemesis Edwards made the appointment, but Benjamin Ashley had been permanently assigned to Hawley as an assistant master and all three had advised the Iroquois in an open meeting to remove their children from the captain's ill-run school, which seven of them promptly did. With only a handful of students left, Kellogg took to coming into Hawley's school and acting as though the boys were his. In his most imperious manner Dwight did the same thing, sometimes removing boys for several days to teach himself. Since the Indians disliked a man of his "sovereign & forbidding aers," they were especially disgusted by his treatment of their young master after Hawley had castigated a Williams associate for coming into his school and caning one of his students, the son of an Oneida chief, without just cause. In response, Dwight flew into Hawley's classroom and, before the alarmed children, berated him for a full three hours. Some of his anger was undoubtedly stoked by the frustration of having watched Hawley appointed just days before he could intrude his own son Henry, a Harvard student, into the school. For the next several months the general kept threatening to underwrite a rival school with Kellogg as steward and young Henry as master, a threat which came to naught. For his part, Ephraim Williams made the most manic gesture of all. One October morning, in an effort to undercut Edward's base of local support, he literally tried, cash in hand, to buy out every English farmer in Stockbridge! Needless to say, he too failed and was soon laughed out of town.[66]

The Williams family's search for autocracy in Stockbridge Indian affairs died in one final act of desperation in 1753, shortly before the colonel moved to Deerfield. After the boarding school had been sufficiently repaired, Hawley had moved in in the fall of 1752 to be near his young linguistic informants. On a bitter New England day in the following February, the school, "in a way unknown, took fire, and was reduced to ashes," along with Hawley's furniture, books, and clothing. Hawley had no doubts that the school had been fired "by design"—and not by the faction adhering to Edwards and Woodbridge. Early in April two-thirds of the Mohawks returned to New York, thoroughly disenchanted with Dwight's stonewalling techniques and the nasty turn of events in the life of their school; the rest followed a year later, ironically, only two weeks after Edwards had been given complete control over the town's Indian affairs. On April 9, 1754, eight days before the Seven Years' War effectively began at the forks of the Ohio, the General Court wrote the epitaph to this long, frustrating experiment in native education by referring to the "late Mohawk School at Stockbridge."[67]

A few months after the Stockbridge Iroquois school was abandoned, the Reverend Eleazar Wheelock opened a free school for Indians in Lebanon, Connecticut. His was a private venture at first, without any government support or exalted political aims, although it quickly acquired both. His initial design was simply to supplement his income: he had been deprived of his ministerial salary by the Connecticut legislature in 1743 for various "disorders in ecclesiastical affairs" stemming from his active promotion of the Great Awakening. Although Wheelock was land rich, the loss of his salary had prompted him to take a few English boys into his house for college preparation. They were soon joined by Samson Occom, a young Mohegan Indian from New London, Connecticut, who came to Wheelock with the hope of improving his self-taught literacy in three or four weeks of tuition. Occom stayed nearly five years, in which time he became a devoted Christian, an affecting public speaker, and a partial convert to the English way of life. Despite his unusual accomplishments, however, there was no place for a man of his color in English society. He returned to a wigwam and spent the next twelve years in poverty, teaching and preaching to the Montauk Indians on Long Island, binding books, and carving spoons, pails, and gunstocks for his white neighbors, most of whom were his spiritual and intellectual inferiors.[68]

If Occom's postgraduate career did not speak well for the conceptual clarity of Wheelock's later design, the doctor was unaware of it. In late 1754 he took two Delaware Indian boys under his wing, which prompted a charitable neighbor, Colonel Joshua More, to endow the fledgling school with several buildings and two acres of land. By the summer of 1761 "Moor's Charity School" had accepted ten Indian students from the "remnant" tribes of the northeastern seaboard. But with the fall of Canada a wide door was

15. Samson Occom (1723–92), the first and perhaps most accomplished Indian pupil of Eleazar Wheelock. The bow and arrows on the wall in the upper left-hand corner suggest that Occom's academic accomplishments could never erase his cultural identity as an Indian. From a 1768 mezzotint in the Dartmouth College Library, by whose courtesy it is reproduced.

opened to the relatively uncontaminated "back nations" of America, and Wheelock entered it with a driving vision of tawny souls blanched by the Bible.

General James Wolfe's victory on the Plains of Abraham was well timed, for Wheelock was becoming increasingly disenchanted with the "little Tribes" of New England. Schools set among them, he felt, had always failed because the natives placed no value on the white man's "Learning," led an unsettled, impoverished existence, lacked any social or familial authority, and resented the English masters who tried to impose a "good and necessary Government" over their children.[69] Most damning of all in Wheelock's eyes was their stubborn ingratitude for the inestimable benefits offered by Protestant saints such as himself. It was simply foolish to waste God's time and the public's money on ingrates while there were "such Vast Numbers intirely without Means of Knowledge and"—he was assured by friends—"continually suing and pleading for Missionaries and Schoolmasters to be sent among them."[70] Turning his back on too-familiar local tribes, Wheelock was quickly captured by the unknown challenge of the Six Nations.

He did not have long to wait before confronting the challenge he had so blindly and blithely accepted. On August 1, 1761, three Mohawk boys sent by Sir William Johnson, the British superintendent of Indian affairs, arrived in Lebanon with "great Caution and Fear." Each brought a horse, "prepared to return in haste, if there should be occasion." One, Joseph Brant, understood a little English and, being the son of a "Family of Distinction," was well dressed. But his teenaged companions, Negyes and Center, were nearly naked and "very lousey." Neither could speak a word of English. Center was visibly ill, his blood "spoiled," according to the local physician, so he was sent home to die—but not before swallowing the bitter pill of white prejudice. "I was very sorry," Wheelock wrote Johnson, "for the Jealousies which the [English] Schollars conceived concerning the Nature of Center's Disorder while I was gone to Boston, and that there was that said or done which gave him a Disgust." Negyes, too, was soon lost to the cause, for when he accompanied Center home he was "captivated by a young Female and married."[71]

Less than four months later two Mohawk boys arrived to take their places, "direct from the wigwams." One had learned "4 or 5 letters in the Alphabet, the other knew not one, nor could either of them Speak a Word of English." Excepting "two old Blankets & Indian Stockins," their clothing was "not worth Sixpence." And as Wheelock had come to expect of such "poor little Naked Creatures," they were "very lousey, which occasioned considerable Trouble." But in other respects they were hardly typical schoolboys. Johannes had carried a gun in the army that captured Montreal the previous year—at the age of twelve.[72]

A scant two weeks after their arrival, Wheelock penned a *cri de coeur* that might well stand as the motto of Moor's Charity School: "Few conceive aright of the Difficulty of Educating an Indian and turning him into an

Englishman but those who undertake the Trial of it." To the Reverend George Whitefield, who had the good sense not to try, he explained his predicament:

> They would soon kill themselves with Eating and Sloth, if constant care were not exercised for them at least the first year. They are used to set upon the Ground, and it is as natural for them as a seat to our Children. They are not wont to have any Cloaths but what they wear, nor will without much Pains be brought to take care of any. They are used to a Sordid Manner of Dress, and love it as well as our Children to be clean. They are not used to any Regular Government, the sad consequences of which you may a little guess at. They are used to live from Hand to Mouth (as we speak) and have no care for Futurity. They have never been used to the Furniture of an English House, and dont know but that a Wine-glass is as strong as an Hand Iron. Our Language when they seem to have got it is not their Mother Tongue and they cannot receive nor communicate in that as in their own. . . . And they are as unpolished and uncultivated within as without.[73]

Predictably, time and experience brought little relief, and Wheelock's list of headaches only grew. Before he moved the school to Hanover in 1770, he tried to turn some sixty-seven native children—forty-nine boys and eighteen girls—into English men and women.[74] Many came from the New England tribes with a helpful modicum of English language, dress, and religion, but the largest number, thirty, were Iroquois, tough adolescents like Johannes and Negyes with an ingrained suspicion of the English and their schemes for reducing them to civility. In his *Narrative* of the school to 1771, Wheelock boasted that he had produced forty "good readers, and writers," all sufficiently masters of English grammar and arithmetic and some advanced in Latin and Greek, who had behaved well in school and left with "fair and unblemished characters." But he also admitted that "I don't hear of more than half who have preserved their characters unstain'd either by a course of intemperance or uncleanness [sex], or both; and some who on account of their parts, and learning, bid the fairest for usefulness, are sunk down into as low, savage, and brutish a manner of living as they were in before any endeavours were used with them to raise them up." Six of the best were already dead.[75]

If these twenty apostates are added to the twenty-seven matriculants who dropped out prematurely (most of them were Iroquois), Moor's Charity School—on its own accounting—enjoyed a success rate in the *short* run of something less than thirty percent. Perhaps this figure fell within the range of Wheelock's expectations after his introduction to the Iroquois. In 1763 he told his public benefactors that "if one half of the Indian boys thus educated shall prove good and useful men, there will be no reason to regret our toil and expence for the whole . . . and if but one in ten does so, we shall have no cause to think much of the expence." In all likelihood the public had somewhat higher hopes for their investments, as well they might at an annual cost of £16 to £20 per boy, the equivalent, some critics said, of that for an English boy at Harvard College.[76]

A satisfactory explanation for this inauspicious record is hard to find. Colonial critics suggested that the native students came too late and left too early, that the curriculum was inappropriate, and that the goal of civilizing the Indians before Christianizing them was unnecessary, if not impossible in the first place. Wheelock's characteristic response was to lament the heart-breaking "Behavior of some I have taken unwearied pains for," and to turn his energies toward a less frustrating project.[77] Rather than redefine his objectives, he merely sought more malleable subjects. But of all people, the Indians—his students and their parents—had the best insights into the cause of Wheelock's failure, a failure magnified by the boundless ambition and unblinking certitude of his goals.

Like those of his pedagogical predecessors, Wheelock's goals were essentially two: to save the Indians from themselves and to save the English from the Indians. The best way to accomplish both was, as he stated so facilely, to turn the Indians into Englishmen. By giving the natives civility for their bodies and Christianity for their souls, he could save them from their savage selves. In the bargain he could promote peace on the frontiers and liberate a great deal of valuable farmland by purging the savage tendencies of unpredictable warriors, particularly their martial ferocity and love of hunting. "For if [the Indians] receive the gospel," admitted Wheelock, "they will soon betake themselves to agriculture for their support, and so will need but a very small part, comparatively, of the lands which they now claim . . . ; and if they will not receive the gospel, they will, as they have done, waste away before it. . . ." Moreover, if anglicized Indians could be sent into their own country as missionaries and teachers, they could do more than English ministers to counteract the "Subtle Insinuations of great Numbers of Jesuits" and "Attach their respective Nations in the English Interest."[78]

Wheelock's way of winning the Indians to Christian civility was to induce native children, usually aged eleven to fourteen, to come to his school in Connecticut, far removed from the "pernicious Influence of their Parents Example." There he proceeded to inure them to "Decency and Cleanliness" in the form of soap and water, English clothes, and, of course, the critical difference between hand irons and wineglasses.[79] In an atmosphere of beetle-browed piety, they were initiated into the arcana of the Westminister Assembly's *Shorter Catechism*, the English alphabet and grammar, arithmetic, and, in still more abstruse languages, the pastoral classics of ancient Greece and Rome. Since they were designed to return to their own villages as preachers, teachers, and interpreters of the English way, they were encouraged to retain their native languages and to teach them as well to their fellow students— Indians from other tribes and English boys preparing for Indian missions. Their spare time was "improved" by learning a trade, such as blacksmithing, from a local master or "husbandry" from the hands on Wheelock's farm. Native girls were apprenticed to local women to learn "the Female Part, as House-wives, School-mistresses, [and] Tayloresses," whereby they, as the helpmates of the native missionaries, would prevent "their turning savage in their Manner of Living, for want of those who may do those Offices for them." Over all, Wheelock sought to spread a benevolent but firm patriarchalism, to treat them as "My [own] Children" and to make them feel at home as "in a Father's House."[80] What the Indians, especially the Iroquois, soon discovered, however, was that English children were treated much differently from children in the longhouse.

One of the reasons, perhaps the main reason, Wheelock preferred to locate his school among the English was that he knew the Indians' "great Fondness for their Children" was incompatible with the birchen government necessary to "humble them, and reform their Manners." "Here," he admitted, "I can correct, & punish them as I please, . . . but there, it will not be born." When in 1772 the Onondaga council rejected for the last time Wheelock's offer to educate their children, they condemned ten years of hard usage of Iroquois children. Grabbing Wheelock's high-handed son Ralph by the shoulder and shaking him, the council speaker replied with unaccustomed anger: "Brother, do you think we are altogether ignorant of your methods of instruction? . . . We understand not only your speech, but your *manner* of teaching Indian[s]. . . . Brother, take care," he warned, "you were too hasty, & strong in your manner of speaking, before the children & boys have any knowledge of your language." And then in a verbal slap that must have stung the Wheelocks' Protestant souls to the quick, he concluded: "Brother, you must learn of the French ministers if you would understand, & know how to treat Indians. They don't speak roughly, nor do they for every little mistake take up a club & flog them."[81]

The sting of the rod was perhaps the sharpest indignity the Indians suffered, but it was not the only one, nor was it the worst. The school's work program, aimed at teaching the boys to farm during play time, seemed to the boys little more than an elaborate ruse for getting the master's chores done at no expense. Wheelock hoped that part-time farm work would "effectually remove the deep prejudices, so universally in the minds of the Indians, against their men's cultivating lands." Instead, it seemed to confirm them and to create new ones against the doctor for taking advantage of his students. Long was Wheelock's list of Indian students who were "reluctant to exercise [themselves] in, or learn any thing about Husbandry." The last word on the subject came from Daniel Simon, a Narragansett and later Dartmouth's first Indian graduate. "If we poor Indians Shall work as much as to pay for our learning," he told Wheelock, "we Can go some other place as good as here for learning."[82]

When Hezekiah Calvin, a Delaware and one of Wheelock's former schoolmasters to the Iroquois, opted out of the doctor's "Design" in 1768, he let it be known around New England that the inmates of Moor's School were not one big happy family. A Rhode Island correspondent told Wheelock that Calvin had given the school a "bad Charracter," complaining (among other things) that "you use the Indians very hard in keeping of them to work, & not allowing them a proper Privelidge in the School, that you . . . Diot & Cloath them with that that's mean, . . . That Mary [Secutor, a Narragansett] ask'd for a small peice of Cloth to make a pair of Slippers, which you would not allow her, [saying] twas too good for Indians &c . . . [and] That you wont give no more of the Indians more learning than to Read, & Write—[alleging] 'twill make them Impudent; for which they are all about to leave you."[83]

Regardless of the accuracy of these criticisms, many of the Indians and their tribesmen *felt* them to be true. What was not in doubt, however, was that the Indian students were surrounded on every side by overt prejudice that often exceeded cultural arrogance and fell clearly into the category of racism. Wheelock instinctively knew that native students could never be mixed with English (except those special few who were preparing for Indian missions), "for it hath been found by some few Instances of Indians educated elsewhere, that the English Students have been apt to look upon them with an Air of disdain, which these Sons of ranging Liberty cannot so well brook." For this reason even Yale, his alma mater, was inappropriate for his Indian graduates; too many sons of Eli would "disdain in their Hearts to be Associates and Companions with an Indian. And what the Consequences of such Contempt of them will be is not hard to guess."[84]

The problem could also be found closer to home. Wheelock had great difficulty in apprenticing his Indian boys because "their fellow Prentices viz. English Boys will dispise them & treat them as Slaves." In 1765 David Fowler, an older Montauk student, received such an "injury" and "provocations" from the Lebanon townies in a sleighing incident that his mentor was somewhat surprised that his new "Christian forebearance" overcame his native spirit of revenge. Even a young English minister turned down Wheelock's offer of an Indian mission because, he said, "[I] should be prodigiously apt to batter some of their Noses, or else Skulk and run for it."[85]

The pestilence of racism, however, infected all of New England, especially during the Seven Years' War and the Indian "rebellion" that concluded it. Wheelock could not raise funds for the school because his potential donors in the colonial legislatures and churches "breath[ed] forth nothing towards [the Indians] but Slaughter & destruction." A collection plate passed in Windsor, Connecticut, in 1763 returned empty save for "a Bullet & Flynt," symbolizing an attitude that survived in Wheelock's own colony long after the frontier hostilities had ceased. Four years later the table conversation of several gentlemen in Middletown was reported to Wheelock, and it could not have pleased, or much surprised, him. They spoke frankly of the hopelessness of converting Indians by anything but "Powder & Ball." On the basis of a wide acquaintance with "human nature," at least as he knew it in New England, one of them declared the doctor's scheme "absurd & fruitlis" because of the "ireconsilable avertion, that white people must ever have to black. . . . So long as the Indians are dispised by the English we may never expect success in Christianizing of them." For their parts, the gentlemen confessed that "they could never respect an Indian, Christian or no Christian, so as to put him on a level with white people on any account, especially to eat at the same Table, no—not with Mr [Samson] Ocham himself, be he ever so much a Christian or ever so Learned."[86] As the cultural competition of the seventeenth century gave way to the racial antipathies of the eighteenth, popular support in America for "Grand Designs" such as Wheelock's evaporated.

There was a slim chance that the Indian students could have withstood the corrosive currents of popular prejudice that swirled about them if Wheelock had shown some sensitivity to their cultural dilemma and sustained his originally high sense of their purpose. Unfortunately he did not, for his cultural and theological assumptions were as ethnocentric and racist as those of his neighbors, and the Indians were quickly relegated to a secondary role in their own salvation. If he was not one before, the Great Awakening turned Wheelock into a seventeenth-century religious Puritan. For the misnamed "New Lights" of the revival, the religious premises of the old covenant theology acquired renewed relevance. Basic to that theology was a dim view of human nature, which had been corrupted at the source by Adam's fall, and a belief that the original sin, pride, must constantly be crushed in man to allow God's omnipotent will full sway. That in Wheelock's eyes the Indians were the proudest people on earth did nothing to make their life in Moor's School an easy one.

Of all the sins committed by his native students, none so angered Wheelock as "Insufferable pride," which he felt to be the foundation of their "Contempt of all Authority," particularly his own. When Jacob Woolley, a twenty-year-old Delaware, got drunk, threw a clench-fisted tantrum, cursed God, and tried to throw his bed out the window, Wheelock judged him not culturally disoriented or personally frustrated but simply guilty of "Pride of Heart," and administered several stripes to "humble & tame him." When he ran away to the Mohegans five months later, Wheelock presented him with an Indian blanket because he had renounced his "polite education" and "herded with Indians (little better than Savages)."[87] In such an atmosphere it was inevitable that Wheelock's need to dominate absolutely would collide with the sons of the Mohawks, who were, he complained, "proud and high in their own Esteem above any other Tribe, having long been reckoned at the head of the Nations." In 1767 he rusticated two Mohawk youths, though, understandably, not without some misgivings. "Great William," the natural son of Sir William Johnson by an Indian woman, had been "too proud, & litigious to consist with the Health & well being" of the school. His traveling companion, who had been at the school only a few months, was "so lifted up with his having been in the Wars, and sent to Hell one or two of the poor Savages with his own hand, that [Wheelock's] House was scarcely good enough for him to live in, or any of the School honourable enough to speak to him. . . . There is," the doctor told Sir William, "& shall be Government in this School."[88]

At the root of Wheelock's unhappy relations with his Indian students was a racial attitude that placed Indians on a level with blacks—on the lowest shelf of humanity. Like many of his contemporaries, Wheelock frequently referred to his "black" children, especially his "black son" Samson Occom, and to the "Black Tribes" on the frontiers who needed his help, a figure of speech that was not lost on his students. Just the way they wrote to him, even as adults, betrays how they must have been treated and taught to think of themselves in his presence. Joseph Johnson must have been taught well. On one occasion he referred to himself as "a Despicable Lump of polluted Clay, as is inclosed in this tawny skin of mine," on another as "your Ignorant Pupil, and good for nothing Black Indian." "If I was an Englishman, & was thus Respected by you," he wrote, "I should be very thankful, but much more doth it now become me, being an Indian, to be humble & very thankfull in very deed." Though Johnson was a Mohegan, he sought temporary relief from his educated self-abasement among the Oneidas in 1768 when "he turn'd pagan for about a week—painted, sung, danc'd, drank & whor'd it, with some of the savage Indians he could find." Hezekiah Calvin, the Delaware dropout, may have chosen an even apter symbol of protest: he is last seen in prison for "forging a pass for a Negro."[89] As an owner of black slaves for much of his life, Wheelock was perfectly capable of distinguishing the two races; that he did not suggests an unconscious reduction of the people he was consciously trying to elevate and a deep ambivalence about his "Grand Design."

Wheelock's innate distrust of the Indians worked to the surface during the course of the 1760s. Originally he felt that Indian missionaries were superior to Englishmen, and gave a dozen reasons why in his first *Narrative* (1763). Yet as early as 1760 he was planning to take "poor & promising [English] Youth" into the school "in case of a failure of Indians." By the time the first Iroquois arrived he was no longer talking privately of Indians as schoolmasters, interpreters, and missionaries—only the first two. He was obviously lowering his sights. In 1762 he had his revised plans confirmed by the Boston Board of the Scottish Society, which funded much of his work. "If the Design is to Educate only a few that shall be qualified, to be Missionaries, Schoolmasters &c," they wrote, "We Apprehend Indians will not be so proper for these Purposes, as Persons Selected from Among the English."[90] After several frustrating years with his Iroquois students, the doctor needed only an excuse to complete his institutional shift to white missionaries.

In the winter of 1769 the Oneidas provided one by abruptly withdrawing their six children. They gave Wheelock an innocuous reason, but he suspected two others: that "an ugly fellow" had spread "Slanders" that "their Children were not well treated" at school, and that, having heard a rumor of an impending Indian war with the colonies, they were "not willing their children should be with the English [as hostages] at such a time." Whatever their reasons, Wheelock considered their action providential; he sent the other Iroquois students home and prepared to move to Hanover, New Hampshire, to found a college for English missionaries. God, he told his English benefactors, had convinced him that "Indians may not have the lead in the Affair, 'till they are made new [spiritual] Creatures." Their "Sloth," "want of Stability," and "doleful Apostasy" disqualified them.[91]

In the future, after the Indian school was transplanted to less fertile New Hampshire soil, Wheelock would prefer native students from the Indian *reserves* of Canada—Saint Francis, Lorette, Caughnawaga—who were descended from adopted English captives, even though most had been raised as Catholics. "Though they were born among the Indians," he wrote, "and have been exposed to partake of their national Vices . . . ; yet they appear to be as sprightly, active, enterprising, benevolent towards all, and sensible of Kindnesses done them, as English Children commonly are." His racial preference was unmistakable, as was his characteristic feeling that the "other" Indians, just over the horizon, were always more susceptible to his designs. These Anglo-Indians, he vowed, were "by far the most promising set of Youths, I have ever yet had from the Indian Country." How quickly he had forgotten his words to Sir William Johnson only a few years before: "The Boys I have from your parts behave very well, better than any I have had from any other Quarter, and it seems to me they are really a much better Breed."[92] Apparently the doctor wished to begin his experiment in cultural transmogrification with subjects who resembled as nearly as possible his desired results. With the unpromising methods and attitudes he employed, that was perhaps the only way to success.

Wheelock's self-confessed failure to produce a cadre of native missionaries made in his own image met with a timely remedy in 1767 upon the return of Samson Occom and the Reverend Nathaniel Whitaker from a fund-raising tour of England and Scotland. Sent by Wheelock to procure donations for his Indian school, the pair raised more than £12,000 during their two-year sojourn.[93] This enormous windfall enabled Wheelock to sever all ties with the missionary societies upon which he had long depended and to begin a serious search for a way to subordinate his involvement in the unrewarding "Indian business" to a project that gave more scope to his energy, political acumen, and need to dominate. He found such an outlet in Dartmouth, a liberal arts college intended primarily for English missionaries, that borrowed the name of the school's ranking English benefactor, the Earl of Dartmouth.

But the idea of founding such a college was not new to Wheelock; the British donations only made it possible for the first time. As early as 1761 Wheelock had begun to cast his eye around the Northeast for a college site. His heart was initially set on the rich farmlands of Iroquois country, "near the Bowells of the Pagan Settlements," where he thought fifteen to twenty square miles would suffice to plant a model Christian community, including a school for Indians and a college for English missionaries.[94] When it became clear that the Iroquois and their Anglican protector, Sir William Johnson, would never countenance an invasion of grasping, grim-lipped New England Congregationalists, Wheelock considered other sites in Ohio, New York, Pennsylvania, and most of the New England colonies before accepting Hanover's offer of land and capital. In that day as in ours, colleges were economic boons to their towns, and Dartmouth simply went to the highest bidder. Wheelock now had the makings of an institution equal to his ambitions and the opportunity to delegate his waning interest in the schooling of Indians. Moor's Charity School continued to admit Indians after the move to New

16. Eleazar Wheelock (1711–79), the minister of Lebanon, Connecticut, founded Moor's Charity School for Indians in 1754 and in 1769, after repeated frustrations in the "Indian business," Dartmouth College for young English men. The rich carpet and appointments of his college study aptly symbolize the Doctor's turn from the small rewards of Indian education. Courtesy of the Dartmouth College Library.

Hampshire, but with increasing admixtures of English students. The dilution of its original purpose and the lengthening shadow of the college finally closed its doors in 1829.

The subordination of the Indians in Wheelock's new design for Dartmouth College was nowhere symbolized better than in his first draft of its charter. Dartmouth was being founded, Wheelock wrote, to educate "Youths of the English and also of the Indian Tribes in this Land in reading, writing & all . . . liberal Arts and Sciences." Then he remembered that several thousand British benefactors had given thousands of pounds to a charity school primarily for Indians, not white colonists, and he scratched out the reference to English youth and added it at the end of the passage, as if to indicate their subordinate position in his design. In its revised form the charter became New Hampshire law, and Doctor—now President—Wheelock proceeded to exhaust his ample treasury, over the protests of his English trustees, on a liberal arts college that graduated only three Indians in the eighteenth century and eight in the nineteenth.[95]

But not everyone was fooled by the doctor's legerdemain, least of all his "black son," Samson Occom. With the frank shrewdness he had shown all his troubled life in his dealings with the English, Occom told his mentor that "your having so many White Scholars and so few or no Indian Scholars, gives me great Discouragement. . . . I am very jealous that instead of your Semenary Becoming alma Mater, she will be too alba mater [white mother] to Suckle the Tawnees, for She is already adorned up too much like the Popish Virgin Mary." In short, he charged, "your present Plan is not calculated to benefit the poor Indians."[96]

The English favored schools as the likeliest means of converting Indians for several reasons. Believing that "savage" peoples must be "civilized" before they could be trusted with the refined beliefs and holy sacraments of Christianity, they turned naturally to the second most familiar agency of education they had known in England. Even in Puritan circles, where literacy was virtually a prerequisite for sainthood, the family, not the school, was the first line of defense against the Devil, the Roman Church, and heresy in every guise. In English societies at home and abroad, families did the most to train up children in the ways of their class culture.[97] Although the English willingly took children from other English families into their own as apprentices and hired laborers, their sense of cultural and, by the eighteenth century, racial superiority prevented them from accepting "savage" children on the same basis. Even if they had been willing, the linguistic, cultural, and disciplinary problems were simply too thorny for most families to handle. Therefore, surrogate families—boarding schools, preferably at a safe distance and overseen by strict paterfamiliae—were chosen as the most viable instruments of civilization.

Schools for Indians appealed not only to cautious or contemptuous colonial families but to private and public benefactors as well. Subsidizing individual families who took in Indian children would have presented sticky accounting problems to funding agencies and reduced the philanthropic appeal of transmuting native copper into English gold. But the idea of underwriting an educational *institution* with a potentially long corporate life appealed greatly to the class of entrepreneurs and gentlemen who had financed most of England's burst of school and college founding in the sixteenth and seventeenth centuries.[98] They and hundreds of other, less affluent Englishmen who had never seen an Indian felt comfortable in contributing to schools that promised to solve America's native problem in a relatively inexpensive and appropriately civilized way.

Finally, Indian schools appealed to the English establishment because neither the dissenting denominations nor the Church of England was capable of committing to the native field sufficient numbers of qualified missionaries. As Sir William Johnson complained, "the very successfull Method practised by the Jesuits seems impracticable with us as I apprehend few English Clergymen could reconcile themselves to a Constant residence in an Indian Town, & a conformity to their Diet, &ca." When more lucrative preferment lay in established colonial parishes, few men of talent would "bury themselves in an obscure Village Surrounded by a parcel of Indians" for the paltry salaries offered by the missionary societies.[99] If English missionaries would not carry the civilized gospel into Indian country, the best alternative was to invite future Indian leaders, particularly chiefs' sons, to attend free schools in English country, where it was hoped their manners would acquire an indelible tincture of "civility" and "virtue."

Unfortunately, English methods were not equal to their aims. Indian boarding schools located in English territory perfectly suited those colonists who cared at all for the Indians' welfare, but the Indians found them wanting. First, the natives had to be motivated—by force or delicate calculations of self-interest—to send their beloved children long distances to a strange and often hostile country and to entrust them to men whose motives they could never fully fathom or trust. When they arrived, the students had to run a gauntlet of European diseases, novel living conditions, homesickness, prejudice, and degrading corporal punishments unknown in their own villages. If the young Indians could survive those tests, they still had to run a curricular course strewn with formidable obstacles such as English grammar (which is not known for its regularity or exciting pedagogical possibilities), catechism (consisting largely of abstract answers to abstract questions), and the prose and poetry of ancient Rome and Greece (two countries implausibly remote from native America).

And where did all of this investment of time, hopes, and money lead? In 1796 two American commissioners of a Scottish missionary society accurately summarized nearly two centuries of Indian schooling with a sad scenario of failure. Typically, they said, the native student

is taught some ornamental and perhaps useful accomplishments. But the degrading memorials of his inferiority, which are continually before his eyes, remind him of the manners and habits of his own country, where he was once free and equal to his associates. He sighs to return to his friends; but there he meets with the most bitter mortification. He is neither a white man nor an Indian; as he had no character with us, he has none with them. If he has strength of mind sufficient to renounce all his acquirements, and resume the savage life and manners, he may possibly be again received by his countrymen; but the greater probability is, that he will take refuge from their contempt in the inebriating draught; and when this becomes habitual, he will be guarded from no vice, and secure from no crime. His downward progress will be rapid, and his death premature. . . . Such has been the fate of several Indians who have had the opportunity of enjoying an English . . . education, and have returned to their native country. Such persons must either entirely renounce their acquired habits, or resume the savage life; or, if they live among their countrymen, they must be despised, and their death will be unlamented.[100]

English classical schooling for Indians fresh from the forest was, in short, the wrong method for the wrong people at the wrong time.

CHAPTER NINE

The Tribe of True Believers

God brake my head.
ANTONY, A MASSACHUSETT INDIAN

Although the English missionaries believed that the spiritual conversion of America could not be achieved until the natives' lawless savagery had been reduced to disciplined civility, they did not postpone their proselyting until that process was completed. Since the civilizing process was not expected to be long or particularly difficult, the missionaries introduced the natives to the "good news" of the gospel as soon as they began to anglicize the secular aspects of native life. When it succeeded, this early introduction to Christianity served two purposes. The first was to convince the "benighted" natives that most of their cultural habits were heinous sins in the eyes of God, who threatened terrible and everlasting punishment if they were not reformed and sanctified in accordance with divine law. The second purpose was to hold out to the Indians the eternal reward of heavenly bliss for their sacrifice of traditional earthly pleasures. The missionaries' hope was, in the words of an eighteenth-century preacher, that "Civility will prepare them to admit Religion, and Religion will prevent them from falling back into barbarism."[1]

Although religion and civility worked in tandem to batter the stubborn foundations of Indian culture, no one doubted for a moment that religion—the search for salvation of native souls—was the more important plank in the missionary platform. The charters of Virginia, Massachusetts, and most of the other colonies founded in the seventeenth century made it perfectly clear that the conversion of America's "infidell people from the worship of Divels to the service of God" was virtually a "national Design" of the highest priority.[2] Why, then, did the colonists take so long to begin missionary work among the natives, particularly in Massachusetts, where the Puritan sense of divine mission informed every other activity after 1630? The first Indians approached by the Puritan missionaries asked the question themselves. In 1647 Wabbakoxets, a Massachusett shaman, asked John Eliot pointedly, "seeing the English [have] been 27. yeers (some of them) in this land, why did [you] never teach [us] to know God till now? Had you done it sooner, said hee, wee might have known much of God by this time, and much sin might have been prevented, but now some of us are grown old in sin."[3]

The English had two replies, the first of which was a theological standard: in His infinite but mysterious wisdom, God had not seen fit "till of late" to give the Indians the grace to recognize their pitiful condition and seek salvation.[4] The other, however, suggests the unreal quality of the colonizers' initial expectations, especially the role that exemplary civility would play. In chartering the Massachusetts Bay Company, King Charles I empowered its governors to make such laws that the colonists' "good life and orderlie conversation maie wynn and incite" the natives of the country to the Christian faith.[5] The initial goal was thus one of passive seduction, not active reduction. If the Indians did not readily convert, the fault was largely their own. Although a few colonists recognized that the English example in the New World might not be as unsullied as their moral leaders could wish, most were eager to sweep any blame for the missionaries' slow start from their own doorstep. Edward Johnson, a founder of Woburn and one of New England's earliest historians, claimed rather imprecisely that "at their first coming" the English did make an effort to introduce the local natives to Christianity, "but yet," he admitted, "very little was done that way, till in process of time they by continuall coming to the English, became better able to understand them." "Apostle" Eliot put it another way: the Indians were "never willing to hear" until he began to preach to them in 1646. By the eighteenth century this particular piece of exculpation had become quite belligerent. In 1723 the Reverend Solomon Stoddard, forced to answer affirmatively the *Question, Whether God is not Angry with the Country for doing so little towards the Conversion of the Indians?*, blamed the initial sixteen-year delay of his Puritan ancestors on the natives' "brutish and sottish spirit." "We gave the Heathen an Example," he snorted, "and if they had not been miserably besotted, they would have taken more notice of it."[6]

When the transcendent superiority of Christianity did not impress itself upon the natives' notice, New Englanders were forced to vend their spiritual wares more aggressively. The logic of the situation was compelling: if the Indians would not come to Christianity, English missionaries, like their Jesuit rivals, would have to take Christianity to the Indians. The black robes of New England, however, began their work with two advantages not enjoyed by their Canadian counterparts, both of which accrued during the long initial period of missionary inactivity.

The first advantage was a decisive edge in population, brought about by crippling epidemics among the natives and by the "Great Migration" and natural fecundity of English settlers. In 1600 the Indian population of New England from the Saco River in southern Maine to the Quinnipiac in western Connecticut may have numbered as many as 144,000.[7] But in 1616–18 a shipborne "plague" carried off between seventy and ninety percent of the coastal Massachusetts—including virtually the whole Patuxet tribe at Plymouth—and struck so many other natives that "they died on heapes, as they lay in their houses." Their unburied remains reminded one early settler of "a new found Golgotha." Of greatest interest to future Puritan missionaries, the Massachusett tribe, once numbering as many as 24,000 people, was reduced to some 750 by 1631, only to be hit two years later by a lethal smallpox epidemic.[8] By contrast, the colonists in Massachusetts alone had swollen to nearly 20,000 by 1646; altogether New England harbored at least 50,000 English souls.[9]

The second English advantage stemmed from the first: their larger population was able to assist the missionaries enormously by politically dominating the natives. Indeed, bona fide attempts to convert the natives of Massachusetts were not made until after March 1644, when five major sachems placed their tribes under the government of Massachusetts and expressed their willingness "from time to time to bee instructed in the knowledge & worship of God." As John Winthrop acknowledged, it was only after the natives' political submission that the Puritans "began to conceive hope that the Lord's time was at hand for opening a door of light and grace to those Indians." Three months later the General Court ordered its new Indian subjects to meet at several designated locations to receive religious instruction from "those whose harts God shall stirr upp to that worke," assisted by "the best interpriter they can gett."[10]

Apparently the supply of inspired preachers was equal to the native demand for them, for in October 1645 the court and the colony's ministers were still trying to sort out the best means to reduce the natives to Christian civility. More than a year passed before a threefold solution was found. In November 1646 the legislature agreed, first, to purchase townships to encourage the Indians to live in an "orderly way" among the English, thus giving rise to the praying towns. Second, although it protested that "we compell them not to the Christian faith" either by force or law, they forbade the natives to "pawwaw, or performe outward worship to their false gods, or to the devill" on pain of a stiff £5 fine. Perhaps this represented a pragmatic reduction in penalty for Indians; Englishmen convicted of blasphemy or of worshipping "any other god but the Lord God" could be put to death. Finally, the legislature decreed that two ministers chosen by the assembled church elders on election day were to be sent each year, in the company of an interpreter and any other saints who wished to go, to preach the Word to the colony's Indians.[11] Just how long these annual missions were to last was not indicated, but the first ones, Eliot's, consumed only a day or two. Unlike the peripatetic Jesuits, Congregational ministers were tied to their congregations, which had called them and given them holy office. Before a minister could go off to preach to a neighboring Indian village, he had to find a substitute to tend his own congregation on the Sabbath and at the weekly lecture. If the size or wealth of his church did not warrant the appointment of a permanent teaching elder, a fully trained ministerial colleague responsible for Christian education, this could be difficult, especially in the middle decades of the seventeenth century, before Harvard produced a surplus of clerical candidates.

Connecticut was the only other English colony in the seventeenth century to lend legislative aid to the Protestant missionary effort, but her Puritan politicians contributed little and late. Characteristically, native groups that exercised a substantial amount of independence, such as Uncas's Mohegans, were not affected by the Englishmen's statutes. Only the Pequots, who had been badly mauled in 1637 by armies from Connecticut and Massachusetts, and some of the small tribes along the Connecticut River and Long Island Sound, who had been dislocated by English settlements, were powerless enough to receive legislative and missionary attention. In 1650 the General Court instructed a single teaching elder to visit the "neighbouring" Indians twice a year to propagate the "Councells of the Lord" through an interpreter. Four years later the lawmakers admitted that these feeble efforts had been attended with little success and called for the education of another interpreter.[12]

The court found the resettled Pequots an easier mark, but not for twenty years. In 1675 the Pequots were given a set of English-style governors and laws, which closely resembled Eliot's prototypes at Natick and Concord. Among the most serious offenses were powwowing, profaning the Sabbath, and failing to give "ready & comely attendance" upon the preaching of the Reverend James Fitch of Norwich "or any other minister sent amongst them." The legislated docility of the Pequots must have compensated Master Fitch somewhat for the frustrations he endured in trying to proselytize his Mohegan neighbors. Before they moved out of his reach, he lamented in 1674, the Mohegans "generally show[ed] an averseness, yea a perverse contempt of the word of God," particularly after their sachems realized that "religion would not consist with a mere receiving of the word" but would "throw down their heathenish idols, and the sachems' tyrannical monarchy."[13]

Since the English missionaries had not bothered to work their way into the Indians' confidence before launching their religious crusade, gaining an initial audience was often difficult. In general, the farther the natives lived from the center of colonial power, the more difficult the missionaries' task became. But even proximity to Boston was no guarantee that natives would turn an attentive ear to the preachers. After Eliot had acquired some confidence in the Massachusett tongue, his first progress into the field was directed to Cutshamekin, the sachem of Neponset (Dorchester), Roxbury's near neighbor to the southeast. Eliot and later Puritan publicists understandably chose to say very little about this inaugural venture in September 1646 because it was an unmitigated failure. The blame, of course, was thrown onto "drunken" villagers who asked derisive questions about Christianity and laughed at the answers.[14]

Six weeks later Eliot reined his horse west toward Nonantum (Newton), where a compliant man named Waban had been appointed "chief minister of Justice" by the Massachusetts authorities, partly for sending his son to a colonial school, largely for his willingness to entertain the new missionaries. When four neighboring clergymen called the colony's subject Indians to a meeting at Waban's wigwam in late October, a gratifying number of men, women, and children appeared for the three-hour service. Even larger groups gathered every other week for the next few months, despite the New England winter.[15]

During the next three years, however, as the Puritans sought to extend their sphere of spiritual influence beyond the Bay, Eliot quickly reached the end of his tether, even though his Roxbury congregation seemed to tolerate his longer absences. In March 1647, when Eliot and two colleagues were called to Yarmouth in Plymouth patent to help compose differences in that "bruised" church, Eliot attempted to proselytize the local Indians on Cape Cod. Although one sachem and several of his men listened courteously to Eliot's stammered Natick dialect, the other groups either had much difficulty in understanding it—dialects sometimes varied within forty or fifty miles—or presented "much opposition against him." A leading sachem, whom the English dubbed Jehu for his "fierce, strong and furious spirit," promised to gather his men to hear Eliot's speech. But on the appointed day he sent them all fishing and arrived at the lecture alone and annoyingly late, where he sat with a "dogged looke and a discontented countenance."[16]

One of Eliot's long-distance targets was the spring fishing camp at the falls of the Merrimack, because such confluences of natives, he said, "are like Faires in England." For three years running he packed his food, bedding, and supplies to seduce listeners nearly sixty miles into the rough domain of Passaconnoway, the renowned shaman and lord of the valley. While Eliot's loaves and the river's fishes kept them in place, the natives tolerated the Puritan presence, at least "in outward appearance," and uttered no profaneness that reached Eliot's ears. After Eliot's third flying visit, however, Passaconnoway allegedly invited him to move permanently to the river to teach his skeptical people the ways of Christ. As Eliot interpreted it, the chief's main reason for the invitation was that "my coming thither but once in a year, did them but little good, because they soone had forgotten what I taught. . . ." Although Eliot was obviously flattered by what he took to be Passaconnoway's invitation, his annual lack of success at the falls led him to redirect his energies into the founding of praying towns closer to home, where "scarcity, cold and want" would not dampen the progress of the gospel.[17]

When the Puritan missionaries managed to gather an audience—by political pressure, material inducement, or force of personality—the difficult work of religious conversion began. Unlike their Catholic rivals, the New England clergy believed that conversion depended ultimately not on human effort but on the grace of God, whose free gift of election enabled a precious minority to experience a process of conversion marked by distinctive stages. Until a candidate had experienced this spiritual regeneration and described it convincingly to the congregation he wished to join or its minister, he could not be admitted to full membership in the visible church. This did not mean that man was totally helpless or that the clergy played no role in the drama of salvation. Although God alone could bring men "home to Christ" through faith, several preparatory stages depended on human volition and an articulate ministry.[18]

Before sinners were capable of receiving God's grace, they had to be "wounded in their hearts for their originall sinne, and actual transgressions." This spiritual heart attack began ordinarily with attendance on "the Word

Written and Preacht," perhaps accompanied by some personal misfortune to subdue "stubborn" natures. Hearing and reading Scripture brought the sinner not only a general knowledge of good and evil but of "his own peculiar and proper sins." Finally convinced of the error of his ways, the sinner could only agonize in despair until God chose to rescue him from the pit of eternal damnation with scriptural assurances and true faith in Christ's redemptive sacrifice. Although no one could ever know with certainty that God had predestined him for salvation, those who had experienced regeneration could with some probability expect to sit at the right hand of God on Judgment Day. If their outward lives conformed to the moral law as well, their chances for heavenly reward were even better.[19]

When Eliot began itinerant missions to his Indian neighbors, he established an order of worship that was followed with only minor variations by English and native missionaries long after his death in 1690. Alterations generally took the form of additions to the service when the growing faith and understanding of the neophytes warranted. In matters large and small, the praying Indians, as Eliot put it, "studiously endeavor[ed] to write after the English copy in all church order," which was only appropriate since the morphology of conversion was essentially the same for the elect of every race.[20]

After an opening prayer to invoke God's blessing upon the proceedings, the missionary catechized the native children in the fundamentals of the Christian faith, sweetening the task with rewards of apples or biscuits. In an English congregation, catechizing could wait until the regular service had ended and the adults had left the meetinghouse to socialize. But Indian novices had to be taught not only the order of worship but the religious meaning of each ritual step. At Waban's village in 1646 Eliot began with only three questions, designed to identify God as "the maker of all the world," Jesus Christ as the source of redemption from "sinne and hell," and the Ten Commandments as the essence of Christian duty.[21] As audiences grew, so did the number and sophistication of the missionaries' questions. Likewise, the repetition of the children's answers served to educate their parents and other adult auditors, who were also catechized separately when time allowed. A Massachusett man named Poquanum acknowledged in 1652 that he came to know God by eavesdropping "when the Children were Catechised and taught the ten Commandements."[22]

As in Puritan culture, the Christian education of Indians soon spread from church to family and school. Once native adults were well catechized, they were expected and usually eager to teach their own children in turn. Weekly lessons and Bible readings were soon heard in bark wigwams as frequently as in clapboard houses. And as quickly as schools were launched in New England's praying towns, the catechism assumed a prominent part in the curriculum. By 1652 Eliot had written a short Natick dialect catechism in the master's book of the Natick Indian school for the guidance of the two Indian teachers. When the pupils were set writing exercises, the copy texts invariably were questions and answers from the catechism.[23] The Natick rudiments were incorporated in Eliot's first published catechism in 1654 and in 1669 became the basis of his popular *Indian Primer*, a dual English-Natick guide to literacy which contained, among other religious material, twenty questions on the Lord's Prayer and a catechism of twenty-four questions and answers with appropriate biblical citations.

The efforts of Eliot and his colleagues to establish native churches on firm foundations of Christian knowledge met with considerable success. On the eve of King Philip's War, Superintendent Gookin boasted, probably with only modest exaggeration, that "there is none of the praying Indians, young or old, but can readily answer any question of the catechism." A year earlier Eliot had reported that while not every Christian Indian family could yet read Scripture, "all christians learn and rehearse catechise." The eight founding members of the Natick church who were grilled before Eliot's Roxbury congregation in 1654 certainly knew their stuff. Through Eliot and three interpreters, they answered an imposing battery of 101 questions to the "comfortable satisfaction" of the hard-nosed church elders.[24]

Not every missionary in New England, however, possessed Eliot's skill in reducing the faith to its plainest elements for people bred in alien modes of thought and religious ritual. Inspired by the appearance of Eliot's catechism in 1654, the Reverend Abraham Pierson of Branford, Connecticut, fashioned a catechism in the Quiripi language for the natives on Long Island Sound which was published by the New England Company five years later. Not only was Pierson inferior to Eliot as a linguist, but his pedagogical approach was the product less of native fieldwork than of his own scholastic nurture in the disputation schools at Cambridge University. For example, in trying to render "God's punishing will" which sinners would feel at Judgment Day, he used *tatággaman*, to strike or beat, which conveyed to the native catechumen the errant notion that God would punish evildoers only by flogging. And to prove that "there is but one true God," Pierson led his Indian reader through a bewildering lesson in Aristotelian logic chopping: "Because the reason why singular things of the same kind are multiplied is to be found in the nature of God; for the reason why such like things are multiplied is from the fruitfulnesse of their causes; but God hath no cause of his being but is of himself therefore he is one."[25] Clearly, Pierson's catechism was no more equal to the spiritual challenge of pagan Connecticut than were its missionaries.

Knowledge gained from catechizing was only the first installment of insight needed to prepare a "dead" soul for an infusion of divine grace. The rest had to come from public preaching of the gospel, which "the Lord hath made . . . the only outward instrumental means to bring home these wandering sinners."[26] For without a full knowledge of divine law, sinners could never recognize the mortal magnitude of their transgressions. Even if they did, despair would overwhelm them if they remained ignorant of Christ's sacrifice and God's mercy.

The preacher's exposition of Scripture was therefore the heart of an Indian service, just as it was in the Puritan churches. Eliot's first two sermons in Nonantum lasted more than an hour, only partly because his newly acquired dialect needed the help of an interpreter. The main reason was the number and difficulty of the Christian messages he had to convey: the Creation and Fall of Man, the Ten Commandments, "the dreadfull torment and punishment" of sinners in Hell, Christ's sacrifice for those who "repent and beleeve the Gospell," the "sore wrath" of God upon those who spurn his covenant of grace, and the "joyes of heaven" for those who accept it. Like their Jesuit rivals, the best English missionaries quickly caught on to the need to employ homely metaphors to adapt the novel Christian tale to native experience. The classic argument for God's existence from design took the form of "a great Wigwam," built not by "Racoones or Foxes" but by a "wise workman." A native basket woven of black and white reeds was made to assure the Indians that God heard their prayers as clearly as Englishmen's. Satan was already known to the auditors as Chepi, the *matchemanitou* who tormented them with misfortune by day and frightening appearances by night.[27]

Although Eliot and several other English missionaries became reasonably fluent in the native dialects of southern New England, they believed that Indian preachers were "the most likely instruments to carry on this work." "An English young man raw in that language, coming to teach among our Christian-Indians, would be much to their loss," Eliot felt, while native missionaries enjoyed the advantages of linguistic fluency, cultural familiarity, and less need for creature comfort. The only skills they lacked—"some of the Liberal Arts and Sciences," "the Art of Teaching," and "the method of Divinity"—Eliot sought to supply in crash courses during the summer and a Natick edition of *The Logic Primer* ("to initiate the Indians in the Knowledge of the Rule of Reason"). But more often English ministers simply conferred with their Indian counterparts from neighboring towns and suggested how they might "lay out into particulars both the Works and Word of God" at the next lecture.[28] The indispensable tool in the preparation of every Indian preacher was, of course, the Bible, which Eliot translated and published first in 1663. Without the Word of the Lord in their own tongue, the natives could not hope to prepare for divine grace or to recognize it when it came.

Indian ministers came to play an increasingly prominent role in the conversion of native New England as low salaries, high frustration, and hard living frightened away English candidates. In 1698 a New England Company census discovered some thirty congregations of praying Indians, which were served by thirty-seven full-time native preachers, teachers, and catechists and only seven or eight native-speaking English ministers, usually on a part-time basis. By the outbreak of the Revolution, at least 133 Indians had ministered to their brethren in southern New England. Most of them, like their Puritan colleagues, were attached to a single congregation, having been "ordained sometimes by the hands of English Ministers, and sometimes by the hands of Indian Ministers in the presence of the English."[29] Although some English congregations were reluctant to allow their Indian neighbors to use their meetinghouses for services, a few Indian ministers were allowed to administer the sacraments to their English neighbors in native churches. Native preachers on Martha's Vineyard seem to have earned the most respect. At the

WUNAUNCHEMOOKAONK NASHPE

MATTHEVV.

CHAP. I.

Ppometuongane *a book* Jesus Chrift, wunnaumonuh David, wunnaumonuh Abraham.

2 *b* Abraham wunnaumonieu Isaakoh, kah *c* Isaak wunnaumonieu Jakobuh, kah *d* Jakob wunnaumonieu Judaſoh, kah weematoh.

3 Kah *e* Judas wunnaumonieu Pharefoh kah Zatahoh wutch Tamarhut, kah *f* Phares wunnaumonieu Ezromoh, kah Ezron wunnaumonieu Aramoh.

4 Kah Aram wunnaumonieu Aminadaboh, kah Aminadab wunnaumonieu Naaſonoh, kah Naaſon wunnaumonieu Salmonoh.

5 Kah Salmon wurnaumonieu Boazoh wutch Rachab, kah Boaz wunnaumonieu Obeduh wutch Ruth, kah Obed wunnaumonieu Jeſſeoh.

6 Kah *g* Jeſſe wunnaumonieu David ketaſſotoh, kah *h* David ketaſſot wunnaumonieu Solomonoh wutch ummittamwuſſuh Uriah.

7 Kah *i* Solomon wunnaumonieu Rehoboamoh, kah Rehoboam wunnaumonieu Abiahoh, kah Abia wunnaumonieu Aſahoh.

8 Kah Aſa wunnaumonieu Joſaphatoh, kah Joſaphat wunnaumonieu Joramoh, kah Joram wunnaumonieu Oziaſoh.

9 Kah Ozias wunnaumonieu Jothamoh, kah Jotham wunnaumonieu Achazoh, kah Achaz wunnaumonieu Ezekiaſoh.

10 Kah *k* Ezekias wunnaumonieu Manaſſes, kah Manaſſes wunnaumonieu Ammonoh, kah Ammon wunnaumonieu Joſiaſoh.

11 Kah Joſias wunnaumonieu Jechoniaſoh, kah wematoh, ut papaume na uttoocheenaſinneohteamuk ut Babylon.

12 Kah *manche* milinneohteohhettit ut Babylon, *l* Jechonias wunnaumonieu Salathieloh, kah Salathiel wunnaumonieu Zorobahtloh.

13 Kah Zorobabel wunnaumonieu Abiadoh, kah Abiud wunnaumonieu Eliakimoh, kah Eliakim wunnaumonieu Azoroh.

14 Kah Azor wunnaumonieu Sadokoh, kah Sadok wunnaumonieu Achimoh, kah Achim wunnaumonieu Eliudoh.

15 Kah Eliud wunnaumonieu Eleazaroh, kah Eleazar wunnaumonieu Matthanoh, kah Matthan wunnaumonieu Jakoboh.

16 Kah Jakob wunnaumonieu Joſephoh, weſſukeh Mary noh mo wachegit Jeſus utteyeuoh ahennit Chrift.

17 Nemehkuh wame pometeongaſh wutch Abrahamut onk yean Davidut, nabo yauwudt pometeongaſh; neit wutch Davidut onk yean ummiſinohkonauh ut Babylon, nabo yauwudt pometeongaſh; neit wutch ummiſinohkonauh ut Babylon nó pajeh uppeyenat Jeſus Chrift, nabo yauwudt pometeongaſh.

18 Kah Jeſus Chrift *m* wunneetuonk yeu no, nagum okaſoh Maryhoh kah Joſeph quoſhkehtit (aſquam naneenhettick ap) miſkauau wutche keteauónat naſhpe Nathanaittooh.

19 Neit weſſukeh Joſephuh wunnomwaenuoh, matta mo wuttenantamoun wutayimauoh muſſiſſewautut, unnantam kemeu nuppogken yeuoh.

20 Webe nitwontog yeuſhog kuſſeh wutangelſunoh Lord wunnaeihtunkquoh ut unnukquomuonganit, no wau, Joſeph ken wunnaumonuh David, ahque wabeſiſh nemunon Mary kummittamwoſ, newutche uttiyeuwoh wachegit, ne naſhpe wunneetupanatamwe Nathauanittooput.

21 Kah woh neechan wuſiaumon woh kuttiſſowen *a* Jeſus, newutche woh wadchanau *n* Luke 1.31. ummiſinninuonuoh wutch ummatcheſeongaſh nooout.

22 Wame yeuſh *n* nihyeupaſh ne woh *n* nih toh anunwop Lord naſhpeu manitt..woh puh nu wau.

23 *o* Kuſſeh peenomp piſh wompequan, kah piſh neechau wunnaumonuh, kah piſh wuttiſſowenoh Emanuel, yeu nauwuttamun, God kuweetomukqun.

24 Neit Joſeph omohket wutch koutnut, wuttuſen uttoh anukqut wotangelſunoh Lord, kah neenunan ummittamwuſſoh.

25 Kah matta onwaheuh na pajeh wunneechanat mohtompeginitchen wunnaumonoh, kah wuttiſſoweunh Jeſus.

CHAP. II.

JESUS *a* neekit ut Bethlem ut Judea uk *a* Luke keiukodtumut Herod Sontim, kuſſeh 2.6. waantomannug wamohettit wutchepooeiyeu Jeruſalemwaut.

A 3 *Na*

ordination of John Tackanash and Hiacoomes in 1670, "many of the English-Church gladly joyned" the native celebrants at the Lord's Supper. According to Matthew Mayhew, missionary successor to his father and grandfather, many more would have attended native services in subsequent years had it not been for the Indian language in which they were conducted.[30]

Christian Indians also served as missionaries to remote tribes and villages. In 1664 Samuel, a churchman on Martha's Vineyard, was called by the natives on Nantucket to teach them, for which he was paid £10 a year by the New England Company. The chief source of missionaries was the large church at Natick, which by 1674 had between forty and fifty full members in a praying population of 145. In 1651, only a year after the Natick church had been founded, Eliot dispatched two "discreet" churchmen to the village of the Narragansett headman "to stir them up to call on Cod." Dressed in the somber coats, neckcloths, shoes, and stockings that Eliot supplied all his missionaries, the native apostles made their pitch. The "great and proud ones" in the audience were unimpressed, but tribesmen some distance from the capital were more inclined to entertain the Christian offer.[31]

Perhaps more receptive were the Nipmucks, who lived sixty or seventy miles west and southwest of Boston near the Connecticut border, where Eliot thought "sundry are willing, and some desire, to be taught and to pray unto God." Natick sent some of its best men on flying missions to these people. In 1674, however, Eliot and Gookin made a progress through seven Nipmuck villages that appeared ready to "subject themselves unto the English" in church and state. At each village they installed a "pious and sober" young man from Natick as minister and moral overseer, to whom the people were to give "obedience and subjection . . . in the Lord." So central to the Puritan mission were these native preachers that they, rather than English missionaries, were the chief spokesmen for Christianity in Eliot's *Indian Dialogues*, which were "partly historical," he wrote, "and partly instructive." The first dialogue featured Piumbukhou, a ruling elder from Natick, trying to convert the skeptics of Nashaurreg, a Nipmuck village in northern Connecticut. Waban's missionary efforts occupy the second dialogue, while the third pits Indian preachers from Natick and Punkapog against the elusive King Philip at his headquarters near Bristol, Rhode Island.[32]

As Eliot's dialogues conveyed with sharply worded realism, the advent of black-robed preachers of an exclusive new god posed a mortal challenge to the spiritual guardians of "pagan" New England. This was no accident. The Christian missionaries knew that in order to inaugurate the kingdom of God in New England they had to destroy the reign of Satan. When they began to preach to Indian audiences, therefore, one of their first tasks was to throw down the spiritual gauntlet before the powwows.

New England's shamans were predominantly male, part-time religious specialists who, by extraordinary visions of Chepi, had become possessed of spiritual "imps" in the shape of serpents, birds, animals, fish, or flying creatures. The powwows "counted their Imps their Preservers, had them treasured up in their bodies, which they brought forth to hurt their enemies, and heal their friends." Like most shamans in the northeastern woodlands, the powwows were thought to have the power to cure both physical and mental illness, foretell the future, control the elements, and bewitch their own or a client's enemies either by magical intrusion of a small physical object or by capture of the victims' souls in dreams.[33] As the missionaries quickly discovered, native traditionalists would give up many beliefs and practices before they would reject the powwows' medical ministrations.

Traditionalists were reluctant for two reasons. First, believing in sorcery, they knew that the powwows wielded most of the spiritual power in the nation and that it was double-edged, capable of both harm and good. Only powwows were thought capable of curing the malevolence of other powwows or witches who inflicted "outward and bodily hurt, or inward pain, torture, and distraction of mind." The second reason was that not all native ailments were psychosomatic. Many were purely physical, and the powwows were the chief physicians, setting broken bones and healing wounds with poultices and internal ailments with herbs and roots. But even these were accompanied by what the English regarded as "diabolical spells, mutterings, [and] exorcisms." "After the violent expression of many a hideous bellowing and groaning," wrote William Wood, the powwow "makes a stop, and then all the auditors with one voice utter a short canto. Which done, [he] still proceeds in his invocations, sometimes roaring like a bear, other times groaning like a dying horse, foaming at the mouth like a chased boar, smiting on his naked breasts and thighs with such violence as if he were mad. Thus will he continue sometimes half a day, spending his lungs, sweating out his fat, and tormenting his body. . . ."[34] Traditional patients were not only grateful for these exertions on their behalf—even when they were not wholly effective—but dependent on them for lack of anything better. The first and most obdurate response to any attack on their powwows was the insistent question put to Hiacoomes in 1644, "What would you do if any of you[r family] should be sick? whither would you go for help?"[35]

The dual nature of the powwows' authority required the missionaries to attack on both fronts. Christians had to offer not only superior medical treatment for sickly bodies but a compelling alternative to the native spiritual etiology of disease. For physical ailments, Eliot and his contemporaries offered a knowledge of European "Physick and Chirurgery" (surgery) and some "wholsome cordialls." Eliot even spent time with some of his "wiser" novices demonstrating human anatomy and the general principles of medicine in order to wean them from the "antick, foolish and irrationall conceits" of the powwows. But realizing his own limitations and the magnitude of the problem, he suggested to his English benefactors that they endow a medical course, presumably at Harvard, where capable Indian and English students could attend autopsies, dissections, and other instructions, and a fund to recompense those who discovered the medicinal properties of American plants, herbs, and roots.[36] Nothing came of his first suggestion until the Harvard Medical School was founded in 1782, when native students were clearly out of the picture; the second would have been costly indeed. About

170 indigenous drugs which have received the imprimatur of *The Pharma-copoeia of the United States* or the *National Formulary of Unofficial Prepa-rations* were used by one or more tribes in North America, and many tribes used even more that failed to win the later approval of the white medical establishment.[37]

The second half of Eliot's challenge to the medical conservatism of the Indians was more effective in both the long and the short run because it worked directly to insinuate Christianity into their spiritual universe: he altered the whole explanation of disease and its cure, thereby rendering the powwows supernumerary. Like all people, he argued, Indians are afflicted with misfortune and disease because they have sinned against God's will, which the English have revealed to them in Scripture. The crimes of the powwows are particularly heinous in the eyes of God because they consort with the Devil and ask their patients to place complete faith in their hubristic manipulations of the cosmos. The only true cure for sin and the hellish death it brings is to "pray unto God, whose gift Physick is, and whose blessing must make it effectuall."[38]

Until the force of Christian logic could penetrate native reasoning, the missionaries relied on the force of personality, law, and nature to undermine the powwows. In the praying towns, of course, powwowing was strictly prohibited on pain of a twenty shilling fine. But by 1674 the penalty had been raised to £5 each for the shaman and his client and twenty pence for every person present, and Superintendent Gookin handled such cases himself rather than entrusting them to local Indian magistrates. Backed by legal sanction, Eliot was free to browbeat a powwow at one of his first meetings with "a sterne countenance," sharp questions, and "unaccustomed terrour."[39] Even more impressive to native spectators, however, was the invulnerability of believing Christians to the malevolent sorcery of the shamans, their resistance to disease, and their apparent enlistment of their God to strike down their enemies. The first sign that the powwows' power was eroding was that whenever Englishmen appeared in Massasoit's village before 1624, the tribesmen could no longer see the "devil" conjured by their powwow. Another sign was the rapid departure of several shamans from the villages visited by Eliot and his colleagues in 1647. Rather than stay and fight the black-robed interlopers, they turned tail, "seeing their imployment and gaines were utterly gone."[40]

It was not only English missionaries who dared to face the powwows down. Thomas Stanton, an early inhabitant of Stonington, Connecticut, and an Indian interpreter for the colony, once bound the hands of a powerful shaman from Long Island, hoisted him onto a hook, and whipped him "untill he promised to desist and go home." The powwow had been hired by a Stonington native to take revenge on one of Stanton's Indian friends. When the sorcerer came to Stanton's house and threatened to "tare [it] in pieces, and himself flye out at the top of the chimney," the old gentleman leaped from his great chair in a fury and pounced on the surprised—and impotent—Indian. The shamans of Martha's Vineyard were equally nonplussed by the daredevil tactics of Hiacoomes, the unprepossessing fellow of low birth and slow speech who became an effective Christian preacher against considerable odds. One Sunday after meeting, a shaman announced to the emerging Indians that he could kill them all with his sorcery if he wished. At which Hiacoomes strode forward and replied that "he would be in the midst of all the Pawwawes of the Iland that they could procure, . . . and when they did their worst by their witchcrafts to kill him, he would without feare set himself against them, by remembering *Jehovah*." When he also pointed to his heel and boasted that "he did put all the Pawwawes under [it]," the shaman was suitably dumbstruck. Having survived devastating epidemics in 1643 and 1645, Hiacoomes concluded that the Englishmen's God "did answer him" when the powwows could not harm him and the sachem who had once struck him in the face for abandoning them was himself struck by lightning.[41]

Blessed with good health and good fortune, the Christian preachers continued to dispense contempt for traditional religion along with their instructions in the new faith. By 1652 eight powwows on Martha's Vineyard had "forsaken their Devilish craft," burned their invisible imps, and converted to the new religion that claimed 283 of their former adherents. Since the advent of God's Word, the shamans confessed, they had killed more patients than they had cured and were incapable of bewitching any of the converts or their children. But withdrawal from traditional beliefs was often painful. Even after cleaving to Christianity, one shaman's imps "remained still in him for some months tormenting of his flesh, and troubling of his mind, [so] that he could never be at rest, either sleeping or waking." Only the elder Mayhew's assurance of divine protection drove the imps away "like Musketoes."[42] Though the contest between old and new was long and perhaps never completely won, Eliot was confident by 1673 that powwowing, at least in the older praying towns of New England, was "abandon'd, exploded, and abolish'd."[43]

Having had the shamans' ancient "yoake of cruelty" lifted from their necks, the natives were potentially ready to put on the new "yoke of Christ," which the missionaries assumed was lighter and somehow more liberating. But Adam's Indian descendants would not easily bow before the English to be fitted for such restraints. Eliot's first task as their self-appointed religious director, therefore, was to "convince, bridle, restrain, and civilize them" by instituting anglicized praying towns and the rule of divine law. His ultimate religious goal, however, was to "humble" them before Christ, to convince them that they were "a company of perishing, forlorne outcasts" riddled with "filthiness and uncleane spirits" and to give them a vivid sense of God's terrible anger at their "sinfull and miserable Estates."[44] He and his Christian colleagues thus bent their rhetorical skills toward moving depictions of original sin, the Indians' particular sins, and the eternal fate of those who failed to reform, repent, and believe in Christ's redemptive death.

Eliot wasted no time. In his first meeting with Waban's people he described "the terrours and horrours of wicked men in hell," hoping to persuade the Indians—"forlorne" remnants of the plague-stricken Massachusetts—to repent for "severall sins which they live[d] in." Two weeks later, after embellishing his verbal portrait of hellfire and damnation, he told the worried villagers "how evill and wicked men may come to bee good": they must lament their "blindnesse and sinfulnesse," seek forgiveness of and "power against their sinnes in the bloud of Jesus Christ," and pray God to pity and accept them should they sin after promising to follow His ways. When the assembly acknowledged that "God is *musquantum, i.e.* very angry for the least sinne in [our] thoughts, or words, or workes." Eliot launched into another passionate description of how unrepentant sinners after death would be "*Chechainuppan,* tormented alive," as in an enemy's fire. As he had hoped, many in his audience suffered "great heartbreakings" and "mourne[d] for sin" tearfully and "exceedingly."[45] Within two months the native villages at Nonantum and Concord had tallied up long lists of traditional practices, declared them offensive to God, and levied fines on perpetrators, hoping that they would thereby cast off those "wild and sinfull courses they formerly lived in." Eliot and his colleagues noted with satisfaction "that mean esteem many of them have of themselves" and their self-identification as *"poore Creatures."*[46]

By the summer of 1647 part of each Indian service was devoted to "admonition and censure," during which the preachers dissected the gruesome anatomy of sin and the auditors "penitently" confessed their trespasses "with much plainnesse, and without shiftings, and excuses." Offences ranged from spiritual generalities to cultural specifics—pride, of course, and stubbornness, but also wife-beating, disobedience to parents, and drunkenness. George, a "malignant drunken Indian" who once asked Eliot the irreverent question "Who made Sack?," was upbraided for killing a Cambridge cow and selling it to Harvard as moose meat.[47]

One confession unwittingly revealed the key to missionary success in New England. Cutshamekin, the sachem of Neponset who had repulsed Eliot's initial foray against native paganism, admitted with some bewilderment that "before I knew God . . . I thought I was well, but since I have known God and sin, I find my heart full of sin, and more sinfull then ever it was before." Early in his preaching career Hiacoomes had witnessed the same phenomenon on Martha's Vineyard. In 1646, when he began to enumerate the islanders' specific sins—he would later name forty-five or fifty—the Indians became "sensible" of sin for the first time; "formerly they did but hear it as a new thing, but not so nearly concerning them."[48] The experience of both parties points to a central challenge for Christian missionaries of every stripe, namely, that people are not born with a sense of sin but must be taught to feel remorse and guilt for having offended an omnipotent God. Raised in a cultural tradition that established community standards of right and wrong, but not sin against divine law, the Indians of southern New England had to be stripped of their former beliefs by strange events and strong teaching and given a plausible set of new beliefs to replace them. Only then would they come to have a "clear sight and sence" of "gross and external" (or cultural) sins but also of spiritual sins of "the Heart and Soul."[49] When circumstances conspired and the black robes taught well, the harvest of converts was often gratifyingly large; when the natives retained their independence and the preachers proved inept, "humiliation" for sin was not forthcoming and the process of regeneration could not begin.

In New England the sharp rod of devastating European diseases, the inexorable growth of the English population, and the marvels of English technology led many natives who had acquired the Christian idiom to acknowledge that "God did justly vex us for our sins" and to seek "Subjection to *Jehovah*."[50] If God granted them the grace to complete the conversion process, they were asked to make a public relation of their spiritual odyssey before being admitted to the visible church. Many of these confessions resemble those of their English counterparts in general style and structure.[51] But almost all are culturally distinctive because of their earnest efforts to document the candidates' escape from "Indianisme." Any number of English men and women might have uttered the confession of Natick's Totherswamp, who admitted that "I break Gods Word every day. I see I deserve not pardon, for the first mans sinning; I can do no good, for I am like the Devil, nothing but evil thoughts, and words, and works. . . . I deserve death and damnation." But only other Indians could have "sinned" by resorting to powwows, refusing to cut their long hair, or joining a praying town "not for the love of God but for the love of the place."[52]

As the title of Eliot and Mayhew's *Tears of Repentance* suggests, Indian confessions seem to have been more lachrymose than most English relations. Natives torn from their cultural roots understandably were emotionally fragile when they were confronted by the depressing tenets of Christian sin. Even before Eliot launched his missions, Indian children who lived in "subjection" to English families would sometimes "tremble and melt into tears" at a preacher's "opening and pressing the Word upon their Consciences." Small wonder, if the Word bore any resemblance to Abraham Pierson's Quiripi catechism, which instructed native children to think of themselves by nature as "filthy loathsome creature[s]" who were by reason of their sin "odious" to the Englishmen's God. Eliot's depiction of sin at Nonantum produced so many "teares in publike" that they splattered the dust of the wigwam where he stood. Such behavior was the more remarkable because Indians were characteristically stoic and little subject to tears, not even under "the sorest torture" or when they were "solemnly brought forth to die." The missionaries attributed converts' tears to "some conquering power of Christ Jesus." They might have looked to more secular conquests as well.[53]

The natives' road to humiliation was seldom short and afforded them many opportunities to question the wisdom of giving up their old ways and the reasonableness of the Christian novelties they were being offered. The missionaries welcomed their doubts and queries because it allowed them to impress the Indians with their formidable book learning, to turn hostile or facetious questions to their own use, and, most important, to enable serious inquirers to "see things really, and not onely have a notion of them." Accordingly, a major part of every Indian service was devoted to answering listeners' questions. As the missionaries quickly discovered, many Indians had "a faculty to frame hard and difficult questions," showing that they possessed enquiring minds capable of grasping the intricacies of Christian theology and European arts and sciences. Even native women were encouraged to express their scruples, but only through their husbands or an interpreter because the English "knew how unfit it was for women so much as to aske questions publiquely . . . by themselves."[54]

An early kind of question probed the consequences of having native practices suddenly declared sinful. In the first few months at Nonantum, Eliot was asked which of two wives an Indian husband should put away—the barren first or the fruitful second? Since gaming was sinful, should a man pay his old gambling debts? Should a woman continue to pray with an angry wife-beater? "Why must we love our enemies, and how shall we do it?" Why did Abraham *buy* a place to bury in? Related questions tested the cultural superiority of the English: "Doe not Englishmen spoile their soules, to say a thing costs them more then it did?" "Why do Englishmen so eagerly kill all snakes?" What will God say about a minister who wears long hair "as some other men do"? In scientific matters the English were regarded less skeptically, to judge by the kinds of "Philosophicall" questions the missionaries received about natural phenomena. One neophyte wanted to know "why God made the Rainbow," another what the sun and moon were made of (Eliot had told them metaphorically that their bodies were made of clay). Such questions were patiently received and answered because they showed that "the Lord Jesus hath at last an enquiring people among these poor naked men."

It was not long before the missionaries' catechizing and preaching generated a range of much tougher questions about biblical history, death, and the problem of evil. Long before the natives were able to read the Scriptures in their own language, they were asking their mentors "whether the devill or man were made first," "how many good people were in Sodome when it was burnt," and why God made Hell before Adam had sinned. With his enemies' or perhaps his own ritual cannibalism on his mind, one warrior wanted to know the meaning of eating Christ's flesh and drinking his blood. Another saw why he should fear Hell but could not fathom why he should fear God. A third inquirer, obviously trying to find his bearings in the new cosmic geography, asked, "when the wicked die, do they first go to heaven to the judgment seate of Christ to be judged, and then go away to hell?"

Death was perhaps the most troubling concern of the natives, evil the most problematic. Tender parents wanted to know where their little children would go when they died, "seeing they have not sinned." The indecisive asked "if one purposeth to pray [convert], and yet dieth before that time, whither goeth his soul?" And many Indians were anxious to learn why God punished sinners in Hell forever, even if they repented, since even English sticklers released malefactors from prison after a finite sentence. Inscrutable divine justice raised several other doubts. "Why doth God make good men sick?" asked the residents of underpopulated Nonantum. "Why did not God give all men good hearts that they might bee good?" And "why did not God kill the Devill that made all men so bad, God having all power?"[55] Whether the missionaries' ready responses to such questions fully appeased the gnawing doubts and intellectual hunger of the natives is doubtful. Whether they did or not, the novices would soon learn that the new religion, like their own, was founded as much on faith as on reason.

Although man could do little to effect his own salvation, he could supplicate God for assurance against doubt and for an infusion of the Holy Spirit. While the missionaries believed that "every true converted believer . . . can pray, and desires to pray, and is ever lifting up his heart to God in prayer," they also knew that Indian converts needed to be taught the rudiments and proper uses of Christian prayer to enable them to participate fully in personal, family, and public worship. The Indian services fashioned by Eliot for the praying towns of New England opened with a prayer for "all men, rulers, ministers, people, young, old, sick, well, English or Indians," and the day's sermon or lesson was bracketed by prayers. Well before they could be regarded as "true believers," the natives were taught that "God is a *God hearing prayers.*" By the second meeting at Nonantum, Eliot's auditors followed his fifteen-minute Indian prayer with their "eies and hands to heaven," and Waban had learned several short prayers, such as "Take away, Lord, my stony heart," "Wash, Lord, my soule," and "Lord, lead mee when I die to heaven."[56]

But even Indians well disposed to the new religion were not entirely sure at first how to pray. Some of the earliest questions directed at Eliot involved the efficacy and form of prayer. The natives' initial concern was that God "understood not what Indians speake in prayer," but Eliot's long prayers in Massachusett and his metaphorical handling of the black-and-white reed basket assured them that God was conversant with all tongues. One man wanted to know whether the quantity of prayers in a day affected his chances of salvation, another whether wicked men could ever pray well. A third asked, "How shall I know when God accepts my prayers?" As to whether God hears a prayer that is only thought, Eliot affirmed that good prayers involved the "inward action of the heart" as well as the "externall action of the lips." The simplest question, perhaps, was what physical posture to assume in prayer. Eliot's patriarchal advice was to "let none lie along or sit, which are postures of unreverence, but either stand like servants, or kneel like sons and daughters before the Lord."[57]

Eliot's novices had to learn other lessons as well. A difficult one was that "when we make our prayers and request[s] unto God," as Waban told a potential convert in *Indian Dialogues*, "we must leave the matter to his love and wisdom, to give us what, and when, and how he will." Another was that the most basic purpose of prayer was to confess and repent sins and to crave God's pardon and mercy. Even when saying grace before a meal the Indians were taught to say something to the effect of: "we are poor worms under thy feet, thou feedest every living creature, and makest our food to be like a staff to sustain our faint and weary bodies. Thou renewest our strength every day and though we are sinners in thy sight, yet thou art merciful to us, and with long patience dost call us to repentance. We confess all our sins before thee, and pray thee for Jesus Christ, his sake, who died for sinners, to have mercy on us, and freely pardon and forgive us all our sins. Bless us at this time, and this food which is set before us. . . ."[58]

The natives obviously learned quickly. By 1651 the leading English missionaries were convinced that their converts prayed "not with any set Form like Children, but like Men induced with a good measure of the knowledg of God, their own wants and the wants of others, with much affection, and many Spiritual petitions, savoring of a Heavenly mind." They also prayed regularly in their families morning and evening, before meals, and even in the fields. Prayer became such a distinguishing mark of the converts that they were known as "praying men" and Christianity in general as "praying to God."[59]

In many religions, music is a major vehicle of prayer, and Protestant Christianity was no exception. As soon as the Indians of southern New England learned to pray, they were taught to sing the Old Testament Psalms of David, the dominant text of religious music in the English-speaking world. Native church services featured psalm singing in at least two places—after the Scripture lesson or sermon and at the closing. In 1651 the Reverend John Wilson attended a service at Natick where "the Indian School-Master read out of his Book one of the Psalms in meeter, line by line, translated by Mr. Eliot into Indian, all the men and women &c. singing the same together in one of our ordinary English tunes melodiously." By the turn of the century the Indian churches of New England, like their counterparts in French Canada, enjoyed a reputation for "excellent singing of psalms with most ravishing melody," "outdoing many of the English, in their meetings."[60]

The comparison with the Catholic choirs of New France is not quite apt, for the musical system dominant in New England until the 1720s severely handicapped even mellifluous Indian voices. As Wilson described, psalms were sung by "lining out." A ruling elder read the psalm one line at a time, a precentor "set a tune," and the congregation put words and music together as best they could without instrumental accompaniment, psalters or hymnals, or a knowledge of musical notation. The tunes were simple and few—less than a dozen all told, and effectively half that in most churches—and even then the precentor had considerable difficulty keeping the congregation and occasionally himself from switching tunes in mid-psalm. When it was not cacophonous, the singing was monotonous. The melodies were ponderous, set for a male tenor, and the chords plain, usually one note per syllable. Many of the psalms were no more than "divinity couched in the sorriest doggerel," especially those from Sternhold and Hopkins's *Whole Booke of Psalmes collected into Englysh metre*, which achieved almost canonical authority in English Protestant circles after its publication in 1562. The *Bay Psalm Book* of 1640—of which Eliot was a cotranslator—was small improvement, as were Eliot's metrical *Psalms of David* in Natick, published in 1663 and reissued in 1680. Not until sight-reading, singing schools, nonbiblical hymns, and increased use of polyphony appeared after 1720 did the music of New England's praying towns begin to compete with the rich motets and soaring anthems of the Laurentian *reserves*.[61]

All of the missionaries' teachings, all of their prescriptions and prohibitions, were aimed at leading the Indians to a strict and regular observance of the Sabbath. Private prayer, family devotions, and the weekly lecture pointed to a special concentration of spiritual activity on the sacred seventh day. For English Puritans, the Sabbath was a day of solemn rejoicing, of rest from earthly labor, a memorial of Christ's Resurrection, and a foretaste of heaven. It was itself a means of grace "for our souls good," indeed the special season of grace and "communion with God." So central was the Sabbath that the Puritans virtually identified it with their religion. "Religion is just as the Sabbath is," Thomas Shepard told the Harvard student body, "and decayes and growes as the Sabbath is esteemed." Half a century later Cotton Mather still maintained that "our whole religion fares according to our sabbaths . . . poor sabbaths make poor christians." The fourth commandment was the "chief hinge of all the rest," argued a Natick preacher. "By profaning the sabbath, we turn all religion and good order out of doors, and set open a door unto all sin and wickedness. . . ."[62]

The way for Indian and other Christians to slam the door on Satan was twofold: they had to labor hard at their personal callings six days of the week and devote the seventh entirely to the service of God in "thought, word, and deed." The Sabbath began at three o'clock on Saturday afternoon and lasted until sunset on Sunday. Long Sunday worship services, at nine in the morning and two in the afternoon, were necessary because "God requires that we should give him a whole day." "When Christ Jesus shall judge the world," an Indian minister told King Philip, "he will examine all men how they spent every sabbath." The missionaries and English laws made it very clear how it was *not* to be spent. In 1652, for example, Plymouth Colony forbade its Indians "to doe any servill worke on the Lords day as by fishing, fowling, planting, hilling [of corn], and carriing of burthens &c." Eliot conveyed a similar message when the people of Nonantum and Concord expressed their willingness but ignorance of how to sanctify the Sabbath. They promptly outlawed Sabbath-breaking—confident that they knew what it meant—and fined the guilty from ten to twenty shillings. If any miscreants happened to slip through the hands of the local constabulary, the colony's superintendent of Indian affairs was ready to nab them and extract the penalty.[63]

At first the natives had some difficulty seeing the wisdom of eschewing all useful activity on Sunday, "it being usuall with them to travaile on that day, as on any other." After all, they did live close to the bone, and the search for food could ill afford a fifteen percent reduction of effort. But the missionaries also made it clear that the Indians spent the other six days of the week in relative ease and sinful idleness. Those who wished to engage in the "heavenly Trade" of New England's "spiritual factory" would have to speed up production during the week, optimally by leaving the chase for civilized agricultural work, in order to earn the spiritual coin for "Gods Market day."[64]

Neophytes took the hint and passed laws to encourage praying town inhabitants to "fall upon some better course to improve their time." And individual saints, zealous in their new faith, blew the whistle on any infractions that attracted notice, including their own. Peter, a Natick ruler, confessed before the elders of the church that despite the biblical injunction to keep the seventh day holy "I did hunt, or shoot, or anything on the Sabbath." In 1647 Nabanton, a teacher at Nonantum, fingered Cutshamekin's wife for "worldly talk" on the Sabbath as she fetched water with a group of women. The lady doubted that it was a sin, "seeing it was early in the morning, and in private," but she had a lot to learn. After a long Sabbath service, another convert came home to his wigwam and a fire almost out. When he split a little dry wood with his hatchet, he found himself accused of profaning the Sabbath by a literal-minded lodgemate.[65]

Hatchets and trees were associated with more than one Sabbath-breaker in native New England. Waban was accused of sending two servants a mile from town to fell a tree containing a fat racoon. He had wanted to entertain two strangers with traditional hospitality, but apparently found his larder bare. Even earlier, before Eliot had begun his ministrations, Indian neighbors of the Puritans had absorbed some of their scruples about Sunday. One of them accosted an Englishman cutting a tree outside the jurisdiction of the Bay Colony and asked him pointedly, "Doe you not know that this is the Lords day, in Massaqusetts? much machet man, that is very wicked man, what, breake you Gods Day?" When some of the English complained to a local sagamore that his men killed pigeons on the Lord's Day, he promised for the future not to allow it. But two of his men chose to defy him and climbed a tall tree in search of nests. When they both fell, one breaking his neck, the other several human limbs, the sagamore sent "two grave old men to proclaime it amongst his Indians, that none of them should kill Pigeons upon the Sabbath day any more." How appropriate it seems that in 1705 Cotton Mather published a digest of laws for New England's praying Indians entitled *The Hatchets, to hew down the Tree of Sin*, particularly since "Sabbath-breaking" was one of the tree's largest branches.[66]

In 1684, after nearly forty years in the field, Eliot looked back on the Sabbatarian performance of his converts and was largely pleased. "They do diligently observe and keep the sabbath, in all the places of their publick meetings to worship God," he told his English benefactors. "The example of the English churches, and the authority of the English laws, which major Gookin doth declare unto them, together with such mults, as are inflicted upon transgressors; as also and especially, the clear and express command of God, which they and their children learn and rehearse daily in their catechism; these all together have fully possessed and convinced them of their duty, to keep holy the sabbath day." Despite the temptation to paint a totally rosy picture, however, Eliot had to admit that "some of the vain and carnal sort among them are not so girt to it, as were to be desired."[67]

Even among the praying Indians, perfection was elusive for various reasons. In 1651 the Commissioners of the United Colonies feared that some of Eliot's recent converts needed more spiritual armor because when they went to Connecticut they mixed with the local pagans and "compl[ied] to[o] much to their way of Sabboth breaking." A century later, the natives of Nantucket blamed their profanation of the Lord's Day on their English employers. "How can we be any ways like christians . . . on the Sabbath day morning," they complained to the Massachusetts General Court in 1747; "then we must be Rowing after whal[e] or killing whal or cutting up whal . . . when we should be at rest on that day and do no worl[dl]y labour, only to do sum holy duties to draw near to God; and when on land we have no time to go to meeting, and then we are to go away again to sea whaling. How can we serve God . . . when our masters lead us to darkness and not in light?" Even when the ideal was beyond their grasp, New England's missionaries and their native followers knew that "all turns upon . . . the Religion of the Sabbath."[68]

Believers also knew that their ultimate goal was to replicate as faithfully as possible the heavenly church of the elect in a "visible Church-state" on earth so as to fortify each other with the "discipline and ordinances" instituted by Christ: the sacraments (baptism and communion), preaching, prayer, the "brotherly watch" of fellow members, and, as a last resort, excommunication. Of course, not every native assembly or praying town could have a church with an ordained pastor, elders, and deacons. The native economy being what it was, Indians met to worship in many different places, a few "stated" (praying towns like Natick and Punkapog) but most "occasional," such as "places of fishing, hunting, gathering chestnuts, in their season" or forts raised against Mohawk incursions. Spots of good land fit for planting corn with "accommodation of fishing" were often five or ten miles apart, and seldom capable of supporting many people. In 1684, for instance, Plymouth Colony, Martha's Vineyard, and Nantucket had some twenty-five places where the Indians congregated for Sunday services, in addition to four major towns and numerous hamlets in the Bay Colony. Each location had its own preachers or teachers, mostly Indian.[69]

The process instituted by Eliot and his colleagues for "inchurching" the natives involved three stages. In the case of the first church gathered, in Natick, the process consumed eight years. The first step was taken in 1652 when Eliot called his most promising converts before him to give "preparatory confessions," which he wrote down and read to the elders of neighboring English churches to get their opinion. Within a month or two, the candidates made somewhat fuller "public confessions" before an assembly of visiting English churchmen; these were the relations published by Eliot in *Tears of Repentance* in 1653, often in both versions. The second stage occurred nearly two years later in Eliot's own Roxbury meetinghouse. There, before an august and somewhat daunting body of saints and elders, the candidates were grilled through interpreters on their knowledge of Christian doctrine and history; Eliot rightly called it *Natootomuhteáe kesuk*, "A day of asking Questions." Finally, in 1660, the eight candidates (one more than the requisite number) subscribed to a covenant of faith and became the pillars of a true church, capable of calling a pastor, receiving baptism (with their offspring), electing officers, sharing communion, and voting in all church affairs. The formal gathering of the first Indian churches at Natick and Mashpee was considered of such spiritual moment that the governor, several English magistrates and church elders, and hundreds of English and Indian neighbors stood as witness.[70]

Why did it take so long to launch the first Indian churches in New England? Eliot and the Reverend Richard Mather, who contributed a long foreword "To the Christian Reader" of *Tears of Repentance*, gave four cogent reasons. The first and most telling, for Eliot at least, was that it was extremely risky to entrust the "Treasure of Christ," the "holy priviledges of Gods house," to people who lived "so unfixed, confused, and ungoverned a life," lest they run away from ecclesiastical censure and "defil[e] the name of Christ among their barbarous Friends and Countrey-men." It simply took time to root the restless natives in permanent praying towns and even longer to "reduce them to civility."[71]

A second reason was Eliot's reluctance to take such a momentous step without the advice and consent of his colleagues and benefactors in England and New England. He particularly wanted their reactions to the native confession in *Tears of Repentance*, which had to be published in London, distributed there, shipped to America, and digested before he could proceed to the second stage. As soon as he received the sanction of a large group of elders and Indian commissioners in Boston, he began to prepare for the convocation at Roxbury. The confessions gathered from the Mashpee candidates by the Reverend Richard Bourne in 1666 were also circulated for comment and approbation.[72]

Another reason for caution, somewhat more predictable than the others, was a medley of English "doubts and jealousies," some of them stemming from cultural arrogance, others from cold fear. Eliot did not proceed to the public examination of his candidates' Christian knowledge in 1653 because a rumor had blazed through the New England countryside that the praying Indians were "in a conspiracy with others, and with the Dutch, to doe mischief to the English." In such circumstances, Eliot thought it best to wait for the troubled waters to calm.[73]

The principal reason for delay, however, especially after the coastal tribes had been suitably "yoked" and "bridled," was the lack of Indian preachers and rulers for new churches. Realizing that the supply of English missionaries could never meet the needs of New England's numerous and scattered plantations of praying Indians, Eliot looked to a native supply. Since it was thought that Indian converts would fare better in their own congregations, they needed their own pastors and elders to be "invested with all Church-power as a Church." Unfortunately, too many of the Indian prospects sent off to English schools or Harvard died before they could qualify or return. Only when Eliot took it upon himself in 1670 to educate promising young men in

Western logic and biblical exegesis were there enough native officers able to "manage the whole instituted publick worship of God among themselves, without the presence or inspection of any English."[74]

Despite delays, the number of Indian churches and ministers grew rapidly after 1670, with only a temporary (but serious) setback during King Philip's War, when English xenophobia was virulent and the Massachusetts praying towns were reduced from fourteen to four.[75] On the eve of the war, southern New England nurtured six Indian churches, each with a full complement of native officers, at least 168 full members, and more than 350 baptized members in a praying population in excess of 2,000. By the end of the century, a New England Company census found 37 Indians and only 7 or 8 Englishmen ministering to 37 Indian congregations. In a native population of over 2,000, Martha's Vineyard allegedly had only two pagan holdouts. Such a record prompted an English friend of the missions as early as 1689 to "challenge the whole world to produce the like instance."[76]

New England's success was earned the hard way, as was that of the Jesuits in New France, under strict requirements for church admission, even after the colonial churches had begun to relax their standards after the Half-Way Covenant and the anglicizing temper of the 1690s. Josiah Torrey, the Harvard-trained minister of Tisbury on Martha's Vineyard and a frequent preacher to the Indians in their language, testified in 1705 that the Indians' method for church admission was "more according to the manner of the churches in primitive times, than is now practised among the churches in most parts." Candidates were still required to make "large and particular" declarations of their Christian knowledge, past sins, and "convictions, awakenings, and comforts" before the assembled congregation.[77]

It seems likely that the native churches on the mainland were able to enforce such rigor after Eliot's death in 1690, given the eagle-eyed solicitude of the Boston commissioners of the New England Company. But some slippage may have occurred by 1711, when Commissioner Cotton Mather proposed "a strict Enquiry, about the late way of Admission into the particular Church-State, practised among our Christian Indians; lest it should (which I hear) degenerate into a very lax Proceedure." If any of New England's primitive rigor was lost in the eighteenth century, it may have been recovered during the Great Awakening by a new generation of English missionaries. When Samuel Kirkland, a protégé of New Light Eleazer Wheelock, ministered to New York's Oneidas and Tuscaroras in the 1770s, the public and private relations that his converts gave toward church membership were, he moaned, *"very long,"* some lasting three hours.[78] No sign of ecclesiastical laxity there.

The history of Protestant missions in colonial America could be—indeed, has been—made to read like a religious romance, in which the spiritual constancy and cultural confidence of two quite different suitors, John Eliot and Thomas Mayhew, Jr., capitalized on fortuitous circumstances to win hundreds of dusky pagans to the true God.[79] Such a reading would not be far wrong, as far as it goes. Unfortunately, it would reduce Anglo-America to a narrow swath of southern New England in the seventeenth century, and effectively ignore not only the other eight English mainland colonies but also New England's own hinterlands in the eighteenth century. New England continued to dominate the evangelical scene in the eighteenth century, but the story line took a dramatic and awkward twist when Protestant missionaries set off on a series of ill-fated errands into the wilderness.

CHAPTER TEN

Errands into
the Wilderness

Heathens they are, and Heathens they will still be.
REV. WILLIAM ANDREWS

In the seventeenth century the only English colonies that enjoyed any evangelical success with the Indians were those in southern New England—Massachusetts, Plymouth, and the adjacent islands of Martha's Vineyard and Nantucket. Even Rhode Island and Connecticut made no headway, in part because they had little interest in doing so. Roger Williams, who knew the Indians as well as any colonist in his day, might have minted many saints if he had not believed that true churches could not be gathered even by the elect on earth and that he did not have divine appointment to an apostolic, converting ministry.[1]

Furthermore, virtually the only Indians the New England missionaries could induce to become "praying men" had been first subjected to English civil authority. As the Indian superintendent of Massachusetts candidly admitted in 1674, all the praying Indians in his colony "did long since, before they began to worship God, actually and solemnly submit themselves unto the jurisdiction and government of the English." Conversely, those who acknowledged English authority usually converted to English religion. After disease and wars had sadly reduced the native population, the Boston commissioners told the New England Company in 1705, "almost all that remain under the influence of the English, in this Massachusetts province, are so far christianised."[2] In other words, Christ's conquests in Anglo-America were made only after pagan resistance had been smashed by microscopic shock troops, waves of covetous plowmen, and an intolerant government of occupation. English missionaries preached most convincingly to a captive audience.

When the black robes ventured out of the settlements where the English enjoyed a demographic and political advantage, however, they were brought up short by the obduracy of native traditionalism and by the inadequacy of their own evangelical methods to make a dent, much less a major difference. Their failure was most conspicuous, perhaps, whenever they challenged the Jesuits for native souls and political allies on the long southern frontier of

New France. If the history of the few English missions in the seventeenth century resembles a religious romance, the eighteenth-century story looks much more like a tragicomedy or farce in four acts.

ACT ONE: "Western" New England

SCENE ONE: *Connecticut, 1713-14*

In the middle of October 1713, Experience Mayhew crossed the choppy sound between Martha's Vineyard and Cape Cod and spurred his horse toward Connecticut. This fourth-generation missionary had been asked by the New England Company to visit the Indians along the southern coast of New England to offer them the gospel. When he reached Stonington, Connecticut, on the nineteenth, he secured the services of an Indian interpreter because the local Pequot dialect was very different from the familiar tongue he carried from the Vineyard. Although at that time of year "most of the young men were gone out a hunting," Mayhew and his local host, the Reverend James Noyes, managed to gather a small group of Pequots from two neighboring towns.

Through the interpreter, Mayhew gave the assembly a two-hour history of the world from Creation to the Crucifixion, and urged them to send their children to English schools to learn to read God's holy book. Then both ministers tried to encourage them to "pray to the same God as the English do" by describing "remarkable Instances of God's hearing & answering prayers," particularly some made for Indians at the point of death and for rain in time of severe drought. Appealing to what he regarded as the listeners' self-interest, Mayhew tried to sweeten the praying pot by showing how Christian Indians lived much better than pagans such as themselves, who went without tame cattle and English clothes. The natives gave all this a polite reception, and Mayhew rode off to New London with a jaunty air to bestow his next blessing upon the Mohegans, the stubborn descendants of Uncas.[3]

The New London episode was a bust from start to quick finish. The essential problem was that the Mohegans were "so universally gone out a hunting that it was not possible to obtain a meeting," even though Governor Saltonstall and the local minister had informed them that they would be accompanying Mayhew. In the place of his sermon, Mayhew left a long letter to the natives explaining the Christian proposition, which the governor promised to have translated and read to them when they returned. "If you refuse to obey God . . . ," the paper ended, pulling no punches, "he will be angry with you, and will sorely punish you: but if you obey him, you will become a happy people."[4] Just how well the returning hunters took this naked threat from a total stranger is not known.

Somewhat dispirited by his Mohegan reception, Mayhew turned toward home. In passing through Rhode Island, however, he decided to pay a pastoral call on Ninnicraft, the head sachem of the Narragansetts. It proved to be the worst move of the trip. Ninnicraft not only denied him permission to speak to his people, but gave him—through two interpreters—a long list of stinging reasons for rejecting his offer and then upbraided him for wasting his day. If Christianity is so good, he asked, why didn't the black robes "make the English good in the first place, for he said many of them were still bad?" The same applied to the praying Indians of Martha's Vineyard, whom the sachem had seen stealing in Rhode Island. Even if the Indians were inclined to pray, they could ill decide between the divided English around Narragansett Bay, some of whom kept Saturday holy, some Sunday, and some no day at all. He also said that natives indebted to the English and living among them as servants would pay him no mind and a missionary even less if he bid them attend a lecture. "If they should go to meeting, their English masters would send constables for them, and take them away." Finally, to rub salt in Mayhew's already wounded pride, the old sachem allowed that if the Pequots and Mohegans would "submit to Religion, it may be he and his people might do so too: but he was not willing to be the first." According to his official report, Mayhew "would have discoursed more with him," but one wonders to what end, unless to play the martyr.[5]

Undaunted by his first venture into darkest Connecticut, Mayhew accepted a second invitation from the Company a year later. When he reached Stonington at the end of September, the Reverend Noyes was sick and could lend no aid. But Joseph, his former Indian interpreter, was found and put to work translating the Lord's Prayer and several sentences of Scripture into Pequot. When Mayhew invited the sachems from the two nearest towns to assemble their people, however, he found them "so out of frame with the trouble they had lately met with, and were still under that he could by no means prevail with them." The trouble began when Groton, Stonington's western neighbor, divided a neck of land on the shore which the Indians claimed. When the new owners erected fences, the natives tore them down, whereupon an English justice assessed the natives damages of £7 or £8 and confiscated as security the smithing anvil and tools of Skuttaub, a sachem. This action, remarked Mayhew with dry understatement, "produced in the Indians a greater aversation to the English and their Religion than otherwise they would have had."[6]

In spite of the legal imbroglio, Mayhew managed to arrange a meeting with Skuttaub and several of his leading men at the house of another justice in Groton. Using an English interpreter, Mayhew gave a brief half-hour speech on the good will he bore the Indians and some fundamental points of the "true Religion." Skuttaub thanked the missionary for his offer, "but objected as a great discouragement to them, the Injuries which they supposed were done them by the English, with relation to the Lands." When he invited Mayhew to return the following April or August, the missionary could only admire his courtesy, since the sachem's tools were being auctioned off that day and he was hurrying off to try to redeem them. Mayhew's parting shot was that if the Pequots became true Christians, "God and Good men" would befriend them and plead their cause at both the civil and the celestial bar.[7]

Two days later the missionary explained "the mysteries of religion" to an assembly of Mohegans, including several of the local sachem's councillors, in a large double wigwam near New London. When his hour-and-a-half sermon was finished, the councillors spent two hours raising objections to Christianity, less by denying its truth than by questioning its utility. The first objection, which nearly all native groups raised, was that "as several nations had their distinct way of worship, so they had theirs; and they Thought their way was Good, and that they had no reason to alter it." Others objected to the unendurable chafing of the yoke of Christ. Their fathers had tried it on at the insistence of the Reverend Fitch, they argued, and "found Religion too hard for them." Another doubting Thomas wanted to know why, if Christianity was so desirable, several praying Indians of their acquaintance had forsaken the English and joined their enemies. Finally, several Mohegans "could not see That men were ever the better for being Christians, for the English that were Christians would cheat the Indians of their Land and otherwise wrong them, and that their knowledge of books made them the more Cunning to Cheat others, & so did more hurt than good." Mayhew's conclusion that "sometimes" the natives "seemed" pleased with his rebuttals undoubtedly put the best light on the situation.[8]

The remainder of Mayhew's errand was hardly more encouraging. A Niantic village in Lyme was crossed off his itinerary because too many people were out hunting, and a scheduled meeting in Stonington was scotched when the Indians spread a rumor that the black robe had canceled it. When fifty natives eventually convened for a farewell sermon, an old powwow stood up to discourage his people from succumbing to the Christian blandishments. Speaking to the missionary's worst fears, he told Mayhew that if any Indians made promises to convert, they would break them as soon as Mayhew left and would soon "be drunk and be as bad as ever." Mayhew set out for Martha's Vineyard the next day with that dark prediction in his ears, perhaps wondering how Christ's kingdom had been enlarged by his peripatetic efforts. He could certainly point to no converts or even warm novices except one: Joseph, his interpreter, with whom he had talked at some length. And even he, it was later reported, soon fell prey to demon rum, after having tearfully confessed his sinfulness to his evangelical employer.[9]

SCENE TWO: *Connecticut, twenty years later*

In 1734, after ten years in the pulpit, the Reverend Richard Treat was dismissed by the first church in Brimfield, Massachusetts. So the forty-year-old graduate of Yale moved his small family back to his hometown of Glastonbury, Connecticut, and began to look for employment. Having preached for a few months after college in Stonington, where Mayhew had had such small success, he had some familiarity with the local Indians and their "benighted" spiritual condition. But working with them, he later admitted, "never was very agreeable" until, on a trip to Boston, he heard the governor of Massachusetts urge the General Court to accelerate the "reformation and Conversion of the heathen in these american parts." He returned home fired up to harvest the savage souls of the Wangunks near Middletown and, coincidentally, a suitable reward from the New England Company. Armed with ten blankets and twenty primers supplied by the Boston commissioners, Treat persuaded the Indians on December 26 to "Submitt" to his instruction in religion and reading.[10]

For the next six months, Treat struggled over English spelling and grammar with a dozen native children and over the mysteries of Christianity with their less adaptable parents. Until April he gave weekly lectures, after which he preached on the Sabbath until he laid his burden down in June for lack of dependable salary and willing audience. Language was a major problem, as it was for all part-time proselytizers. Treat, of course, was a stranger to the Wangunk dialect, and the Indians were "Such Strangers to the written word of God," he complained, "that whatever I Quoted from them had but little effect." "Besides," he continued, "it was very difficult to Impart to them anything of this nature by reason of their brokeness of Speech in the English dialect, and their unacquaintedness with things, as also an aversion thereunto, in Some of them." He painfully remembered the day when he was preaching on resurrection at the Judgment and a native scoffer asked him if a pig lying by the fire "would rise again after it was dead as well as wee." Not very quick on the uptake, Treat silenced the fellow "for the present," but, he confessed, "it was a great while before I Could do it."[11]

Even less repressible were the local traditionalists and their Mohegan and Niantic brethren, who continued to bedevil the preacher well after he had ceased his regular, apparently fruitless labors among them. Late in the summer of 1735 Treat tried to attend one of their great dances, partly to obtain an accurate count of their numbers for the Company and partly "to prevent no little wickedness which they are Commonly Guilty of at Such times." When he approached close enough to hear their forlorn "Singing, dancing, yelling, [and] huming," he was accosted, told he had no business there, and "bid . . . begone." One of them, wrote Treat, "with no little fury, told me that I was Come to see if I might not preach to them the next day, which he said I should not do." The occasion was salvaged only by a group of Niantics and Mohegans who promised to listen to a sermon the next day in a nearby house.[12]

The following morning Treat went to the house but found no audience except a sick child. Thinking to be of some service to the child, he stayed until several of the missing Indians returned and "did what they Could (Except violence) to Drive [him] away." In order to divert his officious attentions still further, a few souls promised to meet him in an apple orchard ten or fifteen rods away. But when he went there, he could hear them at a distance launching into a powwow with "Grunting, Groning, Sighing, &c. . . . Caused by their smiting upon their breast[s]." Apparently, they were trying to divine whether a recently deceased tribesman had been poisoned by witchcraft. Although Treat was "at a Great loss what to do at that time," his missionary instincts propelled him into their midst to break up the "hellish rout." And not without some reasonable fear, for two years later he still remembered "the rage Some of them were in" who seemed as though they would "Immediatly fall upon and rid the world of me." After he interrupted the proceedings a second time that day and allowed them to cool off, he held a Christian service at which, he said, "they were very orderly."[13]

But the natives had obviously decided that if their ex-missionary would not leave them alone, they would leave him to seek the freedom to worship as they wished. "The next morning they went off and dispiersed," Treat noted, perhaps with some relief, "and I Cant learn that they have Ever been there since upon any like occasion." Because he lacked civil sanctions, economic inducements, or personal charisma, Treat's brief mission had done no more than drive the natives' "paganism" underground, where it would remain for most of the century.[14]

ACT TWO: Northern New England

SCENE ONE: *Maine, 1689-1716*

The colonial competition between France and England in the seventeenth century was largely commercial, thanks to the *entente cordiale* between the last two Stuart kings and Louis XIV. England's navy had all it could do to contend with the Dutch, who moved aggressively into the world economy. But the accession of William of Orange to the English throne in 1689 smothered the Anglo-Dutch rivalry and suddenly rekindled England's Protestant animus toward their mutual Catholic arch-enemy. Within months the conflagration had spread to North America, where a sparse French population sought to check the growing demographic superiority of its English neighbors. The only way the eleven thousand inhabitants of New France could hope to keep Massachusetts's thirteen thousand militia from their doors was to rally the intervening Indian tribes as staunch allies.

Fortunately, the French had been forced to cultivate their native neighbors since settlement and had learned the most effective ways to engage the native heart: they fostered the Indians' sovereignty, urged them to preserve their lands, sought to give them the best trade goods at the lowest prices, and drew them tightly to the Catholic faith. Although they were usually better at speaking native languages and adapting themselves to native protocol, French traders could not always beat English prices, material quality, or proximity to markets. In Maine, as Father Râle admitted, Abenakis on the Kennebec had only a two- or three-day journey downriver to an English truckhouse or trading ship, while Quebec was fifteen hard days away.[15] But as missionaries the French had no rivals, and the religion they taught proved to be the strongest link in the covenant chain that prevented the English from sweeping into Canada from northern New England.

The intercolonial wars between France and England thus took on a decisively religious character, particularly in Maine, where European treaty makers and ineffectual conference committees had left the boundary between New England and old Acadia dangerously undefined. Whenever war broke out in America, both parties scrambled to confirm or enlist Indian allies with liberal presents, promises of aid, or doomsday propaganda, but typically and most confidently with preachers or priests. Upon his return to France in late 1689, the marquis de Denonville, recent governor-general of Canada, put the French case succinctly for the Ministry of Marine: "Though the interests of the gospel should not engage us to keep missionaries in all the Iroquois and other Indian villages, the interest of Civil Government for the good of Commerce must see to it that we always have some there, for these native peoples cannot be governed except by missionaries who alone are able to maintain them in our interests and to prevent them from revolting against us. I am convinced by [four years'] experience," he continued, "that the Jesuits are the most capable of controlling the spirit of all the Indian nations, for beside their skillful management, they alone are masters of the different languages because of their long experience among them. . . ."[16]

Ten years later the earl of Bellomont, Denonville's counterpart in New York and New England, gave voice to similar thinking. As a solution to the "Eastern Indian" attacks on the English in the last war, which "insolence" no one doubted was prompted by the French missionaries, Bellomont offered that "the most natural and proper way would be to send Protestant ministers among 'em."[17] By the outbreak of Queen Anne's War in 1702, neither side, French or English, would have argued with the French minister who told the Jesuit superior in Quebec that "the interests of religion and those of the King . . . are in fact inseparable. . . . If the English chase the French out of [Maine], the Catholic religion will not remain there long."[18]

But the French enjoyed one inestimable advantage over their Protestant rivals: Catholic missionaries were ensconced in Abenaki villages long before the English realized the strategic need for native allies, and had converted most of native Maine to the Roman faith. The process had been well begun in the interior by Father Druillettes in the late 1640s and by Capuchins at the mouth of the Penobscot in the early 1650s. In 1687 Abbé Pierre Thury, a graduate of the Quebec Seminary, established a mission on the Penobscot, followed seven years later by Vincent Bigot and Sébastien Râle, who founded the Jesuit mission at Norridgewock on the upper Kennebec. By 1699 at least six Jesuits were living with and administering the sacraments to Abenaki villagers on the Saco, Androscoggin, and Kennebec rivers, all in territory claimed by Massachusetts.[19] Within a short time they built impressive belfried churches and often schoolhouses just outside the village palisades and insinuated themselves into the political and cultural life of the tribes. The longer they stayed, the more indispensable they became to the Indians, whose sovereignty and land became virtually inseparable from what the natives called "prayer." The Abenakis "are not indifferent to their own [economic] interests," Father Râle noted, "but their faith is infinitely dearer to them. . . . This is the bond that unites them to the French." Which explains why Bellomont had the New York and Massachusetts assemblies pass laws in 1700 outlawing all "Jesuits, priests and popish missionaries" from "his Majesty's territories" on pain of perpetual imprisonment or, in case of escape and recapture, death.[20]

The greatest threat to Abenaki land and therefore Catholicism was English settlements eastward up the coast and northward up the rivers. Pushed by imperial demands for pine masts, the steady continental appetite for fish, and local needs for lumber, immigrants and discharged soldiers from Massachusetts, New Hampshire, and (after 1716) Ireland spread inexorably into the territory left in dispute by the treaties of Ryswick and Utrecht. After 1713 Massachusetts (whose jurisdiction included Maine) instituted its own colonial system to buffer itself from New France with its own citizens rather than unreliable native allies. Townships were granted, tax incentives offered, and trading posts and forts built at the mouths of key rivers.[21] When the alarmed Abenakis protested the building of forts on their ancient lands "in peace as though 'twere war," Lieutenant-Governor Dummer replied with a straight face that the forts were built "only against Pirates that might otherwise take away the goods [which the government] had a mind to send that way to trade. . . ."[22]

One sure solution to the steady and dangerous alienation of the Abenakis was well known as early as 1700, when Judge Samuel Sewall urged the province to set aside inalienable reserves for the Indians of Maine. "Except this be done," he warned, "I fear their own Jealousies and the French Friars will persuade them that the English, as they increase, and think they want more room, will never leave till they have crowded them quite out of all their lands. And it will be a vain attempt for us to offer Heaven to them if they take up prejudices against us, as if we did grudge them a living out of their own earth." Even Lord Bellomont thought it "a great scandal to our religion and nation that justice is not done to these poor creatures."[23]

Fair-minded and farsighted officials were few in eighteenth-century New England, however, so the English turned reflexively to the less but still expensive solution of last resort—posting to Maine Protestant ministers whose civilizing program would sharply reduce the natives' need for land and whose religious offerings would seduce them from the Jesuits' "Inchantments and vile Superstition."[24] Yet even for healthy salaries of £100 to £120 a year, full-blooded Harvard graduates were loath to commit themselves to lives of quiet desperation in frontier posts on the frigid Maine coast, much less in squalid native villages where years might pass before they could even learn to speak. Since trading was forbidden and marriage unlikely, the self-denial entailed by such a life could not compete with plusher preferments in English-speaking Bay towns. Those who signed on for two- or three-year stints in Maine were either fresh out of college or hard pressed for work, often both.[25]

While the Indians did not object to the simultaneous English policy of underselling the French at their truckhouses, they did take great umbrage at the official intrusion of Protestant ministers and the ad hoc proselyting of settlers. When the Abenakis captured the English fort at Pemaquid in 1689, one of their chief motives was to expel the settlers who had "interfered with them in the exercise of their religion and prayers." And this was five years before a minister was sent to the fort to establish a school for Indian children.[26]

Even more grievous to the Abenakis were English attempts to replace their beloved Jesuits with Protestant strangers. In November 1699 the Indians assembled to treat at Casco Bay expressed extreme surprise when the English tried to give them "other missionaries than those who now teach them," announcing in no uncertain terms that "the Abenaki will never pray like the Englishman." A year and a half later, at another Casco parley, they slammed the door on an offer to send some of their children to Boston for schooling and to unite with the English in "the true Christian Religion, separated," as the officer so tactfully put it, "from those foolish superstitions and plain Idolatries with which the Roman Catholicks and especially the Jesuits and Missionarys have currupted it." Such effrontery astonished the Abenakis, and they proceeded to put the English in their place. "The English formerly neglected to instruct us in Religion," they jabbed, "which if they had then offered it to us, we should have embraced it and detested the Religion which we now profess; but now being instructed by the French we have promised to be true to God in our Religion, and it is this we profess to stand by."[27] In such a climate, the two green Harvard graduates who had already been posted to Saco and Casco forts must have been thoroughly frustrated in the Indian half of their mission for the remainder of their brief stays.

The English, it seems, were slow learners, even in peacetime, when the need to undercut the Jesuits was somewhat less urgent. Early in 1714 the Norridgewocks approached the governor of Massachusetts for English workmen (whom they would pay) to rebuild their church, which had been torched in an English raid some nine years before. Ever the shrewd diplomat, Governor Dudley offered to foot the whole bill if they would put a Protestant minister in the pulpit when it was finished. To which the Abenakis, through their spokesman, again expressed their astonishment. "When you came here you saw me a long time before the French Governors did; neither those who preceded you, nor your Ministers, ever spoke to me of prayer or of the Great Spirit," the spokesman said. "They saw my furs, my beaver- and elk-skins, and of those alone did they think. . . . If, when you first saw me, you had spoken to me of Prayer, I would have had the misfortune to pray as you do. . . . Therefore," he concluded, "I tell thee that I hold to the prayer of the Frenchman; I accept it, and I shall keep it until the world shall burn and come to an end."[28]

SCENE TWO: *Maine, 1717–1718*

The world certainly had not come to an end by the late summer of 1717, when the Reverend Joseph Baxter was introduced to the Abenakis at the treaty of Arrowsic Island. With characteristic unctiousness, Governor Shute of Massachusetts told the natives that since King George and the people of New England were Protestants, they "would gladly have [them] of the same Religion." Along with an English and an Indian Bible (which unfortunately was rendered in the Natick dialect, unfamiliar to the Abenakis), Baxter was presented as the instrument of this generous English policy. The Abenaki spokesman acknowledged that they revered all men of God, but as for the Bibles, they asked to be excused: "GOD has given us Teaching already," he said, "and if we should go from that, we should displease GOD."[29]

Despite his cool reception, Baxter set up shop at Fort George at the mouth of the Kennebec. The rugged frontier communities he visited during the next eight months must have seemed a far cry from his comfortable congregation in Medfield, where he had served for the past twenty-one years. Ignorant of any Indian language and destined to remain so, he wisely did not attempt to sell his wares in the native villages upriver, in the center of Father Râle's gravity. Instead, he tried to coax Abenaki children into school with toys and "curiosities" supplied by the Massachusetts Assembly, and he pressed the superiority of Protestantism upon any adults who wandered into the English towns. Ten days after he arrived, he told the largest assembly of Abenakis he would ever face—four men and a woman—that the Bible was the only religious guide they would ever need, that they need confess their sins only to God, not man, and that forgiveness came from God alone. Undoubtedly, in the process "he turned into derision . . . all the pious customs that are so sacredly observed in the catholic Religion," as Râle later charged. The only other taste of Protestantism he gave the few natives he met was impressing them with the utter seriousness of shooting a gun on the Sabbath.[30]

To judge by his own journal, Baxter does not seem to have earned his £150 salary in quite the way his legislative employers would have wished. They were probably impressed initially that some Androscoggins requested him to be sent to them, where an interpreter lived, and craved a "small Praying house" for their use with the English of the local fort. But they cannot have been much pleased by his slow linguistic progress, his utter lack of political clout among the Abenakis, or his extracurricular ventures in real estate. The full extent of his Indian vocabulary after eight months consisted of four pronouns, twenty-nine numbers, and three tell-tale phrases: "How do you, I do not care, [and] I forgot." The numbers were of no use in counting his converts because they began with "*Pesegu*—1," and he had none, but they may have aided his land investments around Brunswick and Topsham, where he often preached. With six children at home to feed, Baxter made the most of his long sabbatical down east.[31]

Although he had a visit from the new Jesuit priest on the Penobscot, Étienne Lauverjat, Baxter never met the formidable Father Râle. But he heard from some of the pro-English faction among the Norridgewocks of two of Râle's clever stratagems to keep his parishioners out of Baxter's reach. In mid-October, as huge forest fires were ravaging parts of Canada, Râle reportedly told his neophytes that "the world is now to be gradually destroyed by fire, and that the fire would come to them"—if they did not exorcise their temptations to heresy?—"by Christmas." Sometime in March following, the old priest, who during his twenty-nine years in America had learned to see, hear, and speak "only as an Indian," described in words familiar to the Abenakis a strong vision he had had one night. Awakened by "a great Light as if his wigwam had been on fire," he felt an invisible hand choking him, and heard a voice saying "it is in vain for you to take any pains with these Indians, your children, for I have got possession of them, and will keep possession of them." He also produced a letter written in Abenaki by a deceased Indian who claimed that he was now "burning in a most terrible fire." Clearly, Râle was threatening to leave the Norridgewocks if they did not resist the economic and religious blandishments of the English; he was also ready to excommunicate anyone who got too cozy with the intruders or accepted a political cruise to London. "You must know," he told the Massachusetts establishment, "a Missionary is not a Cipher like a Minister. . . . A Jesuit is not a Baxter. . . ."[32]

But Baxter did not get away scot-free. Just as he was leaving Maine, he felt the full force of Râle's ire for his audacious if unsuccessful irruption upon "Catholic soil." Râle was convinced that his converts "knew how to *believe* the truths which the catholic Faith [taught] but that they did not know how to *dispute* them" with men trained in the scholastic art of logic chopping. So he took it upon himself to "prove by Scripture, by tradition, and by theological arguments the truths which [his Protestant nemesis] had attacked by such stale jests."[33] The chagrin written on Baxter's face when he opened Râle's Latin treatise, which was a full hundred pages long, can easily be imagined, particularly since the Indian messenger was waiting to carry his reply the next day.

The best Baxter could do was to send a curt Latin reply to the effect that he could not be scared off by Râle's "puerile and ridiculous" arguments and would continue to bring the Abenakis into "the straight path of salvation." In a letter to France, Râle, a former professor of rhetoric and Greek, sniffed that the Harvard man's style was so obscure and his Latin so extraordinary that he was forced to read the letter several times "in order to comprehend its meaning." So confident was Râle of his own linguistic and theological advantage that he pursued Baxter, who returned to Massachusetts twelve days later, with another letter chastizing him for the philological errors in his reply. It was two years before Baxter recovered from that insult to play the pedant with Râle's Latin. Although he paid one short and equally fruitless visit to Maine in 1721, partly to inspect his property, Baxter never responded to the Jesuit's hundred-page challenge, perhaps because, as he told Râle, he wished to "Make no friendship with an angry man." The more likely reason is that he felt out of his element in arguing from the history of church fathers and councils rather than the Bible alone. This is the impression he gave when he told Râle that "there are many of us" (meaning Congregational ministers) "who can reply to your arguments and show them to be empty and vain."[34]

One of those capable of standing in for the unpublished and unprecocious Baxter was Cotton Mather, who actually daydreamed about converting Râle, of all people, to Protestantism by "writing largely in the Latin Tongue unto him." He must have soon realized the fatuity of such a plan, for in five months he was backing an Irish Protestant minister in Maine for the slightly less ambitious job that Baxter had had. And the man's qualifications? He had Indian interpreters nearby, and he was so expert in Latin and polemical theology that he "need not be shy of encountering" the dreaded priest.[35] Another of Baxter's surrogates was Governor Shute himself, who felt obliged to defend his missionary's performance from the priest's "Unchristian as well as unkind Treatment." To Râle he wrote, "Certainly, you Cannot Suppose the Main or principal Qualification of a Gospel Minister, or Missionary among a Barbarous Nation, as the Indians are, to be an Exact Scholar as to the Latin Tongue."[36]

Clearly the old Jesuit did not, but he must have relished the discomfort his learned attacks were causing his English adversaries. Although in 1724 they pillaged his church, drove his converts to Canada, and carried his scalp back to Boston, the thought that he had completely foiled their foolish scheme to steal his converts gave him obvious and abundant satisfaction while he lived. Even more gratifying was the knowledge that for a quarter of a century he had helped the Abenakis maintain their political independence and land base

18. Pewter communion vessels from the Norridgewock Indian church, which were hurriedly buried before the church was burned in 1705 and again in 1722 by English troops. The *pyx* or container for communion wafers (center) bears the seal of the Collège de Lyons, where Father Sébastien Râle completed his education before coming to Canada in 1689. Courtesy of the Maine State Museum, Augusta; photo by Greg Hart.

from the incessant grasping of the English. The pity is that this man—and three New England ministers—who wanted nothing more than to live by the cross were made to die by the sword because both France and England subordinated religion to politics in their struggle for continental hegemony.[37]

ACT THREE: The New York Frontier

SCENE ONE: *Iroquoia, 1686–1703*

When the first English missionary to the Iroquois was appointed in 1703, he was neither a Harvard man nor on the payroll of the New England Company. Neither of these negative facts is particularly surprising, but to a long line of colonial officials and Indian leaders they were at least unexpected. For the last fourteen years of the seventeenth century, English governors and legislators had slowly come to realize that Protestant missionaries were badly needed in New York and had launched a feeble search at home and abroad, assuming that the preachers would hail from Harvard and be paid from the "Corporation" coffers. Only after 1701, with the founding in London of the Society for the Propagation of the Gospel in Foreign Parts (SPG), was the institutional apparatus in place for putting an English Protestant in the New York field in the middle of a hot war.

The New Yorkers' major problem was due to the Five Nations' position in the geopolitical center of the Northeast. The Iroquois straddled two major drainage systems (the Mohawk and the Delaware-Susquehanna) within shooting distance of a third (the Champlain Valley or the "Mahican Channel"), which enabled them to reach trading partners—or targets—on the Mississippi, Hudson, or St. Lawrence.[38] Through most of the seventeenth century the Dutch and then the English in New York had little to fear because the Iroquois directed most of their martial energies against the French and their native trading partners and allies. But the advent of Jesuit missionaries in Iroquoia in the interstices of war put a permanent crease in New York's brow. The Iroquois-at-peace not only allowed the "Western" tribes of the Great Lakes to increase the size and frequency of their fur brigades to the St. Lawrence, but began to peddle their own pelts in Montreal rather than Albany.

Even more serious was the demographic depletion of Iroquois villages that occurred when the priests bred religious factions and many of the neophytes withdrew from pagan kinsmen and demon rum to Catholic sanctuaries along the St. Lawrence. This simultaneously gave the French a formidable phalanx of tested warriors for defense and reduced the supply of potential English allies and customers. As early as 1686 Governor Thomas Dongan worried that he had already lost six or seven hundred Iroquois to the French, a concern that ballooned after the outbreak of King William's War in 1689. Within two years New York officials informed the king that the loss of so many natives not only greatly diminished their "hunting" and his "revenue" but gravely endangered the preservation of New York and the rest of the English mainland colonies, since the Iroquois were "the only bullwarke and wall of defence both against other Indians and the French."[39] By the close of hostilities with the French in 1698, the once-dreaded Iroquois war machine had been cut in half by death and emigration; the tribes nearest the English settlements, the Mohawks and Oneidas, had lost six of every ten warriors. Even the peace of Ryswick did little to staunch the human flow. Robert Livingston, the knowledgeable secretary to the colony's commissioners of Indian affairs, complained in 1700 that the Mohawk population grew weaker by the day, "more," in fact, "since the peace." Nearly two-thirds of the nation was "actually at Canada with their familyes, who are kindly received, being cloathed from head to foot, are secured in a Fort guarded with souldiers, & have Priests to instruct them."[40]

Although English officials recognized that the warrior population of Caughnawaga had soared from 80 to 350 since the start of the war, they had some difficulty swallowing the fact—confirmed by numerous Caughnawaga prisoners, traders, and ambassadors—that the Iroquois had migrated to Canada strictly "for Religion's sake."[41] One common way to sugarcoat the bitter truth was to deny the Jesuits' sincerity. When Peter Schuyler and Godfriedus Dellius, the Dutch minister at Albany, went to Canada in 1698 to exchange prisoners, they told the Jesuit superior that his priests were "prompted rather by the desire to seduce our Indians [to Canada] and to enfeeble us . . . than by charity and a design for their salvation."[42]

Another tactic was to insinuate that the French bought their converts. At an important council with the fifty League chiefs in 1700, Lord Bellomont was told that they could not persuade their Catholic brethren to return home because the governor of Canada "has many wayes to draw and keep them; he feeds them when they are hungry and cloaths them when they are naked: for it is the French custome to cloath all those that are baptiz'd and receiv'd into their Church." Bellomont did not have to be told. "Tho' it is the Jesuites' custome by bribes and rewardes to purchase proselites," he replied, "Protestants . . . hold that those only are good Christians who profess Christianity out of faith and a good conscience and not upon the score of worldly interest."[43]

Keen capitalists that they were, the English could at least appreciate how the poor Indians might be seduced by Mammon. But they obviously had trouble understanding why the neophytes would stay in Canada under a religious regime believed to be authoritarian and severe. For this is the picture of Catholicism painted by the Iroquois traditionalists who remained behind. The Onondagas convinced Robert Livingston that the "cunning" Jesuits cozened their converts into giving them a share of every hunt, laying it before the image of the Virgin Mary in church for remission of their sins and her prayers for good luck in the next hunt. Bellomont was even readier to believe that the Jesuits "whip their Proselytes with an iron chain, cut the women's haire of[f], put the men in prison, and when the men commit any filthy sin . . . beat them when they are asleep." To English minds it was indeed "strange to think what authority these priests have over their Indian proselites."[44]

Just how to counter that priestly authority was the English problem; for even after the Jesuits left Iroquoia in anticipation of Denonville's major attack on the Senecas in 1687, one "large Thorn" in the English side—Father Pierre Millet—returned to Oneida as an adopted League chief.[45] One approach was to induce the Canadian Iroquois to return to New York, by hook or by crook. When two Protestant members of a Mohawk war party returned two prisoners to Caughnawaga in 1691, they made overtures to their Catholic brethren about reunion. The Caughnawagas allowed that they would return to the Albany area only if a priest there would teach them the six essential points of religion: "1. forgiving of sins By the preist. 2. prayers for the dead. 3. That the mother of Christ must be worshiped. 4. That the signe of the Crosse must be Used. 5. That the pope alone is ord[a]ined to speak with god. 6. That prayers must be used befor the Images." Apparently, they knew little about the Calvinist theology of Dominie Dellius—or perhaps they knew a great deal and feigned ignorance to stay put. Five years earlier Governor Dongan, a Catholic who had once fought for the French on the continent, had offered to give the Caughnawagas an English Jesuit if they would move to a large reservation at Saratoga, forty miles north of Albany, but they had not bitten on that offer either.[46]

In 1692, some three hundred and fifty Iroquois warriors headed for Canada were instructed to sing essentially the same siren song, but only after a rousing overture of destruction. Peter Schuyler, the mayor of Albany, told the raiders to abandon all thoughts of treating with the praying Indians or their priests, who were "too cunning" for them, and to "give them a Blow at once & Destroy their Indian Corn." Then, he thought, they would be receptive to the English offer of land, provisions for a year, equal treatment with their Iroquois brethren, freedom from pressure to wage war on the French, and, not least, a minister "to Instruct them in the true Christian Religeon."[47] Needless to say, the New York psychology did not work on the Caughnawagas, whose numbers (rather embarrassingly) continued to grow rather than diminish.

Since the English were singularly unsuccessful in luring Catholic Iroquois back to the fold, they threw their energies into ensuring that the rest of the flock did not wander off in search of diviner pastures. The first step was to persuade the Iroquois to remove the jesuitical temptations from their midst. Before the Iroquois took a beating from the French and their native allies in King William's War, English requests and warnings were paid little heed. But after some serious losses in the late 1690s, the Iroquois suddenly realized that they were "overwhelmed and tormented by [the Jesuits] against their will." So in September 1698 the League council at Onondaga agreed not to "suffer any Jesuits to come among us to live."[48]

Yet by February 1700, after the Iroquois waved the white flag, Lord Bellomont was certain that Father Bruyas "and a great many Missionaries besides" were among the Five Nations "practising to alienate them totally from their obedience to His Majesty." His solution, he told the Board of Trade, was to offer the Mohawk and Onondaga sachems "mony or extraordi-

nary presents" to deliver up all the Jesuits they had among them, which
"Vermin" he would send prisoners to England. If he succeeded, "the Jesuits
would never trust themselves again among those Nations." The governor was
wrong—at that date the Jesuits merely *threatened* to put a priest in every
Iroquois village—so his emissaries to Onondaga in April simply expressed his
displeasure that young Mohawks went to Canada "daily" to be instructed by
the Jesuits.[49] But by the end of August Bellomont was ready to get tough with
any priests found among "his" Iroquois. At a major council in Albany, he
privately offered two trusted chiefs from each nation one hundred pieces of
eight for every Jesuit they delivered to him. This followed the spirit if not the
letter of the "Act against Jesuits and Popish priests" passed by the New York
Assembly a month earlier, which in turn was patterned after a law passed by
Parliament in March.[50] The Iroquois spokesmen wisely replied that they
could not arrest the Jesuits until they enjoyed firm peace with their Western,
pro-Catholic enemies, several groups of whom had agreed to move to Iroquoia, and until their Caughnawaga kinsmen had returned home. Whatever
their motives in 1700, after the grand settlement with the French the following year, the Onondagas and Senecas felt free to accept Black Robes during
the winter of 1702–3.[51]

Simultaneously, the English talked of putting their own black robes in
the field to beat the Jesuits at their own game. But English Protestants were
in short supply in heavily Dutch New York, so the governors initially were
forced to enlist the services of the Dutch ministers of Albany and Schenectady—Dominie Dellius from 1689 to 1698 (when a fraudulent land grab
alienated the Mohawks and got him fired) and Bernardus Freeman and
Johannes Lydius after 1700. Although they never left their urban pulpits, the
Dutch enjoyed three advantages as missionaries: they knew the Mohawk
language, their Protestant theology (if not practice) was acceptably rigorous,
and they were familiar with many of the Iroquois who regularly came east to
trade. In the 1690s Dellius used these advantages to baptize 131 natives and
to admit 16 adults to communion, after haphazard instruction from Mohawk
translations he had made of the Ten Commandments and various prayers,
creeds, liturgies, and psalms. As if to emphasize the intimate connection
between religion and political economy, most of their godparents were Indian
commissioners or well-heeled merchants related to one.[52]

The Dutch dominies, however, could do little to sustain the new converts
in their native villages; peripatetic English missionaries were clearly needed to
checkmate the stealthy moves of the Jesuits. Moreover, pro-English factions
among the Five Nations, particularly the Mohawks, begged for visible symbols of English alliance. Most persistent after 1691 were the Protestant
Mohawks who settled at the confluence of Schoharie Creek and the Mohawk
called Tiononderoge, some thirty-five miles northwest of Albany. In their
first year there they petitioned the governor for "ministers to instruct as well
as the French send Preists to instruct their Indians," reminding him that the
Jesuits thought nothing of traveling three hundred leagues to establish a
mission.[53] For the next twelve years the English promised to send ministers to

promote the king's interests and true religion, thereby forfeiting the moral superiority they once claimed over the French who made religion a "pretence" for imperial ambition. But as it turned out, most of the Iroquois were interested less in high English preaching than in low English prices.

Lord Bellomont most clearly focused English desires and frustrations in the missionary business. In 1698 he urged the Board of Trade to procure £300 a year from the New England Company (of which he was a member) to "encourage Protestant Divines to instruct these Indians, and thereby oblige them to the interest of the Crown of England as well as save their Souls." The following summer he heard an angry Iroquois delegation complain not only of high prices and chintzy gifts but the nonappearance of the promised black robes. A year later the three eastern nations of Iroquois renewed their complaint, "admir[ing] that the English cannot as well send a Minister . . . as the French do so many Jesuits among their Indians."[54] When Bellomont met for a week with the fifty chiefs in a "close chamber" in August, he did so with a "heavy heart," less because his guests were ripe with bear grease, smoke, and rum than because he could not gratify them with ministers. But not for want of trying; his offers of £100 a year found no takers, so he renewed his request that the New England Company send two Church of England men of sober lives, young enough to learn the Indian tongue yet scholarly enough to "encounter the Jesuits in point of argument." He also entered a plea with Whitehall for a fort to be built at Onondaga, for "without a Fort," he was certain, " 'tis next to impossible to prevail with the Ministers to live among the Indians." The natives' "nasty" hygiene and "loathsome" food were apparently too much for delicate Protestant stomachs; inebriated Indians brandishing tomahawks definitely were.[55]

Bellomont preferred Anglican priests for several reasons, not the least of which was that "in New England the Ministers pray extempore and mightily decry set forms of prayer." He was also unhappy with the temporary quality of the offer he had received from the New England Company, which offered £80 a year to five ministers—one to each Iroquois nation—for only three years, "provided the ministers be taken out of Cambridge Colledge in New England." The Indians, he thought, needed to know that their missionaries were permanent investments, not future economic casualties. For these and other reasons the Board of Trade pressed upon the archbishop of Canterbury and the bishop of London the urgent need for a separate fund to send Church of England missionaries to America to combat the Jesuits.[56]

In 1701 their wish was granted with the founding of the SPG, but another two years elapsed before a suitable cleric could be found for the New York job. In the meantime, the Iroquois, enjoying the security of the peace with New France and the English competition for their trade, gave voice to their growing disenchantment with empty promises and the religious imbroglio of the previous seventeen years. In June 1701 the League council told the French and English spokesmen at Onondaga, "You are both to[o] dear with your goods. I would have accepted of his [wampum] belt [offering missionaries] who sold the cheapest pennyworth. . . . Wee are sorry we can not pray, but now wee are come to this conclusion: those that sell their goods cheapest, whether English or French, of them will wee have a Minister. . . ." A year later at Albany the chiefs again complained of high prices, trader cheating, and finicky pelt preferences. "As soon as the goods are cheaper here," they lectured Bellomont's successor, "then we will consult about having ministers in our Castles . . . for then we can afford to buy a good honest Coat to go to Church withall, which we cannot now, for it would be scandalous to come to Church with a Bear Skinn on our backs." Only the Protestant Mohawks from Tiononderoge submitted a religious request—for "a good large Church" to replace their "little Chappell made of barke."[57]

And so it would be for much of the eighteenth century. A few of the remaining Mohawks continued to practice their reformed faith as best they could, while the vast majority of "Longhouse People" sought to "come to [them]selves again" after the European contenders had made them "drunk with all [their] noise of praying."[58]

SCENE TWO: *Fort Hunter, 1712–19*

When William Andrews arrived in Albany in November 1712 to assume the post of SPG missionary to the Tiononderoge Mohawks, the sky quite literally seemed to be the limit. Having had previous experience in America, he had some sense of the peculiar strengths and difficulties of an Indian language. His sole predecessor, an impatient, ham-handed man with no cultural sensitivity, had left the post in 1705 after less than a year in the comparatively cozy confines of Albany, which the Mohawks did not seem to hold against him. Thanks to Queen Anne, Fort Hunter had just been completed next to Tiononderoge with four blockhouses for its twenty-man garrison, a chapel, and a house for two missionaries. "King" Hendrick and the principal Mohawk sachems greeted him cordially, and the Albany Indian commissioners took him under their experienced wing. Lawrence Claessen, the government interpreter, was assigned to him to translate from Mohawk to Dutch, and John Oliver, his schoolmaster, from Dutch to English. As the *pièces de résistance*, the queen had donated to the Mohawk chapel a handsome six-piece set of communion plate, an altar cloth, a tasseled cushion for the pulpit, two Books of Common Prayer, and a painted canvas of Her Majesty's imperial arms, symbolizing, of course, the firm union of native church and foreign state. With the additional gift of a dozen large Bibles and painted tables of the Creed, Lord's Prayer, and Ten Commandments from the archbishop of Canterbury, the president of the SPG, Andrews was more than ready to do the Lord's work among the heathen.[59]

During his first year among the Iroquois, Andrews enjoyed a measure of evangelical success. By the spring of 1713, after twice-weekly catechizing and prayer, he had baptized one young man and eight children of baptized parents, and admitted to communion fourteen adults—after repairing the holes in their Christian knowledge left, he assumed, by the Jesuit priests who had baptized them; sixty or seventy regularly attended chapel. A schoolhouse was built and by fall forty boys and girls were grappling with the mysteries of orthographic Mohawk.[60]

But his success was already tempered by a growing apprehension of the obstacles he faced. His most formidable opponents were the Dutch traders of Albany and Schenectady, who "never did very well like of a Minister Settling among them, Except one of their own way, for fear their Trading should be interrupted or their Gaines lessened." Their "Extortion, deceitfull Dealing, lyeing and Cheating" was an odious example of Christian behavior, and they continually poisoned the Indians' minds against the English, "telling that the design of the English in building of Forts among them [was] only to get their Land from them." Even before he arrived, they spread the rumor that Andrews would be an economic burden by demanding "the Tenths of everything [the natives] had." They also equated his Low Church latitudinarianism with "a Popish Religion," and some even suggested that "instruction in Religion [would] do them no good" at all. Perhaps the worst legacy of the traders was the rotgut rum they peddled in native villages, which all too often turned the men particularly into "mad distracted Creatures" who tried to brain the nearest missionary, stab their own wives and children, or burn their houses.[61]

Operating from the relative security of his holy fortress, Andrews did his best to outflank his Dutch rivals and to breach the walls of Iroquois tradition, which in the 1710s were being repaired and raised after years of internecine factionalism provoked by competing European powers. In some theaters his victories continued. By the spring of 1716 he had baptized 16 adults, 54 children, and 54 infants; about 50 Mohawks attended chapel "pretty Constantly . . . . when at home," 38 of whom received the sacrament, and "a great many others" were "Casual hearers." For a village population of 360, these figures were not unimpressive. Yet a year and a half later Andrews was fulminating against the "vile Wretches" in his church who masqueraded as Christians, bemoaning his "ill success," and begging to be transferred to Virginia.[62] What happened to the bright promise of 1712?

Ironically, the first casualty was the school, which from the beginning offered the best of everything except, perhaps, relevance. The sole language of the classroom was Mohawk. The SPG sent great numbers of hornbooks and primers "in Indian" as well as leather inkhorns, penknives to cut quills, and assortments of paper. The birchen regime found in the typical English classroom was jettisoned for fear that fond parents would not think the acquisition of civilized "Learning" worth "the least displeasing" of their young. On the contrary, gifts of all sorts were distributed liberally to promote attendance: food, glass beads, scissors, mirrors in gilt leather cases, rings, buttons, buckles, large-toothed combs, and ear-bobs. When attendance slipped, Andrews requisitioned blankets, shirts, and stockings to persuade ten or twelve children to return to their books.[63]

But slip it did. As early as May 1714, the missionary lamented that "after three or four months most of [the pupils] grew weary of learning and left off coming." Young Mohawks, perhaps more than most children, he admitted, "had rather be at their play than their books." A year later the school population had dropped to twenty, whom Andrews had to feed "or else wee should have but very few," especially during the lean summer months. By the spring of 1716 only six or seven attended—one lame boy who could not hunt and the rest girls—and "they C[a]me so seldom" that progress was glacial. Andrews blamed the traders for telling the Indians that "Learning would doe them no good, that it requir'd much time to attain to it, that it took their Children of[f] from their hunting, or at least if their Children went to School that the [SPG] should maintain them." Whatever the reason for this pedagogical fiasco, a year later the schoolmaster was relieved of his duties and the oversupply of Indian books sent home because they were clearly "of Noe Use here."[64]

Andrews's hopes for the adult generation of Iroquois dimmed as quickly and as completely as did those for the young. By the fall of 1717 chapel attendance had slipped to twenty-five diehards, eighteen or twenty of whom took communion; only two were men, and they were not ashamed to sleep through church in the morning and "be drunk in the afternoon." Six months later the faithful were reduced to fourteen or fifteen. Christian marriages fell off equally sharply, after the spring of 1716, to none; the Mohawks apparently preferred "their own loose way [of] takeing and leaving one another at pleasure." On their sick and death beds putative Christians failed to show any signs of penitence, "no affectionat[e] Expressions, prayer[ful] acknowledgment of sins and sorrow for them, sighs or tears or so much as lifting up of an hand or Eye." To Andrews's jaundiced eye, they all seemed to be in "a very Stupid hardened Condition." After watching such declension with mounting sadness, it occurred to Andrews that even the baptism of their infants, which most parents insisted on to the very end, meant something quite different to the Mohawks. "They are indeed pretty carefull of their Children's Baptism," he noted, because they "conceive that alone is sufficient to make them fit for Heaven, and that there is but little need of doing any thing more excepting a few, who think they are also obliged to receive the sacrament of the Lord's supper once." Good Protestant that he was, Andrews blamed one of his Jesuit predecessors for the Mohawks' dismaying faith in the sovereign "vertue" of baptism because they had seen him baptize enemies about to be burned to death with little or no instruction.[65] But there is no reason to rule out the quick-handed Dutch ministers or the natives' own syncretic creativity as likely causes. Except in extremis, the Jesuits were as scrupulous about baptizing adults as the most hidebound Puritan.

Occasionally Andrews felt obliged to extend his Christian outreach to neighboring villages and tribes, but he was no more successful there. In the spring of 1714 he managed to reach Oneida, where he preached to a hundred and baptized eighteen children and one adult, all of whose parents on one side or the other had been baptized by the Jesuits. But when a number of the infants died soon thereafter, he was accused of the same malevolent shamanism the Jesuits often were charged with during epidemics, and threatened with death if he ever returned. By 1717 the other three Iroquois nations were equally hostile to Christian proselytizing. When any of them passed Fort Hunter en route to Albany, they did not attend services but merely stuck their painted faces in the chapel door to "mock and deride" the participants. Simultaneously, the two hundred Mohawks at the second castle of Canajoharie forbade Andrews and Claessen to visit them again. When the missionary forced the issue and began to preach to a half dozen hardy souls, the traditionalists beat a drum up and down the village to drown him out.[66]

Some of the hostility to Andrews in Tiononderoge and most of it abroad was due to three events that overlapped from 1716. The first was the recent arrival in Iroquoia of fifteen hundred pugnacious Tuscaroras who had been driven from North Carolina after repeated injustices and an abortive uprising. Carrying "an Implacable hatred against Christians at Carolina" and a distrust of Englishmen in general, they soon were adopted by the Iroquois as the sixth fire of the Longhouse, and fostered a spirit of independence and a revival of traditionalism in the confederacy during the 1710s. Andrews concluded in 1717 that the Tuscaroras were "a great Occasion of Our Indians becoming so bad as they are, [so that] they now take all Occasions to find fault and quarrel, wanting to revolt."[67]

The Tuscarora irruption coincided with a deadly outbreak of smallpox in the summer of 1716, which encouraged the Iroquois to resume their traditional mourning wars to assuage grief and replace fallen kinsmen by going on the warpath and torturing or adopting captives. The chief targets were the southern "Flatheads"—the Catawba, Cherokee, and Creek allies of the North Carolinians who had ousted the Tuscaroras. When these traditional enemies coincided in 1715–16 with the military needs of South Carolina, which was trying to put down a revolt of the Yamassees and other "Flathead" trading Indians, New York officials even egged the Iroquois on with powder, shot, and fair words.[68]

To a Protestant missionary, however, this concatenation of revivals meant the resumption of "Old Heathenish practices" that were by definition anathema to the reformed creed. Many communicants had to be debarred from the sacrament because they returned to "their former Evill practices, like the dog to his vomitt, and the sow that was washed to her wallowing again in the Mire." Interpreter Claessen, who had been captured and adopted by the Iroquois as a child, persuaded Andrews that the Indians were practiced hypocrites who played along with missionaries only "as long as they get or are like to get any thing by it." Even the more successful Jesuits were thought to win converts chiefly by pardoning their manifold sins, often for "pay" from the sinners. Mohawks with Canadian connections asked the interpreter why their minister "could not pardon their Sins as well as the Ministers at Canada." This theological liability, coupled with a much smaller budget for native gifts and the eschewing of "beads, Crossing and Pictures," put Andrews at what he regarded as a decisive disadvantage.[69]

Andrews's real nemesis, however, was not less rigorous clerical competitors or gross native materialism but the renewed faith of the Iroquois in their ancient communal ceremonies. When disease cut deeply into a population already decimated by the wars of the seventeenth century, war parties had to be mounted to capture replacements. Before the warriors left, dreams and sweat lodge conjurations had to be consulted about probable outcomes, and offerings of appeasement made to the "Devil." When warriors were killed, their manes too had to be propitiated in elaborate rituals of mourning and condolence between collateral clans and in communal torture, ritual cannibalism, or family adoption of prisoners. Andrews never saw a prisoner burned or eaten at Tiononderoge, but he heard of such grisly rites in other villages and had to deny communion to a Mohawk sachem for biting off a prisoner's nails, conjuring the Devil, and planning the execution of an Indian widow and her two daughters for "bewitc[h]ing his wife's Sister." When it came to savage torture, he lamented, professed Christians were "as bad as the Others, for which thing in particular I never Could have so good Opinion of them as before."[70]

Renewing his plea to be transferred, Andrews projected his growing frustration onto his native neighbors in the spring of 1718. Perhaps the act that finally threw him into despair was the Mohawk sale to a trader of a piece of land they had once promised to the church for the use of a resident minister. Andrews fairly exploded: "They are a sordid, mercenary, beggerly people having but little sense of Religion, honesty or goodness among them, liveing generally filthy, brutish lives . . . through their own sottishness, sloth and laziness. . . . They are [moreover] of an inhumane savage Nature [who] Kill and Eat one another." "Heathens they are, and Heathens they will still be," he concluded, carving an appropriate headstone for his evangelical labors of six years. A year later he consigned the chapel plate and furniture to the fort's commander, packed his saddlebags, and moved to Virginia. There he died within two years, not of mortifying native indifference but of an indifferent mortal disease.[71]

ACT FOUR: The Ohio Country, 1772

Between June 19, 1772, and October 1, 1773, the Reverend David McClure made a 4,268-mile round trip from New Hampshire to the Delaware Indian towns on the Muskingum River in northeastern Ohio, wore out three horses, and converted no one. A bright, twenty-four-year-old Yale graduate and protégé of Eleazar Wheelock, at whose Indian school and new college he taught, McClure had been expected to do better. But like most of his Protestant colleagues who ventured into the western Indian business, he arrived too late and offered too little to entice the Delawares away from their traditional faith or their adherence to the Moravian missionaries who had preceded him by thirty years. The failure of his mission, however, was due less to his personal inadequacies than to the determination of the recently united Delawares to control their own destiny as long as possible, free from the inevitable interference of the English, German, and Scotch-Irish immigrants who were spilling over the Alleghenies at an alarming rate. They knew that to allow an English minister to settle among them was to allow a large spurred boot into the door of their sovereignty, so they gently but firmly closed it on Master McClure while they had the chance.

McClure's preparation for his mission was certainly more adequate than that of most Protestant missionaries. After a softer preparation in the Latin schools of Boston, he attended Wheelock's Indian school in Connecticut, where he played and learned with native boys from several different eastern tribes. Like the Indians, who resented it, he was put to work on Wheelock's farm to learn practical husbandry, "lodge[d] hard" on straw bunks, and lived on plain boiled dishes and Indian corn pudding to inure him to the rigors of his future calling in the wilderness. The summer following his freshman year at Yale he accompanied Samuel Kirkland to Oneida to teach school and to learn some of the native tongue. There, being adopted by the widow of the late sachem, he got his first taste of traditional native culture, but particularly of "the aversion of the human heart to the holy religion of the Saviour." He also learned how to cope with the terrors of drunken Indians, knowledge that would stand him in good stead six years later in the Ohio country.[72]

In 1769 he took his Yale degree and returned to Wheelock's school, first in Lebanon and then in Hanover, to teach three classes of English boys and the handful of remaining Indians. By the spring of 1772, then, when he and a Yale classmate received the invitation of the Scottish Society of New Jersey to introduce Christianity to the Ohio Delawares, he was relatively well prepared except in years and knowledge of the Algonquian dialect of the Delawares. A month after their ordination the two apostles set off for Fort Pitt via Brotherton, the New Jersey village of Christian Delawares under John Brainerd, whom they expected to accompany them west.[73]

In Brotherton the young missionaries got some good news and some bad. The bad news was that Brainerd could not leave, and that a series of recent frontier murders by whites and Indians made the Pittsburgh area distinctly unhealthy for travelers, especially greenhorns. But the good news was that a large group of more docile Susquehanna Delawares was moving to the Ohio to join their brethren, and among the migrants was Joseph Pepee, an able interpreter who had been converted by Brainerd. If the frontier cooled down by the time the ministers arrived, Pepee would see them safely to the Delaware capital at New Comer's Town, where Nettautwaleman presided. So they set off in the August heat, happily unaware of the unfavorable omens that would greet them.[74]

A few days later they met one in the august person of Kayahsota, the powerful Seneca chief, and his interpreter, the soon-to-be-infamous Simon Girty, who were on their way to Philadelphia. When McClure asked the old chief what he thought of their mission, he replied that "he was afraid it would not succeed, for the Indians are a roving people, & they will not attend to your instructions." Moreover, he added, another minister had recently been at one of the Delaware towns on Beaver Creek and had "one half of the Indians . . . offended with the other for hearkening to him." Unhappily for McClure, the social fissure opened at Kuskuskies by the Baptist missionary

David Jones would prompt the council at New Comer's Town to close ranks against his black-robed successors.[75]

At Fort Pitt, McClure put his sick companion under a doctor's care, equipped himself with a wampum belt and speech from George Croghan and a tent and supplies from an officer at the fort, and signed up his Delaware interpreter Pepee and a resourceful manservant who also spoke Delaware, a former captive who interpreted for the garrison. On September 7 the company reached Kuskuskies, a neat Moravian village with houses along a single street and a log church. There McClure attended evening prayer, surrounded by candlelight, paintings of the life of Christ, and melodious Delaware hymns, and decided that the Moravians had adopted "the best mode of christianizing the Indians." "They go among them without noise or parade," he wrote admiringly, "& by their friendly behaviour conciliate their good will. They join them in the chace, & freely distribute to the helpless & gradually instil into the minds of individuals, the principles of religion. They then invite those who are disposed to hearken to them, to retire to some convenient place, at a distance from the wild Indians, & assist them to build a village, & teach them to plant & sow, & to carry on some coarse manufactures." They even built outhouses for them, so attentive were they to the cleanliness of their converts. Impressed as McClure was, a conversation with his Moravian counterpart must have unsettled him somewhat. The principal object of the Moravians, the Reverend Entwine noted, without needing to draw an invidious comparison, was to "carry the knowledge of Jesus Christ among pagans, & not to build on other's foundation, or enter on other men's labors." While he approved of McClure's general design, "he thought it would scarcely be safe for a missionary to venture among the [Ohio] Indians . . . for he had been there & found many of them much opposed to the Gospel." Oblivious to the gentle reproof and warning he had received, McClure set out for the heart of Indian country.[76]

Had he listened to the old Moravian hand he might have saved himself a trip. Fifteen days after he presented his wampum credentials and proposal to "teach them the way to happiness & to heaven," the Delaware council at New Comer's Town ordered the black robe to return whence he came. The tactics they used to reject his offer were numerous and classically native. For starters, they produced an unsigned letter from the Quakers in Philadelphia which promised the Delawares that acceptable missionaries would always bear a certificate from them, which, needless to say, McClure did not have. As the spiritual heirs of William Penn, "the Great *Onas*," the Quakers exercised "unbounded influence" over the Indians of the region; having contributed $100 to aid the migration of the Susquehanna Delawares did nothing to diminish their reputation. Then for two weeks the council made the young minister cool his heels and prohibited him from visiting other villages while the townsmen careened through an interminable drunken "frolic," made possible by eighteen gallons of rum brought from Pittsburgh. Having drunk their fill from wooden bowls, the bacchanalians tore off their clothes and "fought like dogs, biting, scratching," and swearing like traders in

English because their own language was destitute of such foul words. McClure narrowly escaped having his head bashed in during one phase of the proceedings, and was presented with "a long bloody lock of hair" shortly after by a grinning native who had ripped it from the scalp of an obnoxious neighbor.[77]

Two days before the frolic McClure had held his first religious service in the council house, during which he had narrated the life of Christ and explained "the atonement which he made for the sins of men." In the preacher's eyes, "the greater part of the audience appeared stupid and insensible of the importance of what was spoken." On the day of the frolic McClure learned why. His interpreter informed him that some of the headmen "wished I would preach of sin, and tell them what it is. They observed that I had said, they must repent and forsake their sins. They should be glad to know what they must forsake." But the rum intervened, as if to provide a text. When the alcoholic haze lifted, McClure launched a three-day course of sermons on sin to steadily dwindling audiences.[78]

At its conclusion, the Delawares had clearly had enough of the killjoy in their midst. One wag commented that "if all the things which [McClure] had mentioned were *sins*, he believed that all were sinners, and no one was free from sin." Then the speaker of the council lit into the preacher. He pointed out first that if the Great Manitou had wanted the Indians to know the Bible, he would have given it to them when he gave it to the white man. As it is, while the white man must consult his black book to know what to do, the Indian can use his head and "think." Another objection was that "if we take your religion, we must leave off war, and become as women, and then we shall be easily subdued by our enemies." Before McClure could rebut satisfactorily, the speaker complained that "the white people, with whom we are acquainted, are worse, or more wicked than we are, and we think it better to be such as we are than such as they are."[79]

In the end, however, the Delawares' rejection of Christian missions revolved around the crucial issues of land and sovereignty. In explaining why they had disinvited him, the council told McClure with some heat that "they did not like that the white people should settle upon the Ohio. They destroyed their hunting." In the dreamy way McClure used to pause to admire the rich soil and luxuriant meadows of the Muskingum the Delawares no doubt saw a real threat to their "uncontrouled independence & almost unbounded liberty" and, as McClure had seen, "the speedy approach of the time when there would be another race of people there." Talk of purchase and sharing was out of the question for these peoples, who had already been squeezed out of Pennsylvania by such means. Land they did not mind "selling," but, they insisted, "the Elks are our horses, the Buffaloes are our cows, the deer are our sheep, & the whites shan't have them."[80]

So on October 6 David McClure's "disinterested and benevolent errand" into the wilderness came to an abrupt end. "The prospect of being instrumental of much good to these poor & perishing heathen," he lamented, "was no more." Not having shared their language, their culture, or their history, the young pedagogue from Dartmouth could not appreciate the Delawares' decision. Nor could he foresee that in four short years the armed clash of white men would once again drag the Indians into misery, death, and dependence. Their bountiful lands on the Muskingum and the freedom they entailed were doomed as soon as the first shots were fired on Lexington Green. It was only a matter of time before populous towns, "Schools and Colleges & Churches" in "honor of the Saviour would be seen through[out] that extensive & now howling wilderness," just as the minister had envisioned.[81]

AMERICA IN
TRANSLATION

CHAPTER ELEVEN

Preachers, Priests, and Pagans

They have no skill of submission. . . .
THOMAS CHURCHYARD

The Christian missions to the Indians of eastern North America have not received a favorable press from either contemporaries or historians close to the scene, much less those of a more secular bent in our own day. We might expect lay observers to be somewhat skeptical of the inflated appraisals of the missionaries themselves, but the consistently low marks given to both Protestant and Catholic efforts come as something of a surprise. What is perhaps equally surprising is that, while marks are freely handed out, the various missions are seldom distinguished from one another and the standards of judgment are never made explicit.

One obvious reason for such negative appraisals is that many of those passing judgment were avowed or situational opponents of the missionaries under scrutiny. New England Puritans sought to puncture the Catholics' record in New France by ridiculing their alleged propensity for baptizing natives sunk in pagan ignorance or on their deathbeds—the thick and the dead.[1] Jesuits fired a double salvo by suggesting that Protestant "depravity" made such a mockery of the labors of the Recollects that in the friars' first ten-year stint in Canada "almost no progress" was made.[2] To which the Recollects—or their hired pens—retorted that even the English and the Dutch were doing better than the Jesuits, who, since they joined the Recollects in 1625, had propagated "scarcely any Christianity among the Indians, except some individuals in very small number."[3] And to top if off, an anticlerical Canadian officer thought that both orders had "lavish[ed] away all their Divinity and Patience to no purpose" because they refused to recognize "the (almost) invincible Aversion of the Indians to the Truths of Christianity."[4]

Another category of unflattering judgments belongs to the missionaries and their countrymen who found their own labors barren. The English were especially prone to this mode of self-scourging for having neglected the conversion of the natives until colonial land hunger, injustice, and "civilized" vices had "unpeople[d] them."[5] The eighteenth-century editor of an optimistic seventeenth-century description of New England believed that "the christianizing of the Indians scarcely affords a probability of success. As every attempt to civilize them since the first settlement of this country hath proved abortive . . . it will rather appear a Utopian amusement than a probable pursuit."[6] In 1772 Samuel Kirkland, arguably the most effective Protestant missionary to the Iroquois, confessed that "religion is very low with us in the wilderness" and prospects "are very small, or rather none at all." After long experience, he had concluded against his fondest hopes that the Indians were "in a peculiar sense & manner under the curse of Heaven" and "as a people or Nation" would never be called to God at the millennium.[7] A visit to Kirkland's Oneida some years later persuaded the Reverend Jeremy Belknap that conversion of Indians was indeed "a hopeless business." "The numbers who have been converted from Paganism to the rational worship of the Deity, and a regular practice of morality," he lamented, "is not by far equal to those who have either retained their native Superstitions, or changed them for some more glittering and refined"—by which he meant Catholicism.[8] But the English were not alone in their pessimism. Even the Catholic bishop of Quebec told the Vatican in 1788 that "there is little that can be done for the salvation of these barbarians. . . . I was myself a missionary among them several years and I saw how little one can expect from them."[9]

The most critical assessments of the colonial missions were made by two early nineteenth-century historians, a Frenchman in the United States and an Englishman in Canada. After extensive travel in the United States, Alexis de Tocqueville concluded that "the Europeans have not been able to change the character of the Indians; and though they have had power to destroy, they have never been able to subdue and civilize them."[10] In 1825 John Halkett, a director of the Hudson's Bay Company and a champion of the Red River colony, published a damning critique of the major missions in North America, Protestant and Catholic alike. Believing that it was far easier to civilize than to convert Indians, he declared after an extensive review of the sources that the Jesuits had effected little, the Puritans even less. Neither group had left behind any "permanent trace of the real conversion" of the natives, he said, for "while the Romish and the Protestant missionaries reviled each other, the Indian lent a deaf ear to both."[11]

Whatever their particular complaints against the missions, most of these assessments shared four characteristics. First, they admitted—however grudgingly—that the major missionary efforts did enjoy some success, however slight. Second, they ignored any appraisal of the missions' effects on the Indians as individuals or societies. Third, they tended to judge the missions by their long-range or "permanent" effects; the farther the critic stood from the seventeenth century, the more likely he was to find the missions wanting. Finally, with a single exception, these assessments were grounded upon the assumption that the Indians had to be "civilized" before they could be converted. The exception was the Jesuits, who, after 1640, abandoned that policy as impossible and undesirable in order to concentrate on converting the natives to Roman Catholicism. For this they were roundly criticized by the Recollects, who before 1629 and after 1670 pursued the former goal, with a marked lack of success. In 1691 a Recollect spokesman in France complained that none of the Jesuits' native converts "are seen living among French Europeans, but only in neighboring villages, cut off from intercourse, living in the Indian way, incompatible with *real* Christianity" (that qualifier again) "giving no signs of religion but the chant of hymns and prayers, or some exterior and very equivocal ceremonies."[12]

The Recollects notwithstanding, the Jesuits consistently received the highest marks from the critics for effort if not effect. Recognized by all as "indefatigable," the Jesuits won points for their adaptations to native life, their well-regulated *reserves*, their positive outlook on native ability, and their political and pedagogical skills. Baron de Lahontan, no admirer of the priesthood, noted that the Recollects branded the Indians as "stupid, gross and rustick Persons, incapable of Thought or Reflection," while the Jesuits entitled them to "good Sense, to a tenacious Memory, and to a quick Apprehension season'd with a solid Judgment."[13] Large and flourishing Jesuit missions, small and languishing Recollect missions were the result. Perhaps the Jesuits were respected most by English Protestants who suffered from their effectiveness. Dr. Belknap of New Hampshire and Sir William Johnson of New York prescribed the Jesuit "reductions" in Paraguay as a cure for English missionary ineptitude, and commended the Jesuits for conforming to the natives' manners and "follow[ing] them in their peregrinations through the wilderness."[14] Jonathan Edwards, recently posted to the frontier mission of Stockbridge in western Massachusetts, credited his Jesuit adversaries not only with zealous pursuit of their religious goals but with using "all the arts & subtle management" of the Roman Church to win the political allegiance of most of New England's Indian neighbors.[15] For better or worse, the Jesuit missions appeared to contemporaries of all persuasions to be the most successful.

From a European perspective, the Jesuits' contemporaries were undoubtedly right. The English missions, which were all based on a "civilize first" philosophy, were confined effectively—in the seventeenth century, exclusively—to southern New England. There, by 1674, John Eliot, the Mayhews, and a number of colleagues had gathered nearly twenty-three hundred "Souls yielding obedience to the gospel" from local tribes which had been battered by disease, frightened by English power, and increasingly deprived of their land by fair means and foul. A sizable minority of these "praying Indians" had been baptized or admitted to full membership in highly selective Indian churches, having been nurtured on the Bible and other devotional works translated into a Massachusett dialect. By the American Revolution, there had been at various times in New England 22 Indian churches, 91 praying towns or reservations, 72 white missionaries, and 133 native preachers and teachers. In the eighteenth century many of the natives dressed in English clothes, lived in English houses, followed English trades or farming, and lived under English laws. Most spoke English, which some acquired in English schools. Perhaps 500 Indians had crossed the cultural divide to become Anglicized Christians in all but color and perhaps memory.[16]

The other colonies fell far short of the Puritan standard for both conver-

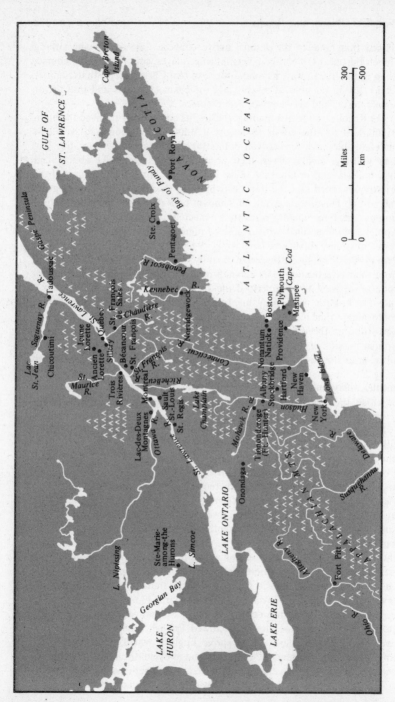

NORTHEASTERN NORTH AMERICA: THE THEATER OF COMPETITION

sion and civilization. Neglecting to send ministers to the natives, the Virginia Company concocted a grandiose scheme for an Indian college and collected a great deal of money toward it, but the Powhatan uprising in 1622 blasted any hopes of implementing it. Early in the eighteenth century Governor Spotswood briefly sponsored a school at a frontier fort, but that too collapsed with the loss of his fur trade monopoly there. In 1724 the College of William and Mary raised a handsome building for Indian students, but the few who attended came too late, left too early, and died or took sick in an urban setting, much like the handful of Indians at Harvard in the seventeenth century.[17] In Pennsylvania the Quakers did not believe in proselyting except by quiet example, but the Moravians, a German sect, met some success in converting Delawares and Mahicans and gathering them in Europeanized towns to farm and to pray. Not surprisingly, many of their missionary methods resembled those of the Jesuits.[18]

Partly to halt further Jesuit inroads upon the Iroquois and partly to keep New England Congregationalism at bay, the Society for the Propagation of the Gospel maintained a broken series of Anglican missionaries at British forts in Mohawk country throughout much of the eighteenth century. Anglican prayer books and Scripture were translated into Mohawk, and Queen Anne handsomely endowed a chapel for the converts, but the New Yorkers did little more than hold a portion of the Mohawks in the British alliance; nearly half the tribe had moved to Sault Saint-Louis opposite Montreal in the last two decades of the seventeenth century to become Catholics.[19] In South Carolina the SPG priests confined themselves to the coastal settlements, where only a few Indians were ministered to among white colonists and black slaves.[20] David Brainerd had a moment of spiritual success in New Jersey during the Great Awakening, but he died at twenty-nine, and his brother John never caught fire in the same way, although he oversaw a dwindling congregation until the Revolution. When another missionary visited him in 1773, he "mourn[ed] the little success of his labours among them"—which might well serve as an appropriate epitaph for the fitful efforts of most of his Protestant colleagues in the eighteenth century.[21]

But even the Puritan performance was not as solid as its statistics seem to suggest. Several tribes in Connecticut and Rhode Island stoutly resisted Christian blandishments well into the eighteenth century. Schools failed notoriously to turn Indian children into English adults. Even Eleazar Wheelock's famous Indian school in Connecticut enjoyed a success rate in the *short* run of less than 30 percent during its sixteen-year life; most of its students dropped out prematurely or apostatized soon after graduation.[22] The great majority of praying towns were also short-lived and soon lost to the Indians because of white land pressure, debts, and ineffective white overseers. The land base of Mashpee on Cape Cod was unique in being inalienable except by unanimous consent of its native inhabitants, a provision inserted by its missionary progenitor that preserved the town in Indian hands until 1870.[23] By contrast, Natick, the centerpiece of Eliot's enterprise, had been overrun by white settlers by the mid-eighteenth century. Likewise, most Indian churches died by the nineteenth century as native populations melted away; only Mashpee (which became solidly Baptist by 1830) and Gay Head on Martha's Vineyard survive today.

Moreover, most of New England's Indian converts had no viable alternative. Surrounded by native enemies and proliferating English settlements, and decimated by inexplicable diseases, they were quickly thrown into political, social, and religious disarray. Eliot's colonial equivalent of the Marshall Plan seemed to many to offer the best or the only hope for demographic survival and cultural regeneration. And finally, the Puritans' goal of extensive "civilization" before conversion inevitably entailed a high rate of failure, even among putative converts. Native social values, dress, housing, work patterns, language, and religious rituals survived and even flourished in many praying towns. While traditional families of "the blood" assumed leadership of the new communities, surrounding English ethnocentrism and later racism helped the natives to maintain enclaves of Indian identity which may have looked English but continued in many respects to feel, think, and believe Indian.[24]

In marked contrast to the lackluster Protestant performance among predominantly small, weakened coastal groups, the Jesuits enjoyed remarkable success with large, powerful, sedentary groups around the Great Lakes and with mobile hunting bands all over New France. Having abandoned early a mission policy that sought to civilize the natives by settling them among the French and transforming every aspect of traditional culture, the Jesuits poured their considerable resources and energies solely into the Indians' religious conversion and the moral reform of those native practices that contravened essential tenets of Catholic dogma, such as polygyny and divorce. Rather than demanding that the Indians move to French territory, where they would inevitably fall from grace at the invitation of French brandy sellers, fornicators, and gamblers, the priests traveled to Indian country to learn enough language and adopt enough customs to become accepted by the natives as one of them. Their ultimate goal was to replace the native shamans, to lead whole tribes and villages to Christianity, and to establish Catholic churches for the sustenance of their neophytes. If that proved impossible, the alternative was to draw Christian factions away from their pagan kinsmen to settle morally guarded *reserves* along the St. Lawrence, though at arm's length from the major French towns.

By the beginning of the eighteenth century, 115 Jesuit fathers and numerous lay brothers had established some thirty missions across New France, from Nova Scotia through Maine, Quebec, Ontario, and New York to Michigan, Wisconsin, and Illinois. In succeeding decades, with the addition of another hundred priests, the Society planted the cross in Louisiana and the Ohio Valley.[25] It is impossible to calculate the number of Indians they converted in this enormous effort. Some idea of its magnitude may be gained from the number of baptisms apparently underrecorded in the Jesuit *Relations* between 1632 and 1672: a careful Jesuit historian counted 16,014 souls who received the rite, about a third of them on their deathbeds. But in 1653

Father Bressani testified from personal knowledge that some 12,000 Hurons alone had been baptized, most of whom had succumbed to epidemics or Iroquois war parties. Whatever the number of moribund baptisms, we are left with an impressive sum of more than 10,000 natives, mostly adults, who chose to become Christians after long and painstaking instruction by the priests.[26] For the Jesuits, consciously avoiding the mass baptisms of the Spanish friars, feared that the natives "would soon show a contempt for [their] holy Mysteries, if they had only a slight knowledge of them."[27] Apostasy was worse than paganism.

Another measure of the Jesuits' success is the number and fidelity of *reserves* established along the St. Lawrence. Excluding the first, Sillery, all seven *reserves* were populated by Indians who had exiled themselves from their kinsmen and communities, many of whom had been or still were deadly hostile to the French. Many converts, particularly Abenakis and Iroquois, were potential English allies and stood to gain economically by turning south. Instead they willingly sacrificed material advantage for the Black Robes' religion, at the same time serving as military counterweights to the imperial designs of the more numerous English. When Montcalm's army assembled in 1757 for the attack on New York's northern forts, 820 warriors from the *reserves* and three of their French priests fell in, including 363 Iroquois into whose former country the army was headed. In another war a missionary had correctly observed that "nothing else than religion retains the Indians in their fidelity to the French." Montcalm's aide-de-camp agreed. Of his native troops he said, "all real control is ecclesiastical."[28]

Indian converts not only left their homelands to embrace Catholicism, but after the fall of New France the vast majority remained in the Faith, at times with no priests to guide them. The Micmacs of Nova Scotia and New Brunswick were typical. After Jesuits had introduced them to Christianity in the seventeenth century, other priests who had thoroughly adopted the Jesuits' time-tested methods completed their conversion in the eighteenth. When these political priests could not stem the English tide, the French were expelled and the Micmacs were subjected to a determined campaign of decatholicization by the transplanted New England Company, which had spearheaded Eliot's missionary thrust and its successors. By conserving Catholic prayers, hymns, and catechisms in homemade books written in the Micmac hieroglyphic, by faithfully celebrating the feast of their patron saint, and by baptizing infants with a special formula designed by the missionaries, the Micmacs preserved their identity as Catholics, which they have maintained ever since.[29] By the same token, the former Laurentian *reserves* are still Catholic, more than two centuries after the British Conquest.

How can we account for the Jesuits' pronounced superiority in the mission field? To survey the question properly we should look at three areas: French colonial settlement, Roman Catholicism, and the Jesuit order itself.

Unlike the swarm of English farmers, the few French colonists in the St. Lawrence Valley and elsewhere did not settle on occupied Indian lands and proceed to alienate the natives by their insatiable demand for more. Although

the Jesuits had to contend with the pernicious example of French traders and
soldiers, the Indians were not deprived of their homelands by the miscreants.
Moreover, the dependence of New France's small and sexually imbalanced
population on Indian trappers, porters, and mercenaries fostered a greater
tolerance of native culture. The French readiness to marry Indians stood in
marked contrast to the ethnocentric disdain of the more balanced English
population for such "mongrel" matches.

Another advantage was the nature of Catholicism. The contrast between
Catholic and Protestant was not a distinction between emotion and intellect,
for both religions were at bottom devotional movements, rooted in religious
experience and aimed at the heart as well as the head. Both were, in that
sense, popular religions, with a common source in Scripture and medieval
Catholic practice. Despite the similarity of methods, however, Catholicism
posited a "divine spark" that survived the Fall and remained unblemished by
Original Sin. While Protestants denied that man could do anything to
achieve his own salvation, Catholics encouraged him to elect God, to seek
salvation through good works, right living, and faithful worship.[30] Although
the Indians originally entertained no well-defined idea of heaven or salvation
in an afterlife, they found more sense in the possibility of earning their future
condition than in having it given or denied them regardless of a lifetime of
intentions and actions.

Catholicism was also highly liturgical, appealing to all the senses as well as
to reason. In native hands the Jesuit priest put attractive medals, rings,
crucifixes, and rosaries as mnemonic devices to recall his oral message. To
their noses he introduced the mysterious fragrance of incense, which resembled their own tobacco offerings to the Great Spirit. To their lips he lifted
holy wafers. To their eyes he offered huge wooden crosses, candlelit altars
rich with silk and silver, long brocaded chasubles, and pictorial images of the
major acts in the historical drama of Christianity. And into their ears he
poured sonorous hymns and chants, tinkling bells, and a steady stream of
Indian words. Although Christianity was a prophetic religion that put a
premium on the faithful adhesion of will to a theology, Catholicism over the
centuries had become more like a religion of tradition, in which practice is
paramount. Indians who practiced their own tolerant traditional religions
found it easier to advance to understanding of the Christian creed through
affective Catholic rituals than through formal Protestant "harrangues" of
"abstract truth."[31]

A third Catholic advantage was the Church's attitude toward women. With
the cult of the Virgin and several indispensable communities of nuns in
Canada, the Church had role models to attract the women of native tribes, in
many of which women enjoyed more status than in European societies and
the founding culture heroes were nurturing women. It may also be that
Indian women who suffered from a lack of men, particularly during the
Franco-Iroquois and intercolonial wars, found in virginity a practical as well
as a spiritual solution.[32]

As important as the character of French settlement and Roman Catholicism were, the major credit for the Jesuit successes must go to the Jesuits themselves. Personally created by the pope and answerable directly to him, the Society of Jesus was blessed with mobility, discipline, and wealth. Although its members took a vow of poverty, the order itself enjoyed substantial revenues from testamentary bequests, lands in France and Canada, and royal subventions. This freed its numerous personnel from parish work to combat heresy and paganism wherever in the world they flourished; Puritan ministers, who were tied to a congregation for ecclesiastical validation, had to rely on the uncertain support of lay societies of English benefactors if they wished to undertake Indian missions in their spare time. And while the Society was a collection of distinct, often strong-willed individuals, they were bound by a vow of unquestioning obedience to their superiors, which gave their teachings more consistency than Protestants could obtain from their atomistic encounters with the Bible. The catechism heard by an Indian in Sault Sainte-Marie would not be contradicted by that taught in Quebec City.

The individual preparation of the Jesuits was also superior. When they arrived in Canada at an average age of thirty-four, they had been educated in the finest schools and colleges of Europe—their own. Most had taken seven years of philosophy and theology beyond the B.A. in classical humanities, and virtually all had taught in Jesuit colleges for some years to sharpen their pedagogical skills for the task ahead. Their linguistic and rhetorical training in the learned languages of Greece, Rome, and France, while it was limited in some technical areas, prepared them well for acquiring the native languages of North America.[33] By contrast, the Harvard graduates who devoted any time to Indian missions were typically in their mid-twenties, with only home study in theology after the B.A. to their credit. Socially and intellectually, they had ranked in the bottom third of their classes.[34]

The Jesuits' final and perhaps most important advantage was their attitude toward native culture. Unlike the Dominicans and Franciscans within their own church and the Puritans and Anglicans without, the Jesuits articulated and practiced a brand of cultural relativism, without, however, succumbing to ethical neutrality. While they, like all missionaries, sought to replace the Indians' cosmology and religion with their own, they were more willing than their Christian counterparts to adopt the external lifestyle of the Indians until their goal could be realized. Rather than immediately condemn and destroy what they found, they carefully studied native beliefs and practices and tried to reshape and reorient them in order to establish a common ground on which to begin conversion. In large measure, whatever success the Jesuits enjoyed was gained not by expecting less of their converts, as the English insisted, but by accepting more.

Although the Jesuits possessed several advantages over their English rivals, by no means did they enjoy universal or permanent success in converting the Indians to Christianity. While the English record was downright poor, except in southern New England, contemporaries were not wrong to suggest that the

French missions too had not fulfilled their founding goals of converting native America to European religion and culture. The reasons are not difficult to find. In fact, they are so plentiful and so overwhelming that we should rather wonder how the missionaries achieved as much success as they did. The usual explanations, those most commonly given by contemporaries in a spirit of halfhearted expiation, pointed to the regrettable but inevitable results of contact with European cultures: disease (to which the Indians had no immunities), avarice (especially for native farm lands and clearings), war (fomented by European trade competition and exacerbated by European firearms), alcohol (for whose use the natives had no cultural sanctions), and the immoral example of false Christians (who, instead of raising the Indians' sights, "reduced them to civility"). Cotton Mather spoke for many when he confessed that the Europeans had "very much Injured the Indians . . . by Teaching of them, Our Vice. We that should have learn'd them to *Pray*, have learn'd them to *Sin*."[35]

While no one would deny that these external forces did much to undermine the missionary program, we will never understand the conversion process unless we shift our perspective to the Indians and ask why they chose or chose not to convert to the new religion. For no matter how skillful, devoted, and energetic missionaries are, conversion is ultimately a personal, voluntary act of individuals, a decisive act of reason, faith, and will that no one can make for them. When the natives came to exercise their options, they found many good reasons why they should hold fast to their traditional beliefs, customs, and rituals.

In native society, change was kept at bay initially by the conservative inertia of habit. Familiar ways were physically softer, psychically safer, and socially smoother than new ones. Unspoken codes of social behavior and cultural understanding were widely shared with kinsmen and tribesmen, and the "fear of what others would say" was a potent factor in the oral intimacy of woodland society.[36] Change also bred competition for material and spiritual resources, and competition bred factions—or fed existing ones—which pinched the placid face of village life. Even the missionaries' promise that converts would go eventually to the Christian heaven carried the implicit threat of separation from loved ones and relatives in the traditional land of the dead. "We are well as we are," protested a Massachuset woman, "and desire not to be troubled with these new wise sayings."[37]

The sharp exclusivity of Christianity in all things—rituals, morality, afterlife—was to Indian thinking not only divisive but foolish. When new Christian gods and spirits could be added to the traditional pantheon without cultural dissonance, it made little sense to put one's whole trust in such novelties until they could be tested by time. The limber pragmatism of native religion was especially attractive when missionaries from many denominations hawked their spiritual wares while proclaiming the one true faith.

For traditional Indians, conversion to Christianity had three other serious drawbacks. First, it diminished their intellectual independence by imposing upon them spiritual directors and culture brokers from an alien, often hostile world. If the natives were forced to swallow greater dependence on European trade goods and military allies, they could at least choose to remain at ideological liberty. Secondly, most of their tribesmen who received a Black Robe's moist benediction upon their foreheads died shortly after, apparently the victims of the white man's sorcery. Not without reason, many natives thought that "believing [in Christianity] and dying were one and the same thing."[38] Finally, it took little time for the Indians to discover that the Christian preoccupation with the future cast a pall on the traditional pleasures of the present. To enter the "narrow way" of scriptural conformity was to submit to a weekly Sabbath and daily abnegation that frowned on familiar feasts, songs, dances, games, and cures, on sexual relations and even economic necessities such as hunting and fishing. Why should we pray to God and believe in Jesus Christ, asked some of Eliot's first auditors, when "our Corne is as good as yours, and wee take more pleasure than you?"[39]

Strengthened by arguments such as these, the Indians' "hereditary prejudices" toward their own religious culture greatly frustrated the missionaries who labored to wean them from it. But when traditionalist arguments were illustrated with examples from "the Contemptible State of the domesticated Tribes" (as Sir William Johnson described them), potential converts dug in their heels even deeper.[40] Those Senecas who listened to a war chief declaim against the foreign presence of Samuel Kirkland and his Holy Book would have thought long and hard before opening their ears to the stranger. "Brethren attend!" intoned Onoongwandikha. "You may be assured, that if we Senecas . . . receive this white man and attend to the Book which was made solely for white people, we shall become a *miserable abject people*. . . . How many remnants of tribes at the East are so reduced, that they pound sticks to make brooms to buy a loaf of bread or it may be a shirt. . . . Why, their grandsons are all become *mere women*! . . . [I]f we change or renounce our religion for that of the white people, we shall soon lose the spirit of *true men*. . . . We shall be sunk so low as to hoe corn and squashes in the field, chop wood, stoop down and milk cows *like negroes* among the Dutch people."[41]

Behind the worried words of the Seneca warrior lay more than two hundred years of cultural resistance by eastern natives who thought their own ways at least equal, if not superior, to those proffered by the missionaries. When the missionaries overstepped the native bounds of courtesy and pressed them to change their thinking, the Indians time and again made a characteristic response. If during a theological debate with the missionary a native leader was not convinced of the wisdom of the Christian position, he would close with a subtle plea for toleration. "All your arguments," warned Pierre Biard from experience with the Micmacs, "and you can bring on a thousand of them if you wish, are annihilated by this single shaft which they always have at hand, *Aoti Chabaya* (they say), 'That is the Indian way of doing it. You can have your way and we will have ours; every one values his own wares.'"[42] By a similar tactic the Hurons tried to dampen Father Brébeuf's ardor for their conversion. "Do you not see that," they asked him, "as we inhabit a world so different from yours, there must be another heaven for us, and another road to reach it?"[43] Sometimes the rejection could be even more pointed. The Iroquois at Shamokin minced no words in spurning the offer of David Brainerd in 1745 to settle among them for two years, build a church, and call them together every Sunday "as the whites do." "We are Indians," they announced, "and don't wish to be transformed into white men. The English are our Brethren, but we never promised to become what they are. As little as we desire the preacher to become Indian, so little ought he to desire the Indians to become preachers."[44] The preacher left the next day.

In the face of so many compelling reasons for standing pat, it might seem strange that Indians even considered changing their religious ways. Yet, to judge from the number of native converts in the colonial period, many obviously entertained the possibility long enough at least to reject it. What impelled them to give a hearing to the missionaries? What was capable of penetrating their cultural complacency and glacial indifference to normative novelty?

Contemporary critics of the missions and historians of a similar disposition have insinuated that many—even most—of the Indians who listened to the missionaries were "wheat and eel" Christians, beggarly hypocrites who grunted assent to the missionaries' preachments only as long as they were offered a pipe of tobacco, a nip of brandy, or a handful of biscuits. Understandably, the critics' suspicions increase when the missionaries or their political benefactors raise the material ante. When converts are given military garrisons in besieged villages, discounts at the company store, elaborate gifts, and exclusive rights to purchase firearms, as they were in Huronia, skeptics' eyebrows fairly soar. The difficulty with such wholesale incredulity is that gifts were the lubricant of all native social interaction, and a missionary who tried to gain an audience without them would have preached to the trees. Moreover, the missionaries in general were keen judges of character and kept a sharp eye on their native neophytes "least they should onely follow Christ for loaves and outward advantage."[45] We can find more bona fide reasons for native interest in the missionary message.

At the top of any list must be simple curiosity. French missionaries, after all, were among the first Europeans seen in Indian country. Not only did they share the white-skinned, hirsute appearance of their countrymen, but they affected dress, speech, and mannerisms that marked them as different even from the other strangers. To be inquisitive about men who carried no arms, avoided sex, and cared nothing for land, beaver, or brandy was, under the circumstances, only natural.

In the cautious conformity of an Indian village, however, mere curiosity might not be enough to draw an audience to the new preachers. Someone needed to take the first step, to take their fingers from their ears when the black robe appeared, preferably a person of respect—an elder kinsman, a hospitable sachem, a shaman sizing up his competition, or a trading captain who had filled his packs and senses with the minor miracles of a colonial town. Where one stepped, others would follow. "Such," reported the Jesuits, "is the influence exerted by the example of the leaders of provinces and cities over the minds and conduct of the people."[46]

Curiosity could turn to respect if the missionary, after a suitable apprenticeship in native ways, proved himself to be a "man of sense." Anyone who was impatient to perfect the native tongue, generous of mind and hand, and polished in the art of protocol stood a good chance of gaining auditors for his religious lessons. If he was also armed with some of the brighter products of European science and technology, his chances increased dramatically. A man who could manipulate a magnetic compass, tell a clock to chime, predict an eclipse, or know the (written) thoughts of a distant colleague was a man worth listening to.

In the end, numbers of native people not only attended the Christian Word to satisfy their curiosity but accepted it to fulfill a serious need. During the colonial period many Indians became Christians, both genuine and nominal, and adopted in some degree European ways. They did so because they were persuaded that the Catholic, Anglican, Moravian, or Congregational faiths spoke more to their spiritual and cultural condition than did traditional religions. It remains to explain the existence and variety of these conversions while at the same time accounting for those Indian groups who remained stubbornly traditional.

Any explanation must begin with the continuous, long-term changes in native religion that occurred before the arrival of Columbus and his successors. As archaeology, folklore, and historical linguistics prove without question, no aspect of pre-Columbian Indian culture was static. Therefore we should resist the temptation to judge postcontact changes as either happy or tragic deviations from a noble norm of savage innocence. Purposeful change and adjustment was the only norm.

The first discernible changes occurred very early in the precontact period, when native groups borrowed particular beliefs, myths, culture heroes, religious artifacts, ceremonies, and even whole cults from other groups, some at considerable distances via long-established trade routes. Through this continuous process of borrowing and transfer, tribes in contiguous culture areas, such as the northeastern woodlands, came to share a large number of religious traits.

The next round of changes took place in response to the bruited arrival of the Europeans in the period of proto- or indirect contact. Before they actually met any Europeans, many tribes encountered often fabulous stories of white "gods" or "spirits," some of the products of their awesome technology, and their selectively lethal diseases. When the invaders finally appeared in Indian villages, thereby inaugurating the period of direct contact, the crisis of intellect precipitated by rampant sickness and death, novel forms of magic, and the unknown was only exacerbated by the need to account for the existence of strange bearded men with pale skin and barbarous tongues who were obviously not, like the natives themselves, "original people."[47]

The Indians responded to this general crisis in a variety of ways, depending largely on their geographical and political distance from colonial authority, their economic independence, the health of their population and the succession of leadership, their strength relative to neighbors who may have become allied with the invaders, and their intellectual and emotional flexibility and morale, which was the product of their recent past experience.

Tribes that still enjoyed relatively healthy populations, stable social structures, and political and economic independence could choose to deal with the Christian missionary in at least four ways. They could, as many groups in New England did, direct a steady stream of searching questions at him about the consistency of his theology.[48] Or they could question its applicability to their culture by unleashing their polite but frustrating "secret weapon" of outer agreement and inner disagreement. On the other hand, if the proselytizer annoyed them enough, they could simply ignore him until he despaired and went home, or if he persisted, they could chase him away with arms or kill him as a troublemaker and witch. Whatever course of action they chose, the result was the persistence of traditional religion and the unimpaired authority of the native priest.

Sooner or later, all the eastern tribes began to lose their aboriginal sovereignty and strength. As colonial settlements drew closer, disease tore at the native social fabric, leaving gaps in the web of kinship, political succession, technological expertise, and corporate memory. Trade goods from the shops and factories of Europe became desirable luxuries, then necessities. Entangling alliances forced the tribes into the periodic embrace of the colonial governments when they could no longer play them off against each other. And missionaries were emboldened to plunge into native cantons in search of converts. In these dangerous though not yet fatal circumstances, the native community split into factions as different individuals and interest groups variously perceived the nature of the problems facing them and the best solutions. A dissident minority always had the option of voting with its feet, as was common in pre-Columbian times, by moving to either a more traditional village or a Christian praying town or *reserve*. More frequently, factions stayed to fight for the political and social control of community resources and its future religious and cultural direction.

Those who saw an urgent need to adjust to post-European conditions without surrendering their ethnic and cultural identity could exercise two options—if both existed. The first was to join a revitalization movement led by a native prophet or charismatic figure who warned the Indians to reaffirm their ancient beliefs and resume their ancient ways before the Europeans captured their spirits as well as their furs. Many of these leaders, such as the eighteenth-century Delaware Prophet and Handsome Lake in the early nineteenth century, incorporated Christian elements in their religions while clearly rejecting Christianity itself. Many others, however, were intolerant of any foreign intrusions, seeking to restore their culture to an imagined precontact purity.[49]

A second option was also to revitalize native culture but through the selective use of Christianity rather than nativism. Tribes who escaped the worst maladies of European contact had little need of the full "civilized" cure offered by the Christian doctors. To have taken it would have brought on cultural suicide. But the complete prescription did contain some useful ingredients, such as political and military alliance, guaranteed land, economic aid, and trade advantages. If to obtain them the Indians had to swallow the bitter pill of religious conversion, the sacrifice was small enough, especially if Christianity truly satisfied some new intellectual or emotional hunger. If there was none to be satisfied, the convert could simply, in time-honored Indian fashion, add the power of the Christian God to that of his own deities and proceed to syncretize the beliefs and practices of the new religion with the deep structures of his traditional faith. By accepting the Christian priest as the functional equivalent of a native shaman and by giving traditional meanings to Christian rites, dogmas, and deities, the Indians ensured the survival of native culture by taking on the protective coloration of the invaders' culture. Obviously, this brand of Christianity often lay very lightly on the surface of their lives, its acceptance largely expedient to ensure their independence and group identity. But many Indians found in Christianity genuine sources of spiritual strength that helped them cope with their rapidly changing world. As John Smith noticed very early, "all things that were able to do them hurt beyond their prevention, they adore with their kinde of divine worship."[50]

Several tribes who responded even more positively to the mission offerings were the coastal Algonquians of southern New England. So seriously were they crippled by a plague in 1616–18, and so thoroughly overrun by the colonial juggernaut in the following two decades, that only John Eliot's complete program of moral rearmament, social reconstruction, and religious revitalization was capable of saving them from ethnic annihilation. Lacking any viable options, large numbers of them, led in many cases by traditional leaders of "the blood," converted to Christianity and the English way of life that accompanied it. Even though their conversion entailed wholesale cultural changes, it preserved their ethnic identity as particular Indian groups on familiar pieces of land that carried their inner history. At the cost of a certain amount of material and spiritual continuity with the past, their acceptance of Christianity, however sincere, not only allowed them to survive in the present but gave them a long lease on life when many of their colonial landlords threatened to foreclose all future options. Ironically, the acute English sense of cultural superiority—which was colored by racism before the eighteenth century—helped the Indians to maintain the crucial ethnic core at the heart of their newly acquired Christian personae. In colonial eyes, they were still Indians and always would be, no matter how "civilized" or Christianized they became. Despite the assimilative goal of the missions, the English had serious limitations as agents of social reconstruction. They were far better at rooting out than transplanting.

In every setting, particularly in Canada, where material seductions were small or nonexistent, Indians converted largely because they were persuaded—by the missionaries and the logic of the situation as the natives saw it—that the Christian answers to the urgent, new questions of life were intellectually and emotionally satisfying, at least more so than the outmoded explanations offered by their traditional wise men. They yielded to no force except the force of their own reason. The most effective missionaries, especially the Jesuits, succeeded largely because they managed to frame the Indians' most vital problems and concerns in compelling, idiomatic terms and then to offer a single solution that seemed to the natives not only efficacious but inexorable. The best missionaries, therefore, were at once the best students of Indian culture and the best teachers of the Christian alternative.

On any frontier, acculturation is normally a two-way process, especially in the early stages of contact. But in colonial North America the direction of religious change—unlike changes in other aspects of culture—was decidedly unilinear, largely because Indian religion was pragmatically incorporative and tolerant of other faiths, and Christianity was aggressively evangelical and exclusive. Indian religious culture was forever on the defensive, trying to minimize the adjustments necessary to group survival and independence; Christianity sought to cajole or strong-arm the natives into spiritual submission. Any changes in colonial religion were minor and self-generated, and not due to native pressure to convert to a False Face or Midéwiwin society. At most, the Indian presence sporadically brought out the evangelical inheritance of some of the colonial denominations and moved them marginally away from their own narrow brand of tribalism.

To be on the defensive, however, does not imply the total loss of initiative. The Indians were tenacious of their culture and lifestyle, but their traditionalism was neither blind nor passive. As the history of the missions clearly shows, the native peoples of the Northeast were remarkably resourceful in adjusting to new conditions, especially in using elements of European religious culture for their own purposes. According to the social and political circumstances in which they found themselves after contact, they accepted the missionaries' offerings in just the amounts necessary to maintain their own cultural identity. They may have made individual or short-term miscalculations of self-interest, white strength, and policy direction—no group is capable of a perfect functionalism—but in general they took what they needed for resistance and accepted only as much as would ensure survival. Because of their creative adaptability and the defects of the mission programs, many Indian people were never fully "washed white in the blood of the Lamb." Although their outer lives could be partially reduced to civility, their inner resources were equal to the invasion within.

CHAPTER TWELVE

The English Apostates

He hated too strongly the English
Nation, where he was almost a slave,
to give up his religion and his liberty.
LT. ALEXANDRE DOUVILLE

In the contest for North America, societies that suffered a demographic disadvantage sought to lessen the odds against them by rearranging the players. In wartime the smallest groups, such as the French, normally took people from the largest and added them to their own, thereby gaining a critical psychological advantage as well as a social bonus. When English settlers in substantial numbers were captured by the French, converted to Roman Catholicism, and naturalized as French citizens, the French not only added hardy *habitants* to their small population but shook the confidence of the English in their own cultural and religious superiority.

The English, enjoying an ample and rapidly growing population, did not have to resort to such tactics, and temperamentally were not capable of executing them. Most French captives were soldiers, largely impervious to conversion in any case, who were sent home under flags of truce as quickly as possible in exchange for more susceptible English civilians. English patrols seldom raided Canadian settlements, except in Acadia, and even less frequently took French women and children captive. And little or no effort was made to convert or naturalize French prisoners during their brief stay in New England or New York; the arbitrary five to ten pound fee that at least one New York governor charged for letters of "denization" could not have made the prospect particularly inviting.[1]

The French, sometimes alone but usually with their Indian allies, took special pains to capture, acculturate, and convert English settlers, and they succeeded at a rate mortifying to English ministers and officials. What was most disturbing to the English establishment was less the number of English converts, substantial though it was, than the symbolic value of such conversions in the contest of cultures. It was one thing to lose the battle of missions to the black-robed "forces of darkness." But if English Protestants could not even maintain their own religious identity in the relatively civilized midst of Catholic Canada, their pretensions to the status of God's "chosen people" and their holy errand into the wilderness would be cast in grave doubt. In the eighteenth-century war for the continent, no side could afford to surrender such a major moral weapon.

The consternation of the English over their inability to recover their kith and kin was most pronounced at the end of each intercolonial war when emissaries were sent to Canada to exchange prisoners. The governors of the respective colonies were usually most cooperative in entertaining and assisting the searchers. English ambassadors to New France were given room, board, and transportation at state expense for as long as their mission lasted, sometimes for several weeks. At the conclusion of the first two wars, governors Frontenac and Vaudreuil ordered their officers, citizens, and the clergy to provide every assistance in assembling English captives in Montreal or Quebec so that they could be questioned openly whether they wished to return. Moreover, they compelled children under the age of twelve to return because the young could not be expected to make sensible decisions about religion.[2] But they drew the line at two other groups: English adults who were officially naturalized and children "born in the country" to one English and one French parent. Confident of the power of love, the French acquiesced easily to the English demand that "French women might go with their English husbands, and English women should not be compelled to tarry with their French husbands." All others had "free liberty" to return or stay. Indeed, in 1714, several English converts exercised the liberty of going to visit their relatives in New England, but all quickly returned to their adoptive northern homes.[3]

Despite the official air of cooperation, however, the French governors were powerless to control the clergy, who had the greatest interest in their captive Protestant audience. Governor Vaudreuil admitted that "he could as easily alter the course of the waters as prevent the priests' endeavors," and the water he knew best was the mighty St. Lawrence, which ran before his door. When John Stoddard and the Reverend John Williams arrived in Canada in 1714 to redeem New Englanders, they discovered just how effective the priests could be. Returning with only twenty-six countrymen, they were understandably peeved that some priests, "not being content with the endeavors they have used with the prisoners for many years during the war, do now make it their business to go from house to house to solicit our people to tarry in this country. Some they endeavor to terrify by suggesting their danger of perdition; some they threaten to take from them their effects, wives, and children." To no avail, the agents laid upon the equally helpless governor their righteous resentment of "the priests' daily practicing with many of our young and simple people, and by a sort of force constraining of them to abide" in Canada. They might have taken some consolation from the knowledge that they had procured one more prisoner than their New York predecessors had at the end of King William's War. When Governor Frontenac rounded up the English in Quebec in 1698, all of them "(except two or three) unanimously refused to return" with Peter Schuyler and Dominie Dellius. Even when the underaged children were granted them, "some still remained, who hid themselves."[4]

The number of Englishmen who remained permanently in Canada was, as colonial officials realized by the end of King William's War, indeed cause for concern. The vast majority had been taken by Indian or French and Indian war parties from New England, at least, 1,641 persons between 1675 and 1763. About 300 had been captured in each of the first three intercolonial wars, well over 500 in the last. Two-thirds of the New England prisoners were male, half of them children.[5] Most of the Indian raids were launched from Catholic *reserves* under or at the instigation of French officers or priests. The traditional military objective of the natives, as we shall see in the next chapter, was to capture replacements for fallen kinsmen, whom they would adopt into their families. But as their dependence on trade goods, immunity to imported diseases, and supply of European war captives grew, the Indians learned that their French allies and priests were eager to redeem English prisoners for generous gifts and even the promise of heaven. So increasingly as the eighteenth century wore on, the Canadian Indians were prompted to capture English settlers less for adoption (though that remained an important motive) than for their ransom value, which was not inconsiderable. In 1714 a St. François Indian family pocketed 160 livres for an Englishman, half paid by the English emissaries, half by Governor Vaudreuil. Although colonial officials worried that purchasing captives would encourage the Indians to continue their "diabolical kidnapping mode of warfare," ransoms were constantly paid by French and English families and governments throughout the wars. Naturally, in a seller's market the prices went up. By 1752 English agents were spending 300 livres per captive; a future revolutionary hero from Vermont cost an Indian pony worth 515 livres.[6]

Thus many English colonists came to spend their captivity in comfortable stone houses in Montreal and Quebec rather than smoky longhouses in St. François or Caughnawaga. And large numbers of them—we will never know for sure just how many—never returned to New England. Thanks to the assiduous research of Alice Baker and Emma Coleman and a careful tabulation by Alden Vaughan and Daniel Richter, we do know that only 46 percent definitely returned to New England. We also know that 451 (and probably 63 more) were last held in civilian Canada, not in military prisons. Of those 451, 117 returned to New England while 202 (44.8 percent) chose to live and die in Canada. The new Canadians were predominantly young and female. Of the cases for which sufficient information exists, only 35 were over sixteen; 118 were fifteen and under. Nearly a third of the female captives but less than a tenth of the males stayed. In short, girls between the age of seven and fifteen were most susceptible to conversion, but all ages and sexes turned their backs on their natal homes.[7] The fifteen columns devoted to the names L'Anglais and Langlois, the French equivalent of *English*, in the current Montreal telephone directory are testimony to the lineal virility of New France's male captives.

Fortunately, the French were excellent record keepers, and the long trails of paper footprints left by the English prisoners allow us to trace a typical journey from Anglo-Protestant to Franco-Catholic. The first step was baptism in the Catholic Church, which followed months of catechetical instruction, church attendance, and an informal abjuration of the false and error-ridden "Calvinistic heresy" in which they had been raised. In the presence of two Catholic godparents, the candidate was anointed with the holy waters in a parish church or convent chapel. Mary Scammon, a fourteen-year-old captive from Maine, was baptized in the Ursuline chapel at Trois Rivières. The corridors were strewn with spring flowers and the chapel was festooned with fragrant garlands. When Mary stepped into a double circle of her friends, she was dressed in a rich gown and blue belt, rings and bracelets adorning her fingers and arms, bright flowers twined through her plaited hair. After she proceeded through the catechism and the words of the rite, the Recollect priest asked her the age-old question, "Do you renounce the pomps of Satan?" "Yes," she replied, "I renounce them with all my heart." Whereupon she removed her bracelets, rings, and belt and handed them to a companion. Then she loosened her hair, dropping the flowers to the floor, and put on a long white veil to signify her complete rejection of earthly vanity. Thus was she reborn Marie Anne Marguerite in the communion of Catholic saints.[8] Not every baptismal ceremony was celebrated with such style, but no candidate could have failed to sense the solemn importance of the step he was taking.

If the priest was not certain whether the candidate had been baptized previously, as he might not with English children, he would administer the rite "*sous condition*," with a mental reservation, making it a true baptism only in case the first was somehow invalid. To the French priests, baptism was no mere formality. A Jesuit asked the Reverend John Williams not long after the latter's capture in 1704 whether all the English captives at Lorette, mostly from Williams's Deerfield congregation, had been baptized. When Williams told him they were, the priest said, "if they be not, let me know of it, that I may baptize them, for fear they should die and be damned, if they die without baptism. . . . When the Savages went against you, I charged them to baptize all children before they killed them; such was my desire of your eternal salvation, though you were our enemies."[9]

The second step on a prisoner's path to conversion was naturalization as a French citizen. As we have seen, the one group of Englishmen French officials would not consider repatriating was those who had received *lettres de naturalité* from the king, who had granted their wish to "be known as French." At no cost, the recipients, "professing the catholic, apostolic and roman religion" and "desiring to end their days as our subjects," were granted "all the rights, privileges and immunities enjoyed by our born subjects, as well as the same rights to hold and dispose of property, real and personal." In return, they promised obedience to the king and not to leave the country without his "express and written permission," to transmit information or to "be employed as go-betweens with foreigners," on pain of forfeiting their new rights.[10]

In 1710 the king issued letters of naturalization to a cadre of eighty-four Englishmen taken in the current and previous war, documents that reveal the third and final step toward conversion—marriage to a Canadian. Of the forty-four males, ten (23 percent) were already married to French women and had children (ten in one instance!); another was married to a country-woman. Even more telling, fourteen of the forty females (37 percent) were married to French men, though only six (15 percent) had children, undoubtedly because they were considerably younger than their male counterparts. Three years later another forty English prisoners received French citizenship. Surprisingly, none were yet married. In subsequent years, especially during the long period of official peace between 1725 and 1744, the supply of candidates for naturalization declined to a few New Englanders caught by revenge-seeking Indian allies. When one came forward, however, the French governor would submit an individual request to the king for the desired privileges. In 1731, for instance, Governor Beauharnois assured His Majesty that Abel Olivier was a "good catholic" and had been established in Quebec for nineteen years and married for ten.[11]

Two other reasons explain why the last two intercolonial wars did not produce a rich harvest of naturalizations similar to that of 1710–13. One is that more soldiers were captured in the latter campaigns, and quickly exchanged in large groups because they were too expensive to feed and house. Another is that after 1722 a hundred-livre fee was required by the Conseil Supérieur from each person seeking naturalization. Only those with a substantial stake in Canada in real or personal property would have found the fee worth the legal protection of their legacies it bought them.[12]

The obvious question posed by the striking number of English apostates is, Why? What prompted these freedom-loving scions of the New Protestant Jerusalem to embrace "the scarlet whore of Rome" and to throw in their lot with a contemptibly small colony of "slaves" who (they believed) wore wooden shoes, ate roots, and lived under an absolute, despotic prince?[13] Though every individual had his private reasons, to which the historian is seldom privy, it is possible to suggest some general reasons of both a worldly and a religious sort.

One reason for choosing to remain with the French was simple gratitude for being delivered out of the hands of the Indians and relief at having survived the painful journey from the English colonies. Those prisoners who survived the initial attack on their homes, the apparently random brutality of their native captors, the rigors of several-hundred-mile treks through seemingly trackless wilderness in all seasons, and the welcoming blows of the gauntlet in native villages were understandably grateful to the French people who paid substantial sums for their redemption, no matter how strange their tongue or manners. Coresidence would soon remove the strangeness but never the sense of obligation they owed to their benefactors.

A related reason for staying was the prisoners' natural reluctance to undertake the arduous trip home, particularly if they knew that their immediate family had been killed or carried to Canada. Many captives were repatriated on ships or horseback, but ship travel in the St. Lawrence and along the coasts of Acadia and New England was notoriously hazardous, and most captives, especially the "low-born," had to retrace their heavy steps on foot. Anyone with any memory of what they had suffered—and 20 percent of the adult women from northern New England were either pregnant or recently delivered when they were captured—could not be faulted for choosing the path of least resistance.[14]

Adult captives had two special incentives to refuse repatriation. Men particularly were welcomed and encouraged to stay in Canada if they possessed skills or trades beyond the ordinary. As late as 1716 Governor Vaudreuil was complaining to his superiors that the small Canadian population effectively "undermined all [economic] enterprises because of the difficulty of finding enough masters and journeymen, who worked only for excessive wages." Skilled English craftsmen filled the void nicely because they often worked for lower wages to repay the cost of their redemption from the Indians. Those who had no debts were allowed to enter the labor market at whatever wage they could command. When Robert Eastburn told his French captor that he was a blacksmith, he was advised to send for his wife when he got to Canada because, said the Frenchman, "you can get a rich living there." After working about nine months for her "mistress," Jean Lowry moved into her own quarters in Montreal and earned her keep by her needlework. Joseph Bartlett lived in Montreal with a rich but gouty captain, and received good fare and a warm room for attending him. In his leisure, the young captive "wrought at shoe-making."[15]

The trades most in demand, however, were weaving and the building of sawmills. Even the *reserve* Indians knew the relative value of their human commodities. In 1704, having just sold a young English child to a Montreal lady, a group of Caughnawagas thought better of it and offered to swap the child for an adult weaver whose service, they argued, "would much advance the design she had of making cloth." The lady in question may have been La Dame de Repentigny, who redeemed several English weavers in order to employ them to teach local inhabitants how to weave heavy coverlets from tree bark, rough linen from nettle fibers, and a kind of rug from sheep's wool. In 1706 the king awarded her two hundred livres for establishing a factory in Quebec. His only concern was that the English workers be made Catholics if they were not already.[16]

Captives who could build sawmills were in such demand that they rarely stayed in Canada long enough to entertain conversion. In 1705 the aptly named Thomas Sawyer was captured in Massachusetts. When he reached Montreal, he told the governor that he had seen an excellent site on the Chambly River for a sawmill, and was willing to build it in exchange for his freedom. But his Caughnawaga captors had their hearts set on sacrificing him to the manes of a dead relative, and actually tied him to a post surrounded by kindling. Only the sudden appearance of the local Jesuit brandishing "the key to the gates of Purgatory" secured his release. Sawyer finished the job in a year and returned to New England, leaving his captive son behind for a brief time to show the French how to use the facility. Within twenty years, five other captives had built sawmills along the St. Lawrence to earn their freedom. By 1719 Canada had nineteen mills; by 1754 there were twelve between Trois Rivières and Quebec alone, modeled after English originals.[17] Fortunately for the French, most English skills did not carry such a high price tag, and many captive craftsmen joined the ranks of the converted.

While English prisoners might have been led by mundane considerations to entertain the possibility of becoming Canadians, in the long run most actually did so out of love—for French spouses, converted kinsmen and friends, or the Mother Church. Falling in love and marrying in Canada is perhaps the easiest scenario to appreciate when we consider that the preponderance of converts were young men and women of marriageable or soon-to-be marriageable age and little prospect of getting home soon. Before 1719 and perhaps for some time after, English women were at something of a premium. The sexes were not in balance in French Canada until that year, and English girls on the whole continued to be slightly better educated than their Canadian sisters and always something of a novelty.[18] But the naturalization list of 1710, with its numerous spouses and offspring, makes it clear that English men enjoyed no special immunity to *l'amour*.

The Canadian marriage of Grizel Warren Otis illustrates not only the centripetal force of conjugal love but a force of nearly equal strength—the social networking of English converts once they decided to make Canada their home. Grizel was a twenty-seven-year-old mother of two when she was captured by an Abenaki war party in Dover, New Hampshire, in the summer of 1689. Having watched her two-year-old daughter and aged husband tomahawked, she and her three-month-old daughter Christine were hustled off to Canada, where they were soon redeemed by the French. Grizel was soon living in service in the Montreal home of Paul Le Moyne de Maricourt, marine captain, interpreter, and adopted son of the Onondagas.

Four years passed as Grizel imbibed the faith of her benefactors and circulated enough to meet Philippe Robitaille, an illiterate cooper. In May she was baptized into the church of her Irish Catholic mother as Marie-Madeleine, to which she added Robitaille five months later in a marriage consecrated by Henri-Antoine Meriel, Sulpician priest, chaplain of the Hôtel-Dieu, and an assiduous proselytizer of English captives. To the new couple five children were born in the next ten years; four were living in 1710 when Madame Robitaille received her *lettre de naturalité* from the king.[19]

As Madeleine's new faith took hold and blossomed, she worked closely with Father Meriel to bring other prisoners to the Church. In December 1705, just two years after her own baptism, she and other English converts secured the conversion of two fellow captives who were dying in the Hôtel-Dieu. Abigail Turbet, a thirty-year-old widow from Maine, made her peace with God by asking Meriel to say a mass for her "that she might have her sins pardoned." Accordingly, she was baptized in the parish church in the presence of her captive cousin, Anne Stilson, and Madeleine Robitaille. Mrs. Turbet prayed to the Virgin Mary, crossed herself, and kissed a crucifix; she died two weeks later. Esther Jones seems to have had a few qualms about the new faith until Mesdames Robitaille and Stilson and Louis Trafton, a gunsmith from Maine, went to work. But she, too, ended by making a confession of faith, kissing a crucifix, and asking for extreme unction, vowing that "if ever she should recover and get home, she would reproach the ministers for their neglecting that sacrament." Two days later she gave up the ghost, wearing a rosary given by the hospital nuns around her neck.[20]

The social networks created or maintained by English prisoners and their new families played an inestimable part in holding the English in Canada and gaining new converts. A surprising number of English captives sponsored each other in baptism, witnessed each other's marriages, and stood as god-parents when children were born. Friendships formed at home, in Laurentian *reserves*, or in Canadian cities were nurtured over lifetimes and served to bind the converts to each other as well as to French Canada. As one example, consider the maze of social connections that developed between Abigail Nims, captured at Deerfield in 1704, and Sarah Hanson, taken twenty years later from Dover, New Hampshire. Abigail was reared by the Indians at Sault-au-Récollet along with Hannah Hurst, another Deerfield girl five years her senior. Both were taught their catechism and prayers by Sister Marie-des-Anges of the Congregation of Notre Dame, the former Mary Sayward of York, Maine. In 1715 Abigail married a boy from across the street in Deerfield, John Rising, and proceeded to have eight children. When their last son, Jean-Baptiste Jérome, was born in 1740, Hannah Hurst stood as god-mother. Five years later their daughter Anastasie married Jean-Baptiste Sabourin, the eldest son of a French father of the same name and Sarah Hanson, who had also lived at Lac des Deux Montagnes (to which the *reserve* of Sault-au-Récollet had moved in 1721). When it came time for young J.-B. Jérome to take a bride, he chose Marie-Charlotte Sabourin, Sarah's youngest daughter. As English captives continued to arrive in Canada, they, like Sarah Hanson, were absorbed by ever-widening circles of engagement that smoothed their entry into French culture and made their decision to remain in Canada altogether understandable.[21]

English officials might sympathize with their countrymen who allowed themselves to be seduced by earthly passion in New France, but they shook their collective heads in disbelief that a Protestant saint would voluntarily give up the "true religion" for the bastardized faith that Calvin and Luther had long ago rejected. Can you imagine in your own lives, the colonial clergy asked their congregations, the calamitous change suffered by your captive brethren—"The Priest taking away your Bibles, Teaching you to count your Beads, Commanding you to fall down before the Host, To worship an Image, To pray to Saints, To adore a Wafer, And shewing the Place of Torment to such as scruple"?[22]

In the safety of their own pews, of course, the religious fate of the Canadian captives was unimaginable or, at worst, a phantom of idle specula-tion to be quickly exorcised. And yet when these same churchgoers were led into the spiritual wilderness by French and Indian war parties, substantial numbers of them defected from Geneva to Rome with deceptive ease. Back home, across the cultural chasm, ministers such as Cotton Mather tried to explain away their apostasy by charging that "the French use all the means imaginable, to Seduce their Captives into the Idolatries and Superstitions of the Church of Rome," and that their successes consisted mainly of "some feeble and easy Children . . . little to be boasted of." But as more of their parishioners failed to come home, rationalizations increasingly failed to satisfy, and closer attention had to be paid to "the Exquisite Methods of the Seducers."[23]

Clerical eyewitnesses were the best source of information, and the Reverend John Williams of Deerfield was the best qualified of all. Captured in 1704 with over a hundred of his townsmen, he experienced at close range, if not always firsthand, the subtle and often raw power of the French priests. To hear "the redeemed captive" tell it, the Catholic Church made most of its converts among the English by bribing, beating, and badgering them into submission. The priests would "take the English children, born among them," he began, "and against the consent of their parents, baptize them." "Some made it their work to allure poor souls by flatteries and great promises, some threatened, some offered abusive carriage to such as refused to go to church and be present at mass." At Chateauviche, where Williams was sent to silence his counsel to the other captives, a gentleman offered Williams, in the presence of "the old bishop" Laval and a priest, "his house, and whole living, with assurance of honour, wealth and employment" if he would embrace their ways. The superior of the Jesuits threw in the promise of a large royal pension. Other captives were "taken and shut up among their religious, and all sorts of means used to gain them." A Deerfield girl in a convent was subjected for more than two years to bribes, "flatteries, threatenings, and abusive carriages" to bring her to turn. When she would not cross herself, "they hit her a box on the ear" and struck her hands with "a rod with six branches full of knots." "They pinched her arms till they were black and blue; and made her go into their church; and because she [again] would not cross herself, struck her several blows with their hands on her face." Williams's own son Samuel was allegedly dealt similar abuse by a French schoolmaster who tried to forcefeed him religion along with the French language. When he would not attend mass, four of the biggest hulks in the school were sent to dragoon him.[24]

Even before *The Redeemed Captive* was reprinted in 1720 and 1758, the minister's catalogue of terrors became the standard English explanation for the apostasy of their countrymen in captivity: the converts were either compelled against their wills, or were too young to know any better. Since the future of Protestantism rested on them, the souls of English children were at greatest risk. Williams reported with open disgust that the Jesuits had told him that "it was a great mercy that so many of our children were brought to them, and that now, especially since they were not like speedily to be returned, there was hope of their being brought over to the Romish faith."

Needless to say, "the consideration of such crafty designs to ensnare young ones, and to turn them from the simplicity of the gospel to Romish superstition, was very exercising" to the minister and his readers.[25]

Yet prisoners of all ages were subjected to persistent proselytizing by Canadian laymen and clerics. The process began in Indian *reserves*, where native captors tried to persuade their newly adopted relatives to attend mass and to perform the standard Catholic rituals. When the captives were "sold" or given to the French, conversion efforts continued in the homes of their redeemers. Thomas Brown, one of Rogers's Rangers captured on a scout near Fort William Henry, was sent to live on a farm outside Montreal. "The Family," he later wrote, "often endeavoured to persuade me to be of their Religion, making many fair Promises if I would. Wanting to see what Alteration this would make in their Conduct towards me, one Sunday Morning I came to my Mistress, and said, 'Mother, will you give me good Cloaths, if I will go to Mass?' She answered 'Yes, Son, as good as any in the House.' She did so, and I rode to Church with two of her Daughters; in giving me Directions how to behave they told me *I must do as they did.* When we came Home I sat at the Table and ate with the Family, and Every Night and Morning was taught my Prayers."[26]

In the Montreal home of his rich master, Joseph Bartlett also had "a great deal of talk on the subject of religion, and the different modes of worship." When he attended church, he allowed, "they were very civil to me, not compelling me to kneel." The ubiquitous Father Meriel even gave him an English Bible (contrary to the worst fears of the Protestant ministers at home) and used to sit with him at his shoemaking to talk of his health and his lack of church attendance. When the young cobbler objected that he could not understand the Latin services, Meriel advised him to try again and to hold fast to that which was good. "Who knows (said he) but that God hath sent you here to know the true way of worship." After a short time the priest came again and asked him how he liked their manner of worship. "I told him it seemed strange to me. He said this was generally the case at first, but after a while it would appear otherwise." They ended their conversation with some spirited sparring over the biblical sanction for Purgatory, venial sin, and intercessory prayers to saints and angels.[27]

As the captors of Jean Lowry discovered too late, the better versed in Protestant scripture a prisoner was, the harder it was to promote conversion. Mrs. Lowry argued with such knowledge and gusto that she claimed to have bested every layman and priest who dared to cross her. When she steadfastly refused to do any servile work on the Sabbath, even though her employers argued that the priests allowed it, she replied, "the Priests is no Example for me, I follow the Example of Jesus Christ." Whereupon "they told me I was a good woman, but had a bad Religion; for if I was a Roman Catholick and would live so strict, I wou'd go streight to Heaven as soon as I dy'd." With a Montreal interpreter, a former candidate for the priesthood, she argued against papal infallibility and apostolic succession so successfully that he allegedly confessed his desire to go to the English colonies to enjoy the freedom of a scriptural religion. Apparently, her devastating critique of a book he gave her on the *Vindication of the Roman Catholick Religion, against the Presbyterian proved out of Scripture* turned his own religious foundations to dust. She even accused her master's family of cannibalism for believing in transubstantiation! "They were silent for some Time," she gloated, before someone admitted, "I never tho't there had been such People among the English, for I thought they had been meer Bruits, but there will certainly be some of them saved as well as us."[28]

Most prisoners, however, were much less resistant than Mrs. Lowry to the intellectual subversion of the French priests. The English were particularly vulnerable without their ministers. The very few clergymen who were captured were prevented from holding prayers or converse with the other prisoners, and correspondence from the English colonies was carefully censored for religious content. The Jesuits of Quebec allegedly circulated a satirical poem about the Reverend Williams, the import of which was that "the king of France's grand-son had sent out his huntsmen, and they had taken a wolf, who was shut up, and now he hopes the sheep would be in safety." By law, the "sheep" could not meet in groups of more than three or leave their masters' houses after sunset on pain of imprisonment. Whenever the Church gained a deathbed convert, the news was broadcast immediately in English circles in hopes that apostasy was contagious. To increase its attractiveness, converts were "honourably buried in the churchyard, next to the church," with the full array of Catholic ceremonies and celebrants.[29]

Of course, the ministers were not wrong to worry that captive children were the main targets of the priests and nuns. For one reason, English children tended to come to the French alone, orphaned by war, redeemed from Indian families, or separated from their parents, who languished in unhealthy military prisons. Quickly adopted by kindly French families or communities of nuns—not the sadistic bugbears of Williams's imagination—they were sent to parish or convent schools as boarding or day students, their fees paid by generous merchants, government officials, or clergymen. Young girls quickly found surrogate mothers and sisters in the nuns and sometimes a viable female calling besides marriage. After baptism and confirmation, lay *confréries* of Catholic women and girls drew them into another extensive network of female and partially English bonds.[30]

For at least eight English girls, their nascent spirituality could be fully nurtured only by taking the veil in a religious order. Two joined the Ursulines, two the Sisters of the Congregation of Notre Dame, both largely teaching orders; four others became nurses in the Hôtels-Dieu of Montreal and Quebec.[31] Perhaps the most incredible odyssey to the Lord was made by Esther Wheelwright, who was captured by Abenakis at Wells, Maine, in 1703.

Esther came from hardy stock, which may partially explain her strength of character. Her great-grandfather had wrestled—successfully—with Oliver Cromwell at Cambridge before moving his Puritan sympathies to Massachusetts and getting into hot water over his and Anne Hutchinson's Antinomian tendencies. Her father was a minor officeholder and retailer of strong liquors in Wells but also a member of Governor Joseph Dudley's council. Esther was one of eleven children.

When the Abenakis hit Wells, killing or capturing thirty-nine inhabitants, Esther was seven. She spent the next six years as the adopted daughter of an Indian family on the headwaters of the Kennebec, where she quickly learned Abenaki and some French from the resident Jesuit. When Governor Vaudreuil heard of her whereabouts, he brought her to Quebec and into his own home to be raised beside his daughter Louise. The following year both girls were boarded with the Ursuline nuns to attend school. By 1710 she had forgotten her childhood speech and wished to be made a French citizen. The resolve of this young girl who had known three cultures never wavered.

By now the English authorities had learned that Esther was alive and well in Quebec and began to pressure Vaudreuil for her return. Upon which Vaudreuil sent her to Montreal, where she stayed with the nuns at the Hôtel-Dieu. There she met Father Meriel, who persuaded her to stand sponsor at the baptism of Dorothée de Noyon, the firstborn child of a former Deerfield captive and her French husband. Esther also stayed for a short time with the Ursulines at Trois Rivières, probably of her own volition, for in June 1711 Vaudreuil told Governor Dudley that "she does not wish to return" because of the "change of her religion."[32]

What that change entailed was made clear a year later when Esther began her novitiate as an Ursuline nun in Quebec. Three months later, the seventeen-year-old girl who had once been baptized in a Congregational church put on the white veil of a bride of Jesus and assumed the name Esther Marie Joseph de l'Enfant Jésus. The Jesuit who had redeemed her from the Abenakis preached the sermon on God's helping hand in rescuing her from "a sterile and ingrate land, where [she] would have been the slave of the demon of heresy." He also rejoiced that "Providence [had] suspended the natural tenderness of [her] father and mother, and abated the eagerness of their first pursuit" of her, allowing her to reach maturity and decide her own spiritual destiny.[33]

But the French were not entirely certain that their new sister was secure. When the Treaty of Utrecht restored peace to the Anglo-Canadian frontiers in 1713, her relatives resumed their pleas for her return, and several of the English emissaries who came to Canada to redeem prisoners brought letters from her family. In fear that her relations might make greater efforts to see her and try to prevent her conversion, Vaudreuil and Bishop Saint-Vallier agreed with the Ursulines to advance her final vows by one year, the first and perhaps only exception the Canadian order ever made. At the age of eighteen she put on the black veil of the Ursulines and never took it off until death came in her eighty-fifth year.

Relations with her family did not cease, however. For a number of years they still entertained hopes that she could be drawn back to New England. When her father died in 1745, he bequeathed her £100 if she would return; ten years later her mother upped the ante to one-fifth of her estate. Eventually, they realized that monastic religious devotion was impervious to their insensi-

19. Esther Wheelwright (1696–1780), captured by the Abenakis in 1703, became an Ursuline nun—Esther Marie Joseph de l'Enfant Jésus—and eventually superior of the order in Canada. Courtesy of the Massachusetts Historical Society, Boston.

tive attempts at bribery and began to send gifts for the convent. Family-crested silver flagons, cups, place settings, and linen from the Wheelwrights can still be seen in the convent, and a portrait of Esther's mother, transformed into a Madonna by the addition of a veil, once graced the wall of the chapel. In return, Sister Esther sent a large and serene portrait of herself, which now hangs in the Massachusetts Historical Society, as well as several presents and the offer of education in the convent to her sister's granddaughter, also named Esther.

When the English finally took Quebec in 1759, Esther helped to bury General Montcalm in a shell hole in front of the Ursuline altar. The following year and for nine of the next twelve years, she was elected superior of the convent, the only English woman to enjoy such an honor. Because of her birth and sweet temper, she established excellent relations with the British command in Canada, perfected the art of embroidery on birchbark, which sold well to the English officers and gentry, and gradually paid off the convent's debt for food advanced by the army. When she renewed her vows on the golden anniversary of her profession in 1764, the New English must have finally realized that their initial loss was humanity's gain. With the generosity of spirit she had shown all her life, Sister Esther Marie might have hoped for their understanding but would have been content with their acceptance.[34]

After the startling success of the French in converting Protestants during the first two intercolonial wars, the colonial English clergy tried to fortify succeeding generations against possible capture and Catholic seduction. In 1707, the same year he published *Frontiers Well-Defended*, the tireless Cotton Mather turned his pen to *The Fall of Babylon: A Short and Plain Catechism, Which Detects & Confutes the Principles of Popery*. Nearly forty years later, another short salvo was fired in the brisk paper war that raged between the religious rivals. This was a standard reissue (the eighteenth) of *A Protestant's Resolution, Shewing his Reason why he will not be a PAPIST: Digested Into so plain a Method of Question and Answer, that an ordinary Capacity may be able to defend the Protestant Religion against the most cunning Jesuit, or Popish Priest*. The forty-four-page tract listed two dozen specific errors of Catholicism, which it characterized as "a superstitious, idolatrous, damnable, bloody, traiterous, blind, blasphemous Religion," and concluded with eight deceptively simple "Directions how you may keep your self from being a Papist."[35]

Between these two Protestant benchmarks, however, appeared an unusual pamphlet entitled *Letter from a Romish Priest in Canada, To One who was taken Captive in her Infancy, and Instructed in the Romish Faith, but some time ago returned to this her Native Country*. Published in Boston in 1729 with an answer by Governor William Burnet himself, the letter was addressed to Christine Otis Baker by François Seguenot, a Sulpician priest from Montreal. The daughter of Madeleine (Grizel) Robitaille, Christine had been educated by nuns, baptized a Catholic, and married at eighteen to a carpenter by the time she was naturalized in 1710. She had also belonged, with her mother, to the select *confrérie* of the Holy Family, which consisted, Seguenot said, of "Two Hundred Women of the best fashion." But in 1713 her husband died, leaving her a young widow with two young daughters.

The following year she lost her heart to Captain Thomas Baker, a former Deerfield captive and interpreter to the Stoddard-Williams mission, who took her back to New England to marry her and to have her rebaptized as a Protestant. In going she lost her Canadian estate and her children, who were placed with their maternal grandmother when Governor Vaudreuil would not allow them to leave the country. Seguenot's doctrinally fulsome letter was an effort to snatch his "poor stray Sheep" from the jaws of apostasy in "a strange Land where there is nothing but Darkness and Irreligion, Schisms, Divisions and Confusions." After relating the sad news of the marriage and death of her eldest daughter, he tried to entice the couple with land on the island or plenty of work if her husband plied a trade. But he had the good grace to acknowledge that "what is most essential is that you shall be here both of you enabled to work out your Salvation" in the "Bosom of the [true] Church."[36]

Letter from a Romish Priest is unique in the colonial history of religious warfare because it documents one of the rare cases in which an English convert to Catholicism did not remain in French Canada and the Church for the rest of her life. Could they have read about Christine Baker's change of heart, the hundreds of converts who did remain would have found it humanly understandable, perhaps, but spiritually pitiful. For as the French always maintained, the English prisoners who stayed in Canada did so because "they embraced our religion," and that, they knew, was "the strongest reason" of all.[37]

CHAPTER THIRTEEN

The White Indians

*It is very easy to make an Indian
out of a white man. . . .*
FRANCES SLOCUM (WELETAWASH)

The contest of cultures in colonial North America was far from one-sided. Despite superior technologies, aggressive religions, prolific populations, and well-articulated ideologies of imperialism, the French and English invaders enjoyed no monopoly of success in converting enemies to their way of life. In fact, the Indian defenders of the continent were more successful, psychologically if not numerically, than either of their European rivals. Partly because of their unrealistic goals, the English had little success in converting Indians to Christian civility and virtually no success in persuading French Catholics to become anglicized Protestants. The French, on the other hand, hit upon a winning combination of methods for drawing large numbers of natives to at least minimal adherence to Catholic Christianity and substantial numbers of English prisoners to both Catholicism and loyalty to French colonial culture. But the Indians, despite all odds, succeeded in seducing French and English colonists in numbers so alarming to European sensibilities that the natives were conceded to be, in effect, the best cultural missionaries and educators on the continent.

An indispensable article in the European faith in the superiority of their own civility was that no civilized person in possession of his faculties or free from undue restraint would choose to become an Indian. "For, easy and unconstrained as the savage life is," wrote the Reverend William Smith of Philadelphia, "certainly it could never be put in competition with the blessings of improved life and the light of religion, by any persons who have had the happiness of enjoying, and the capacity of discerning, them."[1]

And yet by the close of the colonial period large numbers of French and English settlers had chosen to become Indians—by walking or running away from colonial society to join Indian society, by not trying to escape after being captured, or by electing to remain with their Indian captors when treaties of peace periodically afforded them the opportunity to return home. Perhaps the first colonist to recognize the disparity between the myth of civilized invulnerability and American reality was Cadwallader Colden, surveyor-general and member of the king's council of New York. In his *History of the Five Indian Nations of Canada*, published in London in 1747, Colden described the Albany peace treaty between the French and the Iroquois in 1699, when "few of [the French captives] could be persuaded to return" to Canada. Lest his readers attribute this unusual behavior to "the Hardships they had endured in their own Country, under a tyrannical Government and a barren Soil," he quickly added that "the English had as much Difficulty to persuade the People, that had been taken Prisoners by the French Indians, to leave the Indian Manner of living, though no People enjoy more Liberty, and live in greater Plenty, than the common Inhabitants of New-York do." Colden, clearly amazed, elaborated:

> No Arguments, no Intreaties, nor Tears of their Friends and Relations, could persuade many of them to leave their new Indian Friends and Acquaintance[s]; several of them that were by the Caressings of their Relations persuaded to come Home, in a little Time grew tired of our Manner of living, and run away again to the Indians, and ended their Days with them. On the other Hand, Indian Children have been carefully educated among the English, cloathed and taught, yet, I think, there is not one Instance that any of these, after they had Liberty to go among their own People, and were come to Age, would remain with the English, but returned to their own Nations, and became as fond of the Indian Manner of Life as those that knew nothing of a civilized Manner of living. What I now tell of Christian Prisoners among Indians [he concluded his history], relates not only to what happened at the Conclusion of this War, but has been found true on many other Occasions.[2]

Colden was not alone. Six years later Benjamin Franklin wondered how it was that

> When an Indian Child has been brought up among us, taught our language and habituated to our Customs, yet if he goes to see his relations and make one Indian Ramble with them, there is no perswading him ever to return. [But] when white persons of either sex have been taken prisoners young by the Indians, and lived a while among them, tho' ransomed by their Friends, and treated with all imaginable tenderness to prevail with them to stay among the English, yet in a Short time they become disgusted with our manner of life, and the care and pains that are necessary to support it, and take the first good Opportunity of escaping again into the Woods, from whence there is no reclaiming them.[3]

In short, "thousands of Europeans are Indians," as Hector de Crèvecoeur put it, "and we have no examples of even one of those Aborigines having from choice become Europeans!"[4]

Several sorts of colonists took to Indian life without any compulsion whatever. In New France, the fur trade took hundreds of young men into the lonely *pays d'en haut* for months, even years, at a time. To cultivate their native trading partners, these wiry *voyageurs* and *coureurs de bois* adopted many aspects of native culture—wearing breechclouts, leggings and moccasins, speaking local dialects, eating native foods, following council protocol, and forging alliances with headmen and important traders by marrying native women *à la façon du pays*. In the colony itself, French officials in the seventeenth century promoted intermarriage in order to create "one people" with the natives. But by the early eighteenth century, a balanced French sex ratio and the tendency of the French spouses and offspring of mixed unions to adopt a native lifestyle prompted both church and civil leaders to bestow their blessing with caution.[5]

Intermarriage in the English colonies was nearly nonexistent, due largely to racial prejudice and early balanced sex ratios. But a few colonists did seek their fortunes among their Indian neighbors. In early New England and on the eighteenth-century western frontier particularly, a handful of notorious "renegades" cast off their civilized ways to join the natives in war and peace. During the intercolonial wars, deserters from the army tended to seek refuge in native villages rather than French forts. A few English traders risked the opprobrium of their less adventurous countrymen by acquiring "sleeping dictionaries" in the woods to better learn the native language and mores. And occasionally English men and (less frequently) women discovered that "a sprightly Lover is the most prevailing Missionary."[6]

By far the largest and most alarming group of "white Indians," however, was the European captives who refused repatriation once they were absorbed by Indian society. They were ordinary men, women, and children of yeoman or *habitant* stock, Protestants or Catholics by faith, a variety of nationalities by birth, English or French by law, different from their countrymen only in their willingness to risk personal insecurity for the economic opportunities of the frontier.[7] There was no discernible characteristic or pattern of characteristics that differentiated them from their captive neighbors who eventually rejected Indian life—with one exception. Most of the colonists who were captured for adoption in Indian families—as opposed to sale, ransom, torture, or enslavement—were children of both sexes and young women, often the mothers of the captive children. They were, as one captivity narrative observed, the "weak and defenceless."[8]

The pattern of taking women and children for adoption was consistent throughout the colonial period, but during the first century and a half of Indian-white conflict, it coexisted with a larger pattern of captivity that included all white colonists, men as well as women and children. When the long peace in the Middle Atlantic colonies collapsed in 1753, however, the Indians of Pennsylvania, southern New York, and the Ohio country had no Quebec or Montreal in which to sell their human chattels to compassionate French families or anxious English relatives.[9] For this and other reasons they captured English settlers largely to replace members of their own families who had died, often from English musketballs or imported diseases.[10] Consequently, women and children—the "weak and defenceless"—were the prime targets of Indian raids.

According to the pattern of warfare in the Pennsylvania theater, the Indians usually stopped at a French fort with their prisoners before proceeding to their own villages. A young French soldier captured by the English reported that at Fort Duquesne there were "a great number of English Prisoners," the older of whom "they are constantly sending . . . away to

Montreal" as prisoners of war, "but that the Indians keep many of the Prisoners amongst them, chiefly young People whom they adopt and bring up in their own way." His intelligence was corroborated by Barbara Leininger and Marie LeRoy, who had been members of a party of two adults and eight children captured in 1755 and taken to Fort Duquesne. There they saw "many other Women and Children, they think an hundred who were carried away from the several provinces of P[ennsylvania] M[aryland] and V[irginia]." When the girls escaped from captivity three years later, they wrote a narrative in German chiefly to acquaint "the inhabitants of this country . . . with the names and circumstances of those prisoners whom we met, at the various places where we were, in the course of our captivity." Of the fifty-two prisoners they had seen, thirty-four were children and fourteen were women, including six mothers with children of their own.[11]

The close of hostilities in Pennsylvania came in 1764 after Col. Henry Bouquet defeated the Indians near Bushy Run and imposed peace. By the

20. Colonel Henry Bouquet defeated the "Ohio Indians" at Bushy Run in 1763. The following year he demanded the return of all white captives and any children they had had by Indian spouses. Most of the captives, especially young children who had become totally assimilated, returned to English society with great reluctance. From [William Smith, D.D.], *An Historical Account of the Expedition against the Ohio Indians, in the Year MDCCLXIV . . .* (Philadelphia, 1765; reprinted London, 1766), engraving by Benjamin West.

articles of agreement reached in October, the Delawares, Shawnees, and Senecas were to deliver up "all the Prisoners in [their] Possession, without any Exception, Englishmen, Frenchmen, Women, and Children, whether adopted in your Tribes, married, or living amongst you, under any Denomination, or Pretence whatever." In the weeks that followed, Bouquet's troops, including "the Relations of [some of] the People [the Indians] have Massacred, or taken Prisoners," encamped on the Muskingum in the heart of the Ohio country to collect the captives. After as many as nine years with the Indians, during which time many children had grown up, 81 "men" and 126 "women and children" were returned. At the same time, a list was prepared of 88 prisoners who still remained in Shawnee towns to the west: 70 were classified as "women and children." Six months later, 44 of these prisoners were delivered up to Fort Pitt. When they were captured, all but 4 had been less than sixteen years old, while 37 had been less than eleven years old.[12]

The Indians obviously chose their captives carefully so as to maximize the chances of acculturating them to Indian life. To judge by the results, their methods were hard to fault. Even when the English held the upper hand militarily, they were often embarrassed by the Indians' educational power. On November 12, 1764, at his camp on the Muskingum, Bouquet lectured the Shawnees who had not delivered all their captives: "As you are now going to Collect all our Flesh, and Blood, . . . I desire that you will use them with Tenderness, and look upon them as Brothers, and no longer as Captives." The utter gratuitousness of his remark was reflected, no doubt purposely, in the Shawnee speech when the Indians delivered their captives the following spring at Fort Pitt. "Father—Here is your Flesh, and Blood . . . they have been all tied to us by Adoption, although we now deliver them up to you. We will always look upon them as Relations, whenever the Great Spirit is pleased that we may visit them. . . . Father—we have taken as much care of these Prisoners, as if they were [our] own Flesh, and blood; they are become unacquainted with your Customs and manners, and therefore, Father, we request you will use them tender, and kindly, which will be a means of inducing them to live contentedly with you."[13]

The Indians spoke the truth and the English knew it. Three days after his speech to the Shawnees, Bouquet had advised Lt. Gov. Francis Fauquier of Virginia that the returning captives "ought to be treated by their Relations with Tenderness and Humanity, till Time and Reason make them forget their unnatural Attachments, but unless they are closely watch'd," he admitted, "they will certainly return to the Barbarians."[14] And indeed they would have, for during a half century of conflict captives had been returned who, like many of the Ohio prisoners, responded only to Indian names, spoke only Indian dialects, felt comfortable only in Indian clothes, and in general regarded their white saviors as barbarians and their deliverance as captivity. Had they not been compelled to return to colonial society by militarily enforced peace treaties, the ranks of the white Indians would have been greatly enlarged.

From the moment the Indians surrendered their European prisoners, the colonists faced a series of difficult problems. The first was the problem of getting the prisoners to remain with the colonists. When Bouquet sent the first group of restored captives to Fort Pitt, he ordered his officers there that "they are to be closely watched and well Secured" because "most of them, particularly those who have been a long time among the Indians, will take the first Opportunity to run away." The young children especially were "so completely savage that they were brought to the camp tied hand and foot." Fourteen-year-old John McCullough, who had lived with the Indians for "eight years, four months, and sixteen days" (by his parents' reckoning), had his legs tied "under the horses belly" and his arms tied behind his back with his father's garters, but to no avail. He escaped under the cover of night and returned to his Indian family for a year before he was finally carried to Fort Pitt under "strong guard." "Having been accustomed to look upon the Indians as the only connexions they had, having been tenderly treated by them, and speaking their language," explained the Reverend William Smith, the historian of Bouquet's expedition, "it is no wonder that [the children] considered their new state in the light of a captivity, and parted from the savages with tears."[15]

Children were not the only reluctant freedmen. "Several women eloped in the night, and ran off to join their Indian friends." Among them undoubtedly were some of the English women who had married Indian men and borne them children, and then had been forced by the English victory either to return with their mixed-blood children to a country of strangers, full of prejudice against Indians, or to risk escaping under English guns to their husbands and adopted culture. For Bouquet had "reduced the Shawanese and Delawares etc. to the most Humiliating Terms of Peace," boasted Gen. Thomas Gage. "He has Obliged them to deliver up even their Own Children born of white women." But even the victorious soldier could understand the dilemma into which these women had been pushed. When Bouquet was informed that the English wife of an Indian chief had eloped in the night with her husband and children, he "requested that no pursuit should be made, as she was happier with her Chief than she would be if restored to her home."[16]

Although most of the returned captives did not try to escape, the emotional torment caused by the separation from their adopted famlies deeply impressed the colonists. The Indians "delivered up their beloved captives with the utmost reluctance; shed torrents of tears over them, recommending them to the care and protection of the commanding officer." One young woman "cryed and roared when asked to come and begged to Stay a little longer." "Some, who could not make their escape, clung to their savage acquaintance at parting, and continued many days in bitter lamentations, even refusing sustenance." Children "cried as if they should die when they were presented to us." With only small exaggeration an observer on the Muskingum could report that "every captive left the Indians with regret."[17]

Another problem encountered by the English was the difficulty of communicating with the returned captives, a great many of whom had replaced their knowledge of English with an Algonquian or Iroquoian dialect and their baptismal names with Indian or hybrid ones.[18] This immediately raised another problem—that of restoring the captives to their relatives. Sir William Johnson, the superintendent of Indian affairs, "thought it best to advertise them [in the newspapers] immediately, but I believe it will be very difficult to find the Freinds of some of them, as they are ignorant of their own Names, or former places of abode, nay cant speak a word of any language but Indian." The only recourse the English had in such instances was to describe them "more particularly . . . as to their features, Complexion etc. That by the Publication of Such descriptions their Relations, parents or friends may hereafter know and Claim them."[19]

But if several colonial observers were right, a description of the captives' physiognomy was of little help after they had been with the Indians for any length of time. Peter Kalm's foreign eye found it difficult to distinguish European captives from their captors, "except by their color, which is somewhat whiter than that of the Indians," but many colonists could see little or no difference. To his Maine neighbors twelve-year-old John Durell "ever after [his two-year captivity] appeared more like an Indian than a white man." So did John Tarbell. After thirty years among the Indians in Canada, he made a visit to his relatives in Groton "in his Indian dress and with his Indian complexion (for by means of grease and paints but little difference could be discerned)." When O. M. Spencer returned after only eight months with the Shawnees, he was greeted with a newspaper allusion "to [his] looks and manners, as slightly resembling the Indians" and by a gaggle of visitors who exclaimed "in an under tone, 'How much he looks like an Indian!'" Such evidence reinforced the environmentalism of the time, which held that white men "who have incorporated themselves with any of [the Indian] tribes" soon acquire "a great resemblance to the savages, not only in their manners, but in their colour and the expression of the countenance."[20]

The final English problem was perhaps the most embarrassing in its manifestations, and certainly was so in its implications. For many Indians who had adopted white captives, the return of their "own Flesh, and Blood" to the English was unendurable. At the earliest opportunity, after bitter memories of the wars had faded on both sides, they journeyed through the English settlements to visit their estranged children, just as the Shawnee speaker had promised Bouquet they would. Jonathan Hoyt's Indian father visited him so often in Deerfield, sometimes bringing his captive sister, that Hoyt had to petition the Massachusetts General Court for reimbursement for their support. In 1760 Sir William Johnson reported that a Canadian Indian "has been since down to Schenectady to visit one Newkirk of that place, who was some years a Prisoner in his House, and sent home about a year ago with this Indians Sister, who came with her Brother now purely to see Said Newkirk whom she calls her Son and is verry fond of."[21]

Obviously the feelings were mutual. Elizabeth Gilbert, adopted at the age of twelve, "always retained an affection toward John Huston, her Indian father (as she called him), for she remembered his kindness to her when in captivity." Even an adult who had spent less than six months with the Indians honored the chief who had adopted him. In 1799, eleven years after Thomas Ridout's release, his friend and father, Kakinathucca, "accompanied by three more Shawanese chiefs, came to pay me a visit at my house in York town (Toronto). He regarded myself and family with peculiar pleasure, and my wife and children contemplated with great satisfaction the noble and good qualities of this worthy Indian." The bond of affection that had grown in the Indian villages was clearly not an attachment that the English could dismiss as "unnatural."[22]

Children who had been raised by Indian parents from infancy could be excused perhaps for their unwillingness to return, but the adults who displayed a similar reluctance, especially the women who had married Indian men and borne them children, drew another reaction. "For the honour of humanity," wrote William Smith, "we would suppose those persons to have been of the lowest rank, either bred up in ignorance and distressing penury, or who had lived so long with the Indians as to forget all their former connections. For, easy and unconstrained as the savage life is, certainly it could never be put in competition with the blessings of improved life and the light of religion, by any persons who have had the happiness of enjoying, and the capacity of discerning, them." If Smith was struck by the contrast between the visible impact of Indian education and his own cultural assumptions, he never said so.[23]

To find a satisfactory explanation for the extraordinary drawing power of Indian culture, we should begin where the colonists themselves first came under its sway—on the trail to Indian country. For although the Indians were known for their patience, they wasted no time in beginning the educational process that would transform their hostile or fearful white captives into affectionate Indian relatives.

Perhaps the first transaction after the Indians had selected their prisoners and hurried them into cover was to replace their hard-heeled shoes with the footwear of the forest, moccasins. When Captain John Lovewell's scout surprised an Indian war party near Lake Winnipesaukee in 1724, each warrior carried two blankets and "a great many spare *Moggasons*, which were supposed for the supplying of Captives that they expected to have taken." Moccasins were universally approved by the prisoners, who admitted that they traveled with "abundant more ease" than before. And on more than one occasion the knee-deep snows of northern New England forced the Indians to make snowshoes for their prisoners in order to maintain their pace of twenty-five to thirty miles a day. Such an introduction to the superbly adapted technology of the Indians alone would not convert the English, but it was a beginning.[24]

The lack of substantial food supplies forced the captives to accommodate their stomachs as best they could to Indian trail fare, which ranged from nuts, berries, roots, and parched corn to beaver guts, horseflank, and semiraw venison and moose, eaten without the customary English accompaniments of bread or salt. When there was nothing to eat, the Indians would "gird up their loins with a string," a technique that at least one captive found "very useful" when applied to himself. Although their food was often "unsavory" and in short supply, the Indians always shared it equally with the captives, who, being hungry, "relished [it] very well."[25]

Sometimes the lessons learned from the Indians were unexpectedly vital. When Stephen Williams, an eleven-year-old captive from Deerfield, found himself separated from his party on the way to Canada, he halloed for his Indian master. When the boy was found, the Indian threatened to kill him because, as Williams remembered five years later, "the Indians will never allow anybody to Hollow in the woods. Their manner is to make a noise like wolves or any other wild creatures, when they call to one another." The reason, of course, was that they did not wish to be discovered by their enemies. To the young neophyte Indian this was a lesson in survival not soon forgotten.[26]

Two other lessons were equally unexpected but instrumental in preparing the captives for even greater surprises when they reached the Indian settlements. Both served to undermine the English horror of the Indians as bloodthirsty fiends who defiled "any Woman they take alive" before "putting her to Death." Many redeemed prisoners made a point of insisting that, although they had been completely powerless in captivity, the Indians had never affronted them sexually. Thomas Ridout testified that "during the whole of the time I was with the Indians I never once witnessed an indecent or improper action amongst any of the Indians, whether young or old." Even William Smith admitted that "from every enquiry that has been made, it appears—that no woman thus saved is preserved from base motives, or need fear the violation of her honour." If there had been the least exception, we can be sure that this champion of civilization would have made the most of it.[27]

One reason for the Indians' lack of sexual interest in their female captives was perhaps aesthetic, for the New England Indians, at least, esteemed black the color of beauty.[28] A more fundamental reason derived from the main purpose of taking captives, which was to secure new members for their families and clans. Under the Indians' strong incest taboos, no warrior would attempt to violate his future sister or cousin. "Were he to indulge himself with a captive taken in war, and much more were he to offer violence in order to gratify his lust, he would incur indelible disgrace." Indeed, the taboo seems to have extended to the whole tribe. As George Croghan testified after long acquaintance with the Indians, "they have No [J]uri[s]diction or Laws butt that of Nature yett I have known more than onest thire Councils, order men to be putt to Death for Committing Rapes, wh[ich] is a Crime they Despise." Since murder was a crime to be revenged by the victim's family in its own way and time, rape was the only capital offense punished by the tribe as a whole.[29]

Equally powerful in prohibiting sexual affronts was a religious ethic of strict warrior continence, the breaking of which was thought to bring misfortune or death. "The Indians will not cohabit with women while they are out at war," noted James Adair, a trader among the southeastern tribes for thirty years; "they religiously abstain from every kind of intercourse even with their own wives, for the space of three days and nights before they go to war, and so after they return home, because they are to sanctify themselves."[30] When William Fleming and his wife were taken from their bed in 1755, the Indians told him "he need not be afraid of their abusing his wife, for they would not do it, for fear of offending their God (pointing their hands toward heaven) for the man that affronts his God will surely be killed when he goes to war." Giving the woman a plundered shift and petticoat, the natives turned their backs while she dressed, to emphasize the point.[31]

Captive testimony also chipped away at the stereotype of the Indians' cruelty. When Mrs. Isabella M'Coy was taken from Epsom, New Hampshire, in 1747, her neighbors later remembered that "she did indeed find the journey [to Canada] fatiguing, and her fare scanty and precarious. But in her treatment from the Indians, she experienced a very agreeable disappointment. The kindness she received from them was far greater than she had expected from those who were so often distinguished for their cruelties." More frequent still was recognition of the Indians' kindness to children. Thomas Hutchinson told a common story of how "some of the children who were taken at Deerfield, they drew upon slays; at other times they have been known to carry them in their arms or upon their backs to Canada. This tenderness," he noted, "has occasioned the beginnings of an affection, which in a few years has been so rivetted, that the parents of the children, who have gone to Canada to seek them, could by no means prevail upon them to leave the Indians and return home." The affections of a four-year-old Pennsylvania boy, who became Old White Chief among the Iroquois, seem to have taken even less time to become "rivetted." "The last I remember of my mother," he recalled in 1836, "she was running, carrying me in her arms. Suddenly she fell to the ground on her face, and I was taken from her. Overwhelmed with fright, I knew nothing more until I opened my eyes to find myself in the lap of an Indian woman. Looking kindly down into my face she smiled on me, and gave me some dried deer's meat and maple sugar. From that hour I believe she loved me as a mother. I am sure I returned to her the affection of a son."[32]

When the returning war parties approached the first Indian village, the educational process took on a new complexion. As one captive explained, "whenever the warriors return from an excursion against an enemy, their return to the tribe or village must be designated by war-like ceremonial; the captives or spoils, which may happen to crown their valor, must be conducted in a triumphant form, and decorated to every possible advantage." Accordingly, the cheek, chin, and forehead of every captive were painted with traditional dashes of vermilion mixed with bear's grease. Belts of wampum were hung around their necks, Indian clothes were substituted for English, and the men and boys had their hair plucked or shaved in Indian fashion. The physical transformation was so effective, said a twenty-six-year-old soldier, "that I began to think I was an Indian." Younger captives were less aware of the small distance between role playing and real acceptance of the Indian life-style. When her captor dressed Frances Slocum, not yet five years old, in "beautiful wampum beads," she remembered at the end of a long and happy life as an Indian that he "made me look, as I thought, very fine. I was much pleased with the beautiful wampum."[33]

The prisoners were then introduced to a "new school" of song and dance. "Little did we expect," remarked an English woman, "that the accomplishment of dancing would ever be taught us, by the savages. But the war dance must now be held; and every prisoner that could move must take its awkward steps. The figure consisted of circular motion round the fire; each sang his own music, and the best dancer was the one most violent in motion." To prepare for the event each captive had rehearsed a short Indian song on the trail. Mrs. Johnson recalled many years later that her song was "danna witchee natchepung; my son's was nar wiscumpton." Nehemiah How could not master the Indian pronunciation, so he was allowed to sing in English "I don't know where I go." In view of the Indians' strong sense of ceremonial propriety, it is small wonder that one captive thought that they "Seem[e]d to be Very much a mind I Should git it perfect."[34]

Upon entering the village the Indians let forth with some distinctive music of their own. "When we came near the main Body of the Enemy," wrote Thomas Brown, a captive soldier from Fort William Henry, "the Indians made a Live-Shout, as they call it when they bring in a Prisoner alive (different from the Shout they make when they bring in Scalps, which they call a Dead-Shout)." According to another soldier, "their Voices are so sharp, shrill, loud and deep, that when they join together after one has made his Cry, it makes a most dreadful and horrible Noise, that stupifies the very Senses," a noise that naturally frightened many captives until they learned that it was not their death knell.[35]

They had good reason to think that their end was near when the whole village turned out to form a gauntlet from the entrance to the center of the village and their captors ordered them to run through it. With ax handles, tomahawks, hoop poles, clubs, and switches the Indians flogged the racing captives as if to beat the whiteness out of them. In most villages, significantly, "it was only the more elderly People both Male and Female wh[ic]h rece[iv]ed this Useage—the young prisoners of Both Sexes Escaped without it" or were rescued from any serious harm by one or more villagers, perhaps indicating the Indian perception of the captives' various educability. When ten-year-old John Brickell was knocked down by the blows of his Seneca captors, "a very big Indian came up, and threw the company off me, and took me by the arm, and led me along through the lines with such rapidity that I scarcely touched the ground, and was not once struck after he took me."[36]

The purpose of the gauntlet was the subject of some difference of opinion. A French soldier who had spent several years among the northeastern Indians believed that a prisoner "so unfortunate as to fall in the course of the bastonnade must get up quickly and keep on, or he will be beaten to death on the spot." On the other hand, Pierre de Charlevoix, the learned traveler and

21. Frances Slocum (1773–1847) was captured at the age of five and raised by the Delawares. Sometime in her late teens she married a Delaware and, when he deserted her, a Miami war chief. By the latter she had two sons (who died young) and two daughters. In 1839 her Pennsylvania relatives discovered her in Indiana. Two years later they had her portrait painted by George Winter, a young English artist traveling in America. One daughter would not show her face, having the widespread Indian fear of lifelike images. From *The Journals and Indian Paintings of George Winter, 1837–1839* (Indianapolis: Indiana Historical Society, 1948); reproduced by courtesy of Mrs. Evelyn Ball.

historian of Canada, wrote that "even when they seem to strike at random, and to be actuated only by fury, they take care never to touch any part where a blow might prove mortal." Both Frenchmen were primarily describing the Indians' treatment of other Indians and white men. Barbara Leininger and Marie LeRoy drew a somewhat different conclusion from their own treatment. Their welcome at the Indian village of Kittanning, they said, "consisted of three blows each, on the back. They were, however, administered with great mercy. Indeed, we concluded that we were beaten merely in order to keep up an ancient usage, and not with the intention of injuring us."[37]

William Walton came closest to revealing the Indians' intentions in his account of the Gilbert family's captivity. The Indians usually beat the captives with "great Severity," he said, "by way of Revenge for their Relations who have been slain." Since the object of taking captives was to satisfy the Indian families who had lost relatives, the gauntlet served as the first of three initiation rites into Indian society, a purgative ceremony by which the bereaved Indians could exorcise their anger and anguish, and the captives could begin their cultural transformation.[38]

If the first rite tried to beat the whiteness out of the captives, the second tried to wash it out. James Smith's experience was typical.

> The old chief, holding me by the hand, made a long speech, very loud, and when he had done he handed me to three squaws, who led me by the hand down the bank into the river until the water was up to our middle. The squaws then made signs to me to plunge myself into the water, but I did not understand them. I thought that the result of the council was that I should be drowned, and that these young ladies were to be the executioners. They all laid violent hold of me, and I for some time opposed them with all my might, which occasioned loud laughter by the multitude that were on the bank of the river. At length one of the squaws made out to speak a little English (for I believe they began to be afraid of me) and said, "No hurt you." On this I gave myself up to their ladyships, who were as good as their word: for though they plunged me under water and washed and rubbed me severely, yet I could not say they hurt me much.[39]

More than one captive had to receive similar assurance, but their worst fears were being laid to rest.

Symbolically purged of their whiteness by their Indian baptism, the initiates were dressed in new Indian clothes and decorated with feathers, jewelry, and paint. Then, with great solemnity, the village gathered around the council fire, where after a "profound silence" one of the chiefs spoke. Even a hostile captive, Zadock Steele, had to admit that although he could not understand the language spoken, he could "plainly discover a great share of native eloquence." The chief's speech, he said, was "of considerable length, and its effect obviously manifested weight of argument, solemnity of thought, and at least human sensibility." But even this the twenty-two-year-old New Englander could not appreciate on its own terms, for in the next breath he denigrated the ceremony as "an assemblage of barbarism, assuming the appearance of civilization."[40]

A more charitable account was given by James Smith, who through an interpreter was addressed in the following words:

> My son, you are now flesh of our flesh and bone of our bone. By the ceremony that was performed this day, every drop of white blood was washed out of your veins. You are taken into the Caughnewaga [French Mohawk] nation and initiated into a war-like tribe. You are adopted into a great family and now received with great seriousness and solemnity in the room and place of a great man. After what has passed this day you are now one of us by an old strong law and custom. My son, you have now nothing to fear. We are now under the same obligations to love, support and defend you that we are to love and to defend one another. Therefore you are to consider yourself as one of our people.[41]

"At this time," admitted the eighteen-year-old Smith, "I did not believe this fine speech, especially that of the white blood being washed out of me; but since that time I have found that there was much sincerity in said speech; for from that day I never knew them to make any distinction between me and themselves in any respect whatever until I left them . . . we all shared one fate." It is a chord that sounds through nearly every captivity narrative: "They treated me . . . in every way as one of themselves."[42]

When the adoption ceremony had ended, the captive was taken to the wigwam of his new family, who greeted him with a "most dismal howling, crying bitterly, and wringing their hands in all agonies of grief for a deceased relative." "The higher in favour the adopted Prisoners [were] to be placed, the greater Lamentation [was] made over them." After a threnodic memorial to the lost member, which may have "added to the Terror of the Captives," who "imagined it to be no other than a Prelude to inevitable Destruction," the mood suddenly shifted. "I never saw . . . such hug[g]ing and kissing from the women and crying for joy," exclaimed one young recipient. Then an interpreter introduced each member of the new family—in one case "from brother to seventh cousins"—and "they came to me one after another," said another captive, "and shook me by the hand, in token that they considered me to stand in the same relationship to them as the one in whose stead I was placed." When the forty-year-old Recollect priest Louis Hennepin was adopted by the Sioux, he wrote, his Indian father told "five or six of his wives . . . that they were to treat me as one of their sons" and then ordered "each one of those assembled to call me by the name I was to hold in our new relationship."[43]

Most young captives assumed the places of Indian sons and daughters, but occasionally the match was not exact. Mary Jemison replaced a brother who had been killed in "Washington's war," while twenty-six-year-old Titus King assumed the unlikely role of a grandfather. Young Margery West even became a mother to an Ohio Mingo family. Although their sex and age may not always have corresponded, the adopted captives succeeded to all the deceased's rights and obligations—the same dignities, honors, and often the same names. "But the one adopted," reported a French soldier, "must be prudent and wise in his conduct, if he wants to make himself as well liked as the man he is replacing. This seldom fails to occur, because he is continually reminded of the dead man's conduct and good deeds."[44]

So literal could the replacement become at times that no amount of exemplary conduct could alter the captive's reception. Thomas Peart, a twenty-three-year-old Pennsylvanian, was adopted as an uncle in an Iroquois family, but "the old Man, whose Place [he] was to fill, had never been considered by his Family as possessed of any Merit." Accordingly, Peart's dress, although in the Indian style, was "in a meaner Manner, as they did not hold him high in Esteem after his Adoption." Since his heart was not in becoming an Indian anyway, and "observing that they treated him just as they had done the old worthless Indian . . . he therefore concluded he would only fill his Predecessor's Station, and used no Endeavours to please them."[45]

When the prisoners had been introduced to all their new relatives and neighbors, the Indians proceeded to shower them with gifts. Luke Swetland, taken from Pennsylvania during the Revolution, was unusually feted with "three hats, five blankets, near twenty pipes, six razors, six knives, several spoons, gun and ammunition, fireworks, several Indian pockets [pouches], one Indian razor, awls, needles, goose quills, paper and many other things of small value"—enough to make him the complete Indian warrior. Most captives, however, settled for a new shirt or dress, a pair of decorated moccasins, and abundant promises of future kindness, which later prompted the captives to acknowledge once again that the Indians were "a[s] good as their word." "All the family was as kind to me," related Thomas Gist, "as if I had realy been the nearest of relation they had in the world." The two women who adopted Mary Jemison were no less loving. "I was ever considered and treated by them as a real sister," she said near the end of a long life with them, "the same as though I had been born of their mother." Even though he tried to escape and killed three of his adoptive tribesmen, Pierre Radisson was confident that his Mohawk parents "loved me as if I were their own natural son."[46]

Treatment such as this—and it was almost universal—left an indelible mark on every captive, whether or not they eventually returned to colonial society. Although captives like Mrs. Johnson found their adoption an "unnatural situation," they had to defend the humanity of the practice. "Those who have profited by refinement and education," she argued, "ought to abate part of the prejudice, which prompts them to look with an eye of censure on this untutored race. . . . Do they ever adopt an enemy," she asked, "and salute him by the tender name of brother?" It is not difficult to imagine what effect such feelings must have had in younger people less habituated to English culture, especially those who had lost their own parents.[47]

The formalities, purgations, and initiations were now completed. Only one thing remained for the Indians: by their daily example and instruction to "make an Indian of you," as the Delawares told John Brickell. This required a steady union of two things: the willingness and gratitude of the captives, and the consistent love and trust of the Indians. By the extraordinary ceremonies through which they had passed, most captives had had their worst fears allayed. From a state of apprehension or even terror they had suddenly emerged with their persons intact and a solemn invitation to begin a new life, as full of love, challenge, and satisfaction as any they had known. For "when [the Indians] once determine to give life, they give every thing with it, which, in their apprehension, belongs to it." The sudden release from anxiety into a realm of affirmative possibility must have disposed many captives to accept the Indian way of life.[48]

According to the adopted colonists who recounted the stories of their new lives, Indian life was more than capable of claiming their respect and allegiance, even if they eventually returned to English society. The first indication that the Indians were serious in their professions of equality came when the adopted captives were given freedom of movement within and without the Indian villages. Naturally, the degree of freedom and its timing depended on the captive's willingness to enter into the spirit of Indian life.

22. This French sketch of 1666 shows an Iroquois war party returning with hooped scalps on a pole and an Indian prisoner, who carries a gourd rattle to accompany himself in his special captivity song. The prisoner tie was adapted from a woman's tumpline or burden strap and was often made like a dog's choke-chain. The neckpiece was a flat band often decorated with colored porcupine quills. From Edmund B. O'Callaghan and Berthold Fernow, eds., *Documents Relative to the Colonial History of the State of New-York*, 9 (Albany, N.Y. 1855).

Despite his adult years, Thomas Ridout had earned his captor's trust by the third night of their march to the Shawnee villages. Having tied his prisoner with a rope to himself the first two nights, the Indian "never afterwards used this precaution, leaving me at perfect liberty, and frequently during the nights that were frosty and cold," Ridout recalled, "I found his hand over me to examine whether or not I was covered." As soon as seventeen-year-old John Leeth, an Indian trader's clerk, reached his new family's village, "my father gave me and his two [Indian] sons our freedom, with a rifle, two pounds of powder, four pounds of lead, a blanket, shirt, match-coat, pair of leggings, etc. to each, as our freedom dues; and told us to shift for ourselves." Similarly, Pierre Radisson was entrusted with a knife, hatchet, and fowling piece. Eleven-year-old Benjamin Gilbert, "considered as the [Indian] King's Successor," was of course "entirely freed from Restraint, so that he even began to be delighted with his Manner of Life." Even Zadock Steele, a somewhat reluctant Indian at twenty-two, was "allowed the privilege of visiting any part of the village, in the day time, and was received with marks of fraternal affection, and treated with all the civility an Indian is capable to bestow."[49]

The presence of other white prisoners complicated the trust relationship somewhat. Captives who were previously known to each other, especially from the same family, were not always allowed to converse "much together, as [the Indians] imagined they would remember their former Situation, and become less contented with their present Manner of Life." Benjamin Peart, for example, was allowed the frequent company of "Two white Men who had been taken Prisoners, the one from Susquehanna, the other from Minisinks, both in Pennsylvania," even though he was a Pennsylvanian himself. But when he met his captive wife and infant son by chance at Fort Niagara, the Indians "separated them again the same Day, and took [his] Wife about Four Miles Distance."[50]

Captives who were strangers were permitted not only to visit frequently but occasionally to live together. When Thomas Gist suddenly moved from his adopted aunt's house back to her brother's, she "imajined I was affronted," he wrote, and "came and asked me the reason why I had left her, or what injury she or any of the family had done me that I should leave her without so much as leting her know of it. I told her it was the company of my fellow prisoners that drew me to the town. She said that it was not so far but I mite have walked to see them every two or three days, and ask some of them to come and see me those days that I did not chuse to go abroad, and that all such persons as I thought proper to bring to the house should be as welcom[e] as one of the family, and made many promises how kind she would be if I would return. However," boasted the twenty-four-year-old Gist, "I was obstinate and would not." It was not surprising that captives who enjoyed such autonomy were also trusted under the same roof. John Brickell remarked that three white prisoners, "Patton, Johnston, and Mrs. Baker [of Kentucky] had all lived with me in the same house among the Indians, and we were as intimate as brothers and sisters."[51]

Once the captives had earned the basic trust of their Indian families, nothing in Indian life was denied them. When they reached the appropriate age, the Indians offered to find them suitable marriage partners. Understandably, some of the older captives balked at this, sensing that it was calculated to bind them with marital ties to a culture they were otherwise hesitant to accept. When Joseph Gilbert, a forty-one-year-old father and husband, was adopted into a leading family, his new relatives informed him that "if he would marry amongst them, he should enjoy the Privileges which they enjoyed; but this Proposal he was not disposed to comply with, . . . as he was not over anxious to conceal his Dislike to them." Elizabeth Peart, his twenty-year-old married sister, was equally reluctant. During her adoption ceremony "they obliged her to sit down with a young Man an Indian, and the eldest Chieftain of the Family repeating a Jargon of Words to her unintelligible, but which she considered as some form amongst them of Marriage," she was visited with "the most violent agitations, as she was determined, at all events, to oppose any step of this Nature." Marie LeRoy's honor was even more dearly bought. When "it was at length determined by the [Indians] that [she] should marry one of the natives, who had been selected for her," she told a fellow captive that "she would sooner be shot than have him for her husband." Whether her revulsion was directed toward the act itself or toward the particular suitor was not said.[52]

The distinction is pertinent because the weight of evidence suggests that marriage was not compulsory for the captives, and common sense tells us that any form of compulsion would have defeated the Indians' purpose in trying to persuade the captives to adopt their way of life. Mary Jemison, at the time a captive for two years, was unusual in implying that she was forced to marry an Indian. "Not long after the Delawares came to live with us, at Wiishto," she recalled, "my sisters told me that I must go and live with one of them, whose name was She-nin-jee. Not daring to cross them, or disobey their commands, with a great degree of reluctance I went; and Sheninjee and I were married according to Indian custom." Considering the tenderness and kindness with which most captives reported they were treated, it is likely that she was less compelled in reality than in her perception and memory of it.[53]

For even hostile witnesses could not bring themselves to charge that force was ever used to promote marriages. The Puritan minister John Williams said only that "great essays [were] made to get [captives] married" among the Canadian Indians by whom he was captured. Elizabeth Hanson and her husband "could by no means obtain from their hands" their sixteen-year-old daughter, "for the squaw, to whom she was given, had a son whom she intended my daughter should in time be prevailed with to marry." Mrs. Hanson was probably less concerned that her daughter would be forced to marry an Indian than that she might "in time" want to, for as she acknowledged from her personal experience, "the Indians are very civil towards their captive women, not offering any incivility by any indecent carriage." An observer of the return of the white prisoners to Bouquet spoke for his contemporaries when he reported—with an almost audible sigh of relief—that "there had not been a solitary instance among them of any woman having her delicacy injured by being compelled to marry. They had been left liberty of choice, and those who chose to remain single were not sufferers on that account."[54]

Not only were younger captives and consenting adults under no compulsion, either actual or perceived, to marry, but they enjoyed as wide a latitude of choice as any Indian. When Thomas Gist returned to his Indian aunt's lodge, she was so happy that she "dress'd me as fine as she could, and . . . told me if I wanted a wife she would get a pretty young girl for me." It was in the same spirit of exuberant generosity that Oliver Spencer's adopted mother rewarded his first hunting exploit. "She heard all the particulars of the affair with great satisfaction," he remembered, "and frequently saying, 'Enee, wessah' (this is right, that is good), said I would one day become a great hunter, and placing her forefingers together (by which sign the Indians represent marriage) and then pointing to Sotonegoo" (a thirteen-year-old girl whom Spencer described as "rather homely, but cheerful and good natured, with bright, laughing eyes") "told me that when I should become a man I should have her for a wife." Sotonegoo cannot have been averse to the idea, for when Spencer was redeemed shortly afterward she "sobbed loudly as [he] took her hand, and for the moment deeply affected, bade her farewell."[55]

So free from compulsion were the captives that several married fellow white prisoners. In 1715 the priest of the Jesuit mission at Sault-au-Récollet "married Ignace shoetak8anni [Joseph Rising, aged twenty-one] and Elizabeth T8atog8ach [Abigail Nims, aged fifteen], both English, who wish to remain with the Christian Indians, not only renouncing their nation, but even wishing to live *en sauvages*." But from the Indians' standpoint, and perhaps from their own, captives such as John Leeth and Thomas Armstrong may have had the best of all possible marriages. After some years with the Indians, Leeth was married to a young woman, "seventeen or eighteen years of age; also a prisoner to the Indians; who had been taken by them when about twenty months old." Armstrong, an adopted Seneca, also married a "full blooded white woman, who like himself had been a captive among the Indians, from infancy, but who unlike him, had not acquired a knowledge of one word of the English language, being essentially Indian in all save blood."[56] Their commitment to each other deepened their commitment to the Indian culture of which they had become equal members.

The captives' social equality was also demonstrated by their being asked to share in the affairs of war and peace, matters of supreme importance to Indian society. One of the Frenchmen Father Simon Le Moyne redeemed from the Iroquois in 1661 was "all ready to give himself up to vice and embrace the life of an Indian, having even cast in his lot with some Iroquois for accompanying them on a hostile raid." When the Senecas who had adopted Thomas Peart decided to "make a War Excursion," they asked him to go with them. But since he was in no mood—and no physical condition— to play the Indian, "he determinately refused them, and was therefore left at Home with the Family." The young Englishman who became Old White Chief was far more eager to defend his new culture, but his origins somewhat limited his military activity. "When I grew to manhood," he recalled, "I went with them [his Iroquois kinsmen] on the warpath against the neighboring tribes, but never against the white settlers, lest by some unlucky accident I might be recognized and claimed by former friends." Other captives, many of them famous renegades, were less cautious. Charlevoix noticed in his travels in Canada that adopted captives "frequently enter into the spirit of the nation, of which they are become members, in such a manner, that they make no difficulty of going to war against their own countrymen." It was behavior such as this that prompted Sir William Johnson to praise Bouquet after his expedition to the Ohio for compelling the Indians to give up every white person, even the "Children born of White Women. That mixed Race," he wrote, referring to first-generation captives as well, "forgetting their Ancestry on one side are found to be the most Inveterate of any, and would greatly Augment their numbers."[57]

It is ironic that the most famous renegade of all should have introduced ten-year-old Oliver Spencer to the ultimate opportunity for an adopted captive. When he had been a captive for less than three weeks, Spencer met Simon Girty, "the very picture of a villain," at a Shawnee village below his own. After various boasts and enquiries, wrote Spencer, "he ended by telling me that I would never see home; but if I should 'turn out to be a good hunter and a brave warrior I might one day be a chief.'" Girty's prediction may not have been meant to tease a small boy with impossible delusions of grandeur, for the Indians of the Northeast readily admitted white captives to their highest councils and offices.[58]

Just after Thomas Ridout was captured on the Ohio, he was surprised to meet an English-speaking "white man, about twenty-two years of age, who had been taken prisoner when a lad and had been adopted, and now was a chief among the Shawanese." He need not have been surprised, for there were many more like him. John Tarbell, the man who visited his Groton relatives in Indian dress, was not only "one of the wealthiest" of the Caughnawagas but "the eldest chief and chief speaker of the tribe." Timothy Rice, formerly of Westborough, Massachusetts, was also made one of the clan chiefs at Caughnawaga, partly by inheritance from his Indian father but largely for "his own Super[io]r Talents" and "war-like Spirit for which he was much celebrated."[59]

Perhaps the most telling evidence of the Indians' receptivity to adopted white leadership comes from Old White Chief, an adopted Iroquois.

> I was made a chief at an early age [he recalled in 1836] and as my sons grew to manhood they also were made chiefs. . . . After my youngest son was made chief I could see, as I thought, that some of the Indians were jealous of the distinction I enjoyed and it gave me uneasiness. This was the first time I ever entertained the thought of leaving my Indian friends. I felt sure that it was displeasing to the Indians to have three of my sons, as well as myself, promoted to the office of chief. My wife was well pleased to leave with me, and my sons said, "Father, we will go wherever you will lead us."
>
> I then broke the subject to some of my Indian relatives, who were very much disturbed at my decision. They immediately called the chiefs and warriors together and laid the plan before them. They gravely deliberated upon the subject for some hours, and then a large majority decided that they would not consent to our leaving. They said, "We cannot give up our son and brother" (meaning myself) "nor our nephews" (meaning my children). "They have lived on our game and grown strong and powerful among us. They are good and true men. We cannot do without them. We cannot give them to the pale faces. We shall grow weak if they leave us. We will give them the best we have left. Let them choose where they will live. No one shall disturb them. We need their wisdom and their strength to help us. If they are in high places, let them be there. We know they will honor us."[60]

"We yielded to their importunity," said the old chief, and "I have never had any reason to regret my decision." In public office as in every sphere of Indian life, the colonial captives found that the color of their skin was unimportant; only their talent and their inclination of heart mattered.

Understandably, neither their skill nor their loyalty was left to chance. From the moment the captives, especially the young ones, came under their charge, the Indians made a concerted effort to inculcate in them Indian habits of mind and body. If the captives could be taught to think, act, and react like Indians, they would effectively cease to be European and would assume an Indian identity.[61] This was the Indians' goal, toward which they bent every effort in the weeks and months that followed their formal adoption of the white captives.

The educational character of Indian society was recognized by even the most inveterately European captives. Titus King, a twenty-six-year-old New England soldier, spent a year with the Canadian Indians at St. François trying—unsuccessfully—to undo their education of "Eight or ten young [English] Children." What "an awfull School this [is] for Children," he wrote. "When We See how Quick they will Fall in with the Indians ways, nothing Seems to be more takeing in Six months time they Forsake Father and mother Forgit thir own Land Refuess to Speak there own toungue and Seemin[g]ly be Holley Swollowed up with the Indians." The older the person, of course, the longer it took to become fully Indianized. Mary Jemison, captured at the age of fifteen, took three or four years to forget her natural parents and the home she had once loved. "If I had been taken in infancy," she said, "I should have been contented in my situation." Some captives, commonly those over fifteen or sixteen years old, never made the transition from European to Indian. Twenty-four-year-old Thomas Gist, soldier and son of a famous scout and Indian agent, accommodated himself to his adoption and Indian life for just one year and then made plans to escape. "All curiosity with regard to acting the part of an Indian," he related, "which I could do very well, being th[o]rougherly satisfied, I was determined to be what I really was."[62]

Children, however, took little time to "fall in with the Indians ways." Titus King mentioned six months. The Reverend John Williams witnessed the effects of eight or nine months when he stopped at St. François in February 1704. There, he said, "we found several poor children, who had been taken from the eastward [Maine] the summer before; a sight very affecting, they being in habit very much like Indians, and in manners very much symbolizing with them." When young Joseph Noble visited his captive sister in Montreal, "he still belonged to the St. François tribe of Indians, and was dressed remarkably fine, having forty or fifty broaches in his shirt, clasps on his arm, and a great variety of knots and bells about his clothing. He brought his little sister . . . a young fawn, a basket of cranberries, and a lump of sap sugar." Sometime later he was purchased from the Indians by a French gentleman who promptly "dressed him in the French style; but he never appeared so bold and majestic, so spirited and vivacious, as when arrayed in his Indian habit and associating with his Indian friends."[63]

The key to any culture is its language, and the young captives were quick to learn the Indian dialects of their new families. Their retentive memories and flair for imitation made them ready students, while the Indian languages, at once oral, concrete, and mythopoeic, lightened the task. In less than six months ten-year-old Oliver Spencer had "acquired a sufficient knowledge of the Shawnee tongue to understand all ordinary conversation and, indeed, the greater part of all that I heard (accompanied, as their conversation and speeches were, with the most significant gestures)," which enabled him to listen "with much pleasure and sometimes with deep interest" to his Indian mother tell of battles, heroes, and history in the long winter evenings. When Jemima Howe was allowed to visit her four-year-old son at a neighboring Indian village in Canada, he greeted her "in the Indian tongue" with "Mother, are you come?" He too had been a prisoner for only six months. In just one year Jasper Parrish, an eleven-year-old Delaware captive, could "understand their conversation very well and could speak so as to be understood by them."[64]

The early weeks of captivity could be disquieting if there were no English- or French-speaking Indians or prisoners in the village to lend the comfort of a familiar language while the captives struggled to acquire a strange one. If a captive's family left for their winter hunting camp before he could learn their language, he might find himself, like Thomas Gist, "without any com[p]any that could unders[t]and one word that I spake." "Thus I continued, near five months," he wrote, "sometimes reading, other times singing, never melancholy but when alone. . . . About the first of April (1759) I prevailed on the family to return to town, and by the last of the month all the Indians and prisoners returned, when I once more had the pleasure to talk to people that understood what I said."[65]

Younger captives probably missed the familiarity of their native language less than the adult Gist. Certainly they never lacked eager teachers. Mary Jemison recalled that her Seneca sisters were "diligent in teaching me their language; and to their great satisfaction I soon learned so that I could understand it readily, and speak it fluently." Even Gist was the recipient of enthusiastic, if informal, instruction from a native speaker. One of his adopted cousins, who was about five or six years old and his "favorite in the family," was always "chattering some thing" with him. "From him," said Gist affectionately, "I learn'd more than from all the rest, and he learn'd English as fast as [I] did Indian."[66]

As in any school, language was only one of many subjects of instruction. Since the Indians generally asssumed that whites were physically inferior to themselves, captive boys were often prepared for the hardy life of hunters and warriors by a rigorous program of physical training. John McCullough, aged eight, was put through the traditional Indian course by his adoptive uncle. "In the beginning of winter," McCullough recalled, "he used to raise me by day light every morning, and make me sit down in the creek up to my chin in the cold water, in order to make me hardy as he said, whilst he would sit on the bank smoking his pipe until he thought I had been long enough in the water, he would then bid me to dive. After I came out of the water he would order me not to go near the fire until I would be dry. I was kept at that till the water was frozen over, he would then break the ice for me and send me in as before." As shocking as it may have been to his system, such treatment did nothing to turn him against Indian life. Indeed, he was transparently proud that he had borne up under the strenuous regimen "with the firmness of an Indian." Becoming an Indian was as much a challenge and an adventure for the young colonists as it was a "sore trial," and many of them responded to it with alacrity and zest. Of children their age we should not expect any less.[67]

The captives were taught not only to speak and to endure as Indians but to act as Indians in the daily social and economic life of the community. Naturally, boys were taught the part of men and girls the part of women, and according to most colonial sources—written, it should be noted, predominantly by men—the boys enjoyed the better fate. The new Mohawk Pierre Radisson boasted that "I took all the pleasures imaginable . . . shooting partridges and squirrels, playing most part of the day with my companions." An Ohio pioneer remembered that the prisoners from his party were "put into different families, the women to hard drudging and the boys to run wild with the young Indians, to amuse themselves with bow and arrow, dabble in the water, or obey any other notion their wild natures might dictate." William Walton, the author of the Gilbert family captivity narrative, also felt that the "Labour and Drudgery" in an Indian family fell to "the Share of the Women." He described fourteen-year-old Abner Gilbert as living a "dronish Indian life, idle and poor, having no other Employ than the gathering of Hickory-Nuts; and although young," Walton insisted, "his Situation was very irksome." Just how irksome the boy found his freedom from colonial farm chores was revealed when the ingenuous Walton related that "Abner, having no useful Employ, amused himself with catching fish in the Lake. . . . Not being of an impatient Disposition," said Walton soberly, "he bore his Captivity without repining."[68]

While most captive boys had "nothing to do, but cut a little wood for the fire," draw water for cooking and drinking, and "shoot Blackbirds that came to eat up the corn," they enjoyed "some leisure" for "hunting and other innocent devertions in the woods." Women and girls, on the other hand, shared the burdens—onerous ones in English eyes—of their Indian counterparts. But Mary Jemison, who had been taught English ways for fifteen years before becoming an Indian, felt that the Indian women's labor "was not severe," their tasks "probably not harder than that [sic] of white women," and their cares "certainly . . . not half as numerous, nor as great." The work of one year was "exactly similar, in almost every respect, to that of the others, without that endless variety that is to be observed in the common labor of the white people. . . . In the summer season, we planted, tended and harvested our corn, and generally had all our children with us; but had no master to oversee or drive us, so that we could work as leisurely as we pleased. . . . In the season of hunting, it was our business, in addition to our cooking, to bring home the game that was taken by the [men], dress it, and carefully preserve the eatable meat, and prepare or dress the skins." "Spinning, weaving, sewing, stocking knitting," and like domestic tasks of colonial women were generally unknown. Unless Jemison was correct, it would be virtually impossible to understand why so many women and girls chose to become Indians. A life of unremitting drudgery, as the English saw it, could certainly hold no attraction for civilized women fresh from frontier farms and villages.[69]

The final and most difficult step in the captives' transition from English to Indian was to acquire the ability to think as Indians, to share unconsciously the values, beliefs, and standards of Indian culture. From an English perspective, this should have been nearly an impossible task for civilized people because they perceived Indian culture as immoral and irreligious and totally antithetical to the civilized life they had known, however briefly. "Certainly," William Smith assumed, "it could never be put in competition with the blessings of improved life and the light of religion."[70] But many captives soon discovered that the colonists had no monopoly on virtue and that in many ways the Indians were morally superior to the Europeans, more Christian than the Christians.

As early as 1643 Roger Williams had written a book to suggest such a thing, but he could be dismissed as a misguided visionary who let the Narragansetts go to his head. It was more difficult to dismiss someone like John Brickell, who had lived with the Indians for four and a half years and had no ax to grind with established religion. "The Delawares are the best people to train up children I ever was with," he wrote. "Their leisure hours are, in a great measure, spent in training up their children to observe what they believe to be right. . . . as a nation they may be considered fit examples for many of us Christians to follow. They certainly follow what they are taught to believe right more closely, and I might say more honestly, in general, than we Christians do the divine precepts of our Redeemer. . . . I know I am influenced to good, even at this day," he concluded, "more from what I learned among them, than what I learned among people of my own color." After many decades with them, Mary Jemison insisted that "the moral character of the Indians was . . . uncontaminated. Their fidelity was perfect, and became proverbial; they were strictly honest; they despised deception and falsehood; and chastity was held in high veneration." Even the Tory historian Peter Oliver, who was no friend to the Indians, admitted that "they have a Religion of their own, which, to the eternal Disgrace of many Nations who boast of Politeness, is more influential on their Conduct than that of those who hold them in so great Contempt." To the acute discomfort of the colonists, more than one captive maintained that the Indians were a "far more moral race than the whites."[71]

In the principled school of Indian life the captives experienced a decisive shift in their cultural and personal identities, a shift that often fostered a considerable degree of what might be called "conversion zeal." A French officer reported that "those Prisoners whom the Indians keep with them . . . are often more brutish, boisterous in their Behaviour and loose in their Manners than the Indians," and thought that "they affect that kind of Behaviour thro' Fear of and to recommend themselves to the Indians." Matthew Bunn, a nineteen-year-old soldier, was the object of such behavior when he was enslaved—not adopted—by the Maumee in 1791. "After I had eaten," he related, "they brought me a little prisoner boy, that had been taken about two years before, on the river called Monongahela, though he delighted more in the ways of the savages than in the ways of Christians; he used me worse than any of the Indians, for he would tell me to do this, that, and the other, and if I did not do it, or made any resistance, the Indians would threaten to kill me, and he would kick and cuff me about in such a manner, that I hardly dared to say my soul was my own." What Bunn experienced was the attempt of the new converts to pattern their behavior after their young Indian counterparts, who, a Puritan minister observed, "are as much to be dreaded by captives as those of maturer years, and in many cases much more so; for, unlike cultivated people, they have no restraints upon their mischievous and savage propensities, which they indulge in cruelties." "The young Indians," noted another minister, "often signalized their cruelty in treating captives inhumanly out of sight of the elder, and when inquiry was made in the matter, the insulted captive must either be silent or put the best face on it, to prevent worse treatment for the future."[72]

Although fear undoubtedly accounted for some of the converts' initial behavior, desire to win the approval of their new relatives also played a part. Pierre Radisson said he "did what I could to get familiarity with them . . . , taking all freedom, which [his Mohawk mother] enticed me to do. . . ." "I had lived in my new habitation about a week," recalled Oliver Spencer, "and having given up all hope of escaping . . . began to regard it as my future home. . . . I strove to be cheerful, and by my ready obedience to ingratiate myself with Cooh-coo-cheeh [his Indian mistress], for whose kindness I felt grateful." A year after James Smith had been adopted, a number of prisoners were brought in by his new kinsmen and a gauntlet formed to welcome them. Smith "went and told them how they were to act" and then "fell into one of the ranks with the Indians, shouting and yelling like them." One middle-aged man's turn came, and "as they were not very severe on him," confessed the new Indian, "as he passed me I hit him with a piece of pumpkin—which pleased the Indians much." If their zeal to emulate the Indians sometimes exceeded their mercy, the captives had nonetheless fulfilled their new families' expectations: they had begun to act as Indians in spirit as well as body. Only time would be necessary to transform their conscious efforts into unconscious habits and complete their cultural conversion.[73]

"By what power does it come to pass," asked Crèvecoeur, "that children who have been adopted when young among these people, . . . and even grown persons . . . can never be prevailed on to re-adopt European manners?"[74] Given the malleability of youth, we should not be surprised that children underwent a rather sudden and permanent transition from European to Indian—although we might be pressed to explain why so few Indian children made the transition in the opposite direction. But the adult colonists who became Indians cannot be explained as easily, for the simple reason that they, unlike many of the children, were fully conscious of their cultural identities while they were being subjected to the Indians' assiduous attempts to convert them. Consequently, their cultural metamorphosis involved a large degree of personal choice.

The great majority of white Indians left no explanations for their choice. Forgetting their original language and their past, they simply disappeared into their adopted society. But those captives who returned to write narratives of their experiences left several clues to the motives of those who chose to stay behind. They stayed because they found Indian life to possess a strong sense of community, abundant love, and uncommon integrity—values that the European colonists also honored, if less successfully. But Indian life was attractive for other values—for social equality, mobility, adventure, and, as two adult converts acknowledged, "the most perfect freedom, the ease of living, [and] the absence of those cares and corroding solicitudes which so often prevail with us." As we have learned recently, these were values that were not being realized in the older, increasingly crowded, fragmented, and contentious communities of the Atlantic seaboard, or even in the newer frontier settlements.[75] By contrast, as Crèvecoeur said, there must have been in the Indians' "social bond something singularly captivating."[76] Whatever it was, its power had no better measure than the large number of French and English colonists who became, contrary to the civilized assumptions of their countrymen, white Indians.

Education and Empire

Soap and education are not as sudden as a massacre,
but they are more deadly in the long run.

MARK TWAIN

Christianity is and always has been an evangelical, a proselytizing religion; missionaries are essential to its nature. Christ aimed at the spiritual conquest of the whole world, not just the Near or Middle East. The earthly realization of the Christian vision entails the conversion of the adherents of all other religions—Muslim, Buddhist, Taoist, polytheist, monotheist. By its very nature, Christianity is exclusive and intolerant; one cannot be a Hindu and a Christian at the same time. In the shadow of the Cross, all other beliefs and practices pale into insignificance.

Christianity is also a historical religion, a faith more of time than place. In the birth, life, and death of Christ it found its origins, vision, and driving purpose. Time for Christians pivots on Christ's axis—B.C. and A.D.—and the Bible, divided into Old and New Testaments, is the telling of that epic story. Historical time is merely the premonition and fulfillment of God's prophecies, which will culminate definitively, if figuratively, on the Last Day of Judgment. The meantime, the here and now, is dedicated to the endless and usually thankless task of saving pagans and heretics from eternal perdition.

It was fitting, if also paradoxical, that Christopher Columbus, who witnessed the final *reconquista* of Spain from the Moors, discovered a New World while seeking in one corner of the Old World (China) the wealth to mount an anachronistic crusade to liberate Jerusalem in another and restore it as the seat of Christendom.[1] Wishing to expand the empire of Christianity by conquering ancient and obdurate enemies, he discovered a whole continent of new, seemingly docile souls perishing without benefit of clergy. By pulling America into the relentless stream of Christian time, Columbus inadvertently redirected the evangelical energies of European Christianity toward the Occident and introduced the American natives to the civilized notion of conquest as conversion. In that deceptive guise, much harm was—and still is—done in the name of philanthropy.

When Spain's European competitors followed her to the New World, they too cloaked their conquests in religious garb. While every small-scale tactical incursion upon native life, land, and liberty was not regarded as divinely inspired, the comprehensive plan of conquest was promoted invariably as the fruit of religious inspiration or rationalization. But the Christian motives behind the invasion were never in any sense pure. Bold-faced crimes could wear the mask of God with easy effrontery, and the Christianity of Western Europe was not a text of high-minded morality and faith so much as a complicated, culture-bound product of the societies that professed it. The doctrinal beliefs found in most catechisms might be considered the refined essence of Christianity, but the missionaries and their secular agents always demanded of native converts more than sincere profession of a creed. Catholic and Protestant creeds alike were surrounded by traditional and cultural requirements that went far beyond belief into the nooks and crannies of behavior and appearance.

Christian scripture spoke of conversion as the shucking of "the old man, which is corrupt" and the putting on of "the new man, which after God is created in righteousness and true holiness."[2] When a European neophyte shucked "the old man," he remained a European in culture. But when an Indian was asked to discard his old self, he was asked to commit cultural suicide, to cease to be an Indian, because *his* evil past was no mere metaphor like original sin and did not consist of a series of easily repentable actions taken in a continuous cultural frame of reference. He was expected to peel off his whole cultural being, his "savagery," in order to prepare for whitewashing in "the blood of the Lamb." "When a man is converted," the Reverend William Crashawe told the new governor of Virginia in 1609, "he is cast in a new mould." Even the dregs of English society could become "new men," the preacher allowed, but only if they were trained up, as the Indians should be, in "severe discipline, sharpe lawes, a hard life, and much labor."[3] For the poor laboring classes from England's urban streets, the "new mould" was still discernibly English, different in degree, perhaps, from their old life, but not in kind. The Indians, on the other hand, had to be given "Civilitie for their bodies" as well as "Christianitie for their soules," which was tantamount to stripping them bare of the last vestiges of their own culture.

The conversion of the natives entailed such a cultural metamorphosis that they became trusted scouts, sentries, and soldiers for the European colony whose churches they attended. The fiercest defenders of colonial borders were the *reserve* and "praying" Indians, who now scalped under the sign of the Cross. Having fomented civil strife in native villages by their proselytizing, the missionaries often instigated civil war by pitting tribesmen, even kinsmen, against each other to honor the Prince of Peace. Having divided Satan's minions, the black robes helped to conquer them all, some by faith, others by fire.

According to the Christian gospel, the dominant mark of Lucifer and his Indian servants was pride, the original sin. One of the striking ironies of the invasion within was that in seeking to crush the natives' "overweening pride," the colonists, missionaries and laymen alike, inflated the same sin to excessive proportions in their own cultures. The blind faith that they were God's "chosen people" prevented them from recognizing the tragic hubris in their national compulsions to "reduce" the natives to less than they were. Born of pride, the European philosophy of conversion spawned the triple terrors of cultural arrogance, dogmatism, and intolerance on a grand scale. Discovering the natives, respecting them, and leaving them to set their own collective courses was not a real possibility for Early Modern man. "The zeal of the conqueror [was] so mixed with the zeal of the missionary that it was hopeless to expect *laissez-faire.* . . ."[4]

In mistaking history for a primer in "the cant of conquest," the invaders missed that comparative opportunity Montaigne spoke of when he described "this great universe" as "the true looking-glasse wherin we must looke, if we will know whether we be of a good stamp, or in the right byase. . . . So many strange humours, sundrie sects, varying judgements, diverse opinions, different lawes, and fantasticall customes teach us to judge rightly of ours, and instruct our judgement to acknowledge [its] imperfections and naturall weaknesse, which is no easie an apprentiship." They missed the chance to learn that "savage" and "civilized" are relative terms without objective authority or content, that "men call that barbarisme" which simply is "not common to them."[5] Such a lesson was badly needed in that fiercely intolerant age, as it still is in our own more subtly intolerant one.

Most of the European colonists, however, were not men of quiet contemplation or philosophical reflection—they were men of action. Indeed, most colonists were only inadvertent or passive invaders who wanted to get on with the job of living in a new place—raising a family, plying a trade, belonging to a community—rather than having anything to do, good or ill, with Indians. The vast majority of colonists were probably unsympathetic or simply indifferent to the missionaries and their reductive plans for the natives, except to the extent that a bloodless solution to "the Indian problem" would prove, at least in the short run, cheaper and safer than cruder, more direct methods. We know that laymen cheered when John Eliot's shallop was rammed in Boston Harbor during the racial tensions of King Philip's War, predicted the failure of Eleazar Wheelock's experiment in Indian education, and put bullets in the collection plate when missionaries sought funds for new missions. This should remind us that while the missionaries and their congregations shared many assumptions about the superiority of "civilization" and the deficiencies of "savagery," the black robes, like their native converts, constituted small factions within larger societies that passively or actively resisted the missions.

These larger societies, French, English, and Indian, waged war with each other on a number of fronts—over trading counters, in courts and councils, in plowed fields and on battlefields, as well as in classrooms and church pews. Eventually, and with very few exceptions, the Indians lost badly, if not to deadly diseases alone. Sooner or later, in different ways and degrees, Indian communities were deprived of sovereignty, land, economic independence, mobility, dignity, and living members. The Christian missions played a prominent part in the European victories, particularly of the English. First, the "civilizing" phase of the missions served effectively to disarm and pacify many natives who might otherwise have resisted the newcomers more forcibly. Second, the agricultural assumptions of the civilizing credo procured from the now-sedentary natives huge tracts of former hunting land for colonial expansion, which had the hidden benefit of postponing or obviating altogether the need for more final solutions and even greater injustice. Finally, "mission Indians" helped the colonists fight their own wars against resistant natives and foreign rivals, often providing the vital margin between survival and defeat. Without the missionaries' sway over armed neophytes, the timing and duration of America's intercolonial conflicts and therefore the history of colonial North America would have been very different indeed.

Though the Indians eventually lost and usually lost badly, the Christian missions also softened the blow. Conversion was, as many natives found, one way of adapting to the invasion of America. For those worst hit by the invaders and their microbes, Natick and Sillery served as halfway houses on the road to recovery. The full civilizing remedy was the colonial equivalent of the Marshall Plan, which offered the hapless natives a complete program of moral rearmament, social reconstruction, and religious revitalization. If racism, disease, lawlessness, and hypocrisy eventually spelled the demise of many Christian Indian groups—as they certainly did—the *initial* effectiveness of the mission program cannot be denied for those Indians faced with accommodation or annihilation.

The missions also provided the natives with practical techniques for coping with the invaders. Literacy and elementary arithmetic, a knowledge of European laws, deeds, and the court system, quarantine and nursing, and a greatly expanded geography all helped the Indians adjust to their own new world. Of greater importance still was the acquisition of a new cosmology and religion which were capable of explaining, predicting, and controlling the larger universe into which they had been yanked. Novel diseases, minor miracles of technology, distant places, and unknown faces could all be explained and safely domesticated by the power of the printed word and the knowledge professed by the black robes. And finally, the praying towns and *reserves*, surrounded by arrogant and eventually racist colonial communities, helped the Indians to maintain the crucial ethnic core at the heart of their newly acquired Christian personae. As a form of protective coloration, conversion—however sincere or complete—preserved their ethnic identity as particular Indian groups on familiar pieces of land that carried their inner history.[6]

In the end the European conquest of America was nearly total, but it was not obtained without a share of deep ironies. One is that the vast majority of Indians in the colonial period, for whom "Example [was] before precept," were not seduced by Christianity because the Christians with whom they were most conversant taught them the vices of Europe and few, if any, virtues. "What great offence hath been given by many profane men," lamented Edward Winslow, "who, being but seeming Christians, have made Christ and Christianity stink in the nostrils of the poor infidels and so laid a stumbling-block before them."[7]

One ironic consequence of the disparity between Christian preaching and practice was, in the words of Sir William Johnson, that "those Indians who have the least intercourse with us, have the most integrity, & possess the best Moral Qualities." Another was the embarrassing opinion of European captives and other persons who knew both cultures well that the natives who were uncontaminated by European vice inadvertently, naturally, lived a purer Christian text than the colonial Christians. A final irony was that the standard native technique for frustrating aggressive missionaries and other reformers, their "secret weapon" of outer complaisance and inner disagreement, was considered "a form of politeness" in native society. Thus, with a happy brand of poetic justice, a piece of savage civility was used to stymie the civilized savagery of men who intruded themselves upon native life and ran roughshod over the bounds of native courtesy.[8]

But the final strategy of the Indians in the uneven contest of cultures was the psychological and moral equivalent of the definitive fencer's move in which he wraps his sword around his opponent's and lets both weapons fly out of their hands to the ground. The Indians' conversion of hundreds of "civilized" captives to "savage" life tore from the hands of the colonists, however briefly, their sharp conceit as the "chosen people" of God and their unexamined faith in the superiority of their own customs and opinions. With Montaigne we can only regret that the invaders, stripped bare and defenseless, did not seize the moment for self-understanding, tolerance, and true humiliation.

Abbreviations

AN Archives Nationales, Colonies, Paris; microfilm in Public Archives of Canada, Ottawa
BAE Bureau of American Ethnology, Smithsonian Institution, Washington, D.C.
Bougainville, *Journals* Edward P. Hamilton, ed. and trans., *Adventure in the Wilderness: The American Journals of Louis Antoine de Bougainville, 1756–1760* (Norman, Okla., 1964). French original: H.-R. Casgrain, ed., *Journal du Marquis de Montcalm durent ses Campagnes en Canada de 1756 à 1759* (Quebec, 1895)
Coll. de Manuscrits *Collection de manuscrits contenant lettres, mémoires, et autres documents historiques relatif à la Nouvelle-France*, 4 vols. (Quebec, 1883–85)
Colls. Conn. His. Soc. *Collections of the Connecticut Historical Society*
Colls. Mass. His. Soc. *Collections of the Massachusetts Historical Society*
Conn. Archives Connecticut Archives, State Library, Hartford
Conn. Col. Recs. J. H. Trumbull and C. J. Hoadly, eds., *The Public Records of the Colony of Connecticut*, 15 vols. (Hartford, 1850–90)
C.S.P.Col. W. Noel Sainsbury et al., eds., *Calendar of State Papers, Colonial Series, America and the West Indies* (London, 1860–)
DCB *Dictionary of Canadian Biography* (Toronto and Quebec, 1966–)
Doc. His. Maine William Willis and James Phinney Baxter, eds., *Documentary History of the State of Maine, Collections of the Maine Historical Society*, 2d ser., vols. 1–24 (Portland, 1869–1916)
Doc. His. N.Y. Edmund B. O'Callaghan, ed., *Documentary History of the State of New York*, 4 vols. (Albany, 1849–51)
Eliot, *Brief Narrative* John Eliot, *A Brief Narrative of the Progress of the Gospel amongst the Indians in New England, in the Year 1670* (London, 1671), reprinted in *Old South Leaflets*, no. 21, 1–9
Eliot, *Indian Dialogues* *John Eliot's Indian Dialogues: A Study in Cultural Interaction* [Cambridge, Mass., 1671], ed. Henry W. Bowden and James P. Ronda (Westport, Conn., 1980)
Eliot, *Late Manifestation* John Eliot, *A Late and Further Manifestation of the Progress of the Gospel amongst the Indians in New-England* (London, 1655), in *Colls. Mass. His. Soc.*, 3d ser., 4 (1834): 261–87
Eliot and Mayhew, *Tears of Repentance* John Eliot and Thomas Mayhew, *Tears of Repentance; or, A Further Narrative of the Progress of the Gospel amongst the Indians in New-England* (London, 1653), in *Colls. Mass. His. Soc.*, 3d ser., 4 (1834): 197–260
Force, *Tracts* Peter Force, comp., *Tracts and Other Papers, Relating Principally to the Origin, Settlement, and Progress of the Colonies in North America from the Discovery of the Country to the Year 1776*, 4 vols. (Washington, D.C., 1836–47)
Ford, *Some Correspondence* John W. Ford, ed., *Some Correspondence between the Governors and Treasurers of the New England Company in London and the Commissioners of the United Colonies in America, the Missionaries of the Company, and Others between the Years 1657 and 1712* (London, 1896)
Gookin, *Historical Collections* Daniel Gookin, *Historical Collections of the Indians in New England* [1674], ed. Jeffrey H. Fiske (Towtaid, N.J., 1970)
Hawley Manuscripts Gideon Hawley Manuscripts, Massachusetts Historical Society, Boston
Hawley Papers The Papers of Gideon Hawley, Congregational Library, Boston, Mass.
HNAI *Handbook of North American Indians*, gen. ed. William C. Sturtevant, 20 vols. (Washington, D.C.: Smithsonian Institution, 1978–)

Johnson Papers James Sullivan et al., eds., *The Papers of Sir William Johnson*, 14 vols. (Albany, N.Y., 1921–62)

JR Reuben Gold Thwaites, ed., *The Jesuit Relations and Allied Documents*, 73 vols. (Cleveland, 1896–1901)

Mass. Archives Massachusetts Archives, State House, Boston

Mass. Col. Recs. Nathaniel B. Shurtleff, ed., *Records of the Governor and Company of the Massachusetts Bay in New England*, 6 vols. (Boston, 1853–54)

NEHGR *New-England Historical and Genealogical Register*

NYCD Edmund B. O'Callaghan and Berthold Fernow, eds., *Documents Relative to the Colonial History of the State of New-York*, 15 vols. (Albany, 1856–87)

OED *The Oxford English Dictionary on Historical Principles*, 13 vols.

ONEAH Original Narratives of Early American History, gen. ed. J. Franklin Jameson

PAC Public Archives of Canada, Ottawa

Pa. Col. Recs. *Minutes of the Provincial Council of Pennsylvania*, 16 vols. (Philadelphia and Harrisburg, 1851–53)

Ply. Col. Recs. Nathaniel B. Shurtleff et al., eds., *Records of the Colony of New Plymouth in New England*, 12 vols. (Boston, 1855–61)

Pubs. Col. Soc. Mass. *Publications of the Colonial Society of Massachusetts*

RAPQ *Rapport de l'Archiviste de la Province de Québec*

RHAF *Revue d'Histoire de l'Amérique Française*

R.I. Col. Recs. John Russell Bartlett, ed., *Records of the Colony of Rhode Island and Providence Plantations, in New England*, 10 vols. (Providence, 1856–65)

Sagard, *Histoire du Canada* Gabriel Sagard-Théodat, *Histoire du Canada et voyages que les frères mineurs Recollects y ont faicts pour la conversion des infidèles* (Paris, 1636), trans. H. H. Langton, University of Toronto Library, MS 7 (pagination follows that of the book)

Shepard, *Clear Sun-shine* Thomas Shepard, *The Clear Sun-shine of the Gospel Breaking Forth upon the Indians in New-England* [London, 1648], in *Colls. Mass. His. Soc.*, 3d ser., 4 (1834): 25–67

[Shepard], *Day-Breaking* [Thomas Shepard], *The Day-Breaking, if not the Sun-Rising of the Gospell with the Indians in New-England* [London, 1647], in *Colls. Mass. His. Soc.*, 3d ser., 4 (1834): 1–23

Sibley's Harvard Graduates John L. Sibley and Clifford K. Shipton, *Biographical Sketches of Those Who Attended Harvard College* (Cambridge, Mass., 1873–)

Va. Co. Recs. Susan M. Kingsbury, ed., *The Records of the Virginia Company of London*, 4 vols. (Washington, D.C., 1906–35)

Wheelock Papers The Papers of Eleazar Wheelock (1728–79), Dartmouth College Library, Hanover, N.H. Calendar number from *A Guide to the Microfilm Edition of the Papers of Eleazar Wheelock* (Hanover: Dartmouth College Library, 1971); the first three digits indicate the year of the manuscript: e.g., 760628 is 1760.

Whitfield, *Light Appearing* Henry Whitfield, *The Light Appearing More and More towards the Perfect Day; or, A Farther Discovery of the Present State of the Indians in New-England* (London, 1651), in *Colls. Mass. His. Soc.*, 3d ser., 4 (1834): 100–147

Whitfield, *Strength Out of Weaknesse* Henry Whitfield, *Strength Out of Weaknesse; or, A Glorious Manifestation of the Further Progresse of the Gospel among the Indians in New-England* (London, 1652), in *Colls. Mass. His. Soc.*, 3d ser., 4 (1834): 149–96

Winslow, *Glorious Progress* Edward Winslow, *The Glorious Progress of the Gospel, amongst the Indians in New England* (London, 1649), in *Colls. Mass. His. Soc.*, 3d ser., 4 (1834): 69–98

WMQ *The William and Mary Quarterly*

Notes

1. THOSE POOR BLIND INFIDELS

1. Charles Horton Cooley, *Life and the Student* (New York, 1927), 201-2; Robert F. Berkhofer, Jr., *A Behavioral Approach to Historical Analysis* (New York, 1969), chs. 2-3.

2. Silas Tertius Rand, *Legends of the Micmacs* (New York, 1894), 225-26. This version was narrated in Micmac by Josiah Jeremy in 1869. For a similar tradition, see Clayton Coleman Hall, ed., *Narratives of Early Maryland, 1633-1684*, ONEAH (New York, 1910), 40, 42.

3. Ella Elizabeth Clark, ed., *Indian Legends of Canada* (Toronto, 1960), 150-51. This story was told by a member of the Bear clan in 1855.

4. *JR* 5:119, 121.

5. John Heckewelder, *History, Manners, and Customs of the Indian Nations Who Once Inhabited Pennsylvania and the Neighbouring States* [1818], ed. William G. Reichel (Philadelphia, 1876), 71-75. Heckewelder received this story from an intelligent Delaware man at the end of the eighteenth century.

6. Lawrence C. Wroth, *The Voyages of Giovanni da Verrazzano, 1524-1528* (New Haven, 1970), 134-35; David Beers Quinn, ed., *The Roanoke Voyages, 1584-1590*, Hakluyt Society Publications, 2d ser., vols. 104-5 (London, 1952), 104:111-12.

7. Emma Helen Blair, ed. and trans., *The Indian Tribes of the Upper Mississippi Valley and Region of the Great Lakes*, 2 vols. (Cleveland, 1911), 1:309.

8. H. P. Biggar, ed., *The Voyages of Jacques Cartier*, Publications of the PAC, 11 (Ottawa, 1924): 56, 62, 162-63.

9. Ibid., 165.

10. Louise Phelps Kellogg, ed., *Early Narratives of the Northwest, 1634-1699*, ONEAH (New York, 1917), 129, 155-56.

11. Quinn, *Roanoke Voyages* 104:378-79.

12. Wroth, *Voyages of Verrazzano*, 137.

13. Blair, *Indian Tribes of the Upper Mississippi* 1:308-9; Kellogg, *Early Narratives of the Northwest*, 45-46.

14. James Axtell, *The European and the Indian: Essays in the Ethnohistory of Colonial North America* (New York, 1981), 370 n. 28.

15. *Father Louis Hennepin's Description of Louisiana* [Paris, 1683], trans. Marion E. Cross (Minneapolis, 1938), 82, 96, 98, 105, 108-9, 130.

16. William Wood, *New England's Prospect* [London, 1634], ed. Alden T. Vaughan (Amherst, Mass., 1977), 96.

17. Quinn, *Roanoke Voyages* 104:375-76.

18. Henry S. Burrage, ed., *Early English and French Voyages Chiefly from Hakluyt, 1534-1608*, ONEAH (New York, 1906), 372.

19. Wood, *New England's Prospect*, 96.

20. Wroth, *Voyages of Verrazzano*, 141.

21. Thomas Morton, *New English Canaan* [London, 1632], in Force, *Tracts* 2, no. 5, p. 21. See also Edward Winslow's premature judgment to the same effect in Dwight B. Heath, ed., *A Journal of the Pilgrims at Plymouth: Mourt's Relation* [London, 1622] (New York, 1963), 83.

22. Philip L. Barbour, ed., *The Jamestown Voyages under the First Charter, 1606-1609*, Hakluyt Society Publications, 2d ser., vols. 136-37 (Cambridge, 1969), 136:143, 137:364. See also William Strachey, *The Historie of Travell into Virginia Britania (1612)*, ed. Louis B. Wright and Virginia Freund, Hakluyt Society Publications, 2d ser., vol. 103 (London, 1953), 88-89; Alexander Whitaker, *Good Newes from Virginia* (London, 1613), 23-24; Hall, *Narratives of Early Maryland*, 44-45.

23. [Edward] *Johnson's Wonder-Working Providence, 1628–1651*, ed. J. Franklin Jameson, ONEAH (New York, 1910), 263. See also Wood, *New England's Prospect*, 100–102.

24. *JR* 8:121.

25. Thomas Hobbes, *Leviathan* [London, 1651], ed. Michael Oakeshott (Oxford, 1946), 69. For example, the Recollect priest Gabriel Sagard thought that the Hurons "do not recognize and worship any real divinity or god in heaven or on earth of whom they could give any rational account and whom we could recognize" (Sagard, *Histoire du Canada*, 396–97).

26. Anthony F. C. Wallace, *Religion: An Anthropological View* (New York: 1966), 107.

27. Jack Goody and Ian Watt, "The Consequences of Literacy," *Comparative Studies in Society and History* 5 (1962–63): 304–45, at 310, 344; Walter J. Ong, *The Presence of the Word: Some Prolegomena for Cultural and Religious History* (New Haven, 1967), esp. ch. 3; idem, *Orality and Literacy: The Technologizing of the Word* (New York, 1982); Marshall McLuhan, *The Gutenberg Galaxy: The Making of Typographic Man* (Toronto, 1962).

28. Anthony F. C. Wallace, *The Death and Rebirth of the Seneca* (New York, 1970), 59–75.

29. Axtell, *The European and the Indian*, ch. 5; Åke Hultkrantz, "The Problem of Christian Influence on Northern Algonkian Eschatology," *Studies in Religion/Sciences Religieuses* 9 (1980):161–83.

30. *David Zeisberger's History of the Northern American Indians*, ed. Archer Butler Hulbert and William Nathaniel Schwarze (Columbus: Ohio State Archaeological and Historical Society, 1910), 132–33.

31. Raymond D. Fogelson and Richard N. Adams, eds., *The Anthropology of Power: Ethnographic Studies from Asia, Oceania, and the New World* (New York, 1977), chs. 11 (Ojibwa), 13 (Seneca), 14 (Cherokee); A. Irving Hallowell, *Culture and Experience* (Philadelphia, 1955), chs. 8, 13–15; Raymond D. Fogelson, ed., *Contributions to Anthropology: Selected Papers of A. Irving Hallowell* (Chicago, 1976), chs. 9–10; Frank G. Speck, "Penobscot Tales and Religious Beliefs," *Journal of American Folklore* 48 (1935):5.

32. Arthur C. Parker, "Iroquois Uses of Maize and Other Food Plants," in William N. Fenton, ed., *Parker on the Iroquois* (Syracuse, 1968), Book One; John Witthoft, *Green Corn Ceremonialism in the Eastern Woodlands*, Occasional Contributions from the Museum of Anthropology of the University of Michigan, no. 13 (Ann Arbor, 1949); Howard S. Russell, *Indian New England Before the Mayflower* (Hanover, N.H., 1980), chs. 14, 16, 17.

33. The preceding paragraphs are based on a large number of primary sources, such as the Jesuit *Relations* (*JR*) and the works of John Eliot and his New England colleagues. The following secondary works are also pertinent: Wallace, *Religion*; idem, *Death and Rebirth of the Seneca*; Hartley Burr Alexander, *The World's Rim: Great Mysteries of the North American Indians* (Lincoln, Nebr., 1953); Ruth M. Underhill, *Red Man's Religion: Beliefs and Practices of the Indians North of Mexico* (Chicago, 1965); Ruth Benedict, *The Concept of the Guardian Spirit in North America*, Memoirs of the American Anthropological Association, vol. 29 (Menasha, Wis., 1923); M. R. Harrington, *Religion and Ceremonies of the Lenape*, Indian Notes and Monographs, 2d ser., vol. 19 (New York: Museum of the American Indian, 1921); Ruth Landes, *Ojibwa Religion and the Midéwiwin* (Madison, 1968); A. Irving Hallowell, *The Role of Conjuring in Saulteaux Society*, Publications of the Philadelphia Anthropological Society, vol. 2 (Philadelphia, 1942); Frank G. Speck, *Penobscot Shamanism*, Memoirs of the American Anthropological Association, 6 (Menasha, Wis., 1919), 239–88; Werner Müller, "North America in 1600," in Walter Krickeberg et al., *Pre-Columbian American Religions* (New York, 1968), ch. 3; Frank G. Speck, *Naskapi: The Savage Hunters of the Labrador Peninsula* (Norman, Okla., 1935); Adrian Tanner, *Bringing Home Animals: Religious Ideology and Mode of Production of the Mistassini Cree Hunters* (New York, 1979); Calvin Martin, *Keepers of the Game: Indian-Animal Relationships and the Fur Trade* (Berkeley and Los Angeles, 1978); Elisabeth Tooker, ed., *Native North American Spirituality of the Eastern Woodlands* (New York, 1979); and the works cited in n. 31.

2. RECONNAISSANCE

1. Marcel Trudel, *The Beginnings of New France, 1524–1663*, trans. Patricia Claxton (Toronto, 1973), 37. See also idem, *Histoire de la Nouvelle-France I: Les vaines tentatives, 1524–1603* (Montreal, 1963), 129–31.

2. Wroth, *The Voyages of Verrazzano*, ch. 9.

3. H. P. Biggar, ed., *A Collection of Documents Relating to Jacques Cartier and the Sieur de Roberval*, Publications of the PAC, 14 (Ottawa, 1930): 42. In 1493 and 1494 Pope Alexander VI, a Spaniard, had divided the New World between Spain and Portugal. Thus Francis, whose son married Clement's niece, asked for an interpretation of the papal bulls to avoid trouble with his political ally and new relative.

4. Brian Slattery, "French Claims in North America, 1500–59," *Canadian Historical Review* 59 (1978): 139–69, esp. 145–53.

5. Biggar, *The Voyages of Jacques Cartier*, 56, 65, 80–81.

6. Ibid., 108, 221.

7. Ibid., 139.

8. Ibid., 153, 164–66.

9. Ibid., 180–81.

10. Ibid., 206–7; Jacques Rousseau, "L'annedda et l'arbre de vie," *RHAF* 8 (1954): 171–201.

11. Biggar, *Voyages of Cartier*, 225–27, 249, 252; Biggar, *Cartier and Roberval*, 82.

12. Biggar, *Voyages of Cartier*, 186; Biggar, *Cartier and Roberval*, 128–29.

13. Biggar, *Cartier and Roberval*, 178–85.

14. Ibid., 72, 277, 289–92; Biggar, *Voyages of Cartier*, 263.

15. Biggar, *Cartier and Roberval*, 77–79, 325.

16. Biggar, *Voyages of Cartier*, 259, 264; Biggar, *Cartier and Roberval*, 451, 456–57, 461, 463.

17. Slattery, "French Claims in North America," 165–68.

18. In the sixteenth century the Catholic calendar included 57 fast days and 108 days of abstinence, a total of five and a half meatless months. Colbert reduced the fish days to 92 in 1666 (Marcel Trudel, *Introduction to New France* [Toronto, 1968], 253; Christopher Hill, *Society and Puritanism in Pre-Revolutionary England* [New York, 1964], 148–49).

19. Biggar, *Voyages of Cartier*, 52, 56; Biggar, *Cartier and Roberval*, 78.

20. Richard Hakluyt, *The Principal Navigations, Voyages, Traffiques & Discoveries of the English Nation* [London, 1598–1600], 12 vols. (Glasgow, 1903–5), 8:145–46; E. G. R. Taylor, ed., *The Writings and Correspondence of the Two Richard Hakluyts*, Hakluyt Society Publications, 2d ser., vols. 76–77 (London, 1935), 76:205–6.

21. Hakluyt, *Principal Navigations* 8:145–46; Taylor, *Hakluyt Writings* 76:205, 77:227, 233, 266, 278; D. B. Quinn, "The Voyage of Étienne Bellenger to the Maritimes in 1583: A New Document," *Canadian Historical Review* 43 (1962):328–43. Hakluyt's account of Bellenger's voyage is also printed in David B. Quinn, ed., *New American World: A Documentary History of North America to 1612*, 5 vols. (New York, 1979), 4:306–8.

22. Quinn, "The Voyage of Étienne Bellenger," 330–31, 333; Taylor, *Hakluyt Writings*, 76:207, 77:227, 278; *DCB* 1:421–22. See Trudel, *The Beginnings of New France*, ch. 4, and idem, *Les vaines tentatives*, 218–21.

23. Trudel, *The Beginnings of New France*, 55–56, 62–63; idem, *Les vaines tentatives*, 217–18, 228–35; *DCB* 1:421–22; Quinn, *New American World* 4:308–11.

24. Trudel, *The Beginnings of New France*, 60; idem, *Les vaines tentatives*, 221–26.

3. BEYOND THE COMPTOIR

1. Marc Lescarbot, *The History of New France* [Paris, 1609], trans. W. L. Grant, intro. H. P. Biggar, 3 vols. (Toronto: Champlain Society, 1907–14), 2:211–16.

2. Ibid. 2:217, 227.

3. Ibid. 2:249–71; *The Works of Samuel de Champlain*, ed. H. P. Biggar, 6 vols. (Toronto: Champlain Society, 1922–36), 1:271–80, 301–11, 367–70. See also Morris Bishop, *Champlain: The Life of Fortitude* (New York, 1948), ch. 5; Marcel Trudel, *Histoire de la Nouvelle-France II: Le comptoir, 1604–1627* (Montreal, 1966), ch. 1; Trudel, *The Beginnings of New France*, ch. 6.

4. Andrew Hill Clark, "The Conceptions of 'Empires' of the St. Lawrence and the Mississippi: An Historico-Geographical View with Some Quizzical Comments on Environmental Determinism," *American Review of Canadian Studies* 5 (1975): 4–27, esp. 13–20.

5. Champlain, *Works* 1:412.

6. Ibid. 1:311–469; Lescarbot, *History of New France* 2:272ff.; Bishop, *Champlain*, chs. 6–8; Trudel, *Le comptoir*, ch. 2.

7. Lescarbot, *History of New France* 2:338; Champlain, *Works* 1:419–23. See also Robert Le Blant and Renè Baudry, eds., *Nouveaux documents sur Champlain et son époque I: 1560–1622*, Publications of the PAC, 15 (Ottawa, 1967); Lucien Campeau, ed., *La première mission d'Acadie* (1602–1616), Monumenta Novae Franciae 1 (Rome and Quebec, 1967); and David B. Quinn, "The Preliminaries to New France: Site Selection for the Fur Trade by the French, 1604–1608," *Wirtschaftskräfte und Wirtschaftswege: Festschrift für Hermann Kellenbenz*, ed. Jürgen Schneider, 4 (Nuremberg, 1978): 9–25.

8. Champlain, *Works* 1:232.

9. *JR* 9:132.

10. H. P. Biggar, *The Early Trading Companies of New France* (Toronto, 1901); Trudel, *Le comptoir*, chs. 5–6, 8–9, 13; Gustave Lanctot, *A History of Canada* [*Origins to 1763*], trans. Josephine Hambleton and Margaret M. Cameron, 3 vols. (Cambridge, Mass., 1963–65), vol. 1, chs. 9–11.

11. Father Christian Le Clercq, *First Establishment of the Faith in New France* [Paris, 1691], trans. John Gilmary Shea, 2 vols. (New York, 1881), 1:109–12, 214, 222, 255–56. See Raphael N. Hamilton, "Who Wrote *Premier Établissement de la Foy dans la Nouvelle France?*" *Canadian Historical Review* 57 (1976):265–88 for serious doubts that Le Clercq was its author.

12. *JR* 7:257; Champlain, *Works* 5:326–27.

13. Sagard, *Histoire du Canada*, 139, 717.

14. Champlain, *Works* 2:326–51.

15. Sagard, *Histoire du Canada*, 64–72; Le Clercq, *First Establishment of the Faith* 1:157–74.

16. Trudel, *The Beginnings of New France*, 128–39; idem, *Le comptoir*, 268–69, 293–94.

17. Le Clercq, *First Establishment of the Faith* 1:224.

18. *JR* 1:87, 171, 183; 3:137. See Campeau, *La première mission d'Acadie*, intro., chs. 6–7, and Campeau, *La première mission des Jésuites en Nouvelle-France* (1611–1613), Cahiers d'histoire des Jésuites, 1 (Montreal, 1972):11–47.

19. Sagard, *Histoire du Canada*, 736–37, 805; *JR* 5:39, 45.

20. *Édits, ordonnances royaux, déclarations et arrêts du Conseil d'État du roi concernant le Canada* (Quebec, 1854), 5, 7, 10. See Trudel, *The Beginnings of New France*, 169–71, and idem, *Histoire de la Nouvelle-France III: La seigneurie des Cent-Associés, 1627–1663. Book I: Les événements* (Montreal, 1979), 1–25.

21. *JR* 23:271 (Barthelemy Vimont), 8:15 (Paul Le Jeune).

22. John Dickinson has shown that between 1608 and 1666 fewer than two hundred French colonists were killed by the Iroquois during attacks or in captivity. All but ten of the victims were men, and only five were alone when they were killed. The greatest number of deaths occurred during the accelerated Iroquois offensives of 1650–53 and 1660–61. Although mortality due to the Iroquois never endangered the demographic existence of the colony, the unpredictable presence of Iroquois raiders and the damage they did to the Laurentian economy caused two-thirds of the single émigrés to return to France and many other Frenchmen who thought of emigrating to stay home ("La guerre iroquoisie et la mortalité en Nouvelle-France, 1608–1666," *RHAF* 36 [1982]:31–54).

23. W. J. Eccles, *France in America* (New York, 1972), 34; Trudel, *The Beginnings of New France*, ch. 18, which summarizes idem, *La population du Canada en 1663* (Montreal, 1973).

24. Richard Colebrook Harris, *The Seigneurial System in Early Canada: A Geographical Study* (Madison, 1966), 42–43; Trudel, *The Beginnings of New France*, 246–56, which summarizes idem, *La terrier du Saint-Laurent en 1663* (Ottawa, 1973). See also idem, *Les débuts du régime seigneurial au Canada* (Montreal, 1974); idem, *The Seigneurial Regime*, Canadian Historical Association Booklet no. 6 (Ottawa, 1971); and R. Cole Harris and John Warkentin, *Canada before Confederation: A Study in Historical Geography* (New York, 1974), ch. 2.

25. Marcel Trudel, *Montréal: La Formation d'une société, 1642–1663* (Montreal, 1976); Louise Dechène, *Habitants et marchands de Montréal au XVII⁰ siècle* (*Paris, 1974*). Gustave Lanctot, *Montreal under Maisonneuve, 1642–1665*, trans. Alta Lind Cook (Toronto, 1969) is uncritically romantic. The best contemporary account is Dollier de Casson, *A History of Montreal, 1640–1672*, ed. and trans. Ralph Flenley (London, 1928).

26. E. R. Adair, "France and the Beginnings of New France," *Canadian Historical Review* 25 (1944):246–78; H. H. Walsh, *The Church in the French Era: From Colonization to the*

British Conquest (Toronto, 1966), ch. 3; Cornelius J. Jaenen, *The Role of the Church in New France* (Toronto, 1976), chs. 1, 5.

27. W. J. Eccles, *Canada under Louis XIV, 1663-1701* (Toronto, 1964), 4.

28. Ibid., ch. 1; Trudel, *The Beginnings of New France*, 268-80; Lanctot, *History of Canada*, vol. 1, ch. 19.

29. Eccles, *France in America*, ch. 3; idem, *Canada under Louis XIV*, chs. 2-5; Lanctot, *History of Canada*, vol. 2, chs. 1-5; Silvio Dumas, *Les filles du roi en Nouvelle-France*, Cahiers d'histoire no. 24 (Quebec: La Société historique de Québec, 1972).

4. THE ART OF REDUCTION

1. Bruce G. Trigger, *The Children of Aataentsic: A History of the Huron People to 1660*, 2 vols. (Montreal, 1976), 1:214-28; James F. Pendergast and Bruce G. Trigger, *Cartier's Hochelaga and the Dawson Site* (Montreal, 1972), 71-92; J. V. Wright, *Ontario Prehistory* (Toronto, 1972), 90.

2. Sagard, *Histoire du Canada*, 321.

3. Harris, *The Seigneurial System in Early Canada*, ch. 2.

4. June Helm, ed., *Subarctic*, *HNAI* 6 (1981):169-95; Kenneth S. Lane, "The Montagnais Indians, 1600-1640," *Kroeber Anthropological Society Papers* 7 (Sept. 1952):1-62; Lucien Campeau, ed., *Établissement à Québec* (1616-34), Monumenta Novae Franciae 2 (Rome and Quebec, 1979), intro., 68-96.

5. Trigger, *Children of Aataentsic* 1:228-34, 361-64, 2:457-58; idem, "Champlain Judged by His Indian Policy: A Different View of Early Canadian History," *Pilot Not Commander: Essays in Memory of Diamond Jenness*, ed. Pat and Jim Lotz, *Anthropologica* 13, nos. 1 and 2, (1971), 85-114.

6. Champlain, *Works* 5:124-25; Trigger, *Children of Aataentsic* 2:630. On the Montagnais trade in general, see Jean-Paul Simard, "La Chasse-Gardée des Montagnais de Tadoussac," in *Démographie du Saguenay et Lac St-Jean* (forthcoming).

7. Sagard, *Histoire du Canada*, 321.

8. Bruce G. Trigger, ed., *Northeast*, *HNAI* 15 (1978):792-97.

9. Father Gabriel Sagard, *The Long Journey to the Country of the Hurons* [Paris, 1632], ed. George M. Wrong, trans. H. H. Langton (Toronto: Champlain Society, 1939), 257.

10. Blair, *Indian Tribes of the Upper Mississippi* 1:176-77 (Nicolas Perrot); Trigger, *Children of Aataentsic* 1:278-86.

11. *JR* 8:29; Trigger, *Northeast*, *HNAI* 15:795.

12. Sagard, *Histoire du Canada*, 701; *JR* 5:33, 193.

13. Sagard, *Histoire du Canada*, 321.

14. Trigger, *Children of Aataentsic* 1:336-37; Sagard, *Long Journey to the Hurons*, 9, 86.

15. Sagard, *Long Journey to the Hurons*, 90-91.

16. Trigger, *Children of Aataentsic* 1:350-58.

17. A comprehensive introduction to Huron culture is Conrad Heidenreich's entry in Trigger, *Northeast*, *HNAI* 15:368-88, which summarizes Elisabeth Tooker, *An Ethnography of the Huron Indians, 1615-1649*, BAE bulletin 190 (Washington, D.C., 1964; reprinted Midland, Ont., 1967); Bruce G. Trigger, *The Huron: Farmers of the North* (New York, 1969); Conrad Heidenreich, *Huronia: A History and Geography of the Huron Indians, 1600-1650* (Toronto, 1971); and Trigger, *Children of Aataentsic*. John A. Dickinson, "The Pre-Contact Huron Population: A Reappraisal," *Ontario History* 72 (1980):173-80, suggests a range of 25,000 to 30,000.

18. Lescarbot, *History of New France* 3:9; Trigger, *Northeast*, *HNAI* 15:346-49, 421, 467-69.

19. Trudel, *Beginnings of New France*, 148-49; W. J. Eccles, *France in America* (New York, 1972), 37.

20. *JR* 45:197 (Jérôme Lalemant).

21. Quoted in W. J. Eccles, *The Canadian Frontier, 1534-1760* (New York, 1969), 42 (1644).

22. Marie de l'Incarnation, *Correspondance*, ed. Dom Guy Oury (Solesmes, 1971), 398 (Aug. 30, 1650), 649 (Nov. 2, 1660); *Word from New France: The Selected Letters of Marie de l'Incarnation*, ed. and trans. Joyce Marshall (Toronto, 1967), 185, 257.

23. *NYCD* 4:905; Richard Haan, "The Problem of Iroquois Neutrality: Suggestions for Revision," *Ethnohistory* 27 (1980):317–30; Yves F. Zoltvany, "New France and the West, 1701–1713," *Canadian Historical Review* 46 (1965):301–22; Anthony F.C. Wallace, "The Origins of Iroquois Neutrality: The Grand Settlement of 1701," *Pennsylvania History* 24 (1957):223–35.

24. See below, Chapter 10, for the Jesuits' important role in frustrating English designs on Iroquois sovereignty, territory, and allegiance.

25. Blair, *Indian Tribes of the Upper Mississippi*; Louise Phelps Kellogg, *The French Regime in Wisconsin and the Northwest* (Madison, 1925); W. J. Eccles, *Frontenac, The Courtier Governor* (Toronto, 1959), chs. 6, 16; idem, *Canadian Frontier*, chs. 6–7; Robert T. Bauman, "The Ottawas of the Lakes, 1615–1766," *Northwest Ohio Quarterly* 30 (1958):186–210; 31 (1959):38–64; 32 (1960):88–101, 138–72; 33 (1961):7–40; 35 (1963):69–100; 36 (1964):60–78, 146–67; Yves F. Zoltvany, *Philippe de Rigaud de Vaudreuil: Governor of New France, 1703–1725* (Toronto, 1974); R. David Edmunds, *The Potawatomis: Keepers of the Fire* (Norman, Okla., 1978), chs. 1–2; James A. Clifton, *The Prairie People: Continuity and Change in Potawatomi Indian Culture, 1665–1965* (Lawrence, Kans., 1977), chs. 3–5.

26. Kenneth M. Morrison, *The Embattled Northeast: The Elusive Ideal of Alliance in Abenaki-Euramerican Relations* (Berkeley and Los Angeles, 1984); P.-André Sévigny, *Les Abénaquis: Habitat et migrations (17ᵉ et 18ᵉ siècles)*, Cahiers d'histoire des Jésuites no. 3 (Montreal, 1976).

27. Le Clercq, *First Establishment of the Faith* 1:82.

28. Ibid., 110.

29. Ibid., 215, 220, 222.

30. The Jesuit *Relations* were published annually between 1632 and 1672, although various missionary reports before and after that period could be considered formal relations and are included in Thwaites's edition of *The Jesuit Relations (JR)*. For the history of these invaluable writings, see Lawrence C. Wroth, "The Jesuit Relations from New France," Bibliographical Society of America, *Papers* 30 (1936):110–49; Joseph P. Donnelly, *Thwaites' Jesuit Relations: Errata and Addenda* (Chicago, 1967), 1–26; and Léon Pouliot, *Étude sur les Relations des Jésuites de la Nouvelle-France (1632–1672)* (Montreal, 1940).

31. *RAPQ* (1926–27), 20, Frontenac to Colbert, Nov. 2, 1672; *NYCD* 9:93 (English translation); Hamilton, "Who Wrote *Premier Établissement de la Foy*."

32. Le Clercq, *First Establishment of the Faith* 1:402–3.

33. Father Louis Hennepin, *A New Discovery of a Vast Country in America* [Utrecht, 1697], ed. Reuben Gold Thwaites, 2 vols. (Chicago, 1903), 2:458, 459, 460, 466.

34. Baron de Lahontan, *New Voyages to North-America* [The Hague, 1703], ed. Reuben Gold Thwaites, 2 vols. (Chicago, 1905), 2:413.

35. Le Clercq, *First Establishment of the Faith* 1:110–11, 214, 222, 256, 377, 379; Hennepin, *Description of Louisiana*, 180.

36. See, for example, Le Clercq, *First Establishment of the Faith* 1:110, 181, 186, 194, 210, 235, 236; and Marie de l'Incarnation, *Correspondance*, 718, 883, 902, 903, 962, 995.

37. See the *Autobiography of Venerable Marie of the Incarnation, O.S.U., Mystic and Missionary*, ed. and trans. John J. Sullivan (Chicago, 1964); and Saint Ignatius of Loyola, *The Constitutions of the Society of Jesus*, ed. and trans. George E. Ganss (St. Louis, 1970). In 1634 Father Paul Le Jeune requested priests for the Canadian mission who were, among other things, "extremely pliant and docile" (*JR* 6:67). See also *JR* 8:183–85, 34:177–79, 35:123, 125, 129, 133, 39:167, 70:277–79.

38. Le Clercq, *First Establishment of the Faith* 1:222; Champlain, *Works* 3:145, 146.

39. *JR* 6:145, 8:15.

40. Sagard, *Histoire du Canada*, 454–55.

41. *JR* 6:146–47.

42. *JR* 16:33.

43. Campeau, *Établissement à Québec*, intro., 49–50; Le Clercq, *First Establishment of the Faith* 1:188; Sagard, *Histoire du Canada*, 52, 59, 72.

44. *JR* 5:109, 6:85–87; *DCB* 1:58–59, 533–34.

45. *JR* 5:197, 6:83–89, 153–55, 12:47. On students as hostages, see also *Word from New France*, 223, 233; Sagard, *Histoire du Canada*, 39; *NYCD* 9:111, 117.

46. In 1636 five Indians were sent to France—a young Iroquois woman, a little boy, and three Montagnais girls. These seem to have been the last children sent specifically for "civilizing" (*JR* 11:95).

47. *JR* 11:221. See also *JR* 8:181, 10:21, 16:169; Camille de Rochemonteix, *Les Jésuites et la Nouvelle-France au XVIIe siècle*, 3 vols. (Paris, 1895–96), 1:280–87.

48. *JR* 12:65; also 9:101, 107, 12:47, 77, 115.

49. *JR* 14:233; also 12:49, 53, 16:187.

50. *JR* 9:233.

51. *JR* 16:169–79, 251, 17:33; see also 15:109, 24:103, 39:129.

52. For the work of the Ursuline seminary, see *Word from New France*; Marie de l'Incarnation, *Correspondance*; *Les Ursulines de Québec depuis leur établissement jusqu'à nos jours*, 4 vols. (Quebec, 1863–66), vol. 1; *Glimpses of the Monastery: A Brief Sketch of the History of the Ursulines of Quebec during the Lifetime of Venerable Mother Mary of the Incarnation* (Quebec, 1872).

53. *JR* 7:289, 9:101.

54. *JR* 19:17, 22:155–77, 25:217.

55. *JR* 9:99, 16:25.

56. *JR* 16:27, 19:11–13, 24:187, 25:221.

57. *JR* 19:23, 25:125, 28:177.

58. *JR* 20:251, 24:185; also 19:25.

59. *JR* 9:101, 24:157–59; also 20:233. For the larger social role of the hospitals in New France, see Jaenen, *The Role of the Church in New France*, 110–16; W. J. Eccles, "Social Welfare Measures and Policies in New France," *XXXVI Congreso Internacional de Americanistas* (Seville, 1966), 4:9–20.

60. Father François Du Creux, *The History of Canada or New France* [Paris, 1664], trans. Percy J. Robinson, ed. James B. Conacher, 2 vols. (Toronto: Champlain Society, 1951–52), 1:92; *JR* 8:57–59. See also *JR* 6:81–83, 9:171, 65:245; *Word from New France*, 185.

61. Lahontan, *New Voyages to North-America* 2:413; *JR* 6:141, 229–31; also 5:33, 16:179.

62. *JR* 7:255, 271, 8:9.

63. Sagard, *Histoire du Canada*, 714. See also Le Clercq, *First Establishment of the Faith* 1:134; *JR* 1:77.

64. *JR* 21:293–307, 6:83; Jean Côté, "L'Institution des donnés," *RHAF* 15 (1961–62):344–78.

65. *JR* 24:103; James P. Ronda, "The Sillery Experiment: A Jesuit-Indian Village in New France, 1637–1663," *American Indian Culture and Research Journal* 3 (1979):1–18; George F. G. Stanley, "The First Indian 'Reserves' in Canada," *RHAF* 4 (1950):178–85; Rochemonteix, *Les Jésuites . . . au XVIIe siècle* 1:244–77; P.-A. Lamontagne, *L'Histoire de Sillery, 1630–1950*, ed. Robert Rumilly (n.p., 1952), 8–19.

66. *JR* 18:91–117; Eleanor Leacock, "Montagnais Women and the Jesuit Program for Colonization," in *Women and Colonization: Anthropological Perspectives*, ed. Mona Etienne and Eleanor Leacock (New York, 1980), 25–42.

67. *JR* 18:111–13, 21:81–105.

68. Campeau, *Établissement à Québec*, intro., 121–28.

69. Axtell, *The European and the Indian*, 257–59.

70. "[François Vachon de] Belmont's History of Brandy," ed. Joseph P. Donnelly, *Mid-America* 34 (1952):52–57.

71. Dollier de Casson, *History of Montreal*, 341, 374. See also *NYCD* 9:883; *JR* 66:149.

72. On Frontenac's hypocritical involvement in the brandy trade, see Jean Delanglez, *Frontenac and the Jesuits* (Chicago, 1939), 101–29; Eccles, *Frontenac*, 61–68.

73. *JR* 62:183, 64:131; "Belmont's History of Brandy," 57–58. See also *JR* 62:140–245, Chauchetière's annual history of the Sault mission from 1667 to 1685.

74. *JR* 58:83, 62:109–49, 203, 63:100–37; Dollier de Casson, *History of Montreal*, 375.

75. "Belmont's History of Brandy," 60; Pierre Boucher, *Histoire véritable et naturelle des moeurs et productions du pays de la Nouvelle France* (Paris, 1664), 116; Dollier de Casson, *History of Montreal*, 375; Marquis de Denonville, "Mémoire d'un plus grands maux de la colonie" (Aug. 10, 1688), PAC, AN C11A, 10:123–24; *NYCD* 9:882; Pierre-François-Xavier de Charlevoix, *History and General Description of New France* [Paris, 1744], ed. and trans. John Gilmary Shea, 6 vols. (New York, 1866–72), 3:55. See also George F. G. Stanley, "The Indians and the Brandy Trade during the Ancien Regime," *RHAF* 6 (1952–53):489–505; Alfred Goldsworthy Bailey, *The Conflict of European and Eastern Algonkian Cultures, 1504–1700* (2d ed., Toronto, 1969), ch. 6; Delanglez, *Frontenac and the Jesuits*, 69–129.

76. *JR* 65:29–31.

77. Eccles, *France in America*, ch. 3; Eccles, *Canada under Louis XIV*, chs. 2–7.

78. *RAPQ* (1930–31), 45 (Jan. 5, 1666), 58 (Nov. 13, 1666).

79. *RAPQ* (1930–31), 72 (April 5, 1667), 84 (Oct. 27, 1667), 95 (Feb. 20, 1668); Delanglez, *Frontenac and the Jesuits*, 40–46; E. M. Faillon, *Histoire de la colonie française en Canada*, 3 vols. (Villemarie [Montreal], 1866), 3:270–84.

80. Delanglez, *Frontenac and the Jesuits*, 44–48; Amédée Gosselin, *L'Instruction au Canada sous le régime français (1635–1760)* (Quebec, 1911), 389–90.

81. *RAPQ* (1926–27), 20 (Nov. 2, 1672), 44 (Nov. 13, 1673), 65–66 (Nov. 14, 1674); *NYCD* 9:108, 111, 117–18, 150.

82. *NYCD* 9:120, 123, 130.

83. Charlevoix, *History of New France* 4:198. See also *Word from New France*, 341; Marie de l'Incarnation, *Correspondance*, 809 (Sept. 1, 1668); Denonville to Minister, Nov. 13, 1685, PAC, AN C11A, 7:46–47; Father Antoine Silvy [Antoine-Denis Raudot], *Letters from North America* [1709–10], trans. Ivy Alice Dickson (Belleville, Ont., 1980), 111. On Raudot's authorship, see *DCB* 2:553.

5. WHEN IN ROME

1. *JR* 13:173, 44:297.

2. *JR* 10:89, 8:85, 12:119; Sagard, *Histoire du Canada*, 148.

3. *JR* 12:121–23.

4. *JR* 50:257.

5. *JR* 8:77, 12:123, 50:259.

6. *JR* 5:37; Sagard, *Histoire du Canada*, 157.

7. Sagard, *Histoire du Canada*, 262–63.

8. *JR* 5:127; Sagard, *Long Journey to the Hurons*, 227. In 1967 the world snowshoe record for the 220-yard dash was 25.6 seconds; a respectable high school runner covers the same distance in only two or three seconds less (William Osgood and Leslie Hurley, *The Snowshoe Book* [Brattleboro, Vt., 1971], 119).

9. *JR* 7:35–65, 51:137, 65:43–49.

10. *JR* 65:43.

11. *JR* 12:123.

12. A. M. D. G. [Arthur Melançon], *Liste des missionnaires-Jésuites: Nouvelle-France et Louisiane, 1611–1800* (Montreal, 1929). The age of the priests when they arrived in Canada ranged between nineteen and fifty-three; the great majority were in their thirties.

13. Allan P. Farrell, *The Jesuit Code of Liberal Education: Development and Scope of the Ratio Studiorum* (Milwaukee, 1938); George E. Ganss, *Saint Ignatius' Idea of a Jesuit University* (2d rev. ed., Milwaukee, 1956); John W. Donohue, *Jesuit Education: An Essay on the Foundations of Its Idea* (New York, 1963); François de Dainville, *Les Jésuites et l'éducation de la société française: La naissance de l'humanisme moderne* (Paris, 1940; reprinted Geneva, 1969).

14. Loyola, *Constitutions*, 213–14; Joseph P. Donnelly, *Jacques Marquette, S.J., 1637–1675* (Chicago, 1968), 21–61; Francis Xavier Talbot, *Saint among Savages: The Life of Isaac Jogues* (New York, 1935), 10–21; idem. *Saint among the Hurons: The Life of Jean de Brébeuf* (New York, 1949), 5–11.

15. See, for example, the biographies of the forty-five Jesuit fathers in *DCB* 1.

16. Joseph de Guibert, *The Jesuits, Their Spiritual Doctrine and Practice: A Historical Study*, ed. George E. Ganss, trans. William J. Young (Chicago, 1964 [Rome, 1953]); A. Lynn Martin, *Henry III and the Jesuit Politicians* (Geneva, 1973), ch. 1; H. Outram Evennett, *The Spirit of the Counter-Reformation*, ed. John Bossy (Cambridge, 1968), chs. 3–4.

17. Thomas V. Cohen, "Why the Jesuits Joined, 1540–1600," Canadian Historical Association, *Historical Papers 1974*, 237–58; idem, "Social Origin and Religious Style: The Jesuit Questionnaire of 1561–68" (Paper delivered at the annual meeting of the American Historical Association, Atlanta, Dec. 28, 1975).

18. *The Spiritual Exercises of St. Ignatius*, ed. and trans. Louis J. Puhl (Chicago, 1951), 43.

19. Loyola, *Constitutions*, 280. On the influence of Massé and other former missionaries, see Talbot, *Saint among Savages*, 20; idem. *Saint among the Hurons*, 15–20; Donnelly, *Marquette*, 64. For examples of lobbying to be sent to Canada, see Campeau, *La première mission d'Acadie*, 19–50 passim.

20. Loyola, *Constitutions*, 96–97, 201, 203, 214, 234–35; idem, *Spiritual Exercises*, 7, 32–33. See Eugen Weber, *Peasants into Frenchmen: The Modernization of Rural France 1870–1914* (Stanford, 1976), ch. 1, "A Country of Savages."

21. Sagard, *Histoire du Canada*, 322; *JR* 6:267, 33:143, 34:159, 51:265.

22. Loyola, *Constitutions*, 275.

23. Sagard, *Historie du Canada*, 151; *Andrew Graham's Observations on Hudson's Bay, 1767–91*, ed. Glyndwr Williams, intro. Richard Glover (London: Hudson's Bay Record Society, 1969), 186.

24. *JR* 1:281, 3:73, 39:183, 44:285–87, 51:45; Sagard, *Histoire du Canada*, 137, 162.

25. Sagard, *Histoire du Canada*, 125–26; *JR* 4:197, 6:67.

26. *JR* 6:7; Sagard, *Long Journey to the Hurons*, 84.

27. Loyola, *Constitutions*, 159, 319.

28. *JR* 7:217; Sagard, *Histoire du Canada*, 702.

29. *JR* 1:173; Cadwallader Colden, *The History of the Five Indian Nations of Canada* (London, 1747), 3; Sagard, *Histoire du Canada*, 226; "Account of the Captivity of William Henry in 1755," *London Chronicle* 23:1,799, June 25–28, 1768, col. 1.

30. *JR* 51:265; see also 5:169, 6:261, 267, 33:143, 51:259.

31. Sagard, *Histoire du Canada*, 322.

32. *JR* 33:143–45. Father Bressani made a similar point in 1653 (39:29).

33. Loyola, *Constitutions*, 201, 214.

34. *JR* 10:91, 14:125–27.

35. Victor Egon Hanzeli, *Missionary Linguistics in New France: A Study of Seventeenth- and Eighteenth-Century Descriptions of American Indian Languages*, Janua Linguarum, Series Maior 29 (The Hague, 1969), 32–44.

36. *JR* 7:27.

37. *JR* 7:31, 10:117, Sagard, *Histoire du Canada*, 286–90[87].

38. *JR* 7:21–31, 10:117–23; Hanzeli, *Missionary Linguistics in New France*, ch. 5.

39. *JR* 39:103–5, 67:147.

40. Sagard, *Histoire du Canada*, 295–96, 476.

41. Sagard, *Histoire du Canada*, 292–96; *JR* 4:179, 209, 5:203; Le Clercq, *First Establishment of the Faith* 1:250.

42. Sagard, *Histoire du Canada*, 292–93; *JR* 67:147. The Recollects fashioned the first Canadian dictionaries or word lists between 1615 and 1629. In 1625 they presented King Louis XIII with copies of their Huron, Montagnais, and Algonquin lexicons. When the Jesuits arrived in Canada in the same year, they launched their own studies with the aid of the Recollect guides. By 1637 the Jesuits had broken through the sophisticated Huron grammar; by 1657 the five Iroquois languages were accessible, as were Algonquin, Montagnais, and Abenaki two years later. So well armed were the Jesuits by 1665 that they asked their French provincial for a printing press and type to mass-produce works in the native languages of Canada, but nothing came of it (Hanzeli, *Missionary Linguistics in New France*, 50; *JR* 49:166).

43. *JR* 13:11, 51:139, 68:55.

44. *JR* 2:219–21, 3:195–97, 7:57; Hennepin, *Description of Louisiana*, 109.

45. *JR* 3:195, 7:93, 51:137, 67:143, 147; Sagard, *Histoire du Canada*, 307–8; Sagard, *Long Journey to the Hurons*, 138.

46. *JR* 39:167, 40:37–39.

47. *JR* 5:191.

48. *JR* 5:287, 16:239–41, 50:129, 171, 197; *DCB* 1:205.

49. Father Joseph François Lafitau, *Customs of the American Indians Compared with the Customs of Primitive Times* [Paris, 1724], ed. and trans. William N. Fenton and Elizabeth L. Moore, 2 vols. (Toronto: Champlain Society, 1974–77), 2:240.

50. *JR* 68:269.

51. *JR* 68:269; Le Clercq, *First Establishment of the Faith* 1:131–32.

52. *JR* 27:97–99, 38:33, 64:91–105.

53. In 1701 the Society of Jesus collected rents in Canada totaling 3,430 livres, which amounted to a return of less than 1 percent on their seigneurial investments. Their total expenses for the year—for 48 priests, 9 donnés, and 14 servants—were 13,145 livres; nearly half of the amount had to come from royal subvention. In the 1680s it was estimated that the clothing and support of a missionary in the field cost 600 livres a year, partly because the Atlantic passage doubled the cost of clothes and the fathers "wear out a great deal of these, in consequence of their frequent journeys and the length of the winter" (Guy Frégault, *Le XVIII*^e

siècle canadien: Études [Montreal, 1968], ch. 3; *JR* 65:181-87; *Coll. de Manuscrits* 1:308; *NYCD* 9:151).

54. Bruce G. Trigger, "The Jesuits and the Fur Trade," *Ethnohistory* 12 (1965):30-53; Cornelius J. Jaenen, "The Catholic Clergy and the Fur Trade, 1585-1685," Canadian Historical Association, *Historical Papers 1970*, 60-80; Lucien Campeau, "Le Commerce des clercs en Nouvelle-France," *Revue de l'Université d'Ottawa/University of Ottawa Quarterly* 47 (1977):27-35.

55. *JR* 44:45, 52:177.

56. See, for example, Trigger, *Children of Aataentsic*, vol. 2, ch. 8.

57. *JR* 2:45, 5:195, 9:233, 10:245, 34:209-11, 67:163.

58. *JR* 5:35, 63, 195, 6:243, 66:179.

59. *JR* 10:219, 257, 51:205.

60. *JR* 41:109-13, 42:105-7.

61. *JR* 2:45, 21:47, 33:241, 49:227.

62. *JR* 5:105, 179; Sagard, *Histoire du Canada*, 87; Sagard, *Long Journey to the Hurons*, 84.

63. Sagard, *Long Journey to the Hurons*, 88-89, 140; *JR* 3:95, 13:147.

64. *JR* 44:49, 49:179.

65. *JR* 4:219, 223, 5:191.

66. *JR* 6:25.

6. HARVEST OF SOULS

1. Loyola, *Constitutions*, 66, 68, 71-72; idem, *Spiritual Exercises*, 43-44.

2. *JR* 5:21, 8:121, 14:125-27.

3. *JR* 1:221, 13:81, 14:107, 149, 17:115, 29:257, 43:135, 297.

4. In "Jesuits and Their Families: The Experience in Sixteenth Century France," *Sixteenth Century Journal* 13 (1982):3-23, A. Lynn Martin has shown that, contrary to the rules of the Society, many Jesuits did not commit social suicide when they entered holy orders.

5. *JR* 2:153, 6:221, 16:41; also 13:79.

6. *JR* 1:277 (Joseph Jouvency).

7. *JR* 6:165, 183, 7:85-87, 161-63, 11:121, 223, 251.

8. *JR* 55:193, 58:43, 60:219.

9. *JR* 8:147, 9:41-43, 10:313, 12:149.

10. *JR* 9:19-21, 43.

11. *JR* 1:275, 6:195, 231, 243, 7:59-63, 117.

12. *JR* 7:57.

13. *JR* 13:115, 181, 213, 15:69, 47:187.

14. *JR* 13:115, 62:95-97.

15. *JR* 11:151, 12:73, 153-59; see also 9:211, 10:39, 31:119, 247, 62:253, 63:89, 68:113.

16. *JR* 12:7.

17. *JR* 12:61.

18. *JR* 11:251-63; see also 9:17, 11:181, 31:203.

19. *JR* 52:147.

20. *JR* 11:261, 12:155, 169.

21. Trigger, *Children of Aataentsic* 2:538, 541-43, 590-96, 646, 657, 694.

22. *JR* 9:69-71, 13:215, 68:49-51; see also 15:137.

23. *JR* 7:147-59, 32:273. In 1637 a Huron captain acknowledged his thanks to "our good God" and attributed to the Jesuits' prayers "the success of his fishing this Autumn" (*JR* 15:125).

24. *JR* 10:35-43, 63:207; see also 17:137, 39:125, 50:191. William A. Starna, George R. Hamell, and William L. Butts have a fascinating discussion of corn infestations in "Northern Iroquois Horticulture and Insect Infestation: A Cause for Village Removal," *Ethnohistory* 31 (1984):197-207.

25. *JR* 8:109-13, 11:261.

26. *JR* 8:111. For other arguments from design, see *JR* 7:103, 10:17, 11:159, 191, 14:191.

27. *JR* 11:159.

28. *JR* 62:199.

29. *JR* 58:181-85.

30. *JR* 30:67, 39:145.

31. *JR* 17:119–21; see also 39:139–41, 62:199–201.

32. Sagard, *Histoire du Canada*, 285.

33. Ibid., 638; see also 707.

34. *JR* 39:149.

35. *JR* 30:63.

36. *JR* 15:121, 67:187.

37. *JR* 30:67–69; see also 44:45, 62:59.

38. *JR* 43:175; see also 17:125, 39:151–55.

39. *JR* 10:245; see also 12:61, 15:121, 43:177.

40. *JR* 9:89.

41. *JR* 6:231, 15:157, 19:39, 28:63, 29:281. See also A. Irving Hallowell, *Culture and Experience* (Philadelphia, 1955), ch. 6, "Some Psychological Characteristics of the Northeastern Indians," esp. pp. 128–32.

42. For some of the northeastern Indian versions of Genesis, see Clark, *Indian Legends of Canada*, 1–9; *JR* 5:153–57, 6:157–63, 10:125–39, 67:153–55; Pierre de Charlevoix, *Journal of a Voyage to North-America* [Paris, 1744], 2 vols. (London, 1761), 2:141–44; William N. Fenton, "'This Island, The World on the Turtle's Back,'" *Journal of American Folklore* 75 (1962):283–300.

43. *JR* 11:157.

44. *JR* 13:169.

45. Campeau, *Établissement à Québec*, 242–57, 266–72. Brébeuf's catechism was published in Rouen in 1630 and reprinted in all the editions of Champlain's works after 1632. Massé's prayers were published only once in the colonial period, also in Champlain's 1632 *Voyages*.

46. *JR* 13:171–73, 16:41, 161; see also 10:27.

47. *JR* 17:129–31, 145.

48. *JR* 33:145–47.

49. *RAPQ* (1939–40), 216.

50. John Gilmary Shea, ed., *A French-Onondaga Dictionary, from a Manuscript of the Seventeenth Century*, Library of American Linguistics, vol. 1 (New York, 1860), under the appropriate French words. I am very grateful to Professor Hanni Woodbury of Columbia University for these translations.

51. Personal correspondence with John Steckley, University of Toronto, Nov. 27, 1982. See also his "Brébeuf's Presentation of Catholicism in the Huron Language: A Descriptive Overview," *Revue de l'Université d'Ottawa / University of Ottawa Quarterly* 48:1–2 (Jan. and Apr. 1978), 93–115.

52. Father Sebastian Rasles [Râle], "A Dictionary of the Abnaki Language, in North America," ed. John Pickering, *Memoirs of the American Academy of Arts and Sciences* 1 (1833):384, 389, 405, 416, 454–55, 486.

53. *JR* 6:137, 10:119–21, 62:239–41.

54. *JR* 1:165–67, 10:121.

55. A. Fraser, ed., "Huron Manuscripts from Rev. Pierre Potier's Collection," *Fifteenth Report of the Bureau of Archives for the Province of Ontario, 1918–19* (Toronto, 1920), 609–22, translated by John Steckley, to whom many thanks.

56. *JR* 10:61.

57. *JR* 32:209–11.

58. *JR* 54:181.

59. *JR* 51:31, 49. For other Christian dreams, see 15:73, 16:175, 41:181, 43:285.

60. *JR* 7:169, 11:203.

61. *JR* 15:181, 17:211, 31:191–93.

62. *JR* 13:233, 16:47, 24:133–35, 32:287; Champlain, *Works* 3:221–24.

63. *JR* 2:19, 10:73, 50:123; Sagard, *Histoire du Canada*, 458–64.

64. Loyola, *Spiritual Exercises*, 25, 158.

65. *JR* 36:245–46; Charles E. Cleland, "From Sacred to Profane: Style Drift in the Decoration of Jesuit Finger Rings," *American Antiquity* 37 (1972):202–10; George Irving Quimby, *Indian Culture and European Trade Goods: The Archaeology of the Historic Period in the Western Great Lakes Region* (Madison, 1966), 76–77; Mary Elizabeth Good, *Guebert Site: An 18th Century, Historic Kaskaskia Indian Village*, Central States Archaeological Societies, Memoir no. 2 (Wood River, Ill., 1972), 80–81; Charles E. Cleland, ed., *The Lasanen Site: An Historic Burial Locality in Mackinac County, Michigan*, Publications of the Museum, Michigan State University, Anthropological Series, vol. 1, no. 1 (East Lansing, 1971), 29–34;

Lyle M. Stone, *Archaeological Investigation of the Marquette Mission Site, St. Ignace, Michigan, 1971: A Preliminary Report*, Reports in Mackinac History and Archaeology no. 1 (Mackinac Island, Mich., 1972), 16–17; Judith Ann Hauser, *Jesuit Rings from Fort Michilimackinac and Other European Contact Sites*, Archaeological Completion Report ser. 5, Mackinac Island State Park Commission (Mackinac Island, Mich., 1982).

66. *JR* 60:137–39.

67. Loyola, *Spiritual Exercises*, 161; *JR* 11:89, 63:89, 113, 68:59.

68. Loyola, *Spiritual Exercises*, 32–33.

69. *JR* 1:289–91.

70. *JR* 18:85–87, 63:67–69.

71. *JR* 13:71; see also 15:117, 185, 49:83, 51:263, 62:135.

72. *JR* 11:89.

73. *RAPQ* (1929–30), 35–37. For Indian opinion about living portraits, see Sagard, *Histoire du Canada*, 554; *JR* 19:203–5, 62:57. Three pictures that echo several of Garnier's suggestions may be seen in François-Marc Gagnon, *La conversion par l'image: Un aspect de la mission des Jésuites auprès des Indiens du Canada au XVIIᵉ siècle* (Montreal, 1975), plates 12, 23, 24.

74. On the work of Nobletz, see Gagnon, *La conversion par l'image*, 67–71 and plates 19, 20.

75. *JR* 62:173.

76. *JR* 52:119–21.

77. *JR* 53:207–13. On other aspects of missionary art in New France, see Gagnon, *La conversion par l'image*; François-Marc Gagnon and Nicole Cloutier, *Premiers peintres de la Nouvelle-France*, 2 vols. (Quebec, 1976); Gérard Morisset, "Les missions indiennes et la peinture," *Revue de l'Université d'Ottawa/University of Ottawa Quarterly* 4 (1934): 308–20.

78. *JR* 11:183, 14:223; also 67:181.

79. *JR* 8:141, 62:25, 63:169. For the converts of the Huron and other captive tribes in Iroquoia, see Daniel Karl Richter, "The Ordeal of the Longhouse: Change and Persistence on the Iroquois Frontier, 1609–1720" (Ph.D. diss., Columbia Univ., 1984), ch. 3.

80. *JR* 7:295, 39:139.

81. *JR* 17:129–31.

82. *JR* 17:131, 51:191–201, 52:23; William Ingraham Kip, ed. and trans., *The Early Jesuit Missions in North America* (New York, 1847), 89–90, 121.

83. *JR* 30:19, 33, 39–41, 63:225.

84. Alan Gowans, *Church Architecture in New France* (New Brunswick, N.J., 1955); Luc Noppen, *Les églises du Québec (1600–1850)* (Montreal, 1978).

85. *JR* 7:149, 15:139, 62:171, 68:109.

86. *JR* 67:87–89, 68:81, see also 16:167, 17:39–41, 63:211, 67:245.

87. *JR* 63:27, 31. For a color photograph of the 1699 belt and a somewhat smaller one from the Hurons in 1678, see Jules B. Billard, ed., *The World of the American Indian* (Washington, D.C.: National Geographic Society, 1974), 125.

88. *JR* 63:193–95. The McCord Museum in Montreal possesses a five-foot-six-inch, twenty-seven-row belt featuring a large cross, an Indian, and a white man that seems to commemorate the conversion of a tribe (M1904), and a two-foot, eleven-row belt featuring a church, a cross, two priests, and three Indians (M1905). The latter is dated 1638 without good evidence and is said to have marked the construction of the first church in Huronia (Ossossané?). Bruce Trigger thinks it more likely that the belt came from Lorette in the 1660s or '70s. It may have had a function similar to that the Lorette belt played among the Saulteurs.

89. *JR* 10:83, 63:217.

90. *JR* 1:211, 2:91, 14:267, 15:225, 32:225, 56:133, 68:273.

91. *JR* 60:145, 63:211, 68:273–75; see 30:141, 60:145, and Bougainville, *Journals*, 76, for other comparisons with choirs of nuns.

92. *JR* 2:213, 36:245, 67:245; Marius Barbeau, *Trésor des anciens Jésuites*, Anthropology Series no. 43, bulletin 153, National Museum of Canada (Ottawa, 1957). See *JR* 42:269–89 for a list of donations to the church of Notre Dame de Recouvrance in Quebec between 1633 and 1657.

93. Sagard, *Histoire du Canada*, 416; Hennepin, *Description of Louisiana*, 105, 107.

94. *JR* 5:265, 17:39, 43, 62:47, 68:63, 69.

95. *JR* 1:161–65, 3:147; Le Clercq, *First Establishment of the Faith* 1:142.

96. *JR* 8:169, 175.

97. *JR* 14:77, 39:143–45; Pouliot, *Étude sur les Relations des Jésuites*; ch. 6, esp. pp. 223–24.

98. *JR* 7:275, 51:235; Pouliot, *Étude sur les Relations des Jésuites*, 224.

99. *JR* 13:167, 14:7, 67, 39:125, 48:123, 51:69, 52:187, 62:61, 137.

100. *JR* 11:119, 13:241, 49:57.

101. *JR* 13:121, 15:125; Dechêne, *Habitants et marchands de Montréal*, 25 n.21.

102. *JR* 10:63, 18:125.

103. Sagard, *Histoire du Canada*, 449; Le Clercq, *First Establishment of the Faith* 1:221; *JR* 25:109, 51:125, 131.

104. *JR* 15:175, 63:185–87, 249.

105. *JR* 47:165, 60:33; Axtell, *The European and the Indian*, ch. 5, "Last Rights: The Acculturation of Native Funerals in Colonial North America."

106. *JR* 3:85, 17:141, 31:217.

107. *JR* 37:187, 63:35; for calendars, see also 23:317, 31:217, 223, 50:33, 43, 62:181, 63:157.

108. *JR* 15:77f., 17:41f., 27:67–69, 35:249, 51:193, 231, 52:217, 237, 62:111–15.

109. *JR* 63:211, 67:87, 68:271; Bougainville, *Journals*, 76.

110. *JR* 31:227, 34:183, 49:27, 77, 49:99, 62:45, 119, 175–79, 63:219; Loyola, *Spiritual Exercises*, 37–38; Kip, *Early Jesuit Missions*, 106–11.

111. Loyola, *Spiritual Exercises*, 157; *Catéchisme de la Vénérable Mère Marie de l'Incarnation* (3d ed., Tournai, 1878), 347–50. For the special devotion to the Virgin in New France, see Adrien Pouliot, *Aux origines de notre dévotion à l'Immaculée-Conception*, La Société historique de Québec, Cahiers d'histoire no. 8 (Quebec, 1956), and Hector Bibeau, "Le climat marial en Nouvelle-France à l'arrivée de Mgr. de Saint-Vallier," *RHAF* 22, no. 3 (Dec. 1968):415–28.

112. *JR* 40:227, 48:125–27, 52:29, 213, 62:51, 179, 63:187, 201–5, 227 (quoted).

113. *JR* 62:179, 63:187–89, 205, 227, 68:273; Cornelius J. Jaenen, *Friend and Foe: Aspects of French-Amerindian Cultural Contact in the Sixteenth and Seventeenth Centuries* (Toronto, 1976), 75.

7. REDUCE THEM TO CIVILITY

1. Taylor, *Hakluyt Writings* 76:164–65; see also 77:223, 339; Richard Eburne, *A Plain Pathway to Plantations* [London, 1624], ed. Louis B. Wright (Ithaca, 1962), 55–56.

2. Robert Gray, *A Good Speed to Virginia* (London, 1609), sig. C1v–C2r.

3. Taylor, *Hakluyt Writings* 77:214 (quoting Jacques Cartier), 339; Eburne, *Plain Pathway*, 56. See also [George Peckham], *A True Reporte of the late discoveries . . . of the New-found Landes . . .* (London, 1583), sig. B3v–B4r: Having "no knowledg of God," the American natives are "in sorte, thirsting after christiantie, (as may appeare by the relation of such as have travailed in those partes)."

4. *Nova Britannia: Offering Most Excellent fruites by Planting in Virginia* (London, 1609), in Force, *Tracts* 1, no. 6, p. 22. See also Thomas Harriot, *A briefe and true report of the new found land of Virginia* [1588], in David B. Quinn and Alison M. Quinn, eds., *Virginia Voyages from Hakluyt* (London, 1973), 68: "If meanes of good governement be used . . . they may in short time be brought to civilitie, and the imbracing of true religion."

5. John Witthoft, "Archaeology as a Key to the Colonial Fur Trade," *Minnesota History* 40 (1966):204–5. Evidence of the nonperishable items are found in Indian graves as far inland as the Senecas from 1550.

6. Gray, *Good Speed to Virginia*, sig. C1v–C2r.

7. *A True Declaration of the estate of the Colonie in Virginia* (London, 1610), in Force, *Tracts* 3, no. 1, p. 6. See also [Peckham], *True Reporte*, sig. F2v–F3r, and Samuel Purchas, *Virginia's Verger*, in *Hakluytus Posthumus; or, Purchas His Pilgrimes* [London, 1625], 20 vols. (Glasgow, 1903–05), 19:232.

8. Winslow, *Glorious Progress*, 83. See also Solomon Stoddard, *Question, Whether God is not Angry with the Country for doing so little towards the Conversion of the Indians?* (Boston, 1723), 10–11; [John] *Winthrop's Journal "History of New England," 1630–1649*, ed. James K. Hosmer, ONEAH (New York, 1908), 2:124, 319; Shepard, *Clear Sun-shine*, 57–58; Whitfield, *Light Appearing*, 112; Wood, *New England's Prospect*, 102; Eliot, *Indian Dialogues*, 65–66.

9. Cotton Mather, *India Christiana* (Boston, 1721), 28–29. See also Eliot and Mayhew, *Tears of Repentance*, 230 (confession of Totherswamp), and Samuel Kirkland to J. Bowdoin, March 10, 1784, Kirkland Papers: "Many Oneidas at the conclusion of the American Revolu-

tion observed the difference between White and Indian lives. The Whites were prosperous and appeared the favorites of Heaven, and so they too wanted Christ and comfort."

10. Richard Hakluyt the younger, "Discourse of Western Planting" [1584], in Taylor, *Hakluyt Writings* 77:216.

11. *New England's First Fruits* [London, 1643], in Samuel Eliot Morison, *The Founding of Harvard College* (Cambridge, Mass., 1935), 421; [Shepard], *Day-Breaking*, 16; Winslow, *Glorious Progress*, 90.

12. Charles Inglis to William Johnson, March 28, 1770, *Johnson Papers* 7:506.

13. William Crashaw, *A Sermon Preached in London before the right honorable the Lord La Warre . . . Febr. 21. 1609* (London, 1610), sig. D4r, Klv. In 1642 Thomas Lechford, a visiting Anglican lawyer, indirectly criticized his Massachusetts hosts when he declared that "in value doe some think of civillizing [the Indians], either by the sword, or otherwise, till (withall) the word of God hath spoken to their hearts." But he was neither a Puritan nor a missionary, and his testimony only underlines the prevailing ideology of conversion (*Plain Dealing; or, Newes from New-England* [London, 1642], in *Colls. Mass. His. Soc.*, 3d ser., 3 [1833]:91).

14. Mather, *India Christiana*, 28–29. See also Gray, *Good Speed to Virginia*, sig. Blv, C2v, C4r–v, and Purchas, *Pilgrimes* 19:231.

15. William Smith to William Johnson, March 16, 1767, *Johnson Papers* 5:511. See Sir Walter Raleigh, *The Discoverie of . . . Guiana* [London, 1596], ed. Vincent T. Harlow (London, 1928), 146, where the English pledged to teach the "liberal arts of civilitie" to the natives when the latter were liberated from the Spanish yoke.

16. *A Letter from the Rev* Mr. Sergeant of Stockbridge, to Dr. Colman of Boston* (Boston, 1743), 3, 5; John Callender, *An Historical Discourse, on the Civil and Religious Affairs of the Colony of Rhode-Island and Providence Plantations* [Boston, 1739], in *Collections of the Rhode Island Historical Society* 4 (1838):138; Jonathan Edwards to Joshua Paine (transcript), Feb. 24, 1752, Andover-Newton Edwards Collection, Yale Univ. Library, folder 1752B.

17. *A Letter from the Rev* Mr. Sergeant*, 5. As Robert Berkhofer pointed out for the nineteenth-century Protestant missions, "To become truly Christian was to become anti-Indian" (*Salvation and the Savage: An Analysis of Protestant Missions and American Indian Response, 1787–1862* [Lexington, Ky., 1965; New York, 1972], 122).

18. Taylor, *Hakluyt Writings* 77:214; *Doc. His. Maine* 7 (Farnham Papers):24; Max Farrand, ed., *The Laws and Liberties of Massachusetts* [1648] (Cambridge, Mass., 1929), 29; *Ply. Col. Recs.* 10:285–86 (1662), 368 (1679); George Washington to Richard Henry Lee, Feb. 8, 1785, American Philosophical Society, B L51 2, fol. 262. See also Gray, *Good Speed to Virginia*, sig. C2v, C4r–v; William Hubbard, *The Present State of New-England* (London, 1677), 86 (2d pagination); Daniel Gookin, *Historical Collections of the Indians in New England* [1674], ed. Jeffrey H. Fiske (Towtaid, N.J., 1970), 5, 60, 129; Christopher Carleill, *A discourse upon the entended Voyage to the hethermoste partes of America* (London, 1583), sig. Blr; Hall, *Narratives of Early Maryland*, 20, 84, 90; Rev. Charles Inglis, "Memorial concerning the Iroquois" (1771), in *Doc. His. N.Y.* 4:669. Appropriately, the phrase first gained currency in the Elizabethan campaigns to bring the "wild Irish" into the English pale. In 1572 Sir Thomas Smith declared that the primary aim of the adventurers in Ireland was "to reduce that countrey to civilitie and the maners of the English" (Nicholas P. Canny, "The Ideology of English Colonization: From Ireland to America," *WMQ*, 3d ser., 30 [1973]:596). In the sixteenth century the Spanish were also speaking of "reducing" American barbarians to real "men" (J. H. Elliott, "The Discovery of America and the Discovery of Man," *Proceedings of the British Academy* 58 [1972]:101–25; Anthony Pagden, *The Fall of Natural Man: The American Indian and the Origins of Comparative Ethnology* [Cambridge, 1982]).

19. *A Letter from the Rev* Mr. Sergeant*, 3: ". . . raise them, as far as possible, into the Condition of a civil industrious and polish'd People"; Eleazar Wheelock, *A Continuation of the Narrative of the Indian Charity-School in Lebanon, in Connecticut, From the Year 1768, to the Incorporation of it with Dartmouth-College . . . 1771* (Hartford, 1771), 20: "endeavours were used with them [his Indian students] to raise them up." The only other reference to elevation I have found comes from Joseph Talcott, the governor of Connecticut, who in 1725 thought it "best to bring [the natives] *up* from their own habits and Customs . . . by degrees" (*Colls. Conn. His. Soc.* 5 [1896]:398).

20. Roy Harvey Pearce, *Savagism and Civilization: A Study of the Indian and the American Mind* (Baltimore, 1965), 5, 31; Gary B. Nash, "The Image of the Indian in the Southern Colonial Mind," *WMQ*, 3d ser., 29 (1972):197–230; Francis Jennings, *The Invasion of Amer-*

ica: Indians, Colonialism, and the Cant of Conquest (Chapel Hill, 1975), part 1; Neal Salisbury, "Inside Out: Perception and Projection in the Puritans' Encounter with the Indians" (Paper delivered at the American Studies Association, San Antonio, Nov. 7, 1975).

21. I have chosen the medical metaphor advisedly. Eleazar Wheelock, the leading exponent of Indian education in the eighteenth century, often said that his goal was to "cure the Natives . . . of their Savage Temper" and to "purge all the Indian out" of his students (Wheelock Papers 762521.1, 764560.1). Even a fleeting acquaintance with eighteenth-century medical practices will convey the full rigor of treatment implied. See also *Doc. His. Maine* 2:9.

22. [Peckham], *True Reporte*, sig. F3r; Gray, *Good Speed to Virginia*, sig. D2r.

23. John Smith, *A Map of Virginia* [Oxford, 1612], in *Jamestown Voyages* 137:371; Gookin, *Historical Collections*, 109; John Eliot to William Steele, Dec. 8, 1652, *NEHGR* 36 (1882):295; Whitfield, *Light Appearing*, 139.

24. Adriaen Van der Donck, *A Description of the New Netherlands* [Amsterdam, 1655], ed. Thomas F. O'Donnell (Syracuse, 1968), 100; *NEHGR* 36 (1882):296; Whitfield, *Light Appearing*, 126, 137.

25. If racism connotes something more precise than mere bias or ethnocentrism, the attribution of racist attitudes to the early English colonists and explorers is a simplistic reduction of historical complexity which ignores chronology and geography. (See, for example, Philip L. Berg, "Racism and the Puritan Mind," *Phylon* 36 [1975]:1–7, and G. E. Thomas, "Puritans, Indians, and the Concept of Race," *New England Quarterly* 48 [1975]:3–27.) If the best historians cannot sharply distinguish the growth of racism and of black slavery, those who treat people neither black nor white should exercise equal if not greater caution. (See Winthrop D. Jordan, *White over Black: American Attitudes toward the Negro, 1550–1812* [Chapel Hill, 1968], 66–71, 85–98; Edmund S. Morgan, *American Slavery, American Freedom: The Ordeal of Colonial Virginia* [New York, 1975], 130, 232–34, 328–32; Joseph Boskin, *Into Slavery: Racial Decisions in the Virginia Colony* [Philadelphia, 1976]; Gary B. Nash, "Red, White and Black: The Origins of Racism in Colonial America," in *The Great Fear: Race in the Mind of America*, ed. Gary B. Nash and Richard Weiss [New York, 1970], 1–26; Karen O. Kupperman, "The Ethnographic Quality of the Early English Response to the American Indian" [Paper delivered at the American Society for Ethnohistory, Albuquerque, Oct. 7, 1976], 9–10; and Alden T. Vaughan, *New England Frontier: Puritans and Indians, 1620–1675* [rev. ed. New York, 1979], 324, 336, 338).

26. *Winthrop's Journal* 2:53; [*Edward*] *Johnson's Wonder-Working Providence, 1628–1651*, ed. J. Franklin Jameson, ONEAH (New York, 1910), 223. See Jennings, *Invasion of America*, ch. 15, for the details.

27. *Ply. Col. Recs.* 5:169 (1675); Hubbard, *Present State of New-England*, 78 (2d pagination).

28. *A Letter from the Rev^d Mr. Sergeant*, 3. For the importance of political sovereignty to the missionary program, see Jennings, *Invasion of America*, ch. 14; Neal Salisbury, "Red Puritans: The 'Praying Indians' of Massachusetts Bay and John Eliot," *WMQ*, 3d ser., 31 (1974):30; Gary B. Nash, "The Political Dimensions of the Seventeenth-Century Missions" (Paper delivered at the International Conference on First Images of America: The Impact of The New World on the Old, UCLA, Feb. 7, 1975; not included in the printed proceedings of the conference, *First Images of America*, ed. Fredi Chiappelli [Berkeley and Los Angeles, 1976], 2 vols.).

29. Whitfield, *Strength Out of Weaknesse*, 171; Eliot, *Late Manifestation*, 269.

30. *Mourt's Relation*, 91–93. See also William Bradford, *Of Plymouth Plantation, 1620–1647*, ed. Samuel Eliot Morison (New York, 1952), 25.

31. *Winthrop Papers* (Boston: Massachusetts Historical Society, 1929–), 2:120. See also [Francis Higginson], *New-Englands Plantation* [London, 1630], in Force, *Tracts* 1, no. 12, p. 12. The English theory of *vacuum domicilium* has a long and distinguished pedigree. Thomas More first adumbrated such a position in *Utopia*, ed. E. L. Surtz and J. H. Hexter, Yale Edition of the Works of St. Thomas More, vol. 4 (New Haven, 1965), 137. See David B. Quinn, "Renaissance Influences in English Colonization," *Transactions of the Royal Historical Society*, 5th ser., 26 (1976):73–93, at 75.

32. John Josselyn, *An Account of Two Voyages to New-England Made during the years 1638, 1663* [London, 1674] (Boston, 1865), 99.

33. Charles Hudson, *The Southeastern Indians* (Knoxville, 1976), 211–18, 269–99; Anthony F. C. Wallace, "Women, Land, and Society: Three Aspects of Aboriginal Delaware Life," *Pennsylvania Archaeologist* 17 (1947), 12; William N. Fenton, "The Iroquois in History," in

352 NOTES

Eleanor B. Leacock and Nancy O. Lurie, eds., *North American Indians in Historical Perspective* (New York, 1971), 134–35; Neal Salisbury, *Manitou and Providence: Indians, Europeans, and the Making of New England, 1500–1643* (New York, 1982), ch. 1.

34. Roger Williams, *A Key into the Language of America* (London, 1643), 46–48; "Rev. William Morell's Poem on New-England," *Colls. Mass. His. Soc.*, 1st ser., 1 (1792):132; Van der Donck, *New Netherlands*, 81–82.

35. Josselyn, *Account of Two Voyages*, 99; Williams, *Key*, 47; Wood, *New England's Prospect*, 113–14. By the nineteenth century, some American writers (males, predictably) were less ready to condemn the Indian man's prerogatives. In 1824 the Reverend James Seaver, the author of Mary Jemison's popular captivity narrative, noted with obvious approval the nature of Indian family government: "One thing respecting the Indian women is worthy of attention, and perhaps of imitation, although it is now a days considered beneath the dignity of the ladies, especially those who are the most refined; and that is, they are under a becoming subjection to their husbands" (James E. Seaver, *A Narrative of the Life of Mrs. Mary Jemison* [Canandaigua, N.Y., 1824], ed. Allen W. Trelease [New York, 1961], 181).

36. Norman H. Dawes, "Titles as Symbols of Prestige in Seventeenth-Century New England," *WMQ*, 3d ser., 6 (1949):69–83; Gary B. Nash, *Class and Society in Early America* (Englewood Cliffs, N.J., 1970); Stephen Foster, *Their Solitary Way: The Puritan Social Ethic in the First Century of Settlement in New England* (New Haven, 1971), ch. 1.

37. Morton, *New English Canaan*, in Force, *Tracts* 2, no. 5, p. 20; *Johnson's Wonder-Working Providence*, 162.

38. *Mass. Col. Recs.* 2:55–56; *Winthrop's Journal* 2:156–57, 160.

39. *Winthrop's Journal* 2:122–26, 156; Whitfield, *Strength Out of Weaknesse*, 178. See also Whitaker, *Good Newes from Virginia*, 40: "If we were once the masters of their Countrey, and they stoode in feare of us . . . it were an easie matter to make them willingly to forsake the divell, to embrace the faith of Jesus Christ, and to be baptized."

40. *Mass. Col. Recs.* 2:84, 134, 166, 176; 3:6–7, 56–57. See Hugh Jones, *The Present State of Virginia* [London, 1724], ed. Richard L. Morton (Chapel Hill, 1956), 116, for the continued English realization that force would defeat the object of conversion.

41. Whitfield, *Light Appearing*, 138–39; Whitfield, *Strength Out of Weaknesse*, 177–78, 190–91; Gookin, *Historical Collections*, 65–66; Josselyn, *Account of Two Voyages*, 115.

42. Gookin, *Historical Collections*, 14–15, 66–68, 73; Wood, *New England's Prospect*, 112. For the praying town laws against bug biting, see [Shepard], *Day-Breaking*, 20–21; Shepard, *Clear Sun-shine*, 40; Oliver N. Bacon, *A History of Natick* (Boston, 1856), 248.

43. Eliot and Mayhew, *Tears of Repentance*, 227; Gavin Cochrane, "Treatise on the Indians of North America Written in the Year 1764," Newberry Library, Ayer MS 176, ch. 7. The natives of Virginia were equally slow to resort to English-style houses. During the seventeenth century, only four "kings" did so (Helen C. Rountree, "Change Came Slowly: The Case of the Powhatan Indians of Virginia," *Journal of Ethnic Studies* 3, no. 3 [Fall 1975]:3).

44. Gookin, *Historical Collections*, 62; Winslow, *Glorious Progress*, 81; John Eliot, *The Christian Commonwealth; or, The Civil Policy of the Rising Kingdom of Jesus Christ* (London, 1660), in *Colls. Mass. His. Soc.*, 3d ser., 9 (1846):127–64; Neal Salisbury, "Prospero in New England: The Puritan Missionary as Colonist," *Papers of the Sixth Algonquian Conference 1974*, ed. William Cowan, National Museum of Man, Mercury Series, Canadian Ethnology Service, vol. 23 (Ottawa, 1975), 258–59.

45. Whitfield, *Light Appearing*, 131; Whitfield, *Strength Out of Weaknesse*, 171–72; John Eliot, "An Account of Indian Churches in New-England, 1673," in *Colls. Mass. His. Soc.*, 1st ser., 10 (1809):128; Gookin, *Historical Collections*, ch. 7, esp. p. 86.

46. Gookin, *Historical Collections*, 56, 59, 80, 84–85, 86; Edmund S. Morgan, *The Puritan Dilemma: The Story of John Winthrop* (Boston, 1958), chs. 7–8; idem, ed., *Puritan Political Ideas, 1558–1794* (Indianapolis, 1965), xvii–xix; T. H. Breen, *The Character of the Good Ruler: A Study of Puritan Political Ideas in New England, 1630–1730* (New Haven, 1970), chs. 1–2; Foster, *Their Solitary Way*, chs. 1, 3, 6.

47. Darrett B. Rutman, *American Puritanism: Faith and Practice* (Philadelphia, 1970), 24–26, 82–83, 125; George Lee Haskins, *Law and Authority in Early Massachusetts* (New York, 1960), 19–20; Michael Zuckerman, *Peaceable Kingdoms: New England Towns in the Eighteenth Century* (New York, 1970), 54–55, 95–96; Richard L. Bushman, *From Puritan to Yankee: Character and the Social Order in Connecticut, 1690–1765* (Cambridge, Mass., 1967), ch. 1.

48. Gookin, *Historical Collections*, 66; Whitfield, *Strength Out of Weaknesse*, 172; Eliot and Mayhew, *Tears of Repentance*, 207. Sometime in the 1660s Eliot published in broadside a

Natick-English *Christian Covenanting Confession* for the use of new praying towns. For a facsimile, see Eliot, *The Indian Primer*, ed. John Small (Edinburgh, 1880).

49. W. H. Whitmore, ed., *The Colonial Laws of Massachusetts* (Boston, 1889), 55; Haskins, *Law and Authority in Early Massachusetts*, ch. 9; [Shepard], *Day-Breaking*, 20–21 (Newton, 1646); Shepard, *Clear Sun-shine*, 39–40 (Concord, 1646); *Conn. Col. Recs.* 2:575–76 (Pequots, 1675); Bacon, *History of Natick*, 247–48 (Natick, 1651).

50. Gookin, *Historical Collections*, 61–62; *Conn. Col. Recs.* 2:575.

51. Edward Howes to John Winthrop, Jr., June 1632, *Colls. Mass. His. Soc.*, 4th ser., 6 (1863):476; Gookin, *Historical Collections*, 96; Winslow, *Glorious Progress*, 83. See also Shepard, *Clear Sun-shine*, 54, and Eliot and Mayhew, *Tears of Repentance*, 252.

52. Rev. Jared Eliot to Rev. Thomas Prince, June 3, 1729, *Colls. Conn. His. Soc.* 3 (1895):291–92; *Extracts from the Itineraries and other Miscellanies of Ezra Stiles, D.D., LL.D., 1755–1794*, ed. Franklin B. Dexter (New Haven, 1916), 151 (hereafter Stiles, *Extracts*). See also Whitfield, *Light Appearing*, 141. If William Strachey was accurate, the Powhatans of Virginia were extremely atypical in paying tribute amounting to 80 percent of their agricultural yield (W. Strachey, *Historie of Travell into Virginia*, 87).

53. Whitfield, *Light Appearing*, 139. See also Gookin, *Historical Collections*, 75–76, and Eliot, *Indian Dialogues*, 120–23.

54. Eliot, *Brief Narrative*, 5–7; Gookin, *Historical Collections*, 64–65, 72, 74.

55. Eliot, *Indian Dialogues*, 120–28. See also Wood, *New England's Prospect*, 98.

56. *Colls. Mass. His. Soc.*, 4th ser., 6 (1863):476; William Kellaway, *The New England Company 1649–1776: Missionary Society to the American Indians* (London, 1961), 268–69.

57. Kellaway, *New England Company*, 253–54, 269.

58. *Ply. Col. Recs.* 10:123 (Sept. 18, 1654); Whitfield, *Light Appearing*, 139–41. See also *Ply. Col. Recs.* 4:80 (Feb. 7, 1665), where six Plymouth Indians were allowed to order themselves "civilly" under a constable provided that "what homage accostomed legally due to any superior sachem be not heerby infringed."

59. Gookin, *Historical Collections*, 83, 109–10.

60. *Doc. His. Maine* 4:294 (I have reversed the last two accusations).

61. Morton, *New English Canaan*, in Force. *Tracts* 2, no. 5, p. 13; Charles Orr, ed., *History of the Pequot War: The Contemporary Accounts of Mason, Underhill, Vincent and Gardener* (Cleveland, 1897), 30, 35, 44, 72–77, 81.

62. Eliot to Steele, Dec. 8, 1652, *NEHGR* 36 (1882): 294. For other native opponents of Christianity, see Hubbard, *Present State of New-England*, 8–9 (1st pagination). As determined as the New England missionaries were, they refrained from going to the lengths advocated by one Virginia clergyman. In 1621 the Reverend Jonas Stockden lamented that the Indians "devoure[d] all the English gifts bestowed in an effort to convert them by "faire meanes." Since the colonists were met only with "derision and ridiculous answers," he concluded that "till their Priests and Ancients have their throats cut, there is no hope to bring them to conversion" (Captain John Smith, *The Generall Historie of Virginia* . . . [London, 1624], 140; also in Lyon G. Tyler, ed., *Narratives of Early Virginia 1606–1625*, ONEAH [New York, 1907], 348).

63. Eliot, *Brief Narrative*, 8.

64. Massachusetts Indian Commissioners (Cotton Mather, author) to the Governor and General Court of Connecticut, Sept. 30, 1706, in *Colls. Mass. His. Soc.*, 6th ser., 3 (1889):347–48; *Conn. Col. Recs.* 2:576 (Pequot laws of 1675): "It is ordered that a ready & comely attendance be given to heare the word of God preached by Mr. [James] Fitch, or any other minister sent amongst them. The cheife [native] officers & constables are to gather the people as they may. And if any be refractory & refuse, or doe misbehave themselve[s] undecently, such shall be punished with a fine of five shillings, or be corporally punished, as the officers shall see most meet."

65. *R.I. Col. Recs.* 1:292–93; Charles H. Lincoln, ed., *Narratives of the Indian Wars, 1675–1699*, ONEAH (New York, 1913), 10.

66. These calculations are based on a 1:5 warrior-to-population ratio. The seven "old towns," founded before 1670, had a combined population of 495 in 1674. The largest town, Natick, had 145 souls. The next largest, Wamessit, had only half as many (Jennings, *Invasion of America*, 251 n. 67; a table drawn from Gookin, *Historical Collections*, ch. 7).

67. Ford, *Some Correspondence*, 13, 20, 26; Mary Pray to James Oliver, Oct. 20, 1675, *Colls. Mass. His. Soc.*, 5th ser., 1 (1871): 106; Douglas E. Leach, *Flintlock and Tomahawk: New England in King Philip's War* (New York, 1958), 243.

68. Shepard, *Clear Sun-shine*, 50; *OED*, s.v. "labour" and "toil"; Samuel Hopkins, *Histori-*

cal Memoirs Relating to the Housatonic Indians [Boston, 1753], in *Magazine of History with Notes and Queries*, extra no. 17 (New York, 1911), 138; Gookin, *Historical Collections*, 61; Cotton Mather, *The Way to Prosperity* (Boston, 1690), 27.

69. *Mourt's Relation*, 91–92; *Colls. Mass. His. Soc.*, 1st ser., 4 (1795):63, 71, 73.

70. *Mass. Col. Recs.* 2:56; *Winthrop's Journal* 1:124; Eliot and Mayhew, *Tears of Repentance*, 246, 247.

71. Jones, *Present State of Virginia*, 62; J. Hector St. John de Crèvecoeur, *Letters from an American Farmer . . .* [London, 1782] (London, 1912), 215. William Wood claimed that the New England Indians had admirable physiques because "they are not brought down with suppressing labour, vexed with annoying cares, or drowned in the excessive abuse of overflowing plenty" (*New England's Prospect*, 82).

72. Van der Donck, *New Netherlands*, 96; *Ply. Col. Recs.*, 10:382 (Aug. 27, 1664).

73. Hill, *Society and Puritanism in Pre-Revolutionary England*, chs. 4–5, esp. pp. 125, 147–49; Edmund S. Morgan, "The Labor Problem at Jamestown, 1607–18," *American Historical Review* 76 (1971):595–611, at 601; Keith Thomas, "Work and Leisure in Pre-Industrial Society," *Past and Present* 29 (Dec. 1964):50–62, and Discussion, 63–66; Peter Laslett, *The World We Have Lost* (New York, 1965), ch. 1. See also Morgan's perceptive chapter on "Idle Indian and Lazy Englishman" in *American Slavery, American Freedom*, ch. 3.

74. Morgan, *American Slavery, American Freedom*, chs. 1, 3, esp. p. 70; Morgan, "Labor Problem at Jamestown," 597–600.

75. John White, *The Planter's Plea* [London, 1630], in Force, *Tracts* 2, no. 3, p. 18.

76. Bradford, *Plymouth Plantation*, 204–10, 216–17. For a modern corrective, see Salisbury, *Manitou and Providence*, 152–62.

77. Charles Chauncy, *Gods Mercy, Shewed to his People* (Cambridge, Mass., 1655), 15–16; *Winthrop's Journal* 1:179–80.

78. James Axtell, *The School upon a Hill: Education and Society in Colonial New England* (New Haven, 1974), 101 and 101 n. 7; Foster, *Their Solitary Way*, 106–7; Haskins, *Law and Authority*, 33, 77, 88, 90, 100, 134.

79. *The Necessity of Reformation* (Boston, 1679), 5, 6; Mather, *Way to Prosperity*, 27.

80. Tyler, *Narratives of Early Virginia*, 18, 101.

81. Force, *Tracts* 1, no. 12, p. 13; Johnson's *Wonder-Working Providence*, 262. See also Jones, *Present State of Virginia*, 55; Captain Bernard Romans, *A Concise History of East and West Florida*, 2 vols. (New York, 1775), 1:64; John Bartram, *Observations on the Inhabitants, Climate, Soil, Rivers, Productions, Animals . . . In his Travels from Pensilvania to Onondago, Oswego and the Lake Ontario, in Canada* (London, 1751), 77; Stiles, *Extracts*, 411; "Morell's Poem on New-England," 131; and Edward Winslow, *Good Newes from New England* [London, 1624], in Alexander Young, ed., *Chronicles of the Pilgrim Fathers of the Colony of Plymouth from 1602 to 1625* (2d ed., Boston, 1844), 363.

82. J. Franklin Jameson, ed., *Narratives of New Netherland, 1609–1664*, ONEAH (New York, 1909), 105, 107; Wood, *New England's Prospect*, 112–16. See also "Morell's Poem on New-England," 136, and "The Indians in Virginia . . . 1689," ed. Stanley Pargellis, *WMQ*, 3d ser., 16 (1959):232.

83. *Diary of David McClure, Doctor of Divinity, 1748–1820*, ed. Franklin B. Dexter (New York, 1899), 68. For a similar hypothesis, see John Peirce, "Notes on a Visit to Several Tribes of [Iroquois] Indians 1796," typescript of MS in Friends' Library, Swarthmore College, Ayer MS NA 692, Newberry Library, 13–14: "In proportion to the Rudeness, and uncultivation of these people, are the Hardships and Difficulties of their Women greatly increased; for where the men think it a reproach for them to work, all the Chopping, Mowing, etc. necessarily fall upon their Women: and as they increase in Civilization . . . the Women are generally relieved from this Drudgery, and their Labours confined more to their Houses, and amongst their Children, where they ought to be." See also *Of the Remarkable Occurrences in the Life and Travels of Colonel James Smith . . .* [Lexington, Ky., 1799], in Samuel G. Drake, ed., *Indian Captivities* (Boston, 1839), 202.

84. Bartram, *Observations*, 77; Wood, *New England's Prospect*, 112–15. See also *Zeisberger's History of the Northern American Indians*, 14, 18: "The Indians who really devote themselves to the chase . . . are at home but a small part of the year. . . . If they are at home and not engaged in the chase they lie all day on their britchen [bunks] and sleep. . . . Whatever time is not devoted to sleep is given to amusements."

85. Williams, *Key*, 99; Harriot, *Briefe and true report*, 56; Romans, *Concise History of Florida* 1:86; Parker, "Iroquois Uses of Maize," 21–22, 31, 33; G. Melvin Herndon, "Indian Agriculture in the Southern Colonies," *North Carolina Historical Review* 44 (1967):283–97, at 288–90. Iroquois women are still responsible for the cultivation of the "three sisters" while the

men care for the imported crops—oats, wheat, and hay (Annemarie A. Shimony, *Conservatism among the Iroquois at the Six Nations Reserve,* Yale University Publications in Anthropology no. 65 [New Haven, 1961], 154–55). See also Charles M. Johnston, eds., *The Valley of the Six Nations: A Collection of Documents on the Indian Lands of the Grand River* (Toronto: Champlain Society, 1964), 308, for a similar division of labor in 1842.

86. Williams, *Key,* 102, 116. See also Whitaker, *Good Newes from Virginia,* 25.

87. Heckewelder, *History,* 154–57; Parker, "Iroquois Uses of Maize," 23.

88. Seaver, *Narrative of Mary Jemison,* 55–56, 184–85.

89. Heckewelder, *History,* 156; Parker, "Iroquois Uses of Maize," 23–24, 29–31; Alex F. Ricciardelli, "The Adoption of White Agriculture by the Oneida Indians," *Ethnohistory* 10 (1963):315–17, 323; *[James] Adair's History of the American Indians* [London, 1775], ed. Samuel C. Williams (Johnson City, Tenn., 1930), 437; Lafitau, *Customs of the American Indians,* 1:lxxxi.

90. *Winthrop Papers* 2:120. In the seventeenth century, "manurance" meant cultivation, tillage, as well as fertilizing, but Winthrop's prescription of cattle dung clearly indicates the latter (OED, s.v. "manurance," "manure").

91. Van der Donck, *New Netherlands,* 96. See also Jameson, *Narratives of New Netherland,* 107; Josselyn, *Account of Two Voyages,* 99; *R.I. Col. Recs.* 1:298.

92. Harriot, *Briefe and true report,* 56; Wood, *New England's Prospect,* 113; Van der Donck, *New Netherlands,* 96. For convincing proof that the natives of eastern America did not widely use fish fertilizer, as the legend of Squanto and the Pilgrims would have us believe, see Lynn Ceci, "Fish Fertilizer: A Native North American Practice?" *Science* 188, no. 4183 (April 4, 1975):26–30, and Letters, ibid. 189, no. 4207 (Sept. 19, 1975).

93. In preindustrial societies, subsistence farming can be seen as a form of social control over its marginal members, whether or not the upper classes consciously intend it as such (Morgan, "Labor Problem at Jamestown," 604, 606). For the paraphernalia required for English-style farming, see Darrett B. Rutman, *Husbandmen of Plymouth: Farms and Villages in the Old Colony, 1620–1692* (Boston, 1967), esp. ch. 2 and appendix.

94. Samuel Stanhope Smith, *An Essay on the Causes of the Variety of Complexion and Figure in the Human Species* [New Brunswick, N.J., 1810], ed. Winthrop D. Jordan (Cambridge, Mass., 1965), 240. See also William Smith to William Johnson, June 22, 1767, *Johnson Papers* 5:569: "I could wish to see them settle in Towns & durable Habitations, & have Property to fix & attach them to us."

95. Robert Beverley, *The History and Present State of Virginia* [London, 1705], ed. Louis B. Wright (Chapel Hill, 1947), 233; *American Magazine and Monthly Chronicle for the British Colonies* (Philadelphia: William Bradford) 1, no. 2 (Nov. 1757):83.

96. *Colls. Mass. His. Soc.,* 1st ser., 4 (1795):68, 72. See also Carl Bridenbaugh, ed., "Patrick M'Robert's Tour through Part of the North Provinces of America," *Penn. Mag. of His. and Biog.* 59 (1935):170. In 1753, several years before Kirkland senior went to the Oneidas, another missionary lamented that "they don't improve a 1/40 of their clear Land" (Gideon Hawley to ——— , Onohquage, June 13, 1753, Hawley Papers).

97. *The Writings of Benjamin Franklin,* ed. Albert H. Smyth (New York, 1907), 10:97; Morton, *New English Canaan,* in Force, *Tracts* 2, no. 5, pp. 39–40; Albert C. Myers, eds., *Narratives of Early Pennsylvania, West New Jersey, and Delaware 1630–1707,* ONEAH (New York, 1912), 233.

98. For some of those who appreciated the laborious nature of hunting, see Josselyn, *Account of Two Voyages,* 106; Williams, *Key,* 116; Heckewelder, *History,* 157–58; and *Adair's History,* 432.

99. Barbour, *Jamestown Voyages* 137:359; "Morell's Poem on New-England," 136; Van der Donck, *New Netherlands,* 96. See also John Lawson, *A New Voyage to Carolina* [London, 1709], ed. Hugh T. Lefler (Chapel Hill, 1967), 176, and *Lieut. Henry Timberlake's Memoirs, 1756–1765,* ed. Samuel C. Williams (Johnson City, Tenn., 1927), 99.

100. *William Byrd's Histories of the Dividing Line betwixt Virginia and North Carolina* [1728], ed. William K. Boyd (New York, 1967), 116; John Witthoft, *The American Indian as Hunter* (Harrisburg: Pennsylvania Historical and Museum Commission, 1967), 2–3.

101. *Doc. His. Maine* 7 (Farnham Papers):50. Early advertisements for New England emphasized that the aristocracy would find settlement pleasant because of "good creatures to hunt and to hawk and for fowling and fishing" (Everett Emerson, ed., *Letters from New England: The Massachusetts Bay Colony, 1629–1638* [Amherst, Mass., 1976], 84). See also Capt. John Smith, *Works, 1608–1631* (Birmingham, 1884), 727.

102. *Zeisberger's History,* 119; "The Indians in Virginia . . . 1689," *WMQ,* 3d ser., 16 (1959):234. According to Bernard Romans, the Creeks scratched their boys "from head to foot

through the skin with broken glass or gar fish teeth, so as to make them all in a gore of blood," then washed them with cold water, to harden them for hunting and warfare (Romans, *Concise History of Florida* 1:96). See also *Timberlake's Memoirs*, 90; Beverley, *History and Present State of Virginia*, 92; Winslow, *Good Newes*, 360; Witthoft, *American Indian as Hunter*, 23.

103. *Adair's History*, 432; Heckewelder, *History*, 157; *Zeisberger's History*, 23; Benjamin Franklin to James Parker, March 20, 1751, in Leonard W. Labaree et al., eds., *The Papers of Benjamin Franklin* (New Haven, 1959–), 4:117–21; *Colls. Mass. His. Soc.*, 2d ser., 3 (1815):6. Fishing seems to have been only slightly less arduous: see Williams, *Key*, 116; Hudson, *Southeastern Indians*, 281–84.

104. Shepard, *Clear Sun-shine*, 50; Winslow, *Glorious Progress*, 81, 90.

105. Axtell, *School upon a Hill*, ch. 3; Steven R. Smith, "The London Apprentices as Seventeenth-Century Adolescents," *Past and Present* 61 (Nov. 1973):149–61; Lawrence W. Towner, "A Good Master Well Served: A Social History of Servitude in Massachusetts, 1620–1750" (Ph.D. diss., Northwestern Univ., 1955).

106. *Colls. Conn. His. Soc.* 5 (1896):405 (Talcott Papers); *Ply. Col. Recs.* 10:251, 398. The law was given more teeth in 1708 when the company required that all Indian indentures contain a provision that "the Master be Obliged to teach the Apprentices to Read, and learn the Catechisme" (Kellaway, *New England Company*, 230).

107. John Daniel Hammerer, *An Account of a Plan for Civilizing the North American Indians*, ed. Paul L. Ford, Winnowings in American History, Indian Tracts, no. 1 (Brooklyn: Historical Printing Club, 1890), 20. See also Gookin, *Historical Collections*, 125, and Jones, *Present State of Virginia*, 62, 115.

108. Gookin, *Historical Collections*, 125; Shepard, *Clear Sun-shine*, 58–59; Kellaway, *New England Company*, 230. See also Lawrence W. Towner, "'A Fondness for Freedom': Servant Protest in Puritan Society," *WMQ*, 3d ser., 19 (1962):201–19. By the mid-eighteenth century, well-developed racism toward Indians also made the native children reluctant apprentices. Eleazar Wheelock complained to a correspondent in 1764 that "I find it Difficult to find Places Suitable for these [Indian] Boys to serve an Apprenticeship at and the greatest Dirty is that their fellow Prentices viz. English Boys will dispise them and treat them as Slaves, which will discourage and Spoil them" (Wheelock Papers 764268.1).

109. Gideon Hawley to Andrew Oliver, Dec. 9, 1760, Hawley Papers; Hawley to Lt.-Gov. Thomas Hutchinson, May 28, 1761, Hawley Papers; "Mashpee Indian Petition to a Committee of the [Massachusetts] General Court to hear their Grievances," August 13, 1761, Hawley Manuscripts; John A. Sainsbury, "Indian Labor in Early Rhode Island," *New England Quarterly* 48 (1975):378–93, at 384.

110. Kellaway, *New England Company*, 230; *Colls. Conn. His. Soc.* 5 (1896):204n, 205 (Talcott Papers); Mass. Archives 33:548–49 (April 1772).

111. Gray, *Good Speed to Virginia*, sig. D3v; *Ply. Col. Recs.* 10:273; *Colls. Mass. His. Soc.*, 5th ser., 9 (1885):45–47; Richard S. Dunn, *Puritans and Yankees: The Winthrop Dynasty of New England, 1630–1717* (Princeton, 1962), 72–73; J. R. Jacob, "The New England Company, the Royal Society, and the Indians," *Social Studies of Science* 5 (1975):450–55.

112. Gookin, *Historical Collections*, 73; *Ply. Col. Recs.* 10:244; Kellaway, *New England Company*, 152–53; Ford, *Some Correspondence*, 114.

113. Daniel Gookin, "An Historical Account of the Doings and Sufferings of the Christian Indians in New England, in the Years 1675, 1676, 1677," in *Archaeologia Americana: Transactions and Collections of the American Antiquarian Society* 2 (1836):495, 530.

114. Gookin, *Historical Collections*, 34, 72, 104, 115; Gookin, "Christian Indians," 532; *Ply. Col. Recs.* 10:382; [Shepard], *Day-Breaking*, 17; Shepard, *Clear Sun-shine*, 59; Winslow, *Glorious Progress*, 80–81; Ford, *Some Correspondence*, 20. In the eighteenth century the Iroquois gathered ginseng for a bullish European market, and the Moravian Delawares in Michigan made birch-bark canoes for Detroiters (*Peter Kalm's Travels in North America* [Stockholm, 1753–61]: *The English Version of 1770*, ed. Adolph B. Benson, 2 vols. [New York, 1937], 2:435–37; *Colls. Mass. His. Soc.*, 1st ser., 4 [1795]:53; *Diary of David Zeisberger, A Moravian Missionary among the Indians of Ohio* [1781–98], ed. and trans. Eugene F. Bliss, 2 vols. [Cincinnati, 1885], 1:159–60, 161, 164, 167).

115. Ricciardelli, "Adoption of White Agriculture," 326–28; Louise S. Spindler, "Menomini Women and Culture Change," *Memoirs of the American Anthropological Association* 91 (1962):14–20; Louise and George Spindler, "Male and Female Adaptations in Culture Change," *American Anthropologist* 60 (1958):217–33; Margaret Mead, *The Changing Culture of an Indian Tribe* (New York, 1932, 1965), 150–51, 155–56, 158–63; Frederick O. Gearing, *The Face of the Fox* (Chicago, 1970), 52–53; Hallowell, *Culture and Experience*, 353, table 10;

Ralph Linton, ed., *Acculturation in Seven American Indian Tribes* (New York, 1940), 245, 295; Ruth Landes, *The Ojibwa Woman* (New York, 1971), 135, 177, 180–81, 187.

116. Gookin, *Historical Collections*, 34. See also Colden, *History of the Five Indian Nations*, 3. Lest it appear implausible that so few could strike fear into the hearts of so many, see Madeleine and Jacques Rousseau, "La crainte des Iroquois chez les Mistassins," *RHAF* 2 (June 1948):13–26.

117. H. H. Brackenridge expressed the prevailing sentiment in 1782: "To live by tilling is *more humano* [the human way], by hunting is *more bestiarum* [the way of beasts]" (*Indian Atrocities: Narratives of the Perils and Sufferings of Dr. Knight and John Slover, among the Indians, during the Revolutionary War* [Cincinnati, 1867], 69). See also *Johnson Papers* 7:965, and Joan Thirsk in *Past and Present* 29 (Dec. 1964):64. Of the seventeenth-century missionaries, Roger Williams seems to have been the exception in thinking that "keeping some kind of cattle" constituted "some degree of civility" (*R.I. Col. Recs.* 1:298). Perhaps the Rhode Island economy, based increasingly on stock raising, overcame his English expectations. See Carl Bridenbaugh, *Fat Mutton and Liberty of Conscience: Society in Rhode Island, 1636–1690* (Providence, 1974).

118. David B. Quinn, *The Elizabethans and the Irish* (Ithaca, 1966), 14–15, 76–78; Canny, "Ideology of English Colonization," 587; James Muldoon, "The Indian as Irishman," Essex Institute, *Historical Collections* 111 (1975):267–89, at 274.

119. Josselyn, *Account of Two Voyages*, 99; Fulmer Mood, "John Winthrop, Jr. on Indian Corn," *New England Quarterly* 10 (1937), 128; James Rosier, *A True Relation of the most prosperous voyage made this present yeere 1605, by Captaine George Waymouth* [London, 1605], in Burrage, *Early English and French Voyages*, 392. Even today, tourists can buy ceramic "moose milk" jars on northern Indian reservations.

120. Shepard, *Clear Sun-shine*, 59, 61; Winslow, *Glorious Progress*, 87; *NEHGR* 36 (1882):296–99; Gookin, *Historical Collections*, ch. 7; Whitfield, *Strength Out of Weaknesse*, 168.

121. John Sergeant, Journal at Stockbridge, April 1739–March 1740, Yale University Library, MS Vault, Stiles, Misc. MSS, 4; Hopkins, *Historical Memoirs*, 61, 83–84, 108, 151–52.

122. *Diary of David McClure*, 7; James D. McCallum, ed., *The Letters of Eleazar Wheelock's Indians* (Hanover, N.H., 1932), 65, 221, 231, 287. Samuel Kirkland, one of Wheelock's best students, carried the English torch for farming to his missionary post among the Oneidas. See his journal for June 3, 1773: "Have attended my people into their fields, to instruct them in their husbandry, am encouraged to hope some few of them will in time make œconomists, at least Indian ones, altho it is no easy task to inspire an Indian with a notion of industry & frugality" (*The Journals of Samuel Kirkland*, ed. Walter Pilkington [Clinton, N.Y., 1980], 83).

123. Gideon Hawley to James Freeman, Nov. 15, 1802; Hawley to Nathan Strong, Aug. 1802, Hawley Manuscripts.

124. Gookin, *Historical Collections*, 73; Josselyn, *Account of Two Voyages*, 115; Jeremy Belknap and Jedidiah Morse, "The Report of a Committee of the Board of Correspondents of the Scots Society for Propagating Christian Knowledge, Who Visited the Oneida and Mohekunuh Indians in 1796," *Colls. Mass. His. Soc.*, 1st ser., 5 (1798):12–32, at 22; John Thornton Kirkland, "Answers to Queries, Respecting Indians," *Colls. Mass. His. Soc.*, 1st ser., 4 (1795):67–74, at 68, 72; Rountree, "Change Came Slowly," 5.

125. In 1955 nutritionist M. K. Bennett estimated that the average intake of animal and bird meat by the southern New England Indians before 1675 was only 10 percent of their total diet, while fish accounted for another 9 percent. (The average American in 1952 ingested about 22 percent meat and less than ½ percent fish.) I would agree with Bennett that before 1675 "the Indians—even the Christianized ones—took to domesticated animals and to European crops only in a small way." But by the Revolution, a shrunken land base, reduced game resources, and acquired taste for colonial staples forced the Indians into somewhat greater changes of diet, chiefly wheat (which they bought) and beef and pork (which they raised on the hoof) ("The Food Economy of the New England Indians, 1605–1675," *Journal of Political Economy* 63 [1955]:392, 395).

126. Jonathan Edwards, *An Account of the Life of Mr. David Brainerd* (Edinburgh, 1798), 520–21. On mixed farming, see Bridenbaugh, *Fat Mutton*, ch. 3; Rutman, *Husbandmen of Plymouth*, ch. 2, esp. 46–49; James T. Lemon, *The Best Poor Man's Country: A Geographical Study of Early Southeastern Pennsylvania* (Baltimore, 1972), ch. 6, esp. 160–67.

127. Shepard, *Clear Sun-shine*, 59; Gookin, *Historical Collections*, 73; *Journals of Samuel Kirkland*, 83 (June 3, 1773).

128. *Journals of Samuel Kirkland*, 24 (April 7, 1765).

129. Gideon Hawley, Journal, March 16, 1754, Hawley Papers. For the advocacy of re-serves, see Samuel Sewall to Sir William Ashurst, May 3, 1700, *Colls. Mass. His. Soc.*, 6th ser., 1 (1886):231–33; John Minot to William Dummer, Oct. 4, 1725, Mass. Archives, 52:294–96; Gideon Hawley to James Freeman, Nov. 15, 1802, Hawley Manuscripts.

130. Jennings, *Invasion of America*, ch. 8. In the New England praying towns, spots of fertile land were "but here and there" at "a great distance from each other; some four or five miles, some eight or nine miles: some ten or twelve miles" (Eliot, *Brief Narrative*, 11).

131. *Colls. Conn. His. Soc.* 4 (1892):319–21 (Talcott Papers); John W. DeForest, *History of the Indians of Connecticut from the Earliest Known Period to 1850* (Hartford, 1851), ch. 11, esp. 427–29.

132. Samuel Sewall to Sir William Ashurst, May 3, 1700, *Colls. Mass. His. Soc.*, 6th ser., 1 (1886):231–33. In Pennsylvania the Conestoga Indians peacefully farmed fifty acres of their five-hundred-acre reserve until the Paxton boys murdered them and took possession of the farm by right of "conquest" (*Penn. Mag. of His. and Biog.* 4 [1880]:119–20).

133. A. Irving Hallowell, "The Nature and Function of Property as a Social Institution," *Culture and Experience*, ch. 12; Mary W. Herman, "The Social Aspects of Huron Property," *American Anthropologist* 58 (1956):1044–58; George S. Snyderman, "Concepts of Land Own-ership among the Iroquois and their Neighbors," *BAE* bulletin 149 (1951): 13–34; A. F. C. Wallace, "Political Organization and Land Tenure among the Northeastern Indians, 1600–1830," *Southwestern Journal of Anthropology* 13 (1957):301–21; Rolf Knight, "A Re-exami-nation of Hunting, Trapping and Territoriality among the Northeastern Algonkian Indians," in Andrew Leeds and Andrew P. Vayda, eds., *Man, Culture and Animals: The Role of Animals in Human Ecological Adjustments* (Washington, D.C., 1965), 27–42; Jennings, *Invasion of America*, ch. 3.

134. *Adair's History*, 436; *A Tour of Four Great Rivers in 1769. Being the Journal of Richard Smith of Burlington, New Jersey*, ed. Francis W. Halsey (New York, 1906), 67; Winslow, *Glorious Progress*, 81.

135. Belknap and Morse, "Report," 22: At Oneida "not more than two or three families procure a subsistence by agriculture; and these have little encouragement to proceed; because their neighbours will live upon them, as long as they have any thing to eat." In 1682 Plymouth Colony tried to reduce the physical movements of its Indians with fines, whipping, and certificates because "by theire disorderly removeing from one Place to another [they] live Idlely and on the Labours of others and spend their Time to Noe Profitt" (*Ply. Col. Recs.* 11:254). See also Smith, *Tour of Four Great Rivers*, 83.

136. Barbara Graymont, *The Iroquois in the American Revolution* (Syracuse, 1972), 38–39; "The Indians in Virginia . . . 1689," 230; Drake, *Indian Captivities*, 205. See also Jones, *Present State of Virginia*, 55; Josselyn, *Account of Two Voyages*, 102; and Wood, *New England's Prospect*, 87.

137. Conn. Archives, Indian Papers, vol. 2, fol. 330a. Traditional Indian ideals of generos-ity and independence from laborious restraints still live on reservations and in cities, thus perpetuating the white myth of the "lazy Indians." See George D. and Louise S. Spindler, "American Indian Personality Types and Their Sociocultural Roots," *American Academy of Political and Social Sciences* 311 (1957):147–57, and Jeanne Guillemin, *Urban Renegades: The Cultural Strategy of American Indians* (New York, 1975), 146–50.

138. Gideon Hawley, Journal, Nov. 2, Nov. 23, 1755, Hawley Papers; Mashpee marriage register, 1764–74, Hawley Papers; Hawley to Nathan Strong, Aug. 1802, Hawley Manuscripts. See also Hopkins, *Historical Memoirs*, 46, 67. For the significance of biblical names to the New English colonists, see Axtell, *School upon a Hill*, 8–10.

139. C. C. Trowbridge, Account of the Delawares [1823–24], in C. A. Weslager, *The Delaware Indian Westward Migration* (Wallingford, Pa., 1978), 179–81; also 100–103; *Zeis-berger's History*, 80; Samson Occom, "An Account of the Montauk Indians, on Long-Island, 1761," *Colls. Mass. His. Soc.*, 1st ser., 10 (1809):108; Heckewelder, *History*, 141; Lawson, *New Voyage to Carolina*, 204; Winslow, *Good Newes*, 363–64.

140. *Ply. Col. Recs.* 3:192. For native preference for English names, see Josselyn, *Account of Two Voyages*, 100, and *Zeisberger's History*, 145.

141. See Daniel F. Littlefield, Jr., and Lonnie E. Underhill, "Renaming the American Indian: 1890–1913," *American Studies* 12, no. 2 (Fall 1971):33–45, for a similar process. Of course, when the colonists were in a distinct minority in Indian country, the natives often gave them Indian names because they could not pronounce their European names easily. The Moravian missionaries who ventured into Iroquois territory were thus renamed, which later worked to their advantage in dealing with other Iroquois. The Indians who received anglicized

names may have enjoyed a similar advantage in English territory (William M. Beauchamp, ed., *Moravian Journals Relating to Central New York, 1745–66* [Syracuse, 1916], 10–11, 58, 89, 128). For the Indian renaming of Jesuit missionaries, see above pp. 83–85.

142. Shepard, *Clear Sun-shine*, 40; *Conn. Col. Recs.* 2:575–76. On July 28, 1674, Joseph Indian of Boston was sentenced to twenty lashes and court costs for having abandoned his wife and two children and "taken another Squaw with whome hee lives & keepes company as his wife." Awk-whew, his new wife, was given fifteen lashes (Samuel Eliot Morison and Zechariah Chafee, Jr., eds., "Records of the Suffolk County Court, 1671–1680," *Pubs. Col. Soc. Mass.*, 29–30 [1933]:485).

143. Wood, *New England's Prospect*, 99; Williams, *Key*, 147; Colden, *History of the Five Indian Nations*, 12; *Zeisberger's History*, 81; "The Opinions of George Croghan on the American Indian [1773]," *Penn. Mag. of His. and Biog.* 71 (1947): 155, 157; "Guy Johnson's Opinions on the American Indians," ibid. 77 (1953): 319.

144. Winslow, *Good Newes*, 557; "Morell's Poem on New-England," 134, 138; [Shepard], *Day-Breaking*, 18, 20; Shepard, *Clear Sun-shine*, 56; *Diary of David McClure*, 72, 91; "Opinions of George Croghan," 156; "Guy Johnson's Opinions," 320; Stiles, *Extracts*, 144–46; Romans, *Concise History of Florida* 1:43, 86.

145. Shepard, *Clear Sun-shine*, 62. For a similar indictment of English housing in the southern backcountry, see Charles Woodmason, *The Carolina Backcountry on the Eve of the Revolution*, ed. Richard J. Hooker (Chapel Hill, 1953), 7, 32.

146. *Mass. Col. Recs.* 2:56; *Winthrop's Journal* 2:124. See also Shepard, *Clear Sun-shine*, 40, no. 19: "If any man lie with a beast he shall die." This was hardly applicable to the Indians before the English introduced domesticated animals. Moreover, it seems to reflect a concern for English rather than Indian morality. In 1642 the Plymouth Colony experienced an epidemic of "notorious sins," especially of the sexual sort. Fornication and adultery were rampant, as were sodomy, buggery, and bestiality. A teenage servant was executed for unnatural relations with "a mare, a cow, two goats, five sheep, two calves, and a turkey," wickedness which "he had long used . . . in old England" (Bradford, *Plymouth Plantation*, 316–21). John Lawson noted that the Carolina Indians had no name for sodomy in their language (*New Voyage to Carolina*, 193).

147. Shepard, *Clear Sun-shine*, 40, no. 24; Winslow, *Good Newes*, 364; Hopkins, *Historical Memoirs*, 63–64; Williams, *Key*, 31–32; Jameson, *Narratives of New Netherland*, 178. The custom of seclusion was not universal. In some of the more sedentary agricultural tribes, such as the Hurons in the seventeenth century and Ottawas in the eighteenth, the women remained in their lodges but used separate utensils for eating and cooking (*Zeisberger's History*, 77–78; Sagard, *Long Journey to the Hurons*, 67). Bernard Romans found in the South that only the Chickasaws "make their females observe a separation at the time of their *Menses*" (*Concise History of Florida* 1:64). For a detailed description of menstrual practices in a woodland tribe, see "The Autobiography of a Fox Woman," ed. Truman Michelson, *BAE 40th Annual Report* (Washington, D.C., 1925), 297–307. The Denver Art Museum exhibits a decorated Naskapi girl's puberty (menstrual) veil made of soft skin. Long fringe prevented her from looking directly at a hunter.

148. Hakluyt, "Discourse on Western Planting," in Taylor, *Hakluyt Writings* 77:235; *Colls. Mass. His. Soc.*, 5th ser., 9 (1885):46. See also Taylor, *Hakluyt Writings* 77:327, 332, 343; [Peckham], *True Reporte*, sig. E2r; Carleill, *Discourse upon the entended Voyage*, sig. A3v–A4r.

149. Wood, *New England's Prospect*, 84; Williams, *Key*, 121. That the native Virginians' dress changed appreciably little during the seventeenth century is confirmed by a comparison of the observations of Smith, *Map of Virginia*, in Barbour, *Jamestown Voyages* 137:355, and Beverley, *History and Present State of Virginia*, 161–66. An important reason for the southern resistance to fitted breeches was that Indian men squatted to urinate (*Adair's History*, 8–9; George Alsop, *A Character of the Province of Mary-land* [London, 1666], 72; Romans, *Concise History of Florida* 1:42). As late as the 1930s, Indian traditionalists could be found who lamented that their ancestors "did not get sick until they commenced wearing White clothes" (Landes, *Ojibwa Woman*, 125). See also Van der Donck, *New Netherlands*, 79; Josselyn, *Account of Two Voyages*, 100–101; Jones, *Present State of Virginia*, 56; Gen. Benjamin Lincoln, "Observations on the Indians of North America [1795]," *Colls. Mass. His. Soc.*, 1st ser., 5 (1798):7; Charles Wolley, *A Two Years' Journal in New York* [London, 1701], ed. Edward G. Bourne (Cleveland, 1902), 35.

150. For the farming costume of the day, see James T. Adams, ed., *Album of American History. 1: Colonial Period* (New York, 1944), 22, 90, 116.

151. Fitz John Winthrop to John Winthrop, Jr., Nov. 1674, *Colls. Mass. His. Soc.*, 6th ser., 3 (1889):445–46.

152. Carl Bridenbaugh, ed., *Gentleman's Progress: The Itinerarium of Dr. Alexander Hamilton 1744* (Chapel Hill, 1948), 98; Stiles, *Extracts*, 108, 114.

153. Bridenbaugh, *Gentleman's Progress*, 112–13, 140–41; *DCB* 3:623, s.v. "Theyanoguin."

154. Smith, *Tour of Four Great Rivers*, 83–84.

155. Shepard, *Clear Sun-shine*, 45; Whitfield, *Strength Out of Weaknesse*, 178. A few of the clothes were newly purchased by the Indians, but many were English hand-me-downs, carefully saved by the natives for Sabbath wear. Eliot's own servant had only a "cast off worne sute of Cloths" for his daily apparel (Shepard, *Clear Sun-shine*, 46; Winslow, *Glorious Progress*, 87). Among the tools Eliot bought with New England Company funds in 1651 were "2 pairs of Taylors sheers" which his brother used "to cut out garments for the Indians" (*NEHGR* 36 [1882]:299).

156. Gookin, *Historical Collections*, 17, 40; *Colls. Mass. His. Soc.*, 1st ser., 10 (1809):130, 132, 133. See also Josselyn, *Account of Two Voyages*, 115; Jaspar Dankers and Peter Sluyter, *Journal of a Voyage to New York and a Tour in Several of the American Colonies in 1679–80*, ed. and trans. Henry C. Murphy (Brooklyn, 1867), 306.

157. Gideon Hawley to Nathan Strong, Aug. 1802, Hawley Manuscripts; *Colls. Mass. His. Soc.*, 1st ser., 4 (1795):72.

158. Wood, *New England's Prospect*, 85; Jameson, *Narratives of New Netherland*, 173. See also Wolley, *Two Years' Journey*, 36. For the rich profusion of native hairstyles, see Wood, *New England's Prospect*, 83; Smith, *Map of Virginia*, in Barbour, *Jamestown Voyages* 137:354, 372; Hall, *Narratives of Maryland*, 43, 86; Williams, *Key*, 49; Jones, *Present State of Virginia*, 56; Beverley, *History and Present State of Virginia*, 159–66.

159. J[ohn] B[ulwer], *Anthropometamorphosis: Man Transform'd; or, The Artificial Changeling* (2d ed., London, 1653), 53. I am grateful to Keith Thomas for introducing me to this fascinating book. See also H. J. Norman, "John Bulwer and his *Anthropometamorphosis*," in *Science, Medicine, and History: Essays . . . in honour of Charles Singer* (Oxford, 1935), 2:82–97.

160. Thomas Hall, *The Loathsomnesse of Long Haire* (London, 1654), 1–2; George Gipps, *A Sermon Preached to the Honourable House of Commons on their Monethly Fast Novem. 27, 1644* (London, 1645), 9–10; William Prynne, *A Gagge for Long-Hair'd Rattle-Heads who revile all civill Round-heads* (London, 1646); [Higginson], *New-Englands Plantation*, in Force, *Tracts* 1, no. 12, p. 12.

161. Gipps, *A Sermon . . . 1644*, 10; Williams, *Key*, 48–49; Hall, *Loathsomnesse of Long Haire*, 23.

162. [Shepard], *Day-Breaking*, 20 (nos. 5, 7); Shepard, *Clear Sun-shine*, 40 (no. 15); Eliot and Mayhew, *Tears of Repentance*, 234, 239.

163. [Shepard], *Day-Breaking*, 22.

164. Shepard, *Clear Sun-shine*, 45; *Winthrop's Journal* 2:324; Axtell, *School upon a Hill*, 160–65.

165. Robert G. Pope, ed., "The Notebook of the Reverend John Fiske, 1644–1675," *Pubs. Col. Soc. Mass.* 47 (1974):134; Winslow, *Glorious Progress*, 91; Morton, *New English Canaan*, in Force, *Tracts* 2, no. 5, p. 94.

166. "Notebook of John Fiske," 133; *Procs. Mass. His. Soc.*, 2d ser., 29 (1895):99; *NEHGR* 1 (1847):369–71; *Mass. Col. Recs.* 4, no. 2:59 (Nov. 3, 1675).

167. Among hostile appraisals, New England views of the Pequots were especially pugnacious. Capt. John Mason, who led Connecticut troops against their Mystic fort in 1637, saw his fiery victory as "the Lord's Doings, . . . Crushing his proud Enemies and the Enemies of his People." Mason's colleague, Capt. John Underhill, was more explicit. He attributed the natives' downfall to "the old serpent," who, "according to this first malice, stirred them up against the church of Christ." They had, at the Devil's instigation, grown to "a *height* of blood, and sin against God and man," both of whom ensured that their wicked "insolency" did not persist (Orr, *History of the Pequot War*, 26, 30, 35, 49, 66, 81, 103, 111). Again in King Philip's War the hostile natives were puffed up with "pride and insolence," and again "the great God" had "rebuked their rage, and broken them in pieces like a potter's vessel" (Gookin, "Christian Indians," 494–95).

168. Shepard, *Clear Sun-shine*, 50; Whitfield, *Light Appearing*, 109, 142; Whitfield, *Strength Out of Weaknesse*, 178; Eliot and Mayhew, *Tears of Repentance*, 208. In the eighteenth century, when the New England missionaries attempted to convert the New York Iroquois, different hair styles posed an ironic but similar problem for the ministers. In 1761

Eleazar Wheelock was told that Samson Occom, the Mohegan he had trained for the ministry, was annoying the Oneidas by insisting that "they must *not* cut their hair, but let it grow as the English do." Although New England had long since fallen from its short-haired ideals, Indian hair still symbolized the antithesis of Christian submission (Wheelock Papers, 761530).

169. Shepard, *Clear Sun-shine*, 40, 50; Eliot, *Brief Narrative*, 8 (my emphasis). See also *Johnson Papers* 7:508; Gookin, *Historical Collections*, 80; Kellaway, *New England Company*, 222; White, *Planters Plea*, in Force, *Tracts* 2, no. 3, p. 6.

170. *Winthrop Papers* 1:158–59; "Autobiography of Thomas Shepard," *Pubs. Col. Soc. Mass.*, 27 (1932), 392. Eliot once explained to an enquiring Indian that God kept some Englishmen, although Christian, in poverty to prevent them from waxing "proud and wanton . . . to depend upon him" (*Winthrop's Journal* 2:319–20).

171. Wood, *New England's Prospect*, 96–97; Morison and Chafee, "Records of the Suffolk County Court," 147–48. The penal use of scissors on Indian inmates, whether in schools, on reservations, or in jails, has a long history in America. On the day he was released from federal prison in March 1976, Leonard Crow Dog, the long-haired religious leader of the Lakota Sioux, had an order to report to the barbershop (Richard Erdoes, "Crow Dog Released from Prison," *Akwesasne Notes*, 8:2 [early summer 1976], 14).

8. THE LITTLE RED SCHOOL

1. Alexander Brown, ed., *The Genesis of the United States*, 2 vols. (Boston, 1890), 1:53, 236; Peter Walne, "The Collection for Henrico College, 1616–1618," *Virginia Magazine of History and Biography* 80 (1972):259–66; Edward D. Neill, *Memoir of Rev. Patrick Copland, Rector of the First Projected College in the United States* (New York, 1871); Robert Hunt Land, "Henrico and Its College," *WMQ*, 2d ser., 18 (1938):453–98; W. Stitt Robinson, Jr., "Indian Education and Missions in Colonial Virginia," *Journal of Southern History* 18 (1952):152–68. The pertinent documents may be found in Edgar W. Knight, ed., *A Documentary History of Education in the South before 1860*, 5 vols. (Chapel Hill, 1949–53), 1:1–31.

2. Knight, *Documentary History of Education* 1:8–11.

3. Smith, *Works*, 929; Land, "Henrico and Its College," 493–94.

4. *Va. Co. Recs.* 3:557. See also William S. Powell, "Aftermath of the Massacre: The First Indian War, 1622–1632," *Virginia Magazine of History and Biography* 66 (1958):44–75; Gary B. Nash, "The Image of the Indian in the Southern Colonial Mind," *WMQ*, 3d ser., 29 (1972): 197–230; J. Frederick Fausz, "The Ideological and Cultural Context of the Virginia Indian Uprising of 1622" (Paper delivered at the Institute of Early American History and Culture, June 1976); Alden T. Vaughan, "'Expulsion of the Salvages': English Policy and the Virginia Massacre of 1622," *WMQ*, 3d ser., 35 (1978):57–84.

5. Knight, *Documentary History of Education* 1:16–17. The book was licensed on March 16, 1620–21, the Virginia Company returned their thanks to the author on Dec. 19, 1621, but the title page gives 1622 as the date of publication.

6. William Lilly, *History of His Life and Times* (London, 1826), 12–13; *Dictionary of National Biography*. Lilly, the astrologer, had been a student under Brinsley.

7. John Brinsley, *A Consolation for our Grammar Schooles* (London, 1622), title page, sigs. A4v, *3v, A3v, A5r, pp. 46–47.

8. Ibid., pp. 7, 12, 57.

9. *Mass. Col. Recs.* 2:203. See also Axtell, *School upon a Hill*, chs. 5–6; Lawrence A. Cremin, *American Education: The Colonial Experience, 1607–1783* (New York, 1970), chs. 1, 6–7; Robert Middlekauff, *Ancients and Axioms: Secondary Education in Eighteenth-Century New England* (New Haven, 1963), pt. 1.

10. Morison, *The Founding of Harvard College*, 313–14.

11. *Ply. Col. Recs.* 10:356; Kellaway, *New England Company*, 114; Margery Somers Foster, *"Out of Smalle Beginings . . .": An Economic History of Harvard College in the Puritan Period (1636 to 1712)* (Cambridge, Mass., 1962), 66, table 9.

12. Gookin, *Historical Collections*, 52–53; *Ply. Col. Recs.* 10:205–6, 218–19, 242–43, 246, 261–63, 275, 277, 296, 317–18, 330, 356, 382–83.

13. [Shepard], *Day-Breaking*, 18, 22; Whitfield, *Strength Out of Weaknesse*, 168–69, 177; Whitfield, *Light Appearing*, 122, 144; *Ply. Col. Recs.* 10:277–78; Eliot and Mayhew, *Tears of Repentance*, 208; Eliot, *Brief Narrative*, 3; Kellaway, *New England Company*, ch. 5.

14. Gookin, *Historical Collections*, 70; Eliot, *Brief Narrative*, 4. In 1672 Eliot published his bilingual *The Logick Primer: Some Logical Notions to Initiate the Indians in the Knowledge of the Rule of Reason* (Cambridge, Mass.). Its Latinate abstractions, scholastic definitions, and foreign examples must have made it a singularly flawed guide to English thinking, except that of the university disputation.

15. Frederick L. Weis, "The New England Company of 1649 and Its Missionary Enterprises," *Pubs. Col. Soc. Mass.* 38 (*Transactions 1947–51*) (1959): 216–18, is a full list of the Indian books printed by the company in the colonial period. Kellaway, *New England Company*, ch. 6, is a detailed account of the same.

16. Gookin, *Historical Collections*, 125–29.

17. Ibid., 128–29. See Stephen J. Greenblatt, "Learning to Curse: Aspects of Linguistic Colonialism in the Sixteenth Century," in Chiappelli, *First Images of America* 2:561–80.

18. Kellaway, *New England Company*, 115, 142, 151, 156–57, 160–61; *Ply. Col. Recs.* 10:368.

19. *Conn. Col. Recs.* 2:574–76; *The Journal of Madam Knight*, intro. Malcolm Freiberg (Boston, 1972), 21.

20. *Colls. Mass. His. Soc.*, 6th ser., 3 (1889):347–48.

21. *Diary of Cotton Mather*, ed. Worthington Chauncey Ford, 2 vols. (reprint ed., New York, 1957?), 1:571, 2:133, 233, 531, 554, 556–57; *Selected Letters of Cotton Mather*, ed. Kenneth Silverman (Baton Rouge, 1971), 144, 265; *Conn. Col. Recs.* 5:7.

22. *Coll. Conn. His. Soc.* ("The Talcott Papers," ed. Mary Kingsbury Talcott, 2 vols.), 4 (1892):81, 83; 5 (1976):413.

23. Ibid. 5 (1896):398, 402; *Diary of Cotton Mather* 2:569; *Selected Letters of Cotton Mather*, 127.

24. *Colls. Conn. His. Soc.* 4 (1892):108; 5 (1896):398, 400–402.

25. *Colls. Conn. His. Soc.* 4 (1892):355–56; 5 (1896): 413, 480.

26. Axtell, *School upon a Hill*, 36–44.

27. Kellaway, *New England Company*, 253; *Colls. Conn. His. Soc.* 4 (1892):107, 283–84, 209; 5 (1896):480n; William S. Simmons and Cheryl L. Simmons, eds., *Old Light on Separate Ways: The Narragansett Diary of Joseph Fish, 1765–1776* (Hanover, N.H., 1982), 41.

28. *Colls. Conn. His. Soc.* 4 (1892):107, 110; Kellaway, *New England Company*, 253–54.

29. Kellaway, *New England Company*, 254.

30. Ibid., 256; *Colls. Conn. His. Soc.* 5 (1896):33–34, 39.

31. See below, pp. 204–15.

32. R. A. Brock, ed., "The Official Letters of Alexander Spotswood, Lieutenant-Governor of the Colony of Virginia, 1710–1722," *Collections of the Virginia Historical Society*, n.s. 1–2 (1882–85), 1:119, 134–35.

33. *WMQ*, 1st ser., 19 (1910–11):423; *WMQ*, 2d ser., 10 (1930):68–69.

34. *Va. Co. Recs.* 3:128–29, 147–48, 228.

35. William Stevens Perry, ed., *Historical Collections Relating to the American Colonial Church. I: Virginia* (Hartford, 1870), 123–24.

36. Brock, "Official Letters of Spotswood" 1:118–19, 121–27, 134–35.

37. Ibid., 1:125; *Va. Mag. of His. and Biog.*, 4 (1897):172.

38. Brock, "Official Letters of Spotswood" 2:88–90, 237; Edward Porter Alexander, ed., *The Journal of John Fontaine . . . 1710–1719* (Williamsburg, 1972), 90–91.

39. *Byrd's Histories of the Dividing Line*, 118, 120; Jones, *Present State of Virginia*, 59.

40. *Journal of John Fontaine*, 91, 93. At some point Griffin may have had an Indian usher, a former student at the college (*C.S.P.Col.* 29 [1716–1717], 142–43).

41. Perry, *American Colonial Church* 1:129, 196; *Journal of John Fontaine*, 97–98.

42. Brock, "Official Letters of Spotswood" 2:281–82; Leonidas Dodson, *Alexander Spotswood, Governor of Colonial Virginia, 1710–1722* (Philadelphia, 1932), ch. 5.

43. J. E. Morpurgo, *Their Majesties' Royall Colledge: William and Mary in the Seventeenth and Eighteenth Centuries* (Williamsburg, 1976), 69: "The Brafferton Building," typescript, William and Mary College Archives, Indian School folder, pp. 11–12.

44. Brock, "Official Letters of Spotswood" 2:91; *WMQ*, 1st ser., 4 (1897):173; Morpurgo, *Their Majesties' Royall Colledge*, 69. The full title of Bishop Wilson's book is *The Knowledge and Practice of Christianity Made Easy to the Meanest Capacities; or, An Essay towards an Instruction for the Indians* (London, 1740); it reached its thirteenth edition by 1781.

45. Jones, *Present State of Virginia*, 114; Wharton Apothecary Account Book (1735–46), Colonial Williamsburg Research Library, Microfilm M-1093, pp. 152, 154; Brafferton Ac-

count with James and William Carter (1765–66), College of William and Mary Archives, College Papers, folder 288. I am grateful to Karen Stuart for the last two references.

46. R. A. Brock, ed., "The Official Records of Robert Dinwiddie, Lieutenant-Governor of the Colony of Virginia, 1751–1758," *Collections of the Virginia Historical Society*, n.s. 3–4 (1883–84), 4:446; Mark Catesby, *The Natural History of Carolina*, 2 vols. (London, 1771), 1:xii.

47. Labaree, *Papers of Benjamin Franklin* 4:482 n. 7; *Pa. Col. Recs.*, 4:733.

48. *Byrd's Histories of the Dividing Line*, 118, 120; Gregory A. Stiverson and Patrick H. Butler III, eds., "Virginia in 1732: The Travel Journal of William Hugh Grove," *Virginia Magazine of History and Biography* 85 (1977):18–44, at 25. See also Jones, *Present State of Virginia*, 59, 61–62, 114–15; Morpurgo, *Their Majesties' Royall Colledge*, 180; Winslow C. Watson, ed., *Men and Times of the Revolution; or, Memoirs of Elkanah Waston* (New York, 1850), 256–57.

49. Hopkins, *Historical Memoirs*, 164–65.

50. Sarah Cabot Sedgwick and Christina Sedgwick Marquand, *Stockbridge, 1739–1939: A Chronicle* (Great Barrington, Mass., 1939), 23, 51, 69; Daniel R. Mandell, "Change and Continuity in a Native American Community: Eighteenth Century Stockbridge" (M.A. thesis, Dept. of History, Univ. of Virginia, 1982), 33–34.

51. Hopkins, *Historical Memoirs*, 39, 46.

52. Ibid., 28, 65–66.

53. Ibid., 81–82.

54. Ibid., 73–76.

55. Ibid., 94–95, 106–11, 148.

56. Ibid., 117–34, 144–47, 154.

57. Ibid., 145, 154–55; Emma Lewis Coleman, *New England Captives Carried to Canada between 1677 and 1760 during the French and Indian Wars*, 2 vols. (Portland, Maine, 1925), 2:97–99, 113.

58. Edmund S. Morgan, *The Gentle Puritan: A Life of Ezra Stiles, 1727–1795* (New Haven, 1962), ch. 5, quotation at 87.

59. *Journals of the House of Representatives of Massachusetts, 1749–1750* (Boston, 1951), 225–26; Mass. Archives 32:30–32; Sereno E. Dwight, *The Works of President [Jonathan] Edwards with a Memoir of His Life*, 10 vols. (New York, 1830), 1:452.

60. Kellaway, *New England Company*, 274–75.

61. *Sibley's Harvard Graduates* 7:62–63.

62. Mass. Archives 32:300, 367–68; Dwight, *Works of President Edwards* 1:480, 491, 494, 527.

63. Mass. Archives 32:206–12, 248–49, 370; Dwight, *Works of President Edwards* 1:486.

64. Mass. Archives 32:299, 303, 305, 366; Dwight, *Works of President Edwards* 1:470, 490–91; *Colls. Mass. His. Soc.*, 1st ser., 10 (1809):148.

65. Jonathan Edwards to Joshua Paine, Feb. 24, 1752, Yale Univ. Library, Andover-Newton Edwards Collection (transcript), folder 1752B; *Sibley's Harvard Graduates* 12:392–411.

66. Dwight, *Works of President Edwards* 1:303–4, 490–91, 504–5; *Sibley's Harvard Graduates* 7:62–63, 13:399; Sedgwick and Marquand, *Stockbridge*, 66–67.

67. *Colls. Mass. His. Soc.*, 1st ser., 4 (1795):54–56; Dwight, *Works of President Edwards* 1:527; Mass. Archives 32:476–77, 508.

68. Edwin Scott Gaustad, *The Great Awakening in New England* (New York, 1957), 74–75; James Dow McCallum, *Eleazar Wheelock, Founder of Dartmouth College* (Hanover, N.H., 1939), ch. 2; Harold Blodgett, *Samson Occom* (Hanover, N.H., 1935), chs. 1–3.

69. *Doc. His. N.Y.* 4:202.

70. Wheelock Papers 760628.

71. Eleazar Wheelock, *A Continuation of the Narrative of the State, &c. of the Indian Charity-School, at Lebanon, in Connecticut; From Nov. 27th, 1762, to Sept. 3d, 1765* (Boston, 1765), 22; idem, *A plain and faithful Narrative of the Original Design, Rise, Progress, and Present State of the Indian Charity School at Lebanon, in Connecticut* (Boston, 1763), 40, 42; Wheelock Papers 762113, 761625.1, 761602.3.

72. Wheelock Papers 761625.1, 762113.

73. Wheelock Papers 761664.3, 761404.

74. Eric P. Kelly, "The Dartmouth Indians," *Dartmouth Alumni Magazine* (Dec. 1929), 122–25.

75. Wheelock, *Continuation of the Narrative* . . . (Hartford, 1771), 19–20.

76. Wheelock, *A plain and faithful Narrative*, 28–29; Wheelock Papers 762165.

77. Wheelock Papers 772174.1.

78. Eleazar Wheelock, *Continuation of the Narrative* . . . ([Portsmouth] N.H., 1773), 12–13; Wheelock Papers 756201, 756900.1.

79. Wheelock, *A plain and faithful Narrative*, 25; Wheelock, *Continuation of the Narrative* . . . (Hartford, 1775), 11.

80. Wheelock, *A plain and faithful Narrative*, 15, 40; Wheelock Papers 767427.1.

81. Wheelock, *A plain and faithful Narrative*, 44; Wheelock Papers 762667.2; McCallum, *Letters of Wheelock's Indians*, 287–88.

82. Wheelock, *Continuation of the Narrative* (1771), 5; Wheelock Papers 774657; McCallum, *Letters of Wheelock's Indians*, 221; also 231, 287.

83. McCallum, *Letters of Wheelock's Indians*, 65.

84. Eleazar Wheelock, *A Brief Narrative of the Indian Charity-School, in Lebanon in Connecticut, New England* . . . (London, 1766), 6; Wheelock Papers 756615.

85. Wheelock Papers 764268.1, 765164.1, 770367.

86. Wheelock Papers 758422, 763581, 767604.1.

87. Wheelock Papers 763666.2, 763659; McCallum, *Letters of Wheelock's Indians*, 255.

88. Wheelock Papers 767265.2, 767163.

89. Wheelock Papers 762516, 761304.1, 769209.2; Eleazar Wheelock, *Continuation of the Narrative* . . . (London, 1769), 16; McCallum, *Letters of Wheelock's Indians*, 131, 141, 148, 183.

90. Wheelock Papers 760566, 762412.1.

91. Wheelock Papers 769255, 769274.2; Wheelock, *Continuation of the Narrative* (1771), 16.

92. Wheelock, *Continuation of the Narrative* (1775), 11, 14; Gordon M. Day, "Dartmouth and Saint Francis," *Dartmouth Alumni Magazine* (Nov. 1959), 28–30; Wheelock Papers 764574.

93. Leon Burr Richardson, ed., *An Indian Preacher in England* (Hanover, N.H., 1933); Blodgett, *Samson Occom*, ch. 6.

94. Wheelock Papers 761129.1, 763204, 763407.2.

95. Wheelock Papers 769663.2; Kelly, "The Dartmouth Indians," 122–25; Leon B. Richardson, "The Dartmouth Indians, 1800–1893," *Dartmouth Alumni Magazine* (June 1930), 524–27. See also Jere R. Daniell, "Eleazar Wheelock and the Dartmouth College Charter," *Historical New Hampshire* 24, no. 4 (Winter 1969):3–44 at 29.

96. Blodgett, *Samson Occom*, 122–23, 135.

97. Axtell, *School upon a Hill*, chs. 2–4.

98. Lawrence Stone, "The Educational Revolution in England, 1560–1640," *Past and Present* 28 (July 1964):41–80.

99. *Johnson Papers* 5:439, 531. See also Gookin, *Historical Collections*, 70; *C.S.P.Col.*, 17:551–56; *An Essay towards Propagating the Gospel among the Neighbouring Nations of Indians in North America* (New London, Conn., 1756), 6–8; Kellaway, *New England Company*, 94, 102, 231–32.

100. Belknap and Morse, "Report," 29–30.

9. THE TRIBE OF TRUE BELIEVERS

1. East Apthorp, *The Felicity of the Times. A Sermon Preached at Christ-Church, Cambridge* . . . (Boston, 1763), 13.

2. *The New Life of Virginea* . . . [London, 1612], in Force, *Tracts* 1, no. 7, p. 18; Thomas Bradbury Chandler, *An Appeal to the Public, in Behalf of the Church of England in America* (New York, 1767), 62–63.

3. Shepard, *Clear Sun-shine*, 55; also Winslow, *Glorious Progress*, 78.

4. Eliot and Mayhew, *Tears of Repentance*, 219 (Richard Mather).

5. *Mass. Col. Recs.* 1:17.

6. *Johnson's Wonder-Working Providence*, 263–64; Shepard, *Clear Sun-shine*, 55; Stoddard, *Question, Whether God is not Angry*, 8.

7. S. F. Cook, *The Indian Population of New England in the Seventeenth Century*,

University of California Publications in Anthropology, no. 12 (Berkeley and Los Angeles, 1976), 84; Jennings, *Invasion of America*, 29; Salisbury, *Manitou and Providence*, 30.

8. Morton, *New English Canaan*, in Force, *Tracts*, 2, no. 5, pp. 18–19; Alfred W. Crosby, "Virgin Soil Epidemics as a Factor in the Aboriginal Depopulation in America," *WMQ*, 3d ser., 33 (1976):289–99; Sherburne F. Cook, "The Significance of Disease in the Extinction of the New England Indians," *Human Biology* 45 (1973):485–508; John Duffy, "Smallpox and the Indians in the American Colonies," *Bulletin of the History of Medicine* 25 (1951):324–41; Henry F. Dobyns, *Their Number Become Thinned: Native American Population Dynamics in Eastern North America* (Knoxville, 1983).

9. Evarts B. Greene and Virginia D. Harrington, *American Population before the Federal Census of 1790* (New York, 1932), 9, 13.

10. *Mass. Col. Recs.* 2:55, 3:6–7; *Winthrop's Journal* 2:156, 160.

11. *Mass. Col. Recs.* 2:166, 176–79; Whitmore, *Colonial Laws of Massachusetts*, 55 (1641).

12. *Conn. Col. Recs.* 1:265, 531.

13. *Conn. Col. Recs.* 2:574–76; Gookin, *Historical Collections*, 108–9.

14. [Shepard], *Day-Breaking*, 4, 11. For the chronology of Eliot's visits, see Vaughan, *New England Frontier*, ch. 9, and Jennings, *Invasion of America*, ch. 14.

15. [Shepard], *Day-Breaking*, 3–8.

16. Shepard, *Clear Sun-shine*, 42–44.

17. Winslow, *Glorious Progress*, 81–83; Whitfield, *Light Appearing*, 123–24.

18. *A Coppy of a Letter of Mr. [John] Cotton of Boston* (London, 1641), 5.

19. Lechford, *Plain Dealing*, 66; Thomas Foxcroft, *Cleansing Our Way in Youth* (Boston, 1719), 176; Edmund S. Morgan, *Visible Saints: The History of a Puritan Idea* (New York, 1963), 68–69.

20. John Eliot to Increase Mather, Aug. 22, 1673, in *Colls. Mass. His. Soc.*, 1st ser., 10 (1809):125.

21. [Shepard], *Day-Breaking*, 9.

22. Eliot and Mayhew, *Tears of Repentance*, 253; Shepard, *Clear Sun-shine*, 51, 53; Winslow, *Glorious Progress*, 80.

23. Whitfield, *Strength Out of Weaknesse*, 169–70.

24. Gookin, *Historical Collections*, 47; *Colls. Mass. His. Soc.*, 1st ser., 10 (1809):125; Eliot, *Late Manifestation*, 276–84.

25. Rev. Abraham Pierson, "*Some Helps for the Indians:* A Catechism in the Language of the Quiripi Indians of New Haven Colony," ed. J. Hammond Trumbull, *Colls. Conn. His. Soc.* 3 (1873):10, 11. Although the title page was dated 1658, the book was not published until the end of 1659 (Kellaway, *New England Company*, 126).

26. Whitfield, *Light Appearing*, 145.

27. [Shepard], *Day-Breaking*, 4, 6, 7, 9; Josiah Cotton, "Vocabulary of the Massachusetts (or Natick) Indian Language" [1707–8], *Colls. Mass. His. Soc.*, 3d ser., 2 (1830):147–257 at 225.

28. *Colls. Mass. His. Soc.*, 1st ser., 10 (1809):128; Eliot, *Brief Narrative*, 3–4; Ford, *Some Correspondence*, 84; Gookin, *Historical Collections*, 70.

29. Ford, *Some Correspondence*, 83–86; Weis, "The New England Company of 1649," 150.

30. Kellaway, *New England Company*, 229–30; Eliot, *Brief Narrative*, 2; Matthew Mayhew, *A Brief Narrative of the Success which the Gospel hath had, among the Indians of Martha's Vineyard . . .* (Boston, 1694), 27–28; Experience Mayhew, *Indian Converts; or, Some Account of the Lives and Dying Speeches of a Considerable Number of the Christianized Indians of Martha's Vineyard . . .* (London, 1727), 15–16.

31. John Eliot to the Commissioners of the United Colonies, Aug. 25, 1664, *NEHGR* 9 (1855):131; Eliot, *Brief Narrative*, 5; Whitfield, *Strength Out of Weaknesse*, 170–71.

32. Gookin, *Historical Collections*, 65, 68, 79–85; Eliot, *Indian Dialogues*, 61.

33. Whitfield, *Strength Out of Weaknesse*, 186; Eliot and Mayhew, *Tears of Repentance*, 202; William S. Simmons, "Southern New England Shamanism: An Ethnographic Reconstruction," *Papers of the Seventh Algonquian Conference 1975*, ed. William Cowan (Ottawa, 1976), 217–56; William S. Simmons, "Conversion from Indian to Puritan," *New England Quarterly* 52 (1979), 197–218 at 198–200.

34. Eliot and Mayhew, *Tears of Repentance*, 204; Gookin, *Historical Collections*, 20–21; Wood, *New England's Prospect*, 101.

35. Whitfield, *Light Appearing*, 110; Shepard, *Clear Sun-shine*, 56; Gookin, *Historical Collections*, 21. The native response has had a long life. When a Russian Orthodox missionary

urged a village of Eskimos to give up their shamans in 1863, they replied, "You Russians have priests and doctors, but we have none. If anyone happens to fall ill, who can help us except the shaman?" (W. H. Oswalt and James W. VanStone, *The Ethnoarcheology of Crow Village, Alaska* [Washington, D.C., 1967], 4).

36. Shepard, *Clear Sun-shine*, 56–57; Winslow, *Glorious Progress*, 84. See Eliot, *Indian Dialogues*, 88–89, for his admiration of native herbalism.

37. Samuel Eliot Morison, *Three Centuries of Harvard, 1636–1936* (Cambridge, Mass., 1936), 168; Morison, *Harvard College in the Seventeenth Century*, 2 vols. (Cambridge, Mass., 1936), 1:281–84; Virgil J. Vogel, *American Indian Medicine* (Norman, Okla., 1970), 6, 267–68.

38. Shepard, *Clear Sun-shine*, 57.

39. Gookin, *Historical Collections*, 21, 61, 83–84; [Shepard], *Day-Breaking*, 19.

40. Winslow, *Good Newes*, 358; Shepard, *Clear Sun-shine*, 50.

41. Simmons, "Southern New England Shamanism," 246; Whitfield, *Light Appearing*, 110–11, 115–16.

42. Whitfield, *Strength Out of Weaknesse*, 186–87; Eliot and ·Mayhew, *Tears of Repentance*, 203, 205.

43. *Colls. Mass. His. Soc.*, 1st ser., 10 (1809):126.

44. Whitfield, *Light Appearing*, 114; Whitfield, *Strength Out of Weaknesse*, 178–79; Eliot and Mayhew, *Tears of Repentance*, 208; Shepard, *Clear Sun-shine*, 50; [Shepard], *Day-Breaking*, 4; *New England's First Fruits* in Morison, *Founding of Harvard College*, 423.

45. [Shepard], *Day-Breaking*, 4, 11, 13, 17.

46. Ibid., 20; Shepard, *Clear Sun-shine*, 38–41.

47. Shepard, *Clear Sun-shine*, 53, 55.

48. Ibid., 55; Whitfield, *Light Appearing*, 112, 115.

49. Eliot and Mayhew, *Tears of Repentance*, 219.

50. Ibid., 207–8.

51. Compare the Indian confessions in Eliot and Mayhew, *Tears of Repentance* and Mayhew, *Indian Converts*, with the English relations in *Thomas Shepard's Confessions*, ed. George Selement and Bruce C. Woolley, *Pubs. Col. Soc. Mass.*, Collections 58 (1981), and *The Diary of Michael Wigglesworth, 1653–1657*, ed. Edmund S. Morgan (New York, 1965), 107–25.

52. Whitfield, *Strength Out of Weaknesse*, 192–93; Eliot and Mayhew, *Tears of Repentance*, 229, 234, 239, 248.

53. *New England's First Fruits*, in Morison, *Founding of Harvard College*, 423; *Colls. Conn. His. Soc.* 3 (1873):43–44; Shepard, *Clear Sun-shine*, 60.

54. Shepard, *Clear Sun-shine*, 41, 42; Gookin, *Historical Collections*, 46.

55. Shepard, *Clear Sun-shine*, 41–42, 45–47, 58, 63–64; Winslow, *Glorious Progress*, 84–86, 91–92; Whitfield, *Light Appearing*, 128–30, 132–33.

56. Eliot to Robert Boyle, April 22, 1684, in Eliot, *Brief Narrative*, 9; [Shepard], *Day-Breaking*, 13, 21; Shepard, *Clear Sun-shine*, 31.

57. [Shepard], *Day-Breaking*, 5, 13; Shepard, *Clear Sun-shine*, 41; Whitfield, *Light Appearing*, 129; Winslow, *Glorious Progress*, 84, 85, 91; Eliot, *Indian Dialogues*, 80.

58. Eliot, *Indian Dialogues*, 73–74, 79, 106.

59. Eliot and Mayhew, *Tears of Repentance*, 206–7; Shepard, *Clear Sun-shine*, 40, 41, 51; Whitfield, *Light Appearing*, 124, 139.

60. Whitfield, *Strength Out of Weaknesse*, 178; Ford, *Some Correspondence*, 87; Cotton Mather, *Bonifacius, An Essay upon the Good* [Boston, 1710], ed. David Levin (Cambridge, Mass., 1966), 155. See also Gookin, *Historical Collections*, 69, 81; Eliot, *Brief Narrative*, 10; Shepard, *Clear Sun-shine*, 62; Whitfield, *Light Appearing*, 118; *The Diary of Samuel Sewall, 1674–1729*, ed. M. Halsey Thomas, 2 vols. (New York, 1973), 2:751; Mayhew, *Indian Converts*, 99.

61. Horton Davies, *Worship and Theology in England. 1: From Cranmer to Hooker, 1534–1603* (Princeton, 1970), ch. 11; Robert Stevenson, *Protestant Church Music in America* (New York, 1966), chs. 1–2; Percy A. Scholes, *The Puritans and Music in England and New England* (London, 1934), ch. 16; Charles E. Hambrick-Stowe, *The Practice of Piety: Puritan Devotional Disciplines in Seventeenth-Century New England* (Chapel Hill, 1982), 111–16.

62. Thomas Shepard, *Theses Sabbaticae; or, The Doctrine of the Sabbath* (London, 1649), preface, sig. A2; Cotton Mather, *Magnalia Christi Americana* [Boston, 1702], 2 vols. (Hartford, 1820), 1:485; Eliot, *Indian Dialogues*, 81, 147; Hambrick-Stowe, *Practice of Piety*, 96–101; Winton U. Solberg, *Redeem the Time: The Puritan Sabbath in Early America* (Cambridge, Mass., 1977).

63. Eliot, *Indian Dialogues*, 93, 144, 147; *Ply. Col. Recs.*, 11:60–61; Shepard, *Clear Sun-shine*, 40, 51–52; Gookin, *Historical Collections*, 61.

64. Shepard, *Clear Sun-shine*, 52; Eliot, *Late Manifestation*, 267; [Lewis Bayly], *The Practise of Pietie* (3d ed., London, 1613), 513–14.

65. Shepard, *Clear Sun-shine*, 39, 52; [Shepard], *Day-Breaking*, 20; Eliot and Mayhew, *Tears of Repentance*, 246.

66. Shepard, *Clear Sun-shine*, 52; *New England's First Fruits*, in Morison, *Founding of Harvard College*, 424; Cotton Mather, *The Hatchets, to hew down the Tree of Sin* (Boston, 1705).

67. Eliot, *Brief Narrative*, 9.

68. *Ply. Col. Recs.* 9:204; Alexander Starbuck, *The History of Nantucket* (Tokyo, 1969), 153–54 (thanks to Daniel Vickers for this reference); Samuel Sewall to Josiah Cotton, Feb. 10, 1713, Ayer MS. N.A. 181, The Newberry Library, Chicago.

69. Whitfield, *Strength Out of Weaknesse*, 171; *Colls. Mass. His. Soc.*, 1st ser., 10 (1809):125; Eliot, *Brief Narrative*, 11.

70. Eliot and Mayhew, *Tears of Repentance*, 228; Eliot, *Late Manifestation*, 272–76; *Colls. Mass. His. Soc.*, 1st ser., 10 (1809):124–26; Gookin, *Historical Collections*, 92–93; [Eliot], *Christian Covenanting Confession.*

71. Winslow, *Glorious Progress*, 89–90; Eliot and Mayhew, *Tears of Repentance*, 227; Eliot, *Late Manifestation*, 285.

72. Eliot, *Late Manifestation*, 271; Cotton Mather, *Magnalia Christi Americana*, 2 vols. (Hartford, 1855), 1:567n.

73. Eliot, *Late Manifestation*, 271, 285.

74. Eliot and Mayhew, *Tears of Repentance*, 221; Eliot, *Late Manifestation*, 285; Gookin, *Historical Collections*, 52–54; *Colls. Mass. His. Soc.*, 1st ser., 3 (1794):186 (the last phrase is missing from Eliot, *Brief Narrative*, 11, as are three paragraphs).

75. Gookin, "Christian Indians," 425–534; Eliot, *Brief Narrative*, 11; Ford, *Some Correspondence*, 52–55.

76. Gookin, *Historical Collections*, 7–9; *Colls. Mass. His. Soc.*, 1st ser., 10 (1809):129–34; Ford, *Some Correspondence*, 83–88; Mather, *Bonifacius*, 154; *Colls. Mass. His. Soc.*, 3rd ser., 1 (1825):101.

77. Ford, *Some Correspondence*, 86; *Sibley's Harvard Graduates* 4:419–20.

78. *Diary of Cotton Mather, 1681–1724*, 2 vols. (New York, n.d.), 2:48 (March 5, 1711); Samuel Kirkland, Journal, Feb. 4, 1771, Kirkland Papers. See also *Journals of Samuel Kirkland*, 69.

79. James P. Ronda and James Axtell, *Indian Missions: A Criticial Bibliography*, The Newberry Library Center for the History of the American Indian Bibliographical Series (Bloomington, 1978), 1–7; Vaughan, *New England Frontier*, chs. 9–11; Henry Warner Bowden, *American Indians and Christian Missions* (Chicago, 1981), 111–33.

10. ERRANDS INTO THE WILDERNESS

1. Roger Williams, *Christenings make not Christians* (London, 1645), in *Complete Writings*, 7 vols. (New York, 1963), 7:29–41; Edmund S. Morgan, *Roger Williams: The Church and the State* (New York, 1967), chs. 1–2.

2. Gookin, *Historical Collections*, 62; Ford, *Some Correspondence*, 84. See also Whitfield, *Strength Out of Weaknesse*, 171, and *Colls. Mass. His. Soc.*, 1st ser., 10 (1809):128.

3. Ford, *Some Correspondence*, 97–102.

4. Ibid., 103–9.

5. Ibid., 110–11.

6. Ibid., 112–14.

7. Ibid., 114–16.

8. Ibid., 117–20.

9. Ibid., 121–27.

10. Franklin Bowditch Dexter, *Biographical Sketches of the Graduates of Yale College [1701–45]* . . . (New York, 1885), 212–13; Kellaway, *New England Company*, 255; *Colls. Conn. His. Soc.* ("Talcott Papers") 5 (1896):479–80.

11. *Colls. Conn. His. Soc.* 5 (1896):481.

12. Ibid., 482–83.

13. Ibid., 483–84.

14. Ibid., 484.

15. *JR* 67:95.

16. *Doc. His. Maine* 5:197 (French); *NYCD* 9:440 (English).

17. *C.S.P.Col.* 17:554–55.

18. Robert H. Lord, John E. Sexton, and Edward T. Harrington, *History of the Archdiocese of Boston . . . 1604 to 1943*, 3 vols. (New York, 1944), 1:84. This deceptively titled book is by far the fullest and fairest treatment of the religious and military conflict in colonial Maine.

19. *Doc. His. Maine* 10:49, 51; Mary Celeste Leger, *The Catholic Indian Missions in Maine (1611–1820)*, Catholic University of America Studies in American Church History, no. 8 (Washington, D.C., 1929), chs. 2–3, 5–6.

20. *JR* 67:95; Lord, Sexton, and Harrington, *History of the Archdiocese* 1:74–75.

21. Charles E. Clark, *The Eastern Frontier: The Settlement of Northern New England, 1610–1763* (New York, 1970), chs. 8–9.

22. Lord, Sexton, and Harrington, *History of the Archdiocese* 1:110–11; James Phinney Baxter, *The Pioneers of New France in New England* (Albany, N.Y., 1894), 343–44.

23. Lord, Sexton, and Harrington, *History of the Archdiocese* 1:77; *C.S.P.Col.* 17:487. See a similar suggestion by John Minot in 1725 (*Doc. His. Maine* 10:343–46).

24. *Doc. His. Maine* 10:55.

25. Ibid., 10:85, 23:29; *C.S.P.Col.* 17:554–55, 18:517; *Sibley's Harvard Graduates* 4:300, 356–57, 421, 527, 550.

26. *Coll. de Manuscrits* 1:480; John Clarence Webster, *Acadia at the End of the Seventeenth Century*, New Brunswick Museum, Monographic Ser. 1 (Saint John, N.B., 1934), 61.

27. Lord, Sexton, and Harrington, *History of the Archdiocese* 1:70; *Doc. His. Maine* 10:94.

28. *Doc. His. Maine* 23:57; AN C11A 35:192ff., Sept. 25, 1715; *JR* 67:210. With a grant from the French governor, the Norridgewocks eventually hired a motley crew of English carpenters and rebuilt their church, though not without directing loud complaints to Bay officials about their poor workmanship and exorbitant wages (*Doc. His. Maine* 23:89–92; Lord, Sexton, and Harrington, *History of the Archdiocese* 1:95–6; Baxter, *Pioneers of New France*, 122).

29. *Collections of the Maine Historical Society*, 1st ser., 3:363–68.

30. *NEHGR* 21 (1867):49 (Baxter's journal); *JR* 67:97.

31. *Doc. His. Maine* 23:82–3; *NEHGR* 21 (1867), 50, 59–60; *Sibley's Harvard Graduates* 4:147, 152.

32. *NEHGR* 21 (1867), 50, 54; *JR* 67:93; *Doc. His. Maine* 9:379; Baxter, *Pioneers of New France*, 96, 103–4.

33. *JR* 67:99.

34. Baxter, *Pioneers of New France*, 145–47 (translation), 397–99 (Latin); *JR* 67:99; *NEHGR* 21 (1867), 54–59. I am grateful to J. W. Jones, Jr., of the College of William and Mary for analyzing the persnickety Latin of the combatants.

35. *Diary of Cotton Mather* 2:554 (Sept. 11, 1718); Silverman, *Letters of Cotton Mather*, 275 (Feb. 3, 1719).

36. *Doc. His. Maine* 9:374–78.

37. For Râle's life and works, see *DCB* 2:542–45; Baxter, *Pioneers of New France*; Convers Francis, "Life of Sebastian Rale," *The Library of American Biography*, ed. Jared Sparks (Boston, 1834–48), 2d ser., 7:157–333; Rochemonteix, *Les Jésuites . . . au XVIIe siècle*, vol. 3, ch. 9.

38. Francis Jennings, *The Ambiguous Iroquois Empire* (New York, 1984), 30–33.

39. *NYCD* 3:394, 796–800.

40. *NYCD* 4:337, 648.

41. *NYCD* 3:436, 4:351, 747–48, 752 (Caughnawaga warriors).

42. *NYCD* 4:349.

43. *NYCD* 4:734.

44. *NYCD* 4:649, 740.

45. *JR* 64:67–107 at 104; *DCB* 2:473–74; Lawrence H. Leder, ed., *The Livingston Indian Records, 1666–1723* (Gettysburg, Pa., 1956), 171; *NYCD* 4:169–70, 349.

46. New York Colonial Manuscripts, 37, no. 56 (April 28, 1691), New York State Archives, Albany; *NYCD* 3:394.

47. Leder, *Livingston Indian Records*, 163.

48. *NYCD* 4:368, 373; Leder, *Livingston Indian Records*, 180, 192.

49. *NYCD* 4:607, 609–10, 656, 659.

50. Lord, Sexton, and Harrington, *History of the Archdiocese* 1:75 n. 31, 76 n. 35.

51. *NYCD* 4:736–37, 1067; Leder, *Livingston Indian Records*, 187.

52. Daniel K. Richter, "The Protestant Mohawks of Tiononderoge" (Paper delivered at the Institute of Early American History and Culture, Williamsburg, Va., May 8, 1984); Lois M. Feister, "Indian-Dutch Relations in the Upper Hudson Valley: A Study of the Baptism Records in the Dutch Reformed Church, Albany, New York," *Man in the Northeast* 24 (1982):89–113.

53. *NYCD* 3:771–72.

54. *NYCD* 4:334, 573, 657.

55. *NYCD* 4:686–88, 717–18; *C.S.P.Col.* 17:554–55.

56. *NYCD* 4:766, 769–70, 774.

57. *NYCD* 4:893, 906, 987.

58. *NYCD* 4:920.

59. John Wolfe Lydekker, *The Faithful Mohawks* (Cambridge, 1938), 13–34; David Humphreys, *An Historical Account of the Incorporated Society for the Propagation of the Gospel in Foreign Parts* (London, 1730), 292–301.

60. SPG Letter Books, Ser. A, 9:123–25 (May 25, 1714), SPG Archives, London (microfilm); Lydekker, *Faithful Mohawks*, 36; Richter, "Ordeal of the Longhouse," 545–47.

61. SPG Letter Books, Ser. A, 9:124, 10:156–57 (Oct. 17, 1714); Lydekker, *Faithful Mohawks*, 35–36, 38, 44; Richter, "Ordeal of the Longhouse," 547–48. I am grateful to Professor Richter for lending me transcripts of four letters either missing or abbreviated in Lydekker, *Faithful Mohawks*.

62. SPG Letter Books, Ser. A, 12:241 (Oct. 11, 1716), 329 (Sept. 1, 1717), 340 (Sept. 26, 1717); Richter, "Ordeal of the Longhouse," 548.

63. Humphreys, *Historical Account of the SPG*, 300; S.P.G. Letter Books, Ser. A, 10:161 (Oct. 17, 1714), 11:319 (April 20, 1716).

64. SPG Letter Books, Ser. A, 9:124–25 (May 25, 1714), 11:318 (April 20, 1716), 12:335–36 (Sept. 1, 1717); Lydekker, *Faithful Mohawks*.

65. SPG Letter Books, Ser. A, 12:338 (Sept. 26, 1717), 13:319–21 (April 17, 1718), 332–33 (Oct. 17, 1718).

66. Richter, "Ordeal of the Longhouse," 552–53; Lydekker, *Faithful Mohawks*, 47; SPG Letter Books, Ser. A, 12:327 (Sept. 1, 1717).

67. SPG Letter Books, Ser. A, 12:310–12 (April 23, 1717); Richter, "Ordeal of the Longhouse," 557–66; David Landy, "Tuscarora among the Iroquois," *HNAI* 15:518–24.

68. Daniel K. Richter, "War and Culture: The Iroquois Experience," *WMQ*, 3d ser., 40 (1983):528–59; Richard Aquila, *The Iroquois Restoration: Iroquois Diplomacy on the Colonial Frontier, 1701–1754* (Detroit, 1983), ch. 7.

69. SPG Letter Books, Ser. A, 12:332–34 (Sept. 1, 1717), 338–40 (Sept. 26, 1717).

70. Ibid. 12:241–42 (Oct. 11, 1716), 328–29 (Sept. 1, 1717).

71. Ibid. 13:319, 323 (April 17, 1718); Richter, "Ordeal of the Longhouse," 555.

72. *Diary of David McClure*, 6–17.

73. Ibid., 19–30.

74. Ibid., 30; Alden T. Vaughan, "Frontier Banditti and the Indians: The Paxton Boys' Legacy, 1763–1775," *Pennsylvania History* 51 (1984):1–29.

75. *Diary of David McClure*, 42; Jones, *A Journal of Two Visits Made to Some Nations of Indians on the West Side of the River Ohio, In the years 1772 and 1773* (Burlington, N.J., 1774; New York: Joseph Sabin, 1865).

76. *Diary of David McClure*, 46–47, 50–52, 55.

77. Ibid., 63, 64–65, 73–76.

78. Ibid., 71, 73.

79. Ibid., 79, 80–81.

80. Ibid., 68, 77, 83, 85.

81. Ibid., 77, 83.

11. PREACHERS, PRIESTS, AND PAGANS

1. See, for example, Williams, *Christenings make not Christians* in *Complete Writings* 7:36; *Collections of the Rhode-Island Historical Society* 4 (1838):138; Lydekker, *Faithful Mohawks*, 36.

2. Du Creux, *History of Canada or New France* 1:19.

3. Le Clercq, *First Establishment of the Faith* 1:255. See also *RAPQ* (1939–40), 216 (1671).

4. Lahontan, *New Voyages to North-America* 1:146, 329, 2:413–14, 438.

5. Gideon Hawley to the Commissioners of the Scottish Society, Feb. 8, 1762 (draft), Hawley Manuscripts.

6. William Wood, *New England's Prospect* [London, 1634], ed. Nathaniel Rogers (Boston, 1764), 94.

7. Samuel Kirkland to the Rev. Mr. Rodgers, June 20, 1772 (draft), Kirkland papers.

8. Gideon Hawley to Jonathan Walter Edwards, Feb. 18, 1801, Yale University Library; [Jeremy Belknap], "Has the Discovery of America Been Useful or Hurtful to Mankind?" *Boston Magazine* (May 1784), 281–85 at 283.

9. Bishop Hubert to Cardinal Antonelli, 1788, quoted in Jaenen, *Role of the Church in New France*, 36.

10. Alexis De Tocqueville, *Democracy in America* [Paris, 1835–40], ed. Phillips Bradley, 2 vols. (New York, 1945), 1:334.

11. John Halkett, *Historical Notes Respecting the Indians of North America with Remarks on the Attempts Made to Convert and Civilize Them* (London, 1825), 256, 293, 354.

12. Le Clercq, *First Establishment of the Faith* 1:256.

13. Lahontan, *New Voyages to North-America* 2:413.

14. *Boston Magazine* (May 1784), 283; *Johnson Papers* 5:389, 439, 531.

15. Jonathan Edwards to Joshua Paine, Feb. 24, 1752 (transcript), Andover-Newton Edwards Collection, file folder 1752B, Yale Univ. Library.

16. Weis, "The New England Company of 1649," 134–218; Kellaway, *New England Company*; Alden T. Vaughan and Daniel K. Richter, "Crossing the Cultural Divide: Indians and New Englanders, 1605–1763," *Proceedings of the American Antiquarian Society* 90 (1980): 23–99.

17. Robinson, "Indian Education and Missions in Colonial Virginia," 152–68; Jerome W. Jones, "The Established Virginia Church and the Conversion of Negroes and Indians, 1620–1760," *Journal of Negro History* 46 (1961):12–23.

18. Elma E. Gray and Leslie Robb Gray, *Wilderness Christians: The Moravian Mission to the Delaware Indians* (Ithaca, 1956); Kenneth G. Hamilton, "Cultural Contributions of Moravian Missions among the Indians," *Pennsylvania History* 18 (1951):1–15; Thomas F. McHugh, "The Moravian Mission to the American Indians: Early American Peace Corps," ibid. 33 (1966):412–31.

19. Lydekker, *Faithful Mohawks*; Frank J. Klingberg, *Anglican Humanitarianism in Colonial New York* (Philadelphia, 1940); Gerald J. Goodwin, "Christianity, Civilization, and the Savage: The Anglican Mission to the American Indian," *Historical Magazine of the Protestant Episcopal Church* 42 (1973):93–110.

20. Frank J. Klingberg, ed., *The Carolina Chronicle of Dr. Francis Le Jau, 1706–1717*, University of California Publications in History 53 (Berkeley and Los Angeles, 1956); idem, "Early Attempts at Indian Education in South Carolina: A Documentary," *South Carolina Historical Magazine* 61 (1960):1–10; idem, "The Indian Frontier in South Carolina As Seen by the S.P.G. Missionary," *Journal of Southern History* 5 (1939):479–500.

21. *Diary of David McClure*, 132.

22. See above, Chapter 8, p. 204–15.

23. Francis G. Hutchins, *Mashpee: The Story of Cape Cod's Indian Town* (West Franklin, N.H., 1979).

24. James Axtell, "Some Thoughts on the Ethnohistory of Missions," *Ethnohistory* 29 (1982):35–41; James P. Ronda, "Generations of Faith: The Christian Indians of Martha's Vineyard," *WMQ* 38 (1981):369–94; Kathleen Bragdon, "American Indian Christianity in Eighteenth-Century Massachusetts: Ritual as Cultural Reaffirmation" (Paper delivered at the 2nd Laurier Conference on Ethnohistory and Ethnology, London, Ontario, May 13, 1983).

25. [Melançon], *Liste des missionnaires-Jesuites*.

26. Pouliot, *Étude sur les Relations des Jésuites*, 223–24; *JR* 39:143.

27. *JR* 7:275.

28. *JR* 66:173; Bougainville, *Journals*, 17, 150–53.

29. L. F. S. Upton, *Micmacs and Colonists: Indian-White Relations in the Maritimes, 1713–1867* (Vancouver, 1979), chs. 2–5, 11; Harold Franklin McGee, Jr., "Ethnic Boundaries and Strategies of Ethnic Interaction: A History of Micmac-White Relations in Nova Scotia" (Ph.D. diss., Dept. of Anthropology, Southern Illinois Univ., 1974), chs. 3–7; Micheline Dumont-Johnson, *Apôtres ou agitateurs: La France missionnaire en Acadie* (Trois-Rivières, 1970).

30. Hambrick-Stowe, *Practice of Piety*, esp. ch. 2.

31. *Boston Magazine* (May 1784), 283; A. D. Nock, *Conversion: The Old and the New in Religion from Alexander the Great to Augustine of Hippo* (London, 1933), chs. 1, 13.

32. Pouliot, *Aux origines de notre dévotion à l'Immaculée-Conception*; Bibeau, "Le climat marial en Nouvelle-France." At Caughnawaga (1685–1716) and Lorette (1685–1698), children (0–14 years) and youths (15–18 years) were predominantly male, but adult females increasingly outnumbered adult males (*The Historical Atlas of Canada*, vol. 1, ed. Cole Harris [forthcoming], pl. 46).

33. See above, Chapter 5.

34. Based on a sample of 29 missionaries who graduated between 1693 and 1731 (*Sibley's Harvard Graduates*, 4–9).

35. Cotton Mather, *The Way to Prosperity* (Boston, 1690), 27.

36. *JR* 7:295.

37. Eliot, *Indian Dialogues*, 73.

38. *JR* 11:239; see also 25:35–37.

39. Eliot, *Indian Dialogues*, 69; Shepard, *Clear Sun-shine*, 57.

40. *Johnson Papers* 12:955; see also 7:597–98.

41. *Journals of Samuel Kirkland*, 24.

42. *JR* 3:123.

43. Charlevoix, *History of New France* 2:79.

44. Beauchamp, *Moravian Journals Relating to Central New York*, 7.

45. *Ply. Col. Recs.* 1:203.

46. *JR* 44:35; see also 44:37, 52:119.

47. Many self-given tribal names simply meant "true" or "original people."

48. James P. Ronda, "'We Are Well As We Are': An Indian Critique of Seventeenth-Century Christian Missions," *WMQ*, 3d ser., 34 (1977):66–82.

49. Charles E. Hunter, "The Delaware Nativist Revival of the Mid-Eighteenth Century," *Ethnohistory* 18 (1971):39–49; Wallace, *Death and Rebirth of the Seneca*, pt. 3.

50. Tyler, *Narratives of Early Virginia*, 108.

12. THE ENGLISH APOSTATES

1. *Coll. de Manuscrits* 2:184; *NYCD* 4:520–21; *NEHGR* 5 (1851):38.

2. *NYCD* 4:350–51; *NEHGR* 5 (1851):28; AN, C11A, 16:12 (Oct. 15, 1698), 99 (July 12, 1698). The English spoke of fourteen years as the dividing line, perhaps as a result of mistranslation.

3. *NEHGR* 5 (1851):28, 33; *Coll. de Manuscrits* 3:64 (Dec. 22, 1721).

4. *NEHGR* 5 (1851):29, 38; *NYCD* 4:350–51.

5. Vaughan and Richter, "Crossing the Cultural Divide," 52–72.

6. Coleman, *New England Captives* 1:119–20; "Journal of Captain Phineas Stevens' Journey to Canada, 1752," in Newton D. Mereness, ed., *Travels in the American Colonies* (New York, 1916), 302–22 at 313–14.

7. C. Alice Baker, *True Stories of New England Captives Carried to Canada During the Old French and Indian Wars* (Cambridge, Mass., 1897); Coleman, *New England Captives*; Vaughan and Richter, "Crossing the Cultural Divide," 52–72. Working from Coleman, Laurel Thatcher Ulrich found that of the captives taken from northern New England, females converted nearly twice as often as males; 58 percent of the girls between twelve and twenty-one stayed in Canada (*Good Wives: Image and Reality in the Lives of Women in Northern New England, 1650–1750* [New York, 1982], 203).

8. Coleman, *New England Captives* 2:114, 147–48; A.M.D.G., *Les Ursulines des Trois-Rivières depuis leur établissement jusqu'à nos jours*, 2 vols. (Trois-Rivières, 1888), 1:191–94.

9. Coleman, *New England Captives* 2:411, 412; John Williams, *The Redeemed Captive Returning to Zion*, 6th ed. (Boston, [1707] 1795), 43.

10. Coleman, *New England Captives* 1:121, 127–28.

11. Ibid. 1:125–29; Pierre-Georges Roy, "Les Lettres de naturalité sous le régime français," *Le Bulletin des Recherches Historiques* 30 (1924):225–32; *RAPQ* (1939–40), 366 (1707); *RAPQ* (1947–48), 252–53 (1714); *Coll. de Manuscrits* 3:158 (quotation), 183 (1737).

12. Vaughan and Richter, "Crossing the Cultural Divide," 53–57, 70; Roy, "Les Lettres de naturalité," 226.

13. John Lowell, *The Advantage of God's Presence with his People in an Expedition against their Enemies* (Boston, 1755), 20. See Sister Mary Augustina (Ray), *American Opinion of Roman Catholicism in the Eighteenth Century* (New York, 1936), and J. M. Bumsted, "'Carried to Canada!': Perceptions of the French in British Colonial Captivity Narratives, 1690–1760," *American Review of Canadian Studies* 13 (1983):79–96.

14. Ulrich, *Good Wives*, 205.

15. *Coll. de Manuscrits* 3:21; *A Faithful Narrative, of the many Dangers and Sufferings . . . of Robert Eastburn* (Philadelphia, 1758), in Samuel G. Drake, ed., *Indian Captivities* (Boston, 1839), 268; *A Journal of the Captivity of Jean Lowry and her Children* (Philadlphia, 1760), 16–17; "Narrative of Joseph Bartlett," in Joshua Coffin, *A Sketch of the History of Newbury, Newburyport, and West Newbury, from 1635 to 1845* (Boston, 1845), 333.

16. Williams, *Redeemed Captive*, 33–34; *RAPQ* (1938–39), 60, 83, 129.

17. Coleman, *New England Captives* 1:310–11, 370, 375, 2:168.

18. Jacques Henripin, *La Population canadienne au début du XVIIIe siècle* (Paris, 1954), 18–19; Amédée Gosselin, *L'Instruction au Canada sous le régime français (1635–1760)* (Quebec, 1911), pt. 1, ch. 8; Kenneth A. Lockridge, *Literacy in Colonial New England* (New York, 1974), 38–42.

19. Coleman, *New England Captives* 1:126, 147–49.

20. Ibid. 1:320–21, 2:8–9; Williams, *Redeemed Captive*, 61–63.

21. Coleman, *New England Captives* 1:239, 2:96, 108–9, 165; Ulrich, *Good Wives*, 208–13; Barbara Austen, "Social Networks among Female New England Captives in Canada, 1689–1763" (Master's thesis, Dept. of History, College of William and Mary, 1985).

22. John Evans, *National Ingratitude lamented* (Charles-Town, S.C., 1745), 25.

23. Cotton Mather, *Good Fetch'd Out of Evil* (Boston, 1706), 21.

24. Williams, *Redeemed Captive*, 43–45, 47, 55, 57–60.

25. Ibid., 43, 47.

26. *A Plain Narrativ[e] of the Uncommon Sufferings and Remarkable Deliverance of Thomas Brown* (2d ed., Boston, 1760), reprinted in *Magazine of History with Notes and Queries*, extra no. 4 (New York: William Abbatt, 1908), 14. John Williams was also told that his conversion would result in a better wardrobe (*Redeemed Captive*, 88).

27. Coffin, *History of Newbury*, 333–34.

28. *Journal of the Captivity of Jean Lowry*, 20, 25, 27–28, 30.

29. Williams, *Redeemed Captive*, 37, 41, 54–55, 62; Pierre-Georges Roy, eds., *Inventaire des ordonnances des intendants de la Nouvelle-France*, 4 vols. (Beauceville, P.Q., 1919), 1:120 (May 30, 1711); "The Journal of a Captive, 1745–1748," in Isabel M. Calder, Ed., *Colonial Captivities, Marches and Journeys* (New York, 1935), 37, 41–42 (burials).

30. Coleman, *New England Captives* 1:153, 2:390–91.

31. Ibid. 1:239, 268–70, 285–86, 356–58, 409, 425–35, 2:389–90.

32. Ibid. 1:427.

33. Ibid. 1:428.

34. Ibid. 1:425–35; Baker, *True Stories of New England Captives*, 45–68; *Au musée du vieux monastère des Ursulines, Québec, 1639–1936* ([Quebec, 1936]), 48.

35. Cotton Mather, *The Fall of Babylon* (Boston, 1707); *A Protestant's Resolution* (18th ed., Boston, 1746), 9.

36. *Letter from a Romish Priest* (Boston, 1729), 1–13; Coleman, *New England Captives* 1:149–54, 2:65–66.

37. *NYCD* 10:215.

13. THE WHITE INDIANS

1. [William Smith, D.D.], *Historical Account of Colonel Bouquet's Expedition against the Ohio Indians, in 1764* [Philadelphia, 1765] (Cincinnati, 1868), 80–81.

2. Colden, *History of the Five Indian Nations*, 203–4 (1st pagination).

3. Benjamin Franklin to Peter Collinson, May 9, 1753, in Labaree, *Papers of Benjamin Franklin* 4:481–82.

4. Crèvecoeur, *Letters from an American Farmer*, 215. Other contemporaries who recognized the disparity between Indian and European conversion results were Charlevoix, *Journal of a Voyage to North-America* 2:108; Joseph Doddridge, *Notes on the Settlement and Indian*

Wars of the Western Parts of Virginia and Pennsylvania, from 1763 to 1783, Inclusive [Wellsburgh, Va., 1824], ed. Alfred Williams (Albany, 1876), 218; *Peter Kalm's Travels* 2:456–57; Johann David Schoepf, *Travels in the Confederation [1783–1784]*, trans. and ed. Alfred J. Morrison (Philadelphia, 1911), 1:283; J. P. Brissot de Warville, *New Travels in the United States of America, 1788*, trans. Mara Soceanu Vamos and Durand Echeverria, ed. Durand Echeverria (Cambridge, Mass., 1964), 420; John F. Meginness, *Biography of Frances Slocum, the Lost Sister of Wyoming* (Williamsport, Pa., 1891), 196; and Felix Renick, "A Trip to the West," *American Pioneer* 1 (1842):79.

Later students of the "white Indians" are John R. Swanton, "Notes on the Mental Assimilation of Races," *Journal of the Washington Academy of Sciences* 16 (1926): 493–502; Erwin H. Ackerknecht, "'White Indians': Psychological and Physiological Peculiarities of White Children Abducted and Reared by North American Indians," *Bulletin of the History of Medicine* 15 (1944): 15–36; A. Irving Hallowell, "American Indians, White and Black: The Phenomenon of Transculturalization," *Current Anthropology* 4 (1963):519–31; and J. Norman Heard, *White into Red: A Study of the Assimilation of White Persons Captured by Indians* (Metuchen, N.J., 1973). All four draw upon western captives as well as colonial in a search for ethnological generalizations. See also Richard Drinnon's *White Savage: The Case of John Dunn Hunter* (New York, 1972).

5. Jaenen, *Friend and Foe*, ch. 5; idem, "Miscegenation in Eighteenth-Century New France" (Paper read at the Second Laurier Conference on Ethnohistory and Ethnology, London, Ontario, May 12, 1983); Olive Patricia Dickason, "From 'One Nation' in the Northeast to 'New Nation' in the Northwest: A Look at the Emergence of the Métis," *American Indian Culture and Research Journal* 6, no. 2 (1982):1–22; Jacqueline Peterson, "Ethnogenesis: Settlement and Growth of a 'New People,'" ibid., 23–64.

6. On intermarriage, see Gary B. Nash, *Red, White, and Black: The Peoples of Early America* (2d ed., Englewood Cliffs, N.J., 1982), 275–80; James Hugo Johnston, *Race Relations in Virginia and Miscegenation in the South, 1776–1860* (Amherst, Mass., 1970), 169–72, ch. 11; J. B. Brebner, ed., "Subsidized Intermarriage with the Indians: An Incident in British Colonial Policy," *Canadian Historical Review* 6 (March 1925):33–36. On renegades, see Hubbard, *Present State of New-England*, 59 (1st pagination); Bradford, *History of Plymouth Plantation*, 2 vols. (Boston: Massachusetts Historical Society, 1912), 2:107–9; *Colls. Mass. His. Soc.*, 4th ser. 6 (1863), 215, 222, 245; *Winthrop Papers* 4:247; Milo Milton Quaife, ed., *The Siege of Detroit in 1763*, Lakeside Classics (Chicago, 1958), 220–21, 249; Consul W. Butterfield, *History of the Girtys* (Cincinnati, 1890). On deserters, see *Johnson Papers* 14 (Index), s.v. "Army, deserters." On traders' wives and lovers, see Lawson, *New Voyage to Carolina*, 190, 192; Ann Maury, ed., *Memoirs of a Huguenot Family* [1852] (New York, 1907), 349–50; *The Journal of Nicholas Cresswell, 1774–1777* (London, 1925), 102–16, 122; J. Leitch Wright, Jr., *The Only Land They Knew: The Tragic Story of the American Indians in the Old South* (New York, 1981), 234–37.

7. This generalization is based on a reading of over 100 captivity narratives and accounts. Primarily because Canada did not have a printing press or a large literary audience in the colonial period, the French did not develop the popular genre of captivity narratives, which provide us with most of our information about English captives. But the process of captivity, adoption, and acculturation was the same for both English and French. Thus what follows, while necessarily English in focus, applies equally to the French captives.

8. [William Walton], *The Captivity and Sufferings of Benjamin Gilbert and His Family, 1780–83* [Philadelphia, 1784], ed. Frank H. Severance (Cleveland, 1904), 27.

9. This is not to say that no expense was involved for the English in securing the release of captive colonists, but it was in the nature of modest presents rather than exorbitant ransoms. Sylvester K. Stevens and Donald H. Kent, eds., *The Papers of Col. Henry Bouquet*, 19 vols. (Harrisburg, Pa., 1940–43), 17:28, 169, 18:182–84.

10. In the 1770s Guy Johnson and George Croghan, both authorities on the Indians of the Middle Atlantic colonies, thought that the English prisoners had been "generally adopted" rather than put to death ("Opinions of George Croghan," 157; "Guy Johnson's Opinions," 322). See also Mary Jemison's remarks in Seaver, *Life of Mary Jemison*, 46–47. While older men and women could be ransomed from the Middle Atlantic tribes, most Indians who had adopted English children could not be persuaded to "sell [their] own Flesh and Blood," not even for "one thousand Dollars," as the Indian father of twelve-year-old Elizabeth Gilbert put it (*Captivity of Benjamin Gilbert*, 103, 107).

11. "Further Examination of Michael La Chauvignerie, Jun'r, 1757," in Samuel Hazard et al., eds., *Pennsylvania Archives* 3 (1853):306; "Examination of Barbara Liningaree and

Mary Roy, 1759," ibid., 634; "Narrative of Marie Le Roy and Barbara Leininger, for Three Years Captives Among the Indians," *Penn. Mag. of His. and Biog.* 29 (1905), 417–20.

12. *Johnson Papers* 11:446, 484–91, 720–21; *Bouquet Papers* 18:253; William S. Ewing, "Indian Captives Released by Colonel Bouquet," *Western Pennsylvania Historical Magazine* 39 (1956):187–203. On his two-month journey to a conference with the western Indians in 1760, John Hays saw 23 English prisoners; at least 14 were children. Their average age was 10 years. Two other prisoners were women, one aged 22 and the other "A[l]most a Woman" (*Pennsylvania Archaeologist* 24 [1954]:63–83).

13. *Johnson Papers* 11:466, 728.

14. *Bouquet Papers* 17:51.

15. Ibid., 38; "Provincial Correspondence: 1750 to 1765," in Samuel Hazard et al., eds., *Register of Pennsylvania* 4 (1829), 390; *A Narrative of the Captivity of John McCullough, Esq.*, in Archibald Loudon, ed., *A Selection, of Some of the Most Interesting Narratives of Outrages, Committed by the Indians, in Their Wars, with the White People*, 2 vols. (Carlisle, Pa., 1808–1811), 1:326–27; *Bouquet's Expedition*, 80.

16. "Provincial Correspondence," 390–91; *Johnson Papers* 11:496–98.

17. *Bouquet's Expedition*, 76, 80; *Johnson Papers* 4:500; "Provincial Correspondence," 390; "Relation by Frederick Post of Conversation with Indians, 1760," *Pennsylvania Archives* 3 (1853):742. I have translated Post's phonetic German spelling.

18. "Prisoners Delivered to Gov. by the Six Nations, 1762," *Pennsylvania Archives* 4 (1853), 100–101; *Johnson Papers* 11:720–21; Coleman, *New England Captives* 1:323, 2:58. In a "List of Prisoners deliv[ere]d up by the Shawanese Nations of Indians at Fort Pit, 10th May 1765," the following names were among those given for 14 captives who had been with the Indians from two to ten years: Wechquessinah ("cant speak Eng[li]sh. knows not from whence taken"), Joseph or Pechyloothume, Jenny or Ketakatwitch, Wapatenaqua, and Nalupeia, sister to Molly Bird (*Johnson Papers* 11:720–21). In an earlier list were Sour Mouth, Crooked Legs, Pouter or Wynima, David Bighead, Sore Knee, Sour Plumbs (*Bouquet Papers* 18:248). It would be important to know if these names were given in derision to resistant, older captives, or in good humor to accepting, younger ones.

19. *Johnson Papers* 11:812; *Bouquet Papers* 17:39–41.

20. *Peter Kalm's Travels* 2:457; Coleman, *New England Captives* 1:296, 2:11; O. M. Spencer, *The Indian Captivity of O. M. Spencer* [New York, 1835], ed. Milo Milton Quaife, reprint of 1917 ed. (New York, 1968), 168–69; Smith, *Causes of the Variety of Complexion*, 70–71n. See also Bernard W. Sheehan, *Seeds of Extinction: Jeffersonian Philanthropy and the American Indian* (Chapel Hill, 1973), ch. 1, esp. 40–42; and Doddridge, *Notes on the Settlement and Indian Wars*, 91.

21. Coleman, *New England Captives* 2:91, 117–18; *Johnson Papers* 10:160, 11:728. O. M. Spencer's Indian father for "several years" paid him an annual visit (*Indian Captivity of O. M. Spencer*, 171).

22. *Captivity of Benjamin Gilbert*, 181; Thomas Ridout, "An Account of My Capture By the Shawanese Indians . . ." [1788], *Blackwood's Magazine* 223 (1928):313.

23. *Bouquet's Expedition*, 80–81.

24. Samuel Penhallow, *The History of the Wars in New-England, With the Eastern Indians* (Boston, 1726), 110; Samuel G. Drake, ed., *Tragedies of the Wilderness . . .* (Boston, 1846), 128; Stephen Williams, *What Befell Stephen Williams in his Captivity [Greenfield, Mass., 1837]*, ed. George Sheldon (Deerfield, Mass., 1889), 5; Williams, *Redeemed Captive*, 14, 30.

25. "Captivity narrative of Joseph Bartlett" in Coffin, *History of Newbury*, 332; *An Account of the Remarkable Occurrences in the Life and Travels of Col. James Smith* [1799], in Howard Peckham, ed., *Narratives of Colonial America, 1704–1765* (Chicago, 1971), 82; Samuel Lee to Nehemiah Grew, 1690, *Pubs. Col. Soc. Mass.* 14 (1911–13):148.

26. *What Befell Stephen Williams*, 6; Drake, *Tragedies of the Wilderness*, 61.

27. Lincoln, *Narratives of the Indian Wars*, 30; Drake, *Tragedies of the Wilderness*, 125, 145; Ridout, "Account of My Capture," 303; *Bouquet's Expedition*, 78; "Provincial Correspondence," 390–91; Colden, *History of the Five Indian Nations*, 8 (1st pagination); John Brickell, *The Natural History of North Carolina* (Dublin, 1737), 320; Jeremy Belknap, *The History of New Hampshire*, 3 vols. (2d ed., Boston, 1813 [1792]), 3:229–30; William Bradford, "Verses" [1654], *Proceedings of the Massachusetts Historical Society* (1869–70), 467.

28. *Johnson's Wonder-Working Providence*, 150, 263; "Morrell's Poem on New England," 135.

29. Charles Thomson in Thomas Jefferson, *Notes on the State of Virginia*, ed. William Peden (Chapel Hill, 1955), 200; "Opinions of George Croghan," 157. See also *Life of Mary*

Jemison, 73, and Sylvester K. Stevens et al., eds., *Travels in New France by J. C. B.* (Harrisburg, Pa., 1941), 69.

30. *Adair's History*, 171.

31. Belknap, *History of New Hampshire* 3:229.

32. Drake, *Tragedies of the Wilderness*, 61, 115–16, 145, 158; Thomas Hutchinson, *The History of the Colony and Province of Massachusetts-Bay*, ed. Lawrence Shaw Mayo, 2 vols. (Cambridge, Mass., 1936), 2:104n; Mrs. Harriet S. Caswell, *Our Life Among the Iroquois* (Boston, 1892), 53. See also *Life of Mary Jemison*, 47, 57, and Timothy Alden, ed., "An Account of the Captivity of Hugh Gibson . . . ," *Colls. Mass. His. Soc.*, 3d ser., 6 (1837):153. The source of Hutchinson's information was Williams, *Redeemed Captive*. Jacob Lunenburg was bound so tightly on his captor's back that he was somewhat crippled for life (Coleman, *New England Captives* 2:215).

33. *A Narrative of the Captivity of Mrs. Johnson*, [Walpole, N.H., 1796], reprint of 3d rev. ed. [1814] (Springfield, Mass., 1907) 62; *Narrative of Titus King* . . . (Hartford, 1938), 10; Meginness, *Biography of Frances Slocum*, 65. See also Peckham, *Narratives of Colonial America*, 89; Howard H. Peckham, ed., "Thomas Gist's Indian Captivity, 1758–1759," *Penn. Mag. of His. and Biog.* 80 (1956):297; *The Indian Captive; or, A Narrative of the Captivity and Sufferings of Zadock Steele* . . . [Montpelier, Vt. 1818] (Springfield, Mass., 1908), 68; Loudon, *Selection of Narratives* 1:303–4; Arthur T. Adams, ed., *The Explorations of Pierre Esprit Radisson* (Minneapolis, 1961), 4–5, 7.

34. *Narrative of Mrs. Johnson*, 57–58; Drake, *Tragedies of the Wilderness*, 129; *Narrative of Titus King*, 8. See also *Explorations of Radisson*, 6.

35. *Plain Narrativ of the Uncommon Sufferings of Thomas Brown*, 8, 12; *The History of the Life and Sufferings of Henry Grace, of Basingstoke in the County of Southampton* [Reading, Eng., 1764] (2d ed., London, 1765), 12. See also Peckham, *Narratives of Colonial America*, 81; "Thomas Gist's Indian Captivity," 298; Drake, *Tragedies of the Wilderness*, 269, 272; *Captivity of Benjamin Gilbert*, 56, 121; "The Story of Captain Jasper Parrish," *Buffalo Historical Society Publications* 2 (1903):527–36 at 528–29.

36. Beverley W. Bond, Jr., ed., "The Captivity of Charles Stuart, 1755–57," *Mississippi Valley Historical Review* 13 (1926–27):66; "Narrative of John Brickell's Captivity Among the Delaware Indians," *American Pioneer* 1 (1842):46. Pierre Radisson also escaped the gauntlet (*Explorations of Radisson*, 10).

37. Stevens, *Travels in New France by J. C. B.*, 68; Charlevoix, *Journal of a Voyage* 1:369–70; "Narrative of Marie Le Roy and Barbara Leininger," 409. See also Bouganville, *Journals*, 21.

38. *Captivity of Benjamin Gilbert*, 56.

39. Peckham, *Narratives of Colonial America*, 81. See also "Captivity of Hugh Gibson," 143; Loudon, *Selection of Narratives* 1:306; and *Life of Mary Jemison*, 44.

40. Steele, *Indian Captive* 70–71; *Narrative of Mrs. Johnson*, 66. Among the Iroquois, only the council of elders could decide the allocation of a captive, but women who had lost kinsmen could request a particular captive. When Pierre Radisson was taken in 1651, "a good old woman" staked a verbal claim to him at the council meeting. When the elders assented with a hearty "ho!" she took off her wampum "girdle" and tied it around her new son (*Explorations of Radisson*, 10). The "Beloved" or war women of the Cherokees had even more direct authority to save or condemn prisoners (*Timberlake's Memoirs*, 94). See also Cara B. Richards, "Matriarchy or Mistake: The Role of Iroquois Women through Time," in Verne F. Ray, ed., *Cultural Stability and Cultural Change: Proceedings of the 1957 Spring Meeting of the American Ethnological Society* (Seattle, 1957), 36–45 at 36–38; and William N. Fenton, ed., "The Hyde Manuscript: Capt. Wm. Hyde's Observations of the 5 Nations of Indians at New Yorke, 1698," *American Scene Magazine* [Gilcrease Institute of American History and Art], 6:2 (1965), [6].

41. Peckham, *Narratives of Colonial America*, 91–92.

42. Ibid.; "John Brickell's Captivity," 46; *Narrative of Mrs. Johnson*, 68.

43. *Life of Mary Jemison*, 44–47; *Captivity of Benjamin Gilbert*, 107, 123; Loudon, *Selection of Narratives*, 307; "Thomas Gist's Indian Captivity," 299; *A Very Remarkable Narrative of Luke Swetland* . . . *Written by Himself* (Hartford, n.d.), 7–8; Hennepin, *Description of Louisiana*, 107–8.

44. *Life of Mary Jemison*, 46; *Narrative of Titus King*, 14; Stevens, *Travels in New France by J. C. B.*, 73. See also *Johnson Papers* 13:191; Charlevoix, *Journal of a Voyage* 1:373; Colden, *History of the Five Indian Nations*, 9 (1st pagination); *Explorations of Radisson*, 11.

45. *Captivity of Benjamin Gilbert*, 126–27, 135.

46. *Remarkable Narrative of Luke Swetland*, 5; "Thomas Gist's Indian Captivity," 299; *Life of Mary Jemison*, 47; *Explorations of Radisson*, 10–11.

47. *Narrative of Mrs. Johnson*, 67–68, 71, 76–77.

48. "John Brickell's Captivity," 44; *Bouquet's Expedition*, 78. The Canadian captors of Titus King told him that he "Should never go hum [home] that [he] was an Indian now and must be and Do as they Did" (*Narrative of Titus King*, 14).

49. Ridout, "Account of My Capture"; John Leeth, *A Short Biography of John Leeth* [Lancaster, Ohio, 1831], ed. Reuben Gold Thwaites (Cleveland, 1904), 28; *Captivity of Benjamin Gilbert*, 109; Steele, *Indian Captive*, 72.

50. *Captivity of Benjamin Gilbert*, 81, 83.

51. "Thomas Gist's Indian Captivity," 301; "John Brickell's Captivity," 54. Joseph Bartlett also lived with other white captives while a prisoner in Canada (Coffin, *History of Newbury*, 332–33).

52. *Captivity of Benjamin Gilbert*, 74, 87, 124; "Captivity of Hugh Gibson," 149. Women were not the only captives alarmed by the specter of forced marriage. When Thomas Gist was first brought to the Huron village where he was to be adopted, he was made to stand naked at a post for an hour "while the Indian Ladies was satisfied as to their sight. For my part," he recalled, "I expected they was going to chuse some of the likeliest of us for husbands, by their standing and looking so long at us in this condition" ("Thomas Gist's Indian Captivity," 298).

53. *Life of Mary Jemison*, 52–53.

54. Williams, *Redeemed Captive*, 131; Drake, *Tragedies of the Wilderness*, 125; "Provincial Correspondence," 390–91. For evidence that at least one Iroquois family tried to compel an adopted Frenchman to marry, see *JR* 47:203.

55. "Thomas Gist's Indian Captivity," 301; *Indian Captivity of O. M. Spencer*, 82, 120, 129.

56. Coleman, *New England Captives* 2:107; *Biography of Leeth*, 39–40; Orlando Allen, "Incidents in the Life of an Indian Captive," *American Historical Record* 1 (1872):409.

57. *JR* 47:203; *Captivity of Benjamin Gilbert*, 135; Caswell, *Our Life Among the Iroquois*, 54; Charlevoix, *Journal of a Voyage* 1:371; *Johnson Papers* 4:620. See also *NYCD* 6:240, and "Story of Jasper Parrish," 531.

58. *Indian Captivity of O. M. Spencer*, 92–93.

59. Ridout, "Account of My Captivity," 295; Coleman, *New England Captives* 1:21, 296, 325–26, 2:190–91.

60. Caswell, *Our Life Among the Iroquois*, 54–55. Old White Chief's three sons—Seneca White, White Seneca, and John Seneca—were prominent in tribal affairs in the nineteenth century (Parrish Papers, Vassar College Library).

61. A. Irving Hallowell has coined the unwieldy term "transculturalization" to denote the process whereby individuals, rather than groups, are detached from one society, enter another, and come under the influence of its customs and values ("American Indians, White and Black," 519–31). Alden Vaughan and Daniel Richter use "transculturation" to mean a virtually complete shift by an individual from one culture to another ("Crossing the Cultural Divide," 24 n. 5).

62. *Narrative of Titus King*, 17; *Life of Mary Jemison*, 57; "Thomas Gist's Indian Captivity," 302.

63. Williams, *Redeemed Captive*, 37; Drake, *Tragedies of the Wilderness*, 169–70.

64. *Indian Captivity of O. M. Spencer*, 120–21; Drake, *Tragedies of the Wilderness*, 161; "Story of Jasper Parrish," 530.

65. "Thomas Gist's Indian Captivity," 300–301.

66. *Life of Mary Jemison*, 48; "Thomas Gist's Indian Captivity," 301.

67. Loudon, *Selection of Narratives*, 1:307; *Indian Captivity of O. M. Spencer*, 65. Jasper Parrish and two Indian boys took the cold water treatment all one winter ("Story of Jasper Parrish," 529).

68. *Explorations of Radisson*, 11; Renick, "A Trip to the West," 78; *Captivity of Benjamin Gilbert*, 98–100. See also "Story of Jasper Parrish," 533, and *Diary of David McClure*, 87.

69. "Narrative of the Capture of Abel Janney by the Indians in 1782," *Ohio Archaeological and Historical Quarterly* 8 (1900):472; *Indian Captivity of O. M. Spencer*, 113, 117–18; "Thomas Gist's Indian Captivity," 300; *Life of Mary Jemison*, 55–56. See also James Axtell, ed., *The Indian Peoples of Eastern America: A Documentary History of the Sexes* (New York, 1981), ch. 4.

70. *Bouquet's Expedition*, 81.

71. Williams, *Key*; "John Brickell's Captivity," 47–49; *Life of Mary Jemison*, 72–73; Douglas Adair and John A. Schutz, eds., *Peter Oliver's Origin & Progress of the American*

Rebellion: A Tory View (San Marino, Calif., 1961), 5; Coleman, *New England Captives*, 2:312. In 1758 four pro-English Delaware chiefs accused the English of treaty breaking and hypocrisy. "We Love you more than you Love us, for when we take any Prisoners from you we treat them as our own children; we are Poor and we cloath them as well as we can, you see our own children are as naked as the first, by this you may see our hearts are better then your heart" ("Journal of Frederick Post," *Pennsylvania Archives* 3 [1853]:534).

72. "Further Examination of Michael La Chauvignerie," 306; *Narrative of the Life and Adventures of Matthew Bunn . . .* [Providence, *c.* 1796] (7th rev. ed., Batavia, N.Y.), 11; Loudon, *Selection of Narratives* 1:311; *Captivity of Benjamin Gilbert*, 112; Belknap, *History of New Hampshire* 3:227.

73. *Indian Captivity of O. M. Spencer*, 86; Peckham, *Narratives of Colonial America*, 108.

74. Crèvecoeur, *Letters from an American Farmer*, 214.

75. Ibid., 215; Charles S. Grant, *Democracy in the Connecticut Frontier Town of Kent* (New York, 1961); Bushman, *From Puritan to Yankee*; Kenneth Lockridge, "Land, Population and the Evolution of New England Society 1630–1790," *Past and Present* 39 (1968):62–80; Gary B. Nash, *Quakers and Politics: Pennsylvania, 1681–1726* (Princeton, 1968); Kenneth A. Lockridge, *A New England Town, The First Hundred Years: Dedham, Massachusetts, 1636–1736* (New York, 1970); Edward M. Cook, Jr., "Social Behavior and Changing Values in Dedham, Massachusetts, 1700 to 1775," *WMQ*, 3d ser., 27 (1970):546–80; Patricia U. Bonomi, *A Factious People: Politics and Society in Colonial New York* (New York, 1971); James A. Henretta, *The Evolution of American Society, 1700–1815: An Interdisciplinary Analysis* (Lexington, Mass., 1973); Kenneth Lockridge, "Social Change and the Meaning of the American Revolution," *Journal of Social History* 6 (1973):403–39; Paul Boyer and Stephen Nissenbaum, *Salem Possessed: The Social Origins of Witchcraft* (Cambridge, Mass., 1974); John Putnam Demos, *Entertaining Satan: Witchcraft and the Culture of Early New England* (New York, 1982); Rhys Isaac, *The Transformation of Virginia, 1740–1790* (Chapel Hill, 1982). Indeed, it may well be that the adults who chose to become Indians did so for some of the reasons that many of their countrymen turned to revolution.

76. Crèvecoeur, *Letters from an American Farmer*, 215.

EPILOGUE: EDUCATION AND EMPIRE

1. Tzvetan Todorov, *The Conquest of America: The Question of the Other* (New York, 1984), 11–12.

2. Ephesians 4:22–24. See also Colossians 3:9–10 and 2 Corinthians 5:17.

3. William Crashaw, *A Sermon Preached in London before the right honorable Lord La Warre . . . Febr. 21.1609* (London, 1610), B1r, D4r–F1r.

4. Paul Horgan, "About the Southwest: A Panorama of Nueva Granda," *Southwest Review* 18 (Summer 1933):350–51.

5. Jennings, *Invasion of America*; *The Essayes of Montagne*, trans. John Florio, intro. J. I. M. Stewart (New York: Modern Library, 1933), 120, 163.

6. Axtell, "Some Thoughts on the Ethnohistory of Missions," 35–41.

7. John Minot to Jeremiah Dummer, Oct. 4, 1725, Mass. Archives 52:294–96; Winslow, *Good Newes*, 274.

8. *Johnson Papers* 5:531 (1767); Hennepin, *Description of Louisiana*, 26–27.

Index

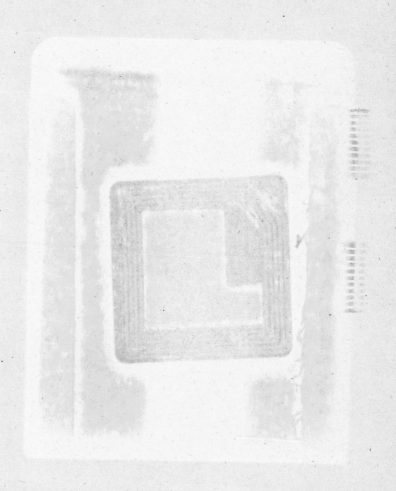